Human Resource Management and Industrial Relations

Human Resource Management and Industrial Relations

Text, Readings, and Cases

Thomas A. Kochan

Sloan School of Management
Massachusetts Institute of Technology

Thomas A. Barocci

Sloan School of Management
Massachusetts Institute of Technology

LITTLE, BROWN AND COMPANY
Boston   Toronto

Library of Congress Cataloging in Publication Data

Kochan, Thomas A.
 Human resource management and industrial relations.

 Includes index.
 1. Personnel management.   2. Industrial relations.
I. Barocci, Thomas A.   II. Title.
HF5549.K64335   1985   658.3   84–29983
ISBN 0–316–50079–8

Library of Congress Catalog Card No. 84-29983

ISBN 0-316-50079-8

9 8 7 6 5 4 3 2 1

BP

Published simultaneously in Canada
by Little, Brown & Company (Canada) Limited

Printed in the United States of America

To Our MIT Students

Preface

This book is the product of more than five years of experimentation and adaptation in search of the right substantive material, cases, and readings to prepare future managers to carry out their responsibilities in human resources and industrial relations. It is fitting, therefore, that we dedicate this book to the Massachusetts Institute of Technology students who were invaluable resources in this project and helped shape the final manuscript.

Throughout the developmental stage our students helped give structure to the basic approach by stating their needs and preferences in ways that only students can: Don't try to train me to be a personnel or human resource specialist; I am planning to be a line manager, or a consultant, or an investment banker, or a financial officer. They were right. Most books in this field are written for the 5 or 10 percent of business school students who choose to major in human resources or industrial relations and who plan to make it their life's work. Meanwhile, the other 90 percent or more lose an opportunity to confront the values, strategies, and practices in human resource management that they will be developing and administering throughout their careers, regardless of their managerial specialization or role. Our student inputs were coupled with those of the business, government, and trade union leaders who offered assistance in the form of sites for case studies and feedback on the relevance of this work to their organizational goals. Confidentiality was often rightfully imposed and precludes thanking them individually here. These organizations face the same issue as the students do. That is, only a few of the managers they hire need expertise in personnel matters, but all must be prepared to contribute to effective and efficient management of human resources.

We address this problem by adopting a line managerial perspective and focusing on the sequence of factors or events that shape human resource strategies, their implementation, and their evaluation. Our model stresses the dynamics of human resource management and industrial relations by starting with a historical perspective to show how all that has come before shapes current policies and practices and *should* inform managers on how to improve policy and practice in the future. We then stress environmental forces and their interactions with the values and business strategies and objectives of top corporate executives. Only within these historical, environmental, and organizational contexts can one begin to explore the more functional aspects of human resource policies. Finally, we stress paying attention to implementation and evaluation of human resource policies and practices.

Organizations are complex political entities. Often, that which is planned or intended will not happen. Moreover, unanticipated secondary effects of actions often cancel out the primary anticipated benefits. Assessing the effects of human resource management and industrial relations policies provides the data needed to begin the planning and deciding cycle once again.

Throughout the book we emphasize the need to face directly the difficult value issues that confront any decision maker operating in a social context in which multiple competing interests are at stake. Casting human resource management policies and practices within the broad framework of industrial relations systems, as we do here, keeps this message at the forefront in case discussions and analyses. We see this message as increasingly significant in teaching human resource management and industrial relations as the American industrial relations system moves through a transition phase in which many basic values, policies, and practices of the traditional system are being questioned and challenged by new approaches. We do not seek to advocate either a return to traditional patterns or blind acceptance of practices currently in vogue. Instead, we want students and practicing managers to make these critical value judgments and choices for themselves.

Authors who seek to fundamentally shift the approach to teaching a subject depend on the judgments and advice of competent colleagues who are willing to react to ideas and provide insights of their own. In this endeavor we were fortunate to receive this type of help from a rich array of friends and colleagues. We especially want to thank Katharine Abraham, David Anderson, Lotte Bailyn, Lee Dyer, Harry Katz, Robert McKersie, and Phyllis Wallace. Helpful reviews of the draft manuscript were provided by Sanford Jacoby, University of California-Los Angeles; Leonard Schlesinger, Harvard University; James Walker, Towers, Perrin, Forster & Crosby; Thomas Bergmann, University of Wisconsin-Eau Claire; Janina Latack, The Ohio State University; George Stevens, University of Central Florida; Thomas Decotiis, University of South Carolina; Gregory Shea, University of Pennsylvania; David Lipsky, Cornell University; Thomas Gutteridge, Southern Illinois University; and Charles Maxey, University of Southern California.

John Chalykoff and Joel Cutcher-Gershenfeld provided needed research assistance at several critical stages in this project. Nancy Mower took on the arduous task of preparing the index. And Michelle Kamin and Karen Humphreys typed and processed this manuscript through its various drafts and at least three stages of technological change — from electric typewriter to word processor to personal computer. We marvel at their resilience and appreciate their competence and dedication to excellence.

Every project needs a manager; complex projects need a facilitator; projects involving academics require someone able to translate tangled ideas into interpretable prose. As this project unfolded, Kirsten Wever took on all these roles, and did so with a style and class the authors may not have deserved. The book would not have been completed in this decade without her help.

A final and very special word of thanks is due to those authors who wrote new material especially for this book. We chose to ask the individuals listed below to do so because we knew that their work was at the cutting edge of research on topics that we needed to cover. We felt it was better to let them present their work and its implications than for us to digest and rework it. This is a pattern that we hope to continue in future editions. For now, however, special appreciation and recognition are extended to Paul Cournoyer, Lee Dyer, Felician Foltman, Ronald Karl, Harry Katz, Ralph Katz, Janice Klein, Robert McKersie, George Milkovich, Anil Verma, and Kirsten Wever.

If our families could have understood what the decision to do a "simple book of readings with short introductions" was destined to become, they would have lobbied against the project. They didn't anticipate the amount of work and time involved any more than we did, but Kathy, Monica, and our children bore the consequences. We appreciate their tolerance and support throughout.

TAK and TAB
Cambridge, Massachusetts

Contents

Human Resource Management
and Industrial Relations

I

Historical and Environmental Contexts

PREVIEW

The starting point for understanding the way human resources are managed within an organization is to recognize the historical and environmental contexts within which managers operate. What managers do is conditioned by the historical, economic, technological, and sociopolitical contexts in which business organizations function, each of which poses particular constraints and offers a limited range of opportunities for the firm, and consequently for its managers.

We therefore begin Chapter 1 with a discussion of the historical evolution of the employment relationship and the emergence of human resource management as it is currently practiced. This chapter includes a *Business Week* article on the so-called new industrial relations, as distinct from the less innovative and generally more adversarial modes of traditional American industrial relations. Following this glimpse of the contrast between the old and the new industrial relations is a case that demonstrates the diverse interests that are affected by reaching and implementing major organizational policy decisions: the case of International Harvester. One of the most interesting aspects of this case is that it illustrates the difficulty of categorizing the various interests affected by these decisions into a labor versus management dichotomy.

The International Harvester case also raises some of the questions that are addressed in more detail in Chapter 2, which focuses on the impact of the environment on the operation and strategies of the organization. This chapter begins with a discussion of the economic, labor market, and sociopolitical (including legal) contexts affecting the operation of a firm. The tensions between an organization's functioning and the limits set by these various environmental factors are then presented in more detail with the case of WWW, Inc.

This case is designed to clarify the ways in which the firm must analyze its environment and then tailor its strategic goals to limits set by the environment. The case also suggests some of the potentially contradictory effects of different environmental constraints.

Chapter 3 narrows the focus to consider the technological environment in more detail. Because of the rapidly changing nature of technologies, this environmental factor merits special attention. The chapter begins with a general discussion of the role of technology, emphasizing the ways in which technological change filters through the human resource management system and affects the key goals of the firm, its employees, and the larger society. Following that discussion is an article addressing some of the sociopolitical choices involved in the introduction of new technologies in the firm, and the ways in which the worker's experience of his or her work (and consequently, the employment relationship) is affected by the management of technological change. Chapter 3 concludes with a case that presents some of the issues and problems posed by the introduction of a specific and widespread new technology — video display terminals.

The organization of Part I of this book moves the reader consciously from the general to the specific. This structure is designed to mirror the theme we wish to emphasize here: that managers carry out their human resource management responsibilities in constantly evolving historical and environmental contexts. An understanding of these changing factors sets the stage for moving on to explore the strategic and organizational contexts that affect the management of human resources.

1

Human Resource Management and Industrial Relations: A Historical Introduction

Historical Approaches to the Employment Relationship

This book combines two historically separate approaches to teaching managers about their roles and responsibilities in designing and implementing the employment policies of an organization. One approach comes from the broad field of industrial relations and takes a multiple interest view, or what is now often called a governance perspective. This approach stresses the need to understand the diversity of interests that workers, employers, labor organizations, and the society at large have in the formation and implementation of employment policies. The other approach focuses more directly on the role of employers as human resource managers seeking both to meet employee expectations and to achieve the economic, or "bottom line," objectives of the firm. The historical separation of these two approaches is unfortunate, and mirrors a similar separation of responsibilities and outlooks among labor relations specialists, personnel specialists, and line managers.

Many firms are struggling to overcome the consequences of the narrowly based training and experience of managers whose careers have tracked them into these distinct roles, whereby it is hard for them to integrate knowledge and experience in business policy and planning, operations or line management, negotiations, communications, and problem solving. Employers have learned that both effective general managers and human resource professionals must be able to combine an understanding of how employment relationships evolve and how they are affected by external forces. Such an understanding requires skills in managing diverse interests, as well as strategies for integrating, wherever possible, the goals of the firm, of its employees, and of society at large. This book blends material from human resource management and industrial relations into a package that is appropriate for all managers, regardless of their specific areas of specialization or responsibility. At the same time, it serves as an introduction for those planning to specialize in human resource management/industrial relations (HRM/IR) as a functional area.

3

A Framework for Analyzing
Human Resource Management/Industrial Relations

It is customary to introduce a book such as this by noting that the practice of HRM/IR is currently undergoing significant change. The dynamic state of this art leads us to focus on some of the most important contemporary changes. At the same time, HRM/IR has never been static, and so the themes of change and transition will continue to be appropriate to the study of HRM/IR in the future. Indeed, we stress throughout this book that HRM/IR policies and practices must constantly evolve as organizations adapt to changing environmental conditions and shifting strategic requirements.

In order successfully to appraise, design, and implement policies that are responsive to current needs, it is necessary to develop an analytical framework for identifying the critical causal links among environmental changes, HRM/IR policies and practices, and the needs and goals of the parties to the employment relationship. We therefore emphasize the importance of developing strong analytical models capable of supporting the HRM/IR planning and evaluation processes that most modern firms are now putting into place to support their human resource management activities.

The general model guiding the organization of this book is presented in Figure 1-1. It begins with an analysis of the key environmental

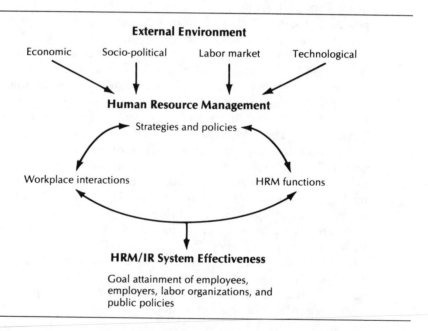

FIGURE 1-1   Framework for Analyzing Human Resource Management and Industrial Relations at the Level of the Firm

factors that influence employment relationships. By reviewing the historical shifts in the *economic, legal, sociopolitical, demographic,* and *technological* contexts affecting the employment relationship, we provide the starting point for an analysis of current policies and their effects.

We next turn to an analysis of human resource management at three levels within the firm. The first sheds light on the development and content of overall organizational HRM/IR *strategies* and *policies.* We emphasize the need to link HRM/IR policies with environmental characteristics and broader business policies and strategies. Second is an overview of the *functional activities* involved in the *implementation* of general policies like recruitment and selection, staffing and development, compensation, and collective bargaining and labor relations. Because of its centrality to an understanding of the American industrial relations system, collective bargaining, as well as the informal aspects of union-management relations, are given particular attention. Third is the micro level of the *workplace*, which allows us to explore relations between individuals and organizations. Here we examine the management of the employment relationship on a more day-to-day basis. Our analysis begins with a discussion of grievance procedures and other mechanisms for providing due process and protection of employee rights at the workplace; it then moves to the organization of work and communications among workers, supervisors, and managers, and the introduction of changes in workplace policies, practices, and behaviors.

Finally, we come full circle by once again moving beyond the policies and practices of a single organization to consider the larger social issues concerning alternative arrangements for structuring the relationships among workers, employers, labor organizations, and the government. By exploring the industrial relations systems of several European countries and Japan, we highlight the uniqueness of many features of the United States system. This contrast raises the obvious question of the extent to which each nation's system should be adapted to fit its specific cultural and political-economic circumstances. At the same time, we consider whether some system features are more effective than others, regardless of the setting.

The Effectiveness of a
Human Resource Management/Industrial Relations System

The diversity of interests, or governance, theme is evident throughout the development of the model, particularly in the outcomes against which the *effectiveness* of an HRM/IR system is assessed. Because workers, managers, labor organizations, and the larger society hold different goals for and expectations about the employment relationship, no single criterion of effectiveness will suffice. Instead, we need to examine the outcomes of an HRM/IR system from the standpoint of each of these different groups.

While it is impossible to list here all the different goals of the various parties, we can highlight some of the more long-standing and stable goals. Workers bring to their jobs a variety of individual goals and needs having to do with job and income security, career advancement, control over the terms under which they work, and the psychological meaningfulness of their work. Although managers share these individual goals and expectations, managers are also ultimately responsible for producing high-quality goods and services in an efficient and predictable manner. Because labor is one of the key factors of production that influences the cost, quality, and predictability of organizational outputs, managers need to control and to economize on the use of human resources. And since managers are held accountable to the owners of the organization (whether private stockholders or public citizens), they want sufficient control to be able to reallocate human resources in response to changing costs and opportunities. These management imperatives translate into the need to control labor costs, enhance productivity, maintain control and flexibility in the use of human resources, and develop an appropriately talented, trained, motivated, and committed work force.

Since both workers and managers want some influence over the terms and conditions of employment, they have both consensual and conflicting views about who should participate in these decisions. Where employees are (or wish to be) represented by a union, the union's right to participate and its other organizational interests also enter into the HRM/IR system. Thus, much of HRM/IR involves *procedural* as well as *substantive* issues and problems.

Finally, society at large has a variety of goals and interests that are affected by the rules and procedures governing employment relationships. For one thing, society depends on organizations to produce economic growth and to distribute the benefits of production as equitably as possible. For another, government must be concerned with the regulation and resolution of conflicts that can occur between workers and employers. In addition, most democratic societies expect the policies and practices governing employment relationships to ensure basic worker rights to due process, fair employment standards, and an effective voice in determining the terms and conditions of employment.

While at times some of these different goals will be in conflict, others will be shared by more than one party. Over time, the balance between consensus and conflict among the parties' goals can change with the nature of the environment and the ways the parties manage their relationship. Ultimately, how one views the effectiveness of an HRM/IR system hinges on a judgment about how well the system protects, balances, and accommodates the different interests of the parties, and how effectively it identifies opportunities for advancing their mutual interests to the fullest possible extent.

Societies and individual firms have approached the design and management of HRM/IR systems in different ways at different stages in history. The next section provides a brief overview of the development of the United States industrial relations system and the varying approaches to the management of human resources at the level of the firm.

Early Views of the Employment Relationship

Moral Foundation for Work

Different societies' approaches to the roles of work and employment have changed drastically over the centuries.[1] These changes reflect changes in the cultural, religious, political, and economic philosophies that have dominated different societies at different times. For example, the early Greeks viewed work as an unpleasant experience — a form of drudgery to be allocated to the lower classes and avoided by members of the aristocratic or leisure classes. Later, Catholic scholars like Thomas Aquinas began to view work as being important to the development of a healthy soul. The development of Lutheranism and Calvinism further extended the notion that work was its own virtue, necessary for a full and complete life. By the seventeenth century, as the industrial revolution began to unfold, this idea developed into what is known as the Protestant ethic, with its emphasis on abstinence and self-discipline. Work was viewed as a means of serving God (Weber, 1930). Thus, the concept of the work ethic was born and became firmly embedded in industrial society. In many respects the Protestant ethic, underscoring discipline, laid the moral foundation for the division of labor common to most modern industrial systems. This ethic also provided a moral basis for the authoritarian structure of modern organizations.

Classical Economic View of Work

The religious views of work fit nicely with the theories of the classical economists who dominated the economic analysis of "labor problems" during the 1800s. The works of people like Adam Smith, David Ricardo, Thomas Malthus, and John Stuart Mill focused on the "natural" laws of economics that were expected to dictate the relationship between labor and capital. The common view articulated by these different writers was that labor could be thought of and treated in the same manner as other physical or financial factors of production. Labor was a commodity subject to the same laws of supply and demand as other commodities; therefore, there was little need to develop labor-specific laws, standards of practice, or managerial policies beyond those required for managing and regulating other aspects of the marketplace.

---

[1]The material presented on the historical development of industrial relations is adapted from Kochan (1980: 2–23).

Instead, the classical economists assumed that in the long run the "invisible hand" of the competitive market would work in the best interest of workers, employers, and society at large.

Challenges to the Classical View

By the late 1800s and early 1900s, two separate challenges to the classical view of the employment relationship were developing. The radical challenge from the left came from Marxists and others who rejected capitalism as a desirable political and economic system. Marx saw an inherent conflict of interest between the working class and the capitalists who owned and controlled the means of production. The employment relationship was one arena in which the inevitable class struggle was played out. The solution to workers' alienation and exploitation could only be found in the overthrow of the capitalist economic and social system and its replacement by a system in which workers owned and controlled the means of production.

While Marxist and neo-Marxist doctrines continue to pose a popular counterforce to classical and neoclassical economic theory, these views never gained sufficient political influence in the United States to have a widespread effect on industrial relations or management practices. Instead, in the United States the challenge by a group of social reform–oriented economists, known as institutional economists, provided a more moderate set of criticisms of the classical economic view. This approach had an important impact on both public policy and private practice. The leading American institutional economists of the early twentieth century, such as John R. Commons, Richard T. Ely, and Thorstein Veblen, shared the Marxist view that labor was more than an economic factor of production, more than a commodity that could be managed and treated as any other. They, too, rejected the economic determinism that was implicit in classical economics; instead, they built their ideas from actual case studies and other direct, empirical observations of working conditions and the behavior of employers and workers. And they, too, shared the view that there was a fundamental conflict of interest between workers and employers.

However, unlike the Marxists, the institutional economists believed that this conflict of interest was inherent in all organizations, regardless of the political or economic context. Instead of searching for a utopian solution, either through revolution or through the "invisible hand" of market forces, the institutionalists stressed the need for periodic negotiations and compromise among the divergent interests of labor, management, and the public. They believed an emphasis on compromise, negotiation, and accommodation was consistent with a pluralist view of a democratic society, and with the principle of freedom to contract, so central to a free enterprise economy.

In short, the American institutionalists argued that a free enterprise economy could effectively balance worker and employer interests.

Achieving an acceptable balance, however, would necessitate an active government policy to regulate employment relations, together with a strong labor movement to represent employees' interests at the workplace and in the political process.

Emergence of the United States Industrial Relations System

The views of the institutionalists provided the intellectual foundation for most of the basic labor laws enacted in the United States in the 1930s, legislation that continues to govern employment relationships today. Through their research and involvement in government affairs, the institutionalists stressed the need for protective labor legislation in such areas as child labor, minimum wages, unemployment insurance, workers' compensation, and social security. For each of these issues, federal laws were enacted during the 1930s as part of the Roosevelt administration's New Deal. The institutionalists also emphasized the need for orderly procedures that protected the rights of individual workers to join trade unions and to engage in collective bargaining. The conflicts of interest among workers, employers, and society were to be accommodated through the combination of legislation, which protected individual rights and established a floor on labor standards, and collective bargaining. The institutionalists sought to legitimize conflict and to promote orderly processes for its regulation and resolution, rather than suppressing the ability of workers to assert their interests either individually or collectively. These arguments provided the intellectual foundation for the National Labor Relations Act of 1935 (the Wagner Act), which states that it is our national labor policy to promote the process of collective bargaining as the primary means of (1) accommodating labor and management interests and (2) introducing a form of industrial democracy into the American workplace.

Perhaps the most lasting contribution of these early industrial relations scholars was their recognition that conflict is a natural and legitimate characteristic of any employment relationship. Overt conflict — in the form of strikes, bargaining impasses, and individual disagreements among individual workers, work groups, and managers — is a logical expression and extension of any democratic society that legitimates the pursuit of pluralistic interests at the workplace. Thus, no system of industrial relations can view conflict per se as pathological. Instead, conflicts of interest must be allowed to be articulated and to surface at the workplace in order to avoid suppression of legitimate differences and goals.

At the same time, as noted earlier, the larger society has a stake in the effective regulation and resolution of conflicts that arise between workers and employers. Society not only values the products and services provided by managers and employees, but also must bear the social, economic, and political costs of workplace conflicts. This makes government in any industrial society not only a mediator of the interests of labor and management, but also an actor in employment decisions, with goals of its own. One of the key roles of government in industrial relations is to balance, on the one hand, the rights of labor and management to assert their individual and collective interests at the workplace against, on the other, society's needs and rights to industrial peace and productivity.

The Perspective of Human Resource Management

If industrial relations and our national labor policies have emphasized diversity of interests and formal laws and procedures for regulating conflict, human resource management and its forerunners of personnel management, human relations, scientific management, and organizational development have tended to deemphasize conflicting interests. Instead, human resource management and its intellectual predecessors have focused on how to manage employees in ways that maximize their commitment and contribution to the goals of the firm, on how to integrate individual workers' goals with the goals of the firm, and on how to increase cooperation within the organization.

Historical Development

The study and practice of human resource management are rooted in the development and application of scientific management principles in the early 1900s. Scientific management attempted to organize work and compensate individual employees in a way that directly linked the employer's needs for productivity to workers' wages. Proponents of scientific management believed that by finding the "one best way" to design jobs and organize work, and then by tying employees' wages to their output, the interests of the firm and its employees could be rendered compatible. Thus, scientific management maintained that the effective application of industrial engineering techniques and incentive wage systems would eliminate any potential conflicts of interest between workers and their employers.

A second phase in the development of human resource management came during and in the decade after World War I, with the growth of employee representation plans, the human relations movement, and what was generally labeled welfare capitalism. The demands of the wartime economy sparked an era of rapid economic growth and the expansion of large-scale manufacturing industries. Between World War I and the Great Depression of the 1930s, many large companies established personnel departments and invested heavily in strategies designed to substitute for trade unions by developing internal, company-run programs for employee participation, representation, and satisfaction of social needs. Whereas the scientific management movement sought to overcome the potential conflict of interest between workers and the firm by linking workers' *individual economic incentives* to the goals of the firm, these new human relations efforts sought to deal more directly with the *social needs* of workers and *work groups*. The expectation was that increased levels of individual and group satisfaction would lead to increased levels of both commitment to the firm and worker performance and cooperation (Roethsberger and Dickson, 1939). In many respects, these early human relations efforts formed the basis for what is currently being described as the development of high-commitment work systems (Walton, 1980) and integrated organizational cultures (Ouchi, 1981).

The human relations movement and employee representation plans were highly successful in the 1920s but collapsed during the Great Depression of the 1930s (Jacoby, 1984). With the subsequent growth of industrial unions between 1935 and 1950, the role of the personnel function shifted from avoiding trade unions to adapting to the presence of unions and collective bargaining. Consequently, between 1935 and the 1960s, labor relations specialists — people responsible for managing relations with unions — rose to the dominant position of influence in personnel departments.

Growth of Human Resource Specialists

Union growth in the private sector of the American economy stopped in the mid-1950s, and the trend reversed to produce a gradual and continuous decline through the 1960s and 1970s. Labor relations specialists continued to play the dominant role in managing relations with unions. At the same time, the period 1960–1980 was one of rapid expansion in other aspects of the personnel function, particularly the management of recruitment, development, and compensation. Because managers and other professional and technical workers in these areas were proliferating in relation to the blue-collar production work force, the ability to attract and retain white-collar and professional employees became a critical function of personnel and human resource management departments. These employees also brought more diverse individual needs and expectations to their jobs, and therefore required new and complex management and motivation systems.

Concurrently, government labor policy shifted away from an emphasis on promoting the collective bargaining process while leaving the substantive terms and conditions of employment either to collective bargaining or to unilateral determination by employers. Greater emphasis was placed on the direct regulation of the terms and conditions of employment. Between 1960 and 1980, for example, new laws were enacted regulating occupational safety and health, equal employment opportunities, pensions, and retirement policies. The regulations produced a demand for new professionals within corporations who could help develop systems for monitoring compliance and ensuring that companies were not exposed to legal sanctions for failing to comply with the law (Janger, 1977). Two important by-products of the development of compliance monitoring systems were, first, the creation of a better base of information about demographic profiles of the labor force and, second, the devising of systems for tracking people's movements across jobs within the firm. The result has been an increase in the application of strategic planning and analysis to the human resource management function.

Contemporary Human Resource Management and Industrial Relations

Based on this historical background, we can now assess the challenges facing human resource management and industrial relations in contemporary organizations. The entire American economy has recently experienced severe pressures as the result of sluggish growth in productivity, high rates of inflation, rapidly increasing energy costs, increases in international competition, and extended periods of high unemployment and high interest rates. Furthermore, American employers have recently been strongly influenced by the arguments of politicians, social critics, and management writers advocating giving greater attention to employee participation, motivation, and job-related decision making. American management in general has been criticized for its focus on short-run profits at the expense of long-run investment needs. Managers have also been urged to engage in longer-run planning and strategy formation with respect specifically to their human resources. Finally, the American industrial relations system must now adjust to the effects of thirty years of declining union membership and union organizing effectiveness, combined with increasing union effectiveness in raising wages and improving fringe benefits in firms that were organized between 1930 and 1960. The result during the 1970s was an increase in the differential between union and non-union workers' wages and benefits (Mitchell, 1980), which in turn put further pressures on unionized firms, leading many of them to become increasingly aggressive at the collective bargaining table.

The combination of severe economic pressures, a shift in the nature of the work force, and the decline of unionization has created two competing systems of industrial relations in the United States economy. One system governs some blue-collar and professional employees, and relies heavily on negotiations and the formal mechanisms for conflict resolution associated with a collective bargaining system. These arrangements tend to be found in the public sector and in those regions, industries, and firms which grew and developed during the period 1930–1950, when union organization was increasing. Thus, unions are now associated with the more mature industries, with older plants, and with older work forces. The other system covers a large, newer, and nonunion set of industries, plants, and regions of the country, those which are usually associated with the high-technology industries that have grown rapidly since 1960. As part of the effort to avoid being organized, many firms in these industries have developed highly innovative and flexible personnel and human resource management systems, while simultaneously matching the basic wage and in some cases fringe benefit programs available to unionized employees.

The battle between the labor movement and unorganized employers continues to be played out today through electoral politics and legislative lobbying and through organizing and counterorganizing efforts at the workplace. Our purpose in this book is not to encourage students to take sides in these ideological debates and tactical maneuvers. Instead, we believe our obligation as teachers and professionals committed to effective human resource management and industrial relations practices is to examine the more generic roles and responsibilities of employers as actors in a constantly evolving industrial relations system. Thus, we will present materials in a framework for analysis that attempts to probe basic issues facing managers who are trying to develop effective HRM/IR policies and practices in their organizations, whether unionized or not.

The View from *Business Week:*
Searching for New Forms of Industrial Relations

We now turn to an article from *Business Week* and an exercise, in order to bring to life the concepts and issues introduced so far. As is true for all the cases and supplementary readings presented in this book, these materials are included both to illustrate and apply the basic concepts introduced in the text, and to provide a basis for classroom discussion and debate.

The *Business Week* article, entitled "The New Industrial Relations," sets the stage for a discussion of the strengths and weaknesses of (1) traditional industrial relations practices and (2) some of the currently popular experiments with "new" human resource management philosophies and practices, which center on high degrees of employee participation in decision making at the workplace. A question to consider while reading the article is whether these experiments render obsolete the "old" or "traditional" industrial relations laws and collective bargaining procedures that are used to regulate or negotiate employment conditions and to resolve conflicts at the workplace. *Business Week* argues that the adversarial system is outmoded. Just what are the sources of the conflicts that underlie the adversarial system? Can these conflicts be eliminated by new managerial styles and strategies, or is this goal naive or utopian? In general, to what extent can these new approaches contribute to the more effective management of human resources? This last question will be primary to our discussion and analysis, not only in this reading but throughout the remainder of this book, as we explore how both the new and the old HRM/IR practices are evolving and shaping the systems of the future.

References

Jacoby, Sanford M., "The Development of Internal Labor Markets in American Manufacturing Firms," in Paul Osterman, ed., *Internal Labor Markets* (Cambridge: MIT University Press, 1984), 23–70.

For a historical analysis of the development of employment policies of American firms see Sanford Jacoby, *Employing Bureaucracies: Unions, Managers and the Transformation of Work in American Industry, 1900–1959* (New York: Columbia University Press, 1985).

Janger, Alan, *The Personnel Function* (New York: The Conference Board, 1977).

Kochan, Thomas A., *Collective Bargaining and Industrial Relations* (Homewood, Ill.: Irwin, 1980).

Mitchell, Daniel J. B., *Unions, Wages and Inflation* (Washington, D.C.: The Brookings Institution, 1980).

Ouchi, William G., *Theory Z* (Reading, Mass.: Addison-Wesley, 1981).

Roethsberger, F. J. and William J. Dickson, *Management and the Worker* (Cambridge: Harvard University Press, 1939).

Walton, Richard E., "Establishing and Maintaining High Commitment Work Systems," in John R. Kimberly and Robert A. Miles, eds., *The Organizational Life Cycle* (San Francisco: Jossey Bass, 1980), 208–90.

Weber, Max, *The Protestant Ethic and the Spirit of Capitalism* (London: Allen and Unwin, 1930).

Suggested Readings

For the broadest introduction to the field of industrial relations, see Neil Chamberlain, Donald E. Cullen, and David Lewin, *The Labor Sector* (New York: McGraw-Hill, 1980).

For the standard classic reference on industrial relations theory, see John T. Dunlop, *Industrial Relations Systems* (New York: Holt, 1958).

For a more complete treatment of the United States collective bargaining system and the industrial relations framework on which much of our work is based see Thomas A. Kochan, *Collective Bargaining and Industrial Relations* (Homewood, Ill.: Irwin, 1980).

For textbooks on labor-management relations, see John A. Fossum, *Labor Relations* (Dallas: Business Publications, 1982) or D. Quinn Mills, *Labor-Management Relations* (New York: McGraw Hill, 1982).

For a more detailed treatment of personnel and human resource management topics, see Herbert H. Heneman III, Donald P. Schwab, John A. Fossum, and Lee Dyer, *Personnel/Human Resource Management* (Homewood, Ill.: Irwin, 1983).

For a historical analysis of the development of employment policies of American firms see Sanford Jacoby, *Employing Bureaucracies: Unions, Managers and the Transformation of Work in American Industry, 1900–1950* (New York: Columbia University Press, 1985).

The New Industrial Relations

The Decline of the Adversarial Approach

Quietly, almost without notice, a new industrial relations system with a fundamentally different way of managing people is taking shape in the U.S. Its goal is to end the adversarial relationship that has grown between management and labor and that now threatens the competitiveness of many industries.

The coming of the Industrial Revolution to the U.S. 150 years ago created a profound shock that is still being felt. From the 1830s well into the 20th century, the nation experienced periodic outbreaks of "the labor problem," troubles that accompanied the acculturation of great masses of pre-industrial immigrants and rural migrants into the harsh discipline of the factories and mines. Today's industrial relations system still contains elements that were jerry-built then to deal with work-force instability: manual jobs fragmented into simple tasks, foremen with awesome disciplinary powers, and a deeply rooted sense that a wide gap separated those who work from those who manage.

But the changed social values and high educational levels of today's younger labor force, combined with economic strains are putting massive pressure on that obsolete system. Increasing numbers of companies and unions are leading a march away from the old, crude workplace ethos and the adversarial relationship it spawns. (See Figure 1-2).

The change will bring current work psychology almost full circle from where it was only 35 years ago, when Elton Mayo, a pioneer work sociologist at Harvard University, accused American management of accepting a "rabble hypothesis" in dealing with workers. Most managers, Mayo wrote, used the wrong incentives to gain labor's cooperation because they viewed employees as a "horde . . . actuated by self-interest" — a money-grubbing rabble with no group loyalty or social goals.

A more enlightened view of worker psychology has taken hold today. It stresses that most people want to be productive and will — given the proper incentives and a climate of labor-management trust — eagerly involve themselves in their jobs. (See Exhibit 1-1). This calls for a participatory process in which workers gain a voice in decision-making on the shop floor. Many companies, some in collaboration with once-hostile unions, are creating new mechanisms to gain worker involvement. Among these mechanisms are "self-managed" work teams, labor-management steering committees in union shops, problem-solving groups — such as "core groups" or the quality circles that are widely used in Japan — and redesign committees that wed social and technical ideas in designing or rearranging plants.

The concepts behind these innovations are not new; social cooperation at work surely predates recorded history. But organized labor's growth as a deeply adversarial institution in the U.S. coupled with management's retention of obsolete methods of controlling workers — Frederick Taylor's "scientific management" approach, for example — have blinded both sides to their mutual interests. Only a few years ago, work innovations were looked upon as slightly bizarre, if interesting, projects that "couldn't produce any bottom-line results," as Jerome M. Rosow, president of Work in America Institute Inc., puts it.

Source: Reprinted from the May 11, 1981, issue of *Business Week*, by special permission, Copyright © 1981 by McGraw-Hill, Inc.

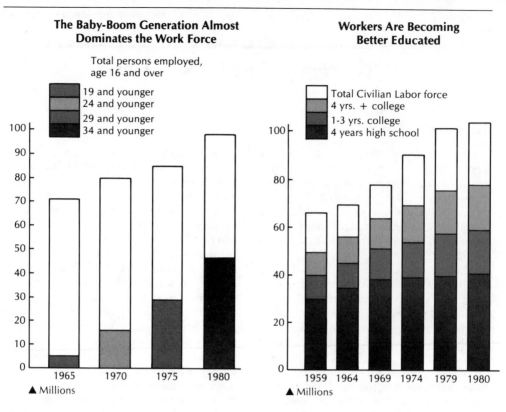

The Baby-Boom Generation Almost Dominates the Work Force

Total persons employed, age 16 and over

- 19 and younger
- 24 and younger
- 29 and younger
- 34 and younger

▲ Millions

Workers Are Becoming Better Educated

- Total Civilian Labor force
- 4 yrs. + college
- 1-3 yrs. college
- 4 years high school

▲ Millions

Data: Bureau of Labor Statistics

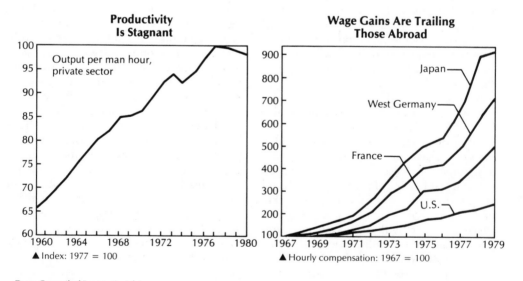

Productivity Is Stagnant

Output per man hour, private sector

▲ Index: 1977 = 100

Wage Gains Are Trailing Those Abroad

Japan
West Germany
France
U.S.

▲ Hourly compensation: 1967 = 100

Data: Council of Economic Advisers

FIGURE 1-2 Fundamental Forces that Are Changing the U.S. Workplace

EXHIBIT 1-1
The Movement's Founding Fathers

There is a common misconception in the U.S. that the theories behind participatory management have been imported from Japan. This could not be further from the truth. American
psychologists have led the way in research on motivational theory, alienation, the impact of
different management styles, and the need for — or lack of — clearly delineated hierarchies
to make things work. This last area is drawing most of the exciting questions today: For
example, do semiautonomous work groups function better than hierarchical organizations that
categorize employees as either order-givers or order-takers?

A partial list of theorists who have contributed to the work innovation movement follows:

Elton Mayo

He reasoned that group activities are effective only when each individual sees his interests as
parallel to those of the group. Individuals, Mayo guessed, see themselves as part of a specific
clan — a family, a community group, and the like — rather than a member of the society as a
whole. He suggested that management try to follow this "clan" principle by encouraging
workers to form stable work groups with specific goals whose attainment would benefit the
group as a whole.

Abraham Maslow

His hierarchy-of-needs theory states that an individual's primary needs, such as food and
shelter, take precedence over emotional needs. But as each primary need is fulfilled, Maslow
theorized, subtler needs such as self-esteem and self-actualization rise to the surface. Maslow's theory points out that when wages are largely high enough to fill basic needs, regular
raises do not satisfy the need for involvement and fulfillment in the job.

Chris Argyris

He believes there is a mutual exclusivity between the total needs of the individual and those
of the corporation. Efficient organizations require highly specialized jobs, which at lower
levels translate into boring and alienating work. Argyris borrowed Maslow's concepts and
called for managers to trust their employees. He stressed job enrichment and limited autonomy for workers.

Douglas McGregor

His famous Theory X vs. Theory Y concepts of management were among the first to suggest
practical applications of some of the earlier concepts of group identification and job enrichment. He claimed old-line Theory X managers — those who believe that people inherently
dislike work and must be ordered to do it — are not as effective as Theory Y managers, who
believe that people want to work and who encourage that basic desire through trust and
cooperation. He advocated sensitivity training and other methods of teaching managers interpersonal skills, and like Mayo, stressed the importance of small working groups led by these
psychologically trained managers.

Rensis Likert

He advocated a system of participative management, as opposed to consultative, benevolent-
authoritative, or exploitative-authoritative management systems. Like others before him, Likert
saw inherent conflicts between strict divisions of labor and cooperative, efficient efforts. He

stressed the need for a corporatewide culture of cooperation. He advocated the establishment of small decision-making groups and suggested there be overlapping memberships among them in order to prevent group rivalries. Many of his theories were the forerunners of modern-day matrix management systems.

William Ouchi

Ouchi recently introduced the idea of a Theory Z organization. It is based on the Japanese-style concepts of long-term employment and participatory decision making but retains individual responsibility for performance. It incorporates such "alien" concepts as slow evaluation and promotion, rotating managers to avoid extreme specialization, consensus decisions, and informal controls. Ouchi has studied several successful companies — including Kodak, Procter & Gamble, International Business Machines, and Hewlett-Packard — and demonstrated how they exhibit definite "Z" tendencies.

But evidence is growing that quality-of-work-life (QWL) programs, as some companies and unions call them, can meet their twin goals of increasing job satisfaction and improving quality and productivity. Moreover, the convergence of two major trends is forcing companies and unions to change their ways.

The 'Baby-Boom' Generation

One trend, social and demographic in nature, consists of increasing demands by better-educated workers at all levels for more challenge on the job and for participation in decision-making. The "baby-boom" generation, which brought radically changed values to the workplace, now just about dominates the labor force. The second trend is economic — the slower growth, declining productivity, and tougher worldwide competition that is shrinking so many basic U.S. industries. These forces must be dealt with, and, increasingly, business and labor are realizing that solving "people problems" is as important as generating capital and introducing new technology. And, as Rosow says, "adversity is a tremendous motivator."

Until recently, the work innovation movement in the U.S. has progressed slowly. The 1950s and 1960s brought increased research and the development of theories on worker psychology. By the early 1970s, corporations such as General Motors, Procter & Gamble, and General Foods had started work improvement programs. Now, the movement has graduated from the experimental phase. Hundreds of companies, profiting from what was learned by forerunners, are trying to redesign jobs and work processes. In the early years, unions feared — and many still do — that these programs would undermine their relevance and position in the workplace. But three of the largest unions — the United Auto Workers, United Steelworkers, and Communications Workers of America — are now involved in what are essentially industrywide projects in their industries.

Richard E. Walton of Harvard, a consultant and an authority on work improvement projects, believes that the last few years have produced a value shift in American industry. In society at large, he says, a return to a "let-the-environment-be-damned" attitude is unlikely. "In the same way, we're not going to treat the psychological and social costs of producing goods and services as if they're the fault of the individuals involved but of the system," he says. "This shift will ebb and flow, but the quality of work will be much more of a concern than it was 10 years ago."

"I'm absolutely convinced that the future of collective bargaining is in quality-of-work-life," says Irving Bluestone, a retired UAW vice-president who is the premier union champion of work innovations. While this is the rhetoric of an advocate, Bluestone's intuition about the growth of the QWL movement has proved correct in the past. In the early 1970s, he was its only supporter on the UAW's 26-member executive board, and he often was criticized for it.

Today, a majority of the board supports worker involvement programs at GM, Ford, Chrysler, and other UAW companies. Labor relations in the entire industry are becoming much more collaborative. But the UAW and the companies have not given up any rights in bargaining contracts. "We can be cooperative on the plant floor and adversarial at the bargaining table," Bluestone says.

Quality Circles

Aside from union-management relations, the workplace is changing in an even more profound way. "It's a real fundamental change in the way we manage people," says Paul W. Chaisson, director of human resources at Malden Mills, a textile manufacturer in Lawrence, Mass. "There's no longer management turf and worker turf," he says. "There's just a sharing of the management of the business, and there's such a thirst among the workers for this process, it's amazing."

The sudden thirst among companies for a quick splash of "consensus management," as practiced successfully in Japan, raises the danger that work redesign will become too faddish. In the 1950s, the Japanese began using an American concept neglected in the U.S. — the quality circle, a committee of workers that analyzes and solves quality problems. Some 200 U.S. companies now have quality circles. Ted Mills, president of the American Center for the Quality of Work Life, warns that a too-hasty application of the concept in U.S. companies would smack of the "American 'quick-fix' mentality" and could harm the entire QWL movement.

But the important work innovations in the U.S. are by no means imitations of a Japanese model; they represent an authentic American movement of employee involvement in production-related decisions on the plant floor. The movement also differs considerably from the European system of codetermination, in which worker representatives sit on corporate supervisory boards. Although UAW President Douglas A. Fraser is a Chrysler Corp. director, his election to the board was a singular quid pro quo for UAW wage concessions. "We want participation from the bottom up," says Glenn E. Watts, president of the Communications Workers. "I don't want to sit on the board and be responsible for managing the business. I want to be free as a unionist to criticize management."

There is no longer any question that significant change in the workplace is under way — and not only in heavy industry. Work improvements are being instituted in supermarkets, schools, banks, and government offices, among other places. Whether this will be a lasting change — a continuing process, instead of a "program" with a termination date — depends on whether American management and labor leaders are willing to risk short-term profits and political gains to produce long-term change.

The Built-in Obsolescence in Today's System

The risks involved in work innovations are worth taking if labor and management hope to respond to the nation's shift in social values and its economic stagnation. The dimensions of the economic problems are well-known: high unemployment and inflation, the decline of basic industries — such as steel, autos, apparel, electrical equipment — because of foreign competition, and a flattening out of a once-high productivity growth.

The social forces that play some part in the productivity slowdown and that call for major changes in the industrial relations system are less well understood. A major factor is the growing influence of the baby-boom generation — people born from 1946 through the early 1960s — on work values. It came to maturity during a period of unparalleled prosperity and social turmoil and therefore brings far different expectations to the job than the generation that grew up during the Depression. Daniel Yankelovich, who heads the research firm of Yankelovich, Skelly & White, describes the younger generation as more concerned with personal growth and enjoyment of work and leisure.

Based on interviews with 3,500 families last year, Yankelovich contends that 40% of the labor force is composed of workers who belong to new work-value groups. One new-value group dislikes formal job structures and rejects money as a substitute for fulfillment; the primary objective of the second group is to earn money not for the sake of money but to buy a certain lifestyle. Once that is achieved, this group tends to hold back on the job. Most important, says Richard Balzer, a vice-president of the Yankelovich firm, a large part of the younger generation "can't return to the traditional 'keeping your nose to the grindstone' when hard times come because they've never known hard times."

Older generations tend to bemoan a perceived loss of the work ethic among younger workers and demand a return to a mythical golden era of hard work. But all studies of people's commitment to productive work indicate a "strong affirmation of the value of work," says Michael Maccoby, director of the Washington-based Project on Technology, Work & Character. However, Maccoby and an associate, Katherine A. Terzi, conclude in a recent study that changes in society "have changed the social character so that it is less frightened and submissive, more self-affirmative and critical of inequity." This suggests strongly that U.S. industry must reorganize work and its incentives to appeal to new worker values rather than try to retrofit people to work designs and an industrial relations system of 80 years ago.

"Living in the 1930s"

This old system, with its built-in conflicts, encouraged the perception that "head work" was the responsibility of managers only. "We're still living in the 1930s world, paying for the use of a worker's hands and not what he can offer mentally," says Alfred S. Warren Jr., industrial relations vice-president of General Motors Corp. Adds Michael Sonduck, corporate manager of work improvement at Digital Equipment Corp., "One of the most dehumanizing assumptions ever made is that workers work and managers think. When we give shop-floor workers control over their work, they are enormously thoughtful."

The rise of industrial unionism in the 1930s reduced corporate power over workers, ended unfair treatment on the job, and gave workers a voice in wages and working conditions through bargaining. But the unions continued to operate with a 1930s philosophy, demanding rules to spread the work and limit management's flexibility. This only strengthened management's resolve to tighten controls over workers. Moreover, unionism has done little to insert the worker into his work or give him pride in quality, largely because the unions have not demanded a voice in reorganizing the work structure — and undoubtedly would have been rebuffed by management if they had.

What resulted was a sharp adversarial relationship between management and labor. "Workers and management are seen to have diametrically opposed interests," writes University of Michigan sociologist Robert E. Cole in *Work, Mobility & Participation*, a 1979 book comparing Japanese and American labor practices. In Japan, workers view the corporation as "the sustaining force" of their lives and therefore eagerly cooperate with management. But in the U.S., Cole says, "management writes off worker cooperation because it is seen as either irrelevant or impossible to achieve."

Increasing numbers of company, union, and academic authorities are coming to believe that a new industrial relations system must include three basic elements:

1. The development of a nonadversarial relationship on the shop floor, so that workers and bosses can collaborate on means and methods of production by circumventing adversarial procedures, such as grievance mechanisms. This need not violate union contracts or prevent unions from negotiating wages and benefits, but greater cooperation at the production level will involve workers in the business to a much greater extent.

2. A reform of bargaining, based on a mutuality of interests developed on the shop floor. This work-level cooperation might well slip over into the bargaining process, particularly if unions — reflecting the concerns of their members — tie themselves more tightly to the success of the individual company, rather than try to keep up with national wage patterns and outdo other unions.

3. A thoroughgoing change in management style in which the traditional top-to-bottom hierarchical form of decision-making is replaced with a participation process. Decisions should be pushed to ever-lower levels, thereby encouraging employees, by extension, to become involved in the business itself. But this would also mean that management must share information with workers, divide with them the gains resulting from increased participation, and work much harder to provide job security and to prevent the catastrophic blows of unexpected plant shutdowns.

A New Way of Managing People

There is a videotape circulating throughout Xerox Corp. in which President David T. Kearns candidly sets forth the company's key strategies, its capital investment plans, the priorities it places on each of its divisions, and the competitive threats it faces. He ends by saying, "I pledge to you that management of this company at [all levels] will listen to you and put your ideas to work."

Over at the Webster (N.Y.) headquarters of Xerox's Reprographics Technology Group, Group President Frank J. Pipp mirrors that approach. He is setting up quality circles, horizontal councils of same-level people from different departments, and vertical work-study groups from different levels within a department. He has gotten the advance agreement of union leaders and has trained hourly workers and foremen on quality circle methods. And he is showing his own videotape back-to-back with Kearns's.

"Both Dave and I honestly believe that most people are naturally innovative, want to work hard, only don't because management doesn't create the kind of environment where they can," Pipp insists. He notes that both he and Kearns have attended quality circle meetings, held dinners with teams, and toured plants together. "We must prove that we really want to listen if [participation] is not to be another passing fad," Pipp says. "Employees always want to be involved — the problem is lack of management involvement."

Indeed, Pipp and Kearns already recognize something that industrial psychologists keep trying to impress on management: A workable participatory management program requires a change in attitude throughout a company, and that change must be supported from the top. "Too many participatory experiments started off well, only to fail because they represented a deviant subculture in a company whose dominant culture was authoritarian," insists William Ouchi, a professor at the University of California–Los Angeles' Graduate School of Management, whose "Theory Z" concept of participatory cultures has been getting widespread recognition.

Paying only lip service to the concept is rarely enough, adds Harry Levinson, head of the Levinson Institute in Belmont, Mass., a psychological consulting group.

"Top management must set a role model and demand that subordinates also set role models," he says. "Just asking for reports once in a while is akin to a father checking his kids' report cards for A's and considering that involvement in their education."

Some managers understand this instinctively. General Motors Corp., which has projects on quality-of-work-life under way in about 90 locations, expects all of its management people to attend an annual conference at which successful programs are described. Last year, Charles L. Brown, chairman of American Telephone & Telegraph Co., sent a memo to the presidents of all 24 Bell System operating companies calling for "an insistence on your part" that quality-of-work-life principles "be tried out and tolerated with the end objective of a spread to the whole organization."

"Because It's Right"

In some cases, a company's philosophy is the personal expression of the chief executive. One of the earliest and largest quality-of-work-life programs involving a union, the United Auto Workers, was implemented by Sidney Harman, now chairman of Harman International Industries Inc., at an automotive mirror plant in Bolivar, Tenn. "It was my conviction I [was responsible for] the development of people who worked for me," Harman says. "You can't create this kind of program as a surrogate for speedup. You do it because it's right."

The program started in 1972, and it was successful in many respects for several years. It doubled productivity on some assembly lines. Harman instituted classes in arts and crafts and business for workers who completed standard output for one shift in less than eight hours, and workers were even involved in costing out contracts. But Harman had basically presented the program to plant management by fiat. In effect, he ordered them to be participatory without being participatory himself. The local management accepted the program but has been much less active

in keeping it going since Harman sold the plant to Beatrice Foods Co. in 1976.

When the consultants who had helped design the program left the Bolivar plant in 1979, the program eroded further because there was nobody left to nourish it. "The local management liked the idea of better relationships with the workers," says Michael Maccoby of the Project on Technology, Work & Character and the chief consultant. "But they didn't look at it in terms of institutionalizing participative management." Adds Harman: "We didn't understand early enough how crucial it was to get middle managers involved at an earlier stage."

Few programs receive the publicity that Bolivar has enjoyed. Thus, failure stories are not easy to ferret out. Nonetheless, many programs die for lack of support. These unsung failures include semi-autonomous work groups that became ineffective because first-line managers feared losing control. They include quality circle groups whose discussions degenerated into a rehash of trivial issues because participants had not been trained to analyze quality problems. And they include potentially effective core groups that lost their stamina the first time management took several months to respond to a suggestion.

The Weakest Link

The basic problem is that the participatory chain is only as strong as its weakest link. If any link breaks, whether it is a first-line supervisor, an engineer, or a plant manager, the process of participative management comes to a halt. Clearly, top management must emphasize that communal problem-solving is an integral part of every person's job.

Harman is now applying the lesson he learned at Bolivar to a participatory program he has started at a North Ridge (Calif.) stereo speaker plant. This time he is holding meetings of all managing personnel to make sure they understand that worker involvement will not usurp their authority. "The role of supervisor as overseer may become redundant with QWL, but why shouldn't the supervisor have a coordinative role and be a teacher?" he asks.

Harman's rhetorical question raises one of the most complex and difficult aspects of instituting an effective program. Polaroid Corp. is grappling with how to persuade the quality-control support staff that allowing workers to inspect their own finished goods is not a direct slap at existing quality inspectors. At General Motors Inland Div., a tug-of-war cropped up between interfunction "product teams" with operating profit responsibility and the sales department over who should have ultimate authority over pricing.

The idea of relinquishing the control they fought so hard to attain is a bitter pill for most supervisors to swallow. They saw their own managers promoted on the basis of bottom-line results, and they are understandably unwilling to risk handing over even some of the authority for those results to underlings. Candid top managers are openly sympathetic. "The toughest job in this system is that of first-level manager," admits Lawrence N. Clark, director of Shaklee Corp.'s Norman plant, where work teams largely manage themselves. Traditional supervisors at the plant are now "management advisers" rather than bosses, Clark notes, and he concedes that it is a difficult transition to make. Similarly, at Ohio Bell Telephone Co., which has one of the most extensive quality-of-work-life programs in the Bell System, Douglas E. Fairbanks, general manager of operations-Southwest region, says that "insecure managers ought not to get involved with QWL."

However, companies can use the same promotion system that once rewarded the take-charge executive to reward the participatory one now. Polaroid recently promoted a supervisor who had been among the first to volunteer for participatory experiments to manager-experimental programs. Xerox's Pipp just created a new job called manager, employee worklife programs.

At GM, the new president, F. James McDonald, is known to be a quality-of-work-life enthusiast. And Alfred S. Warren

Jr., who had been a prime mover in GM's development of quality-of-work-life as a member of the personnel staff, was promoted to vice-president, industrial relations last fall. It was the first time in GM's history that the industrial relations head — who becomes the corporation's chief labor negotiator — did not advance up the ranks in labor relations. GM insiders say this was a clear signal to all of GM that cooperation was to replace conflict in the company's dealings with labor. To get into top management, says one source close to GM, "you now have to show that you can work cooperatively with the union."

GM began experimenting with participatory programs in 1970. Few other companies have had time to develop a cadre of top managers dedicated to quality of work life. But there can be other visible gestures of support. Matsushita Industrial Co. and Quasar Co. have created a "family atmosphere" through company-sponsored recreational activities, educational programs, and the like, notes MIC President Richard Kraft. Numerous CEOs are holding shirtsleeve luncheons with randomly selected workers from all levels to prove that they consider the ideas and questions of all employees to be important.

Creating the Environment

But such simple approaches are by no means sufficient. "It's not just a matter of techniques but of real philosophies," notes James J. Renier, who, since becoming president of Honeywell Inc.'s control systems business in 1978, has been proselytizing the virtues of participatory management throughout the company. "You can't just put out a memo saying 'You will be participative, you jerk,'" Renier insists.

Renier is clearly putting his money where his words are. Honeywell already has 350 quality circles involving about 4,000 employees, or 5% of the total work force. An additional 100 teams are scheduled for this year. But simultaneously, Renier has established a task force, part of whose mandate is to figure out what attributes the ideal bosses of the coming decade will need to motivate employees. "I believe people with high self-esteem are productive," Renier says. "Without a good feeling for the environment we have to create we probably don't do all we can to maximize that self-esteem."

Honeywell is actively training and encouraging managers at all levels to take the quality circles in deadly earnest. Quality circle groups are normally launched by specially trained supervisors. A plantwide steering committee of third-level managers gives prompt responses to requests for capital expenditures and makes sure that the quality circles get the support they need from manufacturing engineers and other technical people. Managers at all levels willingly attend quality circle meetings. "We simply invite them to our meetings, and they come," says Kathy Woehler, a quality circle member.

Renier, for one, candidly admits that this emphasis on participation is requiring a pretty severe change of culture at Honeywell. By contrast. Polaroid managers insist that Edwin Land fostered the idea of a participatory atmosphere since the company's inception. "The support comes by their allowing money to be spent, by their making personal appearances, and by their creating a philosophy of permissiveness that allows experiments to fail without penalty," says Mansfield Elkind, a senior manager.

Indeed, a participatory setup at the managerial level can send clear signals to workers that authoritarianism at the top will not scuttle experimentation with shared control at lower levels. At Sperry Corp., decisions that in most companies would be made by corporate vice-presidents are instead made by management councils composed of a rotating cadre of line people from each of Sperry's divisions. Council members are not necessarily the heads of their departments and thus are often faced with informing their own bosses about decisions.

The councils have been operating for well over a decade, and Sperry Chairman J. Paul Lyet notes that managers are quite used to voicing their opinions. Thus, Sperry's new quality circle program is proceeding smoothly. "You've got to have the proper corporate environment so people do not feel in awe [of authority]," he says.

Companies that are truly committed to making participation work might well heed the lessons of the 1970s. In that decade, scores of companies enthusiastically sent their managers to sensitivity training (T-group) sessions, conflict-resolution encounter groups, and the like. Their well-intentioned but nonetheless naive goal was to turn these managers into exemplary communicators and consummate "nice guys" overnight. That they would then be receptive to sharing authority seemed inevitable.

But one rarely hears about T-groups and such anymore. Their track record in changing managerial behavior was poor. And managers whose attitudes did change all too often returned to unchanged workplaces. Peer pressure — as well as the economic and promotional reward systems — caused them to revert to their old authoritarian management styles. Unless management in the 1980s continues actively to change those long-lived cues, "participatory management" could well degenerate into yet another chic catch-phrase.

The New Approach Is Already at Work

In a cramped, noisy section of a General Motors plant near Dayton, an experiment involving an eight-member work crew is testing the effectiveness of sophisticated form of worker participation. The crew is stationed at the end of a production line in which foam-rubber car seats are formed in aluminum molds. Bending over a hot conveyor line, the workers use short hoe-like tools to scrape off excess rubber "buns" that have extruded through bleeder holes in the molds. Then they remove the cushions and toss them on to another conveyor for shipping. All day long they scrape and toss, a job that plant manager Donald W. Birdsall describes as "demeaning."

To relieve the monotony of this job and to reduce costs, GM two months ago implemented a worker suggestion that had been made through a process known as the Socio-Technical System. The STS concept, developed some years ago in Britain, is a method of integrating workers' ideas for improving a job with technical requirements set by engineers. At GM's Inland Div. plant in Dayton, this process meshes the ideas of 30 hourly and salaried workers who serve on social and technical task forces, and often the "human" considerations carry equal or greater weight than the technical.

Improved Morale

In the early years of work innovations, complex projects with twin goals such as those at Inland were rare. Some managers and consultants designed programs with the primary goal of improving the human aspects of work; others insisted on an "economic" goal, such as increasing productivity. And some companies wanted to shower workers with paternal attention to keep the unions at bay. The improvement projects of the past 15 years have helped narrow the focus of the programs and have provided many lessons for today's programs.

The Socio-Technical System, for example, has mostly been used in designing new plants where planners can start from scratch. It is more difficult to apply it to an existing plant, but Inland's management thought STS would be a useful method of getting worker involvement in redesigning the seat cushion department. General Manager George Johnston believes strongly that "you gain the commitment of people when you involve them in decisions."

Local 87 of the United Rubber Workers, which represents 5,400 workers at Inland, is cooperating with GM in implementing the system. Management pledged that it would not undermine the union's contract or result in job loss. It took two years of exploratory discussions before union and management leaders decided that they could work together in complete trust. But now, says Local 87 President William Hutchins, known as "Red," "there's a less hostile environment than there's ever been."

Hutchins and two assistants, along with several plant superintendents, serve on a Redesign Committee that makes the final decision on task force proposals. Two months ago, it approved a plan by Robert Gibson, an 11-year veteran of the boring job on the so-called demold line, for improving the job and reducing costs — an example of how human and economic goals can coincide.

Gibson suggested that GM expand the work crews from seven to eight members and create the new job of a trouble-shooting monitor who would chart material usage and scrap production. The crew members rotate as the monitor, serving a week at a time before returning to the production line. Gibson contends that a hoped-for reduction in absenteeism, along with material and scrap savings, will more than offset the $30,000-per-year cost of adding a member to the crew. If the plan proves out in a current trial run, it will be used on four production lines involving 100 workers.

"Before STS started, it was always us against them [management]," Gibson says. "Now it's only us." His enthusiasm illustrates another benefit of the participation process: For workers who become involved — attending meetings and learning how to analyze problems — there is a significant improvement in job content.

Both union and company officials feel that morale has improved in the seat cushion department, and they note with some surprise that the workers' suggestions more often focus on improving the product than on personal complaints. As for sustaining the current labor-management cooperation, plant manager Birdsall asks: "If it has become a process, how can you stop it?"

The Inland program shows that management and labor can retain their adversarial systems, such as the grievance procedure, and still work cooperatively through "parallel structures," such as the Inland task forces. Many other lessons about instituting work improvements can be cited:

Human and Economic Goals. If a work improvement aims only at improving productivity, it quickly loses worker support. But a program that has only a vague plan of making workers feel better about themselves is likely to collapse for lack of business perspective. "Improved job satisfaction and improved productivity go hand in hand, and both are as important to workers as they are to managers," says Michael Sonduck of Digital Equipment.

Sidney Harman's Bolivar program, for example, was closely evaluated for a period of 56 months in the mid-1970s by Barry A. Macy, director of the Texas Center for Productivity & Quality of Work Life at Texas Tech University. Macy calculated that, after deducting the costs of implementing the program and providing benefits to workers from savings generated by higher output and other factors, the cost benefit for the company amounted to $3,000 per hourly worker. Not all programs will show such a clear benefit. "If a company goes at this merely to ring the cash register, it's going to be disappointed," concludes Inland Div.'s Johnston.

A Team Concept. In most participation programs, only a relatively few workers' representatives who volunteer for the job are actually involved in the process. But when an entire work force is organized into teams, everybody is a direct participant. Most such programs have taken place in small, nonunion plants engaged in light assembly work.

Shaklee Corp. of San Francisco adopted the "self-managed" work team concept when it opened a plant to produce nutritional products, vitamins, and other pills at Norman, Okla., in 1979. Some 190 of the nonunion plant's 230 employees are organized into 13 teams with 3 to 15 members. With a high degree of autonomy, the teams set their own production schedules based on management's volume goals. They decide what hours to work, select new team members from a pool approved by the personnel department, and even initiate discharges if necessary (three people have been fired since the plant opened).

Salaries now average $300 per week, and workers receive increases partly by demonstrating proficiency in a new skill for six months — a provision included in most team approaches that is calculated to make workers adept at many skills and thus interchangeable. William A. Ayers has worked at the Norman plant since it opened. "You aren't just told what to do," he says. "You have a sense of owning the job, and it makes you want to do a better job."

Robert L. Walter, vice-president of operations, claims that the Norman plant produces an average of 88 units (largely pills and powders) per man-hour, compared with only 30 at an older Shaklee plant. "We're producing the same volume at 40% of the labor costs," Walter says, adding that two-thirds of the production increase can be attributed to the management style and one-third to better equipment.

Butler Mfg. Co., a Kansas City-based producer of pre-engineered industrial buildings and agricultural equipment, has used work teams at a Story City (Iowa) plant since 1976. The plant, which manufactures grain driers, has 93 employees organized into teams of 5 to 12 workers. These teams set their own production goals. "The whole idea is that people adhere more to the goals they set themselves," says Michael R. Simmons, vice-president of corporate personnel. He says that man-hours required per unit were reduced by 30% to 35% in the first two years, compared with production in two other plants of the company.

Worker Receptivity. Most work innovation experts say that the diversity of worker needs must be respected. People should not be pressed into innovative work relationships against their will. Digital Equipment has made similar findings at a

Westminster, Mass., computer assembly plant. DEC started a four-member team in 1977 to assemble standup computers. The team is made up of volunteers from four different skill areas. Each taught the others his job, and now they can switch jobs at random.

Joseph B. Daly, a production manager, says to assemble a computer the team needs only 25% the space an assembly line takes. Cycle time improved by 60%, and output per employee increased "slightly," he says. The team manages its own workplace without close supervision, and its members seem to like the responsibility that comes with directing their own work. "It's better to work under these circumstances because you have a feeling of companionship," says 57-year-old Roy W. Bouley.

But the company has found that only about 65% of other workers are interested in team work. Since it involves defining their own workplace, "some people were complaining that it wasn't clear what their responsibilities were," Daly says. The company plans to extend the concept this summer where it can.

Institutionalizing Changes. "You have to allow time for people to adjust to new relationships," says Gene Kofke, director of work relationships at AT&T. "The worst enemy that quality of work life has is the impatience for quick and finite results." AT&T and the Communications Workers agreed last year to create a national committee to help CWA locals and Bell System companies establish problem-solving committees and other innovations. On Apr. 24, after many months of talks, the company and the union agreed on a set of guiding principles. "You measure the success of these things in years," Kofke adds. "Our management is willing to wait."

Even with projects that show results relatively quickly, management must display patience during the early stages of problem-solving meetings as workers test the company's sincerity. At Malden Mills's Lawrence plant, Paul Chaisson, who heads the innovation efforts, says both management and the union must make "a very long-term commitment, or the new process will die." The $200 million-a-year textile manufacturer wants to improve its work relationships because it foresees a shrinking labor pool in Lawrence as more high-technology companies move into the area. The International Ladies' Garment Workers Union agreed to cooperate in setting up problem-solving groups, and the company brought in the Northeast Labor-Management Center, a Boston-based organization with experience as a "facilitator" of work innovations.

Malden Mills first established seven core groups with about 15 members each in its Retail Div., where fabric manufactured in the mills is inspected, packed, and shipped. This division had had high turnover and absenteeism and other labor problems, and it was decided to allow the workers to raise issues of importance to them when the core groups started meeting last year. The first six months was a purgative period; the workers focused on long-festering complaints about working conditions, apparently testing management's commitment to solve problems.

But last fall the groups suddenly began addressing problems involving cost reductions and improved quality. "When it gets started, people have an appetite for improving the work that explodes," Chaisson says. "Every place we've started this, it goes like a flash fire."

The workers made suggestions about the use of materials and tools, and by last January the percentage of correct fabric inspections had risen to 94%, up from 88% a year ago. One group of 17 inspectors formed a semi-autonomous team and set their own weekly production goal of inspecting 13,500 lb. of cloth — a target 1,500 lb. higher than that management had previously set — and met it. Turnover was cut from an annual rate of 200% two years ago to less than 10% this year.

One of the packers in the Retail Div., 20-year-old Jack O'Keefe, says that "people are getting involved and staying on the job because management is listening to them. They know they can speak up now without worrying about getting fired." Carolyn O'Brien, 24, a department manager, says: "I used to be very autocratic and thought that if people were given a lot of leeway, they'd take advantage of it. Now the people are supervising themselves, and I can be more creative in finding new ways to improve quality."

Union Involvement. The work-innovation movement will continue to grow without organized labor's cooperation although union involvement would help immeasurably. Many union officials, including the AFL-CIO's top leaders, are still reluctant to advocate openly and strongly any concept that tastes of the hated word "collaboration." Within individual unions, small pockets of resistance exist among radical leftists who oppose what they perceive as quality-of-work-life's surrender of shop-floor worker power to management.

But the evidence is growing that rank-and-file workers for the most part want to be more deeply involved in their work and have an unerring ability to spot exploitative schemes. As Sidney Harman says: "You can't fraudulently create a program without being seen through sooner or later." While it is true that workers do not specifically ask their union leaders to negotiate a provision called "quality of work life" in their contracts, most recent surveys of workers' attitudes confirm that they want something more from their jobs — and of their unions — than wages, benefits,

and job security. Most of all, says the UAW's Bluestone, they do not want to go to work merely to be "an adjunct to a tool."

Almost universally, effective work-innovation programs result in a dramatic speedup in management's settling of grievances — and this means quicker justice for workers. And Bluestone cites a striking piece of evidence for the growing rank-and-file support for quality of work life: In every plant where the UAW is cooperating in a successful program, local UAW leaders who pushed it have been reelected.

In Dayton, the UAW's Red Hutchins perceives another important benefit for workers. About 90% of his members, who are not "perennial grievers," see little relevance of the union to their day-to-day lives at work. "This is the guy who wants to do a good job and who will be helped most by quality of work life," Hutchins says. "When we participate on these committees, it's a way of giving service to a guy who's never had service before."

Clearly, a changed social and economic environment in the U.S. demands that labor and management create a new relationship. The lessons provided by the pioneers of work innovations prove that changes in work processes and structures are not only possible, they can be highly successful. Most of all, they show that the U.S. industrial relations system, so long arrested at primitive levels of development, can now evolve into a third stage — a participative stage.

Questions for Discussion

To focus the classroom discussion, assume that you are the vice president of HRM/IR for a typical Fortune 500 firm that operates in a diverse array of markets and has both unionized and nonunion plants. Your chief executive officer has read the *Business Week* article and asked you for your views on its potential relevance for your HRM/IR strategy. The CEO would like to discuss with you the following questions:

1. Should our firm develop a new HRM/IR strategy along the lines suggested in the article?
2. If so, what goals should guide it and how should we go about implementing it? How should we evaluate its effectiveness?
3. If not, why not?

Multiple Interests and Human Resource Management

This case describes a critical set of decisions faced by the International Harvester Company as it went through a difficult restructuring process in the early 1980s in an effort to stave off bankruptcy. The case is presented at the outset of our study of HRM/IR because it illustrates the diverse sets of interests that are affected by any major strategic business decision, especially one that involves the closing of a plant. While the severity of the economic crisis and the magnitude of the organizational restructuring this firm experienced were extreme, similar decisions have confronted most manufacturing firms as they attempt to adapt to changing markets and increasingly competitive environments in the 1980s. The case also illustrates that the different interests affected by major decisions do not always fall neatly into a labor versus management dichotomy.

CASE

The International Harvester Company

THE BACKGROUND

In 1977 Archie McCardell left his position as first in command at the Xerox Corporation for the top spot at the International Harvester Company (IH). In April 1978 he told *Dun's Review,* "I took the job . . . for three reasons: more money, the immediate chance to run a multibillion-dollar corporation, and the challenge of improving the performance of one of the stodgiest companies in the industry." The money was substantial: $460,000 base salary, a $1.5 million up-front bonus, and a $1.8 million loan (at 6 percent) to buy IH stock. The loan would be forgiven if financial ratios were brought up to the level of IH's competitors.

As detailed in the accompanying series of clippings and articles, McCardell's time at IH was tumultuous and rather short-lived. After approximately forty-five months at the helm of IH, McCardell was replaced as Chairman and CEO in May 1982. Several temporary victories for McCardell in his restructuring and new management style were overshadowed by, among other things, his failure successfully to negotiate a contract with the United Automobile Workers (UAW). A six-month strike followed, which further hobbled the ailing company.

IH was not in an enviable industry position from either the perspective of its labor contract with the UAW or that of its financial position and credibility with the banking community.

Labor relations at IH were rarely peaceful or harmonious, and certainly never cooperative. An early low point occurred in 1886 when several persons were killed in a demonstration that was due in part to a strike at the Chicago plant of IH's McCormick works. The strike coincided with organized labor demonstrations for an eight-hour day, culminating in the Haymarket Riots, during which a number of police officers and some demonstrators were killed as a bomb was set off. Exactly who set off the bomb and for what reason were never settled to the satisfaction of historians, although several labor leaders were convicted and several hanged.

The UAW organized its first IH plant in the early 1940s and negotiated its first "master contract" in 1950. The relationship could be characterized as paternalistic, in that the company initiated liberal policies on voluntary overtime and on bumping and transfer rights. These policies essentially allowed employees to turn down overtime and to move upward, downward, or laterally within their bargaining unit any time an opening occurred. These practices were not followed by IH's main competitors, John Deere and Caterpillar, who retained the right to assign overtime, to limit transfers, and to require temporary layoffs. Over the years, the liberal policies led to a competitive disadvantage for IH. For example, in some instances the union would declare a ban on overtime in response to a pending grievance, and often management would back down on the grievance so that the union would withdraw the ban. Moreover, the policies on bumping caused great disruption in the plants. Whenever an employee switched jobs, it created a domino effect, as illustrated at one plant where there were 4,500 bargaining unit employees and no less than 28,000 job moves based on employee requests in the space of a single year.

During the 1960s a "new look" was proposed at IH plants with the aims of reducing the number of written grievances and encouraging their settlement at the shop-floor level. Although the new approach worked to a certain extent, IH was still in an adversarial relationship with the UAW, while Deere and Caterpillar were considered the "innovator" and the "good-faith follower," respectively.

Business strategy also began to affect IH negatively in the 1960s and 1970s with the firm's increasing focus on diversification rather than innovation within existing product lines. Further, older plants were not modernized, investment levels were low, and Deere began to gain a share of the market in one of IH's most profitable lines, farm implements. IH's Board of Directors felt that hiring McCardell away from Xerox in 1977 would turn things around. McCardell had a reputation as a tough manager, and Xerox had experienced relatively quiet and cooperative labor relations with its union, the Amalgamated Clothing and Textile Workers Union. Yet McCardell made little attempt to get to know the UAW leadership, or personally to hammer out agreements that might turn IH around. Pat Greathouse, the UAW vice president in charge of IH, commented, "McCardell didn't know any of us."

After the six-month strike in 1979, the situation at IH worsened, as illustrated by Exhibit 1-2, excerpted from an April 1982 article in *Fortune*. Not only did IH's stock prices drop dramatically, but worldwide employment at IH fell from 93,358 in October 1979 (before the strike) to about 45,000 just three years later.

EXHIBIT 1-2
Forgiveness Comes Hard

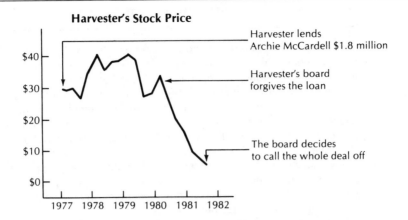

Harvester's Stock Price

Harvester lends
Archie McCardell $1.8 million

Harvester's board
forgives the loan

The board decides
to call the whole deal off

It may have seemed sound when it was drafted in 1977, but Harvester's incentive contract with Chief Executive Archie McCardell has since become a running embarrassment that has antagonized investors and employees. In February the board decided in exasperation to "unwind" the whole bollixed affair.

In winning McCardell from the presidency of Xerox, Harvester gave him a cash bonus of $1.5 million and also lent him $1.8 million with which to buy Harvester stock. In each of the next seven years the board would have the option of forgiving a portion of the loan, never more than a quarter in any one year. Whether the board could exercise its option depended on a formula measuring Harvester's performance against that of six competitors. McCardell would pay 6% interest on the unforgiven balance.

Harvester's 1978 results didn't measure up, but 1979's results were deemed to be so good that the board forgave the *entire* loan, with the forgiveness to take effect in five equal annual installments — essentially paper transactions.

Outrage over the forgiveness grew as Harvester's fortunes fell, and the board has now decided to return to the way things were before it made the loan. It hasn't said how it plans to get back to square one, however, and it won't be an easy trip. One apparent solution would be for McCardell to give back the stock and call things even. But that won't work because the board specified that the unwinding can't leave the company worse off — and McCardell's stock is now worth only a small fraction of the $1.8 million Harvester lent him (see chart).

McCardell could simply be required to pay back the $1.8 million, but that might be more punishment than the board wants to inflict. After getting dividends from his stock, paying interest on the unforgiven balance of the loan, and paying taxes on the two annual forgiveness installments he has received, he's out $320,000 after taxes, assuming a 50% tax rate. If he sold out, he'd just about get his $320,000 back and would have a huge capital loss to offset any capital gains he might have — but he'd still owe $1.8 million.

However the matter is settled, it will probably cost McCardell plenty. Given the condition of the company, some would argue that the contract has done its work after all.

Source: "International Harvester's Last Chance," in *Fortune,* April 19, 1982, p. 108. Copyright © 1982 by Time, Inc. All rights reserved.

EXHIBIT 1-3
States Court Harvester

The state governments of Indiana and Ohio are dangling multimillion-dollar financing packages before the International Harvester Company in a duel over which state will lose a truck-assembly plant operated by Harvester.

At stake in Indiana is a truck-assembly plant in Fort Wayne that employs about 4,500 workers. The Ohio plant, located in Springfield, employs about 2,200.

Indiana's governor, Robert D. Orr, met Monday with Harvester officials in Chicago. Allen County, in which Fort Wayne is located, is seeking $15 million in aid from the state.

In Ohio, state officials are considering a $30 million financing package.

Harvester, anticipating losses of about $1 billion this fiscal year, recently announced it must close or consolidate more operations and obtain greater concessions from lenders to pay off its $4.2 billion debt.

A Harvester spokeswoman, Annette De Lorenzo, said the company would make a decision in the next two to four weeks on which plant to close.

Source: The New York Times, August 10, 1982. Copyright © 1982 by The New York Times Company. Reprinted by permission.

By the summer of 1982 the remaking of IH was still under way, with several crucial decisions yet to be made. The manufacturing facilities had been somewhat streamlined, some divisions had been sold or closed, and the debt structure had been changed to allow for continued operations.

THE CHOICES

Among the decisions the corporation still faced were whether and how to close one of two truck assembly plants — one located in Springfield, Ohio, and the other in Fort Wayne, Indiana. (A third plant, located in Chatham, Ontario, was not involved.) Pressures from creditors and stockholders mandated action to prevent further losses in the truck business. Retail sales of heavy trucks had declined 17.6 percent between August 1981 and August 1982. Exhibits 1-3 and 1-4 offer snapshots of IH's decision-making parameters in 1982.

Springfield, with a total population of 75,000, had an unemployment rate of 13.5 percent. The IH truck assembly plant in Springfield employed 2,200 workers, down from 5,000 about a year before. In an effort to save the plant, the state of Ohio, together with a consortium of eleven local banks, developed a $30 million financing package that entailed purchasing the plant and then leasing it back to IH. The Springfield plant, fifteen years old, was newer than the Fort Wayne plant and had lower long-range operating expenses and lower fringe benefit costs.

Fort Wayne, with a total population of 175,000, had an unemployment rate of 12 percent. Community leaders in Fort Wayne similarly wanted to save

EXHIBIT 1-4

Harvester Changes Structure as It Tries to Pare Operations

International Harvester Co., announced a corporate restructuring as the first step in its previously reported plan to shrink operations and concentrate on making trucks and farm machinery.

The ailing company, which is currently negotiating the sale of its construction-equipment business, said it will reorganize into a Truck Group, an Agricultural Equipment Group and Administrative Services Group. In addition, it said, a new Diversified Group will carry out the planned disposal of various operations.

The restructuring comes less than a year after a previous reorganization. Under that plan, Harvester was organized into a Manufacturing Group responsible for all North American manufacturing operations, a Truck Group responsible for truck sales and overseas manufacturing and an Equipment Group responsible for farm and construction-equipment sales and overseas manufacturing.

In announcing the latest reorganization, Harvester said J. Patrick Kaine, executive vice president of the company and president of the Truck Group, was named executive vice president for truck and agricultural-equipment operations: Neil A. Springer, vice president and general manager of North American truck operations, was named president of the Truck Group and Jack D. Michaels, president of the former Equipment Group, was named president of the Agricultural Equipment Group.

In a separate development, Fort Wayne, Ind., officials yesterday presented Harvester with a new $22 million aid proposal they hope will persuade the company to keep making trucks there. Details weren't immediately available.

Harvester has said it will close one of its three North American truck plants, situated in Fort Wayne, Springfield, Ohio, and Chatham, Ontario, and has indicated that the choice is between Fort Wayne and Springfield. The company is a major employer in both cities.

Springfield has proposed a $30 million aid package: Fort Wayne earlier offered a $9.5 million plan. Both call for combined private-sector and local-government initiatives centering on purchase of a local Harvester plant, which would then be leased back to the company.

Source: The Wall Street Journal, August 18, 1982. Reprinted by permission of *The Wall Street Journal,* © Dow Jones & Company, Inc. (1982). All Rights Reserved.

---

the plant and had put together a financial package to do so. After learning of Springfield's plan, the Fort Wayne group raised its package from $9 million to about $30 million (borrowed from local and state government). Like the Springfield package, the Fort Wayne proposal provided for purchase and lease-back.

With IH, the UAW has traditionally negotiated a master contract covering all UAW-represented employees of IH. Although local unions have negotiated supplemental agreements covering plant-specific issues like seniority, major contract language, including wage levels, have been negotiated by the international union. Historically, the UAW has used pattern bargaining similar to that used in the automobile industry, where bargaining is targeted at one company and then extended to the main competitors. In this industry, the UAW has attempted to retain relative parity among IH, Deere, and Caterpillar.

The parties of interest in the decision to close one of the plants included the top management, the UAW, two state economic development committees and their governors, two UAW local unions, the creditors of IH, and the employees in each plant.[2]

Questions for Discussion

Assume that you are the spokesperson for one of the groups affected by the company's decision. What policy option would you recommend to the Board of Directors of IH? What data would you use to support your recommendations? The various groups are as follows:

1. The corporate management of IH
2. The creditors of IH
3. The national office of the UAW
4. The UAW local union at the Springfield plant (representing 2,200 workers)
5. The UAW local union at the Fort Wayne plant (representing 4,500 workers)
6. The governor's office in Ohio (with the state economic development committee)
7. The governor's office in Indiana (with the state economic development committee)

[2]More details on the financial position of the company and the targeted plants can be found in the following series of articles published in *Fortune*.

"The Strike That Rained On Archie McCardell's Parade," by Carol J. Loomis, *Fortune*, May 19, 1980.

"Archie McCardell's Absolution," by Carol J. Loomis, *Fortune*, December 15, 1980.

"Hard Times For Truck Makers," by Andrew C. Brown, *Fortune*, September 7, 1981.

"International Harvester's Last Chance," by Geoffrey Colvin, *Fortune*, April 19, 1982.

2

The Environment of
Human Resource Management
and Industrial Relations

The environment represents those interrelated factors that are external to a firm and are capable of affecting the conduct and results of HRM/IR, and therefore the firm as a whole. Any organization must acquire resources from its environment (capital, labor, customers, clients, social or political support, etc.) and must return outputs to the environment (goods and services, jobs, clean air, safe products, etc.). The outputs must be sufficiently valued by enough people to attract the inputs needed for survival and growth. While we will not attempt to provide an exhaustive list of all the environmental forces that can affect HRM/IR, we will focus here on three key factors: (1) economic conditions and policies, (2) the laws and public policies governing employment, and (3) the demographic characteristics and work values of the labor force. (In Chapter 3, we will examine a fourth and increasingly important external factor, new technology affecting the workplace.) All these factors influence HRM/IR policies and can stimulate the need for changes in those policies over time.

Implicit in our model is the view that there is no single best set of HRM/IR policies; rather, the test of a good set of policies is the extent to which the policies are congruent with and suited to their environment. *Variations* in the environment help produce *diversity* in the policies and practices as seen across firms and labor organizations. Over time, *changes* in environmental characteristics in turn put pressure on firms, unions, government policymakers, and workers to *adapt*, thus giving the HRM/IR system its dynamic character.

Yet changes in the environment do not automatically translate into changes in HRM/IR policies and practices. Indeed, as we will see later in this book, inertia and resistance to change are often built into the practices and behaviors of organizations, groups, and individuals. Thus, it is necessary to monitor and interpret the current environment and to predict future environmental changes in order to assess current practices, initiate policy revisions, or establish longer-term planning processes. In some organizations these activities are referred to as environmental scanning. But whatever the term, those activities are the first step in any HRM/IR planning process, and as such provide the next stage in our study of HRM/IR systems.

The Economic Environment

The economic environment can be viewed as made up of micro- and macro-level factors. While no single group of workers is always affected in the same way by broad macroeconomic trends, these economywide developments set the outside limits on the ability of the parties to control their own destinies.

Macroeconomic Forces

Four sets of macroeconomic policies of the federal government are shown in Figure 2-1 as being particularly important to the conduct of HRM/IR: (1) government fiscal, or spending, policy; (2) monetary policies of the Federal Reserve Board; (3) formal or informal incomes policies adopted from time to time by different administrations; and (4) federal policies that influence international and domestic trade and investment, often called industrial policies. These four kinds of policies influence the overall rates of inflation, unemployment, and economic growth, which in turn influence HRM/IR activities in four key ways. First, the macroeconomic context shapes the expectations of workers and employers about future economic events, such as the appropriate level of compensation increases for a given year, or the net increases or decreases in staffing or employment levels that will be required. Second, macroeconomic conditions influence the bargaining power of

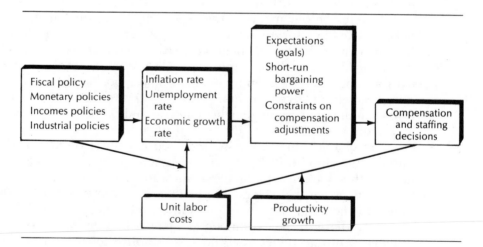

FIGURE 2-1   Simplified Model of Macroeconomic Policies on HRM/IR Decisions

individuals and collective groups in the labor market, since those conditions determine the supply of alternative job opportunities available in the economy. Third, macroeconomic policies and conditions either directly or indirectly constrain workers' and employers' discretion in making compensation decisions. This effect is illustrated by incomes policies whereby federal government wage and/or price "guidelines" may directly limit the increases in compensation allowable in a given year. Fourth, industrial policies are targeted at specific industries or firms, and therefore also have a direct effect on the employment prospects of companies operating in these industries.

A full discussion of the implications of firm-level compensation and employment decisions for the performance of the economy at large lies beyond the scope of this book. However, it is important to keep in mind that the combined decisions of employers, labor organizations, and individual workers feed back to affect these macroeconomic variables and the efforts of the federal government to control them. For example, Figure 2-1 illustrates how compensation and employment-level changes influence unit labor costs if they are not offset by corresponding increases in productivity. To the extent that compensation growth outpaces productivity growth throughout the economy, "cost push" inflation may result. This in turn will put pressure on federal policymakers to tighten the money supply and/or reduce the rate of government spending in order to bring down the rate of inflation. In this manner the interrelated cycle of events between firm-level decisions and macroeconomic policies and conditions comes full circle, and its effects carry over into the future.

Recent Macro Trends and Micro Responses

To illustrate the relationship between broad movements in the macroeconomy and HRM/IR decisions at the micro level, let us briefly review the economic history of the post-1960 period. Table 2-1 presents some basic summary data on movements in prices, unemployment, productivity, unit labor costs, and compensation for the period 1964–1982, and relates them to the general macroeconomic policies in effect during each year.

Between 1962 and 1968 the economy enjoyed sustained economic growth, largely as a result of a tax cut in 1962 and increased government spending to finance the war in Vietnam and the expansion of President Johnson's Great Society programs. The early to mid-1960s also benefited from a continuation of the post–World War II trend in productivity growth — roughly 3 percent (a rate that, as we will see, could not be sustained through the 1970s and into the current period). During the Kennedy-Johnson years the prevailing wage and price (or "incomes") policies consisted either of voluntary guidelines or of a form of not-so-gentle persuasion euphemistically known as jawboning. Partly as a result of these policies, collective bargaining settlements and compensation increases remained rather modest, staying below 7 percent

TABLE 2-1 Macroeconomic History, 1964–1982 (All numbers are in percents)

Year	Inflation Rate (Consumer Price Index)	Unemployment Rate	Increase in Average Hourly Compensation	Wage Increase in Collective Bargaining in Major Settlements*	Productivity Increase (Output per Worker-hour)	Unit Labor Cost Increases
1964	1.2	5.2	5.2	3.2	4.3	0.8
1965	1.9	4.5	3.9	3.8	3.5	0.3
1966	3.4	3.8	7.0	4.8	3.1	3.8
1967	3.0	3.8	5.3	5.6	2.2	3.0
1968	4.7	3.6	7.8	7.4	3.3	4.4
1969	6.1	3.5	7.0	9.2	0.2	6.7
1970	5.5	4.9	7.3	11.9	0.8	6.4
1971	3.4	5.9	6.6	11.7	3.6	2.9
1972	3.4	5.6	6.5	7.3	3.5	2.9
1973	8.8	4.9	8.0	5.8	2.6	5.3
1974	12.2	5.6	9.4	9.8	2.4	12.1
1975	7.0	8.6	9.6	10.2	2.2	7.3
1976	4.8	7.7	8.6	8.2	3.3	5.1
1977	6.8	7.0	7.7	7.8	2.4	5.1
1978	9.0	5.8	8.6	7.6	0.6	8.0
1979	13.3	5.8	9.7	7.4	-0.9	10.7
1980	12.4	7.1	10.4	9.5	-0.7	11.2
1981	8.9	7.6	9.6	9.8	1.8	7.7
1982	3.9	9.7	7.3	3.8	0.4	6.9

*Figures for 1964–1967 are median increases, since averages were not available for these years. All figures are wage increases in the first year of the contract for bargaining units of 1,000 or more employees.

Source: All data are taken from Bureau of Labor Statistics reports except those for Productivity Increase and Unit Labor Cost Increases, which are taken from the *Economic Report of the President,* January 1983.

through 1968, even though the rate of inflation was beginning to rise to what at the time appeared to be unacceptably high levels — more than 4 percent! As a result, by 1966 and 1967 union leaders began to be pressured by rank-and-file workers whose expectations were fueled by the rising cost of living, and whose bargaining power was strengthened by low levels of unemployment and the strong demand for the goods they were producing. (Employers are always hesitant to take a strike during periods of growing demand, since production losses result in an inability to capitalize on markets that are ready to absorb as much as can be delivered.)

By 1968 union leaders and employers in both the union and the nonunion sectors began to respond to rising employee expectations and labor market pressures by granting more liberal wage and benefit increases. This response was facilitated by the shift to the more conservative economic policies of the Nixon administration, which lifted wage and price guidelines and incomes policies of all kinds. The 1970s then saw an explosion in wages, starting in the unionized construction industry and spreading to other parts of both union and nonunion sectors of the economy. Combined with this development was a gradual upward movement in consumer prices and unemployment, the rise in unemployment resulting from the government's efforts to use tight monetary and fiscal policies to control the rate of inflation. However, as the data in Table 2-1 indicate, these aggregate policies did not have the desired effects on the compensation policies of firms, unions, and workers. The pressures became great enough by mid-1971 that the Nixon administration shifted to a strong, mandatory form of incomes policy: wage and price controls.

Thus, mid-1971 marked the beginning of another key historical period, one of experimentation with direct controls, and one that lasted until early 1974, when controls were lifted. During the period of controls, wages were somewhat restrained, particularly in the more visible sectors where collective bargaining took place. However, as the rate of increases in compensation for the post-controls period of 1974–1976 illustrates, a catch-up process followed when the controls were lifted. Once again, employers and unions could satisfy the pent-up expectations of workers without triggering any strong governmental reactions.

Experimentation with looser forms of incomes policies continued during the later part of the 1970s, as the federal government struggled to cope with the perplexing effects of persistent inflation and high unemployment, which derived partly from the oil price increases of the 1970s. These efforts were, however, largely ineffective. The result was a return to higher levels of wage increases through collective bargaining and, by 1980, an expansion of the union/nonunion wage and labor cost differential.

The legacy of the macroeconomic policies of the 1970s appears to be relatively unimpressive. Neither the rises in unemployment caused by tight monetary and fiscal policies nor the periodic use of incomes policies had more than marginal, temporary effects on the compensation policies of United States firms or on the collective bargaining behaviors of workers, unions, and employers. Accordingly, as the nation entered the 1980s, a great debate ensued among economists and policymakers concerning future economic policies for controlling inflation, restoring productivity growth, and more generally regaining the country's international competitive position, which had diminished incrementally during the 1970s.

In the early 1980s the Reagan administration resolved this debate with the most controversial and drastic set of changes in economic and social policies encountered since the New Deal. A tight monetary policy was accompanied by deep cuts in social spending, a 25 percent cut in income taxes spread over three years, and large increases in defense spending. The theory behind the approach, known as supply-side economics, was that tax cuts would unleash sufficient economic activity to restore productivity and economic growth rates to their 1960 levels, and that this in turn would make up for the drop in governmental revenues caused by the tax reduction.

In fact, the American economy witnessed an increase in unemployment to a post-Depression record of 10.8 percent by December 1982, as well as record governmental budget deficits. The Reagan policy did, however, send sufficient shock waves through the economy to change the compensation behavior of firms, the collective bargaining behaviors of employers and unions, and the expectations of workers. As Table 2-1 illustrates, the annual rate of wage increase in collective bargaining settlements in 1982 was only 3.8 percent, compared with 9.8 percent in the previous year. Later in this book we will refer to 1982 as part of an era of concession bargaining, in that major unions were forced by high levels of unemployment and by severe economic crises to accept wage freezes, and in some cases wage cuts. Nonunion firms in those sectors hit hardest by the economic environment were similarly forced to freeze or cut wages in response to the economic climate.

Consequently, in the present period of the mid-1980s, one central issue has emerged for both macro policymakers and the decision makers responsible for compensation and staffing policies within organizations. The questions are whether the "inflationary expectations" of the 1970s have finally been broken, and whether the pressures affecting the core rate of inflation are sufficiently moderate to usher in a period of sustained economic growth, once more allowing for moderate price increases. Alternatively, is the nation simply facing another temporary period of wage and price restraints, which will end as soon as the economy recovers?

The answers to these questions have been clouded by the effects of another macroeconomic development of the 1970s, one not captured in the preceding review of cyclical events: the growing internationalization of the world economy. The decline of American exports and the growth of imports in such domestic industries as steel, autos, and machine tools have produced a debate about the future viability of American "smokestack industries." This has resulted in widespread consideration of the need for another type of macroeconomic policy, namely an industrial policy. While the phrase "industrial policy" is used in a variety of ways, it essentially refers to trade, tax, and investment policies designed to promote certain sectors of the economy. Tax credits for capital investment; import quotas on steel, garments, autos, and other goods; and loan guarantees to firms in specific industries are all examples of industrial policies.

The debate over whether the United States should have a comprehensive industrial policy (*Business Week*, 1982) centers on two issues: (1) Should the government play an active role in promoting some industries over others, and (2) if so, which industries should be favored? Proponents of a formal policy argue that our major trading partners and competitors, such as Japan and leading European countries like Germany and France, have conscious national strategies that subsidize key sectors and that place United States firms at a competitive disadvantage. Proponents further argue that there is already an implicit set of industrial policies in the Reagan administration's increases in the defense budget during the early 1980s. But critics respond that any government interventions designed to promote or subsidize specific sectors are bound to distort market forces, and ultimately will reduce economic growth by misallocating resources.

Microeconomic Forces

How do these broad macro forces and policies get translated into specific impacts on particular companies? Answering this question serves as the second step in the planning process — the assessment of the specific product and labor market conditions that will influence the HRM/IR plans and policies of a given organization.

Product Market Issues.   A full treatment of the economics of product markets, or even of the effects of differential market characteristics on employment policies, lies well beyond the scope of this book; indeed, those issues provide the central focus of the study and practice of corporate strategy and policy. Since we are stressing the need for a closer connection between corporate business strategies and HRM/IR policies and practices, we will concern ourselves with two key variables that influence this linkage: the effects of product market characteristics and their interactions with general business strategies.

The product market is external to an organization and influences HRM/IR policies in two general ways. First, the degree of competition in the product market sets the upper limits on a firm's discretion in pricing any factor of production, including human resource wages. This leads to the general proposition that the more competitive the product market, the more pressures there will be on the firm to economize on the use and the cost of its human resources. This proposition has implications both for the acceptable level of costs and for the availability of resources for experimentation with innovative policies having uncertain payoffs. Thus, we tend to see higher compensation levels and a higher degree of innovation and human resource policy experimentation in firms operating in less competitive environments. Such firms experience a certain measure of discretion, or, as the organizational behavior literature refers to it, organizational slack (Schein, 1979).

Second, the priorities given to different HRM/IR functions and goals tend to vary over the life cycle of a product or an industry. Specifically, these priorities vary with the type of competitive strategy driving the firm (Porter, 1980). Although this point is developed in greater detail in Chapter 4, it is sufficient to note here that in the early stages of a product cycle, innovation in all areas of the organization is key to the start-up and take-off of the firm. Later, the ability to produce at high volumes in a predictable and reliable fashion, and to meet delivery goals for an expanding market, take on greater importance. Finally, in the mature stages of a product or industry, cost minimization tends to form a more critical part of the competitive strategy of the firm. HRM/IR practices become a focal point for cost control, since compensation and staffing are typically among the largest controllable and semivariable costs of production.

Labor Market Forces.   The labor market exerts an obvious impact on the design and implementation of HRM/IR plans and policies through the supply and demand conditions for different types of labor. Variations in the *supply* of labor are treated more fully in the next section of this chapter. The critical issues on the *demand* side of the labor market are the number of jobs required to meet the goals of the organization, the mix or design of those jobs (and their interrelationships), and the duration of the employment opportunities the firm has to offer.

Traditional economic analysis would consider these issues simple derivatives of the demand for an organization's products and the state of existing technology. For our purposes, however, it is more useful to recognize that the firm has a range of choices in how to mix different levels of technology or capital together with workers of different skill levels, and how to set employment levels and entry-level hiring standards in ways that consider both short-run production needs and long-run prospects for employment continuity. That is, increasingly labor is being viewed more as a fixed or quasi-fixed obligation that cannot be adjusted to each short-run fluctuation in product demand without incurring significant costs and severe human hardships. Indeed, one of the most impressive and progressive innovations in human resource management policies to emerge in recent years is some firms' growing commitment to employment continuity (see the reading by Dyer et al. in Chapter 6). At the same time, the use of temporary help, consulting and related services, and part-time employment has been increasing.

Both sets of developments leave firms with a broad array of choices in organizing the human resources required to produce a given set of products or services. Thus, forecasting the demand for labor to meet an organization's future needs requires an assessment of the consequences for organizations and individual workers with respect to alternative production functions, organizational designs, forms of work organization, job and career structures, and employment relationships.

Labor Force Demographics

The influence of the demographic characteristics of the labor force permeates all aspects of HRM/IR. Changes in the age, education, and occupational and regional distribution of the labor force tend to occur in long and slow but relatively predictable patterns. Therefore, these trends can be tracked reasonably easily and assessed with respect to their implications for the supply of labor available to an organization in the short and medium run. What makes the analysis of demographic trends more challenging, however, is the interaction among these relatively predictable numerical trends, on the one hand, and the following factors, on the other: (1) changes in the labor force participation decisions of different cohorts (particularly females, the very young who must decide between additional schooling and employment options, and the very old who must decide between work and retirement); (2) variations in the work values and expectations of different cohorts; and (3) shifts in technology, market conditions, and government policies that affect the demand for labor. Understanding the movements and pressures associated with the demographic characteristics of the work force is fundamental to HRM/IR planning. Thus, in this section we will begin by reviewing the key demographic trends affecting the current and future work force, and then present an up-to-date analysis of the values, expectations, and attitudes of various groups in the work force.

Figure 2-2 presents a framework for tracing the effects of demographic characteristics through the HRM/IR system of a given organization. The model builds on earlier research on the process of work adjustment (Lofquist and Dawis, 1969). Worker characteristics like age, education, race, sex, and prior work and family experiences interact with workers' values and expectations and with their decisions about whether to enter the labor force on a permanent, temporary, part-time, or full-time basis. These characteristics place varying demands on the HRM/IR policies of an organization. Employers, in turn, have expectations of workers and place demands on new employees to adapt to organizational norms and needs (Van Maanen and Schein, 1980). If there is a match between work force expectations and demands, on the one hand, and the policies supplied by the employer, on the other, a smooth work adjustment process can be expected. To the extent that there is a mismatch, and either workers are not socialized into the existing system or the system fails to adapt to the existing work force

Demographic Content

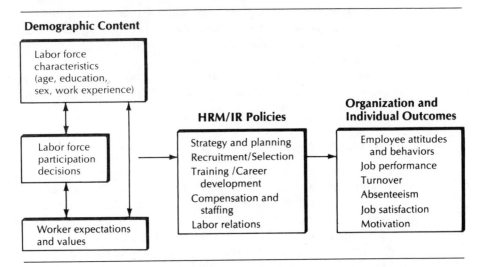

FIGURE 2-2   Effects of Demographic Characteristics on a HRM/IR System

expectations, we can expect problems concerning the attitudes and behaviors of workers and malfunctions in the HRM/IR system (Kanter, 1978). We will trace several examples of this process of adjustment as we review recent trends in work force demographics and worker values.

Labor Force Trends

The labor force has grown at unprecedented rates since World War II because of a combination of the postwar baby boom of the late 1940s and early 1950s and the increase in the labor force participation rate of women (i.e., the percentage of the female population choosing to work or looking for work). The dominant change in the characteristics of both males and females entering the labor force over this period, in comparison with their predecessors, is their higher levels of formal education. Although it is popularly believed that workers who entered the labor force over the past decade or so have different social values and expectations from those of their predecessors — largely because they did not experience the hardships of the Depression, and grew up in the turbulent sociopolitical climate of the 1960s — the evidence does not strongly support this notion, as we shall see.

The rapid rate of growth in the labor force during the 1970s has now subsided somewhat, mainly because the baby boom has been absorbed into the labor force. We are now experiencing the effects of the slowdown in population growth that began in the late 1950s and continued into the early 1980s. The labor force grew at an annual rate of 2.3 percent in the first half of the 1970s but slowed to 1.9 percent near the end of the decade, and has fallen to approximately 1.0 percent in the first half of the 1980s. Given the low birthrates of the past two decades, we can expect a continued real decline in the number of workers between the ages of sixteen and twenty-four for some time to come. Thus, while the problems of coping with large numbers of new entrants into the labor force dominated public and private policy discussions in recent years, we can expect that the central problem facing organizations in the future will be coping with the baby boom bulge as it moves through its prime working and career development years. (As the selection from *The New York Times* in Box 2-1 notes, however, the problem of teenage unemployment will continue to be severe and potentially explosive.)

Two problems will intensify the difficulties experienced by the baby boom cohort as its members compete to move up their career or job ladders. First, the sluggish rates of domestic and international economic growth over the past decade have led to a slower rate of job creation than was seen in the 1960s. Thus, while in the 1970s MBAs, for example, watched with enthusiasm as their job opportunities expanded and compensation levels rose, the MBAs of the 1980s will find a large "plug" created by their immediate seniors, who are now moving more slowly up the corporate ladder and creating fewer entry-level and middle-management positions and opportunities for promotion. Second — and this factor has not shown any significant effect yet, but is a potential deterrent to promotional opportunities — is the elimination of mandatory retirement at age sixty-five, as required by a 1979 amendment to the Age Discrimination in Employment Act of 1967. The labor force participation rates for both men and women continued their downward trends during the early years of this law. But the potential for workers to stay in the labor force longer is clearly increasing, particularly as the health and longevity of the population increases.

What does this gradual aging of the population and labor force imply for HRM/IR? For one thing, in the next decade competition for scarce jobs and fewer promotional opportunities among those in their prime working years will increase. For another, workers' demands for disposable income will increase as well, since large groups of workers will soon be moving through their peak consumption years. Thus, we are likely to see new pressures imposed on compensation and career development policies, particularly those affecting people in their mid-career stages: middle managers; technical specialists and professionals who are anxious to move into more responsible, better-paying supervisory and managerial positions; journeymen craft workers; experienced blue-collar workers; and so on. These workers will also feel the burdens of supporting an aging population as the ratio of the elderly to the working population increases. Unless we are fortunate enough to experience a new period of sustained economic growth, one of the central challenges to human resource management in the next decade will be to assist workers and employers in adjusting to the problems associated with moving this large group of workers through their careers.

BOX 2-1
Teenage Employment Prospects

Outlook for Jobs for Youths in City is the Worst Ever

New York City's teen-agers face the worst employment picture in the city's history and the situation shows no sign of improving, according to city officials, economists and social workers who deal with job seekers.

"Compared to the country, to other central cities, youngsters in New York aren't making it in the labor market," said Samuel M. Ehrenhalt, the regional commissioner of the Federal Bureau of Labor Statistics.

For five of the last seven years, the unemployment rate for teen-agers in the city has been over 30 percent, a third higher than the national average. The officials say this has created a generation of teen-agers who have no jobs, who have become discouraged from looking for jobs and who have sometimes turned to crime or work in the illicit underground economy.

A Shift in Economy

A fundamental mismatch between the city's economy and its teen-age labor force has developed in recent years, Mr. Ehrenhalt said, as the economy has shifted from manufacturing to white-collar service jobs. Between 1947 and 1981 the city lost 55 percent of its manufacturing jobs, according to the Bureau of Labor Statistics.

The service industries that have brought new jobs to the city's economy often require employees to have college or high school degrees, Mr. Ehrenhalt said, and teen-agers are increasingly underqualified for those jobs.

Five out of six job openings in the city require that applicants have high school diplomas, officials say, but 45 percent of high school students drop out before graduating.

Many teen-agers who have left school are looking for full-time, rather than part-time, employment. It is this group that most dramatically shows the difficulty the city's young people have in finding jobs, city officials and educators say.

"We are living through a period of a teen-age employment disaster," said Herbert Bienstock, director of Queens College's Center for Labor and Urban Problems Research and Analysis, and former regional commissioner for the Bureau of Labor Statistics. "What has it done to the teen-agers and the city? We have created a lost generation."

Of the 497,000 men and women between the ages of 16 and 19 in the city, more than 410,000 do not have jobs, the largest number of unemployed young people in any city in the country, according to the Bureau of Labor Statistics.

Such a high number indicates that many teen-agers have become discouraged from looking for jobs, Mr. Ehrenhalt said.

Fewer than one in five 16- to 19-year-olds held either full-time jobs in New York City in the second quarter of 1983, and fewer than 10 percent of the city's black teen-agers were working.

Discouragement in City

Nationally, 40 percent of teen-agers held jobs in that period, and about 18 percent of black teen-agers were working, double the rate in New York, according to the Bureau of Labor Statistics.

Source: William R. Greer, *The New York Times*, July 31, 1983, p. 1. Copyright © 1983 by the New York Times Company. Reprinted by permission.

The unemployment figures "are certainly not getting better," Mr. Ehrenhalt said. "They display for black teen-agers a particularly discouraging situation."

The official unemployment rate for black teen-agers in the city in the second quarter of 1983 was 60 percent. For all teen-agers, the figure was 33.1 percent. Chicago, however, had a higher teen-age unemployment rate — 45 percent — in 1982.

But the unemployment rate does not indicate the number of people who have been discouraged from looking for a job or have not looked recently, officials say.

"Jobs Going to Commuters"

"The city has improved since the mid-1970's and unemployment is less for everyone, but not for teen-agers — they have not participated in the improvement," Mr. Ehrenhalt said. "The job growth since 1977 has all been taking place in Manhattan, below 60th Street, and many of the jobs have gone to commuters who have the educational requirements, rather than the New York City residents."

Dennis Vega, who is 21 years old, dropped out of high school in the 10th grade when his mother died. Mr. Vega, who lives in the Williamsburg section of Brooklyn, said he had found that not having a high school diploma often prevented him from even applying for jobs.

Now, he spends many of his evenings playing handball in a park near the Williamsburg Bridge. He enrolled in a trade school last month, where he is studying security for businesses.

"There ain't nothing out there," he said. "A diploma ain't worth anything. Now you need a college degree to get a job."

Shortage of Schooling

In addition to lacking job experience, Miss Garry (a youth center coordinator) said, most of the young people she sees have left school after only 10 years. "That amounts to a fifth-grade math level" and a reading level slightly above the fifth grade, she said.

"Traditionally you either went to school or you went to work," she said. "What we're finding is that, particularly with minorities, going to school is not as viable an option as it was. One of the reasons we're looking at such a high unemployment rate is that we have such a high dropout rate."

To help meet some of the problems, Schools Chancellor Anthony J. Alvarado has begun reorganizing the way the city's schools offer teen-agers vocational education, said John Tobin, an executive assistant to the Chancellor.

"There is an unemployment rate among teen-agers that is in part caused by the end product of the school system," Mr. Tobin said, "but there are also other reasons. We have a public school system that has a highly minority student body. We know that in the hiring practices of many groups there is prejudice."

But one man, 22-year-old Joseph Bond, is a success story among his friends at the Jefferson Houses. He works in the mail room of Young & Rubicam, an advertising agency on Madison Avenue, and at night he takes classes at York College in Jamaica, Queens. His dream is to get a degree in business administration and open his own business in East Harlem.

Labor Force Participation of Women

As noted earlier, one of the most significant developments since World War II has been the increase in the labor force participation rate of women; the rate rose from approximately 32 percent in 1948 to more than 53 percent in 1982. Not only have women entered the labor force in greater numbers, but more women are remaining in the labor force through their childbearing years. And partly as a result of the enactment and enforcement of equal employment opportunity laws, many women are gradually moving into more jobs and positions of authority traditionally dominated by men. Women's increasing numbers, higher educational levels and career aspirations, and greater political and organizational effectiveness will continue to require adaptations in HRM/IR policies and their implementation to ensure that equal opportunity is institutionalized in practice, rather than remaining dependent solely on legal enforcement.

Educational Attainment

The theory of human capital development (Becker, 1964) maintains that the quality of the labor force, and therefore the productivity of the national economy, increases as the societal level of educational attainment rises. It is clear that on average society has become more highly educated; by 1979 more than 77 percent of the working population had completed high school and just under 20 percent had completed at least four years of college. These percentages have been increasing slowly but steadily for decades.

It may be necessary, however, to reconsider the relationship between aggregate increases in educational attainment and aggregate increases in productivity. It is clear that severe problems exist in the quality of education being provided in the United States, particularly in our large urban public school systems. Furthermore, the high school dropout rate in urban schools continued to hover between 15 and 20 percent throughout the 1970s. A Presidential Commission on Excellence in the Public Schools warned in a widely publicized 1983 report that the entire public educational system in the United States may be failing to provide the quality of education that an increasingly technologically sophisticated and competitive economy requires. Increased education has also historically produced increased worker expectations about challenging work, professional growth, and general upward mobility. To the extent that we are creating a society of individuals who are overeducated as measured by years of schooling but undereducated in terms of the actual skills required for the job opportunities available, we face a major challenge in responding to workers' needs for continuing and/or remedial education and training.

Shifts in Occupations, Industries, and Regions

The changes we have noted in the characteristics of the work force have been accompanied by major shifts from blue- to white-collar occupations, from goods- to service-producing industries, and from the Northeast and Midwest to the southern and western regions of the country. In 1981 white-collar workers accounted for approximately 53 percent of the labor force, compared with about 44 percent in 1961. In 1981 workers in the service sector accounted for more than two-thirds of the labor force. Between 1970 and 1980 the population of the Northeast and the north central regions of the country grew at annual rates of only 0.2 percent and 4.0 percent, respectively, compared with 20.0 percent for the South and 23.9 percent for the West. The movement of jobs from the North to the Sunbelt has been greatest within the manufacturing sector, where employers have sought the advantages of lower cost labor markets and of regions traditionally more difficult for unions to organize.

One implication that this geographic, occupational, and industrial mobility has for HRM/IR policymakers is that employers now face a wider range of choices in selecting a location for their operations. Accompanying the geographic shifts are changes in technology that make less widely dispersed manufacturing and service facilities more economical and a growing belief among managers that smaller settings are easier to manage effectively (Peters and Waterman, 1982). These circumstances point out the depth of problems facing the large urban manufacturing centers of the North as they struggle to adapt to the various changes. Coping with the current and future consequences of these structural transformations and demographic shifts poses major challenges for both private and public HRM/IR policymakers.

Worker Values and Expectations

What effects have all the recent demographic and societal changes had on the values and expectations workers bring to their jobs? Has the work ethic diminished? Have attitudes toward employers, unions, traditional modes of work organization, and motivational incentives changed in fundamental ways?

Clearly, we have witnessed a good deal of popular theorizing. As pointed out in the *Business Week* article, "The New Industrial Relations," in Chapter 1, we are seeing more and more experimentation with new forms of employee participation and involvement designed to meet the needs and expectations of a work force presumed to be more responsive to these processes now than in the past. At the same time (and as in any time of rapid change and social innovation and experimentation), misinformation and overstatement abound with respect to the changes that have occurred in worker values, expectations, and attitudes. We therefore need to look carefully at the available data to distinguish between real and imagined trends. Unfortunately, we have no single, reliable source of data tracking the history of worker views on a broad range of employment issues over substantial amounts of time. Thus, we need to rely on multiple sources of data to obtain a profile of current worker views.

TABLE 2-2 Views of the Work Ethic Compared with Ten Years Ago: In the United States

Question: I would like you to think back ten years ago and tell me how you think a number of things today compare with the way things were then.

| | Total Public | U.S. Sample | | | |
		Business Executives	Labor Union Leaders	Congress	Environmental and Consumer Activists
Base	1201 %	405 %	61 %	81 %	62 %
Do you think most people today work harder or not as hard as they did ten years ago? Not as hard	63	62	62	62	50
Do you think most people today have more pride in their work, or less pride in their work than they did ten years ago? Less pride	76	70	74	77	88
Do you think employees today are more loyal or less loyal to their employers than they were ten years ago? Less loyal	76	74	70	69	73
Do you think that, in general, workmanship today is better or worse than it was ten years ago? Workmanship better	71	73	53	72	71
Do you think that people's motivation to work today is stronger or not as strong as it was ten years ago? Not as strong	73	77	67	69	60

Note: Not all response categories are represented.

Source: "A Sentry Study: Perspectives on Productivity; A Global View." Reprinted by permission of Center for Policy Research, NY, NY.

The Work Ethic

What about the work ethic? Has it declined in American society, as many people seem to believe? Table 2-2 indicates that a majority of representatives from business, labor, government, and public interest groups believe that there has been a decline in the work ethic as measured by how hard people work, the pride they take in their work, loyalty to employers, workmanship, and motivation. However, close inspection of the behavioral and attitudinal evidence produces no convincing support for this view. On the basis of a comprehensive review of trends in workers' expressed views of the importance of work in their lives, as well as behavioral data on work effort (labor force participation rates, number of workers holding dual jobs, number of workers working long hours, etc.), Kanter (1978) has concluded that there is no diminution of the American work ethic. What does appear to be occurring, however, is a gradual transformation and expansion of the expectations workers bring to their jobs and careers. Kanter's summary of these longer trends, published in 1978 (see Box 2-2), serves as perhaps the most accurate description available of overall trends in worker values and expectations.

BOX 2-2
The Long Term Trends in Work Values

Two themes can be said to characterize the ambiance of work in America in 1977 — some parts of which represent continuous threads and ongoing trends since World War II, but others of which are new developments or stronger tendencies. One theme can be called cultural or expressive: the concern for work as a source of self-respect and nonmaterial reward — challenge, growth, personal fulfillment, interesting and meaningful work, the opportunity to advance and to accumulate, and the chance to lead a safe, healthy life. The other can be called political: the concern for individual rights and power, for a further extension of principles of equity and justice into the workplace and into the industrial order, for equality and participation both in their general symbolic manifestations and in the form of concrete legal rights. Neither theme denies the extent to which concerns about income and basic material security still dominate the lives of many Americans and propel them into long hours and second jobs. . . .

A more educated work force — as ours has become — is simultaneously a more critical, questioning, and demanding work force, and a potentially more frustrated one if expectations are not met.

Source: Rosabeth Moss Kanter, "The Long Term Trends in Work Values," *Daedalus,* Vol. 107, No. 1 (Winter, 1978), pp. 53–54. Reprinted by permission of *Daedalus,* Journal of the American Academy of Arts and Sciences, Boston, Mass.

TABLE 2-3   Top Five Work Values

Rank	Managers	Professionals	Clerical	Hourly
1	Pay and benefits	Advancement	Pay and benefits	Pay and benefits
2	Advancement	Pay and benefits	Advancement	Security
3	Authority	Challenge	Supervision	Respect
4	Accomplishment	New Skills	Respect	Supervision
5	Challenge	Supervision	Security	Advancement

Source: Opinion Research Corporation, Princeton, N.J.: *Managing Human Resources/1983 and Beyond.*

Motivational Incentives

Table 2-3 summarizes data from a large number of surveys of worker values conducted by the Opinion Research Corporation (1983) throughout the 1970s and early 1980s; these findings both support and update Kanter's conclusions. For each survey workers were asked to choose from among fourteen job attributes those characteristics which were most important to them. The most interesting finding extending across occupational groups (ranging from hourly workers to managers) is that the issue of pay and benefits continued to be ranked first or second in importance; indeed, it was given top priority by all groups except professionals, who ranked it second. These data, along with numerous other surveys (Lawler, 1971) should put to rest any arguments that pay has somehow lost its motivational potential or become less important or less valued as a reward among contemporary workers.

But is pay a sufficient reward or motivational tool for managing the current work force? The data presented in Table 2-3, along with data such as those displayed in Table 2-4, suggest that while the issue of pay and benefits is important, so too are a wide range of other job attributes. Particularly important, as Kanter has suggested, are those characteristics of the work setting which influence the amount of control workers have over their immediate job environment and career prospects. For example, the Opinion Resource Corporation data show that managers value opportunities for advancement and the authority to make decisions almost as highly as they value pay. Similarly, professionals and clerical workers rank opportunities for advancement very highly. The survey data in Table 2-4, collected in 1982 from four different groups of blue-collar workers and one group of white-collar professionals, show that more than three-fourths of all respondents express a strong desire for having some say, or for having a lot of say, in the ways they do their work and in the quality of the work they produce.

It seems clear that the majority of contemporary workers are concerned with *both* the traditional bread-and-butter issues of pay,

TABLE 2-4 Interest in Participation by Areas of Concern
Total Sample
(Percent of respondents agreeing they want "some say" or "a lot of say")

| Concerns | Blue Collar Workers | | | | White Collar Professionals |
	Case 1	Case 2	Case 3	Case 4	Case 5
Quality of Worklife (QWL)					
The way the work is done — methods and procedures	83	83	91	87	95
The level of quality of work	83	78	88	87	96
How fast the work should be done — the work rate	72	70	81	76	85
How much work people should do in a day	55	43	64	61	70
Who should do what job in your group or section	46	57	51	63	61
Bread and Butter					
When the work day begins and ends	50	33	63	65	76
Pay scales or wages	67	78	82	73	92
Who should be fired if they do a bad job or don't come to work	39	38	39	35	42
Who should be hired into your work group	35	23	32	37	45
Handling complaints or grievances	67	70	72	59	79
Who gets promoted	39	27	42	41	48
Strategic					
The use of new technology on your job	69	70	68	77	79
Management salaries	27	22	13	41	22
Hiring or promotions to upper management	27	8	25	31	44
The selection of your supervisor	42	18	39	52	58
Plant expansions, closings, or new locations	45	22	51	70	40
The way the company invests its profits or spends its money	46	52	41	43	32

Source: Worker Participation and American Unions: Threat or Opportunity? by Thomas A. Kochan, Harry C. Katz, Nancy R. Mower, unpublished manuscript.

benefits, and security *and* the opportunity to participate in decisions affecting their immediate jobs and future career prospects. Nevertheless, it can be misleading, even dangerous, to abstract from these conclusions. It is by no means clear that we now have a new breed of younger workers who are less interested in work, more willing to challenge the formal authority of their supervisors, or more rebellious against organizational rules that promote conformity. Accurate assessments of these characteristics require examination of specific work organizations and groups.

Worker Priorities

The priorities assigned to different work values are not completely stable over time, nor do they necessarily move uniformly in a single direction. Consider, for example, the difference between the 1960s and the 1950s: In the 1960s the widespread view was that not only our youth but society in general was rebelling against the overt demands for conformity thought to be prevalent in the 1950s. The "organization man" was the stereotype of the 1950s, while the "Lordstown syndrome" (the rebellion of assembly line workers in auto plants) was the legacy of the late 1960s and early 1970s. But by the early 1980s some social critics and academicians were admiring the economic and organizational prowess of Japanese and American firms in which the emphasis was on a strong and homogeneous set of values, or their own "organizational culture."

It is therefore important to recognize that work values vary greatly across groups and individuals, over time in response to changing economic and social conditions, and across organizations. All workers possess a combination of traditional interests and expectations and a more modern concern for participation in and influence over their work environment. As education and income go up, so do the priorities workers attach to career advancement, professional autonomy, and influence in organizational decision-making. But economic changes in the environment that threaten income or employment security quickly demonstrate that as workers' interests expand into new areas, there is no concomitant decline in their traditional expectations. Therefore, specific priorities attached to these different values or interests can vary considerably, and should be specifically assessed for each group of workers before predictions or generalizations are offered.

Worker Satisfaction

Another issue that has been debated widely within the popular press and among academicians and managers is whether workers' satisfaction with their jobs, their companies, and their unions has changed in recent years. Here again, the Opinion Research Corporation data are illuminating. Figure 2-3 presents trends in satisfaction with employers and jobs as observed in various occupational groups. There has clearly been a marked decline in workers' satisfaction with their *employers* but no corresponding decline in satisfaction with their *jobs*. The decline in

"How would you rate this company as a place to work compared with other companies you know or have heard about?" (Percent responding "one of the best" or "above average")

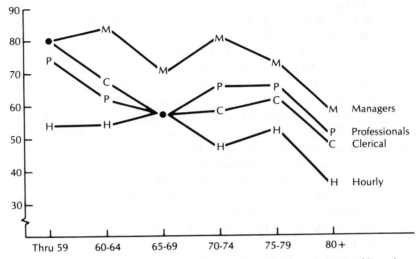

Source: Opinion Research Corporation, Princeton, NJ: *Managing Human Resources/1983 and Beyond.* Reprinted by permission.

FIGURE 2-3   Ratings of Company as a Place to Work

satisfaction with employers cuts across all occupational groups, including managers, professionals, clerical workers, and hourly workers. Less than 50 percent of the hourly workers and less than 70 percent of the managers rate their companies either as "above average" or as "one of the best" places to work. Other data from the Opinion Research Corporation indicate that the drop in satisfaction with employers extends to more specific job attributes, such as career prospects, communication and information sharing, equity in the administration of rules and policies, and the traditional HRM/IR policies covering pay, benefits, and job security. The evidence thus suggests that workers are not becoming more disenchanted with the specific work they do or with the occupations they pursue; instead, they are becoming less satisfied with the ways in which employers are managing.

What about worker attitudes toward labor unions? Do contemporary workers believe there is still a need for unions? Or, as some social critics have suggested, have unions outlived their usefulness? Unions, and especially union leaders, have never enjoyed very favorable public images. Opinion polls taken since the 1940s have consistently shown that the American public ranks the status of union leaders below that of their counterparts in religious, business, governmental, and educational occupations (Bok and Dunlop, 1970). Furthermore, the majority of the population has viewed unions as having too much political power, and more recently, has blamed unions for increasing wages beyond a competitive level (Kochan, 1979; Opinion Research Corporation, 1983). Despite these negative images of unions, the vast majority — somewhere between two-thirds and four-fifths of the American population — continues to agree that unions play a valuable and necessary role in protecting the interests of workers. In a national survey conducted in 1977 for the U.S. Department of Labor, more than 80 percent of respondents agreed that unions improved the wages and job security of their members (Kochan, 1979), and represented their members against unfair treatment by employers. Similarly, in 1983 the Opinion Research Corporation, in conducting a national telephone sample survey, found that 64 percent of respondents disagreed with the statement that "unions in this country are no longer necessary to protect the interests and well-being of the average worker." Moreover, 80 percent of current union members in that sample disagreed with the statement (Opinion Research Corporation, 1983). Other survey data suggest that between 50 and 75 percent of union members rate their unions as doing a "good" or "very good" job in representing their members (Kochan, 1979; Kochan, Katz, and Mower, 1984). Thus, while unions generally lack positive social images, the majority of the American public regards them as useful and necessary institutions at the workplace.

The values, expectations, and aspirations employees bring to the employment relationship will continue to be one of the popular topics for debate in the public media, as well as among HRM/IR professionals. The point of the preceding discussion is that most sweeping generalizations about workers' priorities and workers' views of their work do not take into account many of the variations that exist across individuals and groups. Since the techniques for measuring attitudes, values, and preferences are well developed and relatively easy to administer, a data base on the views of a given set of employees can be built and periodically updated at relatively low cost. Such information can also be used in planning, designing, and evaluating HRM/IR policies. Indeed, the periodic collection of these types of data has become standard practice in many large organizations (for an exploration of the uses of these kinds of attitude data, see Chapter 9).

The Public Policy Environment

Public policy concerns the legal environment in which HRM/IR activities occur. This environment is constantly evolving, both through legislative changes and, increasingly, through court decisions and changes in the administrative practices of government agencies. Table 2-5 outlines the chronology of major public policy developments since the 1930s, a decade that produced most of the legal doctrines and statutes governing employment relationships today. In this introduction to the legal environment, we will first consider the various roles that government plays as both regulator of and actor in our industrial relations system, and then trace some of the key changes in those roles over time. Our purpose is not to provide a comprehensive treatment of law and public policy governing employment practices, but rather to provide a picture of how the government influences decisions and practices at the levels of the firm and the workplace.

The Roles of Government in Industrial Relations

The government of any democratic society must balance several roles, ones that often conflict, in the industrial relations system. First and foremost, the government must serve as a mediator between the multiple interests present in employment relationships. The role of mediator entails balancing the conflicting interests of workers and employers by establishing procedures that govern collective bargaining, and by adopting minimum standards for safety, health, working hours, and so on. As mediator, the government must also set standards that define the rights of individual workers as workers compete with one another for scarce job opportunities. Thus, legislation ensuring equal employment opportunity and prohibiting various forms of discrimination represents government intervention on behalf of certain groups in society that lack sufficient power or influence to achieve equitable job outcomes on their own. As we will see, the role of mediator has become increasingly important in the past several decades.

Second, the government must determine how much autonomy to delegate to private management and/or labor decision makers at the workplace, and must determine to what extent the government should intervene in labor markets and employment decisions in order to assert the government's own goals in such matters as inflation, industrial peace, and unemployment. All democratic societies espouse the philosophy that private individuals should be free to shape the decisions affecting their lives without interference from government. Capitalist democracies further emphasize the rights of freedom to contract and the rights of private property, both of which argue for a relatively autonomous industrial relations system. Yet governments do intervene in various decisions to protect the larger public interests affected by employment decisions, and to respond to the shifting balance of political influence among labor, business, and other interest groups having stakes in those decisions.

While the rhetoric guiding public policy in the United States has traditionally been to promote freedom of decision making in employment relationships, there has been a long-term trend toward a more directly interventionist role for the government in shaping both the substantive terms of employment and the processes by which those terms are established. Thus, a key role for the government is to balance its interest in directly asserting its priorities — through regulating wages, hours, and working conditions — against its interest in adhering to the philosophy of allowing workers and employers the freedom to shape their own destinies at the workplace and in the labor market. Let us briefly review how various administrations have balanced these different roles and objectives over time.

TABLE 2-5 Overview of Major Developments in American Labor Policy

Period	Date	Event	Description
The Common Law Approach	1806	Cordwainer's Case	A combination of workers seeking a wage increase is a criminal conspiracy.
	1842	*Commonwealth v. Hunt*	Unions are lawful. Combination of workers was allowed as long as lawful means were used to gain lawful ends. Courts still hostile to unions.
The Business Law Approach	1890	Sherman Antitrust Act	"Every combination . . . or conspiracy in restraint of trade or commerce among the several states . . . is hereby declared to be illegal." Used by employers seeking injunctions for union activity.
	1894	*Debs Case*	A famous use of the injunction. Eugene Debs jailed for refusing to obey a court back-to-work order in the American Railway Union Strike.
	1906	*Danbury Hatters*	Boycott of goods in violation of the Sherman Act. Union was assessed triple damages.
	1912	Lloyd-La Follette Act	Allowed public employees to request raises from Congress. Allowed Postal Workers to organize, but not strike.
	1914	Clayton Act	"Labor is not a commodity" . . . but courts continued to find union acts illegal.
The Labor Law Approach	1926	Railway Labor Act	Railway workers could now organize and bargain collectively.
	1932	Norris-LaGuardia Act	Federal courts severely restricted in issuing injunctions against unions; yellow-dog contracts "shall not be enforceable."
	1933	National Industrial Recovery Act	Extended to workers the "right to organize and bargain collectively through representatives of their own choosing . . . free from interference, restraint, or coercion of employers." (sec. 7a)
	1935	*Shechter Poultry Case*	Supreme Court Decision: NIRA is held unconstitutional, 295 U.S. 495, 55 S. Ct. 837.

	Year	Act	Description
	1935	NLRA: Wagner Act	Established organizing rights, unfair (employer) labor-practices and the National Labor Relations Board. (NLRB).
	1935	Social Security Act	Includes OASDHI (old age, survivors, disability and health insurance) and OAA (old age assistance).
	1938	Fair Labor Standards Act	Established minimum wage and related wage and hour regulations.
	1947	Taft-Hartley Act	Amended the NLRA. Added unfair union labor practices. Section 8(b).
	1959	Landrum-Griffin Act	Established a bill of rights of union members. Required financial disclosing by unions. Listed guidelines for trusteeships and elections.
The Social and Economic Policy Approach	1962	Executive Order 10988	Encouraged public sector bargaining. Required maintenance of management rights. Orders added by Kennedy in 1963, Nixon in 1969 (Exec. Order 11491). Followed by passage of state laws giving employees of local and state governments the right to bargain.
	1962	Wage-Price Policies	Guideposts 1962–1966; Controls 1971–1973; Guidelines 1978–1980
	1964	Civil Rights Act Title VII	Unlawful for employer or union to discriminate on the basis of race, color, religion, sex, or national origin.
	1970	Occupational Safety and Health Act	Established standards for safety and health; Occupational Safety and Health Administration.
	1972	Supplementary Security Income	Effective January 1, 1974. Replaced OAA of 1935 Social Security Act.
	1974	Employee Retirement Income Security Act (ERISA)	Established minimum standards for private pension plans.
	1978	Mandatory Retirement Act	"Age Discrimination in Employment Act." Outlawed mandatory retirement rules prior to age 70.

Source: Adapted from Thomas A. Kochan, Collective Bargaining and Industrial Relations, pp. 63–64. Copyright © 1980 by Richard D. Irwin, Inc. Reprinted by permission of Richard D. Irwin, Inc., Homewood, IL.

Stages in the Development of Public Policy

United States government policies toward the regulation of employment relationships can be classified into four general categories, corresponding to four different time periods: (1) the common law approach, running roughly from the fashioning of the Constitution to the 1890s; (2) the business law approach, which lasted from the 1890s to the 1930s; (3) the labor law approach, from the 1930s to the 1960s; and (4) the social and economic policy approach, from the 1960s to the present.

Common Law Approach. In the first century of our country's existence, neither our Constitution nor any of our federal statutes explicitly addressed the philosophical and legal doctrines that are expected to govern employment relationships. It was therefore largely up to the state and federal courts to develop a body of common law to guide behavior and to adjudicate disputes between workers and employers. Building on the traditions inherited from British common law, the courts tended to give primacy to the rights of private property and freedom to contract. It was, then, during these formative years that the doctrine of "employment at will" prevailed, a doctrine implying that employees can be discharged by employers for any reason or for no reason (Jacoby, 1983). Since there was no specific legislation to govern the role of labor unions, the courts had to invent the appropriate legal doctrines.

In 1806 a famous case, involving shoemakers in Philadelphia, was handed down. The court ruling viewed unions as "criminal conspiracies" because their purpose was to raise wages above the level employers were willing to pay voluntarily; unions were thus seen as inherently illegal because they interfered with the workings of the free market. This doctrine prevailed until 1842, when a Massachusetts court adopted a "means-end" interpretation of union behavior, stating that unions were illegal only if they engaged in unlawful means to achieve their goals. Still, in the absence of specific legislation governing workers' individual or collective rights, most court decisions tended to favor the protection of employers' property rights over claims of unfair treatment by workers or efforts by unions to gain a permanent place in industry.

Business Law Approach. The passage of the Sherman Antitrust Act of 1890 opened a relatively short era in which labor was regulated as a commodity, similar to other factors of production, leaving the labor market to be regulated as any other market would be. The basic objective was to avoid the building of "monopoly power" on the part of either labor organizations or combinations of employers acting collectively to hold down the free flow of wages and human resources. The principal effects were to increase the use of antitrust laws and of court injunctions against labor unions, and to make it clear that unless specific state or federal legislation was enacted to establish labor standards, market forces would govern all employment relationships.

Emergence of Labor Law. Gradually, the laissez-faire doctrines implicit in the common law and business law approaches began to give way first to state legislation and then, by the 1930s, to federal legislation. In the early 1900s a number of states, including New York, Massachusetts, and Wisconsin, began enacting protective labor laws governing children's and women's hours of work. By the 1920s, Wisconsin, for instance, was pioneering the passage of unemployment and workers' compensation statutes, and establishing state industrial commissions to regulate safety and health conditions in the workplace.

It was the 1930s, however, that ushered in the modern-style regulation of employment relations through federal statutes. The New Deal legislation of the 1930s included the Social Security Act, the National Labor Relations Act, and the Fair Labor Standards Act. These statutes (as amended several times through the years) remain in force today, and were joined in the 1960s and 1970s by the Occupational Safety and Health Act, Title VII of the Civil Rights Act of 1964 (outlawing discrimination in employment), the Employee Retirement Income Security Act of 1974 (establishing fiduciary standards for private pensions), and the Age Discrimination in Employment Act. An overview of the major provisions of these statutes is provided in Table 2-5. All of them depart from the theory that labor should be regulated just as any other factor of production — that is, neither common law nor business law are deemed appropriate for regulating these issues. Further, the free play of market forces has not always produced outcomes that are acceptable to society. Labor-specific legislation was therefore enacted to change the results produced by market forces.

Social and Economic Policy Approach. With the 1960s and 1970s came a second wave of employment relations law. The era witnessed the passage of additional pieces of labor legislation that supplemented those of the New Deal, and signified the introduction of a different philosophical approach. The National Labor Relations Act of 1935 (the Wagner Act) had regulated the process by which workers and their employers established the terms and conditions of employment through collective bargaining, free from government intervention. For years that law had been considered the cornerstone of national labor policy, the basic approach being to regulate the process of collective bargaining and to leave the determination of the actual terms and conditions of employment to the private parties involved. But the legislation of the 1960s and 1970s was aimed more directly at regulating the *substantive* terms of employment. To some extent, the newer legislation reflected a dissatisfaction with the outcomes of collective bargaining on issues like equal employment opportunity; in some measures, it also reflected the fact that less than 25 percent of the nation's workers were covered by a collective bargaining agreement. In any event, the 1960s and 1970s might be characterized as an era in which the government was prone to legislate direct standards and conditions of employment when sufficient political pressure demonstrated the need for a change in the employment policies of private decision makers.

Consistent with this trend have been an expansion of employment and training programs, beginning in 1962 (see Chapter 3, Figure 3-2), and a growth in experimentation with active wage-price or incomes policies. In the 1980s, however, the Reagan administration has slowed the trend toward more direct intervention and toward expansion of government regulation of employment practices. But it is still unclear whether those developments will prove to be (1) a short-run departure from the longer-term trend toward a more active governmental role, or (2) the beginning of a sustained movement away from an expanded governmental role and toward greater roles for the unilateral discretion of employers, for the outcomes of "free collective bargaining," and for the dynamics of private market forces.

It is not our intent to predict the direction in which labor or human resource policy will move in future years. But it is clear that there are increasing concerns with the rights of individuals, on the one hand, and increasing desires to minimize the role of government in society, on the other. We thus have a number of state courts challenging and weakening the long-standing doctrine of employment at will, by questioning the ability of employers to dismiss workers without first demonstrating just cause. At the same time, the expansion of federal statutes protecting worker rights came to a halt in the late 1970s.

The relative dominance of these competing political and social pressures on the legislative process will influence whether or not the federal government will enact laws and regulations governing such issues as plant closings and large-scale layoffs; the introduction of technological change; employment, training, and related human resource development programs; and unfair dismissal of employees not protected by the due process and just cause provisions of collective bargaining agreements or by antidiscrimination statutes. In addition, if the labor movement is successful in regaining some of the political influence it has lost in the past decade, we may see a major effort to revamp the basic labor laws governing union recognition and the collective bargaining process. All these topics are high on the agenda of the labor movement, liberal politicians, and other groups concerned with the interests of workers. But business and other more conservative groups in society may continue to be successful in limiting the expansion of government regulations and increasing the role of market forces. HRM/IR decision makers at the level of the firm need to prepare plans for either contingency. The worst mistake would be to make long-term plans based on the short-run balance of power among the forces that influence public policies governing employment relationships.

References

Becker, Gary S., *Human Capital* (New York: Columbia University Press, 1964).

Bok, Derek C., and John T. Dunlop, *Labor and the American Community* (New York: Simon and Schuster, 1970).

Business Week, "Industrial Policy: Is it the Answer?" July 4, 1982, 54–62.

Jacoby, Sanford, "The Duration of Indefinite Employment Contracts in the United States and England: An Historical Analysis," *Comparative Labor Law*, 5, Winter 1983, 85–128.

Kanter, Rosabeth Moss, "Work in America," *Daedalus*, 107, Winter 1978, 47–75.

Kochan, Thomas A., "How American Workers View Labor Unions," *Monthly Labor Review*, 102, April 1979, 23–31.

Kochan, Thomas A., Harry C. Katz, and Nancy Mower, *Worker Participation and American Unions: Threat or Opportunity?* (Kalamazoo, Mich.: The Upjohn Institute, 1984).

Lawler, Edward E., *Pay and Organizational Effectiveness* (New York: McGraw Hill, 1971).

Lofquist, Lloyd H., and Rene V. Dawis, *Adjustment to Work* (New York: Appleton Century Crofts, 1969).

Peters, Thomas S., and Robert H. Waterman, Jr., *In Search of Excellence* (New York: Harper and Row, 1982).

Porter, Michael E., *Competitive Strategy* (New York: Free Press, 1980).

Schein, Edgar H., *Organizational Psychology* (Englewood Cliffs, N.J.: Prentice Hall, 1979).

Van Maanen, John, and Edgar Schein, "Toward a Theory of Organizational Socialization," in Barry M. Staw, ed., *Research in Organizational Behavior*, Vol 1 (Greenwich, Conn.: JAI Press, 1980), 209–64.

Suggested Readings

Barry Bluestone and Bennett Harrison, *The Deindustrialization of America; Plant Closings, Community Abandonment, and the Dismantling of Basic Industry* (New York: Basic Books, 1982).

Peter F. Drucker, "The Next American Workforce: Demographics and U.S. Economic Policy," *Commentary*, October 1981, 3–10.

Richard B. Freeman, *The Over-Educated American* (New York: Academic Press, Inc., 1976).

William B. Gould, *A Primer on American Labor Law* (Cambridge: MIT Press, 1982).

Clark Kerr, Jerome M. Rosow, Editors, *Work in America: The Decade Ahead* (New York: Van Nostrand Reinhold Co., 1979).

Sar Levitan and Diane Werneke, *Productivity: Problems, Prospects and Policies* (Baltimore: The John Hopkins University Press, 1984).

Scanning the External Environment

Following is a brief profile of WWW, Inc. In examining this case, you are asked to consider the major trends in several environmental categories, and to assess the probable impact of those trends on the company in general and on the human resource planning process in particular.

CASE
WWW, Inc.

WWW, Inc. was founded in the late 1940s as an engineering-oriented, research and development company with primary emphasis on the development of electronic defense systems and subsystems for the U.S. Department of Defense. During its first three and a half decades, WWW, Inc: has proved to be a successful and growing company, attaining gross sales of about $200 million in the early 1980s.

WWW, Inc. is a wholly owned subsidiary of a conglomerate whose annual sales total $2 billion. WWW, Inc. operates as an independent profit center, with specific return-on-investment requirements imposed by the parent company.

WWW, Inc. is located in a high-technology center of the Northeast. Throughout its existence, the firm has relied almost exclusively on high-technology engineering. The company's work force is currently made up of some 2,900 employees, as follows: 2,000 engineers in various subspecialties, 200 skilled and semiskilled production workers (primarily technicians and assemblers), and 700 support staff and clerical workers.

The company's expansion plans call for attaining gross sales of $1 billion by the late 1980s. Meeting that sales goal will depend primarily on (a) the expansion of the firm's research and development work for the Defense Department, entailing mostly one-of-a-kind prototype production of electronics systems, and (b) the establishment of a manufacturing operation that for the first time will put the company in the manufacturing business. About half the production will be for military applications, and the other half for industrial markets; the products for the industrial markets will be commercially applicable offshoots of products developed for the Defense Department.

Establishment of the manufacturing operation is now in the first phase of implementation, the facility under construction. Plans call for a fully automated, computer-controlled factory that uses Manufacturing Resource Planning systems with Materials Requirements Planning (MRP), CAD and CAM systems (Computer Aided Design and Manufacturing), and flexible machining and robotics. The computer system will require that *all* employees be able to input and read computerized reports. The company has purchased the appropriate hardware and software, which are now being implemented, and has the strategic objective of becoming "an entirely paperless factory by the mid-to late-1980s."

Over the next five years, about 2,000 new production workers will be hired. Production requirements call for about 320 of these workers to be solderers, plastics technicians, or electronic specialists (certified to military specifications). The remaining production workers will require company-specific training, but will not need military certification. Additional engineers, systems analysts, and high-level technicians will number about 500 over the next five years.

In considering these growing personnel needs, WWW's management has been assessing whether it might be fruitful to explore the regional vocational schools or other publicly funded or publicly run training institutions. In the industrial Northeast, these schools commonly have excess capacity and thus could expand their enrollments if sufficient demand for trainees could be demonstrated. The management of WWW, Inc., is aware that various local management associations have been publicizing and promoting a public-private partnership in solving employment problems, an effort encouraged by the U.S. Department of Labor as it replaced the Comprehensive Employment and Training Act with the new Jobs Partnership and Training Act.

The market for the Defense Department products is uncertain, since defense expenditures are always subject to change with political priorities. Moreover, WWW's market for the industrial products is also uncertain, since such products have not yet been tried; however, marketing studies have shown substantial potential demand.

Company officials have decided that the production facility should remain close to the parent firm to further cooperation and communication among the various divisions and support staff. Close proximity should also make it easier for corporate management to oversee operations at the new site.

At WWW, Inc., the Personnel Department finds, screens, and if necessary tests prospective employees; hiring decisions are made by the manager(s) in charge of the functional area. The Training Department, which is under the head of Industrial Engineering, is responsible for the training and certification of all direct labor.

Over the past eighteen months, the company has begun implementing quality circles, has invested heavily in communications and other managerial education programs, and plans to extend these activities to involve the entire organization. The quality circles are part of an overall effort to improve productivity, an effort that also includes a detailed work measurement program, performed in-house by the Industrial Engineering staff.

The company has always been quick to adopt design enhancements, since the Defense Department tends to want, and often insists on, the highest quality that current thinking and technology can provide. Top management has risen from the engineering ranks, and is almost exclusively homegrown.

Although reporting and cost accounting are important control mechanisms at WWW, many employees in the organization have never been involved in the production of anything other than one-of-a-kind prototypes. The planned MRP system will for the first time fully integrate the design and production departments under one managerial accounting system. The emphasis will be on "just-on-time" delivery of components, using subcontractors and jobbers. In short, WWW's expansion plans will entail substantial changes in the firm's inventory, reporting and control, and budgetary systems.

The success of WWW's expansion will hinge on careful and long-range–oriented scanning of the environment in which the company operates. Given the firm's current growth strategy, the environmental aspects that will be of particular concern include the following domains: (1) technological trends and changes, (2) economic conditions, (3) the sociopolitical climate and its inherent constraints, and (4) the labor market for skilled, semiskilled, and unskilled workers.

Questions for Discussion

In order to assess the probable impact that each of these environmental domains will have on the company and its plans for expansion, you are asked to undertake an environmental scanning exercise projecting at least three years into the future. The result should be a clear, but not overly detailed, report of anticipated trends — ready to be presented to WWW's General Manager, who will rely on it heavily in the formation of the human resource planning component of the firm's strategic plan.

As you begin in your environmental scanning, consider the following questions, which should provide the basis for your report:

1. What are the current and projected key trends in each of the environmental domains of concern to the firm in its plans for expansion?
2. What will be the probable impact of these trends on WWW, Inc., as a company?
3. More specifically, how are these trends likely to affect the firm's human resource planning strategies and requirements?
4. Finally, what plan of action would you recommend in addressing the situation as outlined in your answers to the previous questions?

3

The Technological Context

The Implications of Technological Change

We now turn to a discussion of the most speculative and uncertain environmental characteristic: technology. Ever since a group of British workers known as the Luddites took hammers to their machines during the industrial revolution, workers, social critics, economic forecasters, and other futurists have warned of the potentially dire consequences of technological change. The early 1960s produced a wave of concern that automation would lead to massive unemployment. But the expanding economy and the unexpectedly slow diffusion of automation quieted those fears by the middle of that decade. We are now in the midst of another era of gloomy speculation regarding job loss, as industry adapts to recent advances in microelectronics.

It is unrealistic to predict that factories of the future will be without people, that middle managers and clerical workers will be eliminated. But each wave of change does alter the number, nature, skill mix, and often the locations of jobs available, as well as the corresponding human-resource requirements. Thus, both public and private human-resource planners and managers need to understand the nature of the new technologies becoming available, the choices they face in adapting to them, and the likely impacts of these choices.

The current wave of technological change is taking the following forms: robotics and computer-aided manufacturing (CAM) systems; computer-aided design (CAD); office automation; and advances in all forms of information processing and analysis and electronic communications. Perhaps the most challenging aspect of introducing new technologies into the workplace is the integration of diverse hardware and software systems. For example, Materials Resource Planning (MRP) systems are fully designed to integrate paperwork, design, purchasing, inventory, and manufacturing into one system. This requires that everyone, from design engineers to warehouse workers, secretaries, and assemblers, interact completely with the system. The training and coordination required present enormous challenges, as demonstrated by the WWW, Inc. case in Chapter 2. Figure 3-1 briefly describes some of

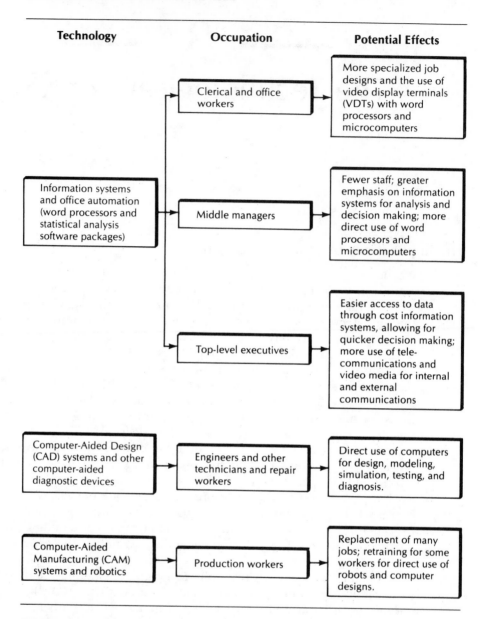

Technology	Occupation	Potential Effects
Information systems and office automation (word processors and statistical analysis software packages)	Clerical and office workers	More specialized job designs and the use of video display terminals (VDTs) with word processors and microcomputers
	Middle managers	Fewer staff; greater emphasis on information systems for analysis and decision making; more direct use of word processors and microcomputers
	Top-level executives	Easier access to data through cost information systems, allowing for quicker decision making; more use of tele-communications and video media for internal and external communications
Computer-Aided Design (CAD) systems and other computer-aided diagnostic devices	Engineers and other technicians and repair workers	Direct use of computers for design, modeling, simulation, testing, and diagnosis.
Computer-Aided Manufacturing (CAM) systems and robotics	Production workers	Replacement of many jobs; retraining for some workers for direct use of robots and computer designs.

FIGURE 3-1   Potential Effects of Microelectronic Innovations on Different Occupational Groups

the new technologies and illustrates the range of effects they are likely to have on different occupational groups. Note that all levels of the labor force are affected by the new technologies, from the high-level executive to the unskilled factory worker.

In this chapter we discuss the rather primitive state of knowledge about some anticipated impacts of these new technologies. Two key messages underlie the material. First, no one has developed an accurate model for predicting the effects of new technologies at macroeconomic, industrial, or occupational levels. There are simply too many unknowns, such as the rate of economic growth, the rate of diffusion of technological innovations, and the organizational choices involved in the introduction of new technology. Thus, professionals within specific organizations need to build their own forecasts on the basis of familiarity with the technologies available and the economic and strategic conditions facing their firms.

Second, decision makers at the level of the firm *do have choices* in how to integrate technological changes into their work environments. There is no necessary or predetermined drive of technology operating here; rather, managers face a set of decisions concerning how to introduce and manage the effects of new systems of work organization. Thus, we need a behavioral model that is capable of predicting and monitoring how new technology affects the firm, its employees, and society at large.

The influence of new technology on the workplace is not limited to the line worker, the line manager, or staff functions. Indeed, top management, to widely varying degrees, will feel the impact. Strategic decisions on automation of production and control functions are often made without full knowledge of the expected costs and benefits (Barocci et al., 1983). These multimillion-dollar investments can have a large impact on the current and future profitability of an organization. There is also the fear that middle-management jobs, particularly staff positions, will be made redundant by powerful analytic tools and by access to remote and in-house data bases. If these tools are effectively utilized by top managers, through personal computers or interactive terminals, managerial skills and organizational structures may change dramatically.

Existing research on these issues is mostly anecdotal and based on case studies and therefore offers widely differing opinions. Michael Scott-Morton predicts a change in the very fabric of management positions, as future managers are called upon fully to utilize new information technology in their day-to-day operations (Scott-Morton, 1983). On the other hand, John Deardon (1983) finds that although top management may find the computer interesting, it will not have a significant impact on the way in which management is carried out. Deardon assumed in his analysis that the more organic silicon chip, which would function much like the human brain, would not be broadly used or even developed in the foreseeable future. Further, Deardon emphasized that the kind of information available to the manager through personal computers is not much different from what has been available through remote terminals for more than a decade. Finally, he contended that staff would supply appropriate data analysis where necessary. Deardon's argument is based on the idea that what we see today is a data explosion, not an information explosion.

Clearly, whether the jobs of top and middle management will be dramatically affected by computers and advances in data processing is uncertain. What is certain is that we will see more and more changes in the technologies that firms choose to invest in. But the impact on job skills and organizational structure is unlikely to be as dramatic for managers as it will be for workers directly engaged in the production of goods and services.

Forecasting the Effects of New Technology

Two important distinctions must be considered in forecasting the effects of technological change on human resources. The first distinction is between the *direct* and *indirect* effects of technological change. The second distinction is between the *macro* and *societal* effects of new technology and its *micro* effects on specific workers and firms.

The direct effects *are* likely to eliminate jobs, since a major reason for introducing technological change is to meet competitive forces by reducing labor costs through increased productivity. However, whether the net effect of new technology is to reduce the number of jobs depends on the indirect effects of technology on productivity, economic growth, and new business opportunities and occupations. For example, productivity growth at the level of the national economy historically has been positively correlated with output growth. Increases in productivity lead to lower prices, which in turn stimulate the demand for goods and services; hence, greater output and employment. Over the long run, therefore, the indirect employment-creating impacts of new technology have tended to compensate for direct employment losses caused by labor-saving technological innovations.

Unfortunately, the jobs created are seldom available to workers who are displaced, since the new jobs may require different skills or training or may arise in new organizations or locations. Thus, we need to examine more closely who will gain and who will lose from new technology and to develop strategies for closing this gap so that the potential long-term benefits of new technology are realized to the fullest. To do this, we must move from the level of economywide technological forecasts to narrower assessments of specific technologies in given regions, industries, and workplaces.

A Region/Industry Example.   One innovative example of this type of region- and industry-specific technological forecast is found in the study of the effects of robotics on the metalworking industries in Michigan (Hunt and Hunt, 1983). Because of the centrality of metalwork manufacturing to the economy of Michigan and the fact that robotics will have its biggest effect on metalworking jobs, the Governor's High Technology Task Force sponsored a study of the direct and indirect employment effects of robotics on various Michigan industries. The aims of the study were to forecast the job losses that were likely to occur in the 1980s and to identify ways to capture some of the new jobs that would be created.

The researchers first interviewed robot manufacturers, potential robot purchasers, and other experts to develop estimates of the number of robots likely to be used in Michigan by 1990. Because of the dominance of the auto industry, they estimated the number of robots auto firms would install by 1990. Based on these rough predictions, they estimated the number of jobs to be eliminated by the purchase of this level of new technology. The results are shown in Tables 3-1 and 3-2.

These forecasts estimate the installation of 7,000 to 12,000 robots in the state by 1990. By using a consensus estimate of the industry (that on average one robot will replace two workers), the authors concluded that 13,500 to 24,000 jobs would be eliminated by 1990 and 75 percent of these job losses would be concentrated in the auto industry. Specifically, 15.2 to 19.5 percent of the welders and 29.2 to 40.6 percent of the painters in the auto industry would be displaced.

On the other hand, the study estimated that manufacturers, distributors, and users of robots could create 5,000 to 18,000 jobs in Michigan by 1990. The wide range in the estimates results from uncertainty over how many of these potential jobs the state can attract. Moreover, a comparison of the skill contents of the jobs lost and created vividly illustrates the human-resource challenge that lies ahead in Michigan. While the major losses are concentrated in semiskilled and low-skilled production work (welding, painting, and general production), the majority of new jobs will either have a highly technical component or require white-collar sales or managerial skills. The number of new jobs is expected to be highest for robotics technicians — workers who install and maintain these machines. Most experts think these technicians will require the equivalent of two years of technical or community college training. Additional jobs will be created for electrical, mechanical, and industrial engineers, occupations beyond the reach of most of those to be displaced.

A Plant-Level Example. A recent study of the effects of a "factory-of-the-future" design in the auto industry in Michigan brings these estimates down to the level of a specific location. The study also demonstrates the upper end of the probable displacement that occurs when all of the new manufacturing technologies — CAD, CAM, robotics, etc. — are integrated into a flexible manufacturing system. The company estimates that these new technologies will reduce the number of workers required to perform this work by 60 percent, with almost all reductions concentrated in the blue-collar ranks (Karl, 1984).

These forecasts at the region, industry, and plant level underscore the need to be cautious in accepting grand aggregate predictions of the economywide effects of technological changes on employment. Even at these specific technology levels, estimates vary widely and are, at best, rough planning guides. Their magnitudes, and the stark evidence for the mismatch between obsolescent and increasingly important skills, clearly indicate that the management of technological transitions can-

TABLE 3-1 Displacement Impact of Robots in Michigan by Application, Cumulative 1978 to 1990

Application	Autos		All Other Manufacturing		Total	
	1978 Employment Level	Displacement Range (Percent)	1978 Employment Level	Displacement Range (Percent)	1978 Employment Level	Displacement Range (Percent)
Welding	14,910	15.2–19.5	22,694	2.0– 3.6	37,604	7.2– 9.9
Assembly	65,764	4.5– 9.5	50,678	0.8– 2.4	116,442	2.9– 6.4
Painting	4,378	29.2–40.6	4,387	6.0–10.3	8,765	17.6–25.4
Machine loading/ unloading	42,149	8.4–13.5	86,906	1.7– 3.2	129,055	3.9– 6.6
All operatives and laborers	206,927	5.1– 8.6	397,598	0.7– 1.5	604,525	2.2– 4.0
All employment	409,506	2.6– 4.3	769,841	0.4– 0.8	1,179,347	1.1– 2.0

Source: Allan Hunt and Timothy L. Hunt, Human Resource Implications of Robotics, 1983. Reprinted by permission of The Upjohn Institute, Kalamazoo, MI.

TABLE 3-2   Current U.S. Occupational Profiles: Robot Manufacturing, Motor Vehicles and Equipment, All Manufacturing, and All Industries

Occupation	Employment Distribution (Percent)			
	Robot Manu-facturing	Motor Vehicles and Equipment	All Manu-facturing	All Industries
Engineers	23.7	2.3	2.8	1.2
Engineering technicians	15.7	1.2	2.2	1.4
All other professional and technical workers	4.2	2.4	4.0	13.5
Managers, officials, proprietors	6.8	3.3	5.9	8.1
Sales workers	3.4	0.5	2.2	6.3
Clerical workers	13.9	6.2	11.3	19.9
Skilled craft and related workers	8.4	20.8	18.5	11.8
Semiskilled metalworking operatives	4.2	15.8	7.2	1.7
Assemblers and all other operatives	19.0	38.6	36.2	13.1
Service workers	—	2.8	2.0	15.8
Laborers	0.7	6.1	7.7	6.0
Farmers and farm workers	—	—	—	1.0
Total[a]	100.0	100.0	100.0	100.0

[a]Columns may not add to total due to rounding.

Source: Allan Hunt and Timothy L. Hunt, *Human Resource Implications of Robotics,* 1983. Reprinted by permission of The Upjohn Institute, Kalamazoo, MI.

not be a solely private affair. Instead, successful adaptation will require an active partnership among leaders in government, education, and the private sector. As Box 3-1 illustrates, this is exactly the type of public-private partnership that the federal government hopes to achieve through the Jobs Partnership and Training Act.

Managing the Introduction of New Technology

While technological forecasts provide a starting point for understanding the potential effects of new technology, they offer little guidance for managers faced with the task of introducing specific technologies into the workplace. These predictions need to be supplemented with models capable of identifying the range of choices in and potential consequences of various new technologies. Figure 3-2 outlines the structure of a general model that is gaining increasing support among researchers and practitioners. The central theme of the model is that the effects of technological change are not determined by technology alone. That is, the design of the work system that accompanies new technology is a result, first, of choices made on the basis of value judgments and,

BOX 3-1
Evolution of Employment and Training Policies

In 1962 the Manpower Development and Training Act (MDTA) was passed and served as the first major entry of the federal government into an active employment and training policy. MDTA was a response to the fear that "structural" unemployment, i.e., a mismatch between job openings and the people unemployed and looking for work rather than a simple "deficiency of demand" for jobs relative to the number of unemployed, was being caused by growth in international trade and technological displacement. Thus the MDTA funded a variety of vocational and other institutional training programs and relocation services largely aimed at unemployed heads of households. Later in the mid 1960s, the target group shifted more toward youth in an attempt to deal with high rates of teenage unemployment and the range of services expanded to link manpower policies with the social services supporting the War on Poverty. By the end of the 1960s, manpower policy took disadvantaged workers — youth, minorities, and other low-income groups — as its target and special efforts were made to involve local community action agencies and other client-advocate groups in the delivery of employment and training programs.

In 1973, the MDTA was replaced by the Comprehensive Employment and Training Act (CETA). While the general objectives remained the same as before, the administration of programs and control over funding shifted to the state and local areas. Each area was to designate a prime sponsor with responsibility for coordinating the various local government, business, and labor groups and organizations interested in participating in employment and training service delivery. Throughout the years of MDTA and CETA, increasing efforts were made to draw the private sector into a stronger partnership in defining job opportunities and training needs and in placing workers who participated in government-sponsored programs.

The twin goals of encouraging local and state control of employment and training policies and drawing the private sector more directly into the process serve as the foundation for the third generation of employment and training legislation in the United States, the 1983 Jobs Partnership and Training Act (JPTA). The key provisions of JPTA are outlined below.

1. The primary responsibility for policy development and oversight has shifted from the federal Department of Labor to the states.
2. Training efforts are to be coordinated with existing education, economic development, employment service, and health and human-service activities to produce a comprehensive state and local employment policy.
3. Private Industry Councils (PICs) are to be established as the primary vehicle for private sector participation in the planning and operation of local employment and training policies and programs. PICs are to be composed of representatives of business (a majority of board members), organized labor, educational agencies, community-based and economic development agencies and state employment and welfare departments.
4. The following are some of the key functions the PICs and the locally based delivery system are expected to perform:

a. Evaluate local labor market needs and identify future opportunities for job growth.
b. Plan, design, and operate training programs to meet these needs.
c. Develop management and evaluation systems for use of JPTA funds.
d. Coordinate JPTA programs with other community services.

JPTA allocates a majority of program dollars directly to the local level. A portion goes to state governments to cover administrative costs to provide governors with discretionary monies for programs of their choosing. Special funds are allocated for youth programs, and another portion is targeted for workers affected by plant closings or other permanent job losses.

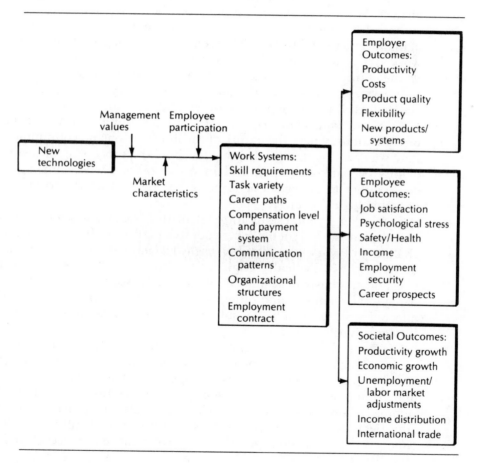

FIGURE 3-2   The Multiple Effects of Technological Change

second, of the characteristics of the markets in which these choices are made. This proposition grows out of the work of "socio-technical systems" (STS) theory (Trist, 1981) and is further elaborated in the Walton paper following this introduction.

STS theory urges managers to involve employees early in the design phase of new technology and to consider the social settings in which the technical innovation is to occur. STS theory predicts that by achieving a sound match between workers' social needs for meaningful, challenging jobs and the technical requirements of the new machinery there will be less resistance to the technology. The result will be work systems that are more responsive to the needs of the organization and its employees. The model in Figure 3-2 posits two stages. The first seeks to explain the effects of technological design decisions on the skill design of the work system; the second relates work systems to a range of outcomes of interest to the firm, its employees, and society.

Those who manage the introduction of new technologies must answer: What type of work system will be most compatible with the technical system, the markets for the firm, and the values and interests of management and workers? Evidence to date suggests that no optimal work system has emerged from new technologies. For example, studies of the introduction of office automation systems showed that while some systems "deskilled" the job of the secretary by establishing specialized word-processing pools, others did not (Adler, 1983; Buchanan, 1982; Glenn and Feldberg, 1977). More deskilling occurred in larger organizations, where the nature of the information and communication flow was routine and predictable (such as the processing of insurance claims or bank deposits), and in organizations where management chose either to disregard or to place low priority on the social effects of technological change.

Another hypothesis is implicit in the model but seldom directly tested; that is, the types of job structures that result from technological change will vary considerably with the individuals engaged in the design process. Typically, engineering professionals make design decisions on the basis of technical efficiency. As Walton argues, however, behavioral scientists and others are urging that representatives of all affected work groups be consulted at earlier stages in the design and implementation process.

New technology sets off a chain reaction of effects. Changes in job design affect skill requirements, compensation levels and payment systems, promotion opportunities and career ladders, social interaction and communication patterns. Further, organizational structures (the number of supervisory and management levels and division of responsibilities), as well as employment structures (use of full-time or part-time workers, subcontractors, or permanent employees), undergo changes.

These characteristics of the work system in turn effect a variety of outcomes of interest to employees, the firm, and society, as indicated in Figure 3-2. New work systems affect not only employees' immediate employment and income security, but also such things as job satisfaction and health and safety conditions. For the firm, the effects can extend far beyond labor costs, productivity, flexibility, and product quality objectives. Some organizations have discovered new market opportunities and businesses after gaining experience with new office systems. Scott-Morton and Rockart (1983) cite an example of a hospital supply firm that placed computer terminals inside hospitals to allow customers to order supplies directly. In time, this led to a new line of business for the supplier as it learned more about, and gradually began serving, the information and data processing needs of hospitals. In manufacturing settings, the introduction of flexible manufacturing systems may open up new, more specialized market opportunities that were previously beyond the reach of firms working with more fixed, mass production-oriented technologies. Finally, the diffusion of new technologies across a large number of settings, the way in which technological change is managed, and the work systems that evolve will affect a variety of broader societal goals. These kinds of effects, many of which appear in Figure 3-2, demonstrate that effective adjustment to new technology requires an active partnership between private and public decision makers.

References

Adler, Paul, "Rethinking the Skill Requirements of New Technologies," Harvard University, Graduate School of Business Working Paper 84–27, October 1983.

Barocci, Thomas A., Mary Thron, Rolf Gaertner, and Kirsten R. Wever, "The Information Systems Decision," Massachusetts Institute of Technology, Sloan School of Management Working Paper 1361–82, January 1983.

Buchanan, David A., and David Buddy, "Advanced Technology and the Quality of Working Life: The Effects of Word Processing on Video Typists," *Journal of Occupational Psychology*, 55, 1982, 1–11.

Deardon, John, "Will the Computer Change the Job of Top Management?" *Sloan Management Review*, Volume 24, Number 1, Fall 1983.

FDA, "An Evaluation of Radiation Emission from Video Display Terminals" (Washington, D.C.: Health and Human Services Publication, FDA 81-8153, February 1981).

Glenn, Evelyn Nakano, and Rosalyn L. Feldberg, "Degraded and Deskilled: The Proletarianization of Clerical Work," *Work and Society*, 25, 1977, 52–64.

Hunt, Allan, and Timothy L. Hunt, *Human Resource Implications of Robotics* (Kalamazoo, Mich.: The Upjohn Institute, 1983).

Karl, Ronald J., *Introducing Flexible Manufacturing in the Auto Industry*. Unpublished Master's Thesis, Sloan School of Management, Massachusetts Institute of Technology, 1984.

"9-5, Campaign on VDT Risks" (Cleveland, Ohio: 9-5, National Association of Office Workers, 1983).

NIOSH, "Potential Health Hazards of Video Display Terminals," June 1981. DHHS (NIOSH) Publication No. 81–129.

Scott-Morton, Michael, "State of the Art Research in Management Support Systems," Massachusetts Institute of Technology Center for Information Systems Research Working Paper 107, July 1983.

Scott-Morton, Michael, and John F. Rockart, "Implications of Changes in Information Technology for Corporate Strategy," Massachusetts Institute of Technology Center for Information Systems Research Working Paper 98, January 1983.

Slesin, L., and M. Zyoko, "Video Display Terminals: Health and Safety," *Microwave News*, 1983.

Trist, Eric, *The Evolution of Socio-Technical Systems* (Toronto: Ontario Quality of Working Life Centre, 1981).

Suggested Readings

William Ascher, *Forecasting: An Appraisal for Policymakers and Planners* (Baltimore: John Hopkins University Press, 1978).

Robert Ayres and Steven Miller, *Understanding and Managing the Productivity, Human Resource and Societal Implications of Robotics and Advanced Information Systems,* (Pittsburgh: The Robotics Institute, 1982).

Martin D. J. Buss, "Managing International Information Systems," *Harvard Business Review,* September–October 1982, 153–162.

Amitai Etzioni, *An Immodest Agenda: Rebuilding America Before the Twenty First Century* (New York: McGraw Hill, 1983).

James L. McKenney and F. Warren McFarlan, "The Information Archipelago — Maps and Bridges," *Harvard Business Review,* September–October 1982, 109–119.

Stephen D. Ruth, "Computer Managers of the 80's: Only Generalists Need Apply," *Journal of Systems Management,* June 1981, 26–29.

New Perspectives on the World of Work
Social Choice in the Development of Advanced Information Technology

Application of advanced information technology will profoundly affect the nature of clerical, professional and managerial work. When these consequences are unplanned, they sometimes are positive and sometimes negative, in human and organizational terms. Referring to the range and importance of these impacts, the author argues why social criteria should be employed in the design and implementation of this new technology. Then, based on the increasingly flexible nature of the technology and its cost profile, he argues why social criteria can be applied without economic sacrifice. Turning to trends in social values, theories of management, and interests of trade unions, the author concludes that social criteria probably will be applied increasingly in the development of information technology in the United States. Finally, the paper reviews some of the methodological issues which will arise in the process.

Introduction

For the past few years, my associates and I have been studying the implications of advanced information technology for white-collar work and how social criteria might be employed to guide development in this area. Based on this research, I will suggest why social criteria should be applied, why they can be, and why it is increasingly likely that they will be. Then I will outline some of the issues that arise when we try to apply social criteria.

Extensive automation of white-collar work has become possible because of two types of technological advances. The first is an explosive growth in computer power per unit of cost — on the order of tenfold increases every four or five years. The second advance is in telecommunications, making it possible to achieve unprecedented movement and integration of electronic information. Consider also two economic facts: (1) the annual growth rate of capital per employee in offices has lagged behind that in manufacturing, and (2) office overhead costs have risen rapidly in recent years. These factors combine to make an extraordinary variety of new applications economically feasible. Experts regard information technology as the most dynamic sector of technical innovations.

Implications for Work And People At Work

My first proposition is that the new information technology has profound implications for the nature of work performed by clerical, professional, and managerial personnel. The potential impact on the work place may be greater than any earlier wave of new mechanization or automation to hit industry. Thus, I propose that the human stakes are high.

The new technical systems [differ] from those of prior generations, particularly because their relationship to human systems has become more pervasive and complex — and more important. Earlier systems utilized large computers, performed a limited number of separate functions, relied upon batch-processing, and were tended by special, full-time operators. The new technologies utilize a network of large and small computers and embrace many activities within a given system, often crossing departmental boundaries. Managers, professionals, and clerical personnel are

Source: Richard E. Walton, "New Perspectives on the World of Work," from *Human Relations*, Volume 35, No. 12, 1982, pp. 1073–1084. Reprinted by permission of Plenum Publishing Corporation and Richard Walton.

required to interact *directly* with computer terminals, often as an integral part of their responsibilities. And because these systems are on-line, the relationship between the user and the system is more immediate. Thus, it is not surprising that the newer systems have the potential for affecting more employees in more ways than ever before, and for influencing work and communication patterns at higher executive levels than previously.

Our studies have covered a number of different applications, including the following three:

1. Electronic mail terminals were placed on the desks of thousands of managers and support personnel in a large firm. This innovation affected the nature of vertical and horizontal communications, access to executives at different levels, decision-making processes, and it modified somewhat the content of the jobs of those who used the tool.

2. A procurement system was installed in a large company, embracing buyers and their clerical support, as well as personnel in the receiving and accounts payable departments. The system made it possible to monitor more closely the performance of purchasing agents, changed the interdepartmental patterns of accountability for errors, and created more tedious clerical work.

3. A phone company automated their local repair bureaus, employing information technology to test phone lines automatically, to monitor the status of all repair orders in the bureau, and to provide telecommunication linkage with service representatives at a new centralized office who received subscriber complaints. Before automation, these service representatives were located in the local repair bureaus. Let us look more closely at this application.

In the *repair bureau*, the new technology reduced the number of personnel and decreased skill requirements. The "test man" is a case in point. In the past, being a test man was a professional job, with a high-status dress code of "starched white shirts

and ties." Mastery required innate ability and experience. Today, the testing function is becoming increasingly automated, and the test man's skills and knowledge have become technologically obsolete. Those holding that position, therefore, have suffered psychologically and economically.

The new system also dramatically affected personnel in the new *centralized answering facility*. The service representatives felt that they had become physically and informationally isolated from other steps in the process of satisfying the customers whose complaints they take. The central facility takes complaints for local bureaus in several states, and the answering personnel neither learn what happens to a particular complaint nor know the people in the bureau to whom they pass along the complaint. Service representatives cannot determine the status of repair work and, therefore, either cannot respond to customers who call back or must provide them with meaningless promises about delivery of services. This has led to tension and mutual fault finding between the service representatives and repair personnel. In these and many other respects the technical system had helped produce "unhealthy" jobs — jobs which failed to meet normal human needs for knowledge and control of the workplace. The result was employee alienation and defective problem-solving.

Not all of the human side effects of these and other systems we studied were negative. I will turn to that point in a moment. But the negative human consequences we found were significant — and largely predictable. The following behavioral generalizations describe some of the common organizational consequences of office applications of the new microprocessor technology.

If the technical system decreases skill requirements, the meaning of work may become trivial, and a loss of motivation, status, and self-esteem may result. This was a common occurrence. In some circumstances those who suffered counterattacked the system.

If the system increases specialization and separates the specialty from interdependent activities, then jobs may become repetitive and isolated, and fail to provide workers with performance feedback. Such jobs produce alienation and conflict.

If the system increases routinization and provides elaborate measurements of work activity, job occupants may resent the loss of autonomy and try to manipulate the measurement system. The fact of measurement itself can put excessive pressure on individuals and can strain peer relationships.

Impact of Technology Varies and Can Be Influenced

My second proposition is that technological determinism is readily avoidable. Technology *can* be guided by social policy, often without sacrifice of its economic purpose. Information technology is less deterministic than other basic technologies that historically have affected the nature of work and people at work.

True, the side effects described above were generally negative, but sometimes the *unplanned* consequences are positive. In each of the areas listed below, the effects were not inherent in the technology. The directional effects resulted, to an important degree, from particular choices made in design or implementation.

1. Work systems based on the new technology often require less skill and knowledge, but sometimes these new systems result in more jobs being upgraded than downgraded. System design can influence that outcome.
2. The technical system can increase the flexibility of work schedules to accommodate human preferences, or it can decrease flexibility and require socially disruptive work schedules.
3. New systems often contribute to social isolation, but sometimes they have the opposite effect. Similarly, they often separate an operator from the end result of his or her effort, but occasionally they bring the operator in closer touch

with the end result. Seldom are these planned outcomes, but they can be.
4. These systems sometimes render individuals technologically obsolete because of changed skill and knowledge requirements, but they also open up new careers.
5. New technology can change the locus of control — toward either centralization or decentralization.
6. New information systems can change — for better or worse — an employee-typist into a subcontractor operating a terminal out of his or her home.

The problem is that those who design applications and those who approve them currently make little or no effort to anticipate their human effects. Thus positive organizational effects are as likely to be accidental as are negative ones.

Why is computer-based technology becoming less deterministic, allowing planners more choice? First, the rapidly declining cost of computing power makes it possible to consider more technical options, including those that are relatively inefficient in the use of that power. Second, the new technology is less hardware dependent, more software intensive. It is, therefore, increasingly flexible, permitting the same basic information-processing task to be accomplished by an ever greater variety of technical configurations, each of which may have a different set of human implications. For example, one system configuration may decentralize decision-making; another may centralize it. Yet both will be able to accomplish the same *task* objectives.

Trends Favor the Exercise of Social Choice

My third proposition is that a number of factors could produce an industrial trend in which human development criteria would be applied to the design of this office technology. I have not yet observed such a trend. But a social revolution affecting work in the manufacturing plant gathered momentum during the 1970s, and the most natural extension of this social revolution to the office would be a movement to seize upon this new office technology and to shape its development. Managements, and unions, where workers are organized, are increasingly acting to modify the way blue-collar work is ordered and managed. And the changes are explicitly in the interest of promoting human development as well as task effectiveness.

The work improvement movement began in the United States and Canada and in some European countries in the early 1970s after several years of sharply increasing symptoms of employee disaffection. Symptoms included costly absenteeism and sabotage, and the media labeled the general phenomenon "the blue-collar blues."

Over the past decade, attention has gradually shifted from symptoms to solutions. Work reform in plants throughout the United States and Canada has grown steadily, and the trend appears to be taking the path of a classical *S* growth curve. Today, the rate of growth in these experiments continues to increase annually, suggesting that we are approaching the steeper portion of the curve.

Work reform reverses many practices launched with the industrial revolution in which tasks were increasingly fragmented, deskilled, mechanically paced, and subjected to external controls. The current trend combines specialized jobs to create whole tasks, integrates planning and implementation, and relies more on self-supervision.

A particularly striking illustration is provided by General Motors (GM) and the United Automobile Workers (UAW), who have jointly sponsored Quality of Work Life (QWL) activities in over half of GM's facilities. Over the course of a decade, political support for QWL activities within each of these organizations grew to the point where such activities have become the official policy of the dominant coalition within each organization. For GM management, policies that favor human development produce a more committed work force; moreover, these policies have come to be regarded by many managers as morally right. For the UAW, these same policies promote industrial democracy and advance unionism. For the work force, such policies allow some discretion where there had been none; they afford human dignity where it had been absent; and they increase the employees' voice in matters that affect them.

The aims of this social revolution are *not* radical in the sense that they challenge either the ownership structure of industry or the basic legitimacy of professional management's current role in deciding where to allocate resources. In this respect, the social revolution in North America differs from some of the forms of industrial democracy developing in Europe.

Some related North American trends *do* have an impact on the ownership structure of smaller enterprises. Professor William F. Whyte and his colleagues at Cornell have documented the experiences of firms which have offered employees stock ownership plans. Moreover, the addition of UAW president, Douglas Fraser, to the Chrysler Corporation Board of Directors is a step toward labor participation in major decisions about resource allocation. But these developments are not typical of the social revolution to which I refer.

The values and behavior patterns which characterize this social revolution have a significance beyond the workplace. More research is needed, but the studies with which I am familiar confirm my own observation that when individuals are able to use a broader range of skills and abilities in their work, they tend to see themselves as capable of making a larger variety of contributions to their community. And when people are afforded a voice in or influence over matters that affect them at work, they will expect the same sort of participation in other social settings. In short, human development at work creates pressures on other institutions to promote similar development. Conversely, human constriction at work is conducive to human constriction in other societal settings.

These observations have been illustrated in a number of American manufacturing plants started in the 1970s where the governing philosophy emphasized human development. Self-supervising work teams were set up which required workers to solve technical and social problems. Members were encouraged to take initiative, to express themselves, and to make constructive use of conflict. The skills and self-confidence gained at work were then exercised in the family setting. For example, their new work roles raised the consciousness of women employees in working-class families and many of them undertook to change their decision-making roles at home from passivity to activity and to move their marriage-role relationships from subordinacy to equality. Many male workers in these innovative plants practiced their own listening skills at home, again with implications for the human development of family members.

Why did this revolution in manufacturing plants gather momentum during the 1970s? Several forces have led to change, at least in North America. One factor, which I mentioned earlier, was the acute rise in worker disaffection during the early 1970s, not unrelated to the unrest which was occurring in the cities and on campuses. Then during the middle 1970s, it became increasingly apparent that American industry was losing its competitiveness in international markets. Management looked for better ways to utilize human resources and recognized that it would have to meet more of the employees' needs and expectations. Unions, fearful about the loss of jobs to foreign competitors, increasingly joined in this venture. Recently American managers, by now somewhat humbled by their own lackluster industrial performance, have adapted Japanese techniques, techniques which also happened to be consistent with Quality of Work Life innovations already developing at home.

No change comparable to that just described is yet underway in the American office. Some clerical workers have been the target of Quality of Work Life activities, especially in large insurance and banking organizations. But for the most part there is little activity in this arena. Ironically, where quality of life has been improved for blue-collar workers, white-collar employees in the same facility often feel neglected by comparison. This feeling of neglect is shared by lower-level managers and professionals, as well as clerical personnel.

Concern within these white-collar groups is growing, as national surveys confirm a decline in job satisfaction among middle managers. Recently, white-collar groups have found themselves almost as vulnerable to massive force reduction as blue-collar workers. In steel, automotive, and rubber companies, for example, tens of thousands of white-collar employees have been cut.

Management is beginning to recognize that it does not tap the fund of skills and knowledge of these white-collar groups. Recently "quality circle," or participative, problem-solving teams have been introduced into white-collar work places, often with beneficial effects on human development. Still, no major pattern of positive social change has emerged affecting those who work in offices.

Now new office technology based on the computer-on-a-chip enters the scene. This new technology either can exacerbate the problem of white-collar disaffection or can be part of the solution. Technology can either constrict human development or promote it.

Although not yet constituting a trend, a significant development is the recent agreement entered into by the American Telephone and Telegraph Company (AT&T) and three unions (including the Communications Workers of America), representing 700,000 employees. The unions and the company have established joint committees to discuss plans for new technology at least six months before new equipment is introduced and to analyze the potential human implications, including job pressures and job organization. In Europe there *is* an established trend for companies and unions to enter into "technology agreements," giving unions and employees an opportunity to modify new technology before it is introduced. The AT&T agreement covers unionized employees, who are mostly blue-collar workers, but the idea probably will be extended to the company's white-collar work force as well.

Implementing Social Choice

The idea that technology has a social impact certainly is not new. Social scientists have long argued that technology can dramatically affect individuals, institutions, and society as a whole. Managers who introduce new work technologies have long appreciated that there will be organizational side effects. But this knowledge has had little influence on the introduction of new work technology.

In the past, considerations of the human impact of innovation have led merely to efforts to overcome workers' resistance. These efforts have emphasized implementation methods, including communication and training, and employment assurances. But efforts to ameliorate the impact should increasingly extend upstream to the design stage itself, where workers could affect the design of hardware, software, and management operating systems.

In the past, where human criteria have been considered in the design of work technology, they have centered on narrow factors, such as ease of learning, operator fatigue, and safety. The criteria should be extended to include a broader array of human needs — for autonomy, for social connectedness, for meaningful work, for effective voice.

But in order to exercise social choice in the significant sense I have just described, one must break new methodological ground.

1. Organizations need explicit normative models, by which designers can judge what human effects are to be considered good, bad, or neutral, and which ones are especially salient. An organizationally specific model would be based both on gen-

eral knowledge about human development and on an understanding of the particular circumstances of the company.

2. Designs should not be approved until an "organizational impact statement" has been prepared and reviewed. The first step would be an examination of the requirements of a proposed technical system. This would clarify the first-order social consequences of the system — how it changes the degree of specialization, locus of control, or skill requirements. The next step would be a prediction of second-order consequences, such as motivational effects, social conflict, and human development. This would require the perspectives of behavioral disciplines not currently involved in systems projects.

3. One needs practical methods for involving those who will eventually use and/ or be affected by a system. While "user involvement" in systems development has been a widely endorsed concept for more than a decade, in that practice users seldom report they have been meaningfully involved.

4. System development should be approached as an evolutionary process. This contrasts with a more typical assumption that the design can and should be completely conceived before implementation. This methodological recommendation is based on the finding that the human impacts of complex information systems are *dynamic*, in the sense that their effects change over time; for example, some initially negative reactions disappear as tasks are mastered, and some initially positive reactions decline as novelty wears off. Complicating the picture is the fact that effects are *reciprocal*, in the sense that the employee will react to the technical system; for example, user reactions may affect the quality of inputs to the system and, in turn, the functionality of the system.

5. My final recommendation is that significantly greater effort must be devoted to evaluation of the operational system, and this evaluation must comprehend social effects as well as economic and technical achievements.

These methodological proposals have an additional implication: management should assign a fraction of every development budget to be used to explore the human implications of these systems, then it should act on this knowledge.

We are only beginning to learn how to exercise social choice in the course of technological development. There are still relatively few instances where designers have paid explicit and comprehensive attention to potential impacts on human systems. In Europe there is growing experience with trade unions which have insisted on being involved in evaluating new computer-based technology before it is installed in the workplace. In the United Kingdom, Enid Mumford and her associates have developed a participative approach to the design of systems which affect clerical groups (Mumford & Weir, 1979; Mumford and Henshall, 1979; and Hedberg and Mumford, 1975). These are pioneering efforts, and though their achievements may be instructive, they are by no means definitive.

Conclusion

To summarize: applications of the new information technology should be guided by human-development criteria; they can be so guided, and now there is decent probability that they will be. If this new work technology is to be shaped by social criteria, we will need new implementation "know-how," and a rich field will be opened for basic and applied research.

The design and implementation of advanced information technology poses major organizational problems, and we must deal with the problems. These innovations also represent the most important opportunity available in the 1980s to introduce constructive changes in clerical, professional, and managerial work. First a few pioneering organizations and then a larger number of progressive ones will exploit this opportunity. The introduction of this technology gives us a chance to rethink the organization and management of professional and clerical work in the office that is analogous to the way green-field plants created an opportunity to pioneer new approaches to managing factory work (Walton, 1979).

The 1980s will be a period of trial and error as we learn how to exercise social choice in systems design. Academic institutions can contribute to the analysis and dissemination of these experiences, but only if some managements, systems developers, and unions choose to lead the way in this uncharted field.

References

Hedberg, B., and Mumford, E. The design of computer systems. In E. Mumford and H. Sackman (Eds.), *Human choice and computers*, North-Holland Publishing Co., 1975.

Mumford, E., and Henshall, D. *A participative approach to computer systems design.* London: Associated Business Press, 1979.

Mumford, E., and Weir, M. *Computer systems in work design.* London: Associated Business Press, 1979.

Walton, R. E. Work innovations in the United States. *Harvard Business Review,* July–August 1979.

Managing the Introduction of New Technology

We now turn to a case designed to illustrate some of the issues involved in managing the introduction of a particularly widespread new technology: video display terminals (VDTs). This case raises questions not only about job design and other structural workplace issues, but also about the physical and mental health of the employees who work with VDTs. The case highlights the range of decisions that managers, government policymakers, and union leaders face as a new technology is introduced into the workplace.

CASE
Video Display Terminals

One of the most controversial work-related health and technology issues of the 1980s centers around the design, introduction, and use of video display terminals in the workplace. These television-like units, based on computer-chip technology, have been installed in offices and factories throughout the United States since the early 1970s. It is estimated that 7 million to 10 million of them are currently in use, and that by 1990 70 percent of all offices will have adopted them. This case considers two issues: technology and health.

TECHNOLOGICAL CONCERNS

The introduction of most kinds of new technology has both direct and indirect effects on the ways in which people perceive their status in the workplace and on the ways in which they actually carry out their jobs. These effects derive from technologically induced changes in job designs and career ladders. For example, VDTs raise questions for secretaries with respect to the potential for job deskilling or downgrading. This kind of change in job design can result from the creation of word-processing pools in offices with several secretaries. In banks or insurance companies, the use of data entry clerks can have a similarly downgrading effect on jobs since their performance can be closely monitored by recording the number of data entries per clerk per hour. Moreover, there is a widespread fear that the computer technology will be used to monitor and measure the performance of VDT operators.

Training is another major concern among employees newly exposed to VDTs. In some cases, employees could be replaced by people who already possess the skills necessary to work with various kinds of VDTs. Even where the existing work force is already or will be trained in VDT-related skills, fears — whether well-founded or not — that employees will be replaced by younger workers or by the machines themselves are commonplace.

VDT-related work in some cases may be farmed out to people working in their homes. Such workers generally complete work on an as-needed piecework basis and cost employers significantly less in wages and fringe benefits than full-time secretaries or clerical staff.

Even without deskilling, downgrading, or the threat of replacement, the introduction of terminals (as with almost any new technology) can have disturbing psychological effects on employees. Task mechanization and routinization can lower an employee's self-esteem. Adjustment to technologically dictated time schedules and performance monitoring can be severely disruptive to an employee who is accustomed to having greater job autonomy and control over the flow of his or her work.

But the introduction of VDT-related tasks often has a beneficial influence on office and staff work. The elimination of tedious and repetitious tasks, the possibility for at-home, flexible working hours, the opening of a port of entry into a new career path, and initiation into the use of application software are among the potential benefits of this new technology. For example, a large computer manufacturer uses word-processing personnel as a labor pool for recruiting new programmer and programmer-analyst trainees. The same firm allows workers with special scheduling problems to work part-time at home, with a terminal connected to the office via telephone. Repetitious tasks such as large mailings and multiple letters can be streamlined, thereby freeing clerical time for other, possibly less tedious, tasks. Finally, application-software usage, such as computer programs for budgeting, can take clerical staff from the processing of words into the intricacies of the budgeting process.

The real questions surrounding the introduction and use of new technology center on the way in which the technology is employed and the degree to which those affected by it will have an opportunity to participate in the basic decisions concerning its utilization.

HEALTH CONCERNS

The health concerns associated with the introduction of VDTs are numerous, including emotional stress, radiation hazards, musculoskeletal factors, and visual problems. A 1981 study by the National Institute for Occupational Safety and Health (NIOSH) found that radiation levels emitted by VDTs were extremely low and would not have an adverse effect on pregnant women or cause cataracts (NIOSH, 1981). Another study, by the Bureau of Radiological Health of the Food and Drug Administration (FDA), reached a similar conclusion (FDA, 1981). But 9 to 5, the national association of office workers, has mounted a campaign to educate the public about the health hazards of VDTs. It maintains that within the past two years eight groups of women operating VDTs in the United States and Canada have experienced an incidence of miscarriages and birth defects significantly higher than would be expected by statistical probability alone (Sleslin and Zyoko, 1983; 9 to 5, 1983). For example, six pregnancies among VDT operators at Surrey Memorial Hospital in Vancouver, British Columbia produced only one healthy baby. Also, at a major Montreal airport, seven cases of spontaneous abortion out of thirteen pregnancies were reported within two years among a group of ticket agents operating VDTs in the same location.

Aside from the issue of radiation hazards, other health-related problems, although less severe, are more prevalent. A study done by NIOSH showed that VDT operators were more likely to complain of physical problems such as burning eyes, fainting, hand cramps, etc., than non-VDT operators (see Table 3-3).

TABLE 3-3   Percentage of Clerical VDT Operators and
Control Subjects with Selected Health Complaints

Health Complaints	Percentage	
	Clerical VDT	Control Subjects
Skin rash	57	31
Irritability	80	63
Fainting	36	17
Nervous	50	31
Fatigue	74	57
Pain down arm	37	20
Stomach pains	51	35
Change in color perception	40	9
Irritated eyes	74	47
Burning eyes	80	44
Blurred vision	71	35
Eye strain	91	60
Swollen muscles and joints	50	25
Back pain	78	56
Painful or stiff arms or legs	62	35
Painful or stiff neck and shoulders	81	55
Numbness	47	18
Neck pressure	57	34
Difficulty with feet from standing long periods	49	35
Sore shoulder	70	38
Loss of feeling in wrists/fingers	33	11
Neck pain into shoulder	56	19
Hand cramps	49	16
Loss of strength in arms/hands	36	14
Stiff or sore wrists	47	7

Source: Michael J. Smith, et al. "An Investigation of Health Complaints and Job Stress in Video Display Operations." In U.S. National Institute for Occupational Safety and Health, *Select Research Reports on Health Issues in Video Display Terminal Operations.* Cincinnati, Ohio, April 1981. Table 9a.

Potential Solutions

Many of the technology and health-related problems connected with VDTs can be overcome by better design and use of the machines. Among the recommendations made by 9 to 5 are:

> All workers should have a break of 15 minutes for every two hours of VDT work, or 15 minutes for every hour of intense VDT work.
>
> Continuous use of VDTs should be limited to 4 hours each day.
>
> All VDT equipment should have adjustable screens, keyboards, and glare-reduction devices; furniture, lighting, and work environment should be designed for the comfort and safety of the operator.
>
> Stress-inducing features of automated jobs such as machine pacing or computer monitoring of tasks should be eliminated.
>
> Employers should provide regular eye exams for all VDT workers.

Exhibit 3-1 presents another list of guidelines for the design, installation, and use of new office technology. These guidelines were prepared by the United Automobile Workers (UAW) New Office Technology Committee as part of its efforts to organize and negotiate on behalf of employees at the Harvard Medical School.

It should be emphasized that this local proposal represents an extreme point of view that has not been adopted at the Harvard Medical School, or anywhere else to our knowledge. The day-to-day operational problems that would result from the enforcement of such proposals would be quite burdensome. For example, the provision that no job will be made monotonous or less satisfying by the introduction of VDTs would present management with a complex and almost unapproachable problem. To date, there have been no minimum federal or state standards required for the design and use of VDTs in the workplace, although legislation to establish such standards has been introduced in some state legislatures (see Exhibit 3-2 for an example of one such bill). The only standard that applies is the 1970 federal standard for X-ray leakage from television sets. Other countries have chosen to enact various VDT standards. In Sweden, the law limits VDT work to four hours a day for any single operator and requires ten-minute breaks every hour. In Canada, pregnant women are not required to work with VDTs. Laws in other countries require eye examinations, adjustable keyboards, nonglare lighting, and other safety measures.

The controversy over the health effects of VDTs will continue, and the role of the principal actors will not only define the outcome for the design and use of VDTs in the workplace, but also may influence the way other new technologies are introduced in the future. The following set of discussion questions is designed to highlight some of the problems and trade-offs involved in the proper introduction of new technologies like VDTs.

EXHIBIT 3-1
United Automobile Workers' Guidelines
for the Use of New Office Technology

Equal Participation

1. All employees who will be affected by a new technology shall have the right to equally participate in the making of decisions about how new technology will be used and policies concerning its use through representatives of their choice.
2. Employees shall be informed of any plans regarding the introduction of new technology, related purchases or changes in job organization at the earliest possible date and no later than that amount of time required for informed participation in decisions.

Health Effects

3. No employee shall be required to use a VDT that does not have all of the following features: detachable keyboard, adequate glare protection, no noticeable flicker, negative results in radiation testing. Work stations shall be flexible and include an easily adjustable table and chair and appropriate lighting. All newly purchased equipment shall include all ergonomically desirable features which are available. Advances in technology shall be monitored and equipment shall be updated on a regular basis.
4. All departments shall be guaranteed school funds to buy ergonomically optimal terminals and furniture for VDTs (see #3) when sufficient funds are not available in the departmental budget.
5. Employees shall not be required to work in an office where a printer is located. If space limitations require that a printer be in the same office, effective noise-dampening measures, such as noise shields, acoustic tiles and carpeting, will be installed.
6. All VDTs shall be regularly serviced at least once a year. The employer shall attempt to secure company-wide maintenance contracts for each brand of machine to make maintenance more affordable. If maintenance cannot be afforded by a department, the cost shall be paid for with university funds.
7. All VDT users shall be entitled to and encouraged to take a minimum of a 10 minute break for every hour of continuous VDT use. No employee shall be required to work more than 2 continuous hours at the VDT or more than 4 hours in any one day.
8. If a woman who is pregnant or intending to become pregnant requests work which does not require VDT use because of unknown, potential radiation hazards, she shall be assigned a comparable job with comparable pay.
9. All employees shall be given employer paid eye exams prior to assignment to VDT work. Employer paid annual eye exams shall be guaranteed to all VDT users. The employer shall guarantee payment for new glasses or a change in prescription needed as a result, at least in part, of VDT use and any special type of glasses (e.g., for those who use bifocals) needed specifically for VDT use.
10. The employer shall maintain occupational health records on all VDT users specifying length of time worked on the VDT, type of terminal and tasks, work conditions and any health problems experienced by the user. Individuals shall have access to these health records.

Job Quality

11. VDT users shall be compensated for new skills and expanded job responsibilities through meaningful salary increases. New job classifications which take into account the changes in skills and responsibilities required in an automated office shall be developed.
12. No job shall be made more monotonous or unsatisfying as a result of the introduction of new technology.
13. New technology shall be implemented so as to create or maintain the number of jobs and enrich the content of jobs.
14. Monitoring devices available on VDTs shall not be used to record the speed, accuracy, or any other aspect of a user's work.

EXHIBIT 3-2
A Legislative Approach to Regulating Video Display Terminals

Employers intending to introduce VDT hardware or software in excess of $5,000 shall give written advance notice of at least 6 months to all affected employees, and shall provide free eye examinations to all affected employees before installation and at least annually thereafter.

If an employee needs new glasses or contact lenses in order to work with a VDT the employer shall provide these. If an eye doctor recommends that an employee stop working with a VDT the employer shall provide other work at equal pay and otherwise similar working conditions. Pregnant employees shall be offered the same for the term of pregnancy.

Employers shall provide VDT operators with flexible work stations, including adjustable back-rests and chair heights; terminal tables with height and tilt options; proper illumination; drapes and/or vertical blinds for windows; and minimal screen glare.

VDT work areas shall be kept at temperatures, humidity levels and ventilation standards prescribed by the American Society of Heating, Refrigeration and Air Conditioning Engineers; VDTs shall be maintained every 6 months; and background noise at VDT work stations shall not exceed 65 decibels.

VDT operators shall have flexible rest periods, including at least 15 minutes of break time per 2 hours of continuous work at a VDT (after 1 hour for employees under unusually high demands); and no employee shall be required to work at a VDT for more than 5 hours per day.

VDT-related jobs shall be designed in such a way as to create motivated and productive employees, to allow for work feedback, and to avoid job fragmentation and the elimination of progress indicators.

Source: Summary of Senate Bill 90 and House Bill 2300 of the State of Massachusetts Legislature, 1984 Session.

Questions for Discussion

1. Should managers involve office workers in the decision-making process involved in the installation of VDT equipment? If so, at what stage of its introduction?

2. What kinds of data should be collected at the workplace before and after VDT introduction in order to determine the various effects of the new technology on employees and on job performance? Who should have access to the data?

3. What should be the role of unions, who represent about 10 percent of American office workers, in the process of the introduction of VDTs? Should union representatives participate in the choice of machinery to be purchased, the specifications of the machinery design, or the layout of offices?

4. What is the appropriate government policy in this type of situation? Is this a case of new technology introduced into the workplace without sufficient study of its effects or adequate safeguards regulating its use? Or are these issues better left to manufacturers, employers who purchase the machines, and collective bargaining? Will the marketplace produce the correct signals to manufacturers so that the recommended safety factors are built into future machines? Or should OSHA review the NIOSH recommendations and other scientific evidence, hold the required public hearings, and issue mandatory standards governing the design and use of these machines? If these federal agencies do not take action, should individual states regulate the use of VDTs along the lines suggested by the bill introduced in Massachusetts?

II

Values and Strategies

PREVIEW

In considering values and strategies, our attention turns to the actions taken within organizations to plan for and design the broad HRM/IR strategies and policies guiding HRM/IR practices. In Part I we suggested how strategies and policies need to take into account the external environment. In Part II, we stress the influence of the values of key organizational leaders, as well as the effects of business strategies and competitive positions of firms. Following our overview is an article by James L. Walker that describes how firms conduct the process of human resource planning. Part II closes with the case of the People Express Company, an airline founded by an entrepreneur who wanted to build a successful organization around specific values and principles. The case provides a good illustration of the fit between managerial values, business strategy, and human resource policies and practices.

Chapter 4 concerns the activities and issues relevant to the top level of our three-tiered framework of HRM/IR within an organization. The discussion highlights the interface between top-management strategy and the HRM/IR system. Activities at this highest level show the organizational contexts of the HRM/IR system and the relationships between that system and other areas of management.

4

Human Resource Management and Its Organizational Contexts

Two themes dominate current research and professional literature on human resource management. First, as an outgrowth of the exploding interest in "corporate culture" (Deal and Kennedy, 1982; Peters and Waterman, 1982), managers and researchers are looking more carefully at the values, norms, and assumptions that underlie an organization's human resource management policies and practices. Second, as a result of the increased emphasis on business strategy and strategic planning, both in practice and in organization and management research, human resource management professionals are being asked to better relate their policies and practices to the broad strategic needs of the firm. Both themes reflect the need to move personnel, or human resource management, out of its traditional, functional mold into a strategic mode by relating HRM/IR practices and policies to the objectives of top executives and line managers.

In this chapter we address the links between top executives' values, philosophies, and business strategies and human resource management. We begin with a discussion of the role of managerial values and move to present a theoretical framework for relating variations in business strategies to human resource management.

The Influence of Management Values

The idea that industry has a human side is gaining more and more attention as management theorists increasingly stress the role of top executives in shaping the internal culture of an organization by clarifying the values at work within a firm. This theme is most obvious in successful organizations whose charismatic founders had clear values that shaped the human resource management policies at every level. Often these values continue to influence human resource policies long after the founder departs (Schein, 1983). Note that not all companies successfully create a culture that facilitates effective HRM/IR policies. Also, some top executives continue to view human resource policies as a low priority that can be left to lower-level personnel specialists. We

95

therefore need to examine the range of values and ideologies that influence the importance attached to the human resources of a firm and the substantive policies guiding their management.

Management Values Versus Competitive Pressures

There is no doubt that the values of top executives have a profound effect on the human resource management strategies and policies of an organization. The question is, to what extent do values represent a stable influence that can be sustained despite changes in the external environment, in business strategies, or in the competitive position of a firm.

In the 1920s many large, growing, innovative United States firms embraced the values of welfare capitalism and the "American Plan" for meeting the social and economic needs of their employees. The values and ideology driving this movement were nicely captured in a 1927 statement of Charles M. Schwab, chairman of Bethlehem Steel Corporation:

> Our job primarily is to make steel, but it is being made under a system which must be justified. If . . . this system does not enable men to live on an increasingly higher plane, if it does not allow them to fulfill their desires and satisfy their reasonable wants, then it is natural the system itself should fail (quoted from Brody, 1980; 48).

The human resource strategies of the 1920s produced increases in profit sharing, personal savings, and stock purchase plans; expansion of various health, welfare, and pension programs; and a variety of social and environmental improvement services, such as sports, recreation, and industrial safety. The executives believed that employees should have greater opportunities to participate in their firms, without resorting to trade unions and collective bargaining. Thus, management promoted company-controlled employee representation plans and union-like organizations.

Although these innovative personnel strategies gained considerable momentum during the high growth years of the 1920s, few survived the Great Depression. Managerial values, it seems, can have important effects in times of economic growth and expansion, when an organization has greater discretion in how it manages its affairs and when labor is more scarce and therefore more valuable. These values, however, are tested as the environment changes from growth to decline, or as a firm's competitive position becomes more precarious. At these critical points the staying power of managerial values is challenged, and the depth of executives' commitment to maintaining the "culture" that was so carefully cultivated in good times meets its most severe test.

Variations in Managerial Values

Some firms have remained committed to their employees through good and bad times. Firms including IBM, Xerox, Polaroid, Digital

Equipment Corporation, Hewlett Packard, Procter and Gamble, and Eastman Kodak represent successful firms whose top executives' values and philosophies produced strategies that place a high priority on innovative human resource management (Peters and Waterman, 1982). Consider, for example, IBM, a firm noted throughout its history for placing a high priority on the management of its human resources. As with many other firms, IBM is experiencing competitive pressures from Japanese and other new entrants into some of its markets. The competition has led IBM to implement new business strategies to become the low-cost producer in those markets. John Opel, IBM's president, stated in an annual message to his managers that, in adjusting to its new business strategies, the company intended to preserve the traditional values underlying its human resource management policies.

> IBM people are our greatest asset. Increased efficiency cannot be paid for by debiting our traditional respect for the individual. There can and need be no compromise on that. The management of people remains paramount.

Box 4-1 summarizes IBM's human resource management philosophy and policies, as described by Walt Burdick, the firm's vice-president of personnel.

IBM has a large, influential personnel staff, approximately one human resource professional to one hundred employees. (This ratio is almost double the average in most United States firms.) In addition, IBM invests heavily in training its supervisors in the art of people management. Each manager undergoes intensive training when first made a supervisor and then receives additional training annually.

A tacit dimension of the IBM philosophy is that unionization or any such formalized group activity is to be discouraged. In this respect IBM is similar to the majority of United States employers. Some firms, also driven by the strong values of their founders, however, have from the start accepted or even encouraged unionization, while both promoting positive labor-management relations and working cooperatively with the union. The Xerox Corporation, driven by the strong values of its founder, Joseph Wilson, is a prominent example of labor-management cooperation and unionization. More recently, the top executives of Ford Motor Company have espoused a similar philosophy; management is joining with the United Auto Workers on strategies to help Ford and its employees adapt to the severe competitive pressures affecting the auto industry.

At the other end of the spectrum, executive values also affect the management of people. Some top managers place a high priority on achieving flexibility and low costs by avoiding long-term employment relationships. These firms prefer to subcontract to others the responsibility of recruitment, selection, and, to some extent, supervision and compensation. For example, Box 4-2, a *Wall Street Journal* article, describes the abuse of temporary laborers in the Houston area.

BOX 4-1
Key Personnel Policies at IBM

1. *Individualism:* Emphasis is placed on managing individuals, recognizing individual differences, and counseling individuals to maximize their career potential. All individual data are regarded as private and confidential.
2. *Staffing and Employment:* The company has traditionally promoted employment continuity. Each hiring decision is made under the assumption that a career is being offered. Most hiring is done exclusively at the entry level with higher level openings filled by promotions from within the organization.
3. *Compensation Policy:* All employees are paid on a salary basis. Salary increases and bonuses are based on merit.
4. *Fringe Benefits:* All benefits are paid 100 percent by the company. All employees receive the same benefits.
5. *Family Relationship:* A paternalistic attitude is maintained, although norms of conformity are less stringent than in earlier years. The company still expects to aid employees in times of stress or tragedy.
6. *Communications:* Open upward and downward communications are encouraged through a variety of programs. Attitude surveys have been done for more than twenty-five years. "Speak up" programs are available to allow anonymous complaints or other messages to be communicated to management. Other ideas and messages can be communicated through IBM's long-standing "Open Door" policy. "Skip level" interviews are held regularly.
7. *Social Responsibility:* Extensive hiring and training of disadvantaged and handicapped workers. Professionals loaned to colleges and community organizations.
8. *Mobility and Flexibility:* Heavy investment in training employees is made to ensure the flexible deployment of people to changes in work organization. Location and production-scheduling decisions are made to smooth out the work flow and stabilize employment. Managers are expected to be geographically mobile. Subcontractors are used for peak work times or for tasks, such as janitorial and food services, which are outside the scope of IBM's main business, and for which the company is unable to provide career opportunities.

Source: Adapted from presentation of Mr. Walter Burdick, Vice President of Personnel, IBM, 1983.

Day laborers supplied by the managers of "flophouses" for drug and alcohol addicts and other homeless people may be the extreme case. They do, however, form part of a large portion of the American work force that is in the so-called secondary labor market (Doeringer and Piore, 1972). If this type of employment relationship were limited to the small percentage of people subjected to the conditions exposed in the *Wall Street Journal* article, the problem could be addressed

BOX 4-2
The Abuse of Temporary Help

The Day Laborer's Toil

It's 5 a.m., and the 120 tenants of Krash Cabin, a filthy flophouse run by one of the many day-labor outfits on the fringes of downtown, are getting their instructions from the burly bunkhouse manager: "Get your asses out of bed before I throw you out," he shouts.

One man, exhausted after digging ditches for 10 hours in 85-degree heat the day before, begs to be allowed to recuperate in his bunk. "I'm too sick to work today," he tells Bob McClarity, the tattoed bunkhouse boss. "I don't give a damn," barks the boss, hauling him out of his bunk. "This ain't a charity hospital."

Indeed it isn't. The men in Krash Cabin are shipped out day and night to unload box-cars, shovel cement, clean coke ovens or handle other dirty, often dangerous, temporary work. The company that runs the operation collects $6 to $15 an hour for the labor but pays the workers the minimum wage of $3.35.

Then it manages to get a good part of that back by deducting from the day's pay voucher assessments for lodging, locker rentals and perhaps work clothes or gloves. To cash the voucher, the worker must go to the company tavern and pay for a drink, whether he wants one or not. Though his work is often hazardous, he is told his employer doesn't have workers' compensation coverage. "It's a slave shop," says the Rev. James Chapman, a local street minister.

Plenty of Takers

Yet this and similar day-labor outfits in this Sun Belt City know their labor pool will be full each day with a growing mob of desperate job seekers willing to endure such conditions. "Sure it's slavery," says Kenneth Sweet, a laid-off auto worker from Detroit with a wife and three children. "But a man's got to feed his family somehow."

Companies providing temporary manual laborers — which operate much differently from suppliers of clerical and other white-collar temporaries — enjoy virtual immunity from supervision. They are not, for instance, considered employment agencies, which in most states face strict licensing requirements and fee reviews. They function under their own rules and have lobbied hard to keep it that way, helping stamp out several federal and state legislative attempts to impose curbs on the industry.

Nobody's Responsibility

Thus, the country's estimated two million day laborers are on their own. Their employers, unregulated and in a highly competitive business, spend little to protect them. The companies to which they are sent feel little responsibility, mostly regarding the workers as a convenient tool to handle fluctuations in demand, union problems or menial tasks.

A four-month investigation, during which this reporter interviewed scores of day laborers across the country and spent time as a worker in several Houston labor pools, including Krash Cabin, suggests that many United States day laborers face some of the same abuses as powerless workers of the 18th century did during the Industrial Revolution.

They frequently work in hazardous conditions. At the same time, there sometimes is scant provision for compensating them if they do get hurt. Various fees may be assessed against their meager wages. Clauses in their contracts may largely preclude them from stepping up to permanent work at a company to which they are sent. And, of course, they can be fired any time.

Liquidated Damages

As many day laborers see it, their best hope is to happen to get a steady "ticket" to one company for several weeks and make such a good impression there that they are offered a job. That has happened to a lucky few, such as Harry Davis, who was hired as a truck driver at a steel-distributing company. But the odds are against it. "Many employers won't hire you." Mr. Davis says, "because they think only tramps and losers work in labor pools."

That isn't the only obstacle. Another is the "liquidated damages clause" found in many day-labor contracts. Such clauses state that if a company gives a full-time job to a temporary worker who was sent over, it must pay the labor pool a fee, either all at once or over a period of weeks.

That fee is $696 for a day laborer at a Houston firm called Quality Temporary Service. The woman who runs the firm, Diane Birch, concedes that liquidated damages clauses may discourage clients from offering employment to temporary workers. But she says the rates are "only fair," given the cost of recruiting and retaining the laborers.

Some temporary workers try to deal with their seemingly inescapable situation by buying beer and other gifts for the bunkhouse bosses, hoping to improve their chances of getting a steady work ticket. But the recent weakening of Houston's robust economy has reduced demand for day laborers. This change has put pressure on the labor pools and forced dozens out of business. It also has meant an even tighter squeeze for workers, because many surviving day labor firms have found a way to keep their profit margins up: by retrieving more of the money they pay out in wages.

Itemized Deductions

For example, most Houston firms have started charging their laborers $1 a day or more for transportation to and from the job site. Many sell the workers used work clothing at a big markup. One company, called Anybody Anytime, even charges its laborers a $1-a-day "maintenance fee" for the cost of cleaning up its hiring hall.

Handy Arrangement

This toll is viewed with indifference by most companies that use temporary laborers. "We have no background at all on these guys," says Robert Houlgrave, an executive of Hughes Tool Co.'s offshore division. "The labor pool just delivers them to us in a van and takes them back when we're done with them." It's a nice arrangement, he adds, "because we don't have the hassle of taking out insurance policies on them, paying benefits or handling a mountain of paper work. The labor pool takes care of all that."

through more vigorous enforcement of existing labor and civil rights statutes. However, the issue of temporary laborers concerns more than just the violation of existing laws by unscrupulous individuals. As suggested in Chapter 3, the country is experiencing growth in the use of a variety of employment relationships: temporary help, subcontracting, employee leasing. Some physicians, for example, are leasing their office and nursing staffs from specialized firms that handle hiring, firing, compensation, and related human resource management tasks for a monthly fee. Although this arrangement frees doctors of many burdensome human resource management responsibilities, such as payroll paperwork, it creates a void in the managerial process — line managers are no longer directly accountable for the management of the people who work with them. As an example of the trend toward subcontracting for services traditionally provided by permanent employees, the U.S. Steel Corporation in late 1983 terminated 4,000 to 5,000 managers and engineers only to hire them back as consultants as needed for specific projects.

The point to be stressed is that the relative importance assigned to human resource management issues within a firm, as well as the choice of HRM/IR policies and strategies, lies in the hands of top executives. These choices reflect the deep-seated values and preferences of organizational leaders; they can permeate every aspect of an organization and have long-term effects. This is the process out of which an organizational culture develops and influences human resource management policies and practices.

The values of key executives can foster innovative policies that are consistent with the values of their employees and the larger society. If executives' values are inconsistent with larger societal goals and values, countervailing forces — laws, regulations, public interest groups, labor organizations — will attempt to limit the discretion of organizational leaders. In addition, technological advances and growing competitive pressures create new opportunities but also place new pressures on firms to treat their human resources as a variable cost similar to other factors of production. Therefore, top executives, and those who report to them, need to constantly examine the effects their values have on their organization's human resource management policies and practices.

The Dynamics of Organizational Life Cycles

Human resource policies and practices vary across different stages of a product life cycle and across firms or strategic business units that follow different competitive strategies. The framework presented here for analyzing these variations is both descriptive and normative. It is descriptive because there is some evidence that the priorities assigned to different human resource activities vary systematically with different product cycles and competitive strategies. (See, for example, the Xerox example in Box 4-3.) It is normative in the sense that by pointing

BOX 4-3
The New Lean, Mean Xerox

The Sept. 23 disclosure by Xerox Corp. that it was planning major cutbacks and a reduction in staff had nothing to do with the current state of the economy. Rather, it was the first stage in a major corporate reorganization aimed at making the copier giant more competitive with the Japanese.

Xerox was burned once by Japanese copier makers, and its management is determined not to let the same thing happen again. When a host of Japanese producers introduced low-price copiers in the U.S. in the mid-1970s, the invasion not only sparked an explosion in sales but also nearly shut Xerox out of a market segment that it had previously ignored. Largely because of this new wave of Japanese competition, Xerox's share of U.S. copier revenues plummeted from 96% in 1970 to just 46% last year — and it is still falling.

Although the reorganization is just getting started, its outlines are already clear. Xerox's huge copier operations will be split into smaller groups, decision-making will be decentralized, and its 125,000-strong work force will be reduced as part of a cost-cutting drive intended to boost productivity in every aspect of the company's business, from manufacturing to marketing.

"This isn't a crash program for 1981 or 1982. It's an attempt to restructure the entire business," explains C. Peter McColough, Xerox chairman. "We're talking about ways to get leaner and tougher throughout the company." In the midst of this reorganization, McColough announced on Sept. 29 that he would step aside as chief executive officer at the company's annual meeting next May. The job of leading the new Xerox through the crucial 1980s will fall to President David T. Kearns, who will take over as CEO. And Kearns leaves no doubt about who will set the corporate pace in the decade ahead. "If you really want to see how good you have to be to compete, the Japanese are the ones to look at," he says. "We want to be remembered as the company that took on the Japanese and were successful."

To squeeze the most out of Xerox's service and sales network, Kearns has divided his huge copier sales force into two separate operations. One group now chases small business sales, while the other handles the large accounts. Service has been taken out of the hands of regional sales managers and set up as a separate group. By increasing the number of sales regions from 5 to 20 and the number of branches from 86 to 145, Kearns intends to increase the flexibility and responsiveness of Xerox's huge, unwieldy U.S. marketing force. He also hopes the move will foster some of the entrepreneurial spirit so visible in many of Xerox's smaller competitors. "I want to pump some excitement back into the [copier] business," says Kearns.

A Corporate Overhaul

This move to decentralized management is also behind a reorganization at Xerox's Stamford (Conn.) headquarters that is just being completed. Kearns is slashing the size of the corporate staff and giving decision-making power — as well as profit responsibility — to the operating units. A small corporate strategy office will look at the long-term issues, but strategic business units

Source: Reprinted from the October 12, 1981 issue of *Business Week*, pp. 126–32, by special permission, © 1981 by McGraw-Hill, Inc.

will manage specific segments of Xerox's broad product range. This shift is aimed at cutting the long product development cycles that have bedeviled Xerox for years.

Kearns knows that his biggest challenge will be to trim Xerox's bloated work force. During its years of breakneck growth, Xerox added new employees as fast as it could hire and train them, with little thought to maintaining productivity. And its obsession with customer service encouraged high staffing levels. "We have too much manpower generally in the company, and we've got to drive up productivity at a much faster rate," Kearns says. "There are too many people and too many layers of management." Major cuts have yet to be made, but Kearns's plans have already sent shudders throughout the organization.

Xerox is also trying to cut manufacturing costs by taking a leaf out of the Japanese book. The company has sent over teams of engineers and managers to study Japanese methods. It has introduced Japanese management techniques, such as quality circles, at its plants throughout the world, and it has adopted many Japanese engineering and procurement practices.

In meeting these challenges, Kearns will be leading a different type of company than his predecessor when he takes over as CEO next year. The easy self-confidence of Xerox's glory days are gone. "They are a far, far better company than they were 10 years ago," says one observer. "It's a stronger management group. They've been made a little bit humble, and they've been learning to compete in an intensely competitive market."

And Kearns himself is a different type of Xerox manager. Says another company watcher, "He is an activist who holds no rules sacred, and that's what you need in the technology business." Kearns is convinced that if Xerox is to meet the next Japanese attack in copiers and if it is to exploit new opportunities in the fast-paced office systems market, the company must continue to change. "I think we can run the company much more efficiently," he says. Restructuring has been painful, admits Kearns, "but it's not been disruptive enough. We've been making changes on an evolutionary basis, and now we're at the point where we have to turn the crank."

---

out how these priorities are likely to shift over time, we are encouraging human resource management decision makers to think about their policies in dynamic terms. That is, it is insufficient simply to build policies that are consistent with the broad values and business strategies of an organization at a given time. Human resource planners also must consider how these values and strategies are likely to change over time in response to changes in employee and corporate needs, in the external market, and in competitive strategy.

Correspondingly, top executives can use the framework for thinking through the human resource issues that will influence the success of a given competitive strategy. The framework can assist all organizational participants to plan for the transitions that occur in business strategy over time and to avoid being victimized by abrupt changes in human resource practices that too often accompany market and organizational transitions.

Consider the experience of the Xerox Corporation summarized in Box 4-3. What does a shift from an environment of growth and market domination to one of maturity and intensified competition mean for the human resource policies and practices of an organization? For Xerox, it meant an abrupt change from a long period of employment expansion and human resource policies appropriate to high-volume production and extensive staff support systems; it meant an emphasis on staff reductions and reorganization, a reallocation of people and resources, and an intensified focus on manufacturing costs, productivity, and employment security. Xerox's experience is not unique: It reflects a generic relationship between the product life cycle or basic business strategy driving a firm's business units, and the priorities and goals assigned to different human resource activities.

A Model of Growth and Decline

In Table 4-1 and the discussion that follows, we have taken a standard, product life-cycle model and extended it to consider the functional areas of human resource management that tend to be given different levels of priority at different stages. Standard models of product life cycles generally distinguish four stages of evolution: introduction, growth, maturity, and decline. We relate these stages to four functional areas of human resource management: (1) recruitment, selection and staffing; (2) compensation and benefits; (3) employee training and development; and (4) labor relations. The descriptions of the life cycle and the functions are not exhaustive; more research is needed about the effects of variations in business strategies and product life cycles on a variety of human resource management activities. In addition, it is important that HRM/IR strategies should cover all four functions, regardless of a firm's or business unit's position on the life-cycle continuum. However, we recognize and emphasize that varying degrees of attention will tend to be accorded to the different functions at different times.

The Introductory Stage.   Perhaps the most common treatment of human resource issues in the early stages of an organization, or of a new product venture, is to ignore them. When the organization expands beyond total control of the founding entrepreneur, however, issues surface concerning the selection and recruitment of technical and managerial talent needed to move new products or services to the marketplace. In the introductory stage of a new business, recruitment and selection of technical and managerial personnel who already possess the basic skills needed to make the product successful are likely to be the most important human resource activities. The control of compensation costs tends to receive a lower priority, as the objective is to recruit the best talent available. The costs of losing or of failing to recruit a key person or group tend to be more serious than the costs of paying something above the market rate. Training and employee de-

TABLE 4-1 Critical Human Resource Activities at Different Organizational or Business Unit Stages

Human Resource Functions	Life Cycle Stages			
	Introduction	Growth	Maturity	Decline
Recruitment, selection and staffing	Attract best technical/professional talent.	Recruit adequate numbers and mix of qualified workers. Management succession planning. Manage rapid internal labor market movements.	Encourage sufficient turnover to minimize layoffs and provide new openings. Encourage mobility as reorganizations shift jobs around.	Plan and implement workforce reductions and reallocation.
Compensation and benefits	Meet or exceed labor market rates to attract needed talent.	Meet external market but consider internal equity effects. Establish formal compensation structures.	Control compensation.	Tighter cost control.
Employee training and development	Define future skill requirements and begin establishing career ladders.	Mold effective management team through management development and organizational development.	Maintain flexibility and skills of an aging workforce.	Implement retraining and career consulting services.
Labor/employee relations	Set basic employee relations philosophy and organization.	Maintain labor peace and employee motivation and morale.	Control labor costs and maintain labor peace. Improve productivity.	Improve productivity and achieve flexibility in work rules. Negotiate job security and employment adjustment policies.

velopment also may receive less attention, because hiring people who already have the required skills is more cost effective.

Equally important to recruitment but often overlooked in the early stages is top executives' development and articulation of a set of values or a philosophy to guide employee relations policies and practices. As noted, the values inferred from the leaders of an organization about how employees are to be treated, what the philosophy toward decision making is to be, or which managerial style is to predominate will determine the climate, or culture, of the organization. Note that the articulation of values is an essential human resource management issue, and it is a function of both the human resource professional staff and top executives. However, it is the actions and value systems of top executives that other organizational participants will use to interpret the values and philosophies that are rewarded within the organization.

The Growth Stage.   The second stage of organizational evolution is often called the growth stage; the organization or business unit has survived its initiation in the marketplace and is expanding beyond the capabilities of the founding team. Additional people must be recruited, hired, and trained in order to keep up with expanding demands for the goods or services being provided. In this stage, the recruitment and selection of needed talent again tends to dominate human resource activities. The numbers and quality of individuals become more significant, and the personnel staff (if any) begins to assume a more important role in developing structured systems for anticipating employment demand and for recruiting and training adequate numbers and combinations of talent. Recruitment and/or development of new managers and executives — or management succession planning — becomes more important as the workload expands and the need for professional management expertise exceeds the limits and interests of the original founder(s). Likewise, the recruitment of marketing talent is also essential because the development of markets for the goods and services of the organization is fundamental to the successful transition through this stage.

Staffing issues take on added importance in this stage because of an active internal labor market develops in which employees rapidly move up the job hierarchy as opportunities become available. The development of orderly career ladders, the specification of minimum standards or qualifications for promotions, and the design of education, training, and development programs to support the career advancement aspirations of existing staff all become more important. Too often, however, these tasks develop more out of necessity than out of a conscious plan. If left unattended, they can create much internal frustration both among employees, who find themselves unqualified for available openings, and among line managers, who are unable to find resources quickly enough to take advantage of growing market opportunities.

Compensation remains below its peak in importance at this stage; the key to an organization's business strategy during periods of rapid growth seldom tends to be cost minimization. Instead, the key to success is the ability to produce sufficient goods and services to meet market demand on schedule. Indeed, both compensation and staffing levels tend to grow erratically during periods of rapid expansion. If ignored, serious problems may result. For example, a major compensation problem likely to be encountered in this stage, particularly if the growth period coincides with rising inflation, is one of internal compensation equity. High rates of recruitment force organizations continuously to upgrade entry-level salaries to compete effectively in the external labor market. Often, entry rates escalate faster than salary increases for those hired in previous years, resulting in salary compression, where the differential between new hires and those with one or more years of service becomes too small to be viewed as equitable by the more senior employees. The differential may even become negative. Thus, the compensation challenge is to develop a plan and a structure that can balance internal salary equity against external labor market pressures.

During the growth stage, the need for both management and organizational development is likely to increase, because the entrepreneur(s) or business unit head can no longer make all the necessary decisions. At this juncture a management group must be formed, and these people must learn to work together as a team. Management development strategies become a normal part of succession planning and career planning for those identified as having the potential to move into key posts. Organizational development techniques (Beckhard, 1969) become useful in attaining the interpersonal and decision-making skills needed to build effective management teams.

Finally, the labor relations objective that tends to receive the most significant attention during the growth stage (as well as during temporary upswings in the business cycle) is the maintenance of labor peace. Pressures to meet expanding product or service demands translate into pressures to avoid strikes, drops in employee motivation that reduce productivity or cause unwanted turnovers, and other manifestations of labor relations problems that divert time and resources from the "mission" of the organization. For this reason, we saw no-strike agreements negotiated between labor and management in firms working under contracts at Cape Canaveral in the early stages of the space race in the 1960s. Similar no-strike agreements have been reached on big construction projects operating under intense time pressures, such as the Alaskan oil pipeline and large power-generating facilities.

The Maturity Stage.   Most organizations eventually reach a stage where numerous competitors have entered their markets and demand for their products or services levels off. At this mature stage, new competitive strategies tend to emerge to differentiate the organization from its competitors and to help define the competitive niche the firm intends to pursue.

The key staffing issue becomes how to cope with a labor force that is larger than necessary, given the existing level of demand, economies of scale, technological improvements, and other productivity advances. In addition, managers face a problem with inadequate turnover as the work force ages and years of seniority build to where the costs of moving to another organization reduce the incentives for employees to leave.

Because demand and growth taper off, the rate of recruitment and selection slows. The focus in human resource management shifts to matching scarce job openings with the talent available within the organization, and to ensuring that sufficient new positions are available to maintain some flow of new employees into the firm. For this reason, employee development activities turn toward additional training, retraining, and continuing education to assure flexibility in allocating existing organizational talent to changing job opportunities.

In the mature stage, compensation issues assume a dominant position in the human resource management function. Labor costs become more important because competitive pressures tend to require more control of variable costs. The labor relations function may be pressured to control labor costs without jeopardizing labor peace. Peace is important because competitors may be waiting to take over customer orders that cannot be met because of work stoppages or declines in product quality, which may result from lowered employee motivation. Finally, it is necessary at this stage to focus on productivity improvement through the more efficient use of human resources and through increased employee involvement. This again reflects the fact that efficiency and control over costs are important to the strategic objectives of a firm in mature markets.

The Decline Stage.   Although most organization executives tend not to want to plan for orderly decline, they must recognize that markets do change and that an organization or business unit must be prepared to adjust by shifting resources from one activity to another. With adequate planning, adjustments can sometimes be made without disrupting the existing work force. More often, however, adjustments require work-force reductions or the transfer of workers to new activities.

During the decline stage, staffing activities turn to planning for work-force reductions or transfers. Training and retraining dominate the activities if new job opportunities are available. Tight controls on compensation costs continue and may intensify during the decline phase, as the organization attempts to survive by conserving costs. Productivity improvement continues as a high priority. In addition, pressure increases for flexibility in the work rules that have evolved during more prosperous times. These pressures may come from top management and newer market competitors, as well as employees. Employees may want improved employment security and adjustment programs (such as early retirement, severance pay, retraining), if these have not surfaced in the maturity stage.

Caveats About the Model.   Several caveats should be kept in mind when using our model. First, although the differences in the priorities assigned to various human resource activities were presented as changes over a life cycle, variations can be found at any given time among different business units of the same firm or across organizations that are following different competitive or business strategies. For example, an organization that follows the competitive strategy of being the lowest cost producer in a given market is likely to place greater priority on minimizing compensation costs and staffing levels and on maximizing productivity throughout all stages of its evolution. Emerson Electric Corporation is an example of such a firm in the highly competitive electronics industry (Peters and Waterman, 1982). Alternatively, a firm that follows a strategy of trying to stay one step ahead of its competitors in product innovation will give priority to recruiting up-to-date technical talent and to updating the technical skills and knowledge of existing research and development specialists.

Second, it is important to note that the model's categories and conceptualization are still in an early stage of theoretical development within human resource management literature. To date, we know of only one empirical study under way that is designed to test the strength of these general hypotheses (Wils, 1984). The arguments presented here should be viewed as theoretical hypotheses generated from case study observations, not as well-grounded facts.

We choose to present these arguments because we believe that human resource management practices need not only to become more closely integrated with the broad strategic plans of the organization, *but also to anticipate the changing human resource needs that occur as business and competitive conditions change.* This message will be reinforced throughout our treatment of various functional areas of human resource management. Meanwhile, the model should provide a substantive foundation for James L. Walker's discussion of the human resource planning process in the reading that follows.

References

Beckhard, Richard, *Organizational Development* (Reading, Mass.: Addison-Wesley, 1969).

Bendix, Reinhart, *Work and Authority in Industry* (New York: Wiley, 1956).

Brody, David, *Workers in Industrial America* (New York: Oxford University Press, 1980).

Deal, Terrence E., and Allan A. Kennedy, *Corporate Cultures* (Reading, Mass.: Addison-Wesley, 1982).

Doeringer, Peter B., and Michael J. Piore, *Internal Labor Markets and Manpower Analysis* (Lexington, Mass.: D. C. Heath, 1971).

Ouchi, William, *Theory Z* (Reading, Mass.: Addison-Wesley, 1982).

Peters, Thomas J., and Robert H. Waterman, Jr., *In Search of Excellence* (New York: Harper and Row, 1982).

Porter, Michael E., *Competitive Strategy* (New York: Free Press, 1980).

Schein, Edgar H., "The Role of the Founder in Creating Organizational Culture," *Organization Dynamics*, Summer 1983, 13–28.

Wils, Thierry, *Business Strategy and Human Resource Strategy.* Unpublished Ph.D. Dissertation, Cornell University, School of Industrial and Labor Relations, 1984.

Suggested Readings

Additional research on business or competitive strategies and human resource activities can be found in:

An Introductory Guide to Human Resource Planning (Toronto, Ontario, Canada: Ontario Ministry of Labour, Office of Employment and Immigration, March 1982).

Dyer, Lee, "Bringing Human Resources into the Strategy Formulation Process," in *Human Resource Management*, 23, Fall 1983, 257–71.

Human Resource Management (this is a professional journal that specializes in human resource strategy issues, published quarterly by John Wiley and Sons, New York).

Human Resources Planning Manual (Toronto, Ontario, Canada: Ontario Ministry of Labour, Office of Employment and Immigration, March 1982).

Lamb, Robert B., ed., *Competitive Strategic Management* (Englewood Cliffs, N.J.: Prentice Hall, 1984).

Linking Human Resource Planning
with Strategic Planning

Key Points

Human resource issues should be considered in the formulation of business plans.

Human resource issues are particularly important in strategic planning — long-range business planning which is aimed at achieving a major change in an organization's direction or emphasis.

Linkages between human resource planning and business planning are made at three levels or time frames of planning: strategic, middle-range, and short-range.

The common approach for considering human resource planning in the context of strategic planning involves addressing a series of pertinent questions as part of the planning process.

The approaches for planning may be informal and highly subjective, or they may be formal, structured, and systematic.

Responsibility for planning lies with operating management. But the analysis work is usually performed with assistance from business planning and human resource staff.

Planning is generally accepted as vital to effective management in most large organizations today. During the past several decades, companies have adopted systematic processes for deciding on objectives, resources needed, and manner of operations. In many instances, this planning is *strategic* in nature. That is, the planning addresses prospective changes in business objectives and the forces affecting the business. Drucker notes that it is necessary in strategic planning to ask: "What is the

business?" "What will it be?" and "What should it be?" With respect to the last question, the usual assumption is that the business will be different.

Natural resources, technological capacities, patents and products, market share and position, and financial capital are all given close consideration in strategic planning. However, human resources are rarely given attention. Consideration of human resource needs is usually limited to annual budgeting and planning, or to analysis and planning conducted by personnel specialists in planning programs such as training and recruiting. Often, human resource planning is viewed as a necessary, but subordinate, process of ensuring that adequate numbers and types of people are available to staff planned operations. Published discussions of planning practices indicate that human resource needs are determined by business programs and strategies, but generally ignore the possibility that human resources may affect business plans.

This chapter presents the concepts and techniques necessary to link human resource planning with business planning. The planning process is first described by drawing distinctions among strategic long-range, middle-range, and short-term or annual planning and budgeting. The issues of human resource management in relation to business planning are identified to suggest the potential impact of human resource issues on business achievements. The balance of the chapter examines specific approaches and techniques used in companies to implement strategy-linked human resource planning.

Source: Chapter 4 of James W. Walker's *Human Resource Planning.* Copyright © 1980 by James W. Walker. Reprinted by permission of McGraw-Hill Book Company and James W. Walker.

The Importance of Planning

Companies often give lip service to the importance of human resources in achievement of business objectives, but rarely is detailed, thoughtful analysis performed. Executives are confident that necessary personnel can always be recruited in the marketplace to meet future needs, should the internal supply prove inadequate. Business planners tend to focus on financial and marketing aspects of planning, often the functional specializations in which they were primarily educated. Personnel professionals, even human resource planning specialists, often are not well informed regarding business planning processes (and rarely have any direct contact with business planners) and are thus ill-equipped to introduce linkages between human resource planning and business strategic planning.

Yet the risks of neglecting this important link are great. In its plans to consolidate product lines, a consumer products company assumed that the same sales personnel could represent all lines. The assumption turned out to be wrong, and previously profitable lines turned sour and were ultimately divested. As another example, a chemicals company rapidly added new production facilities and expanded existing plants to meet demand without planning for the grooming of necessary managers. As a result, start-ups were sometimes delayed and problems were encountered due to inadequate experience and training of key personnel.

On the positive side, a major lumber and paper products company anticipated its requirements for new mill managers and senior technical personnel and systematically rotated prospective candidates among mills and pertinent headquarters and regional staff positions to satisfy the projected needs. As another example, a bank staffs its offices to satisfy work-load demands as projected in its business plans and develops banking office managers according to plans for long-range banking expansion. Positions are authorized in the offices (branches) to support specific business plans such as a new business "call" program desired as part of a specific marketing program.

Objectives and Benefits

Companies commonly prepare annual forecasts of staffing needs as a basis for external recruitment, personnel reassignments and promotions, and annual training program planning. But the one-year planning horizon fails to take into consideration longer-range business plans and needs, such as new facilities, new products, retrenchment, expansion, or gradually changing talent requirements of a qualitative nature. Effective human resource planning involves longer-range *career* development of talent and longer-range planning for utilization and control of human resources in an organization.

The need for a strategic perspective in human resource planning was stated in a manufacturing company as follows: "As the company grows larger and more complex, we recognize a need to plan more systematically for the people needed to staff the business. A lack of adequate talent may be the single major constraint in our ability to sustain future company growth. This (process) is a practical step toward more comprehensive employee planning and development."

In this same company, the benefits anticipated from longer-range human resource planning include the following:

1. An improved understanding of the human resource implications of business strategies
2. Recruiting experienced talent well in advance of needs, both from campuses and from the market
3. Improved planning of assignments and other employee developmental actions such as lateral moves to permit longer-range broadening of managerial perspective
4. Improved analysis and control of personnel-related costs, by providing more objective criteria concerning payroll, turnover, relocation, training, and other costs

These benefits were perceived from shorter-range planning. The link with strategic planning was seen as the logical next step in human resource planning in this company.

What Is Strategic Planning?

Strategic planning is the process of setting organizational objectives and deciding on comprehensive programs of action which will achieve these objectives. In a major oil company, strategic planning includes:

Formulating corporate and regional company objectives and operating charters (statements of identity or purpose)

Choosing the mix of business which will make up the operating entity and will reflect that entity's objectives and its concepts of its own identity

Determining the organization structure, processes, and interrelationships appropriate for managing a chosen mix of businesses

Developing appropriate strategies for carrying out the objectives and directing the evolution of the chosen mix of businesses within the organizational structures thus established

Devising the programs which are the vehicle for implementing the strategies

Strategic planning should not be confused with shorter-range operational or tactical planning. Strategic planning is concerned with those decisions aimed at achieving a major change in direction or velocity of growth. For example, a company may review its various product lines or component businesses and conclude that one or more should be discontinued because they no longer fit the company's overall objectives and plan. New business may be sought, new investments made, or new management approaches adopted. Operational or tactical planning deals with the normal ongoing growth of current operations or with specific problems, generated either internally or externally, which knock the pace of normal growth temporarily off the track.

Strategic planning decisions involve major commitments of resources, result-ing in either a quantum jump in the business along the path it is traveling or a change in the fundamental direction itself. Because assumptions must be made about an unpredictable future (and the resources committed could be lost), strategic planning involves a significant amount of risk. As a result, strategic planning is more complex, more conceptual, and less precise than shorter-range operational planning. Typically, it involves consideration of not just one but several possible scenarios about the future business environment and consideration of several alternative courses of action for the enterprise.

Operational planning, on the other hand, generally assumes a fairly constant business environment and considers changes concerning only such factors as immediate tactics; production efficiency; fine tuning of ongoing systems and practices; adjustment of levels of business activity; responses to customer or other demands; and modification of products, advertising, services, or other business processes. The central difference is the degree of change resulting from the planning — hence the degree of impact on human resource planning.

Steps

New directions in management do not come about easily. Strategic planning, therefore, involves a series of steps, each of which may involve considerable data collection, analysis, and iterative management reviews. The important elements of strategic planning and their potential effects on human resource planning are as follows:

1. *Define the corporate philosophy.* As a first step, fundamental questions regarding the nature of the corporation are addressed, including: "Why does the business exist? What is the unique contribution it makes or can make? What are the underlying motives or values of the owners or key managers?" In a large electronic equipment manufacturing firm, for example, providing employment and pro-

motional opportunities for employees is held to be an important purpose of being in business and therefore an important guide for future growth and change. The dependence of the community on the company is an overriding factor in the minds of the key executives.

2. *Scan the environmental conditions.* The question here is, "What economic, social, technological, and political changes are occurring which represent opportunities or threats?" Labor supply, increasing legal demands governing human resource policies and practices, and rapidly changing technology may, for example, have significant impact on a business. Additionally, the question is asked: "What are the competitors' strengths, strategies, etc.?" Even human resource strategies of other companies may affect the future direction of a business (for example, the ability of a DuPont to attract and retain the best available talent).

3. *Evaluate the corporation's strengths and weaknesses.* Next it must be asked, "What factors may enhance/limit the choice of future courses of action?" Human resource factors such as an aging work force, overspecialization (immobility) of key managers, a lack of promotable "high-potential" talent, and past failure to develop broadly experienced general management talent are common problems that may constrain strategic planning.

4. *Develop objectives and goals.* Other important questions are, "What are the sales, profit, and return on investment objectives? What specific time-based points of measurement are to be met in achieving these objectives?" Too often, the organization structure and the styles of management applied in a company are not supportive of specific objectives and goals. Where commitment is difficult to attain, strategies suffer. Also, important qualitative goals give way to more easily defined and measured quantitative objectives even though strategic objectives frequently involve commitment to changes in quality of service, quality of management, quality of research and development, etc.

5. *Develop strategies.* Last it is important to find answers to these questions: "What courses of action should the corporation follow to achieve its objectives, while meeting specific operational goals along the way? What types of action programs are required in the pursuit of these strategies? What changes in organization structure, management processes, and personnel are required?" Here the focus is sharply on human resource planning and the acquisition, assignment, development, utilization, and (frequently) termination of employees to properly staff the organization. It is at this point that human resource planning most directly links to the strategic planning process.

Three Levels of Planning

The different levels of planning suggested in the above discussion are illustrated in Exhibit 4-1. As shown, strategic planning deals with a long-range perspective and flows into operational planning. This level of planning has a midterm perspective and is concerned with the specific programs planned, the kinds and amounts of resources required, the organizational structure, and management succession and development, as well as specific plans for implementing the strategic plans. Finally, an annual budgeting process provides specific timetables, assignments, allocations of resources, and standards for implementation of actions. Simply, the detail in planning moves into sharper focus as the time frame telescopes into the shorter term.

Human resource planning logically parallels the business planning process. Some companies hold that the annual budget is all they need, particularly for human resource planning. In practice, their "strategic planning" is really vague operational planning. "Any people we need we can hire when the time comes from outside," they state. And in some instances, such as construction, retailing, or project-oriented engineering (or aerospace) firms, the lead time for planning is

EXHIBIT 4-1

Links Between Business Planning and Human Resource Planning

	Strategic Planning: Long-range Perspective	Operational Planning: Middle-range Perspective	Budgeting: Annual Perspective
Business Planning Process	Corporate philosophy Environmental scan Strengths and constraints Objectives and goals Strategies	Planned programs Resources required Organizational strategies Plans for entry into new business, acquisitions, divestitures	Budgets Unit, individual performance goals Program scheduling and assignment Monitoring and control of results
	Issues Analysis	Forecasting Requirements	Action Plans
Human Resource Planning Process	Business needs External factors Internal supply analysis Management implications	Staffing levels Staffing mix (qualitative) Organization and job design Available projected resources Net requirements	Staffing authorizations Recruitment Promotions and transfers Organizational changes Training and development Compensation and benefits Labor relations

necessarily short. But even in these kinds of organizations, engineering talent, managerial talent, and specialized skills required in support of strategic objectives may not be readily available on the market and may require lead time for recruitment or development.

College recruitment plans, for example, are not always reliable if they are developed solely on an annual basis. Rather, they are more accurate when based on a rolling plan involving a multiple-year forecast of needs as part of operational planning which, in turn, is based on strategic planning. Similarly, training and development activities are often budgeted and scheduled on a short-term basis without a long-range context defining the needs that are to be satisfied. As a result, training programs often represent a smorgasbord for employees with little assurance of either cost-effectiveness for the business or career relevance for the employees.

Linking human resource planning with strategic planning involves focusing on

major changes planned in the business — critical issues: "What are the implications of the proposed business strategies? What are the possible external constraints and requirements? What are the implications for management practices, organization, development, and succession? What can be done in the short term to prepare for longer-term needs?"

The Impact of Human Resources

The capacity of an organization to achieve its strategic objectives is influenced by human resources in three fundamental ways:

Cost economics
Capacity to operate effectively
Capacity to undertake new enterprises and change operations

The factors contributing to these three impact areas are listed in Exhibit 4-2. The factors identified are useful as a basis for helping business planners and executives

EXHIBIT 4-2
The Strategic Impact of Human Resource Factors

Sales and net earnings per employee Compensation and benefits costs as a percentage of total costs and expenses Employee replacement costs including recruitment, training Legal and regulatory expense vulnerability (for example, EEO, OSHA) Labor relations vulnerability for cost increases Other	Cost economics	
Technical complexity specialization required Stability and motivation of work force employed Employee competencies relative to job requirements Organizational effectiveness Managerial style and philosophy Other	Capacity to operate effectively	Capacity to achieve strategic objectives
Untapped/undeveloped potential of human resources Depth of management resources Adaptability/receptiveness to change Competitiveness for talent Other	Capacity to undertake new enterprises and to change operations	

think about the relevance of human resource planning. They also serve as the basic elements comprising the approaches commonly used to bridge the two planning processes.

Personnel costs are significant in many organizations, frequently ranking below the cost of financial capital or the cost of goods and materials. Costs of capital, equipment, and materials are increasingly difficult to control due to their scarcity and to inflation. Accordingly, control over staffing levels, compensation and benefits, and staffing mix are important focal points of management attention. In one instance, a midwestern manufacturing firm established a plant in Europe as a step toward increasing its penetration of that market. But when the plant was operating, it was found that local managers with the necessary expertise could not be found, or at least corporate management back home felt more comfortable having individuals personally known to them managing the foreign operations. As a result, the costs of maintaining the United States expatriates were extremely high, and yet the individuals were not as effective as they needed to be because they did not adequately understand the market, language, or customs. After five years, the plant was sold to a European company, with management problems cited as a principal factor.

This suggests the importance of the second group of factors — the positive benefits human resources may have on business plans. The talents and efforts of employees can have tangible effects on productivity, organizational effectiveness, management competencies, organizational stability, external relations, adaptivity to changes, and other changes supportive of a company's strategic objectives. Such effects are often taken for granted, but companies that fail to grow and change are frequently characterized by an absence of such positive support by their employees. An electronics company holds that its phenomenal record of growth and technological innovations is due in large part to the quality and motivation of its employees.

The assumption of positive "people impact" is used in an oil company as a way to stimulate management thinking about human resource issues in relation to business plans. In this company, oriented toward technology, capital, and natural resources, the impact of human resources was identified through "zero-base analysis." "We assume there is no impact at all in any area of human resource management, and then through the strategic planning process examine each potential cost and benefit factor on its actual merits. If human resource planning is found to have no relevance to strategic planning, we won't require any further attention to the subject." This null hypothesis worked well in getting the attention of the managers, and now a procedure of considering human resource needs is an integral aspect of the company's strategic planning.

Approaches for Implementation

What specific techniques may be used to do this kind of analysis and planning? How have companies implemented the planning approach to link with strategic planning? Few companies have had very much experience in this area. Most companies limit their human resource planning to short-term forecasting. But the feasibility of longer-range strategic planning focused on human resource issues has been clearly demonstrated by major corporations. (See Exhibit 4-3).

The approaches usually involve strong staff support to management in the analysis of business plans and objectives and in the examination of pertinent human resource information (forecasting of turnover, retirements, transfers, and promotions, etc.). But the primary responsibility for identifying emerging trends and changes in business requirements relating

EXHIBIT 4-3
A Human Resource Planning Process

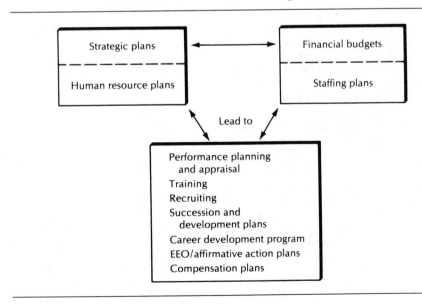

to business strategies rests with the operating managers. In some instances corporate planning staff professionals also get into the act and assist in the human resource planning efforts.

The efforts are typically modest at the start, but attract management interest and attention. In successive years, greater depth is achieved in the analysis and planning as managers perceive the benefit of such planning and become comfortable with the planning process. It has taken many companies years to become proficient in financial planning and budgeting, capital allocation, and other functional planning processes. Adoption of new approaches for "people planning" is also slow. As one executive observed, "It is the first time we have put down on paper our thinking about the long-range needs in this area. Our managers are simply not accustomed to answering questions like these and I think they did a pretty good job for a first time effort."

Application of an Approach

A chemicals and plastics manufacturing company guided its division managers through an analysis of human resource issues through the use of a simple printed guidebook. Exhibit 4-4 presents the essential pages of this guidebook consisting of a series of questions regarding human resource factors relating to strategic plans. The information presented in the exhibit in response to the questions is a synthesis of actual responses and is provided for illustrative purposes only.

The approach called for each division's management to analyze and plan its future human resource needs, organizational changes, and other programs and actions. Assistance was provided both by business planning staff assigned to work with the divisions and the corporate human resource planning staff. Responsibility for the process was given to the division managers for several reasons:

Corporate management did not want the process to be viewed as a staff exercise.

The division managers are most familiar with their own units' strategic plans and related human resource circumstances, and therefore they were the best source of reliable information.

This approach focused the attention of line managers on important human resource issues, increasing their appreciation for them and potentially influencing their judgment in business planning.

The process focused attention on the need for employee development as an ongoing process and not merely a once-a-year appraisal exercise.

Also, the process was viewed as a way to present to managers the full gamut of human resource functions as a single, unified system. As illustrated in Exhibit 4-4, the company's various personnel programs and the process of human resource planning fit together logically with the ongoing business and financial planning cycles.

Each section of the human resource planning guide in Exhibit 4-4 lists a series of questions relating to issues affecting business strategies. The four sections are:

A. Business needs — the human resource implications of planned expansion, contraction, or other changes indicated in the strategic plans

B. External factors — the business impact of governmental regulations, union activity, and human resource availability

C. Internal analysis — the implications of professional turnover, employee mix, and performance patterns

D. Management implications — the changing managerial staffing needs and management skills required

Finally, a format for forecasting exempt staffing needs is included on the last page. This calls for a projection of staffing levels planned for a five-year period, by year, for departmental and functional groups. This rough long-range forecast reflects the general parameters suggested by strategic and operational plans. The first two years of the forecast serve as a basis for planning specific requirements in the annual budget.

EXHIBIT 4-4
Human Resource Planning Guide

Identify below those strategic plans having human resource implications.	*Possible areas for action. What could be done?*

A. Business Needs

1. Expansion of existing business activities?
☐ Recruitment
☐ Training/development
☐ Organization changes
☐

2. Addition of new capacity (new plants, distribution facilities, etc.)?
☐ Recruitment
☐ Training/development
☐ Organization changes
☐

3. Deemphasis or discontinuance of any business activities?
☐ Reassignments
☐ Terminations
☐ Retraining
☐

4. Ventures, acquisitions, or divestitures?
☐ Management reassignments
☐ Recruitment
☐ Organization/position changes
☐ Training/development
☐

5. New products or services?
☐ Training/development
☐ Recruitment
☐ Organization/position changes
☐

6. New technologies or applications?
☐ Training/development
☐ Recruitment
☐ New specializations
☐ Organization/position changes
☐

7. Changes in operating methods or productivity improvements?
☐ Organization/position changes
☐ Training/development
☐ Reassignments
☐

8. Changes in administrative, information, or control systems?
☐ Orientation/training
☐ Organization/position changes
☐ Staffing changes
☐

Identify below those strategic plans having human resource implications.	*Possible areas for action.* *What* could *be done?*

9. Changes in management or organizational structure (matrix management)?

☐ Reassignments
☐ Communications/training
☐ Staffing changes
☐ Recruitment
☐ Terminations
☐ Reassignments
☐

10. Other:

☐
☐

B. External Factors

1. Are qualified (competent) recruits available in the market?

☐ Modify recruitment approach
☐ Modify staffing requirements
☐ Develop more talent from within
☐

2. Are you able to recruit competitively the desired talent?

☐ Modify compensation/job evaluation
☐ Modify recruitment approach
☐ Modify job requirements
☐

3. Are there changes in the personnel relations climate?

☐ Employee communications
☐ Management orientation/training
☐ Fact finding
☐

4. Are there new EEO/affirmative action requirements?

☐ Modify recruitment
☐ Training/development
☐ Modify job requirements
☐ Performance appraisals
☐

5. Are there new OSHA or other regulatory requirements affecting human resources?

☐ Management orientation/training
☐ New systems/procedures
☐ Additional staffing
☐ Fact finding
☐

6. Are there new international business demands?

☐ Management orientation/training
☐ Recruitment
☐ Adapt management systems
☐ Fact finding
☐

7. Other:

☐
☐

Identify below the human resource issues *pertinent to the strategic plans.*	Possible areas for action. *What could be done?*

C. Internal Analysis

   1. Do we have excessive turnover in any group?

   ☐ Modify recruitment/selection
   ☐ Accelerate career advancement
   ☐ Organization/position changes
   ☐ Reassignment/lateral moves
   ☐

   2. Is there too little turnover or mobility in any group?

   ☐ Terminations
   ☐ Reassignment of work
   ☐ Organization/position changes
   ☐ Improved employee appraisals
   ☐

   3. Are age patterns imbalanced in any group, suggesting high future attrition or career path blockage?

   ☐ Modify recruitment/selection
   ☐ Reassignments
   ☐ Accelerate career advancement
   ☐ Terminations
   ☐

   4. Is there a proper balance (employee mix) of managerial, professional/technical, and supporting personnel in each group?

   ☐ Organization/position changes
   ☐ Reassignment of work
   ☐ Modify recruitment/selection
   ☐

   5. Are there noteworthy performance problems in any group (or appraisal results signaling significant problems)?

   ☐ Organization/position changes
   ☐ Reassignments
   ☐ Improved employee appraisals
   ☐ Modify job requirements
   ☐

   6. In what areas are levels of technical competency potential shortcomings?

   ☐ Modify recruitment/selection
   ☐ Reassignments
   ☐ Career counseling
   ☐ Training/development
   ☐

   7. Is the employee mix desired for EEO/AA being achieved? (women and minorities)

   ☐ Modify recruitment/selection
   ☐ Modify job requirements
   ☐ Career counseling
   ☐ Training/development
   ☐

   8. Other:

   ☐
   ☐

Identify below the human resource issues *pertinent to the strategic plans*.	Possible areas for action. What could be done?

D. Management Implications

1. Are there enough employees who could become general managers? (pool of successors)

☐ Modify recruitment/selection
☐ Improved employee evaluation
☐ Special career development plans
☐ Organization changes for future
☐

2. Do the present managers have adequate technical competence in the face of changing demands?

☐ Training/development
☐ Reassignments
☐ Specialized recruitment
☐ Specialization
☐ Career counseling
☐

3. Do they have adequate managerial skills to meet the changing demands of a growing company? (leading, planning, decision making, etc.)

☐ Training/development
☐ Organization/position changes
☐ Reassignments
☐ Recruitment of managerial talent
☐

4. Do key managers and successors have adequate management experience (multiple function exposure)?

☐ Training/development programs
☐ Job rotation among functions
☐ Recruitment of management talent
☐ Evaluation of successors
☐

5. Is the management structure and staffing appropriate for the achievement of our business objectives?

☐ Organization/position changes
☐ Reduce/increase staffing levels
☐ Accelerate management development
☐ Study of strategy implications
☐

6. Other:

☐
☐

	Current	9/79	9/80	9/81	9/82	9/83	9/84
Summary Forecast of Exempt Staffing Needs as of							
Departments							
TOTALS							
Functions							
TOTALS							

The managers are asked to consider each question and briefly note pertinent factors, observations, or assumptions. Questions that are not considered pertinent are deleted, and additional questions may be added where appropriate. The guidebook is intended to be a workbook to direct and stimulate management thinking, and not a rigid procedure.

The second column lists possible responses to stimulate thinking about the human resource implications of each question. Other possible actions may be considered practical under the circumstances as known to the managers. The third and fourth columns call for a translation of the long-range strategy-related needs into specific near-term needs and planned actions. The interpretation of strategic issues into near-term objectives and programs for human resource management is an important step in making the whole human resource planning effort worthwhile.

The guidebook is disseminated to the operating divisions as part of the overall strategic planning guidelines and instructions. In this way the two planning processes are conducted concurrently. The resulting responses indicate to management the important human resource issues that need to be considered in the future.

Alternative Approaches

In a major oil company, the manpower planning staff provided a summary analysis of the previous year's strategic plan, highlighting the pertinent facts and issues for each division. These summaries, together with tabulations of present employment, past and projected attrition (due to turnover, retirements, etc.), and appraisal statistics provided "substantive starters" to the divisions for use considering pertinent human resource issues. The analysis of strategic issues was termed a "situational analysis," as a first step in the company's manpower planning cycle. Questions similar to those presented in Exhibit 4-4 were posed in four areas:

Impact of people on the growth or profitability of the business

Personnel-related costs having a substantial impact on the profitability of the business

Avoidable people-related problems that require inordinate time and attention by management

Management values requiring emphasis on certain human resource programs

In this case, employee relations staff in the divisions performed much of the necessary analysis and completed the planning submissions. The quality of the responses varied, therefore, with the experience, skills, and time availability of these staff, and with their access to the line executives in their divisions for purposes of discussing the human resource analyses.

In a packaging company, guidelines were included as a section in the annual one- to three-year planning process. The initial request for information was minimal, the response was positive, and "the seed was planted from which a full-size human resource planning process can grow." Each division in this company was able to pinpoint issues that were important and that needed attention which had not been explicitly considered before.

Subsequent cycles yielded more comprehensive plans regarding the human resource issues. Submissions were reviewed and synthesized as a corporationwide plan by the human resource staff; highlights and issues of corporatewide concern were brought to the attention of senior management in a formal presentation. This corporatewide plan also provided the basis for targeting of objectives, priorities, and resource requirements for corporate programs and staff activities. Exhibit 4-5 presents excerpts from one year's corporate human resource plan.

The link between human resource planning and business strategic planning is vital if personnel programs and systems are to be attuned to the changing needs of an organization. This chapter has examined the qualities of such an effective linkage

EXHIBIT 4-5

Excerpts from a Corporate Human Resource Plan Presentation

The human resource plan is presented against a background of significant changes in the corporation. Fundamental to these changes is an earnings goal of 10% growth per year. Growth will be achieved by expansion of existing businesses that are sound, reshaping of lower-potential businesses, and acquisitions. Major capital investments will occur in some business areas. International markets will account for an increasing share of our earnings goal achievement.

The plan, therefore, represents a synthesis of issues and activities aimed at supporting the objectives of the businesses as well as a guide for the respective human resource activities in the businesses. Activities must fit business unit needs, but must also be responsive to corporate, legal, and societal needs.

Focus of Major Strategies

I. The demands for managerial and professional talent resulting from changing business strategies require improved management quality and improved salaried employee productivity.

Strategic actions planned	*Representative programs or activities*
A. Terminate low performers	Train managers in more effective appraisals. Extend emphasis of termination program to marginally satisfactory performers.
B. Motivate top performers	Establish program to make sure outstanding performers are being rewarded proportionately under the incentive compensation program. Develop a long-term incentive program.
C. Upgrade managerial capabilities	Establish coordinated program for executive-level search/recruitment and placement. Extend management program (training) to 700 managers and supervisors.
D. Influence retirement plans	Conduct management-level retirement preparation program. Provide appraisal guidelines to managers regarding age discrimination risks and appraisal of low performers and the use of termination versus early retirement.

II. Control rapidly rising human resource costs.

A. Hourly labor costs	Reduce certain job security provisions. Negotiate staffing reductions, productivity improvements. Establish uniform data base for planning negotiations. Establish uniform benefits for nonunion employees across businesses. Reduce accident ratios by 10%, thus reducing lost time and accident costs.

Strategic actions planned	*Representative programs or activities*
B. Salaried pay and benefit costs	Introduce variable benefits program on a pilot basis (to provide cost-control mechanism against future escalation). Consolidate insurance carriers for administrative savings. Reorganize corporate compensation function to provide better services to business human resource staffs. Develop a corporate compensation philosophy. Implement a manpower control reporting system to track staffing changes. Implement controls over use of search firms. Establish central relocation procedure and service. Expand attitude survey programs and follow-up communications programs (to detect and allay concerns in units with high risk of unionization).

III. Manage the impact of external legal factors.

A. Manage ongoing legal compliance	Establish training program for field management to improve handling of arbitration cases and on-site EEO audits. Implement toxic substances control program in XYZ divisions. Conduct comprehensive noise-abatement cost and feasibility evaluation study.
B. Affirmative action plans	Establish an improved reporting system for surveillance of female/minority progress. Negotiate a combined compliance plan covering handicapped, veterans, females, and minorities to reduce administrative costs. Step up women-in-management program to advance females into management positions.
C. Upgrade legislative surveillance	Direct attention of legal staff and public affairs staff to emerging governmental initiatives and to address them.

IV. Improve organizational effectiveness

A. Upgrade personnel data system	Complete implementation of phase I and design for phase II.
B. Upgrade business organization effectiveness	Restructure businesses undergoing major growth or contraction. Assign new managers to key functions where called for; utilize assignments as corporate management development moves.
C. Upgrade human resource staff effectiveness	Corporate staff provide more functional leadership to business staff counterparts. Conduct quarterly reviews of all programs, emerging demands, and budget compliance.

and its practical importance. Approaches were described for implementing the link, using a formal process of questioning business managers, usually as part of the normal business planning process. In some organizations, where the process has been applied for several annual cycles, human resource issues are now routinely addressed as a component of business planning.

In other organizations, human resource issues are studied solely by staff personnel, who present their findings to management or to the business planning staff as inputs to strategic or operational planning. In several instances, committees or task forces have been appointed to consider long-range human resource issues and needs, usually on a one-time basis. Particularly in the task of scanning the environment to identify emerging legal, competitive, labor supply, and other constraints, such a study group has proven a useful tool. Of course, some companies rely on consultants or outside experts to advise on trends, issues, and needs warranting company attention.

Perhaps the most common approach applied, however, is the informal planning process. While not always thorough or systematic, informal management thinking about business strategies often leads to recognition of human resource issues. Planning for the management of corporate resources, including human resources, is a process inherent in the role of a manager. And few managers would admit that they do not consider human resource issues in strategic or operational planning.

Moving from Values to Concrete Policies

We now turn to the case of People Express Airline, which was founded on the basis of a particularly explicit and innovative set of values and principles. As the company moved from its introductory stage to a period of rapid growth, the translation of these values into concrete human resource policies became an increasingly difficult matter. The case illustrates many of the critical human resource management issues that are raised as an organization's overall strategy changes.

CASE
People Express

We're now the biggest air carrier in terms of departures at any New York airport. We've flown almost three million passengers and saved the flying public over one quarter of a billion dollars (not including the savings from fares reduced by other airlines trying to compete with us). We expect to see a $3 million profit this year. . . . We have a concept that works and is unique.

But with no growth horizon, people have been disempowered. We've started slowing down, getting sleepy. So, we've decided to set a new growth objective. Instead of adding 4 to 6 aircraft as we planned for this year, we are now thinking in terms of 12 or more new aircraft a year for the next few years.

With this announcement, Don Burr, founder, president and CEO of People Express airline, concluded the business portion of the company's third quarterly financial meeting of 1982, graciously received rousing applause from several hundred of his stockholder/managers there to hear about and celebrate the success of their young company, and signaled for the music to begin.

ORIGINS AND BRIEF HISTORY

People Express had been incorporated on April 7, 1980. In July of that year it had applied to the Civil Aeronautics Board (CAB) for permission to form a new airline to be based in the New York/Newark metropolitan area and dedicated to providing low-cost service in the eastern United States. Organized specifically to take advantage of provisions of the 1978 Airline Deregulation Act, People Express was the first airline to apply for certification since its passage. (The act, which was designed to stimulate competition, allowed greater flexibility in scheduling and pricing and lowered the barriers to new entrants.)

In applying to the CAB for a "determination of fitness and certification of public convenience and necessity," People Express committed itself to:

1. provide "a broad new choice of flights" with high-frequency service,
2. keep costs low by "extremely productive use of assets,"
3. offer "unrestricted deep discount price savings" through productivity gains,
4. focus on several high-density eastern U.S. markets which had yet to reap the pricing benefits of deregulation,
5. center operations in the densely populated New York/Newark metropolitan area with service at the underutilized, uncongested, highly accessible Newark International Airport.

The Civil Aeronautics Board was sufficiently impressed with this stated intent that it approved the application in three months (compared to the usual year or more). On October 24, 1980 People Express had its certificate to offer air passenger service between the New York/New Jersey area and 27 major cities in the eastern U.S.

START-UP

People Express's managing officers proceeded to work round the clock for the next six months to turn their plans and ideas into a certificated operating airline. They raised money, leased a terminal, bought planes, recruited, trained, established routes and schedules, and prepared manuals to meet the FAA's fitness and safety standards. "We were here every night . . . from November until April when they (the Federal Aviation Administration [FAA]) gave us our certificate. . . . It was hell" (Burr). People's operating certificate was granted April 24, 1981.

OPERATIONS BEGIN

Flight service began on April 30, with three planes flying between Newark and Buffalo, New York; Columbus, Ohio; and Norfolk, Virginia. By the following year, the company employed a work force of over 1,200, owned 17 airplanes, and had flown nearly 2 million passengers between the 13 cities it was servicing. People Express had grown faster than any other airline and most businesses. It had managed to survive a start-up year filled with environmental obstacles, a severe national economic recession, a strike of air traffic controllers, and bad winter weather — all of which had serious negative effects on air travel. By June 1982, though the airline industry in general was losing money, and though competition resulting from deregulation was intense, People had begun showing a profit. Exhibit 4-6 lists milestones in the growth of People Express.

In the spring and summer of 1982 People underwent an extensive review of its infrastructure, added resources to the recruitment function so as to fill a 200-person staffing shortfall, and modified and attempted to implement more

EXHIBIT 4-6
People Express

Major Events

April 1980	— Date of incorporation
May 1980	— 1st external financing — Citicorp venture
October 1980	— CAB certificate awarded
November 1980	— Initial public offering — $25.5 MM common
March 1981	— 1st aircraft delivered
April 1981	— 1st scheduled flight
August 1981	— PATCO strike
October 1981	— Florida service emphasized
January 1982	— One millionth passenger carried
March 1982	— 17th aircraft delivered
April 1982	— Reported first quarterly operating profit
July 1982	— Filed 1,500,000 shares of common stock

systematically a governance and communication system for which there had been little time during start-up. By the fall of 1982, 3 more planes were about to arrive and three more cities were scheduled to be opened for service.

BACKGROUND AND PRECURSORS

Donald Burr had been president of Texas International Airlines (T.I.) before he left it to found People Express with a group of his colleagues. The airline business was a "hobby business" for Burr; his love of airplanes went back to his childhood and he began flying in college, where as president of the Stanford Flying Club he could get his flight instruction paid for. After receiving an MBA from the Harvard Business School in 1965 he went to work for National Aviation, a company specializing in airline investments, thus combining his affinity for aviation with his interest in finance. In 1971 he was elected president of National Aviation. While at National Aviation, Burr began a venture capital operation which involved him in the start-up of several companies, including one which aimed at taking advantage of the recently deregulated telecommunications industry.

Eighteen months later he decided he wanted to get into the "dirty fingernails" side of the airline business. He left Wall Street and joined Texas International Airlines as a director and chairman of the executive committee. In June 1973 he became executive vice president and in 1976 assumed the responsibilities of chief operations officer. Between 1973 and 1977, Texas International moved from a position close to bankruptcy to become a profitable business. Burr was largely credited in the media for managing the turnaround. In June 1979 he was made president of Texas International. Six months later, he resigned.

Looking for a new challenge, one option he considered at that time was starting a new airline. The day after Burr left T.I., Gerald Gitner, his VP of planning and marketing, and Melrose Dawsey, his own and the CEO's executive secretary at T.I., both submitted their resignations and joined Burr to incorporate People Express.

By the fall of 1980, 15 of Texas International's top managers and several more experienced staff from the ranks followed Burr to become part of the People Express management team and start-up crew. Some gave up their positions even before they knew where the new company would be based, how it would be financed, whether they would be able to acquire planes, or what their exact jobs would be. In spite of the personal and financial risks, the opportunity to start an airline from scratch, with people they liked and respected, was too good to pass up. It was an adventure, a chance to test themselves. Burr at 39 was the oldest of the officers. Even if People Express failed, they assumed that they could pick themselves up and start again.

According to Hap Paretti, former legal counsel and head of government relations at Texas International, who became the fifth managing officer at People Express,

> We weren't talking about my job description or what kind of a budget I would have. It was more, we're friends, we're starting a new airline, you're one of the people we'd like to have join us in starting the company . . . what you do will be determined by what your interests are. The idea of getting involved and letting my personality and talents come through to determine my job appealed to me. I'm not happy doing just one thing.

Bob McAdoo, People's managing officer in charge of finance, had been corporate comptroller at Texas International. For McAdoo, joining People Express "was an easy decision, though I was having a good time at Texas International. . . . I happen to be a guy driven by things related to efficiency. This was a chance to build an airline that was the most efficient in the business."

Lori Dubose had become director of human resources at T.I. — the first female director there — within a year after being hired.

> When Burr called to offer me the "People" job he explained that we would all be working in different capacities. I'd get to learn operations, get stock — I didn't know anything about stock, never owned any. At 28 how could I pass it up?

She came even though she was married and her husband decided not to move with her to Newark.

FINANCING AND AIRPLANE ACQUISITION

To finance this adventure, Burr put up $355,000, Gitner put in $175,000, and the other managing officers came up with from $20,000 to $50,000 each. Burr secured an additional $200,000 from FNCB Capital Corp., a subsidiary of CitiCorp. The papers for the CitiCorp money, People Express's first outside funds, were signed on May 8, 1980, Burr's 40th birthday. Subsequently, the investment firm of Hambrecht & Quist agreed to help raise additional start-up funds. Impressed with Burr's record and the quality of his management team, and aware of the opportunities created by airline deregulation, William Hambrecht agreed to Burr's suggestion of taking People Express public. (No other airline had ever gone public to raise start-up money.)

As soon as the CAB application was approved in October 1980 all eight managing officers went on the road explaining their business plan and concepts to potential investors throughout the country. They were able to sell over $24 million worth of stock — 3 million shares at $8.50 per share.

The official plan stated in the CAB application had called for raising $4–$5 million, buying or leasing one to three planes, and hiring 200 or so people the first year. According to Hap Paretti, "We thought we'd start by leasing three little DC-9s, and flying them for a few years until we made enough money to buy a plane of our own." According to Burr, however, that plan reflected Gitner's more cautious approach and what most investors would tolerate at the beginning. Even with the additional money raised, Gitner thought they should buy at most 11 planes, but Burr's ideas were more expansive. From the beginning he wanted to start with a large number of planes so as to establish a presence in the industry quickly and support the company's overhead.

With cash in hand they were able to make a very attractive purchase from Lufthansa of an entire fleet of 17 Boeing 737s, all of which would be delivered totally remodeled and redecorated to People's specifications. While other managing officers recalled being a bit stunned, Burr viewed the transaction as being "right on plan."

BURR'S PERSONAL MOTIVATION AND PEOPLE'S PHILOSOPHY

Government deregulation appeared to provide a "unique moment in history," and was one of several factors which motivated Burr to risk his personal earnings on starting a new airline. At least as important was his strong conviction that people were basically good and trustworthy, that they could be more effectively organized, and if properly trained, were likely to be creative and productive.

> I guess the single predominant reason that I cared about starting a new company was to try and develop a better way for people to work together . . . that's where the name People Express came from (as well as) the whole people focus and thrust. . . . It drives everything else that we do.
>
> Most organizations believe that humans are generally bad and you have to control them and watch them and make sure they work. At People Express, people are trusted to do a good job until they prove they definitely won't.

From its inception, therefore, People Express was seen as a chance for Burr and his management team to experiment with and demonstrate a "better" way of managing not just an airline but any business.

While Burr recognized that his stance was contrary to the majority of organized structures in the United States, he rejected any insinuation that he was optimistic or soft.

> I'm not a goody two-shoes person, I don't view myself as a social scientist, as a minister, as a do-gooder. I perceive myself as a hard-nosed businessman, whose ambitions and aspirations have to do with providing goods and services to other people for a return.

In addition, however, he wanted PE to serve as a role model for other organizations, a concept which carried with it the desire to have an external impact and to contribute to the world's debate about "how the hell to do things well, with good purpose, good intent, and good results for everybody. To me, that's good business, a good way to live. It makes sense, it's logical, it's hopeful, so why not do (it)?"

Prior to starting service, Burr and the other managing officers spent a lot of time discussing their ideas about the "right" way to run an airline. Early on, they retained an outside management consultant to help them work together effectively as a management team and begin to articulate the principles to which they could commit themselves and their company. Over time, the principles evolved into a list of six "precepts," which were written down in December of 1981 and referred to continually from then on in devising and explaining company policies, hiring and training new recruits, structuring and assigning tasks. These precepts were: 1) service, commitment to growth of people; 2) best provider of air transportation; 3) highest quality of management; 4) role model for other airlines and other businesses; 5) simplicity; 6) maximization of profits.

From Burr's philosophy as well as these precepts and a myriad of how-to-do-it-right ideas, a set of strategies began to evolve. According to People's management consultant, the "path" theory was the modus operandi — management would see what route people took to get somewhere, then pave the paths that had been worn naturally to make them more visible.

Thus, by 1982, one could articulate fairly clearly a set of strategies that had become "the concept," the way things were done at People Express.

THE PEOPLE EXPRESS CONCEPT: THE PHILOSOPHY OPERATIONALIZED

The People Express business concept was broken down and operationalized into three sets of strategies: marketing, cost, and people. (Over Burr's objections, the presentation prepared by investment company Morgan Stanley for PE investors began with the marketing and cost strategies rather than the people strategies.)

Marketing Strategy

Fundamental to People's initial marketing strategy was its view of air travel as a commodity product for which consumers had little or no brand loyalty. (See Exhibit 4-7 for a representative advertisement.) People Express

EXHIBIT 4-7
People Express

SHOULD AN EXPERIENCED TRAVELER LIKE YOU FLY A NEW AIRLINE LIKE US?

Particularly a new airline, with the audacity to consistently charge two-thirds less than you're accustomed to paying.

For example, before we flew to Columbus, the standard air fare was $146. People Express charges $40 off peak and $65 peak. What's more, our price to Florida is just $75 off peak and $89 peak.

In short, People Express offers low prices every seat. Every flight. Every day.

And we always will.

But even if paying much less takes a little getting used to, you'll appreciate our other attributes. In no time flat.

OUR SCHEDULES ARE GEARED TO YOUR SCHEDULE.

Because we know how hectic your life can be, instead of the usual frequent excuses, we give you frequent flights — 98 non-stops each business day.

And, unlike any other major airline, People Express doesn't accept freight or mail. So you don't sit on a plane cooling your heels while mail bags and freight cartons are loaded and unloaded.

ALL OUR PEOPLE TREAT YOU AS ATTENTIVELY AS IF THEY OWNED THE AIRLINE. BECAUSE THEY DO.

At People Express, we don't offer jobs. We offer careers. From the person who welcomes you on the plane to the person who pilots the plane, each and every full time member of our staff owns an average of — amazing as it sounds — $13,000 of our stock. (And the stock of the company founders was not averaged in.)

The result quite simply, is the first airline where attitude is as important as altitude.

NON-STOP CHECK IN.

And to save a little more time and hassle, we've done away with another nemesis: the ticket counter. Purchase your ticket through your travel agent.

Or phone in your reservation in advance with us and purchase your ticket right on the plane.

YOU AND YOUR LUGGAGE NEED NEVER BE SEPARATED.

Someone whose time is as valuable as yours has no intention of wasting it waiting for luggage. So instead of hassling you about carry-on luggage, we actually encourage you — by providing unusually spacious overhead and underseat areas. But if you have luggage you want us to handle, we're happy to do it for $3 a bag.

TASTEFUL BOEING 737's. WITHOUT THE INDIGESTION OF AIRLINE FOOD.

People Express flies the finest equipment in the air. Boeing 737's. Easy on your eyes...thanks to our clean, tasteful appointments. Easy on your weary bones...thanks to our comfortable seats. And easy on your stomach...because we don't serve airline food. Of course, if you're willing to spend a little of all that money you're saving, you can get a first rate beverage or snack on board.

THE FASTEST MOVING AIRLINE IN THE WORLD.

People Express offers more flights out of convenient Newark Airport than any other airline.

And we've already flown over a million passengers.

After only ten months of operation.

Perhaps it was our attitude. Or our prices. Or our frequency to all ten cities.

But no other airline has come this far this fast. Which proves we've offered the public something it's been waiting for a long time...a better way to fly.

And nobody will appreciate us more than someone who has been around as much as you.

PEOPLExpress
FLY SMART

defined its own version of that product as a basic, cut-rate, no-nonsense, air trip. A People Express ticket entitled a passenger to an airplane seat on a safe trip between two airports, period. The marketing strategy was to build and maintain passenger volume by offering extremely low fares and frequent, dependable service on previously overpriced, underserviced routes. In keeping with this strategy, the following tactics were adopted:

1. *Very low fares* — On any given route, People's fares were substantially below the standard fares prevailing prior to P.E.'s announcement of service on that route. For instance, People entered the Newark-to-Pittsburgh market with a $19 fare in April 1982, when U.S. Air was charging $123 on

that route. Typically, peak fares ran from 40% to 55% below the competition's standard fares and 65% to 75% below, during off-peak hours (after 6 p.m. and weekends).

2. *Convenient flight schedules* — For any route that its planes flew, People tried to offer the most frequent flight schedule. With low fares and frequent flights, People could broaden its market segment beyond those of established airlines to include passengers who would ordinarily have used other forms of transportation. In an effort to expand the size of the air travel market, People's ads announcing service in new cities were pitched to automobile drivers, bus riders, and even those who tended not to travel at all. People hoped to capture most of the increase as well as some share of the preexisting market for each route.

3. *Regionwide identity* — People set out to establish a formidable image in its first year as a major airline servicing the entire eastern U.S. Large established airlines could easily wage price wars and successfully compete with a new airline in any one city, but they would probably have to absorb some losses and would be hard pressed to mount such a campaign on several fronts at once.

4. *Pitch to "smart" air travelers* — In keeping with its product definition, People's ads sought to identify People Express not as exotic or delicious or entertaining, but as the smart travel choice for smart, thrifty, busy travelers. The ads were filled with consumer information, as well as information about PE's smart people and policies. Unlike most airlines, for instance, every People Express plane had roomy overhead compartments for passengers' baggage thereby saving them money, time, and the potential inconvenience of loss.

5. *Memorable positive atmosphere* — Burr's long-term marketing strategy, once the airline was off the ground financially, was to make flying with People Express the most pleasant and memorable travel experience possible. The goal was for passengers to arrive at their destination feeling very well served. Thus, People Express's ultimate marketing strategy was to staff every position with competent, sensitive, respectful, up-beat, high-energy people who would create a contagious positive atmosphere. The message to staff and customers alike was: "At People Express, attitude is as important as altitude."

Cost Structure

People's cost structure was not based on a clear-cut formula so much as on an attitude that encouraged the constant, critical examination of every aspect of the business. According to Bob McAdoo, the management team "literally looked for every possible way to do things more simply and efficiently." McAdoo could point to at least 15 or 20 factors he felt were important in keeping costs down while preserving safety and quality. "If you look for one or two key factors, you miss the point." Cost savings measures affecting every aspect of the business included the following:

1. *Aircraft* — Since fuel was the biggest single cost for an airline, People chose, redesigned, and deployed its aircraft with fuel efficiency in mind. Its twin engine Boeing 737-100 planes were thought to be the most fuel-efficient planes for their mission in the industry. By eliminating first-class and galley

sections, interior redesign increased the number of all coach-class seats from 90 to 118 per plane. Overhead racks were expanded to accommodate more carry-on baggage. The planes were redecorated to convey a modern image and reassure potential passengers that low fares did not mean sacrificing quality or safety.

P.E. scheduled these planes to squeeze the most possible flying time out of them, 10.36 hours per plane per day, compared with the industry average of 7.08 hours. Finally, plane maintenance work was done by other airlines on a contract basis, a practice seen as less expensive than hiring a maintenance staff.

2. *Low labor costs* — Labor is an airline's second biggest expense. Though salaries were generally competitive, and in some cases above industry norms, People's labor costs were relatively small. The belief was that if every employee was intelligent, well-trained, flexible, and motivated to work hard, fewer people (as much as one-third fewer) would be needed than most airlines employed.

People kept its work force deliberately lean, and expected it to work hard. Each employee, carefully selected after an extensive screening process, received training in multiple functions (ticketing, reservations, ground operations and so on) and was extensively cross-utilized, depending on where the company's needs were at any given time. If a bag needed to be carried to a plane, whoever was heading towards the plane would carry the bag. Thus, peaks and valleys would be handled efficiently. This was in sharp contrast with other airlines which hired people into one of a variety of distinct "classes in craft," (such as flight attendants, reservations, baggage), each of which had a fairly rigid job description, was represented by a different union, and therefore was precluded from being cross-utilized.

3. *In-house expertise and problem solving* — In addition to keeping the work force small and challenged, cross-utilization and rotation were expected to add the benefits of a de facto ongoing quality and efficiency review. Problems could be identified and solutions and new efficiency measures could be continually invented if people were familiar with all aspects of the business and motivated to take management-like responsibility for improving their company.

The Paxtrac ticketing computer was commonly cited as a successful example of how P.E. tapped its reservoir of internal brain power rather than calling in outside consultants to solve a company problem. Many of P.E.'s longer routes were combinations of short-haul flights into and out of Newark. The existing ticketing system required a separate ticket for each leg of the trip, resulting in higher fares than P.E. wanted. Burr spotted the problem when he was flying one day (he tried to spend some time each month on board the planes or in the ground operations area). An ad hoc team of managers was sent off to a hotel in Florida for a week to solve the problem. They came up with a specially designed microprocessor ticketing machine with the flexibility to accommodate the company's marketing plans and fast enough (7 seconds per ticket vs. 20 seconds) to enable on-board ticketing of larger passenger loads.

4. *Facilities* — Like its aircraft, People Express's work space was low cost and strictly functional. The main Newark terminal was located in the old North Terminal building, significantly cheaper to rent than space at the West and South terminals a mile away. People had no ticket counters. All ticketing was done either by travel agents in advance, or by customer service managers on board the planes once they were airbound. Corporate headquarters, located upstairs over the main terminal had none of the luxurious trappings associated with a major airline. Offices were shared, few had carpeting, and decoration consisted primarily of People Express ads, sometimes blown up poster size, and an occasional framed print of an airplane.

5. *Reservations* — The reservations system was kept extremely simple, fast, and therefore inexpensive. There were no interline arrangements with other airlines for ticketing or baggage transfer; no assistance was offered with hotel or auto reservations in spite of the potential revenue leverage to be derived from such customer service. Thus, calls could be handled quickly by hundreds of easily trained temporary workers in several of the cities People served, using local lines (a WATS line would cost $8,000 per month) and simple equipment ($900 vs. the standard $3,000 computer terminals).

6. *No "Freebies"* — Costs of convenience services were unbundled from basic transportation costs. People offered none of the usual airline "freebies." Neither snacks nor baggage handling, for example, were included in the price of a ticket, though such extras were available and could be purchased for an additional fee.

People

Burr told his managers repeatedly that it was People's people and its people policies that made the company unique and successful. "The people dimension is the value added to the commodity. Many investors still don't fully appreciate this point, but high commitment and participation, and maximum flexibility and massive creative productivity are the most important strategies in People Express."

STRUCTURE AND POLICIES

As People moved from a set of ideas to an operating business, People's managers took pains to design structures and develop policies consistent with the company's stated precepts and strategies. This resulted in an organization characterized by minimal hierarchy, rotation and cross-utilization, work teams, ownership, self-management, participation, compensation, selective hiring and recruitment, multipurpose training, and team building.

1. *Minimal Hierarchy* — People's initial organizational structure consisted of only three formal levels of authority. At the top of the organization was the president/CEO and six managing officers, each of whom provided line as well as staff leadership for more than one of the 13 functional areas (see Exhibit 4-8 for a listing of functions).

Reporting to and working closely with the Managing Officers were eight General Managers, each of whom provided day-to-day implementation and

EXHIBIT 4-8
People Express

ORGANIZATIONAL STRUCTURE, 11/82 — AUTHOR'S RENDITION

CEO, President* — Chairman of the Board
Don Burr

Managing Officers

Primary Responsibilities	Lori Dubose	Hap Paretti	Bob McAdoo	Melrose Dawsey	David McElroy	Don Hoydu
Staff	Human Resources	Legal/Govt. Affairs, Marketing	Administration: Planning, Finance	Administration: Pay Roll, Compensation	Administration: Information Systems	Administration: Facilities
Line	In-Flight	Flight Ops.	Reservations	In-Flight	Maintenance	Ground Ops.

General Managers

Primary Responsibilities	Geoff Crowley	Larry Martin	Steve Schlachter	Fred de Leeuw	Jim Barrall	Gil Roberts**	Ron McClelland	John Schaper	Jack Browning
Staff	Human Resources	Marketing	Marketing	Finance Accounting		Chief Pilot Compensation		Human Resources	Service/Vendor Relations Newark
Line	Manpower Scheduling	Reservations		Revenue Accounting	In-Flight	Flight Ops. Facilities & Equip.	Maintenance	Maintenance	Ground Ops.

Team Managers — 30 appointed 10/82

Customer Service Managers | Flight Managers | Reservation Workers | Maintenance Managers

---

*Original President, Gerald Gitner, resigned 3/82 and Burr assumed Presidency.

**Gil Roberts appointed Chief Pilot 11/82.

leadership in at least one functional area, as well as planning for and coordinating with other areas. People's Managing Officers and General Managers worked hard at exemplifying the company's philosophy. They worked in teams, rotated out of their specialties as much as possible to take on line work, filling in at a gate or on a flight. Several had gone through the full "inflight" training required of Customer Service Managers. They shared office furniture and phones. Burr's office doubled as the all-purpose executive meeting room; if others were using it when he had an appointment, he would move down the hall and borrow someone else's empty space.

There were no executive assistants, secretaries, or support staff of any kind. The managers themselves assumed the activities that such staff would ordinarily perform. Individuals, teams, and committees did their own typing, which kept written communications to a minimum. Everyone answered his or her own phone. (Both practices were seen as promoting direct communication as well as saving money.)

Beyond the top 15 officers all remaining fulltime employees were either flight managers, maintenance managers, or customer service managers. The titles indicated distinctions in qualifications and functional emphasis rather than organizational authority. *Flight Managers* were pilots. Their primary responsibility was flying, but they also performed various other tasks, such as dispatching, scheduling, and safety checks, on a rotating basis or as needed. *Maintenance Managers* were technicians who oversaw and facilitated maintenance of P.E.'s airplanes, equipment, and facilities by contract with other airlines' maintenance crews. In addition to monitoring and assuring the quality of the contracted work, maintenance managers were utilized to perform various staff jobs.

The vast majority of People's managers were *Customer Service Managers,* generalists trained to perform all passenger-related tasks, such as security clearance, boarding, flight attending, ticketing, and food service, as well as some staff function activities (see Exhibit 4-8).

By and large, what few authority distinctions did exist were obscure and informal. Managing officers, general managers, and others with seniority (over one year) had more responsibility for giving direction, motivating, teaching, and perhaps coordinating, but *not* for supervising or managing in the traditional sense.

2. *Ownership, Lifelong Job Security* — Everyone in a permanent position at P.E. was a shareholder, required as a condition of employment to buy, at a greatly discounted price, a number of shares of common stock, determined on the basis of his or her salary level. It was expected that each employee in keepng with being a manager/owner, would demonstrate a positive attitude towards work, and participate in the governance of the company. As Managing Officer Lori Dubose pointed out, "We'll fire someone only if it is (absolutely) necessary. . . . For instance, we won't tolerate dishonesty or willful disregard for the company's policies, but we don't punish people for making mistakes." In exchange, People Express promised the security of lifetime employment and opportunities for personal and professional growth through continuing education, cross-utilization, promotion from within the

company, and compensation higher than other companies paid for similar skills and experience.

3. *Cross-Utilization and Rotation* — No one, regardless of work history, qualifications, or responsibility was assigned to do the same job all the time. Everyone, including managing officers, was expected to be "cross-utilized" as needed and to rotate monthly between in-flight and ground operations and/or between line and staff functions. (The terms "line" and "staff" in P.E. differentiated tasks which were directly flight-related from those related to the business of operating the company.)

Seen by some as unnecessarily complicated and troublesome, cross-utilization and rotation where justified by PE in several ways. According to Burr, they were conceived primarily as methods of continuing education, aimed at keeping everyone interested, challenged, and growing. Bob McAdoo appreciated the flexible staff utilization capability which eventually would result from everyone having broad exposure to the company's functions. Rotation did create some difficulties:

> It takes people a while to master each job. It might seem better to have an expert doing a given job. Cross-utilization also means you need high-quality people who are capable of doing several jobs. This in turn limits how fast you can recruit and how fast you can grow.

These were seen, even by McAdoo, the efficiency expert, as short-term inconveniences well worth the long-term payoff.

> When you rotate people often they don't develop procedures that are too complicated for newcomers to learn and master fast. This forces the work to be broken down into short simple packets, easily taught and easily learned.

4. *Self-Management* — People were expected to manage themselves and their own work in collaboration with their teams and coworkers. According to Jim Miller, coordinator of training, "We don't want to teach behaviors — we want to teach what the end result should look like and allow each individual to arrive at those results his or her own way. . . . When desired results aren't achieved, we try to guide people and assist them in improving the outcome of their efforts."

The written, though never formalized, guidelines regarding "self-management" read as follows:

> Within the context of our precepts and corporate objectives, and with leadership direction but no supervision, individuals and/or teams have the opportunity (and the obligation) to self-manage, which encompasses the following:

> Setting specific, challenging, but realistic objectives within the organizational context.

> Monitoring and assessing the quantity/quality/timeliness of one's own performance ("how am I doing?") by gathering data and seeking input from other people.

> Inventing and executing activities to remedy performance problems that appear and exploiting opportunities for improved performance.

> Actively seeking the information, resources and/or assistance needed to achieve the performance objectives.

When it came time for performance reviews, each individual distributed forms to those six coworkers from whom feedback would be useful. Again, growth rather than policing was the objective.

5. *Work Teams* — Dubose observed that "even with smart, self-managed people, one person can't have all the components to be the answer to every situation." People therefore had decided to organize its work force into small (3–4 person) work groups as an alternative to larger groups with supervisors. "If you don't want a hierarchical structure with 40 levels you have to have some way to manage the numbers of people we were anticipating." Teams were seen as promoting better problem solving and decision making as well as personal growth and learning.

Every customer service manager belonged to a self-chosen ongoing team with which he or she was assigned work by a lottery system on a monthly basis. Though monthly staff assignments were made individually according to interests, skills, and needs, staff work was expected to be performed in teams. This applied to flight managers and maintenance managers as well as customer service managers. Each team was to elect a liaison to communicate with other teams. Each staff function was managed by a team of coordinators, most of whom were members of the start-up team recruited from Texas International. Managing officers also worked in teams and rotated certain responsibilities to share the burden and the growth benefits of primary leadership.

6. *Governance, Broad-Based Participation* — People's governance structure was designed with several objectives: policy development, problem solving, participation, and communication.

While Burr was the ultimate decision maker, top management decisions, including plans and policies, were to be made by management teams with the assistance of advisory councils. Each of the 8 managing officers and 8 general managers was responsible for at least one of the 13 functional areas (see Exhibit 4-8) and served on a management team for at least one other function. The 13 function-specific management teams were grouped into 4 umbrella staff committees: Operations, People, Marketing, and Finance and Administration. For each staff committee, composed of managing officers and general managers from the relevant functional areas, there was an advisory council made up of selected customer service managers, flight managers, and maintenance managers serving on relevant line and staff teams. The councils were intended to generate and review policy recommendations, but until August 1982 they followed no written guidelines. A study done by Yale University students under the direction of Professor Richard Hackman, showed considerable confusion as to their purposes (influencing, learning, solving, communicating issues) and role (advising vs. making decisions).

To minimize duplication and maximize communication, each advisory council elected a member to sit on an overarching "coordinating council" which was to meet regularly with Don Burr (to transmit information to and from him and among the councils). These ongoing teams and councils were supplemented periodically by ad hoc committees and task forces which could be created at anyone's suggestion to solve a particular problem, conduct a study, and/or develop proposals.

In addition to maximizing productivity, all of the above practices, teams, and committees were seen essential to promote personal growth and keep people interested in and challenged by their work.

7. *Compensation — High Reward for Expected High Performance —* People's four-part compensation package was aimed at reinforcing its human resource strategy. Base salaries were determined strictly by job category on a relatively flat scale, ranging in 1981 from $17,000 for customer service managers to $48,000 for the managing officers and CEO. (Competitor airlines averaged only $17,600 for flight attendants after several years of service, but paid nearly double for managing officers and more than four times as much for their chief executives.)

Whereas most companies shared medical expenses with employees, People paid 100% of all medical and dental expenses. Life insurance, rather than being pegged to salary level, was $50,000 for everyone.

After one year with P.E. all managers' base salary and benefits were augmented by three forms of potential earnings tied to the company's fortunes. There were two profit-sharing plans, 1) a dollar-for-dollar plan, based on quarterly profits and paid quarterly to full-time employees who had been with P.E. over one year, and 2) a plan based on annual profitability. The former was allocated proportionally, according to salary level, and distributed incrementally. If profits were large, those at higher salary levels stood to receive larger bonuses, but only after all eligible managers had received some reward. The sustained profits were distributed annually and in equal amounts to people in all categories. Together, earnings from these plans could total up to 50% or more of base salary. The aggregate amount of P.E.'s profit-sharing contributions after the second quarter of 1982 was $311,000.

Finally, P.E. awarded several stock option bonuses, one nearly every quarter, making it possible for managers who had worked at least half a year to purchase limited quantities of common stock at discounts ranging from 25% to 40% of market value. The company offered five-year interest-free promissory notes for the full amount of the stock purchase required of new employees, and for two-thirds the amount of any optional purchase. As of July 1982, 651 employees, including the managing officers, held an aggregate 513,000 shares of common stock under a restricted stock purchase plan. Approximately 85% were held by employees other than managing officers and general managers. The total number of shares reserved under this plan was, at that time, 900,000.

8. *Selective Hiring of the People Express "Type" —* Given the extent and diversity of responsibilities People required of its people, Lori Dubose, managing officer in charge of the company's "people" as well as in-flight functions, believed firmly that it took a certain type of person to do well at People Express. Her recruiters, experienced CSMs themselves, looked for people who were bright, educated, well-groomed, mature, articulate, assertive, creative, energetic, conscientious, and hard working. While they had to be capable of functioning independently and taking initiative, and it was desirable for them to be ambitious in terms of personal development, achievements, and wealth, it was also essential that they be flexible, collaborative

rather than competitive with co-workers, excellent team players, and comfortable with PE's horizontal structure. "If someone needed to be a vice-president in order to be happy, we'd be concerned and might not hire them" (Miller).

Recruiting efforts for customer service managers were pitched deliberately to service professionals — nurses, social workers, teachers — with an interest in innovative management. No attempt was made to attract those with airline experience or interest per se (see Exhibit 4-9). Applicants who came from traditional airlines where "everyone memorized the union contract and knew you were only supposed to work x number of minutes and hours," were often ill-suited to People's style. They were not comfortable with its loose structure and broadly defined, constantly changing job assignments. They were not as flexible as People Express types.

The flight manager positions were somewhat easier to fill. Many pilots had been laid off by other airlines due to economic problems, and People Express had an abundant pool of applicants. All licensed pilots had already met certain intelligence and technical skill criteria, but not every qualified pilot was suited or even willing to be a People Express flight manager. Though flying time was strictly limited to the FAA's standard 30 hours per week (100/month, 1000/year), and rules regarding pilot rest before flying were carefully followed, additional staff and management responsibilities could bring a flight manager's work week to anywhere from 50 to 70 hours.

Furthermore, FMs were expected to collaborate and share status with others, even nonpilots. In return for being flexible and egalitarian — traits which were typically somewhat in conflict with their previous training and job demands — pilots at P.E. were offered the opportunity to learn the business, diversify their skills and interests and benefit from profit sharing and stock ownership, if and when the company succeeded.

9. *Recruitment Process* — As many as 1600 would-be CSMs had shown up in response to a recruitment ad. To cull out "good P.E. types" from such masses, Dubose and her start-up team, 8 CSMs whom she recruited directly from T.I., designed a multistep screening process.

Applicants who qualified after two levels of tests and interviews with recruiters were granted a "board interview" with at least one general manager and two other senior people who reviewed psychological profiles and character data. In a final review after a day-long orientation, selected candidates were invited to become trainees. One out of 100 CSM applicants was hired (see Exhibit 4-10 for a CSM profile).

In screening pilots, "the interview process was very stringent. Many people who were highly qualified were eliminated." Only one out of three flight manager applicants was hired.

10. *Training and Team Building* — The training program for CSMs lasted for five weeks, six days a week, without pay. At the end, candidates went through an in-flight emergency evacuation role-play and took exams for oral competency as well as written procedures. Those who tested at 90 or above were offered a position.

The training was designed to enable CSMs, many without airline experience, to perform multiple tasks and be knowledgeable about all aspects of

EXHIBIT 4-9
People Express

EXHIBIT 4-10
People Express

Profile of a Customer Service Manager

Look for candidates who:

1. Appear to pay special attention to personal grooming.
2. Are composed and free of tension.
3. Show self-confidence and self-assurance.
4. Express logically developed thoughts.
5. Ask intelligent questions; show good judgment.
6. Have goals; want to succeed and grow.
7. Have strong educational backgrounds, have substantial work experience, preferably in public contact.
8. Are very mature, self-starter with outgoing personality.
9. Appear to have self-discipline, good planner.
10. Are warm, but assertive personalities, enthusiastic, good listeners.

Appearance Guidelines

Well-groomed, attractive appearance.
Clean, tastefully worn, appropriate clothing.
Manicured, clean nails.
Reasonably clear complexion.
Hair neatly styled and clean.
Weight strictly in proportion to height.
No offensive body odor.
Good posture.
For women, make-up should be applied attractively and neatly.
Good teeth.

 Above listed guidelines apply to everyone regardless of ethnic background, race, religion, sex, or age.

---

an airline. Three full days were devoted to team building, aimed at developing trainees' self-awareness, communication skills, and sense of community. "We try to teach people to respect differences, to work effectively with others, to build synergy" (Miller).

On the last team-building day everybody chose two or three others to start work with. These groups became work teams, People's basic organizational unit. Initially, according to Miller, these decisions tended to be based on personalities and many trainees were reluctant to choose their own work teams. They were afraid of hurting people's feelings or being hurt. Trainers would remind them that People Express gave them more freedom than they would get in most companies, more than they were used to, and that "freedom has its price . . . it means you've got to be direct and you've got to take responsibility" (Kramer).

Over time, trainers learned to emphasize skills over personalities as the basis of team composition and to distinguish work teams from friendship groups. Choosing a work team was a business decision.

BOTTOM LINES: BUSINESS INDICATORS

As of the second quarter of 1982 People was showing a $3 million net profit, one of only five airlines in the industry to show any profit at that time. In addition to short-term profitability, Burr and his people enjoyed pointing out that by several other concrete indicators typically used to judge the health and competitive strength of an airline, their strategies were paying off and their innovative company was succeeding.

> *Marketing Payoff.* Over three million passengers had chosen to fly with People Express. The size of air passenger markets in cities serviced by People had increased since People's entrance. In some instances the increase had been immediate and dramatic, over 100%. Annual revenue rates were approaching $200 million.
>
> *Cost Containment.* Total costs per available seat-mile were the lowest of any major airline (5.2¢ compared to a 9.4¢ industry average). Fuel costs were ½–¾¢ per-seat-mile lower than other airlines.
>
> *Productivity.* Aircraft productivity surpassed the industry average by 50% (10.36 hours/day/plane compared to 7.06). Employee productivity was 145% above the 1981 industry average (1.52 compared to .62 revenue passenger miles per employee) for a 600-mile average trip. Return on revenue was 15.3%, second only to, and a mere .9% below, Southwest — the country's most successful airline. (Exhibit 4-11 shows operating statements through June 1982 and Exhibit 4-12 presents industry comparative data on costs and productivity.)

EXPLANATIONS OF SUCCESS

How could a new little airline with a funny name like People Express become such a formidable force so fast in such difficult times? Burr was fond of posing this question with a semipuzzled expression on his face and answering with a twinkle in his eye! The precepts and policies represented by that "funny" name — People — had made the difference. To back up this assertion, Burr and the other managing officers gave examples of how the people factor was impacting directly on the company's bottom line.

Consumer research showed that, notwithstanding heavy investments in award-winning advertisements, the biggest source of People's success was word of mouth; average customer ratings of passenger courtesy and personal treatment on ground and on board were 4.7 out of 5.

Several journalists had passed on to readers their favorable impressions of People's service: "I have never flown on an airline whose help is so cheerful and interested in their work. This is an airline with verve and an upbeat spirit which rubs off on passengers." Others credited the commitment, creativity,

EXHIBIT 4-11
People Express

STATEMENT OF OPERATIONS*

	From April 7, 1980 to March 31, 1981	Nine Months Ended December 31, 1981	Six Months Ended June 30, 1982
Operating revenues:			
Passenger	$ —	$37,046	$59,998
Baggage and other revenue, net	—	1,337	2,302
Total operating revenues	—	38,383	62,300
Operating expenses:			
Flying operations	—	3,464	4,240
Fuel and oil	—	16,410	22,238
Maintenance	21	2,131	3,693
Passenger service	—	1,785	2,676
Aircraft and traffic servicing	—	7,833	10,097
Promotion and sales	146	8,076	7,569
General and administrative	1,685	3,508	2,498
Depreciation and amortization of property and equipment	6	1,898	3,087
Amortization — restricted stock purchase plan	—	479	434
Total operating expenses	1,858	45,584	56,532
Income (loss) from operations	(1,858)	(7,201)	5,768
Interest:			
Interest income	1,420	1,909	763
Interest expense	14	3,913	5,510
Interest expense (income), net	(1,406)	2,004	4,747
Income (loss) before income taxes and extraordinary item	(452)	(9,205)	1,021
Provision for income taxes (Note 4)	—	—	(470)
Income (loss) before extraordinary item	(452)	(9,205)	551
Extraordinary item — utilization of net operating loss carryforward (note 4)	—	—	470
Net income (loss)	$ (452)	$ (9,205)	$ 1,021
Net income (loss) per common share:			
Income (loss) before extraordinary item	$ (.20)	$ (1.92)	$ .11
Extraordinary item	—	—	.09
Net income (loss) per common share	$ (.20)	$ (1.92)	$ .20
Weighted average number of common shares outstanding	2,299	4,805	5,046

*Unaudited. In thousands, except per share data

EXHIBIT 4-12
People Express

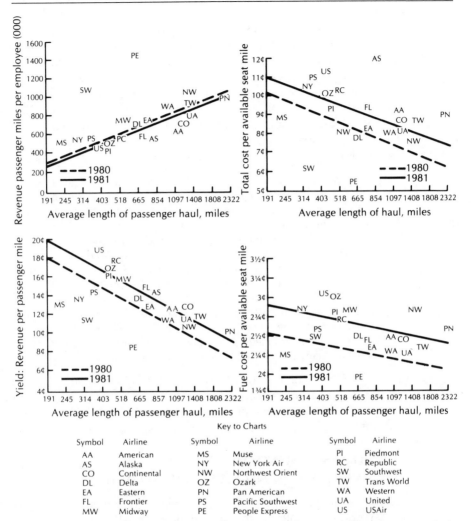

Key to Charts

Symbol	Airline	Symbol	Airline	Symbol	Airline
AA	American	MS	Muse	PI	Piedmont
AS	Alaska	NY	New York Air	RC	Republic
CO	Continental	NW	Northwest Orient	SW	Southwest
DL	Delta	OZ	Ozark	TW	Trans World
EA	Eastern	PN	Pan American	WA	Western
FL	Frontier	PS	Pacific Southwest	UA	United
MW	Midway	PE	People Express	US	USAir

All data has been drawn from calendar 1981 results, except People Express and Muse, for which the first quarter of 1982 is used in order to offer comparisons not influenced by the start-up of operations.

Notes:
— Total cost is operating cost plus interest expense net of capitalized interest and interest income.
— Yield represents passenger revenues divided by revenue passenger miles (RPM).
— Average length of passenger haul is plotted on a logarithmic scale.
— The average line in each graph is a least-squared linear regression curve, based on 16 carriers which evolved in the regulated environment. Southwest, People Express, New York Air, Muse, and Alaska were not used in the calculations to determine the average. The 16 carriers were assigned equal weightings in the average.

Source: Hambrecht and Quist, June 1982.

and flexibility of People's people with the company's very survival through its several start-up hurdles and first-year crises.

Perhaps the biggest crisis was the PATCO strike which occurred just months after P.E. began flying. While the air traffic controllers were on strike, the number of landing slots at major airports, including Newark, were drastically reduced. This made People's original hub-and-spoke short-haul route design unworkable. To overfly Newark and have planes land less frequently without reducing aircraft utilization, People Express took a chance on establishing some new previously unserviced, longer routes between smaller, uncontrolled airports, such as Buffalo, New York to Jacksonville, Florida. This solution was tantamount to starting a new airline, with several new Florida stations, new advertising, and new route scheduling arrangements. The costs were enormous. According to Hap Paretti:

> We could have run out of $25 million very quickly and there wouldn't be any People Express. The effort people made was astronomical, and it was certainly in their best interest to make that effort. Everybody recognized truly and sincerely that the air traffic controllers strike was a threat to their very existence. They rearranged their own schedules, worked extra days, really put the extra flying hours in, came in on their off days to do the staff functions, all things of that nature, people just really chipped in and did it and did a damned good job. So when we went into these markets from Buffalo to Florida, we could go in at $69. If we went in at $199 like everybody else we wouldn't have attracted one person. We could go in very low like that because we had a cost structure that allowed us to do that. That's where the people strategy, from a cost standpoint, resulted in our survival. If it wasn't there we'd be in the same situation many other carriers are today, hanging on by a toenail.

By way of comparison, New York Air, a nonunion airline started by others from Texas International around the same time as People Express with plenty of financial backing, economical planes, and a similar concept of low-cost, high-frequency service, but different people policies, was losing money.

THE HUMAN DIMENSIONS: POSITIVE CLIMATE AND PERSONAL GROWTH

In addition to becoming a financially viable business, People Express had shown positive results in the sphere of personal growth, the number one objective of its "people strategy." High levels of employee satisfaction showed up in first-year surveys done by the University of Michigan. Less tangible but nevertheless striking were the nonverbal and anecdotal data. A cheerful, friendly, energetic atmosphere permeated the planes and passenger terminals as well as the private crew lounge and hallways of corporate headquarters. Questions about the company were almost invariably answered articulately, confidently, and enthusiastically. Stories of personal change, profit and learning were common:

Ted E., customer service manager:

> I was a special education teacher making $12,000 a year, receiving little recognition, getting tired, looking for something else. I started here at $17,000,

already have received $600 in profit sharing, and will soon own about 800 shares of stock worth $12 on the open market, all bought at very reduced rates. (Two months after this statement the stock was worth $26 a share.)

Glenn G., customer service manager:

> I was running a hotline and crisis program, then was assistant manager of a health food store before seeing the People Express recruitment ad in the newspaper and coming to check it out. I'm about to sell my car in order to take advantage of the current stock offer to employees.

Both Glenn and Ted had worked primarily in training but had also done "in-flight" and "ground-ops." jobs. They wanted more responsibilities, hoped to get them but even if they didn't get promoted soon they expected to continue learning from and enjoying their work.

Michael F., a flight captain:

> I'm making $36,000. With my profit-sharing checks so far I've got $43,000 and on top of that I'll get sustained profit-sharing deals . . . I'm doing O.K. . . . Granted, at [another company] a captain might be making $110,000 working 10 days a month [but] they're not really worth it. [In other companies] the top people might make over $100,000 but they throw on 200 guys at the bottom so they can continue to make their salary. Is that fair? [Also, the seniority system would have kept Michael from being a captain at most other airlines.] We're radically different and I believe radically better.
>
> Most pilots know very little about what's going on in their company. In a People flight manager position, the knowledge people gain in this ratty old building is incredible. It's a phenomenal opportunity. It's very stimulating and exciting. I never thought I would have this much fun.

The stories of People's start-up team members and officers were even more dramatic. Each had profited and diversified substantially in their two years with People.

Melrose Dawsey, Burr's secretary at Texas International, was a managing officer at People with primary responsibility for administration. She owned 40,000 shares of stock, purchased at $.50 a share and worth, as of November 1982, over $20/share. For her own career development, she had also begun to assume some line management responsibilities in the in-flight area. In her spare time, she had earned her in-flight certification and run the New York marathon (as had Burr).

Lori Dubose, the youngest officer, had come to People to head the personnel function. In addition, she had taken on primary responsibility for the "in-flight" function as well as assuming the de facto role of key translator and guide vis-à-vis the company's precepts. As others came to see the value and purpose of People's precepts and human resource policies, Dubose's status among the officers had also risen.

Jim Miller had been a flight attendant for a year and base manager of in-flight services for four years at Texas International. As part of Dubose's start-up team, he had been coordinator of training, played a key role in recruitment, and then took on added responsibility for management and organizational development as well.

Hap Paretti, who began as legal counsel and head of government relations, quickly became involved in all aspects of the marketing function, and then went on to head flight operations, a move he acknowledged was "a little out of the ordinary" since he didn't have a technical background as a pilot. He spoke for all of the officers in saying, "As a managing officer you're expected to think about virtually every major decision that comes up for review."

Many spoke of the more subtle aspects of their personal development. Hap Paretti enjoyed the challenge of motivating other people and "managing by example" so as to enhance the growth of others.

Geoff Crowley, general manager in charge of ground operations and manpower scheduling, talked of becoming "less competitive" and "less uptight about winning alone" and more interested in working together with others to accomplish group and company goals.

THE DOWNSIDE OF PEOPLE'S GROWTH AND STRATEGIES

People Express's growth rate and strategies were not without significant organizational, financial, and human costs. By Burr's own observation,

> I would say at best, we're operating at 50 percent of what we'd like to be operating at in terms of the environment for people to do the best in. So we're nowhere near accomplishing what we would really like to accomplish in that regard. [But] I think we're better off today than we ever have been. And I think we're gaining on the problem.

Chronic Understaffing

Lori Dubose saw the hiring rate as the most difficult aspect of the company's growth process, causing many other problems:

> If we could get enough people to staff adequately in all three areas of the company so that people got some staff and some line responsibility and would have some time for management development . . . I think things would be a lot different. [There's been] constant pressure to hire, hire, hire, and we just haven't gotten enough.

She was adamant, however, about not relaxing People's requirements.

When Dubose came to P.E. she expected to have to staff a company flying three planes which would have required rapid hiring of perhaps 200–300 people. The purchase of the Lufthansa fleet meant five to six times as many staff were needed. Given the time consumed by the selective recruiting process, and the low percentage of hires, the staffing demands for supporting and launching 17 planes stretched People's people to the limit. The result was chronic understaffing even by People's own lean staffing standards.

As of November 1982 the 800 permanent "managers" were supplemented with over 400 temporaries, hired to handle telephone reservations, a function trained CSMs were originally expected to cover. Some of these "res"

workers had been there a year or more, but still were not considered full-fledged People people, though many would have liked to be. They received little training, did not work in teams, own stock, receive profitsharing bonuses, or participate in advisory councils. They were just starting to be invited to social activities. For a while those wishing to be considered for permanent CSM positions were required to leave their temporary jobs first on the theory that any bad feelings from being rejected could be contagious and have a bad effect on morale. That policy was eventually seen as unfair, and dropped. Indeed, some managers saw the res area as a training ground for CSM applicants.

In August 1982 several MOs estimated that aside from reservation workers, they were short by about 200 people, though the recruiting staff was working 10 to 12 hours daily, often 6 days a week, as they had since January 1981. This understaffing in turn created other difficulties, limiting profits, policy implementation, and development of the organization's infrastructure.

> If we had another 100 to 150 CSMs without adding an additional airplane we could just go out and add probably another half a million to a million dollars a month to the bottom line of the company. . . . There is additional flying out there that we could do with these airplanes . . . we could generate a lot more money . . . almost double the profits of the company. (McAdoo)

The policy of job rotation, critical to keeping everyone challenged and motivated, had been only partially implemented. Initial plans called for universal monthly rotations, with 50% of almost everyone's time spent flying, 25% on ground line work and another 25% in "staff functions." Due to staffing shortages, however, many people had been frozen in either line jobs without staff functions or vice versa. Some had become almost full-time coordinators or staff to a given function like recruiting and training, while others had done mostly line work and had little or no opportunity to do what they expected when they were hired as "managers." Since neither performance appraisal nor governance plans had been fully carried out, many felt inadequately recognized, guided, or involved.

There were also certain inherent human costs of People's people strategies. Rotating generalists were less knowledgeable and sometimes performed less efficiently than specialists on specific tasks. High commitment to the company plus expectations of flexibility in work hours could be costly in terms of individuals' personal and family lives. For many who were single and had moved to Newark to join People Express, there "was no outside life." As one customer service manager described it, "People Express is it . . . you kind of become socially retarded . . . and when you do find yourself in another social atmosphere it's kind of awkward."

For those who were married, the intense involvement and closeness with coworkers and with the company was sometimes threatening to family members who felt left out. Of the initial 15 officers, three had been divorced within a year and a half. The very fact of People's difference, in spite of the benefits, was seen by some as a source of stress; keeping the hierarchy to a minimum meant few titles and few promotions in the conventional sense.

You might know personally that you're growing more than you would ever have an opportunity to grow anywhere else but your title doesn't change, (which) doesn't mean that much to you but how does your family react? (Magel)

Even People's biggest strengths, the upbeat culture, the high-caliber performance, and positive attitude of the work force could be stressful. "It's not a competitive environment, it's highly challenging. Everybody's a star . . . but, you know," said one customer service manager, "maintaining high positive attitude is enough to give you a heart attack."

High commitment and high ambition, together with rapid growth and understaffing, meant that most of People's managers were working long hard hours and were under considerable stress. Said one CSM, "Nobody is ever scheduled for over 40 hours (a week), but I don't know anybody who works just 40 hours."

Dubose recognized that the situation had taken a toll on everybody's health. "I was never sick a day in my life until I worked for People Express and in the last two years I've been sick constantly." Other managing officers, including Burr, had also been sick a lot, as had general managers. "And start-up team members — oh my God, they've got ulcers, high blood pressure, allergies, a divorce . . . it's one thing after another . . . we've all been physically run down." She adds, however, "It's not required that we kill ourselves," asserting that personality traits and an emotionally rewarding workplace accounted for the long hours many worked.

Burr's stance on this issue was that there were no emotional or human costs of hard work. "Work is a very misunderstood, underrated idea. In fact human beings are prepared and can operate at levels far in excess of what they think they can do. If you let them think they're tired and ought to go on vacation for two years or so, they will."

By the Fall of 1982, though people were still generally satisfied with their jobs and motivated by their stock ownership to make the company work, many of People's managers below the top level were not as satisfied or optimistic as they once were. A University of Michigan 18-month climate survey taken in September 1982 showed signs of declining morale since December 1981. "People are feeling frustrated in their work (and feel they can't raise questions), cross-utilization is not being well-received, management is viewed as less supportive and consultative, the total compensation package (including pay) is viewed less favorably. Clearly there is work to be done in several areas." (Exhibit 4-13 contains excerpts from the 1982 survey.) The report found significant differences in the perceptions of FMs and CSMs: Flight managers were more skeptical of cross-utilization and more uncertain of what self-management meant; they felt most strongly that management was non-consultative.

When questioned about such problems, those in leadership positions were adamant that both business and personal difficulties were short term, and the costs were well worth the long-term benefits. They felt that virtually every problem was soluble over time with better self-management skills — including time management and stress management, which everyone was being helped to develop — and with evolving improvements in organizational

EXHIBIT 4-13
People Express

Excerpts from the 1982 Survey

Changes Since the December 1981 Climate Survey

In comparing the responses from the December 1981 and September 1982 surveys, the following significant changes have apparently taken place:*

Getting help or advice about a work-related problem is not as easy

What is expected of people is not as clear

People are not being kept as well informed about the performance and plans of the airline

Satisfaction with work schedules has decreased

The number of perceived opportunities to exercise self-management is lower

The process used to create initial work teams is viewed less favorably

The work is generally perceived to be less challenging and involving

The overall quality of upper management is being questioned more

Fewer opportunities for personal growth and career development are apparent

People are not very comfortable about using the "open door" policy at People Express

People feel that their efforts have less of an influence on the price of People Express stock

The buying of discounted company stock is being perceived as less of a part of the pay program

The compensation package is thought to be less equitable considering the work people do

People feel they have to work too hard to accomplish what is expected of them

The team concept at People Express is being questioned more

Officers and General Managers are thought to be nonconsultative on important decisions

People Express is thought to be growing and expanding too fast

There is a stronger perception that asking questions about how the airline is managed may lead to trouble

All of these changes are in a negative direction. Clearly, people are frustrated with the "climate" at People Express: morale and satisfaction are on the decline.

On the positive side, people's expectations of profiting financially were somewhat greater.

*Responses on many of these items were still quite positive in an absolute sense, though, showing statistically significant decline from earlier studies.

---

structure. Even those responsible for recruitment insisted, "The challenge is that it seems impossible and there's a way to do it." (Robinson)

> I don't think the long-term effects on the individual are going to be disastrous because we are learning how to cope with it. And I think the short-term effects on the organization will not be real bad because I think we're trying to put in place all the structure modifications at the same time that we're continuing

the growth. That makes it take longer to get the structure modifications on the road. Which isn't real good. But they'll get there. Long term I think they will have a positive effect. I think. I wish I knew, for sure. (Dubose)

Within two months of the climate survey report, Dubose and others from the People advisory council made a video presentation to address many of the items raised in the report. For almost every major item a solution had been formulated.

In spite of all the new initiatives, each of which would entail considerable time and energy to implement, People's officers did not believe they should slow down the company's rate of growth while attending to internal problems. Their standard explanations were as follows:

> If you don't keep growing then the individual growth won't happen. People here have a very high level of expectation anyway, I mean unrealistic, I mean there's no way it's going to happen. They're not going to be general managers tomorrow, they're not going to learn each area of the airline by next month. But they all want to. And even a reasonable rate of growth isn't going to be attainable for the individual if we don't continue to grow as a company. And the momentum is with us now we're on a roll. If we lose the momentum now we might never be able to pick it up again. (Dubose)

Burr put it even more strongly:

> Now there are a lot of people who argue that you ought to slow down and take stock and that everything would be a whole lot nicer and easier and all that; I don't believe that. People get more fatigued and stressed when they don't have a lot to do. I really believe that, and I think I have tested it. I think it's obvious as hell and I feel pretty strongly about it.

He was convinced that the decrease in energy and decline in morale evident even among the officers were not reason to slow down but to speed up. For himself, he had taken a lot of time to think about things in his early years and had only really begun to know what was important to him between his 35th and 40th years. Then he had entered what he hoped would be an enormous growth period, accelerating "between now and when I get senile. It's sensational what direction does. The beauty of the human condition is the magic people are capable of when there's direction. When there's no direction, you're not capable of much."

Approaching 1983, the big issue ahead for People Express, as Burr saw it, was not the speed or costs of growth. Rather, it was how he and People's other leaders would "keep in touch with what's important" and "not lose sight of their humanity."

Questions for Discussion

1. Assess the match between People Express's HRM policies and its current stage of evolution. Will the company be able to maintain its current policies or will some changes be needed in order to meet its future strategic objectives?
2. How much can the HRM policies and practices of People Express be generalized to other firms? Would you recommend them to other existing firms? To other new firms that are about to start up?

III

The Functional Responsibilities of Human Resource Management

PREVIEW

A firm's human resource or personnel department is traditionally responsible for establishing the systems and procedures for the efficient and equitable management of the firm's employees. The department functions to attract, select, retain, develop, and utilize the firm's employees. But a personnel department does not work in a vacuum. Its responsibilities are shared with all managers in the organization, from the highest level executives to the foreman and lead secretary. Just as the marketing function is a staff responsibility that can only be effectively carried out through careful understanding of customers, as well as a close connection to line managers, personnel staff must be in close contact with employees and managers who carry out daily the human resource policies and procedures. In this part, we discuss the activities, acumen, and skills needed by both line and staff to manage human resource activities efficiently and equitably.

Line managers are becoming more aware of their human resource management responsibilities and, consequently, are realizing their need to understand how their behavior affects the management of employees. This has become increasingly important in recent years as more and more organizations put the responsibility for basic human resource management activities directly into the jobs of line managers.

A recent Conference Board survey (Freedman, 1985) of major firms documented the trend toward greater involvement of line managers in human resource policies. The survey results (see Table P-1) show that line management's role has grown most in the areas of human resource planning, employee development and training, and

TABLE P-1 Line and Staff Responsibilities for Human Resource Management Activities

N = 504	Line Exe		HR Exe		LR Exe		C Exe		Line Role Is Increasing %
	R + A %	Primary[b] %	R + A %	Primary %	R + A %	Primary %	R + A %	Primary %	
Human resources planning	24.4	20.3	17.4	67.5	10.3	8.6	71.4	4.4	55.6
Development and training	34.2	18.6	15.4	70.7	8.8	8.6	50.4	2.4	53.8
Salary budget decision	19.3	16.1	19.6	58.4	8.6	5.1	66.5	21.3	23.4
Introduce employee participation programs	34.7	27.1	22.0	51.8	14.9	18.1	37.4	2.7	55.7
Strategies vs. government regulation	31.8	5.9	10.8	70.4	12.2	24.7	53.3	1.2	24.9
Developing wage and benefit goals	28.6	7.6	13.2	64.8	14.2	25.9	73.3	9.0	27.1
Set wage bargaining limits	26.4	18.1	22.5	26.9	16.6	40.6	57.0	17.1	21.5
Set policy toward unions	28.1	6.1	22.5	37.9	10.0	48.4	60.9	11.5	23.9
Directing union avoidance	32.3	9.5	22.0	35.9	8.1	49.6	43.3	1.0	30.4

[a]R + A means authority to review and/or approve policies.
[b]Primary means the primary responsibility for developing and implementing policy.

Source: Conference Board 1984 survey of employee relations practices of major U.S. firms. See Audrey Freedman, *Changes in Managing Employee Relations, 1984.* (New York: The Conference Board, 1985).

the start-up of employee participation processes. The survey also demonstrates the shared responsibility of personnel staff and line managers for all of the human resource and industrial relations activities listed. In most firms surveyed, human resource professionals were responsible primarily for developing and implementing policies in each area, while line managers or the chief executive officer retained the authority to review and approve policies. In short, the effective management of human resources increasingly requires a high degree of cooperation and teamwork between the staff and the line.

The following is a brief overview of the contributions human resource management specialists in modern organizations are expected to make, and alternative ways of structuring industrial relations and human resource management departments.

Human Resource Professionals: Serving Multiple Clients

One way to view the role of human resource professionals is to ask: What do they contribute to the various clients they are expected to serve at different levels within an organization? Table P-2 presents a schematic framework for considering this question at the strategic, administrative, and operational levels of organizational activity. At each level, human resource professionals must be held accountable to at least three sets of clients, each of whom embodies different sets of interests and perspectives. These clients are line managers and executives, employees, and society, whose interests are reflected in laws, public policies, and general social values.

Strategic Roles

We have already discussed the need to link human resource plans and strategies to the larger business plans and strategies of an organization. But the contributions of human resource specialists to long-term strategy must go beyond responding to the strategic plans of top management. Top-level human resource professionals are expected to provide a link between their organization and relevant developments in the external environment. They are called upon to contribute sound professional judgment about external environmental trends and thereby help ensure that internal plans and policies are congruent with — or perhaps help shape — political, economic, and social trends. These top professionals are the organization's link to the outside world in which employment and labor policies are debated and enacted, compensation trends and patterns are established, and the values and educational backgrounds of the labor force are developed. Sorting and interpreting these external events is a key contribution human resource professionals make to the long-term welfare of an organization.

TABLE P-2 Contributions and Client Expectations
of Human Resource Professionals

Organizational Level	Client's Expectations	Contribution of HRM/IR Professionals
Strategic	Line Managers: HRM/IR policies and practices should contribute to long- and short-run organizational performance goals of unit or organization	Provide professional judgment on how environmental trends and organizational strategies intersect with short- and long-range business plans, employee expectations and the values, goals, and laws of society
	Employees: HRM/IR policies should contribute to personal career objectives and needs	
	Public: HRM/IR policies should reflect societal values and public policy goals	
Administrative	Line Managers: HRM/IR technical systems should be suited to specific needs	Use professional expertise to design and implement technically sound and organizationally relevant HRM/IR systems
	Employees: HRM/IR procedures should be administered fairly and equitably, and they should be understandable and available to employees when needed	
	Public: HRM/IR policies should carry out the intent of public policies and societal values	
Operational/ Workplace	Line Managers: HRM/IR function should serve as a problem-solving resource, not a bureaucratic obstacle to getting work done	Effectively administer and coordinate the day-to-day procedures of HRM/IR systems
	Employees: HRM/IR should promote safety issues and ensure equity, due process, and protection of employees' rights	
	Public: HRM/IR should promote social goals of safety and health, equal opportunity, industrial peace, and individual dignity and growth	

Playing this role will always require a balancing act. Sometimes human resource professionals need to prod their managerial colleagues to adjust to changing demands of the external environment, such as encouraging changes in attitudes and behavior toward women and minorities in order to comply with equal employment opportunity laws. Sometimes human resource professionals must negotiate with external interest groups or government agencies on behalf of the organization to change the environment in ways that accept an organization's philosophy or strategies, such as urging changes in educational curricula to prepare students for jobs in the firm.

Client expectations for human resource professionals at the strategic level are likewise relatively straightforward. Line managers expect advice and information useful in focusing their efforts on the human resource activities affecting their short-run performance goals *and* adequate warning of future developments to incorporate into their longer-term plans. Employees look to human resource professionals to represent their interests either directly or indirectly in high-level managerial decisions. Here the boundary-spanning function of the professional again comes to the fore: He or she must negotiate hard with employees and their representatives to achieve written or unwritten bargains and agreements over employment terms and policies, and then aggressively advocate these agreements and the interests of employees within the managerial decision-making process (Walton and McKensie, 1965; Kochan, 1975). This role goes beyond collective bargaining; it is generic to all aspects of human resource management or any other staff function that deals with external groups and multiple internal constituents.

Administrative Contributions and Expectations

The administrative level of an organizational system corresponds to the stage where specific policies are designed and implemented. The primary contributions of human resource professionals at this level are (1) to provide the technical expertise needed to design policies that are consistent with current theory and practice, and (2) to adapt these technical systems to fit the specific needs of the organization. Human resource staff must work with line managers to implement systems being purchased by the organization. All line managers expect to get sound technical advice and not be overburdened with formal systems and programs that do not meet their needs or that are operationally cumbersome.

Employees will judge the effectiveness of the human resource staff at the administrative level by their perceptions of the fairness, accessibility, and clarity of personnel policies. Are the skills offered in training programs relevant and useful? Is the compensation system understandable, and are salaries comparable to those in similar organizations? Are the rules governing promotions and compensation clear and fair? Are candidates really given a fair chance in competing for promotions?

Similarly, public policy representatives may be the most critical observers of the technical adequacy of personnel practices. Are selection procedures consistent with equal employment opportunity laws? Are the wage-and-hour laws being enforced? Are safety and health standards being observed? Is the firm complying with the provisions of prevailing labor relations laws? Again, the technical, occupation-specific skills and training are central to this aspect of the personnel function.

Operational Expectations and Contributions

At the operational, or day-to-day workplace level, the primary contribution of human resource specialists lies in their efficient administration of personnel procedures, in the day-to-day paperwork associated with personnel processes. Line managers, in turn, expect efficiency and a minimization of the bureaucratic paperwork often associated with performance reviews, hiring and promotion decisions, grievance and complaint handling, and so on. They also expect personnel staff to be good problem solvers, able to find the exception to the rule if needed to get things done. Employees want efficiency and problem solving, too, but they also rely on human resource professionals to protect their individual rights on the job and to ensure due process in decision making and industrial jurisprudence. Finally, the public expects human resource professionals to promote safety and health, equal opportunity, industrial peace, individual worker dignity and personal growth, as well as high levels of productivity and quality in the goods and services produced.

Structure of Human Resource Departments

Organizations structure (and restructure) their human resource departments in a variety of ways. In most large firms, the top human resource executive is on the staff of the corporate office and is very often a vice-president. In some firms, he or she also serves as an officer of the firm. Reporting to this executive at the corporate level may be one or more directors of various subfunctions, such as compensation and benefits, training and development, human resource planning, labor relations, safety and health, and equal employment opportunity. The size of the corporate staff depends on the extent to which management authority is decentralized to division or plant/office levels. A 1977 Conference Board survey (Janger, 1977) found, for example, that more than 60 percent of major United States firms have personnel or human resource staff specialists at plant or division levels.

In structuring the reporting relationships of lower-level staff professionals, the question arises whether to have them report directly to corporate staff or to their division or plant general managers. Although no quantitative estimates are available of current reporting patterns, the general management trend toward greater decentralization of decision making seems to be carrying over to the role of human resource staff. That is, the majority of firms today appear to have plant and/or division human resource staff report to their general managers while having a secondary or "dotted line" reporting relationship with their corporate-level human resource counterparts. Regardless of the specific, formal reporting relationships, the generic responsibilities of the corporate human resource staff are to coordinate and plan overall human resource management policies to assure their compatibility with the basic values of the firm and society. Staff at decentralized levels are responsible primarily for tailoring organization policies to the specific strategic and operational needs of their units.

In the four chapters in this part, we examine these human resource management functions, beginning in Chapter 5 with the procedures used to recruit and select new employees. In Chapter 6 we discuss the staffing and development functions; readings and case studies explore the choices firms face as they manage the use and the flow of people through the organization, and as they adapt to changing market and business conditions. The materials describe the differences in policies and practices governing the movement of different groups of workers; blue-collar factory workers are governed by seniority systems, whereas high-level managers and professionals tend to be directly influenced by shifting labor and product market forces and by changes in the direction of their business units. Chapter 7 is devoted to compensation issues, specifically compensation for executives, managers, and non-union employees. Discussion of the functional activities continues in Chapter 8 with the roles and processes of collective bargaining and labor relations.

References

Freedman, Audrey, *Changes in Managing Employee Relations, 1984* (New York: The Conference Board, 1985).

Janger, Alan, *The Personnel Function* (New York: The Conference Board, 1977).

Kochan, Thomas A., "Determinants of the Power of Boundary Limits in an Interorganizational Bargaining Relation," *Administrative Science Quarterly* 20, September 1975, 234–52.

Walton, Richard E., and Robert B. McKensie, *A Behavioral Theory of Labor Negotiations* (New York: McGraw Hill, 1965).

5

Recruitment and Selection

The administrative partnership between personnel staff and line managers begins with recruiting and selecting employees for the organization. In this chapter, we review the tasks and decisions involved in managing a recruitment and selection system and the various ways organizations perform these tasks. Figure 5-1 outlines the sequence of recruitment and selection tasks.

Forecasting Needs and Specifying Job Requirements

The first stage in a recruitment process is to determine the demand for staff far enough in advance to allow time to bring people into the organization, yet close enough to assure reliable forecasts. The process of forecasting demand begins with business plans and estimates of expected changes in the volume of production or services, changes that will influence productivity and the number of people required for the volume of work, and expected changes in organizational structure, which will influence the mix of jobs to be filled. Forecasting supply begins with estimates of the rate of turnover for current jobs. Most forecasting systems start with an inventory of current jobs and job incumbents and proceed to project changes in the business, in the jobs, or in the incumbents, which may trigger a need for recruits.

A variety of informal and formal forecasting methods exist. One informal system simply relies on judgmental forecasting. The most commonly discussed judgmental system is managerial succession planning. Most firms keep track of the expected movements of high-level executives and maintain a record, often computerized, of potential mid- and upper-level managers who may be available to fill executive positions as they become vacant. The management inventory for each manager charts the variety of jobs held in and out of the organization, performance review records, specialized training and general education, and any other information pertinent to assessing whether sufficient managerial talent is being developed to assure orderly succession to the top posts in the organization. If, in reviewing a succession plan, it is discovered that sufficient high-caliber managerial talent is not

Recruitment Phase		Selection Phase		Evaluation and Planning Phase
Assessing Internal Sources	Choosing Recruitment Channels $\rightarrow$	Screening Initial Applicants $\rightarrow$	Selecting Among Finalists $\rightarrow$	Evaluating and Reviewing
Forecasting Staffing Needs $\rightarrow$				
Business plans $\rightarrow$ Turnover estimates $\rightarrow$ Productivity assumptions $\rightarrow$ Job and organizational changes $\rightarrow$ Job analysis $\rightarrow$ Job description $\rightarrow$ Job qualifications	*Informal sources* Employee referrals Direct applicants Direct contacts *Formal sources* Advertising Private search firms College recruiting Public employment service	*Qualification screens* Education Experience Initial interviews	Interviews Tests Reference checks Application blank analysis	Tracking and record-keeping Yield, cost, quality reviews Selection validation EEO audit Client satisfaction

FIGURE 5-1   Recruitment/Selection Sequence

being developed, either the internal development process needs to be revised, or new high-potential talent must be recruited from outside the organization for the mid- to upper-level managerial positions. Although the informal systems used for the lower levels of an organization tend to be more ad hoc and less closely monitored, the principles and general procedures are similar to managerial succession planning.

The keys to effective informal and formal forecasting are the abilities to anticipate how changes in the external environment or the direction of the business will alter historical flow rates and to adjust recruitment plans accordingly before the changes occur. Adjustment is especially necessary in formal, statistical forecasting systems. Chapter 6 demonstrates the uses and limitations of one such formal system, the Markov model, which computes the probability of various types of internal personnel movements on the basis of historical patterns of promotions, transfers, and turnover. Although useful in stable organizational settings where past movement is an accurate approximation of the future, the model will err if predictions are not adjusted to account for changes in turnover rates, hiring rates, and job openings that occur when business conditions or plans change. Thus, even formal models require an element of professional judgment.

Another prerecruitment task involves an analysis of the specific jobs to be filled. Jobs change over time as a result of changes in technology and in the way work is organized. Before recruiting for new positions, or at some periodic interval, HRM needs to reanalyze the organizations' jobs to update job descriptions and qualifications to be used in advertising a position. Conducting a job analysis is usually the first step in drawing up job qualifications and planning a recruitment strategy. Job analysis also provides the initial information needed to validate selection procedures and evaluate job performance.

The final prerecruitment step before embarking on a costly external search and selection process is to consider filling job openings from within the organization. More will be said about this option in Chapter 6 as we discuss the make (internal development and recruitment) or buy (external recruitment) decision.

Choosing Recruitment Channels

Organizations tend to use different recruitment channels for different occupational groups. All organizations rely on formal advertising of positions, both because public announcement is required to comply with equal employment opportunity laws and procedures and because advertising is one of the cheapest means of reaching a large, diverse group of potential applicants. For high-level executives and managers, and increasingly for professional and technical employees, private search firms (often referred to in the trade as headhunters) are used. Although expensive (fees often range between 25 percent to 50 percent of the recruit's annual salary), search firms provide more intensive private data on a more specialized or narrower band of potential recruits. Executive search firms also can contact potential candidates currently employed in other companies on a confidential basis. For blue-collar and clerical recruits, advertisements, direct applications, and employee referrals serve as the primary sources. The U.S. Public Employment Service historically has tried to strengthen its role as a source of recruits for all occupational groups, but for most firms the service is viewed as a secondary source for blue-collar and clerical employees.

Several criteria are relevant to the choice of one or more recruitment channels. Labor market analysts (Rees and Shultz, 1970) have noted that formal channels such as advertising, listing jobs with the Public Employment Service, or recruiting at colleges and vocational schools provide *extensive* information on the entire labor market. On the other hand, informal channels such as employee referrals, direct application, or direct solicitation of a potential candidate can provide more *intensive* information on specific individuals. Thus, alternative channels should be used to evaluate the *numbers and diversity* of viable candidates and the *quality* of information available on individual candidates. It is especially important to ascertain whether recruitment channels are attracting a sufficient number of qualified women and minority candidates to meet equal employment opportunity and affirmative action policy objectives. If not, then new recruitment channels or sources are needed to generate more of these candidates.

Beyond these criteria, most organizations will review the *costs* of alternative channels against their *yield ratios*. A yield ratio is the number of applicants from a recruitment channel divided by the number hired through that channel. Table 5-1 presents yield ratios for college

TABLE 5-1 1982–83 College Recruitment Yield Analysis for a Large Engineering Firm

	Number	Yield Ratio*
Résumés reviewed	3,144	
		31:1
Campus interviews	1,089	
		11:1
Interviews on company site	509	
		5:1
Offers extended	263	
		2.6:1
Offers accepted	115	

*Yield ratio = Number of candidates/number hired. Yield ratios will vary from year to year as the labor market changes. For example, the labor market for college graduates deteriorated between 1981 and 1983. As a result, the percentage of this firm's job offers accepted by college graduates increased from 39 percent in 1981 to 41 percent in 1982 to 44 percent (115 of 263) in 1983. Thus, anticipated yield ratios need to be adjusted periodically to account for labor market changes.

recruiting for a rapidly growing engineering firm. To hire 115 new graduates, the firm conducted 1,089 campus interviews, brought 509 candidates to the firm for interviews, and extended 263 offers. The yield ratio of campus interviews to new hires was 11 to 1, and the ratio of offers to acceptances was 2.6 to 1.

One study has shown that informal recruitment channels, such as employee referrals and direct applications, are somewhat better than formal recruitment channels in retaining employees (Schwab, 1982). Although this finding may not apply to all groups of employees, it suggests that *retention ratios* are also worth considering when evaluating the utility of alternative recruitment channels for a given job.

Validating the Selection Process

After a pool of potential candidates has been recruited, the selection process distinguishes those likely to perform successfully from those likely to perform poorly. In the selection process, the factors used to choose among candidates must be *valid*, accurate predictors of effective job performance. In addition, the selection system itself must meet society's standards of *fairness*.

In a narrow sense, a selection system is fair if candidates who have equal probabilities of performing successfully have equal probabilities of being hired (Guion, 1966). This technical definition of fairness has been broadened somewhat by the adoption of an *adverse impact* standard for enforcing equal opportunity policies. Adverse impact occurs when a selection system produces a disproportionate number of rejections of women, minorities, or other protected groups. If such rejections occur, either the selection process needs to be changed or the employer must be able to prove that sex, age, or other criteria are bona fide occupational qualifications (BFOQs). That is, the burden is on the employer to demonstrate, for example, that being male is a BFOQ for working as a guard in a men's prison. Race is excluded specifically by law from use as a BFOQ.

The validation process involves the following three steps: (1) defining the appropriate job performance measures or criteria, (2) assessing the applicant's likely performance, and (3) analyzing the correlation between job criteria and applicant predictors.

First, the results of job analyses should be used to define measures of effective job performance, referred to as criterion measures in the human resource management literature. Typical measures of job performance for different types of jobs are shown in Box 5-1. For executives, criterion measures might include, among others, an ability to make sound judgments, solve complex problems, communicate effectively, handle stress, and lead and supervise employees. In all cases, whatever dimensions of job performance are chosen, reliable measures of them must be available or developed for use in the selection validation process.

BOX 5-1
Examples of Performance Dimensions
Used for Various Occupations

Store Salesperson

Planning and organizing
Sensitivity
Tolerance for stress
Energy
Attention to detail
Integrity
Oral communication

Administrative Assistant

Grammar, editing, proofreading
Cooperation
Sensitivity
Work standards
Job motivation
Administrative control
Administrative recall
Initiative
Ability to learn

Supervisor

Analysis
Judgment
Planning and organizing
Control
Sensitivity
Leadership
Direction
Recognition of employees' safety needs
Tolerance for stress
Work standards
Initiative
Oral communication

Production Worker

Technical proficiency
Troubleshooting
Work standards
Work planning
Job motivation
Initiative
Tolerance for stress
Work safety

Executive

Analysis
Judgment
Decisiveness
Organizational awareness
Organizational sensitivity
Extra-organizational awareness
Extra-organizational sensitivity
Development of subordinates
Leadership
Adaptability
Independence
Job motivation
Range of interests
Energy
Tolerance for stress
Oral presentation
Written communication

Business Machine Sales Representative

Technical knowledge
Oral fact-finding
Planning and organizing
Tenacity
Sales ability/persuasiveness
Impact
Behavioral flexibility
Resilience
Energy
Motivation for sales
Ability to learn
Oral communication

Source: William C. Byham, *Targeted Selection* (Pittsburgh: Development Dimensions International, 1981).

Second, techniques should be chosen to identify and measure reliably applicant characteristics that can predict effective job performance (referred to as *predictors*). The common techniques for uncovering these predictors are (1) employment interviews, (2) tests, (3) information collected on application forms, such as education, experience, tenure on previous jobs, and, to a lesser extent, (4) reference checks.

Third, an analysis of the correlation between the criterion measures and the predictors of job performance should be made to test empirically the validity of the predictors used to judge candidates. Ideally, such analysis should be done on a sample of applicants who were hired at random, or at least without using the predictors to screen out people. The technique is called *predictive validation*, as it does not limit the sample to current employees who were judged to be high on the predictor variables (and would fall in the upper level of the job performance range). The sample for predictive validation is difficult to arrange. An alternative approach, called *concurrent validation*, involves using current employees to collect data on both predictors and criterion measures. One must infer that those characteristics of current employees that predict job performance will also be valid predictors of the potential job performance of future applicants. A third form of analysis, *content validation*, is perhaps the most common approach in use. Content validation is judgmental rather than statistical. Judgments are made by knowledgeable managers about the likely relationship betwen applicant characteristics and eventual job performance. This approach is used in situations where too small a sample of employees exists in a job classification to warrant statistical analysis, or where jobs change over time so that new skills or qualifications are needed for employees to perform effectively.

The design of a proper validation analysis is a highly technical exercise that we will not dwell on here. However, several caveats of caution about the use of alternative selection techniques are important to note. First, although it remains an important part of most selection procedures, the employment interview consistently is one of the least reliable, least valid techniques for making selection decisions when compared to application form information, work samples, and standardized tests (Arvey and Campion, 1982). In general, interviewers are unable to elicit specific enough job-related information in a form that allows for reliable comparisons across candidates. Instead, most interviewers form initial positive or negative impressions of candidates early in the interview process, and multiple interviewers of the same candidates often form very different impressions on the basis of different interviewee characteristics or statements. Thus, the interrater reliability or agreement is often low.

Marginal improvements in the reliability and validity of interviews can be made by using multiple interviewers who have been trained to avoid common interviewing errors, by structuring the interviews to focus more directly on specific job-related issues and experiences, and by standardizing the scoring or rating methods interviewers use to compare candidates (Arvey and Campion, 1982). Even with these precautions, however, the research evidence is conclusive: At best, only marginal improvements in validity are likely. Interviews must be supplemented with additional information on candidates.

Various tests have been constructed to overcome some of the limitations of the employment interview. The tests range from personality or vocational interest/aptitude tests to cognitive or achievement tests that measure general intelligence or job-specific knowledge, work sample tests such as typing exams for secretaries, mechanical ability and dexterity tests for repair workers, tryouts for baseball players, and in-basket exercises for managers. As one moves from general personality and aptitude tests to more specific job-related exercises, the costs of test development increase along with test validity, assuming the tests are carefully designed and implemented (Heneman, Schwab, Fossum, and Dyer, 1982). Thus, cost effectiveness must be judged on the basis of the numbers of people to be hired and the costs of making wrong decisions.

Before investing in complex test development, however, it may be wise to examine the predictive validity of information collected on standard application forms. Personnel researchers have found background information such as experience, education, previous job tenure, and other data to perform reasonably well in predicting job performance for a wide range of blue-collar, clerical, and technical jobs (Reilly and Chao, 1982).

Evaluating Recruitment Efforts

The final phase of any recruitment and selection process should be to evaluate and audit the strategies and procedures used and to plan future recruitment efforts. While not exhaustive, the following criteria are relevant to such an evaluation: (1) selection system validity and fairness, (2) compliance with equal employment opportunity and affirmative action objectives, (3) administrative efficiency, (4) cost effectiveness, and (5) client satisfaction. As we have introduced most of these topics already, we close this overview of recruitment and selection with a brief paragraph about the need to assess the satisfaction of line managers and job applicants with the procedures followed.

Too often human resource managers focus too narrowly on the legal requirements and technical details of the design of recruitment and selection systems, and they fail to notice how the systems work. The best-designed system cannot achieve its objectives if HRM staff and line managers do not apply it. Over time, managers may adapt recruitment and selection procedures to meet their specialized needs and modes of operation. Indeed some adaptations will be needed in order to fit diverse organizational settings. The challenge for the system's designers is to anticipate the adaptations and various shortcuts, to encourage those that make the system more efficient and more relevant to different jobs and organizational settings and to discourage those that defeat the purposes of the system. Thus, monitoring the process by formally obtaining feedback from line managers and applicants represents an evaluation activity as important as the assessment of the results produced by the system. Both activities provide useful data for planning the next cycle of recruitment.

References

Arvey, Richard D., and James E. Campion, "The Employment Interview: A Summary and Review of Recent Research," *Personnel Psychology*, 35, 1982, 281–322.

Guion, R. M., "Employment Tests and Discriminatory Hiring," *Industrial Relations*, 5, 1966, 20–37.

Heneman, Herbert G. III, Donald P. Schwab, John A. Fossum, and Lee D. Dyer, *Personnel/Human Resource Management* (Homewood, Ill.: Irwin, 1983).

Rees, Albert, and George P. Shultz, *Workers and Wages in an Urban Labor Market* (Chicago: University of Chicago Press, 1970).

Reilly, Richard R., and Georgia T. Chao, "Validity and Fairness of Some Alternative Employee Selection Procedures," *Personnel Psychology*, 35, 1982, 1–62.

Schwab, Donald P., "Recruiting and Organizational Participation" in Kenneth Rowland and George Ferris, eds., *Personnel Management* (Newton, Mass.: Allyn and Bacon, 1982).

Suggested Readings

For a thorough discussion of the technical aspects of selection system design and evaluation, see Wayne F. Cascio, *Applied Psychology in Personnel Management* (Reston, Va.: Reston Publishing Company, 1982).

For an overview of federal policies that regulate recruitment and selection, see James Ledvinka, *Federal Regulation of Personnel and Human Resource Management* (Boston: Kent, 1982).

Evaluating a Selection Process

The following case illustrates some of the common, substantive aspects of the design of an effective selection system and raises important questions about the implementation of such a system. This study demonstrates the importance of having an adequate information base that allows managers to evaluate personnel programs.

CASE
Engineering Systems Unlimited

Janet Hooper, a senior consultant at Evaluation Research Associates (ERA), faced the task of writing the conclusions and recommendations for a consultants' report that she and her staff had prepared for Engineering Systems Unlimited (ESU). Her task would be especially difficult because (1) the quantitative and qualitative results of the study offered conflicting interpretations for how the selection system they had evaluated was working, and (2) the client's staff had many different interests and diverse views on the merits and problems of the selection system. Thus, the phrasing of her recommendations and the means she would suggest for implementing them were as important to their acceptance and use as the substance of her conclusions and recommendations.

BACKGROUND

ESU is a large, rapidly growing engineering and systems development firm. It has been expanding for the past several years, taking advantage of the growing market for its software and related computer systems engineering expertise. Approximately 30 percent of its revenues come from government contracts, and all indications were that this, along with the private sector market, would continue to support high rates of growth.

Because of its rapid growth, the biggest challenge facing the firm's human resource department was to recruit and select a sufficient number of engineers and supporting managers and staff to meet the growing market demand. The director of recruitment for ESU indicated that the firm had been hiring 200 technical employees per month for the past year and a half, and this rate was expected to continue into the foreseeable future.

Because of pressures on the recruiting process, in 1981 the vice-president of human resources and his staff began a search for better ways to structure the company's selection process. After careful study, they signed a contract with Consulting Services of America (CSA), a consulting firm specializing in the design and implementation of personnel systems. CSA had developed a process called professional hiring (PH), which took the best evidence from theoretical and empirical research and applied it to the personnel selection process. The firm had established structured procedures to carry through from the initial employment interview to the final selection decision. ESU hired CSA to adapt professional hiring to the needs of ESU, to train ESU managers in the use of the process, and to help implement the process. The PH system looked particularly attractive to the human resource staff at ESU because it promised to bring more structure to the hiring process — something the engineering managers wanted.

The PH system was installed, the training process was under way, and a number of people were hired. After eight months, however, line managers were grumbling that the procedure was too time-consuming and cumbersome. They were not sure it was worth the time and resources needed to train more managers or to use the process in selecting new hires.

ESU's president heard of the grumbling and called a meeting to decide what to do. At the meeting, the vice-president of human resources suggested that an independent firm be commissioned to evaluate the PH process at ESU. (An outside evaluator was suggested because any evaluation done by the human resource department or by CSA ran the risk of bias.)

Additional training of managers in the PH process was suspended pending the evaluation, and ERA was hired to conduct the study, which took three months. Janet Hooper was in charge of the study. The report follows.

RESEARCH OBJECTIVES AND METHODS

Professional hiring (PH) was developed by Consulting Services of America (CSA) to strengthen the interviewing and decision-making stages of the personnel selection process. The design of PH responds well to the accumulated evidence of the common problems with the interview portion of personnel selection processes. To overcome the generally low reliability that interviews have been shown to have, the personnel literature suggests that selection interviews should (1) focus on specific past job behaviors and/or experiences, (2) identify specific dimensions of the jobs to be filled and focus the interview questions around those dimensions, (3) use multiple interviewers, (4) use a common format to record interviewer evaluations of candidates to facilitate cross-interviewer comparisons, and (5) be conducted by individuals who have been trained in interviewing skills and techniques. To apply these principles, CSA worked with ESU officials to develop job-specific dimensions suited to the company's professional needs. CSA also designed a training program for managers who would conduct interviews and developed a common set of interview guides, scoring formats, and procedures for integrating the interviewers' evaluations so that a consensus could be reached on whether to extend a job offer.

The first PH training at ESU took place in mid-1981 and, shortly thereafter, the first individuals were hired under the PH procedures. Since then, more than 147 managers have been trained in PH and more than 110 technical employees (excluding new college graduates) have been hired via the PH process. The objectives of this study are to see if the use of the PH process has (1) improved the recruiting performance at ESU by increasing the ratio of candidate acceptances to job offers, (2) improved interviewees' perceptions of the quality of the interviewing process, (3) improved the quality of the candidates hired, and (4) achieved acceptance among managers who are actively involved in the recruitment and selection process.

Four sets of data were collected to address these questions:

1. Recruitment files were examined to compare acceptance-to-offer ratios of PH and non-PH groups.
2. Questionnaires were distributed to a sample of PH and non-PH ESU employees to determine whether PH interviews were evaluated more favorably than non-PH interviews.
3. Measures of the job performance of PH and non-PH employees were compared after controlling for differences in education, tenure with the company, tenure on the job, and years of professional work experience.
4. Interviews were held with a sample of managers with PH experience to learn how PH was practiced, to obtain managers' views of the PH process, and to collect ideas about whether and how PH should be used in the future.

QUANTITATIVE RESULTS

Interview/Offer/Acceptance Ratios

Data from the college recruiting files for 1981 and 1982 allow a comparison of both the interview-to-offer and the offer-to-acceptance ratios. According to ESU's Final Report on College Recruiting, between the 1981 and 1982 college recruiting seasons,

> Recruiters received a full day's training in the use of the "Professional Hiring" method of interviewing. . . . In addition to training recruiters, the job dimensions for the Engineer I position were determined and an on-campus interview guide was designed.

A definite improvement in college recruiting performance was achieved in 1982, as shown in Figure 5-2. In 1982, 55 percent of the college interviews for technical recruits led to offers, compared to 44 percent in 1981. In addition, 41 percent of 1982 offers were accepted, compared to 31 percent in 1981. Overall, this meant that "the number of candidates interviewed in-house for each acceptance dropped from 7.2 in 1981 to 4.5 in 1982." While some of these differences may be due to changes in the labor market between these two years, the ESU college recruiters believe that "this improvement in efficiency can be partially attributed to the better 'up front' on-campus interviewing and screening" in 1982. Thus, some of this improvement is attributable to the PH training and procedures.

Although there are no data on the number of PH interviews for technical personnel in 1982, there are data that allow a comparison of offer-to-acceptance ratios for PH and non-PH personnel who were not recruited from college campuses. These data are summarized in Figure 5-3. Seventy-eight percent of

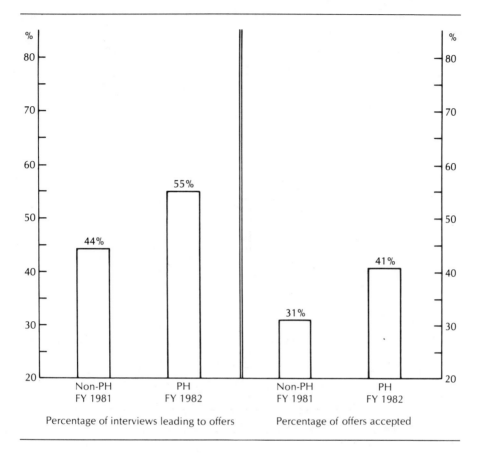

FIGURE 5-2   1981–1982 College Recruiting Data

the offers made under the PH procedure were accepted, compared to 50 percent of non-PH offers. For the noncollege group, therefore, a substantial difference was observed.

Interviewee Questionnaires

To assess whether employees hired through the PH process evaluated their interview experiences more favorably than employees hired through the normal process, a questionnaire was distributed to a sample of current employees. Responses were received from 32 of 51 employees hired under the PH process and 28 of 63 hired under the traditional process. The response rate was slightly above 50 percent and somewhat higher for PH hires.

The employees were asked to what extent they agreed or disagreed with eleven statements about the interviewing process they underwent at ESU. The questions were based on the following objectives of the PH process: (1) to focus on specific prior job experiences, (2) to avoid straying into irrelevant issues, (3) to elicit relevant information the company and the candidate needed

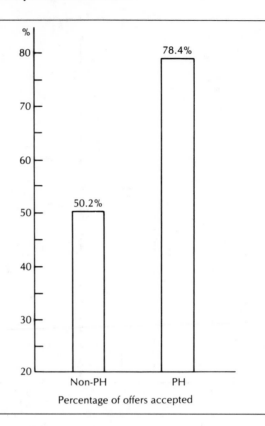

FIGURE 5-3   1982 Noncollege Recruiting Data

to judge the fit of the candidate and the job, and (4) to provide a realistic preview of the job and the employment policies of ESU.

The data in Figure 5-4 indicate that employees hired under the PH process did not rate their interviewing experiences significantly higher than the non-PH hirees. In fact, on ten of the eleven questions, a slightly higher percentage of non-PH hirees agreed with the statements about their interviews. Thus, we cannot conclude from these data that the PH training produced any perceptible improvement in the quality of the interviewing process.

Job Performance Comparisons

Job performance and demographic data were collected on 113 current employees for the analysis of whether the use of PH had increased the quality of employees selected. Of the 113, 51 were PH hirees and 62 were hired under the traditional procedures. One of the limitations of comparisons across these two groups was that the non-PH sample, on average, had much longer tenure with ESU. Average tenure for the PH group was eight months compared to two years for the non-PH group. Thus, before any meaningful assessment of differences in performance could be made, these differences in length of tenure

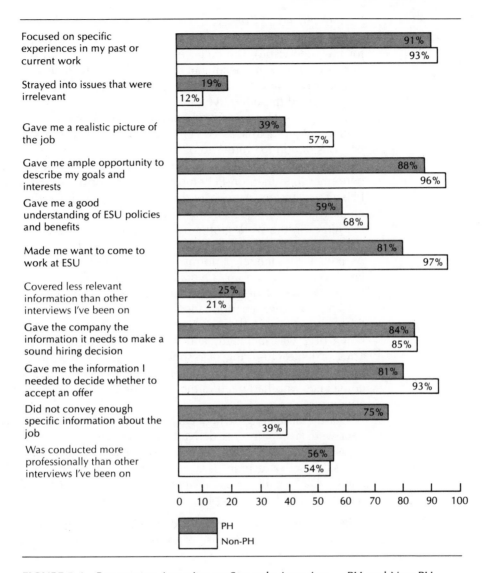

FIGURE 5-4   Percentage Agreeing or Strongly Agreeing — PH and Non-PH

had to be controlled. The analysis used multiple regression equations to explicitly control for (1) tenure with ESU, (2) time in present job grade, (3) education, and (4) length of professional work experience as measured by years since the completion of formal education.

Four sets of performance measures were collected and analyzed:

1. Supervisors were asked to make paired comparison rankings of a sample of six subordinates, some of whom were PH hires and some of whom were a randomly selected set of non-PH hires. Data are available from nineteen supervisors. (Nineteen supervisors should

have produced 114 observations for this analysis; however, one sub-ordinate could not be ranked because he had not actually worked for the supervisor.) The value of this measure ranged from zero to five. A value of zero meant that the five other individuals were ranked as better performers, while a value of five meant that the individual outperformed the other five in the work group.

2. Another measure was derived from the paired comparisons by elim-inating any comparisons of PH hirees to other PH hirees and com-parisons of non-PH hirees to other non-PH hirees. This measure was the percentage of times each PH hiree was rated as being a better performer than the non-PH employees in his or her group. For non-PH hirees this measure was the percentage of times the non-PH employee was ranked as being a better performer when compared to PH hirees in the work group. Thus, this measure could vary from a minimum value of zero to a maximum value of 100.

3. As part of the annual performance appraisal process, each exempt employee was given an "Overall Performance Assessment" on a 1-to-5 scale, with 1 describing "marginal" performance and 5 describ-ing "distinguished" performance. Although the theoretical range of this measure was 1 through 5, no rating of 1 was given, only one rating of 2 was included, and only 6 ratings of 5 were achieved. Thus, a large clustering of response ratings occurred in the 3-to-4 range of this scale. Data on this measure were available for 61 employees who had been in their jobs long enough for performance appraisals.

4. A measure of salary growth of each employee in the sample for whom data were available was derived by calculating the percentage in-crease in salary per month of service with ESU. This measure assumes that salary advancement is a valid indirect measure of job perfor-mance. Data on this measure were available again for 61 observations out of the 113 in the sample.

A multiple regression equation that controlled for differences in tenure, education, time in grade, and years of experience produced the following results:

1. No significant differences in the paired comparison rankings were observed between PH and non-PH employees. The regression esti-mate showed a negative sign, however, indicating that PH employees tended to receive somewhat lower performance rankings than non-PH employees.

2. The same result was obtained for the alternative paired comparison measure that eliminated the PH to PH and the non-PH to non-PH comparisons. That is, the sign of the regression coefficient was neg-ative, indicating slightly higher rankings for non-PH employees, but again the difference between the two groups was insignificant.

3. The results for both the performance ratings obtained from the per-formance appraisal sheets and the salary growth measures produced

the same negative but insignificant result. That is, controlling for differences in tenure, experience, and education, PH employees received slightly, but not significantly, lower performance ratings and salary increases than non-PH employees.

An additional check on these results was performed by limiting the sample to employees with sufficient ESU tenure to have received at least one performance appraisal review. None of the results reported above was changed by limiting the analyses to this more experienced subsample. Thus, the basic conclusion to be derived from these regressions is that no significant differences exist between PH and non-PH employees on the four measures of job performance available for these analyses.

MANAGER INTERVIEWS

Interviews with managers trained in PH and experienced in using it were conducted to (1) determine how PH has been implemented, (2) assess the managers' views of the PH process and its results, and (3) obtain suggestions for improving the selection and recruitment process. The twenty-three managers interviewed were from the divisions of Computer Systems Engineering (CSE), Regional Support Engineering (RSE), Human Resource Management (HRM), Military Operations (MO), Data Processing Services (DPS), and Electronics and Technology Engineering (ETE).

Implementation and Current Use of PH

Of the twenty-three managers, only one indicated that he was currently using PH in the basic way it was introduced in the PH training sessions. Nineteen managers indicated that they were currently using PH in a modified way. Three indicated that they were no longer using PH. Six reasons were cited for modifying or abandoning the PH procedures.

1. Some managers reported that not all of the individuals who participated in the interviewing process had completed training and, therefore, it was impossible to follow the PH process in its complete form.
2. The PH interviews were judged by many to take too long. One group judged that the PH interviews were taking up to two hours each — a length at least double the maximum tolerable.
3. A common, almost universal, complaint was that the PH dimensions were too general in nature, focused too much on interpersonal skills, and failed to focus on the technical dimensions of the jobs, judged by these managers to be crucial to successful performance.
4. Some managers felt uncomfortable with the degree of overlap or repetition in the questioning built into the design of PH.
5. Managers were generally uncomfortable putting highly structured and detailed questions to experienced candidates being recruited for senior positions. These candidates tended to be insulted by the formal structure, detailed note-taking, and recording of responses. As a re-

sult, few managers used more than the general format of PH for interviews with senior-level candidates.

6. Conversely, some managers believed that the PH questions about prior job experience did not fit well with new college recruits, since many lacked experience in jobs directly relevant to the positions for which they were being recruited.

PH procedures were modified by various managers to accommodate these problems. The more important changes are listed below.

1. CSA made the following modifications:
   a. Shortened the interviews to a maximum of one hour (including time needed to answer candidates' questions and promote ESU);
   b. Eliminated almost all overlap in questions asked by different interviewers;
   c. Replaced some of the more general questions with specific ones that reflected the more technical requirements of the jobs.
2. DPS modified the process by establishing permanent interview teams of three people each. Last year, ten teams were established; each team evaluated seven candidates. Data-integration meetings produced rankings within each team, and team captains met to evaluate all the candidates. Some teams used the basic interview guide to develop their own procedure, while others did not. The team captains participated in the final selection meeting with the Data Processing Committee. The team captains used the data generated in the interviews to support their recommendations to the committee.
3. The most common modification among the managers was using the general interview guide to focus questions around specific behaviors and experiences. However, fewer dimensions were used than the PH training specified. The data-integration meetings also tended to follow a less structured and more open-ended process for achieving consensus than the PH training anticipated.

Summary of Interview Findings

Conclusions from these interview data are that the majority of managers endorse the principles of PH and attempt to follow them in practice, but few trained in PH found it possible or useful to implement the system in its original form. All sought to shorten, simplify, and adapt PH to meet their specific needs.

The managers' belief in the value of the basic principles and design of PH were reinforced by their responses to additional questions in the interviews. When asked if they believed PH had resulted in the selection of employees who were better, worse, or not significantly different, none of the managers reported that worse candidates were hired, five reported that PH had no effect, and seventeen (74 percent) reported that they believed PH resulted in the hiring of better candidates. The belief that PH produced better hiring decisions was strongest among managers whose top manager had completed PH training and where the best efforts had been made to adapt PH to the group's specific needs.

Further endorsements of the concept and the goals of PH were found in responses to the question of whether the use of PH should be continued. Nineteen of the twenty-one responding managers endorsed the continuation of PH in some modified fashion. Only two stated they believed it was not worth continuing. Those endorsing its use strongly agreed that PH should be simplified and adapted to the technical nature of the jobs. None endorsed the full or original design of the PH process.

Questions for Discussion

1. How would you evaluate the design of PH?
2. How would you evaluate the implementation of PH at Engineering Systems Unlimited?
3. What conclusions and recommendations would you put in your report to Engineering Systems Unlimited?
4. What should (a) the human resources department and (b) senior management at ESU do differently when implementing personnel programs similar to this one?

6

Staffing, Development, and Employment Stabilization

When the recruitment and selection process is completed, the human resource management responsibilities of line managers intensify. Their task becomes the matching of the organization's staffing needs and budgetary constraints with the career aspirations and employment security needs of the employees. In this chapter we explore some of the challenges managers face in achieving an effective match. In keeping with the themes of earlier chapters, we stress the need for managers to understand and model the dynamics of the "internal labor market" (Doeringer and Piore, 1971). This understanding can be used to develop long-term policies that are adaptable to short-term economic fluctuations in the external environment, shifts in markets and business strategies, and the basic values top executives seek to diffuse throughout the organization. Because the readings that follow describe mostly staffing and employment stabilization policies, we have used a career perspective in this overview.

The Job Longevity Cycle

Recent behavioral science research argues that just as organizations and products move through evolutionary stages, employees also move through evolutionary stages both in their lifetime careers (Dalton, 1977; Hall, 1976; Schein, 1979) and in their specific jobs (Katz, 1980). Managers need to be aware of these evolutionary patterns because the responses employees make to changes in job designs, opportunities for promotions, or other human resource policies may vary depending on their stage in job and career cycles.

Katz (1980) introduced the concept of a job-longevity cycle by suggesting that employees move through three distinct stages in a given job: socialization, innovation, and adaptation. In the socialization stage, employees are busy learning specific tasks to be performed, as well as the norms, values, and customs of the job, their coworkers, and the organization (Van Maanen, 1975). In defining for themselves their relationship with their job, coworkers, and organization, new employees begin to develop what has been called a "psychological contract" with their supervisors and the organization (Barnard, 1938; March and Simon, 1958; Schein, 1978). That is, they form an implicit understanding of what the organization expects from them and what they can expect from the organization in return for good job performance.

Following socialization, employees are ready to accept more challenging assignments and to make their mark on their job and on the organization. In the innovation stage, employees are likely to seek and accept more task variety, autonomy, and responsibility. Also, their interest in training and promotional opportunities peaks.

In the adaptation stage, employees' concerns gradually shift toward consolidating influence and maintaining established work patterns and a stable work environment. There emerges a tendency for complacency and, perhaps, resistance to change. As Katz (1980) stated, managerial advice or efforts to introduce change may elicit the response: Leave us alone; we're doing just fine.

No simple rule of thumb can predict how long each stage will last for any given job or employee. Indeed, important variations will occur in the degree to which individuals take on stage-specific characteristics. Employees with high needs for growth and challenge may leave a job before the adaptation phase begins, or perceptive managers may promote or transfer employees who have reached their full learning and performance potential. By understanding these tendencies, managers will be more able to develop effective policies for motivating and developing the full potential of employees in different phases of their job-longevity cycle.

Group Longevity

Studies of research and development groups suggest the longevity cycle applies not only to individuals, but also to work groups, task forces, and project teams. Figure 6-1 shows this phenomenon by graphing the trends in group performance and communication for a sample of 61 research and development groups in a large United States corporation. Group performance was measured by asking department managers and laboratory directors to rate the technical performance of each group on various dimensions.

It appears that group performance builds to a peak between the first one and a half to three and a half years and then declines for the following four to five years or more. One explanation of this decline in group performance is that the levels of communication among project members, across project teams, and between teams and the larger organization all followed the same cycle of peaking during the middle years of longevity, with decline thereafter.

Allen (1977) has shown that communication is crucial to group performance. Ways to avoid decline in performance include: (1) the gradual infusion of new people with new ideas into project groups, (2) the encouragement of external or cross-group communication through

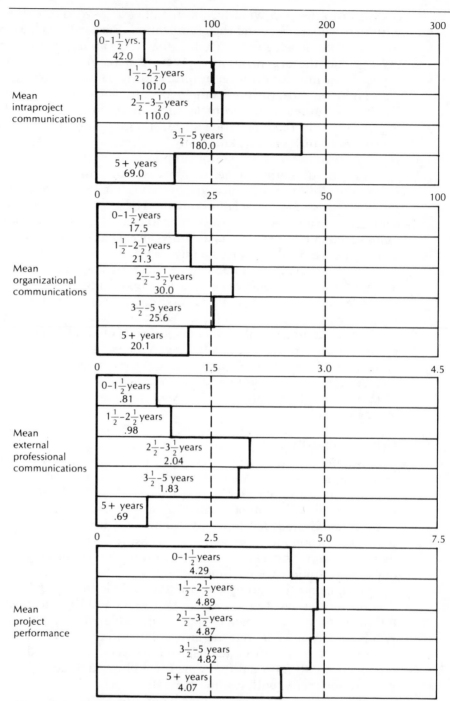

Source: Adapted from Ralph Katz, "Managing Careers: The Influence of Job and Group Longevity," *Career Issues in Human Resource Management* (Englewood Cliffs, N.J.: Prentice-Hall, 1982). Reprinted by permission.

FIGURE 6-1 Communications and Project Performance
of Research and Development Groups

physical proximity or temporary cross-project assignments, and (3) the restructuring of groups before tendencies toward isolationism set in.

Career Stages

Behavioral scientists are building on the work of developmental psychologists to identify a sequence of stages through which employees move during their careers. Table 6-1 depicts four career stages. Although the stages indicate chronological ages, evidence for fixed career stages corresponding to particular age ranges is quite weak (Milkovich and Anderson, 1982).

Most models begin by noting that basic work habits and orientations are formed early in life; through the guidance and role modeling of adults around them, children and adolescents first encounter the responsibilities and rewards of work. In transition to adulthood, they make important vocational choices, decide how much additional education and/or training to pursue, and take entry-level jobs.

In early adulthood, people are expected to establish what Schein (1978) refers to as career anchors. Career anchors are the underlying, and often unconscious, (1) motives that indicate what individuals want to achieve in their careers, (2) talents and skills that suggest their strengths and weaknesses and what they have a chance of achieving, and (3) values that they are prone to follow as they progress through their careers.

TABLE 6-1   Modal Stages in Career Progression

Stage 1 (usually up to age 25)	Stage 2 (usually in 20s and early 30s)	Stage 3 (usually from mid to late 30s through 50s)	Stage 4 (usually from late 50s through 70s or even 80s)
Development of work habits and of one's orientation toward work Basic education and/or vocational training	Initial career choices Socialization in the organization Learning and apprenticeship Development and clarification of career anchors	Advancement Attainment of independent status levels Independent contributions Mentoring and taking responsibility for the development of others Mid-career assessment and questioning	Maintenance in and gradual withdrawal from the organization Transition to postretirement roles and activities

Source: Adapted from models in Hall (1978), Schein (1978), and Milkovich and Anderson (1982).

Popular literature on aging is replete with discussions of the next stage: mid-career struggle. This stage, which can occur anywhere from the early thirties through the fifties, entails intense self-examination and questioning of personal accomplishments.

Finally, as they approach the age of sixty, most people are expected to go through a period of career maintenance, followed by withdrawal. Some, however, continue to search for and achieve new opportunities for personal growth and reward, in a sense, by fighting the physical aging process with new vigor.

Researchers generally agree that an employee's career stage is likely to affect his or her job-related aspirations, attitudes, and behaviors. For example, as with the job-longevity cycle, employees in the earlier developmental stages are generally more willing to consider geographic transfers that offer greater responsibility and upward mobility than are employees in the later maintenance and withdrawal stages.

But there is also a growing skepticism among career researchers about the wisdom of automatically applying these models to the work force of the future (Bailyn, 1984). Two caveats should be kept in mind before making such generalizations. First, most of these staging models were derived from research on male, professional employees who were supported by "traditional" marriage and family lifestyles and support systems. Therefore, the assumptions or findings of these models may not generalize to the more heterogeneous work force of the future. Dual career families and the growing recognition of the interplay of family cycles with career cycles were not anticipated in these models and need to be considered in career planning models of the future. Second, extrapolating these models to future employees implies that future careers *should* conform to the average or modal expectations organizations placed on previous generations of professionals. Again, changes in societal values and family-work life interaction patterns may force managers of the future to critically reassess their expectations for their employees' careers and to change their policies accordingly. Thus, these staging models should be viewed only as general guides to broad, time-related shifts in employee expectations and approaches to their work and careers.

Career/Staffing Management Models

Although job, group, and career stages models have obvious intuitive appeal, there is little empirical evidence as yet to indicate that these stages can be associated with clearly specified age ranges. Yet, most professional career planners argue that sensitivity to the time-related dynamics of individual career aspirations is the key to successfully matching individual needs with organizational needs. A typical model of a matching process (Walker, 1976) is shown in Table 6-2. The model suggests that *individual* career planning and *organizational* staff planning proceed on parallel tracks.

TABLE 6-2   Career Planning Processes: Organizational and
Individual Perspectives

Organizational Processes	Individual Processes
1. Determine job requirements (tasks, skills, qualifications) for each job	1. Form personal career anchors (motivations, talents, and values)
2. Group jobs into job families	2. Assess organizational career paths, promotional opportunities and potential for meeting career objectives
3. Determine typical career paths within and across job families	3. Search for development opportunities (task assignments and training) needed to progress up the career paths in the organization and/or profession
4. Determine training and development needs to support movement up and transitions across job families	4. Assess prospects for match between personal career anchors and organizational career/staffing patterns
5. Provide career counseling	5. Adjust to organizational career patterns or search for career opportunities in other organizations

Human resource specialists and line managers begin the organizational planning process by determining through job analysis, job design, or more informal techniques the tasks, skills, and qualifications required for each job. Jobs are grouped into "job families," and those jobs with closely related requirements and expected career or progression paths within each family are specified. These decisions can be made before hiring anyone by specifying progression paths that appear logical, given the skills and experience required of each job. Alternately, the groupings can be made by following the actual progressions of employees. The reading on Markov modeling, which follows this overview, introduces an analytical technique that helps portray actual internal movements across jobs.

The next step in an organizational career planning model is to determine the boundaries of job families. Boundaries occur at significant breaks in the tasks, skills, or qualifications required to move up the organizational hierarchy or across to a family at the same level in the organization. The boundaries help suggest training and development programs that can provide employees the opportunities to attain the skills and requirements needed to avoid reaching a plateau at the top of their job families and being unable to move. Positions at the top of job families are also important to identify because these have been shown to predict turnover rates (Scholl, 1983). As employees approach their highest job level, they begin to search for promotions outside the organization. Again, the Markov analysis can aid in identifying job family boundaries on the basis of current and former employees' internal progression and prior rates of organizational exit or turnover.

The final stage in an organizational career planning model involves career counseling and development. Using the information on jobs and boundaries, human resource managers can advise employees on how to maximize their chances of achieving their career objectives in the organization. Career counseling becomes the link between organizational and individual planning processes; as Table 6-2 illustrates, individuals undergo a process parallel to the organization when assessing the fit between their career objectives and the opportunities available within the organization. Developmental counseling such as this is often a formal part of performance appraisal procedures (see Chapter 9).

Contemporary Challenges in Career Management

Many trends in the environment, in organizational strategies, and in labor force characteristics suggest that managers need to pay particular attention to staffing and career management responsibilities. Factors that are forcing more emphasis on career issues include (1) the increase in the labor force of women and the growing prevalence of dual-career families, (2) the need to attend to equal opportunity and affirmative action principles, and (3) the desire to design alternative career progression ladders for technical and professional staff.

The increase in the number of dual-career couples is rapidly turning the nature of job choices and related decision-making processes from an individual activity to a joint one. Universities located in isolated or rural areas, for example, are among the kinds of organizations experiencing greater difficulty in recruiting and retaining professionals in dual-career families. Other organizations with high percentages of professional and managerial employees are experiencing similar pressures to adjust their transfer, relocation, and recruitment strategies to accommodate this trend (Hall and Hall, 1978).

Another aspect of dual-career pressures is the need for organizations to adapt their promotion and performance evaluation systems to accommodate temporary career breaks for women who want to have children or parents who must adjust their schedules, turn down travel assignments or geographic moves, and make other career decisions in deference to family responsibilities. Most organizations are uncertain about how to interpret such choices. Do these kinds of actions demonstrate a lack of professional commitment? Or does such a view inevitably place an inequitable burden on women and on parents of young children in general, rendering such an approach inconsistent with the emerging social values and equal employment opportunity requirements of contemporary society?

BOX 6-1
Affirmative Action Guidelines for Promotion Systems

1. Post or otherwise announce promotional opportunities.
2. Make an inventory of current minority and female employees to determine academic, skill, and experience level of individual employees.
3. Initiate necessary remedial job training and work study programs.
4. Develop and implement formal employee evaluation programs.
5. Make sure "worker specifications" have been validated on job-performance-related criteria. (Neither minority nor female employees should be required to possess higher qualifications than those of the lowest qualified incumbent.)
6. When apparently qualified minority or female employees are passed over for upgrading, require supervisory personnel to submit written justification.
7. Establish formal career counseling programs to include attitude development, education aid, job rotation, buddy system, and similar programs.
8. Review seniority practices and seniority clauses in union contracts to ensure such practices or clauses are nondiscriminatory and do not have a discriminatory effect.

Source: Office of Federal Contract Compliance, Revised Order No. 4, 1971.

Chapter 12 covers in more detail the equal employment opportunity and affirmative action requirements of employers. It is worth noting here, however, that federal contractors must comply with many requirements that also affect internal promotion policies. For example, as Box 6-1 notes, employers with federal contracts must post promotion opportunities, collect data on the distribution of women and minorities, and take other steps to ensure that staffing policies promote the internal progression of women and minorities.

The problem of how to establish career ladders that reward scientists and professionals for their technical contributions without forcing them to shift their career orientations into managerial tracks has challenged organizations for years. One strategy, called the *dual ladder*, or the *technical ladder*, is described in Box 6-2. The dual ladder attempts to reward technical expertise and accomplishment on an equal basis with managerial competence. Many high technology organizations have followed this dual strategy in principle, but, as Katz noted (see Box 6-2), this approach has not been particularly successful in compensating talented and ambitious scientists and technicians for staying in technical job families and career paths. Such employees forego both the potential for moving up the managerial hierarchy within the organization and the experience that would allow them to move into management or executive positions in other organizations. Thus, it continues to be difficult to avoid reaching a plateau in technical career paths. Solving this problem is a challenge to technology-driven organizations.

BOX 6-2
The Dual Ladder: Technical or Managerial Careers

One organizational arrangement that has been developed to provide meaningful rewards and alternative career paths for organizational professionals is the "dual ladder system of career advancement." The concept is quite simple (Kaufman, 1974). The dual-ladder approach established two parallel hierarchies: One provides a managerial career path, the other, advancement as a professional or staff member. Each promises equal status and rewards to equivalent levels in the hierarchy. Also known as the "technical," or "individual contributor" ladder, the dual ladder was first developed around 1960 to reward professionals (especially scientists and engineers) for good scientific or technical performance, without removing them from their professional work (Shepard, 1958). By providing professionally oriented individuals with the opportunity and incentive to remain in their fields and stay up-to-date, the dual ladder aims to secure an adequate pool of technical talent for the high technology organization.

While the dual ladder promises equal status and financial rewards to those at equivalent levels in the managerial and professional hierarchies, the sets of incentives associated with the two ladders differ sharply. Movement up the managerial ladder leads to positions of power and participation in the affairs of the organization. By clear contrast, advancement up the professional ladder usually leads to increased autonomy in the practice of one's specialty, but often at the expense of organizational influence.

In general, the objectives of the dual ladder are (1) to attract, retain, and motivate high quality technical and other professional personnel, (2) to provide individual opportunities to follow more optimal career paths, and (3) to focus strong technical skills on important projects with minimum distraction caused by administrative details. As summarized by Katz (1984), few dual-ladder programs have succeeded in achieving all of these goals, especially when the technical ladder has often (1) been used as a "dumping ground" for displaced managerial personnel, (2) lagged in terms of influence, salaries, or other perks, and (3) led personnel to perceive little positive reinforcement after promotion to that ladder. Despite these problems, dual ladders remain popular in high technology settings, and variations on the theme have been adopted in other types of organizations engaged in creative professional work.

Source: This summary of the dual ladder research was written especially for this book by Ralph Katz, Northeastern University.

Training and Development Issues

That staffing and career management policies need the support of training and development policies designed for the specific needs of the firm is almost a truism, one which human resource specialists have always promoted. Training and retraining, or continuous education, increasingly will become central components of human resource strategies in the future. Managers may need to revise a pattern followed by many organizations in the past, that is, to vary directly with the business cycle the resources allocated to management development and employee training. The trend is clearly visible in national statistics on the numbers of people enrolled in apprenticeship training. The auto industry case that follows illustrates the reasons for this pattern. Budgets for management development and training, however, are often among the first to be cut during times of organizational retrenchment.

Training and development will grow in importance because (1) rapid technological change and shifting market demands require updating of professional and technical expertise, and (2) human resource management systems in both the office and the factory demand flexible, multiskilled, and adaptable work forces. Managers will confront the question of whether to continue to treat training as a variable cost, subject to short-term budgetary decision making, or whether to consider such training as a long-term investment in human capital.

Line managers are potential consumers of the many training and development services available both within their organizations, as designed by human resource management professionals, and outside the firm, as offered in professional conferences, workshops, and seminars. Line managers must consider two fundamental questions: Is the training or development program consistent with the future needs of the organization? Is it based on sound theoretical principles of *adult* learning? The latter is essential, as so much of the learning theory available to the designers of training programs is based on concepts of child development (Lacey, Lee, and Wallace, 1982). One expert (Knowles, 1978; 110) stressed the need to recognize that adults learn in very different ways from children. He summarized these differences as follows and urged managers to demand that these distinctions be taken into account in adult training and education.

> Adults see themselves as self-directed and independent; children are dependent on parents, teachers, and others.
>
> Because they simply have not acquired much of it, experience may be of little value to children in the classroom. With adults, experience is an important resource for learning. In training, we must recognize that adults have significant experience. Indeed, they often define themselves as the sum of their experiences. Good training draws from this experience and builds on it.
>
> Children must postpone the application of much of their formal learning. Adults need to see an immediate application of the learning if it is to be meaningful.
>
> Children's readiness to learn is determined by biological development and social pressure. Adults' readiness is based on the development tasks that result from social roles.
>
> Children's orientation to learning is subject-centered; adults' orientation to learning is problem-centered.

Preview of Readings and Cases

We now move to selected readings and a case study for this chapter. Emphasis is on the staffing challenges that organizations face in adjusting to environmental changes and business strategies. The first paper describes Markov analysis, a management tool that helps analyze the dynamics of internal labor markets. The point of this reading is not to train managers in statistical techniques or skills that underlie the conduct of modeling and analysis, but to demonstrate how to use these data in reviewing ways that staffing and related human resource policies affect the movement of people within an organization.

The following paper, by Dyer, Foltman, and Milkovich, summarizes emerging strategies that leading firms use to stabilize employment. These strategies seek to generate greater internal flexibility in the use of employees and high levels of employee commitment to the firm in return for the firm's efforts to promote, if not guarantee, employment security. This paper provides a useful analysis of the policies and practices needed to make an employment stabilization strategy work during the ups and down of business cycles.

We next turn to a question that plagues managers in any organization or functional area experiencing rapid growth — how to manage high turnover. Typically, the question is whether high turnover rates should simply be tolerated and compensated by frequent, active recruitment, or whether more investment in career planning, training and development, and other human resource strategies can reduce turnover costs and enhance the effectiveness of human resource management. The authors of the third reading call this the make or buy trade-off and analyze it in the context of one of the most rapidly growing and changing occupational groups of our time: computer professionals.

The two case studies examine staffing challenges during a decline in a business cycle, and in the life cycle of a business unit. Both cases focus on how much of an investment in surplus human resources an organization should make, given its market position and prospects for the future. The first case views the problem in a blue-collar factory environment, the auto industry, and the second case in the context of a professional, technical, and managerial work force at Polaroid.

References

Allen, Thomas J., *Managing the Flow of Technology* (Cambridge, Mass.: MIT Press, 1977).

Bailyn, Lotte, "Issues of Work and Family in Organizations: Responding to Social Diversity," in M. Arthur, L. Bailyn, D. Levinson, and H. Shepard eds., *Working With Careers* (New York: Columbia School of Business, 1984).

Barnard, Chester I., *The Functions of the Executive* (Cambridge, Mass.: Harvard University Press, 1938).

Dalton, G. W., P. H. Thompson, and R. L. Price, "The Four Stages of Professional Careers: A New Look at Performance by Professionals," in *Organizational Dynamics*, Vol. 6, 1977, 19–42.

Doeringer, Peter B., and Michael J. Piore, *Internal Labor Markets and Manpower Analysis* (Lexington, Mass.: Heath, 1971).

Hall, Douglas T., *Careers in Organizations* (Pacific Palisades, Calif.: Goodyear, 1976).

Hall, Francine S., and D. T. Hall, "Dual Careers: How Do Couples and Companies Cope with the Problem," in *Organizational Dynamics*, Vol. 6, 1978, 57–77.

Katz, Ralph, "A Longitudinal Study of the Dual Ladder in a High Technology Organization." Paper presented at the ORSA-TIMS Conference in San Francisco, May 1984.

———, "Time and Work: Toward an Integrative Perspective," in B. Staw and L. Cummings, eds., *Research in Organizational Behavior*, Vol. II (Greenwich, Conn.: JAI Press, 1980).

Kaufman, H. G., *Obsolescence and Professional Career Development* (New York: American Management Association, 1974).

Knowles, M., *The Adult Learner: A Neglected Species* (Houston: Gulf Publishing, 1978).

Lacey, D. W., R. J. Lee, and Lawrence J. Wallace, "Training and Development," in K. M. Rowland and G. R. Ferris, eds., *Personnel Management* (Boston: Allyn and Bacon, 1982).

March, James G., and Herbert A. Simon, *Organizations* (New York: John Wiley and Sons, 1958).

Milkovich, George T., and John C. Anderson, "Career Planning and Development Systems," in K. M. Rowland and G. R. Ferris, eds., *Personnel Management* (Boston: Allyn and Bacon, 1982).

Schein, Edgar G., *Career Dynamics: Matching Individual and Organizational Needs* (Reading, Mass.: Addison-Wesley, 1978).

Scholl, R. W., "Career Lines and Employment Stability," in *Academy of Management Journal*, Vol. 26, No. 1, 1983, 86–103.

Shepard, H. A., "The Dual Hierarchy in Research," *Research Management*, Vol. 1, No. 3, Autumn 1983, 177–187.

Van Maanen, John, "Police Socialization," in *Administrative Science Quarterly*, Vol. 20, 1975, 207–28.

Walker, James, "Let's Get Realistic About Career Paths," in *Human Resource Management*, Vol. 15, 1976, 4.

Suggested Readings

Derr, C. Brooklyn, ed., *Work, Family, and the Career: New Frontiers in Theory and Research* (New York: Praeger Publishers, 1980).

Katz, Ralph, ed., *Career Issues in Human Resource Management* (Englewood Cliffs, N.J.: Prentice-Hall, 1982).

Van Maanen, John, ed., *Organizational Careers: Some New Perspectives* (New York: John Wiley and Sons, 1977).

Analyzing Human Resource Flows:
Uses and Limitations of the Markov Model

This paper introduces an analytical tool for human resource planners, the Markov modeling of flows of people across jobs and through career ladders. The paper uses a personnel information system from a large high technology firm to introduce the uses and limitations of Markov modeling and to illustrate the effects that changes in the environment have on the movement of people within the firm. The distribution of employees and their probabilities of movement into new jobs are depicted for January 1981 to January 1982, a year in which the company was growing rapidly, and compared to data from September 1982 to September 1983 in which the company imposed a hiring freeze because of a severe recession.

Role of Statistical Models

A basic function of a human resource management planning system is to match the anticipated demand for workers in different job categories with a supply of employees possessing the required skills and experiences to fill these positions. In small organizations with few job categories, this can be done on an informal basis. In somewhat larger firms where skills are interchangeable, training time is short, and/or an ample supply of workers is available in the external labor markets to fill the positions, an informal analysis of the internal labor market may be all that is needed. Informal forecasting methods range from subjective judgments derived from line managers, to historical staffing ratios that relate the number of workers to produc-

Source: Thomas A. Barocci and Paul Cournoyer. Paul Cournoyer is a Senior Information Systems Manager at Digital Equipment Corporation. This Reading was adapted from a section of his dissertation at the Sloan School of Management, MIT.

tion levels, to the succession tables normally kept for key managers and executives (Walker, 1980).

More formal modeling of labor market flows is needed in larger firms with multiple jobs and particularly in firms that prefer to promote from within. In these situations a personnel information system is needed to provide a basis for more formal planning and tracking of internal labor market movements. A variety of statistical techniques can be used to fit different needs. Multiple regression techniques are well suited for estimating the *change* in the number of workers needed (or alternatively the number of workers expected to turn over) in response to changes in product demand. More complex linear, nonlinear, dynamic, or goal programming models can be used to identify the optimal staffing strategy for achieving a specified goal, given a number of constraints. These models can be used, for example, for identifying steps needed to meet affirmative action targets, given the constraints of an expected level of production and historical staffing ratios (Walker, 1980; Milkovich and Mahoney, 1978).

The Markov model is a statistical technique commonly used to track and describe the behavior of an internal labor market and to aid formal and judgmental planning processes. Essentially, by using the model one counts the number of employees in each job within an organization in a time period, follows each employee into the next period, and calculates the probability of promotion, demotion, transfer, and exit from the organization, given the position from which an employee started. Fuguitt (1965; 404) formally described the Markov model as follows:

This model assumes a set of observations which may be classified into a finite number of different states. A given observation may move from one state to another over a time period t, and there are a sequence of such time periods [sic]. The probability that an observation will move from state i to state j between t and $t + 1$ is given by pij. Thus the probability of moving from i to j depends only on the state at time t, and is assumed to be constant over the sequence of time intervals.

The pijs may be arranged in matrix of transition probabilities, commonly denoted as P. The ith row of P gives the probability of going from i at time t to each of the states (including the ith) at time $t + 1$. If one started with a distribution of observations in different states at time t, one could apply the matrix of transition probabilities to obtain the distribution expected in $t + 1$. Since it is assumed that these probabilities do not change over time, successive applications of P would give the expected distribution at time $t + 2$, $t + 3$, . . . $t + n$.

By observing the transition probabilities, one is able to describe the flow of workers within the internal labor market as well as recruitment from and exit to the external labor market.

Assumptions of the Markov Model

The Markov model makes two assumptions in tracing occupational mobility: (1) no more than one occupational change occurs from t_1 to t_2, and (2) all individuals within an occupation have an equal probability of moving to another occupation. The first assumption is usually approximated by using a one-year time span between t_1 and t_2. This has the added advantage of producing annual turnover and hiring rates for each occupation as part of the Markov output.

The second assumption is more problematic and controversial. It assumes there are no individual differences in pro-

motional potential among the inhabitants of a job category. Rosenbaum (1979) challenged this assumption by showing that movement within some internal labor markets is not random. Rather, a "tournament" model better predicts occupational promotions and career floors and ceilings. That is, the chances for promotion can be viewed as a series of competitions in which each outcome affects future outcomes. The winners in each round or time period have the opportunity to continue to compete for upward promotions, whereas the losers may compete only for the opportunity to stay in their present positions or move to lower-level jobs. Rosenbaum concluded that "mobility in the earliest stage of one's career bears an unequivocal relationship with one's later career." Schein's (1978) work on career anchors further supports the thesis that career movement is not random. March and March (1977), on the other hand, reached the opposite conclusion when using Markov models to study the mobility of school superintendents. The point of this debate is that the Markov model's assumptions may be acceptable for predicting *average* movement probabilities within occupations but is less accurate for predicting *which specific individuals* will move.

An Illustration

Table 6-3 illustrates the transition probability matrix of a Markov model for eight information systems (IS) occupations in a large high technology company. These data were collected from January 1, 1981 to January 1, 1982, when the firm experienced increasing demand for its products and, consequently, a moderate rate of employment growth. The eight occupations represent a small fraction of the jobs in the corporation but illustrate the main features of the model and its output.

Each of the eight IS occupations (four systems occupations and four programmer occupations) corresponds to a Markovian state (x). The states are arranged in a transition matrix where the numbers in each

TABLE 6-3 Markov Transition Probability Matrix
During Rapid Growth Period, January 1981–January 1982

January 1, 1981		December 31, 1981										
(512)		P29	P28	P27	P26	S41	S42	S43	S44	T	O	Other IS Jobs
(94) Associate programmers	P29	.297	.531			.016			.016	.106	.042	.000
(237) Programmers	P28	.012	.527	.278			.012	.004	.004	.097	.059	.004
(196) Senior programmers	P27		.005	.556	.132			.061	.025	.071	.112	.035
(99) Principal programmers	P26				.474				.060	.070	.060	.333
(11) Associate analysts	S41			.090		.636	.181	.090				
(40) Systems analysts	S42			.050	.025		.350	.325	.050	.075	.100	.025
(70) Senior analysts	S43				.071		.028	.371	.214	.057	.042	.213
(65) Principal analysts	S44				.015				.476	.061	.030	.412
(76) Other occupations (transfers)		.276	.184	.092	.053	.171	.053	.092	.078			
(259) Recruits		.201	.402	.181	.062	.015	.039	.058	.042			
(977) Active		132	298	231	100	26	36	77	77			

cell represent the probability (p_{ij}) of moving from state x_i to state x_j. The diagonal of the matrix represents the probability of remaining in a given job between times t_1 and t_2. Since the number of moves is finite and the states are mutually exclusive, the p_{ij} must equal one. Finally, the number of transfers to other IS jobs, the number of recruits from the external labor market, the number of voluntary job terminations (T), the number moving to other information systems jobs (0), and the number transferring out of the information systems department (transfers) are all shown as separate states in the matrix.

Each cell in the matrix represents the proportion of employees in the given state on January 1, 1981, who occupied a specific state on December 31, 1981. The diagonal cells show the percentage of employees who remained in a given occupation throughout the year. For example, in cell P28,P28 the number .527 indicates that 52.7 percent of the programmers who were in that position at the start of the period were still there at the end of the period. Associate systems analysts exhibited the highest degree of occupational stability (63.6 percent), associate programmers the lowest degree (29.7 percent).

The off-diagonal cells present the probabilities of different types of moves associated with each job. For example, the diagonal cell P26,P26 indicates that 47.4 percent of the principal programmers remained in their positions over the year. Therefore, 52.6 percent moved to a different job in the matrix, transferred to a different job family or department, or left the organization. A reading to the right of the diagonal indicates that 6 percent were moved to S44 positions and 33.3 percent to other information systems jobs. Similarly, the next to last column (labeled O for other job family) indicates that 6 percent transferred to this state. The column T indicates that the turnover rate for principal programmers during the year was 7 percent.

The bottom three rows indicate the percentage of transfers into these information systems jobs from other job families, the

percentage of new recruits from the external labor market, and the number of personnel in each job category at the end of the period. Thus, 5.3 percent of all transfers into these information systems jobs were placed as principal programmers, whereas 6.2 percent of the new recruits were placed in this position. In contrast, the associate programmer and programmer jobs served as the more common ports of transfer and external entry into the programmer job family.

The Markov matrix also allows one to see breaks in career paths. Consider, for example, the probabilities of promotion from the top programmer job. Although there appear to be predictable, orderly career ladders in programmer jobs and in systems jobs, only 6 percent moved from the top programmer job (principal programmer) to a systems job. An interesting task for further research would be to explore the range of jobs to which the 33 percent of the principal programmers transferred.

One can also compare variations in promotion rates to the next occupation on the hierarchy, across the programming and systems clusters. For the programmer jobs the rate varied from a low of 13 percent for senior programmers to a high of 53 percent for entry-level associate programmers. (It should be noted that people in the P28 position could have had higher promotion rates, but that we cannot determine this because they are at the highest level of the model.) In contrast, the systems analyst cluster showed a slower movement between positions and a somewhat more compact variance (from a low of 6 percent to a high of 32 percent).

Demotion rates are shown in the cells to the left of the diagonal. The data show a low demotion rate ranging from less than 1 percent for senior programmers to 2.8 percent for senior analysts.

Effects of Environmental Change

In addition to tracking movement during a given period, the Markov model can generate predictions of flows and steady states for future periods. To use the model for predictive purposes, however, one must assume that the external product and labor markets remain stable enough to support stable promotion, hiring, and turnover rates. Alternatively, one needs to supplement the Markov predictions with judgments on how environment or organizational policy changes such as a hiring freeze, a salary freeze, or a shift in product mix will modify the traditional patterns of movements. To illustrate how environment and organizational policy changes affect the accuracy of predictions of the model, compare the rates of movement shown in Table 6-3 with those shown in Table 6-4.

The data in Table 6-4 show actual movement for the same jobs between September 1, 1982 and August 31, 1983, a period of declining product demand in which the company imposed a hiring freeze. Although Table 6-3 shows that 259 individuals were recruited from the external labor market, Table 6-4 shows that exceptions were made from the hiring freeze policy for only 73 individuals, leading to a net overall increase in the head count of 11 (from 989 to 1,000) during that year. The hiring freeze also affected those already in the organization, albeit in diverse ways. On the one hand, the probability of remaining in one's existing job increased for all jobs but one (associate systems analyst). The turnover rate went down for all the programming positions, but only for some of the systems analysts. This rate is consistent with a theory of turnover that predicts a general recession, combined with a hiring freeze that limits managers' ability to fill job vacancies, will reduce turnover in occupations with the fewest transferable skills and, therefore, the poorest external labor market prospects, but will increase turnover for skilled professionals who have favorable external labor markets prospects.

Before using the Markov model for predictions, one must assess the viability of the assumption that neither changes in the environment nor changes in organizational policies will significantly affect transition probabilities. Mahoney and Milkovich (1971; 90) reached a similar conclusion in an early study of the use of this technique for equal employment opportunity tracking.

Our results suggest that the Markovian model holds more potential for the analysis of internal labor market structures and the generation of implications of alternative market structures than it does for the more practical matter of generating forecasts. . . . Our results confirm that even relatively minor alterations in the transition probability matrix compound into sizable differences in the distributions of manpower forecasts over a few time periods.

Despite the caveat, formal modeling of the internal labor market can produce useful information on the distribution of males and females, racial minorities, older and younger workers, and so on for equal employment opportunity monitoring and planning. It can also demonstrate what future distributions of these groups will look like if no affirmative action is taken to modify historical rates of promotion or hiring. Finally, modeling the internal labor market produces a clear picture of the actual career ladders and progression prospects at work in the organization and provides a good test of the viability of the career expectations of workers and policies of the organization. This information is central to the design of employee development and training policy.

When formal statistical modeling is combined with careful judgments about the effects of potential changes in the external environment and the business and human resource strategies of the organization, managers are in a good position to assess the match between a future supply of employees with expected demand. If there is a poor match between estimated supply and demand, more complex linear, dynamic, or goal programming models may be called upon to simulate the effects of alternative strategies (e.g., doubling of

TABLE 6-4 Markov Transition Probability Matrix during Slow Growth Period or "Hiring" Freeze, September 1982–September 1983

September 1982		September 1983										Other IS Jobs
(989) Head Count (t_1)		P29	P28	P27	P26	S41	S42	S43	S44	T	O	
(150) Associate programmers	P29	.380	.440	.007			.027			.053	.093	.000
(272) Programmers	P28		.522	.276	.011		.004	.018		.066	.092	.011
(240) Senior programmers	P27			.554	.175			.025	.038	.058	.088	.063
(102) Principal programmers	P26				.559				.059	.049	.107	.225
(23) Associate analysts	S41	.043				.391	.261			.087	.217	.000
(46) Systems analysts	S42			.087	.022		.370	.217		.087	.130	.087
(77) Senior analysts	S43			.039				.480	.195	.039	.156	.091
(79) Principal analysts	S44				.013				.519	.114	.114	.241
(176) Other occupations (transfers)		.392	.108	.080	.040	.136	.097	.068	.080			
(73) Recruits		.192	.493	.151	.027	.055	.041	.027	.014			
(1000) Active total count for a year later (t_2)		140	263	241	113	37	48	72	86			

recruiting efforts, tripling training time, altering career paths) for meeting the organization's needs. In the end, however, the human resource planning loop is only closed when managers combine the results of these analyses with their judgments and choose a course of action that is responsive to the interests of the organization and its employees.

References

Fuguitt, G. V., "The Growth and Decline of Small Towns as a Probability Process," *American Sociological Review*, Vol. 30, 1965, 403–411.

Mahoney, Thomas A., and George T. Milkovich, "An Empirical Investigation of the Internal Labor Market Concept," Proceeding of the Annual Meetings of the Academy of Management, Minneapolis, 1971, 122–142.

March, J., and C. March, "Almost Random Careers: The Wisconsin School Superintendency, 1940–1972," *Administrative Science Quarterly*, Vol. 22, No. 3, September 1977, 377–409.

Milkovich, George T., and Thomas A. Mahoney, "Human Resource Planning Models: A Perspective," *Human Resource Planning*, Vol. 1, 1978, 19–30.

Rosenbaum, J., "Tournament Mobility: Career Patterns in a Corporation," *Administrative Science Quarterly*, Vol. 24, No. 2, June 1979, 220–241.

Schein, Edgar, *Career Dynamics: Matching Individuals and Organizational Needs* (Reading, Mass.: Addison-Wesley, 1978).

Vroom, V., and K. MacCrimmon, "Toward a Stochastic Model of Managerial Careers," *Administrative Science Quarterly*, June 1968, 26–46.

Walker, James W., *Human Resource Planning* (New York: McGraw-Hill, 1980).

Questions for Discussion

Suppose this company is faced with a severe decline in demand for its product because of a recession. Top management is considering the following actions:

1. a hiring freeze
2. a salary freeze
3. both a hiring and a salary freeze
4. a 10 percent layoff by inverse seniority within broad job groupings

Summarize what the data from Tables 6-3 and 6-4 tell you of the likely consequences for:

1. turnover
2. shortages of skills or other personnel bottlenecks
3. training policies
4. internal movements and transfers

Contemporary Employment Stabilization Practices

This paper summarizes our inquiry into the practices of large United States firms that explicitly attempt to stabilize employment, variously called job security, employment security, income security, continuous employment, lifetime employment, full employment, guaranteed employment, and employment stabilization.

We believe that employment stabilization (ES) is being practiced when the following minimum conditions are met:

Top management is committed — or required by labor contract — to make every effort to provide continuous employment or income for at least some segment of its work force, and has put in place at least some activities or programs to support this commitment.

Note that this definition excludes certain arrangements — layoffs with severance pay or seniority recall, outplacement assistance, and supplementary unemployment benefits (SUB) — that some observers would include. It does not exclude dismissing employees for cause.

Employers with ES commitments variously refer to them as philosophies, policies, or practices. These are communicated in a number of ways: published in employee handbooks, spoken during employee meetings and to the press, and expressed by the employers' actions over time.

Perhaps the firmest public commitment we encountered among United States employers is the public pledge by the chairman of Materials Resource Corporation

never to lay off anyone at the company (as cited in *The New York Times* on April 17, 1983). Another relatively firm commitment is found at Lincoln Electric Company, which promises all full-time employees who have at least two years' continuous service a minimum of 49 working weeks of at least 30 hours per week each year; the remaining three weeks are paid vacation. Bank of America is committed to explore all practical business alternatives to layoffs for employees who are performing satisfactorily, but it does not guarantee specific jobs, locations, or pay scales. Nevertheless, in late 1983, the bank experienced its first layoff.

Still another approach is that of Hewlett-Packard; a company brochure states: "Job security is an important HP objective. . . . The company wants HP people to have stable, long-term careers — depending, of course, upon satisfactory job performance." Similar in tone is a statement from Eli Lilly's employee handbook: "It is the company's intent to provide the opportunity for continuous employment for all employees who work on permanent jobs full-time."

Materials Resources Corporation has practiced ES for 26 years, Lincoln Electric for 25, Hewlett-Packard for 44, and Eli Lilly for 107. Bank of America has done so for 79 years.

Historical Developments

Employers' concerns with ES are not new. These concerns were especially high immediately after World War II when memories of unemployment during the Great Depression were still fresh. In his postwar book, *The Guarantee of Work and Wages*,[1]

Source: Lee Dyer, Felician Foltman, and George Milkovich. The authors are faculty members at the New York State School of Industrial and Labor Relations, Cornell University. They wish to thank Madeline Dennis and Ahmed Maher for their research assistance. This piece was prepared especially for this book.

[1]Joseph Snider, *The Guarantee of Work and Wages* (Cambridge, Mass.: Harvard Business School, 1947).

Snider documented the successful efforts of the "big three" in wage guarantees — Procter & Gamble, Hormel, and Nunn-Bush — as well as those of several lesser lights such as the Edwards Motor Company, Parker Manufacturing Company, and Spiegel. He also did a postmortem on several abandoned plans, most of which were dropped because of the Great Depression, the passage of the Social Security Act in 1935, or employee apathy. Two other noteworthy books of the time were published by the American Management Association and the then National Industrial Conference Board.[2] The latter contained the results of a survey that uncovered 125 employers who claimed to be or to have been ES employers. Given the self-report nature of the data and the likelihood that many of these companies would not meet our minimum definition of an ES employer, however, this figure, small as it is, probably overstates the case.

Since the late 1940s, no surge in the number of ES employers, up or down, is apparent. The emphasis has changed from wages then to employment (especially layoff avoidance) now. The cast of characters has changed too. Many of the earlier practitioners are now defunct. P & G, Hormel, and Nunn-Bush have survived, but are no longer ES employers. Some others — Tektronix, Kodak, Dana Corporation, Polaroid, Control Data Corporation, and Bank of America — have tried ES but have been unable to avoid layoffs.[3] Eli Lilly's more successful efforts predate the Great Depression; most of the other companies we identified as ES employers are relatively new and/or relatively recent converts to the concept.

[2]American Management Association, Research Report #1–12, *Annual Wages and Employment Stabilization Techniques* (New York: AMA, 1945) and National Industrial Conference Board, Studies in Personnel Policy #76, *Annual Wage and Employee Guarantee Plans* (New York: NICB, 1946).

[3]We were unable to obtain interviews with Tektronix and Kodak for this study.

The Current Pattern: Managing Employment Stabilization

We estimate that now no more than two or three dozen ES employers can be found in the United States. One authority on plant closings estimated that no more than one in a thousand employers operates this way.[4] Many of these companies are in so-called high-tech industries; some are in service industries (airlines, banking); none is in a basic industry (autos, steel, tires).

The major challenge to ES is change, especially change that either reduces the quantity or alters the skill composition of an organization's human resource requirements — that is, its demand for labor. Employment instability tends to result when changes in demand are unanticipated or occur so rapidly as to preclude, or make difficult, an appropriate adjustment in human resource availabilities — that is, the supply of labor. A drop-off in business — that is, in the demand for a firm's products or services — is the most obvious source of decline in the quantity of human resources required. Another is an increase in labor productivity brought about through better management, technological change, and the like. Also, organizational, strategic, and technological changes often alter an organization's skill needs.

When trying to maintain ES, it is helpful to distinguish between change that is cyclical and change that is long-term and irreversible. Almost all organizations face periodic declines in business volume, and these must be anticipated and managed. Most public attention paid to ES stems from such periods (e.g., the early and mid-1970s and the early 1980s) when strategies for avoiding layoffs are of particular concern.

Many of the company representatives we interviewed indicated that periodic downturns have a less serious impact on

[4]Harold Oaklander, *Workforce Reductions in Undertakings* (New York: Lubin Graduate School of Business, Pace University, 1982).

TABLE 6-5   Actions to Maintain ES—Demand Side

Increasing	Actions Taken When Output Is Variable	Declining
Avoid business that appears to be short-run or cyclical (HP)	Call in vendored work (HP, IBM, Lilly)	Call in vendored work (HP, IBM, Lilly)
Gear up slowly (IBM, LE, Lilly)	Move work to people (IBM)	Produce for inventory (LE)
Vendor some work (HP, IBM, Lilly)	Stretch productivity improvement programs	Create work (HP, LE, Lilly)
	Pressure suppliers for more reliable deliveries (LE)	

ES than do ongoing structural and technological changes. This is especially true now, given the anticipated long-term effects of new microelectronic and related information-processing technologies. In virtually every industry, competitive pressures are expected to intensify cost pressures that will, in turn, alter business strategies and force firms to do more with less. In some cases, phenomenal increases in output and sales are expected to result in only modest increases in the number of employees but significant transformations in skill mixes. None of this is new, although the pace probably is quicker now than in the past. It makes clear, however, that the task of managing ES involves much more than being ready to avoid layoffs when the next recession comes.

Managing the Demand Side

Managing ES requires actions to cope with fluctuations in both the demand and the supply of labor. The demand-side options are shown in Table 6-5.

When output is (or could be) increasing, major tactics are to avoid (1) taking on short-run or cyclical business and (2) undertaking rapid, short-run buildups in personnel that are unlikely to be sustainable. Hewlett-Packard (HP) has consistently used the former approach, initially eschewing most government contracts, but more recently ensuring that such contracts

constitute only a small percentage of total sales. Lincoln Electric (LE)[5] uses the latter tactic, explicitly foregoing some business that requires rapid delivery times rather than taking it and then having to add people to meet these demands. Still another tactic that HP, IBM, Eli Lilly, and others have used during good times is vendoring or subcontracting. By subcontracting, product demand can be met without adding employees, and flexibility is retained when the demand lessens.

When output is variable, the situation is one of work-load imbalance. Demand-side tactics to manage such imbalance include (1) calling in vendored work, (2) moving available work from a busy location to a less busy one (used by IBM in 1974–75), and (3) stretching out productivity improvement programs in some areas until demand picks up.

Critics argue that the act of calling in vendored work simply transfers the unemployment risk to vendors' employees. For this reason, employers such as Control Data and HP limit the amount of work given to any subcontractor. This makes it easier for the subcontractors to practice ES themselves if they are so inclined.

Sometimes output varies not because of

[5]The information on Lincoln Electric comes from Robert Zager, "Managing Guaranteed Employment," *Harvard Business Review*, May–June 1978, 103–115.

variations in product demand, but because suppliers fail to deliver needed parts on time. This is unacceptable to a firm trying to practice ES but is likely to increase with the spread of just-in-time manufacturing. For ES, as well as for cost control, Lincoln Electric holds suppliers to tight schedules and drops those who prove to be unreliable. Managers and purchasers are held responsible for planning deliveries and being ready with alternative sources of supply. Because the company is a highly reliable customer, suppliers strive to meet its demands. When suppliers do fail, the adjustment costs are charged to Lincoln Electric's purchasing department and reflect on merit ratings and annual bonus awards.

When output is decreasing, again, the major tactic is to call in vendored work. Other tactics involve artificially creating a demand for labor by continuing to produce products for inventory or by assigning employees to work that otherwise might never be done. Lincoln Electric uses the former approach, arguing that it not only protects ES, but also is cheaper than stopping and restarting production. During a recent recession, the same company sent a number of blue-collar workers on the road to sell welding equipment; more than $10 million in new orders were generated.

Several ES companies make work for underutilized employees. Materials Resource Corporation, for example, used some scientists and engineers to call on customers and assigned others to projects previously considered of low priority. HP, Lincoln Electric, Eli Lilly, and Control Data also had employees do routine maintenance, mow lawns, or paint fences at one time or another.

The process of managing output and work loads to maintain ES is not a piker's game. Turning down business, vendoring potentially profitable business, moving work to people, stretching productivity improvement programs, producing for inventory, and creating work are all risky and potentially expensive tactics that re-

quire considerable management commitment. That they may be necessary no doubt partly explains why the ES concept is not more widespread.

Managing the Supply Side

Tactics designed to manage labor supply are more commonly used than those aimed at the demand side. Many of the options are shown in Table 6-6.

When output is increasing, it is perhaps uncommon to think of managing ES. Bad decisions, however, create exposures when product demand stabilizes or turns down. Many ES companies make the creation of new positions a tortuous experience even in the best of times. At Lincoln Electric, all such requests go through the chief executive officer (CEO). At Eli Lilly, they must be cleared through the corporate personnel department and, often, through the executive committee. At HP, computerized systems guard against overhiring.

To get the work done without creating new jobs, most ES employers rely on the use of overtime and temporary employees (buffers). In the mid-1970s, Lincoln Electric had employees work fifty-hour weeks for nearly two years rather than add new people in a period of high economic uncertainty. Most ES companies restrict the number of temporaries used at all levels well below those found in Japan, although the ceilings vary widely. Fifteen percent of total employment is the highest figure we heard; one company with more than thirty thousand employees usually has no more than one hundred temporaries. Housewives and students are the two most popular sources of temporaries; the use of retirees is increasing, and no doubt will continue to do so.

Most ES employers seem to hire only those who are highly qualified and seem to spend large sums on training when times are good. Both tactics are intended to enhance employee flexibility, which will be needed as times get tougher or conditions change.

When output is variable, the supply-side solution to work-load imbalances is

TABLE 6-6   Actions to Maintain ES — Supply Side

Increasing	Actions Taken When Output Is Variable	Declining
Add new jobs only as a last resort (HP, IBM, LE, Lilly)	Move people to work/train — sometimes with ultimatum: take it or leave (all)	Freeze hiring (all)
		Cut overtime (all)
Use overtime (LE)		Lay off temporaries
Hire temporaries (all)		Use attrition (all)
Train to meet the future (HP, IBM, Lilly)		Share the work — short week, fortnight, month (HP, LE)
		Encourage voluntary leave of absence, vacations (DG, HP, IBM)
		Encourage voluntary retirement (DG, IBM, Kodak, Polaroid)
		Encourage voluntary termination (Kodak)
		Cut pay (HP)
		Tighten performance standards

to move employees to the work and train them to do the new jobs. This moving requires flexibility. It also requires employees to be geographically mobile, which apparently has always been a problem at the nonexempt level and now is one among exempts as well. To cope with mobility, several ES employers take the position that they are responsible only for offering redundant employees one reasonable employment alternative; refusal is tantamount to resignation. Others make more of an effort to work with employees to find mutually satisfactory arrangements.

Most large ES employers maintain some kind of centralized employment service to locate available jobs within their companies and to provide hiring managers with candidates from among redundant employees. These services may lie dormant most of the time, being activated only as imbalances are identified. When they are used, hiring managers usually are required to fill their jobs from among the candidates the service refers. Control Data, for example, experienced a reduced

need for highly skilled electronic testers. More than one hundred testers were placed on a special work-force action team, which is essentially a labor pool for doing special assignments and maintenance work on older equipment. Part of the assignment, however, is training to prepare qualified employees to return to the regular work force in other capacities.

When output is decreasing, the most common supply-side tactics are associated with layoff avoidance. A typical case of decline involves a hiring freeze (usually centrally controlled), the elimination of overtime, layoffs of temporary employees, and reliance on attrition to reduce the number of employees.

In more serious cases, companies such as Data General and HP have variously used voluntary leaves of absence or timely vacations temporarily to decrease the number of employees. Others — Kodak provides a recent and well-publicized case — have provided incentives to encourage voluntary terminations and early retirements, although some, such as Eli Lilly, have eschewed these as being inconsistent with the ES philosophy. Work sharing and pay cuts (or foregoing pay increases) are also used, although more sparingly. In the early 1970s, HP went to nine work days per fortnight with an accompanying 10 percent cut in pay.

Although not eager to discuss them, some ES companies also tighten performance standards and increase the number of involuntary terminations during decline. These tactics appear in companies that have ongoing marginal employee programs that are less than fully enforced in normal times.

Another approach is to develop hierarchies of actions, or strategies, to prevent — or at least delay — layoffs. Following World War II, the larger Japanese firms informally adopted a three-stage process that more recently has been supported in judicial decisions. The first stage calls for the following tactics:

1. Dismissal of temporary employees
2. Elimination of overtime among regular employees
3. Work sharing
4. Hiring freeze
5. Training during slack times
6. Compulsory paid vacations for those with accumulated time
7. Suspension of pay increases

In stage two the firms invite voluntary resignations, first from employees under 25 and over 50, chronic absentees, and those with alternative means of support, and then from all others. Stage three involves the dismissal of permanent employees.

Variations on this theme occur in United States firms. In the early 1980s, for example, Data General created an array of fifty-two possible actions to cope with its business downturn; the last option was layoff. More formally, CDC has developed a "rings of defense" and an "inner rings of defense" approach, parts of which are shown graphically in Figures 6-2 and 6-3. The strategy has been communicated to top- and mid-level managers, but it has not been widely disseminated.

Support Mechanisms and Conditions

No ES effort exists in isolation, and it is our impression that ES works best when it is properly supported and in the appropriate culture or climate. Significant support mechanisms include the following:

1. *Forecasting and planning.* If the essence of ES is successful adjustment to change, it follows that the effort will most likely succeed when change is anticipated well in advance. In most cases, the primary responsibility for planning for change lies with line managers; in some instances (e.g., Eli Lilly) the personnel function plays a strong role, but in others (e.g., HP) it does not.

2. *Hiring.* Most successful ES companies seem to overhire in the sense that they look for the capacity to do more than simply perform the entry-level job. This appears essential to achieving the flexibility needed to make ES work, although it carries some obvious affirmative action risks.

3. *Training.* Another element to achieve flexibility and to forestall obsolescence is training, although apparently it is not absolutely essential. Most ES employers spend considerable sums on training; it is claimed, however, that Lincoln Electric manages ES in the absence of any formal training program beyond on-the-job training.

4. *Internal staffing.* In ES companies one finds a strong career orientation discouraging job ownership while encouraging growth, development, and flexibility. Promotion from within is the norm. Moving allowances usually apply to all employees.

5. *Communication.* ES firms emphasize up and down communication. Open communication is partly organizational culture; but it also reflects the needs constantly to indoctrinate new cadres of

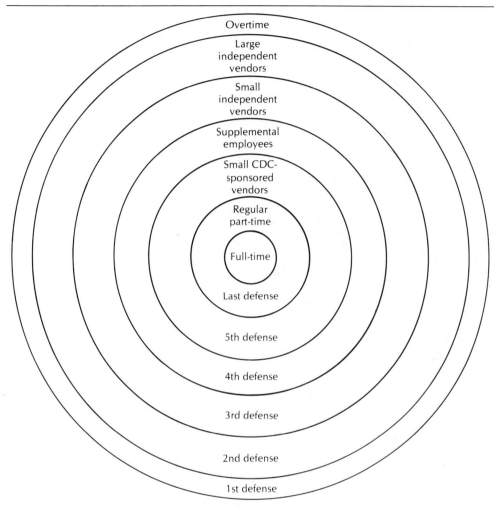

Source: Control Data Corporation, Bloomington, MN. Reprinted by permission.

FIGURE 6-2   Rings of Defense Strategies

managers concerning the inviolability (and perhaps the merits) of ES and continually to remind employees that security is a *quid pro quo* for their forebearance and flexibility on job tasks, work assignments, and geographic mobility.

6. *Control.* Personnel matters in most ES firms are highly centralized, especially when product demand eases. Actions are tracked against plans, the addition of new positions is tightly controlled, training is mandated, managers whose bailiwicks are expanding are sometimes forced to take on redundant employees from elsewhere in the firm, and no one is let go without multiple reviews. Usually this control is exercised by the personnel function and backed up by those at the top.

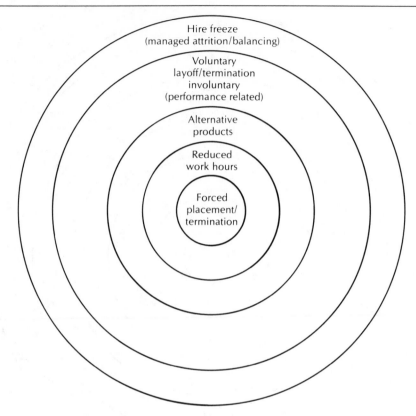

Hire freeze
(managed attrition/balancing)

Voluntary
layoff/termination
involuntary
(performance related)

Alternative
products

Reduced
work hours

Forced
placement/
termination

Source: Control Data Corporation, Bloomington, MN. Reprinted by permission.

FIGURE 6-3   Inner Rings of Defense

Necessary Conditions for Employment Stabilization

ES programs and support mechanisms are important, but we are convinced that two conditions are absolutely essential if an ES effort is to be successful: top management commitment and long-term profitability.

All ES efforts, at some point, will be tested and, we believe, will be found wanting unless top management is totally committed to the concept and has successfully communicated this commitment down the line. It is no accident that many of the more successful ES efforts were put in place by strong founders who have achieved folk-hero status or are still active

in their firms, men such as A. P. Giannini (Bank of America), W. Hewlett and D. Packard, T. Watson (IBM), Eli Lilly, J. F. Lincoln, and S. Weining (Materials Resource Corporation). In the absence of an uncompromising position on ES by top management, subordinates cannot be expected to turn down potentially profitable business because of longer-run employment ramifications.

Long-term profitability is also essential. Even the most committed firm will relent on ES before letting the business fail (witness events at Bank of America). Some will hold on longer than others, as Delta Airlines and Material Resources Corporation have shown, but eventually profitability must be restored if the ES commitment is to be kept.

In addition to top management commitment and long-term profitability, other conditions appear to increase the feasibility and success of ES. These include a supportive culture, growth, the existence of multiple product lines and multiple facilities located close to one another, as well as nonunion status.

The dominant culture in most ES companies is what we have come to call performance-oriented paternalism (POP). Performance expectations are high, rewards and punishments are based on merit, and policies and rules are strictly enforced. At the same time, however, there is extreme concern for the welfare of individual employees: Pay and benefits are generous, working conditions are exceptional, grievance outlets and employee assistance programs abound, egalitarianism is practiced with respect to such amenities as parking spots and cafeterias, and ritual and hoopla are common as means of recognizing, rewarding, and socializing those "lucky enough to belong."[6]

Growth, multiple product lines, and multiple and proximate facilities provide flexibility with which to work to preserve ES. Nonunion status provides the same advantage, although in this case the questions of which is the cause and which is the result are uncertain.

Results

What do ES firms get? What does it cost? Are the benefits worth the costs? Surprisingly, little effort has been made to answer these questions by the companies we studied. Others have researched some aspects of these issues, but the results are far from conclusive. In the end, except in extreme cases, it is clear that to ES companies benefits and costs do not matter all that much.

[6]For more on this, see Peters and Waterman, *op. cit.*, chapter 8, in which several ES companies — Data General, Delta, DEC, HP, IBM — are prominently mentioned.

Benefits and Costs

We found no explicit attempt to model the organizational benefits and costs associated with ES. We were able, however, to construct our own model by mapping out the cause-and-effect statements inherent in the responses to our questions and in the literature. This model is shown in Figure 6-4. On the benefits side, the argument seems to be that employment stabilization leads to perceptions of employee security which, in turn

1. makes it easier for the organization to recruit, because word gets out into the community;
2. makes employees more willing to accept change and to increase their productivity, because they feel little need to protect their turf and are not afraid of working themselves out of a job;
3. reduces the perceived need for third-party representation (unionization); and
4. makes employees more committed to the organization.

As a result, the reasoning goes, the organization has better, more highly motivated employees and a flexible work environment; these, in turn, result in increased productivity. The organization also has lower voluntary and involuntary turnover, which means lower administrative costs for such things as recruitment, the orientation and training of new recruits, and unemployment compensation taxes. Higher productivity and lower administrative costs, in turn, contribute to greater profitability.

Offsetting these apparent benefits, however, are some obvious costs. Turning down or losing business because of slow start-ups, vendors, excess inventory, and excess people can all directly result in lower short-term profitability. Eli Lilly, for example, in the mid-1970s was carrying some five hundred surplus employees at an estimated annual cost of $15 million. It has been estimated that Delta Airlines, which lost $61.2 million in the first nine

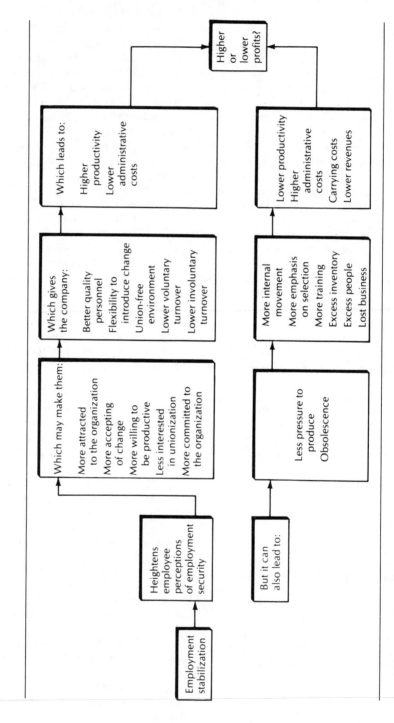

FIGURE 6-4   Model of the Benefits and Costs of Employment Stabilization

months of fiscal year 1983 (ending March 31, 1983), was at one time carrying as many as one thousand underutilized employees.

Further, productivity can be adversely rather than positively affected by perceived employment security, especially if performance is not effectively managed and little resort is made to termination. Frequent internal moves, if necessary, can result in reduced efficiency. An ES organization may experience higher-than-average costs associated with selection and training, especially among longer-service employees.

The Dearth of Research

No one knows for sure the extent to which the putative benefits and costs of ES are, in fact, realized. In general, the benefits often seem vague and ephemeral, while the costs seem real. Pieces of the puzzle, however, have been studied. Research shows, for example, that higher perceived job security tends to lead to a greater acceptance of change.[7] Also, a few comparisons have been made of the relative costs of layoffs vis-à-vis various alternatives to layoffs.[8] The results of the latter studies tend to vary. ES, for example, is cost effective during short downturns but not over longer periods.

More definitive research is possible, although it is difficult to do. In actual work settings, for example, it would be difficult to separate the effects of ES from the effects of other factors on employees attitudes, behavior, and productivity. Further, the links between employee attitudes and behavior, on one hand, and organizational results, on the other, are often difficult to sort. Finally, there is the problem of recip-

[7]F. Fox and B. Staw, "The Trapped Administrator: Effects of Job Security and Policy Resistance Upon Commitment to a Course of Action," *Administrative Science Quarterly*, 24, 3, 1979, 449–471.

[8]See Leonard Greenhalgh, *A Cost-Benefit Balance Sheet for Evaluating Layoffs as a Policy Strategy*, Mimeo, n.d.

rocal causality: Managerial flexibility, for example, contributes to an organization's ability to manage ES successfully, and it also appears to be significantly enhanced by the successful management of ES. Research to tease out the effects of such roundabout patterns is intricate and arduous to design and carry out.

Despite the difficulty, however, more — and more convincing — research on the effects of ES would be helpful. We were surprised to find little such research under way on ES. On the other hand, it is doubtful that further research would have much influence on the decision to begin or to abandon ES. It appears that in most cases this decision is based on values ("It is the only morally acceptable way to manage") or logic ("How can you claim respect for the individual and then not commit to making every effort to protect his or her job?"), not on perceptions of benefits and costs. Such research could affect the nature of the ES commitment and especially the way it is carried out. Once the ES decision is made, the task is to manage the business so that the commitment is maintained while profitability is enhanced, or at least not jeopardized. More needs to be known about the ways in which this has been, and can be, successfully done.

Summary and Conclusions

Employee security is a subject of long-standing interest to employers, labor union leaders, and public policymakers. Over the years, this elusive goal has been defined in many ways and pursued through a plethora of programs under a variety of labels. Here, we focused on firms whose top management is committed, at a minimum, to make every effort to provide continuous employment or income for at least some segment of its work force and in which specific activities or programs have been instituted to support this commitment.

The exact number of firms fitting our definition of ES is unknown. Because of the recession of the early 1980s, an apparently severe case of structural unemployment among those formerly employed in the basic industries, and the success of the Japanese economy, interest in ES in the United States is now relatively high. This interest is manifest in the management literature, more directly in bargaining proposals put forth by a few of the major labor unions, and in federal and state legislative proposals. The nature and the prospects of the proposals being advanced, however, make it highly unlikely that the next few years will see either a noticeable increase in the number of ES employers or a significant change in the nature of activities in which these employers now engage.

It appears that the major challenges to ES will continue to come from traditional sources. Principal among these are changes in business strategies and new technologies, both of which often alter the number and nature of employees that organizations need, and the uncertain state of the United States economy, which puts nearly all enterprises at some risk. In most instances, successfully dealing with these challenges requires more than a simple contingency plan for avoiding layoffs. It involves the formulation and implementation of a comprehensive strategy that includes (1) mechanisms for managing an organization's demand for and supply of labor when its output is increasing, variable, or declining; and (2) support activities, such as forecasting and planning, hiring, training, internal staffing, communication, and control. The impetus to do all this, it appears, must come from a highly committed top management bent on developing within the firm a distinctive culture that we have labeled performance-oriented paternalism (POP).

Clearly, ES requires considerable commitment and concentration, and no small amount of cost. Are the results worth it? No one knows for sure. One can find ES firms that are highly successful, non-ES firms that are equally successful, and ES firms that have not survived. Research on the economic effects of ES is sparse. In part, we suspect, this paucity reflects the difficulty of such research. It also reflects the fact that most ES employers seem to justify their efforts on the basis of morality and values rather than economics. Thus, rather than asking if their efforts are worth it, they accept the concept as a given and concentrate instead on making it work.

Questions for Discussion

1. What groups in society would benefit most if the majority of firms adopted employment stabilization policies? Specifically, consider the effects adopting those policies would have on careers and employment experiences of young workers accepting their first job after completing their education; young professionals three years out of business or engineering school, who are looking for their next major professional growth opportunity; mid-career professionals who sense limited promotional opportunities within their firm; and employees of small firms that subcontract to larger firms.

2. What questions would you ask a company's chief executive officer who says to you, "I've been hearing a lot about the benefits firms get when they agree not to lay people off and would like to try out that idea with my employees"?

3. How would you determine whether the managers and employees of a specific company are ready for the adoption of an employment stabilization program?

Make or Buy: Computer Professionals in a Demand-Driven Environment

The director of the Information Systems (IS) Department was feeling frustrated. Three of his top thirteen managers had resigned to take positions with competitors and each had received a 20 to 30 percent salary increase in their new job. When he complained about his turnover problem to the personnel director, an equally frustrated response came back: "All your people are outliers on our salary schedule, if we keep making exceptions for them we may have to redo our entire pay structure. Whenever we move one of your IS people into another functional department we get complaints from their colleagues because their salaries are so much higher."

The problem in the above dialogue is not new. In each decade, technological, organizational, or demographic changes seem to produce a new set of skills in short supply. In the 1950s, the postwar baby boom created a teacher shortage. In the 1960s, the space race created a shortage of aeronautical engineers and related technicians. In the 1970s, skilled machinists, nurses, and professional managers, especially MBAs, were in short supply. In the 1980s, information systems professionals are needed to support the growing number of applications for computer and information technologies.

In this paper, we draw on data collected from a study of the internal labor markets for information systems professionals and managers to illustrate how employers can respond to occupational or skill shortages. We begin by examining the costs of turnover, because high turnover rates are often

Source: Thomas A. Barocci and Paul Cournoyer. Paul Cournoyer is a Senior Information Systems Manager at Digital Equipment Corporation. The piece was written especially for this book.

a signal that some aspect of an organization's human resource policies is not working well. We then analyze two options firms have for responding to skill shortages: (1) to "make" new managers by training, developing, and providing career ladders for professionals, and (2) to "buy" trained talent from the external labor market. Finally, we examine the roles of training, career ladders, and compensation systems in a human resource strategy designed to develop talent within a firm.

Turnover and Its Costs

Although turnover in high-growth occupations is nothing new, it is currently a serious problem in information systems (IS) departments. It is exaggerated, moreover, because computer professionals have tended to be more attached to their occupations than to their companies. During the last ten years, great strides have been made in developing career paths for nonmanagerial IS professionals, but few organizations have addressed the career issues for supervisors and managers in these departments (Idema, 1978). The problem is becoming more acute as functional specialists in other parts of the organization become more closely linked with the IS department, and more IS managers get placed directly into functional area positions (Keen, 1980).

Recently, the IS department manager in a large electronics manufacturing company asked one of the authors rhetorically, "What can I do to convince my chief financial officer in this company that I need a budgetary increase to allow for increased salaries, increased education, increased amenities, and increased equipment purchases?" He continued, "Turnover in the department was 35 percent last year and 25 percent at the top, and it's killing me."

The response was simple: Let's demonstrate how much it costs in the short run if we do NOT do anything about the high turnover.

To analyze the turnover and its costs, we first talked with personnel staff. They offered a list of recruiting, advertising, moving, interviewing, and other costs associated with filling vacant positions. These can be high, often amounting to almost 40 percent of a person's starting salary. These costs, however, are only the beginning; indirect costs, such as training and related start-up activities, can dwarf these costs (Hall, 1981).

The method of estimating the costs of turnover within an organization can be illustrated by the following example. Figure 6-5 shows the organizational chart of the firm's IS department. For simplicity, only the top of the structure is shown, but the principles are the same as one moves down the organization. In fact, one study estimated the turnover costs of low-level computer professionals and found the recruitment costs of one systems project leader to be $10,339, while the training costs were $15,735. The total was 87 percent of the project leader's average annual salary of $30,000 (Tessier, 1982).

Of the thirteen top positions in the IS department, three required replacements during the previous year: senior manager of software engineering, manager of software engineering, and systems consultant. Their combined salaries ($105,000, $75,000, $60,000) was $240,000, or about 25 percent of the total top management

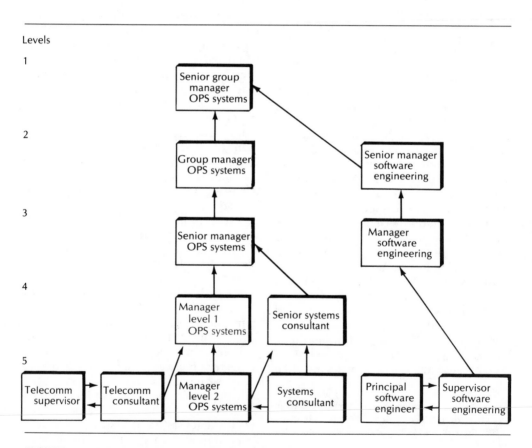

FIGURE 6-5   I.S. Department Organizational Chart

salary budget of $985,000. The turnover rate was three of thirteen, or 23 percent — actually lower than the average for IS units we have found in other fieldwork.

Exhibit 6-1 shows the calculation of the direct costs in replacing the three people who left. Advertising search costs include agency and finder fees. To this we must add the recruitment expenses of bringing personnel to the area and the firm for interviews, and in the final selection, bringing spouses to the area for a visit. Relocation expenses are also included, as is the allocation of 20 percent of the time of a senior person on the organization's personnel staff. Estimated by the personnel department, the latter includes the time spent shuffling the pay-point scheme to allow for the red-circle rates (individual pay rates set for some special reason but not to be treated as a precedent for future incumbents in that position) necessary to offer the new hires the 20 percent (average) salary increase required to lure them from their old jobs. Total direct costs equalled $197,000, a conservative estimate that does not include bridge loans and mortgage subsidies. Obvious, but noteworthy, is that no output to the firm is directly related to this expenditure.

In addition to direct costs, indirect costs include an estimate of existing management time spent interviewing and convincing candidates that this was the right place to work. Interviews with managers indicated that approximately 2 percent of their total yearly hours were spent on this activity. The same interviews obtained managers' estimates of the time it takes new personnel to arrive at a 90 percent productivity level. Exhibit 6-1 shows the results of these estimates. During the first 7 weeks the productivity of the new hires was only 20 percent, during the next 7 weeks the figure rose to 32 percent, and during the last 7 weeks their productivity reached an estimated 86 percent. In total, the learning curve productivity losses cost the company an additional $62,000.

By adding direct and indirect costs, we arrived at a total cost of turnover for these executives of $279,000, or 116 percent of

the annual compensation paid for these positions — and this is a *conservative* estimate. It does not account for the time that management had to spend training the new hires.

One more consideration should be noted. These same costs were incurred not only by the firm under study here, but also by the other firms that hired those who left the company. The same expenses pervaded all levels of IS departments and all other high-demand occupations in the economy. Such expenses will not diminish until serious attention is focused on ways to lower turnover through effective management of human resources. Preventing all turnover is unrealistic and probably undesirable, but preventing the turnover of valued people with firm-specific skills can be the single largest productivity enhancement program available. Turnover prevention requires the institution of a systematic program explicitly considering the make-buy decision.

The Make–Buy Choice

The scarcity of computer-related personnel and the corresponding increase in wages generally result in an increase in turnover. To alleviate a firm's shortage of computer professionals, an organization has three options: (1) train existing employees in data processing and provide a way of upgrading existing skills, (2) hire unskilled personnel and offer training development programs, (3) recruit personnel with the requisite skills from the outside. The decision about which option or combination to use is a basic choice a firm must face.

The short-run approach is often to try to maximize profits by minimizing the cost of training by paying recruitment fees and salary premiums for external personnel with the requisite skills. Although this approach may alleviate internal equity pressures and appear to keep compensation costs down, it is short-sighted and does not solve the critical, long-term problem.

The long-run strategy is to determine if

EXHIBIT 6-1
Corporate IS Dept: Top Management — 13 Positions
Estimation of Yearly Turnover Costs

(Total Compensation for 13 Positions = $985,000/Year)

Salaries

Turnover	3 Jobs	1 Year	=	23%
Job A	Level 5	60K/yr		
Job B	Level 3	75K/yr		
Job C	Level 2	105K/yr		

Estimation Calculation

Direct

1. Employment advertising	$ 6,000
2. Agency and finder fees	
(30% of A, B, C) + 20%	86,000
3. Applicant expenses with spouse ($2,000 × 3)	6,000
4. Relocation expenses ($13,000 × 3)	39,000
5. Employment staff compensation (20% × 60,000)	12,000
6. Salary increases (20% of 240,000)	48,000
Direct hiring costs (sum of 1–5)	$197,000

Indirect (estimated)

7. Cost of existing management time — Interviewing, etc. (2 percent of total yearly "billable" hours)	$ 20,000
8. Learning curve productivity losses:	

Average Weekly Pay (3 People)	Weeks Learning To 90% Productivity	% Effective During Learning Curve		
		First 1/3	Second 1/3	Third 1/3
$5,500	21	20%	32%	86%

A. First third loss ($5,500 × .80 × 7 wks.)	$ 30,800
B. Second third loss ($5,500 × .68 × 7 wks.)	26,180
C. Third third loss ($5,500 × .14 × 7 wks.)	5,390
Total learning curve productivity losses	$ 62,370
Total indirect ($20,000 + $62,370)	

Grand Total

Direct + indirect ($82,370 = $197,000)	$259,370

*Not including existing management on-the-job training time.

turnover is lower for personnel hired at average or below average salaries as trainees, trained and developed, and promoted within the organization's internal career ladders — a "make" decision as opposed to a "buy" decision. In the "buy" decision, personnel are recruited at higher salaries from outside the organization, receive little training, and experience little or no career mobility. One might argue that by "making" computer professionals, the employees would feel a sense of loyalty to the firm providing the training and benefit from a higher salary through having increased their firm-specific skill level. As a result, one would expect turnover to decrease. The opposite argument is that after employees undergo training, they become more attractive to competing firms, who then bid them away. This assumes that their training will be useful in competing firms. In this case, an organization's decision to "make" personnel would cause turnover to increase.

The buy decision seems to be the most likely approach during a labor shortage situation, especially when the time for meeting the organizations' technical needs is short. Most firms, it appears, buy the talent to meet their IS needs. Once employees are bought, however, chances are they will have few inhibitions about being bought again; therefore, the propensity to change jobs is higher.

Doeringer and Piore (1971) warn that how a firm reacts to the external labor market (i.e., the make or buy decision) has various implications for the industry. Reacting to labor shortages by bidding up salaries (the buy strategy), without accompanying adjustments in other policies such as training, may not relieve the labor scarcity as existing talent simply moves around. Buying talent creates an inflationary salary spiral. Consequently, we need to examine how a make strategy, which offers intensive training, career planning, and appropriate compensation, might be used to alleviate firm and industry skill shortages.

Firms might argue that by providing primarily firm-specific training, employees will not be able to sell these specific skills in the labor market, so the turnover rate will not increase. The returns to specific training accrue to the trainee and the firm providing the training. An example of firm-specific training would be company-specific, higher-level computer languages. In this case, it makes sense to invest in specific training, as there is a a greater likelihood of reaping the rewards and a lower chance of turnover (Becker, 1964). Providing general training that competitors could use (e.g., standard, data-base management systems) may be viewed as a less valuable investment, because it would render the employee more attractive to competitors; the result is an increased risk of turnover. In cases where turnover reaches an excess of 30 percent per annum (implying that more than half the employees may quit their current organizations two years from now), the distinction between general and specific training becomes more important. Organizations have, on average, less than two years to tie a person to the firm with investments in specific training and to obtain a return on those investments through employee retention.

Using a data base of approximately 800 IS professionals, we constructed Table 6-7, which offers rank orders for the managerial and nonmanagerial categories and percentage of each occupational group who indicated that the reason for leaving their last job was "important" or "very important." As shown, the lack of growth opportunity within the organization was the primary reason for both the managerial and nonmanagerial categories. Salary was the second most important reason and the category of "attractive offer from another firm" (closely akin to "salary") was third in priority. These data illustrate a strong need to provide growth opportunity and challenging work to this group of professionals in order to maintain their tenure with the organization.

TABLE 6-7 Respondents' Reasons for Leaving Their Jobs; Managerial and Nonmanagerial

Percentage Considering Important Reason	Nonmanagerial					Managerial				
	Ranking	Programmer	Systems Analyst	Technical Staff	Project Leader	Ranking	Project Manager	Systems Development Manager	Technical Staff Manager	I/S Director
Boring work	4	9.0	7.6	10.3	3.6	5	10.3	3.6	6.6	4.0
Salary	2	10.3	13.0	13.6	16.3	2	12.3	15.6	12.0	13.6
Too little growth opportunities	1	14.3	15.6	12.3	22.3	1	18.3	15.0	23.6	19.6
Attractive offer at another firm	3	12.3	9.6	9.3	8.3	3	10.4	12.0	10.6	14.0
Not enough challenges	8	6.0	6.3	3.3	6.0	4	7.6	9.0	7.3	5.6
Personal reasons	7	4.3	6.3	10.0	5.6	8	5.6	1.3	10.0	4.0
Bureaucracy	10	5.0	3.3	4.3	2.6	10	3.0	3.3	2.6	2.6
Management problems	5	5.3	7.3	7.6	9.3	7	6.6	6.3	3.6	5.0
Work environment	9	5.6	6.0	2.0	6.0	9	2.0	5.6	4.0	5.0
Not enough career development	6	10.0	5.3	4.3	8.3	6	3.3	5.0	4.0	10.0

Source: Human Resource Policy Project, CLSR, MIT, 1983.

Role of Career Paths

The development of structured career paths is one aspect of the make decision that firms can adjust to provide an incentive for their professionals to stay with the firm, thereby reducing voluntary turnover. Goldfarb Haber (1978) used 1970 census data to show that few data-processing occupations developed along a structured career path. Only 10 percent of those who were programmers in 1965 had become systems analysts by 1970. Movements were usually lateral rather than vertical. Data from a Center for Information System Research study showed that by the early 1980s the paths had become more structured and vertical. The modal path, increasing path, and outlier path are offered in Figure 6-6. These paths were established during the 1970s, but the data confirm that the paths must change again. Figure 6-7 shows our speculations on future career path changes (see Barocci and Wever, 1983).

The first step in designing career paths is to choose a limited number of entry positions, or initial hiring jobs, and to promote workers from within through well-defined, internal career ladders supported by appropriate training. To ensure that sufficient advancement opportunities open up and to meet the needs of the overall organization, flexible policies for intraorganizational transfer and adequate information on position openings across the company are needed. IBM, for example, has an extensive retraining and relocation program (*Business Week*, 10 November 1975). Such employee policies will foster a higher level of commitment to the firm, and presumably lower turnover. McLaughlin (1979) wrote:

> Again and again, shops that reported no problems struck some common chord. They hired from within other departments of their own firm to find employees whose allegiance was to the company rather than to the (data processing) profession. They found ways to challenge and to add interest to jobs.

Conclusion

Given that IS departments are being asked to increase their orientation toward end-user management support systems (MSS) and given that these occupations will continue to evolve in a demand-driven environment, we must explore the human resource planning, training, and educational prescriptions for firms, as well as IS professionals and managers. Scott-Morton (1983) characterized the issue as follows:

> This proliferation of information power in the hands of users, in particular, is transforming the Management Support Systems (MSS) field from an interesting, but somewhat isolated use of information systems by a small core of creative individuals to a central position among management tools. One increasingly finds Management Support Systems woven into the very fabric of management. This transformation has just begun and the enormity of its impact has not yet been felt.

If indeed MSSs are "woven into the very fabric of management," the implications for the duties, responsibilities, and careers of those who hold the lead in skill in this area may have to change dramatically.

References

Alloway, Robert, and Judith Quillard, "User Manager's Systems Needs," Working Paper #86, Center for Information Systems Research, Sloan School of Management, MIT, 1982.

Barocci, Thomas A., and Kirsten R. Wever, "Managing Information Systems Career Paths," Working Paper #1481-83, Sloan School of Management, MIT, 1983.

Becker, Gary, *Human Capital* (New York and London: Columbia University Press, 1964).

Doeringer, Peter, and Michael Piore, *Internal Labor Markets and Manpower Analysis* (Lexington, Mass.: D. C. Heath, 1971).

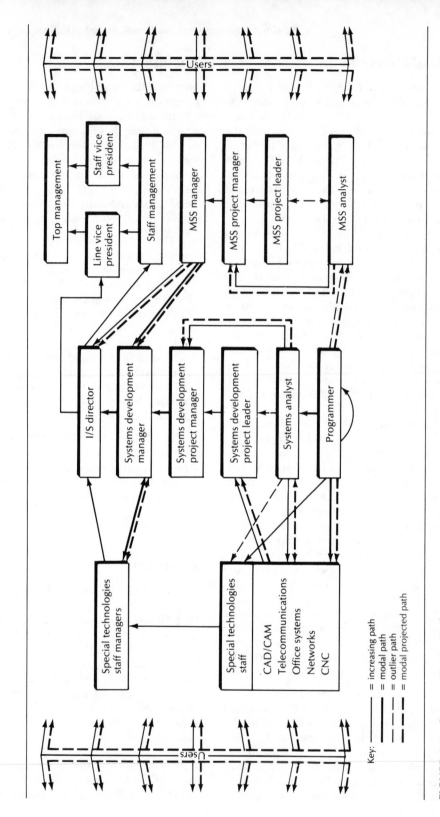

FIGURE 6-6 Current Career Paths

Key:
——— = increasing path
▬▬▬ = modal path
– – – = outlier path
▬ ▬ ▬ = modal projected path

222

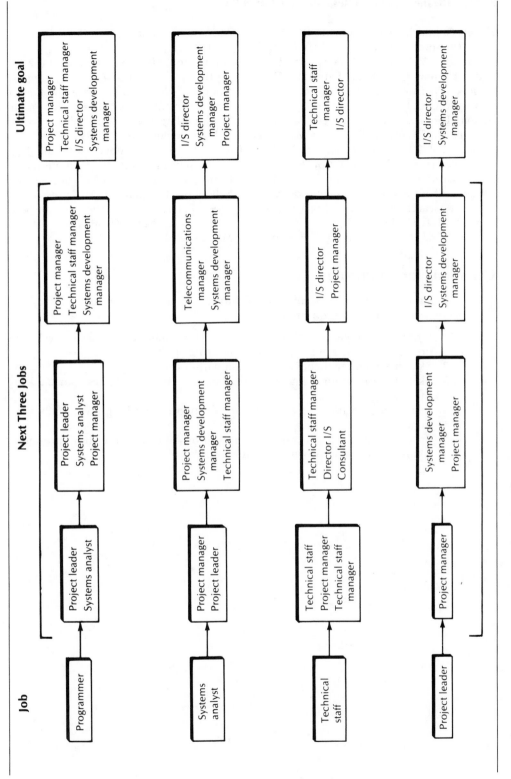

FIGURE 6-7 Job Aspirations; Nonmanagerial Respondents

223

Haber, Goldfarb, "Labor Market Response for Computer Occupations," *Industrial Relations*, Vol. 17, No. 1, February 1978.

Hall, Thomas, "How to Estimate Employee Turnover Costs," in *Personnel*, July–August 1981.

Idema, Thomas, "*Systems Career Path Development*," Journal of Systems Management, Vol. 29, No. 4, April 1978, 30–39.

Keen, Peter G. W., "Information Systems and Organizational Change," Working Paper #55, Center for Information Systems Research, Sloan School of Management, MIT, 1980.

McLaughlin, R. A., "That Old Bugaboo Turnover," *Datamation*, October 1979, 97–101.

Scott-Morton, Michael S., "State of the Art of Research in Management Support Systems," Working Paper #107, Center for Information Systems Research, Working Paper #1473–83, Sloan School of Management, MIT, 1983.

Tessier, Debara, "Turnover Costs for Project Managers," May 1982, unpublished term paper for course 15.663, Sloan School of Management, MIT.

Wegner, Peter, *Research Directives in Software Technology* (Cambridge, Mass.: MIT Press, 1979), 224.

Questions for Discussion

Using our data and speculation on future career paths for IS professionals, answer the following questions.

1. From the perspective of an IS director, formulate a strategy for using IS professionals within a large manufacturing operation.
2. Sketch a plan for turnover reduction within this firm.
3. Sketch an operational plan for hiring and training of IS professionals during the next five years.
4. Establish priorities for an educational program for IS professionals/functional managers.
5. Speculate on the organizational implications of the data we have presented coupled with Scott-Morton's prediction.

Layoffs and Training in the U.S. Auto Industry

In this paper we examine changes in human resource management policies at a General Motors (GM) division complex in mid-Michigan, changes induced by a reduction in the numbers of apprentices and journeymen in skilled trades. Hourly employees in the division, as in all of GM, are represented by the United Auto Workers (UAW). Factors shaping the choices of labor and management in the reduction-in-force (RIF) decision included the contractual rules governing training and layoffs, which are in the national UAW-GM collective bargaining agreement. This case study also describes the role of the contractual rules governing human resource management practices for a typical group of blue-collar factory employees.

CASE
General Motors

DIVISION CHARACTERISTICS

This GM division produces component parts for automobiles, trucks, farm machinery, and aircraft; most of the products are not highly technical. Its plants, located in the United States and overseas, include a major manufacturing complex in mid-Michigan. Domestic employment for the division peaked in the mid-1970s at more than 13,000 blue-collar and 2,000 white-collar employees. By 1981, employment had been reduced to less than 6,400 blue-collar and 1,800 white-collar employees.

The division has been in the forefront of manufacturing technology. Innovations such as laser hardening, computerized matching of parts at assembly, and metal-forming improvements have been brought into its mass production operations. These highly technical processes require a trades work force that is skilled in traditional and new industrial manufacturing technologies. In addition, future advances in technology, such as computer numerical control (CNC), integrated flexible automation (robots), and programmable controllers, will require further training of the work force in this division.

CONTRACTUAL AND PROCEDURAL RULES

The United States auto industry has undergone large-scale cyclical flux in sales and production since World War II. A detailed contractual system has developed through collective bargaining to guide adjustments in employment and

Source: Harry C. Katz and Ronald Karl. Harry Katz is Associate Professor of Industrial Relations, Sloan School of Management, MIT. Ronald Karl is a Senior Engineer at General Motors. This case was written especially for this book.

work hours in response to that flux. At the heart of this system is a seniority-based layoff procedure, which is linked to supplementary unemployment benefits (SUB). Contractual rules also regulate training and other aspects of human resource allocation.

Layoffs and Seniority

Layoffs and associated employment rights follow departmental seniority, which is guided by job ladders outlining departmental lines within a specific plant. The general outline of this system is provided in each national company-UAW agreement, while the specific layout of the job ladder is set in supplementary plant agreements.

Introduced in the 1955 agreements and expanded in 1967, the supplementary unemployment benefits that laid-off auto workers receive in addition to state unemployment insurance benefits are an important part of the layoff system. Companies contribute to a SUB fund on a per-hour basis, with a current contribution rate of roughly thirty cents per hour worked. SUB, in combination with unemployment insurance benefits, can be as high as 95 percent of take-home pay; as of the 1982 contract, workers can accumulate up to 104 weeks of SUB entitlement.

Within the contractual system, workers can use their seniority rights to bid on job openings in other departments in the same plant. A history of grievance cases and arbitration awards has established the practice that seniority governs intraplant transfer rights unless management can prove that another less senior worker has abilities that far exceed those of the more senior worker. In practice, however, this criterion is rarely invoked because management finds it both difficult to substantiate such claims and costly to adjudicate the disputes that might arise from them.

Skilled-Trades Jobs and Training Systems

A sharp differentiation exists within the blue-collar job-classification system between skilled-trades jobs and production jobs. Trades workers receive significantly more pay (on average $3.00 per hour) than production workers; further, their duties are outlined in detail in local agreements, which helps maintain craft demarcation lines. At GM, trades workers made up 20 percent of all blue-collar workers in 1980. Exhibit 6-2 summarizes the nature of skilled-trades work.

A worker can attain journeyman trades (craft) status (1) through a formal four-year apprenticeship program, or (2) by working eight years on the job as an employee-in-training (EIT). The apprenticeship program entails 576 hours of class work concurrent with three and one-half years of on-the-job experience. The program's curriculum covers basic math and science as well as theory and laboratory practices of the trade. At national and plant levels, joint union-management committees closely monitor the program. The number of apprentices is regulated through contractual language stipulating that appren-

EXHIBIT 6-2
Organization of Skilled Trades Work

The skilled trades at the division are made up of traditional facilities maintenance, machine maintenance, and tooling fabrication trades. Their functions include the following:

1. Maintain production equipment on an as-required basis, as in the case of break-downs. This entails most downtime maintenance of the equipment and is done at the request of the production department. This type of work comprised 20 percent of the skilled trades work in 1981.

2. Check and maintain production equipment on a periodic basis to prevent un-planned machine downtime. This involves periodic checks and replacement of machine components, and nonoperator service to equipment (such as oiling). This type of work (known as PM, for planned maintenance) comprised 8 percent of the skilled trades work in 1981; it is scheduled by a maintenance engineer in the plant.

3. Perform project work such as plant rearrangements, machine design changes, and tooling fabrication. These projects may be large rearrangements or simple machine changes (such as installing a light at a work station). This type of work made up the remaining 72 percent of the 1981 trades work load; it is scheduled by a maintenance planner at each plant.

---

tice-journeymen ratios cannot exceed 1:5 (1:8 during specified exceptional conditions) to allay union fears that apprentices earning lower wages could be replacing journeymen. Another contractual stipulation is that for every applicant to the apprenticeship program from outside the company, two must be accepted from within the company. In practice, the percentage of external recruitment of apprentices is much below 33.3 percent and has been dropping to 1 or 2 percent in recent years because of layoffs of production workers and heightened pressures for internal promotion. Observers of the apprenticeship system suggested that recent external applicants have been recruited only as a way to increase the number of female and minority applicants in accordance with affirmative action guidelines.

Employees-in-training are workers who have demonstrated proficiency in skilled-trades work but who lack either proof of trade experience or valid journeyman certificates. These employees are allowed to function as learners for the time it takes to become a journeyman (up to eight years on the job). They can be used rapidly to supplement the journeyman work force, because they normally have significant practical experience in the trade. They are not bound by the apprentice program rules concerning classroom hours. EIT programs are managed at local levels.

There is no corporatewide formal planning of long-term skill needs or training requirements, nor are there any companywide skills inventories for the blue-collar work force. By contrast, GM tracks white-collar employees and uses an information system to fill job openings with employees possessing particular skills. Any blue-collar skills planning that occurs is limited to the plant level, and to short-term responses to the introduction or anticipation of new machinery.

Recent Job Security Innovations

In response to large layoffs, gloomy sales forecasts, and significant compensation concessions, the contracts reached at GM and Ford in March 1982 introduced a number of new programs that affect personnel planning and training. One of those is a joint labor-management "National Employee Development and Training Program" at each company, funded by company contributions (ten cents per worker hour at GM). Another innovation in the 1982 agreements at GM and Ford, with major implications for personnel planning, is the guaranteed income stream (GIS) benefit. This program provides that permanently laidoff workers with more than 15 years of seniority receive 50 percent of their last year's earnings (an additional 1 percent for each year of seniority beyond 15 years up to 75 percent of the previous year's pay) until they reach the normal retirement age. The 1982 national agreements also included a novel effort to experiment with employment guarantees at select plants (four at GM and three at Ford). At these plants 80 percent of the existing work force is guaranteed employment during the term of the agreement (until September 1984).

Another novel feature of the new agreements at Ford and GM was a promise by management not to close any plants for 24 months "as a result of outsourcing the components manufactured in the facility." Then, in 1984, the parties negotiated a job security program that provides income support and retraining for all workers affected by new technology or outsourcing. All of these programs put further pressure on the companies to engage in more extensive personnel planning and to develop policies that better use the existing work force.

In response to the severe economic pressure of massive layoffs, and as part of a strategy to improve competitiveness through cooperative solutions, worker participation programs have expanded significantly in the auto industry during the last three years. These participation programs represent a further development affecting personnel planning and administration. The participation effort includes formal programs that engage workers in production decision-making at the shop level via quality circles, and at corporate and plant levels through so-called mutual growth forums where labor and management discuss business responses to competitive pressures. In addition, workers and union officials have begun to receive information regarding new technologies, business plans, extensive supplier relations, and personnel policies, via direct communication with management through channels that lie outside the traditional collective bargaining system. The net effect of this worker involvement and information sharing is to move labor and management away from formal, contractual rule making, and toward decentralized, flexible procedures.

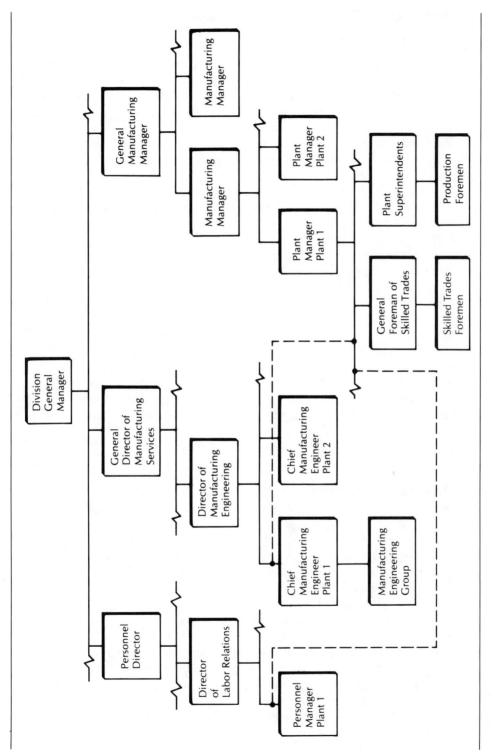

FIGURE 6-8 Partial Organizational Chart of Divisional Operations

MANAGEMENT AND SUPPORT SYSTEMS

The Division's Training System

As mentioned, a sharp differentiation exists between skilled and production job classifications in the auto industry's blue-collar work force. This differentiation is also reflected in the management organization of the GM division. Figure 6-8 shows the organization of the GM component division as related to the skilled trades. Each plant within the division's functions is almost autonomous with respect to changes in work force and assignments of employees. A typical plant in the division has 800 to 1,200 blue-collar employees.

The craft worker reports to an assigned foreman, often a former craft worker. Foremen report to the skilled-trades general foreman for their plant. The skilled-trades general foreman is the top manager of the crafts and reports to the plant manager. There is no collective hierarchy for the skilled-trades management across the division, in contrast to other manufacturing managerial structures in the corporation. This feature entails some trade-offs between the coordination of skilled-trades policy throughout the division, on the one hand, and autonomy in the allocation of individual plant resources, on the other.

To provide the necessary coordination across the division, the general foremen in the mid-Michigan location began to meet weekly as a group in 1978 to discuss common problems, strategies, and future requirements. Topics include labor relations strategies such as line of demarcation, policy problems such as the interplant "bumping" of tradesmen, and training programs such as in-plant training and apprentices.. General foremen are responsible for the performance and the training of the trades at their plants, with the exception of the apprentice program.

Planning and Budgeting Systems

Planning and budget systems at the division constitute the main quantitative tools for skilled-trades management. The planning of skilled-trades work loads for periodic and project work is based on a simple, computerized, job-modeling system. This system uses worker-hours, availability of parts and material, and timing constraints to produce labor requirements and loading forecasts.

The budgeting of skilled-trades work takes two forms. First, plant expense accounts are established to accrue operating expenses for the plant. Operating expenses, such as normal maintenance of plant and equipment, are charged to these accounts. Because these accounts directly affect the plant's profits, managers watch them carefully. Second, major rearrangements and retooling are charged to appropriations that are received from the corporation. Examples include retooling for product-line changes, such as the all new domestic models of the last five years. Budgets are set at the beginning of a year and calculated as a given percentage of the direct (productive) labor used at the plant.

New Training Initiatives

By 1980, management saw that the level of training in the division (and throughout GM) was inadequate; the corporation had to increase its commitment to training its employees to enable them to handle emerging technologies. Two methods were used to meet this goal: New journeymen who were trained or trainable in the new technologies were brought into the expanding work force, and some of the existing workers were retrained.

To expand the number of tradesmen, the division's human resource strategy traditionally had been to develop journeymen internally, rather than to recruit actively from other area employers. Mid-Michigan is heavily dominated by GM and by auto industry suppliers. Management did not like to strip workers from suppliers, as this tended to create ill will among area employers, including GM suppliers. Within the division, both the apprentice program and the EIT method were used to train employees or new hires to become journeymen. The preferred method was to use apprentices.

Two methods are used to retrain the existing work force in response to the introduction of new technologies. The first is in-plant classes on new technology soon to enter the plant. The second consists of on-the-job training with a vendor representative. This approach has been used only as a last resort because so few tradesmen can participate in such training.

Budgets for training were handled on a plant-by-plant basis. All of the plant's operating budget accounts paid for all training, including all the hours an apprentice spent at work. Thus, these learners were charged to the plant at the same rate and to the same accounts as journeymen. Training seminars by vendors were also charged to the plant, so that all training funds, except the tuition of apprentices, drained the plant operating budget and were subject to fluctuations in production schedules.

The rapid pace of technological change and a lack of up-to-date training among a significant portion of the existing work force made skilled-trades management recognize the full value of the apprentice program. Thus, skilled-trades general foremen began to expand the use of the apprentice program for employee training whenever possible, to discourage the use of EIT's where an apprentice program existed, and to improve both the classroom and in-plant curricula within the apprentice program. They also recognized that existing journeymen needed to update their own skills, as many had entered the trade years before.

1981 SKILLED-TRADES LAYOFF: THE SYSTEM IN ACTION

During the summer of 1981, the automobile industry in the United States was experiencing a deep recession and heightened international competition. Some plants in the component division had laid off more than 40 percent of their production employees due to lack of work and a changing product mix. The cut in production had not affected the skilled trades in this division because only 28 percent of the skilled-trades work was dependent on production. The remaining 72 percent consisted of project rearrangement and retooling, as part of GM's $40-billion capital investment program. By fall 1981, however, much of the changeover for the 1983 model year was complete, and some programs for 1984 and beyond had been postponed, sometimes indefinitely. The abrupt loss of work for the skilled-trades resulted in the decision to lay off more than one hundred skilled tradesmen.

The question facing the skilled-trades managers was how to achieve the reduction in force (RIF). Their most immediate problem was the fate of the apprentices.

The traditional solution was to take first all apprentices and nonseniority EITs (having less than four years of training) out of the trades. This had been done since 1970, and skilled tradesmen had been laid off in the 1974 recession. Apprentices and EITs would be removed from in-plant training and sent back to former production jobs if they held seniority in other departments in the plant. Most apprentices were low-seniority workers (less than five years) who did not hold production seniority; thus most would be laid off. The second group to be cut back would be seniority EITs; the third would be journeymen. This sequence, however, would effectively eliminate the apprentice class for a given trade and thus reduce or eliminate the number of employees with the most up-to-date training (albeit low experience).

General foremen were apprehensive about this method of reducing the work force, particularly with respect to its long-term effect on the apprentice program, for the following reasons.

1. Talented younger apprentices might be lost permanently.
2. The local community college where class work was conducted had made sacrifices to schedule classes for the apprentices and might be reluctant to recommend the program in the future if it were terminated now.
3. The skills taught to the apprentices were state-of-the-art for the plant and would become necessary as the apprentices became journeymen. The alternative method of training journeymen — in-house training — was expensive and often inefficient, because journeymen generally have less time for training.
4. The general foremen saw many good workers in the 1981 group of apprentices and in many cases would have preferred to keep these employees rather than certain other tradesmen. (This was not a determining factor in the end, but it did spur the investigation of alternatives to the traditional layoff approach.)
5. The general foremen saw the apprentice program as the best method of providing for future trained craftsmen and judged that the program should not be subject to cyclical flux, as it had been in the past. The circumstances provided a good opportunity to change the standard practice of reducing apprentices during low ebbs in the business cycle. In fact, 75 percent of the apprentices were close to completion of the training program.

These factors illustrate the changing focus of the division's human resource policy toward the generation of a well-trained, highly motivated future work force. The skilled-trades managers recognized this need and judged that the apprentice program should continue to provide the majority of the new tradesmen. Their judgment was based on several considerations, including the inadequate supply of a local skilled-labor pool. Outside hiring was less attractive as an alternative because new hires often came with bad habits, and because stealing workers from other local facilities was politically taboo. At the same time, however, scheduled production and corporate policies would not allow the maintenance of employees who did not have sufficient work.

The problem was how to carry out the RIF without losing the apprentices, many of whom would be journeymen within a year. This task had to be accomplished without alienating the remainder of the work force, without violating the union contract, and preferably with the cooperation of the local union.

As mentioned, the traditional method of accomplishing a RIF was unsatisfactory to the skilled-trades managers. Further, the union was not in favor of losing the apprentice class. First, many of the apprentices soon would graduate to journeyman status. Second, if outside journeymen were hired as in the past, they might be nonunion workers, whereas the apprentices came from the ranks of union-represented production workers. Third, the removal of the apprentice program was distasteful to union leaders, who had a long-standing commitment to the apprentice program.

Alternative Choices

The skilled-trades managers conferred with the divisional labor relations department about how best to address the problem. These managers indicated that they strongly supported the apprentice program, and that they did not favor traditional layoff practices in this case. With these criteria in mind, two options were proposed. The first was to lay off journeymen. The GM-UAW national agreement stipulated that maximum ratios of apprentices to journeymen must be maintained (1:8), and the mid-Michigan plants were well below this ratio. They could lay off journeymen in the seniority group without violating the contract, because journeymen were in a different seniority group than apprentices within the plant's local seniority agreement. This is typical of auto plant agreements.

However, this method had some serious shortcomings. Although the contract did not specifically recognize journeymen's seniority rights over apprentices, the corporation in the past had argued that experienced workers were more desirable than inexperienced ones. That is one of the rational bases for the seniority system from both union and management perspectives. In the national collective bargaining agreement, the corporation also had agreed to a "Statement on Technological Progress," which pledged that training would be provided as new technologies emerged (see Exhibit 6-3). The union might argue that the layoff of journeymen would reduce the number of trained employees while increasing the use of cheaper apprentice labor.

EXHIBIT 6-3
UAW and GM Statement on Technological Progress

Important recent changes in the contractual system that affect training include a "Statement on Technological Progress," introduced in the 1976 agreements at Ford and GM and elaborated in the 1979 agreements. This statement used the following language to commit the companies to rely on existing UAW-represented employees as a work force for any new technologies.

It is recognized that advances in technology may alter, modify, or otherwise change the job responsibility of represented employees at plant locations and that a change in the means, methods, or process of performing a function, including the introduction of computers or other new or advanced technology, will not serve to shift the work function from represented to nonrepresented employees.

The second alternative, which the labor relations department suggested, was to use the seniority rules for apprentices to maximum advantage. This option hinged on four key circumstances in this case.

1. The division had hired journeymen from the outside during the previous four years because of internal work-load requirements and the death of craftsmen in the area labor pool. These tradesmen had low divisional seniority.
2. The skilled-trades seniority rules as applied to the apprentice program stipulated that upon graduation the trades date of entry is set to *the beginning* of the apprentice program.
3. Most apprentices were within one year of completing the program. If they were laid off, they would not finish the program until they were rehired and placed back in the program.
4. The local union was sympathetic to both the apprentice program and the principle of equity for apprentices nearing the end of training.

This second option would allow apprentices to stay in the program, if on graduation they could hold seniority with the current journeymen, and if they were reasonably close to graduating. Thus, some journeymen could be laid off while apprentices in the same trade were kept, assuming that the journeymen's divisional date of entry was later than the date on which the apprentice had entered the apprentice program.

Course of Action

Division management chose to offer the union the second alternative, because it best satisfied the criteria set out by the general foremen and the labor relations staff. The plan was submitted to the management of each plant, and approval was given to approach the union with the proposed scheme. The labor relations staff spoke for the company in presenting the proposal informally to the president of the UAW local. A verbal agreement was reached at a subsequent meeting. The union agreed that it was more equitable to allow

TABLE 6-8   Trades Populations after Reduction in Force

	Journeymen — All Trades	Apprentices — Total and Less Than One Year to Completion
November 1981	1449	98 (74)
November 1982	1283	2 (0)

the short-term apprentices to finish where possible, in lieu of keeping an employee with less divisional skilled-trades seniority.

The layoffs resulting from the new policy initially included nine journeymen; nine apprentices in the same trades were retained. Later, because of further volume reductions, many more apprentices and journeymen were laid off. The population of tradesmen in the components division one year after the RIF decision is shown in Table 6-8.

Implications for Training/Apprenticeship Policies

The RIF policy that was adopted symbolized a compromise between the need to maintain a stable work force and the need to incorporate a younger work force with state-of-the-art technical skills. The results of the change in policy were not numerically spectacular. Of more than one hundred employees who were laid off, only nine were journeymen who would normally have stayed. From the skilled-trades managers' point of view, the overall scale of recession-induced layoffs had essentially killed the apprentice program. Those employees who had been attending classes at the local college were allowed to finish the semester, and many continued to attend classes while laid off. Yet, the policy clearly failed to attain the goal of keeping the apprentice program active even in the face of layoffs.

From the union's perspective, whenever employees who were nearing the completion of a long training process were laid off, an equity problem emerged. The new policy resolved this problem by allowing apprentices who were near completion to finish. However, the union continued to face the dilemma of how to represent all employees equally. The journeymen who were to be laid off because of the new policy were members of the same local union as the apprentices and other more senior journeymen. Yet, these people were laid off in lieu of nonjourneymen who had considerably less experience in the trade. The new policy was clearly not in the best interests of these employees, though their union representatives had agreed to it.

For the employees, then, the results appeared mixed. On the one hand, the new agreement recognized the special nature of training programs, and especially the apprentice program. On the other hand, the clear signal received by the laid-off journeymen was that the management and the union were concerned with protecting employees who had been with the company for some time. The laid-off journeymen probably would not stay in the area to await recall, because they had highly marketable skills even in the midst of economic downturn.

The chosen policy resolved a difficult dilemma in the short run: It allowed a number of young apprentices to complete their training and stay with the firm, but lost some skilled workers who will be needed when business conditions improve. Thus, the cyclical nature of the investment in training of blue-collar workers was not altered in this case. Indeed, tying the training budget directly to annual production levels predetermines the cyclical pattern of training. A question the managers of this division (and managers of blue-collar workers in many other United States firms) must yet answer is whether the training of skilled workers should remain a variable cost tied to production levels, or whether training should be budgeted and scheduled as a long-term capital investment.

Questions for Discussion

1. Each of the alternatives had certain advantages and risks. Other steps were also possible. Assess the alternative chosen. What are the implications for the union-management relationship?
2. In light of the pressures for change in this industry, what would you recommend as a *long-run* strategy for the training system in the component division? Specifically, what policy changes, if any, would you recommend for (a) information and planning, (b) budgeting, (c) training/retraining, and (d) staffing of this division?

Voluntary Severance Programs

The case of the Polaroid Corporation should provoke thinking about ways in which an organization can approach the problems involved in a massive scaling down of a work force. As the case illustrates, traditional solutions, while safe with respect to their likely consequences, are not always as effective as innovative approaches. However, the different interests of the affected employee and management groups render new and unfamiliar severance policies quite risky.

CASE
Polaroid

In the first nine months of 1981, Polaroid's profits plunged by 45 percent to $29.4 million on a 2 percent drop in sales of $974 million. Senior management found itself in the unenviable position of having to devise strategies to reduce its operating costs by 6 percent. To do this, it would have to reduce its work force by approximately 8 percent. This translated to almost one thousand

TABLE 6-9   Polaroid's Domestic Work Force — 1981

	Population	Percentage of Population
Exempt	4,418	34
Nonexempt	8,563	66
Total	12,981	100

persons from both exempt and nonexempt categories. (Table 6-9 shows a breakdown of the work force in 1981.) The options considered to achieve this goal included layoffs, early retirement, and a new retirement program called the voluntary severance program.

COMPANY BACKGROUND

Polaroid was founded in 1937 by Edwin H. Land who built and managed the company for forty-three years. In 1980 Land stepped down as chief executive officer to devote his time and energies to pure research. He was succeeded by William J. McCune, Jr. During Land's tenure, Polaroid expanded into the design, manufacturing, marketing, and distribution of three broad categories of products: (1) cameras and films used primarily by nonprofessionals, (2) photographic lines for professionals and industrial users, and (3) polarizing filters used in sunglasses and technical applications. It was Land's genius in research and development (R & D) that led to the phenomenal growth of the company during the 1950s and 1960s. Land's organizational philosophy was that "factory experience is a continuation of research experience." He stated:

> I have learned that every significant invention has several characteristics. By definition, it must be startling, unexpected, and must come to a world that is not prepared for it. If the world were prepared for it, it would not be much of an invention. (Polaroid, 1983)

Many observers of the company thought that Land's emphasis on R & D left the company without the strategic planning and marketing emphases necessary to flourish in the extremely competitive environment of the 1970s and 1980s. Consequently, when McCune, a Polaroid veteran with 41 years of service to the company, succeeded Land in 1980, new hopes flourished for the future of the company.

CONDITIONS, PHILOSOPHY, ALTERNATIVES

In 1980–81, United States companies were absorbing early recessionary shocks, but the ensuing recession forced many to lay off workers. Polaroid was no exception; the company quickly realized that normal attrition and an extremely low rate of hiring would not trim costs sufficiently. Any alternative, however, would have to be consistent with the company's philosophy toward personnel. Polaroid's genuine concern for the welfare of its employees is implicit in the founder's statement of purpose:

> . . . to give everyone working for Polaroid personal opportunity within the company for the full exercise of his talents; to express his opinions, to share in the progress of the Company as far as his capacities permit, to earn enough money so that the need for earning more will not always be the first thing on his mind — in short, to make his work here a fully rewarding important part of his life. (Polaroid, 1983)

Layoff

The first alternative management considered was layoffs. Polaroid's layoff policies were based strictly on seniority for nonexempt (hourly) employees. Department managers declared certain members of their areas surplus. A surplus member then had the right to bump any less senior employee in order to keep his or her job. The surplus member had to be qualified to bump into a new position, but during a layoff, *qualified* was interpreted loosely. These bumping rights meant that a surplus of even a small number of employees would ripple through the corporation over a period of several months. Three or four times the original number of employees could be affected.

During the last large-scale layoff in 1974, some areas had two or three new people a week moving into the same job. Training the new people was an almost worthless task since many were bumped a few days later from the jobs for which they had just been trained. The hidden cost of all this disruption was difficult to measure but clearly substantial.

Among exempt (salaried) workers, the situation was somewhat different. Polaroid's layoff policy granted no bumping rights to salaried employees (except those who had once been nonexempt), but it did guarantee that anyone with ten years' seniority in an exempt job would not be laid off. Hence, a job had to be found for any senior exempt employee declared surplus, and the burden of any exempt layoff would thus fall on the 33 percent of the exempt members with less than ten years' seniority.

A summary of seniority and exempt/nonexempt status is shown in Table 6-10. Two-thirds of the salaried employees had more than ten years' seniority and were protected from being laid off. Exempt employees with ten or more years seniority could, however, be required to change jobs as part of the organizational restructuring. Forty percent of the nonexempt employees had more than ten years and, although not specifically exempted from layoff, these

TABLE 6-10 Seniority Breakdown of Work Force

	Population	More than Ten Years' Seniority
Exempt	4,418	2,896 (66%)
Nonexempt	8,563	3,461 (40.4%)
Total	12,981	6,357 (49.2%)

members would not be likely layoff candidates. Many of these workers would also be subject to job changes as part of the realignment. Management estimated that approximately 25 percent of Polaroid's work force with less than 10 years' seniority would have to leave for the corporation to make the necessary 6 percent reduction in payroll. This estimate reflected both the limited number of low seniority people and the lowest salary levels.

Another possibility in terms of layoffs was to change the current policy by removing the ten-year exemption from the exempt group's layoff policy. Although this change would allow Polaroid to cut its total exempt work force, there was strong concern about making such a move immediately prior to a cutback.

Early Retirement

The second possibility was an early retirement program used at Polaroid in 1980. This early retirement program encouraged older workers to leave before the usual retirement age of 65 by offering a package of financial incentives. It had been limited to employees 55 and older with 15 or more years at Polaroid. Early retirement programs had become quite popular, and many companies had used them to trim their work forces and make way for younger workers. Polaroid had been pleased with the results of its program. A good mix of workers chose to leave, and Polaroid, which has no mandatory retirement age, did not find (as some feared it would) that only the most productive older workers left.

Voluntary Severance Program

The third alternative, a voluntary severance program, was a new twist on the early retirement program. It would allow anyone with more than ten years' seniority to leave the company, no matter what their age. Fully 66 percent of exempt personnel and 40.4 percent of nonexempt personnel met this requirement. These numbers accounted for almost half of the total work force. The details of this option as proposed by corporate staff were as follows. Full pay would be continued for five to thirty months depending on age and seniority. Those under 45 years of age would receive one month's pay for every two years' seniority. Those between 45 and 55 would receive gradually increasing amounts per year of seniority. From 55 to 62, one month's pay would be received for each year of seniority. After the age of 62, pay benefits would be reduced because of eligibility for social security, but no less than a full month's pay from the combined sources of income was allowed for each month of eligibility. The maximum number of months was thirty (two and one-half years of full pay). Participants could choose to receive the payments as a full month's pay, a half-month's pay for twice as many months, or a discounted (at 12 percent) lump sum.

In addition to these pay benefits, participants could maintain their medical, dental, and life insurance programs for up to two years by continuing to pay the same premium a current employee would pay. Those near retirement age would make a transition to Medicare and supplements when appropriate.

Accumulated vacation time would also be paid, and all vested benefits in the profit sharing plan and the pension plan would be made available.

The anticipated cost of this program was approximately $30,000 per employee. A total cost of approximately $30 million was anticipated if this option were selected.

Costs were not management's only concern with this alternative. In a way the program was a self-selected layoff, and as such had good and bad points and a high level of uncertainty. No other company had tried this sort of policy for employees of all ages, and Polaroid would be treading in unknown territory. What reaction would the employees have to the proposal? Of those eligible, would only the best (those with other job opportunities) leave? What would be the effects on those ineligible for the program? Lastly, would the business and financial communities view the program as forward thinking or foolhardy generosity that might damage the corporation's financial position?

ACTIONS AND RESULTS

Polaroid decided to implement the voluntary severance program (VSP) in order to cut Polaroid's payroll by 6 percent. The unusual nature of the program made it impossible to project whether it would achieve that goal. The program was voluntary and risky, and many in top management waited anxiously for the February 15, 1982, deadline, after which the program's impact in both monetary and nonmonetary terms could be evaluated.

As of the cutoff date, 934 employees, or 7.2 percent of the domestic population, had elected to participate in the voluntary severance program. This number represented almost 15 percent of those eligible; in terms of payroll reductions, it was close to the 6 percent Polaroid was seeking. The average age of VSP participants was 53.4 years, and the average seniority was 18.4 years.

Shortly after the program deadline, Polaroid, through an independent firm, conducted a telephone survey about the VSP. The survey included eligible members who had participated in the program, eligible members who had not participated, and noneligible employees. More than 600 people were interviewed. The employees overwhelmingly accepted the need for a cutback and were genuinely pleased that a form of self-selection was used to make the cuts.

More than 50 percent of the eligible members who did not participate said that they had made the decision to stay with the company before the end of November 1981. About 25 percent of the eligibles who stayed did not make their decision until January or February. Some of these people wanted to leave but could not make satisfactory arrangements before the deadline. A rash of resignations in the spring and early summer of 1982 confirmed that some of these people continued their job searches, and that although they received no benefits from VSP, it had served as a catalyst in their decision to move.

Of those who did leave, only 30 percent had announced their decision by the end of December. More than 40 percent announced their decision in the last two weeks of the program. Those who left did so for a variety of reasons; mentioned most often were age, the chance for early retirement, and the desire to do something new. Important contributing factors were limited growth potential, the chance to accumulate money, and general job dissatisfaction. Only 24 percent of the people who had left considered themselves retired, 44 percent were going to a new job, looking for a new job, or starting their own business. About 29 percent indicated they had made no future plans.

Across all categories of interviewees (leavers, stayers, or noneligibles), the survey found a high level of approval for the VSP package. Fully 83 percent thought the total package was either too generous (10 percent), generous (52 percent) or just right (21 percent). Little variation was found among the groups, although one might predict that the stayers would feel the package was not enough while the noneligibles might think it was too much. The noneligibles also said that the program made them feel positive about the future of the company.

Although a corresponding survey of Polaroid management has not been done, discussions indicated that many managers were skeptical of or entirely opposed to the program at the outset, but most were enthusiastic supporters by the deadline. First, and possibly most important, all the superstars did not leave the company. This result was predicted by the early retirement program of 1980, but nevertheless, many managers breathed a sigh of relief on February 16 when they realized that few, if any, of their outstanding employees had made the decision to leave.

Areas where new jobs were easy to find, such as data processing and electronics, took some losses, but these areas were predicted as problem areas before the program began. In most areas of the company, enough employees of high rank and pay left so that additional cutbacks were unnecessary. Rearrangement of the work force was necessary, but most managers looked at this as an opportunity to improve prior practices and try new approaches.

Finally, Polaroid recovered its costs by the third quarter of 1982. A traditional layoff may have appeared to recover costs a few months earlier, but from the point of view of most managers, the hidden costs of the bumping in a traditional layoff would have delayed the payback point further than the accounting numbers would indicate.

More Than Success

The success of the voluntary severance program for Polaroid has been undeniable. It was difficult to imagine how such a serious reduction in work force could have been made under more positive conditions. The company reduced its payroll by the required amount, but in doing so, it did not send employee morale crashing to new lows.

Management might not have taken the risks involved in the VSP without the experience of the early retirement program in 1980. Even with that experience, management was not sure what would happen. The results sold most of the skeptics, and if the need arose, Polaroid would probably be ready to try a similar program again. No company wants to face Polaroid's situation, but the method chosen to cope with the problem left both the corporation and its employees with a positive attitude toward the future — something a traditional layoff never could have done.

References

Land, Edwin H., "Selected Papers on Industry," Polaroid Corporation (Cambridge: Polaroid Corporation, 1983).

Questions for Discussion

1. Who are the major interest groups in this type of decision? What might their preferences be among the three alternatives?
2. Evaluate the three alternatives (pros/cons) from the perspective of the major interest groups.
3. What strategy would you have recommended? Why?
4. What would you recommend if in March 1982 it became clear that another $8 million labor cost reduction would be necessary on the basis of sales projections for the remainder of the year?

7

Compensation: Wages, Salaries, Benefits, and Incentives

No human resource management activity receives more attention and discussion among employees than compensation. It follows that no other human resource activity is likely to be a bigger potential asset or liability to the organization than its compensation policies. Yet, because the design and management of compensation systems involve much technical detail, top management and line managers are often only too willing to delegate responsibilities for these policies to human resource staff specialists. Often top management asks only, what is the overall cost of our wage, salary, and benefit plan, and can we get these costs down in some way? In times of austerity or crisis, line managers inevitably turn quickly to such devices as salary freezes or bonus suspensions, because labor costs are normally one of the largest "controllable" costs under their discretion.

In this chapter we introduce the basic principles of compensation management in a way that provides line managers with the information necessary to avoid the quick-fix approach to their compensation responsibilities. Consistent with the themes introduced in Chapter 4, managers will experience different pressures on their compensation systems when operating under different competitive conditions or when guided by different strategies. By understanding the basic principles that underlie effective compensation practices, line managers can better understand the adjustments their wage and salary policies will undergo during periods of organizational transition.

Most experts stress the following questions for assessing an organization's compensation system: (1) Is it equitable? (2) Does it satisfy legal requirements? (3) Is it competitive in the context of the external market? (4) Does it foster employee motivation and work performance? This chapter explores these four questions, which human resource professionals and line managers must consider in designing and administering compensation systems.

Importance and Scope of Compensation Systems

Compensation systems encompass the entire range of financial rewards employees receive from their employers, from direct wages and salaries to fringe benefits, and from product or service discounts to severance or retirement payments. The importance of the level, mix, and administration of compensation cannot be overemphasized. As noted in Chapter 2 (Figure 2-5), most occupational groups consistently rank pay first in importance in a long list of job attributes. Compensation determines an individual's and a family unit's standard of living, has a great influence on physical and psychological health, and can shape a person's perceptions of self-worth and social standing in the community.

Aside from its obvious importance to individual employees, effective compensation management can have important organizational consequences as well. Increases in compensation can contribute to work motivation and effort *if* employees see an explicit causal link between their job performance and their financial reward. This is the central proposition of *expectancy theory*, the most widely cited psychological model for explaining employee motivation (Vroom, 1964). Moreover, behavioral research has documented the organizational consequences of employee dissatisfaction with pay. Figure 7-1, adapted from Lawler (1971), summarizes the consequences, which include grievances, absenteeism, and strikes. Given the multiple individual and organizational consequences, managers should design and administer compensation policies with considerable care.

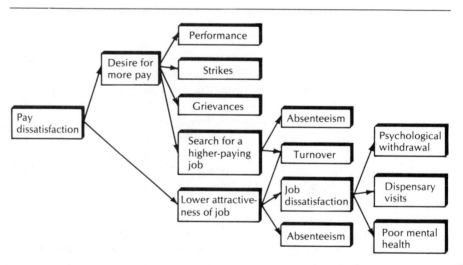

Source: Lawler, Edward, *Pay and Organizational Effectiveness* (New York: McGraw-Hill, 1971), 233. Reprinted by permission of McGraw-Hill Book Company.

FIGURE 7-1   Consequences of Pay Dissatisfaction

Issues in Wage and Salary Administration

Like other aspects of a human resource management system, compensation policies evolve in response to changes in the external environment and in the needs of the organization. As discussed in the life cycle model in Chapter 4, in the early stages of the life of an organization or business unit, compensation levels and policies tend to be ad hoc and driven by what the external market demands to attract needed talent. Over time, however, pressures for internal equity and for organizational efficiency require more formal compensation structures supported by administrative rules, external salary surveys, job evaluations, pay progression principles, and so on. After a compensation system is established, changes are usually made only at the margins; fundamental changes, such as changing from an individual piece rate to an hourly pay rate or changing the commission schedule for sales personnel, require tremendous effort, education, and communication. Thus, it is important that managers incorporate their concerns for equity, competitiveness, legality, and motivation into the compensation systems from the start.

Legal Considerations

The federal government sets minimum compensation levels under the Fair Labor Standards Act, the core of which establishes the federal minimum wage. The current minimum is \$3.35 per hour. This minimum has been adjusted upward periodically over the years; this level was set in legislation passed in 1978.

Some states have their own minimum wage laws, which can set a minimum higher than the national minimum. Most state laws cover employees who fall outside the scope of the federal act (mainly employees of state and local governments and of small firms that do not engage in interstate commerce). Federal wage-and-hour laws also specify requirements for overtime pay for nonexempt workers (nonsalaried, nonsupervisory employees). Currently federal law requires that overtime be paid at a rate of 150 percent of the normal pay for time worked over forty hours a week.

Levels of Compensation

Different levels of compensation for various employee groups derive from the quality of employees needed for effective operation, the availability of the employees deemed necessary for the job, the competition for these employees, and the financial soundness of the organization. Existing compensation levels for specific groups can be changed in marginal ways by external factors, such as competition that bids up the salaries and wages in occupations with a shortage of certain skilled workers. Increases in the consumer price index, on the other hand, put pressures on the compensation levels of all employees.

Uses of Surveys

Formal data-gathering and reference to published materials will tell an organization where it stands in relation to the competition and guide the establishment of rates for new positions. Sources of information include compensation consulting firms, leading employers in the area, employer associations, and government agencies, or, if resources and expertise are available, ad hoc and company-specific surveys.

Even if the goal is simply to match the competition, anecdotal evidence alone cannot provide all the necessary data. A compensation survey shows if the listed jobs are similar in content to those in the organization of interest. For example, a survey of pay rates for systems analysts requires complex analysis. In one company, a person with this job title might be the system architect in charge of programming and system implementation; in another firm, the position may consist only of programming in FORTRAN or BASIC. The personnel department often cooperates with local, regional, or national associations, depending on the labor market for the occupational areas in question.

A firm's position in relation to its competition should be based on an explicit decision, not on happenstance. When a firm has accurate knowledge of the going rate, it can decide whether to meet it, to exceed it, or to offer lower rates while using other means to attract and retain employees. The efficiency and effectiveness of the value-added processes within a firm may be crucial to the establishment of its rates; higher work force productivity should be met with higher pay. If productivity is to be an important criterion for compensation decisions, it will need to be measured and assessed periodically, both for the organization as a whole and for specific work groups and departments (see Chapter 9).

A firm's ability to pay will be a primary determinant of its position in the wage hierarchy in a community. In recent years, the ability-to-pay issue has gained attention in basic industries such as auto and steel. The unions, in exchange for greater job security, have made concessions to managements by accepting salary cuts or only small increases. Moreover, in response to increased variability in market conditions and ability to pay, the uses of various contingent forms of compensation, such as profit sharing, have increased in an effort to tie variations in compensation costs more directly to the economic performance of the firm.

Although published survey data can aid in starting the process of setting or adjusting compensation, it is also necessary to go beyond the numbers and job titles and to tailor the data to the organization in question. Tables 7-1 and 7-2, for example, show a comparison of rates for persons in some high technology jobs. The data show different levels and changes for different areas of the country.

Setting compensation levels for job classifications within a company is contingent upon the work to be performed (job descriptions), industry and area pay levels, and the supply and demand for workers.

TABLE 7-1 Average Salaries: Programmers/Analysts

	1982			1983			1982–1983 % Change		
	United States	Metropolitan Areas	Establishments Employing 2,500 Workers or More	United States	Metropolitan Areas	Establishments Employing 2,500 Workers or More	United States	Metropolitan Areas	Establishments Employing 2,500 Workers or More
Programmers/Programmer Analysts I	17,535	17,527	19,056	19,777	19,621	21,396	12.7	11.9	12.2
Programmers/Programmer Analysts II	20,629	20,663	22,332	22,148	22,229	23,640	7.3	7.5	5.8
Programmers/Programmer Analysts III	25,192	25,306	27,432	26,224	26,258	27,444	4.0	3.8	0.04
Programmers/Programmer Analysts IV	29,165	29,415	31,368	31,444	31,532	32,496	7.8	7.2	3.4
Programmers/Programmer Analysts V	35,430	35,485	36,768	38,125	38,196	39,096	7.6	7.6	6.3

Source: Bureau of Labor Statistics, national survey of professional, administrative, technical and clerical pay, March 1982 and September 1983.

TABLE 7-2   Median Salaries: Computer Professionals

	1982 ($000)	1983 ($000)	% Change
Engineering/Scientific Programmers and Programmer Analysts			
6 months–1 year	20.1	20.7	2.9
1 year–2 years	22.0	24.4	10.9
2 years–4 years	26.2	28.8	9.9
More than 4 years	32.0	33.8	5.6
Mini/Micro Computer Programmers and Programmer Analysts			
6 months–1 year	19.7	20.9	6.0
1 year–2 years	22.9	24.0	4.8
2 years–4 years	26.6	27.7	4.1
More than 4 years	32.8	34.5	5.2
Telecommunications Programmers and Programmer Analysts			
1 year–2 years	25.3	26.6	5.1
2 years–4 years	30.6	30.7	0.3
More than 4 years	36.2	37.5	3.6

Source: EDP, Computer Salary Survey and Career Planning Guide, 1982 and 1983.

Some of these factors are illustrated in Tables 7-1 and 7-2, which give average and median salaries for programmer analysts in 1982 and 1983. Tables such as these are helpful in providing general information on trends, but for a particular company to set salary levels, it is necessary to compare job descriptions, experience, geographical area, and size of company.

Table 7-1, which compares programmers/programmer analysts job levels, indicates that programmers in metropolitan areas make slightly more than programmers in the United States as a whole. Programmers in companies with 2,500 or more employees earn significantly more (approximately 10 percent) than programmers in the United States as a whole.

When the programmer/analyst job is broken down into the three job classifications in Table 7-2, both the job descriptions and demand for these workers help explain the significant differences in pay among telecommunications, mini/micro computer, and engineering/scientific programmers. Both demand and requirements for telecommunications programmers are higher. A bachelor's degree in electrical engineering or computer science and at least one year of assembly language are highly desirable. The other two classifications do not require such degrees. Thus, the median salaries of telecommunications programmers are higher than the salaries of other types of programmers.

Cost of Living

The rate of change in the cost of living is often reflected either formally or informally in wage and salary adjustments. The failure of compensation to keep pace with changes in the cost of living can cause serious dissatisfaction within an organization, as employees find it harder to maintain their standards of living. About 60 percent of major collective contracts include cost-of-living adjustment clauses (C.O.L.A.), which automatically trigger increases in base rates to reflect all or, more likely, part of the increase in the consumer price index over the previous period. In nonunion firms, cost of living tends to affect salary increases more subtly by reducing the pool of money available for merit increases. As discussed in the following section, the combination of rapid inflation and growing market competition for entry-level employees can create severe salary compression between entry-level workers and longer-service employees.

Wage and Salary Equity

Organizational status is often determined by wage and salary levels, as well as by the benefits and perquisites associated with key positions. Even more important to employees than comparability with people in other organizations is the knowledge that compensation is equitable *within* their organization. When employees compare themselves with others in the organization on the basis of skill, type of work, span of control, seniority, work conditions, or other factors and find that they are not at least equal to others in the categories most relevant to them, they can become extremely dissatisfied. The principle of internal equity was captured by William H. Davis (1943), in a War Labor Board report issued during World War II:

> There is no single factor in the whole field of labor relations that does more to break down morale, create individual dissatisfaction, encourage absenteeism, increase labor turnover and hamper production than obviously unjust inequalities in the wage rates paid to different individuals in the same labor group within the same plant.

Although Davis was referring only to nonexempt employees, his statement holds true for salaried and technical employees. Although some organizations keep wage and salary information confidential, most firms tacitly or explicitly recognize that this information moves through the grapevine if it is not offered formally. This *grapevine effect* heightens the importance of internal pay equity; office or shop floor communication is usually quite good. Often wage information is explicitly public, such as in labor contracts, in job postings, or through other communication channels. For exempt positions, this information is more likely to be private, but it still manages sometimes to move through the organizational grapevine.

Salary compression problems producing internal inequity recently have occurred in occupations where the demand for employees is extremely high. Some organizations have made offers to recently graduated electrical engineers at salaries equal to or even exceeding those of long-time employees. Although recruiters make high starting offers only to meet competition in the labor market, often no one considers appropriate adjustments in the internal labor market. The result has been labeled *salary compression*. Compensation policies often involve such dilemmas, but problems like salary compression must be dealt with if an organization is to avoid lowering employee morale and increasing turnover.

Most firms deal with the equity issue through some form of job evaluation, but this method does not directly address what each job is worth to the organization. This latter issue is connected with the equal employment opportunity question of comparable worth (see Chapter 13), which most often arises when jobs are typically occupied by one sex, such as nursing or plumbing (Livernash, 1980).

Job Evaluation

Job evaluation, which differs from employee performance appraisal, begins with a job description and analysis (Pigors and Myers, 1981; Heneman et al., 1983), and allows for a comparison of a given job with other jobs in the organization. Some job criteria, such as education needed, weight lifted, working conditions, and the like, can be calculated objectively; others, such as the complexity of duties, ingenuity, mental demands, strategic responsibility, or negotiation results, cannot. As such, the process is always partially subjective, though it never involves the evaluation of employees.

Although almost all firms will use the same criteria (education, experience, initiative, physical demand, safety of others, and working conditions) for hourly jobs, firms will assign different weights to these criteria when evaluating salaried jobs. For example, "physical effort" would not show up on most managerial job evaluation schemes, although it may be essential to assessing the worth of a manual job. On the other hand, education and experience would hold greater weight in evaluating a managerial job.

Four main types of job evaluation systems are currently in use in major United States companies. These include evaluations by rank, by classifications, by points, and by factors. Each is suitable for certain types of organizations, depending on their size, the complexity of their production functions, and the preferences of top managements.

The *rank method* is the simplest. Managers rank positions in terms of complexity, job requirements, working conditions, or other elements relevant to the organization. Inherent in this method is a large degree of subjectivity; as such, ranking cannot be effectively used in organizations with more than fifteen or twenty job classifications. The ranking process by definition produces an ordinal scale whereas the difference between, say, jobs ranked 3 and 4 may not be the same as the difference between jobs ranked 11 and 12. Inequities in ranking may result in pay scales that do not reflect the differences among jobs on the variables of interest. For example, if the ranking system were used for the jobs listed in Table 7-3, the pay difference between 1 and 2 might be the same as that between 5 and 6; but this assessment probably would be less accurate than an assessment based on a formal job analysis.

Classification systems rely more heavily on detailed data obtained in a job analysis. The job analysis is used to establish pay grades (or groups) and to develop written definitions of each grade. The grades are then arranged in a hierarchy, and every position in the organization is assigned to a particular grade. This process essentially extends the rank method with grades or classifications within each rank. The federal government's pay scheme is built around this type of system. Ranks and classifications are built into a matrix, with ranks on the vertical axis and grades or classifications on the horizontal axis. Each division or functional area within an organization sets various skill or experience bench marks for the classifications and sets the pay at an appropriate rate.

An example of the matrix for a small information systems department is given in Table 7-4. With skill enhancement or experience, those ranked *programmer* might move from grade 1 through grade 6, or they might jump to the programmer analyst rank without going through all the grades in the programmer rank.

The *point system* is most commonly used in large organizations (see Table 7-5. The features to which points are assigned include skill, effort, job conditions, and responsibility. Each of these can contain many different subsets; for example, responsibility can be subdivided

TABLE 7-3   Simple Ranking Method from Lowest to Highest

1. Secretary/Key Punch
2. Assistant Programmer
3. Programmer
4. Programmer/Analyst
5. Systems Analyst
6. Project Manager

TABLE 7-4   Weekly Pay Rate by Grade or Classification

Ranking	1	2	3	4	5
1. Secretary/Key Punch	$182.00	$215.00	$240.00	$302.00	$353.00
2. Assistant Programmer	$196.00	$229.00	$290.00	$346.00	$384.00
3. Programmer	$272.00	$326.00	$383.00	$475.00	$547.00
4. Programmer/Analyst	$380.00	$425.00	$504.00	$604.00	$733.00
5. Systems/Analyst	$434.00	$474.00	$564.00	$668.00	$826.00
6. Project Manager	$515.00	$548.00	$654.00	$764.00	$965.00

TABLE 7-5   Point Method: Job Evaluation Rank Points

	Skill	Effort	Job Con- ditions	Res- ponsi- bility	Total	Competitive Position Value (Bench Mark $/Year)	(Bench Mark $/Week)
1. Secretary/Key Punch	30	30	40	30	130	$12,480	$240
2. Assistant Programmer	40	40	40	40	160	$15,080	$290
3. Programmer	50	50	35	75	210	$19,960	$383
4. Programmer Analyst	75	70	30	100	275	$26,208	$504
5. Systems Analyst	90	80	30	105	305	$29,328	$564
6. Project Manager	100	100	30	125	355	$34,008	$654

into span of control, number of employees supervised, budgets, product responsibility, geographic area, and so on. Each element and subelement has degrees associated with it, as well as an explicit number of points. To arrive at a total number of points, the elements are weighted according to company priorities and managerial judgments and are added up. The total might then be multiplied by a dollar amount for each point. In this manner, all of the elements of each position are built into the salary figure.

We emphasize that the point system is only as accurate or objective as the rating scales built into it; the scales likewise are only as objective as the conceptions of jobs and the responsibilities of the people who construct them. Over time and with considerable effort, this system can become more objective than the rank and classification methods. The processes of reliability testing and validation, however, can be time-consuming and costly.

The *factor method* is another refinement of the rank system; this fourth system ranks separately the various factors required for each job rather than the job as a whole. The factor method usually is limited to five *compensable factors*. Because factoring is hinged to key jobs within an organization by way of comparison on compensable factors, it is almost always custom-made for a specific organization.

The compensable factors are usually: (1) mental requirements, (2) physical requirements, (3) skill requirements, (4) responsibility, and (5) working conditions (see Table 7-6). *Key jobs* serve as the standards against which other jobs in the organization can be compared. Key jobs usually are performed by a significant number of people within

TABLE 7-6 Factor Comparison Method*

$ Per Hour Per Factor	Mental Requirements	Skill Requirements	Physical Requirements	Responsibility	Working Conditions
$1.00	Secretary/Key Punch	Secretary/Key Punch		Secretary/Key Punch	Assistant Programmer Programmer Programmer/Analyst
$1.50	Assistant Programmer	Assistant Programmer	Assistant Programmer Programmer Programmer/Analyst	Assistant Programmer	Secretary/Key Punch
$2.00	Programmer	Programmer	Secretary/Key Punch	Programmer	
$2.50	Programmer/Analyst			Programmer/Analyst	
$3.00		Programmer/Analyst			
$3.50					
$4.00					

*By adding up the dollars-per-hour values associated with each factor shown in this table, we would get the following hourly wages for these jobs: secretary/key punch operator, $6.50; assistant programmer, $7.00; programmer, $9.00; and programmer/analyst, $11.00.

the organization and have relatively standard external comparisons, so they remain stable in content over time. For example, in a manufacturing operation, tool maker and electrician might be key jobs; in a data processing shop, computer operator and systems analyst might fill this role. Job descriptions and specifications must be carefully assembled for key jobs. The relative importance of the factors must then be assessed for each job, and money values per hour assigned to each factor. An example of this method is shown in Table 7-6.

After the factors are assembled, each job within the organization is compared to the key jobs on each of the dimensions and is judged to be higher, lower, or the same. In this way, the entire wage or salary structure is constructed. It can be altered by reassessing the monetary amounts for each of the key job attributes. The structure may be altered, for example, by meeting the salaries for these jobs in competing organizations, or by changing key jobs or creating new ones for emerging functions within the organization.

The main advantage of the factor system is that it is firm-specific; yet, it also allows for a comparison with the external labor market. The system must reflect the skills and attributes that are considered most important to the organization, and the points assigned should produce a wage that is competitive in current market conditions. The main disadvantage of this system is that it focuses on only five factors, which can lead to an underestimation of differences among jobs, especially in modern, complex organizations. The technique is most suited to traditional, stable technology organizations where the key jobs have remained unchanged for a relatively long period.

One can find many other methods of job evaluation, but they are essentially variations on these four types. Some specific schemes, such as the Hay system, have been developed by private firms and then sold to other organizations. The Hay system compares jobs across an array of client organizations and assigns job points on the basis of three factors: accountability, problem solving, and know-how. Every job is given a maximum number of points across the three dimensions, and a dollar amount is assigned to each point. The range of points can be wide. For example, a low-level clerical worker may have a point total of only 150, whereas the chief executive in the same company may rate 3,000 points. The advantage of the Hay system is that it offers comparability across organizations on the basis of the Hay organization's data base, as well as continued updates using the standardized job dimensions.

All organizations have job evaluation systems, though sometimes only tacitly. As firms grow and attention must be paid to internal equity as well as to the external labor market, a more formalized job evaluation structure becomes imperative. All four evaluation systems, however, inherently contain a certain amount of subjectivity and must be viewed as such. Also, because of this subjectivity, different job evaluation systems will result in different wage and salary scales. For this reason, an organization's choice about which to use will have important consequences for internal and external pay equity as well as the morale and motivation among its employees.

Finally, some organizations have moved from the practice of paying blue-collar workers on the basis of specific jobs performed or job assignments toward a pay-for-knowledge system. Under this new approach, employees in a given work unit or team are trained in all the jobs performed by the team, and job rotation is encouraged. An employee's pay rate is based on the number of skills or jobs that he or she has mastered. Usually, the team or the team's supervisor certifies when an employee has mastered a new skill or job. Although this system still requires some form of job evaluation, the pay depends on the range of skills mastered, rather than on the specific job performed on a specific day. This pay system is discussed more fully in Chapter 11.

Indirect Compensation and Incentive Systems

The term *fringe benefits* is widely used, but in the 1980s it has become a misnomer. Before 1930, fringe benefits accounted for less than one percent of payroll; by 1980, fringes had risen to more than 40 percent of payroll, and the increase continues. In all job categories shown in the U.S. Chamber of Commerce data in Table 7-7, we see a significant increase in fringes as a percentage of payroll.

Even more dramatic, as Table 7-8 shows, from 1955 to 1975 the

TABLE 7-7 Benefits Costs: 1959, 1969, 1980 (as a percentage of payroll)

	1959	1969	1980
Total benefit costs	24.7	31.1	41.4
Legally required benefits	3.5	5.3	8.1
Pension, insurance, and other agreed upon payments	8.5	10.4	15.2
Rest periods, lunch breaks	2.2	3.1	3.8
Payments for time not worked (holidays, vacations, etc.)	8.4	10.1	11.9
Profit sharing, bonuses	2.1	2.2	2.4

Source: Employee Benefits, 1980. Chamber of Commerce of the United States, Washington, D.C., 1980, 27. Reprinted by permission.

TABLE 7-8 Cost Changes for Selected Factors: 1955–1975

Factors	Rise in Cost 1955–1975
Average base annual income	+92%
Consumer price index	+98.6%
Corporate taxes	+100%
Benefits	+397%

TABLE 7-9   Benefit Program Objectives and Criteria

Objectives	Criteria
1. Reduced turnover	1. Cost
2. Improved morale	2. Ability to pay
3. Enhanced security	3. Need
	4. Union power
	5. Tax considerations
	6. Public relations
	7. Social responsibility
	8. Work force reactions

annual base income for workers rose by 92 percent, the consumer price index went up by 99 percent, and benefits rose by almost 400 percent (Hanna, 1977). According to the Chamber of Commerce, the total price for United States employee benefits in 1980 was $435 billion. The increasing popularity of indirect compensation stems from legal requirements, paternalistic employer policies and/or competitive pressures, economies of scale, trade unionism, and tax considerations.

The objectives and criteria of benefit programs are shown in Table 7-9; the most ubiquitous benefits are shown in Table 7-10. These are divided into four categories: (1) employee security payments, (2) payments for time not worked, (3) bonuses and awards, and (4) service programs. Some of the more important emerging benefits include dental insurance, legal insurance, home-financing aid, loan funds, health facilities or club membership subsidies, and a variety of stock-option plans. Payment for time not worked, such as personal days, vacation time, and holidays, is also on the increase.

Yet another important trend is toward cafeteria-style benefit programs, where a company allows employees to choose from a list of benefits that may total the monetary level tied to a particular job classification. This trend evolved in response to the dramatic increase in two-earner families and to differing priorities among employee groups regarding current versus future income. The pros and cons of flexible benefit programs are shown in Table 7-11.

Employers are legally required to offer all employees old age, survivors, and disability insurance (OASDI); workers' compensation; unemployment compensation; and often state disability insurance. OASDI is commonly called Social Security; together with Medicare, it is jointly funded by employer and employee contributions calculated as a percentage of gross earnings (to a maximum individual tax for each year). In 1984, the rates were 7 percent for the employer and 6.7 percent for the employee. In 1965, Medicare was added to Social Security; Medicare is divided into health insurance, financed directly by OASDI deductions, and supplementary medical insurance (SMI), financed by participants at an $11-per-month rate and matched by the federal government. SMI aids in the payment of medical bills and other health-related goods and services.

TABLE 7-10   Common Employee Benefits

Employee Security Payments	Payments for Time Not Worked	Bonuses and Awards	Service Programs
1. Legally required employer contributions: old age, survivors, disability, and health insurance; unemployment compensation; workers' compensation; state disability insurance	1. Call-back and call-in pay	1. Holiday premiums	1. Annual reports to employees
2. Supplemental unemployment benefits	2. Clean-up time	2. Overtime premiums	2. Athletic teams
3. Accident insurance	3. Dental-care time	3. Shift premiums	3. Beauty parlors
4. Disability insurance	4. Death-in-the-family leave	4. Weekend premiums	4. Cafeteria and canteen services
5. Hospitalization insurance	5. Downtime	5. Anniversary awards	5. Club membership payments
6. Life insurance	6. Family allowances	6. Attendance bonus	6. Company housing
7. Medical insurance	7. Holiday pay	7. Christmas bonus	7. Company newspaper
8. Surgical insurance	8. Jury duty time	8. Quality bonus	8. Company stores
9. Pensions	9. Layoff pay	9. Safety awards	9. Credit union
10. Contributions to savings plans	10. Medical time	10. Profit-sharing bonus	10. Dances
11. Contributions to stock purchase plans	11. Military service allowance	11. Service bonus	11. Dietetic advice
12. Home financing	12. National Guard duty	12. Suggestion award	12. Discount on company products
13. Payment of optical expenses	13. Lunch periods	13. Waste-elimination bonus	13. Educational assistance
14. Health and welfare funds	14. Portal-to-portal pay	14. Year-end bonus	14. Food subsidies
	15. Religious holidays		15. Income tax service
	16. Reporting pay		16. Legal aid
	17. Rest periods		17. Library and reading room facilities
	18. Room and board allowance		18. Loan funds
	19. Severance pay		19. Lunch period entertainment and music at work
	20. Sick leave		20. Magazine subscription payments
	21. Supper money		21. Medical examinations
	22. Time spent on collective bargaining		22. Nursery
	23. Time spent on grievance		23. Parking
	24. Vacation time		24. Parties and picnics
	25. Voting time		25. Purchasing service
	26. Witness time		26. Savings plans

Source: Andre F. Sikula and John F. McKenna, *The Management of Human Resources* (John Wiley and Sons, 1984), 298–301. Reprinted by permission.

TABLE 7-11   Advantages and Disadvantages of Flexible Benefit Programs

Advantages	Disadvantages
Employees choose packages that best satisfy their unique needs.	Employees make bad choices and find themselves uncovered for predictable emergencies.
Flexible benefits help firms meet the changing needs of a changing work force.	Administrative burdens and expenses increase.
Increased involvement of employees and families improves understanding of benefits.	If employees pick only benefits they will use, the high level of use drives up the cost of the benefit.
Flexible plans make introduction of new benefits less costly. The new option is merely added as one among a variety of elements from which to choose.	

Source: George T. Milkovich and Jerry Newman, *Compensation* (Plano, Tex.: Business Publications, forthcoming 1984).

Unemployment insurance is administered primarily by the states and is funded solely by employer contributions. Premiums are based on an employer's experience rating: Employers with stable work forces pay low rates; those with cyclical or seasonal businesses pay higher rates. Employees who are laid off can collect a certain amount of compensation for a specified period, as determined by the state. The maximum benefit levels vary by states.

Workers' compensation pays medical bills and at least partial wages or salaries for workers injured on the job. Employers pay all costs of this coverage, and private carriers or state insurance funds administer the claims and payments. Several states require disability insurance coverage as well.

Buying insurance can be significantly less expensive when done on a group basis. Indeed, an individual with certain health problems may not be able to acquire certain kinds of insurance alone. By providing insurance benefits, a company reduces the cost for each employee, since the risk is spread over a large number of people. Moreover, the purchase of benefits can be deducted as an expense by the employer and is not counted as taxable income for the employee. Tax laws thus make the provision of insurance benefits especially attractive for both employer and employee.

Tax advantages apply to the wide array of benefits listed in Table 7-10, except those in the pay-for-time-not-worked category. The higher the tax bracket, the more important and the more cost effective the provision of benefits becomes. It is not surprising, therefore, that surveys constantly show that, in direct proportion to salary level, employee preferences tend toward fringe benefits as opposed to salary increases.

Recognition of the particular value of long-term and loyal employees has led some firms to extend their benefit programs. The Dyer et al. reading in Chapter 6 illustrated this point with reference to employment stabilization policy. Some employers have gone beyond the provision of health insurance, jointly funded pension programs, and disability benefits by providing such exotica as physical fitness facilities, stress reduction programs, marital counseling, and the like.

As we stressed in Chapter 4, employers' inclination toward a paternalistic view of employees develops from top management's values, the rate of growth and the scarceness of talent in the industry, and a firm's ability to pay. An array of benefits, in conjunction with activities that foster friendship and familial attitudes, can provide long-term stability in the work force and, by reducing turnover, may enhance the firm's profitability.

Note that most firms that employ these policies do so from the beginning of the organization's history. Thus, the full fringe-benefits policy is both engrained in the value system or culture and helpful in retaining key talent during the growth stages of the firm's life cycle — times when turnover costs are high and retention of talent is crucial to the firm's strategies.

The recent increase in benefits derives from another factor that is of increasing importance in the 1980s. The attraction and retention of employees in emerging occupations that are in short supply often depend on the ability of the company to offer competitive salaries *and* benefits. Society's increased emphasis on leisure time, physical fitness, and careers mandates careful, fully competitive planning of the packages offered to new and continuing employees.

Trade unions historically have obtained a variety of benefits for their members. Before the 1930s, unions did not bother to push for government provision of unemployment and disability insurance. Rather, they viewed such insurance as an element of the contribution of collective bargaining to social welfare. At the same time, this arrangement enhanced the attractiveness of unions in the eyes of both members and nonmembers. Since the 1930s, however, unions have pressed for improvements in social insurance and fringe benefits through both collective bargaining and legislative lobbying. Studies have consistently shown, for example, that unions have achieved significantly better fringe benefit packages for their members through collective bargaining than are provided to comparable nonunion members (Freeman, 1981).

Most companies fail to educate and update employees on the cost changes for benefits (particularly health insurance), or to communicate effectively the usage and complexity of their benefit packages. Some firms, however, design communications strategies to address this problem; for example, IBM's dental plan pays a fixed fee for certain dental procedures. Over a set period the amount paid will not cover 100 percent of the cost of those procedures, a fact noted by employees. Periodically and with great fanfare, IBM announces increases in payments for various procedures, which the company believes will increase awareness of the cost of provision and have an immediate positive effect on employees.

Finally, benefits can also consist of perquisites, or perks — benefits available to top executives. Perks reflect the notion that rank has its privileges. They can include special parking places and dining rooms, legal and personal counseling services, vacation homes, and memberships in country clubs. The provision of perks depends to a great extent on an organization's values and past practices. For example, some of the remaining large railroad companies still offer their executives the use of personal railcars for their travels. Although expensive, this service reflects a time-honored tradition. Other organizations, operating under more egalitarian philosophies, choose not to provide special parking places or dining facilities for their executives. These sorts of perks may diminish because of the Internal Revenue Service's current attention to such benefits. If perks are converted to cash for the purpose of income tax payments, compensation experts and executives alike may reconsider more seriously their inherent liabilities.

The trend toward more indirect compensation should continue, along with an increasing emphasis on its creative, efficient use as a method of motivation and retention. We emphasize, however, that little empirical research supports the notion that the provision of benefits directly increases the motivation and productivity of workers. Nonetheless, because many people still believe deeply in the positive relationship between bottom-line results and competitive benefit packages, present trends are likely to continue.

Long-Term Incentives and Bonuses

Executive compensation plans usually differ from other compensation plans in the organization. Executive packages often provide both short-term (usually one year) and long-term incentive plans, which typically include stock-option or equity components. Some firms also apply bonuses and incentives to lower-level employees, but these tend to be tied to production quotas, sales incentives, or group performance (such as the Scanlon plan, discussed in Chapter 11).

Yearly bonus plans have been gaining popularity in all but nonprofit and regulated industries. Organizations want top management's pay to be more directly tied to the economic performance of the firm. According to a 1978 Conference Board survey, bonus plans are most popular in manufacturing, construction, and retail trade industries and least popular in utilities and insurance companies (Fox, 1978). The belief that there is a relationship between effort, motivation, and pay has even permeated the federal government, which has instituted a bonus plan (CITATION) for certain cadres of high-level executives. Although short-term bonus plans have become more common, a number of critics have stressed the need to restructure top-management compensation incentives. Such restructuring should encourage greater attention to long-term asset-building objectives, while discouraging short-term profit or income-per-share objectives.

Sometimes companies create bonus pools to be divided among a group of executives; these are limited by the company's performance.

Small bonuses or no bonuses will reflect years of poor performance; high bonuses will reflect good years. Bonuses typically are worth less than 25 percent of salary but can rise to 100 percent or more in certain industries.

Long-term incentive plans and discounted purchases of stocks or stock surrogates are currently gaining even more popularity. Box 7-1

BOX 7-1
Overview of Stock Plans

Incentive Stock Options

Employees can purchase up to $100,000 worth of company stock per year at the market value of the stock and can declare income from the stock's appreciation as nontaxable long-term capital gain, as long as they hold the stock for at least two years after they are granted this option, and at least one year after they buy the stock.

Nonqualified Stock Options

Employees can purchase as much stock as they want, sometimes at prices below the stock's market value. They can consider appreciation in the value of the stock as long-term capital gain if they hold it for at least a year, and they can take a tax deduction for the full amount of the purchase.

Stock Appreciation Rights

Employees do not need to make an investment in stock, but are paid some percentage (up to 100 percent) of the value of the stock's appreciation over time. They must declare the income as taxable.

Performance Share/Unit Plans

Employees are paid the value of a certain amount of company stock, usually every one to two years, contingent on their ability to meet specific company goals, usually over a three-to-five-year period. This income is taxable, but if payment is in stocks rather than simply their value, the appreciation can be declared as long-term capital gain if the stocks are held for at least a year.

Restricted Stock Plans

Employees are awarded stock or can purchase stock at lower than market rates, at the end of a certain period of employment with the company. They can declare the stock's appreciation as long-term capital gain if they hold it for more than a year, but they must pay taxes on dividends.

Phantom Stock Plans

Employees are awarded units that mature parallel with stock appreciation, which they are paid at the end of some period of employment. If held for more than a year, the units can be declared as long-term capital gain.

summarizes the current mix of stock plans and their tax advantages to employers and employees.

The recent increase in the number of mergers and acquisitions in American industry has led to the golden-parachute practice in which an executive protects his or her income with an agreement that provides a lump sum or salary continuity if he or she is displaced after an unfriendly takeover by another firm. Myers's article following this chapter describes an increasing number of recent critiques of this type of plan.

Summary

The wages or salaries an organization pays its employees comprise only the most visible parts of its compensation policies. The mixture of the various elements in a compensation package, together with that package's relative standing in the market, consists of a diverse range of factors, all of which must be balanced carefully to meet the criteria of equitability, legality, competitiveness, and motivation.

Whether a compensation package is equitable depends not only on comparative pay levels, but also on employees' and managers' perceptions of fairness with respect to the internal labor market and to the firm's ability to pay. The legal requirements affecting compensation packages entail consideration not only of federal and state minimum-wage laws, but also of the rules governing employers' and employees' contributions to and benefits from the government's social programs. The competitiveness of a compensation package hinges not only on pay levels, but also on the company's benefits, work environment, internal promotional possibilities, and a host of other factors. Finally, whether a compensation package motivates employees and improves work performance depends not only on the qualities of the work force, but also on how a company chooses to balance the equitability, legality, and competitiveness of its compensation policies.

The single most dramatic change in the compensation policies of most firms since World War II has been the explosion of benefits as a percentage of total compensation. This trend has forced compensation experts and human resource managers to reassess more traditional means of recruiting and retaining the employees necessary to fulfill a firm's strategic objectives. Competitive salaries are no longer sufficient to attract and hold employees in occupations that have a high demand for and a short supply of candidates. The increasing complexity and size of benefit packages represent attempts to comply with this trend.

The challenge of providing attractive compensation packages will be greatest for firms that are still expanding, especially because growing companies are likely to need employees with scarce skills and abundant job opportunities. The challenge also will be prominent in more mature firms, as these must pay greater attention to the ability-to-pay issue by devising successful compensation packages that balance market-competitive salaries, wages, and benefits with firm specific considerations.

The elements that will begin to address these challenges will be wide-ranging. It will be necessary to pay careful attention to link the components directly to the firm's longer-term growth and cost-control objectives. This linkage, in turn, will require the close coordination of compensation planning and administration by those responsible for the broader human resource and strategic planning functions.

The overall effectiveness of compensation policies will be illustrated by an organization's medium- and long-term abilities to keep its employees motivated and satisfied. More broadly, the prescriptions translate increasingly into careful human resource planning processes.

References

Davis, William H., "West Coast Airframe Co. Case," *War Labor Reports,* National War Labor Board, March 31, 1943, Vol. 6, 594.

Fox, Harland, *Top Executive Compensation,* Conference Board, 1978.

Freeman, Richard B., "The Effect of Unionism on Fringe Benefits," *Industrial and Labor Relations Review,* (34) July 1981, 489–509.

Hanna, John P., "Can the Challenge of Escalating Benefit Costs Be Met?" *Personnel Administration,* 22(9), November 1977, 50–57.

Heneman, Herbert G., et al., *Personnel/Human Resource Management* (Homewood, Ill.: Richard D. Irwin Co., 1983).

Lawler, Edward E., *Pay and Organizational Effectiveness: A Psychological View* (New York: McGraw-Hill, 1971).

Livernash, Robert E., *Comparable Worth Issues and Alternatives* (Equal Employment Advisory Council, Washington, D.C., 1980).

Opinion Research Corporation, *Managing Human Resources: 1983 and Beyond,* 1983.

Pigors, Paul, and Charles A. Myers, *Personnel Administration* (New York: McGraw-Hill, 1981).

Vroom, Victor, *Work and Motivation* (New York: Vroom, 1964).

Suggested Readings

For an excellent overview of the job evaluation process, see Paul Pigors and Charles A. Myers, *Personnel Administration* (New York: McGraw-Hill, 1981).

For a comprehensive up-to-date treatment of compensation issues, see George T. Milkovich and Jerry Newman, *Compensation* (Plano, Tex.: Business Publications, forthcoming 1984).

For practical guidelines for building compensation packages, see Richard I. Henderson, *Compensation Management* (Reston, Penn.: Reston Publishing Company, 1979) and Kenneth Wheeler, Marc J. Wallace, Jr., N. Fredrick Crandall, and Charles H. Fay, *Practicing Human Resource Administration* (New York: Random House, 1982).

For designing sales compensation systems see John K. Moynahan, *Designing an Effective Sales Compensation Program* (New York: American Management Association, 1980).

Top Management Featherbedding?

There is a fairly widespread belief among practitioners and students of management that unions encourage "featherbedding" by production workers. There are many well-known examples of such practices, including diesel firemen on freight locomotives who shoveled no coal and the "bogus type rule" in printing which required copy to be reset after one use in order to force the hiring of more workers. According to some observers, it took difficult economic times and unemployment to force unions to accept concession bargaining, which froze wages, removed "restrictive work rules," and suspended cost-of-living clauses. Some unions, however, have resisted these concessions, and some companies have found that they are forced to reduce employment by closing uneconomic plants. It is generally believed that union "featherbedding" will result in reduced productivity and higher labor costs.

However, what new costs will companies incur for the recently publicized "protections" sought by an increasing number of top managements with the support of their boards of directors? A "double standard" may be emerging — that is, in difficult times, top executives are protected while blue- and white-collar employees and "redundant" middle managers receive less generous farewells.

The Golden Parachute

If a company is acquired in an "unfriendly" takeover, "golden parachutes" can provide top managers with their full salaries (and often other benefits) for up to

Source: Charles A. Myers, *Sloan Management Review,* Vol. 24, No. 4, Summer 1983, 55–8. Massachusetts Institute of Technology. Used by permission of the author.

five years. These benefits, which come with "merger mania," are said to facilitate the transition between old and new managements. It is further argued that such benefits provide executives with financial protection against possible ruthless action by the acquiring firm. However, in an October 4, 1982 editorial, *Business Week* called these parachutes "The Gilded Ripoff." It found that they are "an outrageous misuse of stockholders' assets and an abuse of management prerogatives" and that they "encourage the public's distrust of business."

A particularly well-publicized example of such benefits involved William M. Agee, chairman and chief executive officer of the Bendix Corporation. Undoubtedly at his suggestion, the Bendix board of directors approved generous golden parachutes for Agee and for fifteen other top executives. Indeed, Agee's parachute alone was estimated to be worth $4 million. Yet Agee and Alonzo McDonald, Jr. (the Bendix president) did not pull the rip cords on their parachutes until after the "friendly" takeover by Allied Corporation. Prior to that, Agee stunned the business world by announcing that he planned to take over Martin-Marietta. Martin-Marietta's president and board resisted, saying that they would seek to acquire Bendix — with the rumored support of United Technologies (a large conglomerate). At that point, Agee sought to be acquired by another large firm, Allied Corporation, and this acquisition did materialize on January 31, 1983. Not long after, Allied's CEO, Edward L. Hennessy, Jr., told Agee and former Bendix president, McDonald, that he could not find suitable jobs for them in the merged company. It was reported that Hennessy told Agee that he could not be "the number two man" and hence his possible successor as CEO of Allied. Consequently, when the two top Bendix executives were "pushed out" in mid-February 1983, they used their Bendix parachutes.[1]

There seems to be a follow-the-leader tendency in this type of executive "featherbedding." In a survey conducted by the president of Ward Howell Associates (a leading executive search firm), it was found that over 60 percent of Fortune 1000 companies have contracts that protect the top executive (and often other high-level executives) from financial loss if they are forced out of a company after an acquisition.[2] *Fortune* published a survey by Ann Morrison which comments on this kind of protection:

> The quality of stockholder mercy is not strained. It allows executives with "golden parachutes" to droppeth as the gentle rain after a takeover attempt. These men are blessed. They are blessed if they win, for they keep their companies, their positions, and their compensation. They are blessed if they lose, for they still keep their compensation even if not their jobs.

This survey covered more than the Fortune 1000 companies; it also polled retailing, financial, service, and other manufacturing companies. According to the survey, the largest industrial companies that have golden parachutes are Phillips Petroleum, Sun, and United Technologies. The survey also showed that the most generous agreements started at $7.8 million (the parachute for the CEO of the American Family Company). The executives with the most coverage were found in eight companies, ranging from 20 protected executives at Emhart Corporation to 234 covered executives at Beneficial.[3]

[1]See *Business Week*, 21 February 1983, 37; "Did Bill and Mary Blunder?" *Newsweek*, 11 October 1982, 94.

[2]See *Forbes*, 22 November 1982, 238. *Forbes*'s editors added, "Now what about Golden Parachutes for lesser mortals who are laid off because their bosses make dumb mistakes."

[3]See A. M. Morrison, "Those Executive Bailout Deals," *Fortune*, 13 December 1982, 82–86.

In contrast with these protected executives are the larger number of middle managers (and even some higher executives) who are dismissed by top management. Although allegedly dismissed for poor performance, many of these managers are laid off because their companies face economic adversity (e.g., the auto industry). However, at the *top* management level, dismissed executives are given a soft cushion.

Generous Settlements for Top Executives

A case at RCA provides an extreme example of this. CEO Edgar A. Griffiths hired Maurice R. Valente as president and then dismissed him six months later because "his performance did not meet the expectations of the board." Several weeks later he also dismissed Jane Cahill Pfeiffer, chairman of RCA's National Broadcasting Company subsidiary. Although these top executives presumably received generous severance contracts, they were not as generous as the one that the board offered Griffiths in order to ease him out of the company. The board found that Griffiths's management style and other attributes were not appropriate for the company. Nevertheless, the board gave Griffiths "a new employment contract" which would pay his $450,000 annual salary for five years following his resignation in return for consulting services.[4] Thornton W. Bradshaw, a board member and CEO of Arco, became the new chief executive officer of RCA.

Another example of this kind of executive compensation is found in AMAX, a large minerals company. AMAX has been adversely affected both by the drop in minerals prices and by reputedly poor business decisions of its CEO, Pierre

[4]See "Why Griffiths Was Forced Out as RCA Chairman," *Business Week*, 9 February 1981, 72–73.

Gousseland. He is quoted as saying: "I have watched 25 percent of my staff leave. Many of these people are my friends." One of these "friends" was the president and chief operating officer of AMAX. Termination benefits no doubt have been paid to these officers that are far more generous than any paid to the 21,000 employees laid off "permanently."[5] They have joined the ranks of the unemployed, contributing to the highest U.S. unemployment rate since 1940.

A third example of generous dismissal compensation for top executives is the case of Robert Aboud, former chairman of the First National Bank of Chicago (now the First Chicago Corporation). Because of Aboud's abrasive management style, a number of the bank's executives had taken positions with other leading banks. Finally, the board dismissed him; later it was revealed that he received $781,349 as part of a "separation agreement." In addition, at age fifty-one, he would draw a pension of $106,267 — the same pension he would have received had he stayed with the bank until age sixty-five. Aboud was later named president of Occidental Petroleum, thus receiving a new salary and perhaps being eligible for a new pension plan.[6] Ironically, when mergers and even bankruptcies occur, this is what happens at the top of the organization while "regular" employees are laid off without much, if any, separation pay.

Middle Management Terminations

The middle manager who has reached a plateau or whose performance is not evaluated very highly is now being "terminated" (a kinder word than "fired"). In progressive firms, such a manager may be provided with "outplacement services" by companies that offer counseling and assist in the manager's job search. These companies also offer advice to managers who must terminate employees. In contrast with the treatment of terminated top executives, one outplacement firm reportedly advises management that arguing with employees during the termination interview is "destructive." Reasons for the termination should be clearly explained, but not discussed. Managers are urged to "let the dismissed employee get things off his or her chest" and to give the dismissed manager a sealed envelope containing the termination benefits, which can be opened and absorbed later.[7]

Compensation and Performance of Top Executives

The process of establishing relative compensation within a company involves some form of job evaluation in order to avoid the inequities which might otherwise creep into the compensation system.[8] Although this process may include middle and upper management, the compensation of the chief executive is usually determined by the board of directors. Data used in comparisons include salary, bonuses, profit sharing, and stock purchase contributions to the chief executive's account by the company.

For example, in 1981 the board of W.R. Grace Company reportedly voted to pay J.

[5]See L. Chavez, "AMAX: Coping with Austerity," *New York Times*, 9 December 1982, 30 and 36. This company was mentioned earlier for paying two of its directors additional compensation. (They were usually paid $16,000 a year, plus $800 for each meeting.); *New York Times*, 12 April 1982. Former President Ford was paid an additional $100,000 a year for his services as a "consultant"; Former Defense Secretary Harold Brown received $75,000 more a year for his consulting services. A *New York Times* editorial concluded: "If a company wants to use outsiders to show that the business is run well, it should not be paying them insider rates."

[6]See "Cushioning the Fall," *Business Week* (editorial), 30 March 1981.

[7]Quoted in the nationally syndicated column of S. Porter, *The Tampa Tribune*, 27 November 1982, 4.

[8]See P. Pigors and C. A. Myers, *Personnel Administration*, 9th ed. (New York: McGraw-Hill, 1981), ch. 20.

Peter Grace (the chairman, CEO, and grandson of the founder) a $1 million special bonus. This award, which was paid in addition to Grace's salary and regular bonus, was made "in recognition of his accomplishments during his thirty-six-year tenure as the company's chief executive." A *Fortune* survey of top executive compensation in 140 large companies provided other striking (although less extreme) examples of compensation. As in the Grace case, these companies' policies bore little relation to company performance in terms of stock price growth or return to shareholders.[9] *Fortune* asserts that "to an extraordinary extent, those who flop still get paid handsomely. In this regard, they have something in common with union members who are able to extract higher-than-market wages from their employers. . . . If directors behaved responsibly, they would handle the stockholders' money as if it were their own, avoiding compensation excess."[10]

A comparison of 1981 salary increases to those paid in 1970 is revealing. Compensation for the chairman of U.S. Steel went up 173 percent, while the salary of the president of the AFL-CIO increased 57 percent and the average hourly wages of auto workers went up 133.3 percent. During the same period, the CPI increased 124.6 percent.

Following the *Fortune* analysis (and probably influenced by its findings), a Tampa, Florida, daily asked: "Does Performance Determine Pay?" It concluded that there was little correlation between the two. The daily compared two retail firms:

a drugstore, Jack Eckard Corporation, and a convenience store chain, Stop & Go, Inc. The CEO of Eckard received $307,398, although 1982 earnings had dropped 13.2 percent and stockholders' equity was 13.3 percent. In contrast, the Stop & Go CEO earned $147,810, even though this firm's earnings per share had risen by 23.6 percent and the stockholders' return on equity was 23.2 percent.[11]

Conclusion

This paper has reviewed three substantial benefits enjoyed by the chief executives of large companies: golden parachutes, generous settlements following dismissals of top executives by boards of directors, and total compensation of top executives that is not closely related to measures of company performance. These practices tend to increase corporate costs at the expense of the stockholders, who generally have little opportunity to object. Furthermore, the treatment of dismissed top executives contrasts sharply with the treatment of dismissed middle managers, white-collar employees, and blue-collar workers.

The examples given in this paper illustrate conclusively that there are, indeed, blatant forms of "management featherbedding" for top executives. There is no doubt that some "union featherbedding" exists — a practice that top executives decry. Yet union typesetters with their bogus type rule have been replaced by computerized typesetting on many newspapers, and diesel firemen have been removed from many freight lines. More recently, concession bargaining has removed restrictive work rules and has sometimes brought about a reduction in wages.

The crucial question which still must be answered is: When will "management featherbedding" for top executives be modified or eliminated either by top executives or by boards of directors acting in the stockholders' interests?

[9]See C. J. Loomis, "The Madness of Executive Compensation," *Fortune*, 12 July 1982, 42–52. This survey has many excellent charts comparing chief executives' compensation with return on stockholders' equity in the following types of industries: conglomerates, chemicals, metal manufacturing, petroleum refining, pharmaceuticals, office equipment, retailing, banking, and processing. These constitute the most extensive published analysis of CEO compensation I have seen.

[10]Ibid., 45.

[11]See *The Tampa Tribune*, 6 February 1983, 1.

Establishing a Compensation System

The following case describes a small but growing research and consulting firm that has set compensation in an ad hoc fashion during its start-up phase. The firm's top executives now realize the need for a formal compensation policy that is consistent with professional standards of effective compensation and that contributes to the strategic objectives of the firm. The case illustrates the application of the general principles of effective compensation design and management to a specific organizational and strategic setting.

CASE
Commodities International, Inc.

In the five years since we set up shop, our business has grown at an average annual rate of 40 percent. I know there are a lot of long-range issues we need to think about, but there just is no time. Everybody here already has a job and a half keeping up with current projects. But it is time we design a compensation plan that rewards people for emphasizing the goals and strategies we want to achieve.

These comments were made by David Gull, the founder of Commodities International, Inc. (CI).[1] During its start-up phase, CI's compensation policies were ad hoc. Hiring salaries were set at prevailing market rates, and annual increases were determined by Gull on the basis of recommendations from other senior managers.

BACKGROUND

Commodities International was founded in 1979 by David Gull, a professor at a leading university, and Jim Ryder, a young entrepreneur who had helped Gull market his book. The two men wanted to capitalize on the reputation Gull had developed as a commodities expert, especially in the field of international raw materials trade, through his academic work. CI incorporated in Delaware and authorized 1,000 shares of stock. Of this, Gull took 300, Ryder 201, and the rest was not issued.

CI's primary product was a series of commodities briefs on fundamental commodity issues and trends. The series included studies of commodity markets, their regulation, and international producer associations. It was sold as a package for an annual subscription fee. In addition, CI organized conferences on the same topics. The conferences were open to the public for a fee

---

[1]The authors would like to thank Deborah Ghose for her help in researching and writing this case.

and tended to feature famous keynote speakers. Finally, CI undertook a few consulting projects for individual clients, including market studies and risk analysis.

To keep overhead costs low, Gull and Ryder initially did not hire any staff. Instead, they asked a number of commodities experts from industry and academia to join the firm as senior associates. Senior associates were paid a $1,000 annual retainer, in return for which they allowed CI to use their names in promotional material. They also contributed one commodities brief per year for a prearranged additional fee. Senior associates wrote and Gull edited most of CI's briefs.

During its first two years, CI established a national reputation for producing objective, timely analyses of commodity trade issues. As result, the company was frequently cited in wire service articles, in *The New York Times*, and in industry publications. In 1979, its first year of operation, CI's revenues totaled $297,000; 1980 revenues rose to $614,000, and by 1983, they had almost reached $2.5 million (see Table 7-12).

THE FOUNDING PARTNERS

David Gull, the president of CI: At 42, Gull had established an international reputation as a commodities expert. He had spent a decade in the field and had written for numerous publications. CI's establishment could be credited largely to his intellectual capital. It was believed widely within the firm that "*David* is the firm's product." Meanwhile, CI had been moving steadily away from this cult of personality. The name Commodities International had been chosen in a conscious attempt to avoid a personality-dependent image.

Jim Ryder, the vice-president of CI: Ryder packaged and implemented Gull's ideas. He boasted a keen eye for detail and a tendency toward organization. Like Gull, he had a strong entrepreneurial drive and an antibureaucratic bias. CI's creation hinged on the combination of Gull's product and Ryder's innate marketing ability.

INITIAL GROWTH

Between 1979 and 1984, CI's revenues grew to nearly $2.5 million (see Table 7-13 for details). The partnership expanded to include three new members,

TABLE 7-12 CI Revenues by Source in Thousands of Dollars

	1979	1980	1981	1982	1983
Subscriptions	172	289	432	506	714
Consulting	125	325	532	874	1,329
Direct mail	—	—	40	153	419
Total	297	614	1,004	1,533	2,462

TABLE 7-13 Commodities International Financial Highlights in Thousands of Dollars

	Actual					Goals	
	1979	1980	1981	1982	1983	1984	1985
Revenues	297	614	1,004	1,533	2,462	3,939	6,302
Cost of sales	276	571	871	1,254	1,630		
Income (loss) before taxes	21	43	133	279	832		
Provision for taxes	8	16	53	112	349		
Net income (loss)	13	27	80	167	483		
Return on sales	4%	4%	8%	11%	20%		

TABLE 7-14 Revenues by Source in Percentages

	1979	1980	1981	1982	1983
Subscriptions	58	47	43	33	29
Consulting	42	53	53	57	54
Direct mail	—	—	4	10	17
Total	100	100	100	100	100

and the number of full-time employees grew from four to forty-one. The roster of senior associates on retainer, part-time professionals, and loosely affiliated student workers grew to two hundred.

Because Gull and Ryder were sensitive to the risks of excessive overhead, they initially brought in new full-time employees only after the work load had become excessive and when they were reasonably certain the new employees could be supported for at least six months. Between 1980 and 1981, three new partners were brought in either to develop planned new products or to manage consulting projects.

In 1980, for example, Gull and Ryder decided to upgrade the price and quality of the subscription service by adding two new products: a quarterly report on world commodity markets and a biannual producer pricing policies update. They brought into the partnership an expert from the European Economic Community, Vladimir Kozinski, to prepare and market the commodities report. At the same time, they persuaded Susan Marke, a professor who had written several commodities briefs for CI, to join the partnership to write the pricing update and to assist as a risk analysis consulting project manager. Marke subsequently hired three MBAs as staff consultants.

In 1981, Ryder brought Tom Carter, a personal friend with a strong marketing background, into the partnership. Carter had proposed that con-

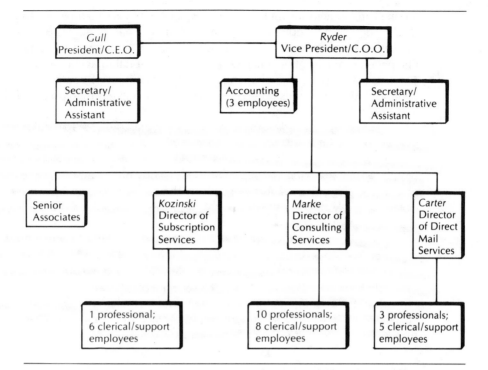

FIGURE 7-2   CI: Staffing Chart (1983)

densed commodities briefs be marketed through broadly targeted, direct-mail campaigns. A typical mailing list could include 30,000 names. These briefs were sold individually for $200 to $400.

During the first two years, CI's revenues had been split almost evenly between annual subscription fees and consulting projects. Between 1980 and 1983, revenues from consulting grew faster than subscription revenues; the new direct-mail service also expanded rapidly. In 1983, consulting, subscriptions, and direct mail accounted for 50, 30, and 20 percent of revenues, respectively (see Table 7-14). The company's staffing chart is shown in Figure 7-2.

STRATEGIC ISSUES

When Gull and Ryder drew up CI's first business plan, their main concern was to develop a client base that would buffer the firm from cyclical movements. The solution they developed was the annual subscription, where companies paid a $4,000 to $8,000 annual fee for a series of reports that as a package would provide clients with a broad understanding of national and international commodity market and pricing trends.

As soon as CI began publishing papers, it became evident that there was an extensive market for the kind of analysis the firm produced, particularly among firms in various metals industries. CI's publications filled a gap created by the recession's depletion of high-level staff departments. Thus, the firm's marketing problem was to respond effectively to the interest generated by its first paper, while establishing a coherent, professional image and product line. The first response to this challenge was the institution of conferences on the commodities brief topics. These served to introduce the firm to potential clients and to solidify its reputation.

The consulting side of CI's business was initiated by a conference participant who needed an extensive risk analysis concerning a potential joint venture in a mineral rich Latin American country. At the time, Gull and Ryder wondered if consulting work would jeopardize CI's reputation as an objective observer of the commodities scene. They debated the subject intensely before deciding to take on the project; its cash-flow benefits enabled the firm to offset significant overhead costs.

The direct-mail service raised yet another strategic issue. As a low-cost, mass market service, this project had a different image from the high-quality, objective, intellectual image CI had worked to establish. Thus, considerable ambivalence about the service spread throughout the firm.

Ryder was particularly concerned about employee compensation. He considered it best to begin by developing an action plan after careful consideration of the roles of each of CI's lines of business.

CONSULTING SERVICES

Susan Marke, director of consulting, was an expert on third world commodity trade. She had built up CI's consulting capacity almost single-handedly but found that while the consulting side of the business had helped maintain a ready cash flow, it was not to be marketed aggressively. The lack of formal commitment to that branch of the business left her understaffed, without any stable overhead facilities, and relying heavily on business school graduate and undergraduate students.

SUBSCRIPTION SERVICES

Vladimir Kozinski wrote CI's oil review; he had an assistant who regularly monitored market journals and reports. Unlike Marke, he was not interested in expanding his staff. Rather, he strongly advocated hiring academics and others on retainer. He also thought the consulting group might be cut back, noting that expansion of the consulting end would place CI in competition with firms that did nothing but management consulting, and did it better.

DIRECT MAIL SERVICES

Tom Carter's direct-mail campaign for the company's commodities briefs had become increasingly lucrative. Carter himself supported the expansion of both the consulting and subscription ends of the business, as well as the growth in his domain. (Recall that in 1983 the consulting, subscription, and direct-mail services accounted for 50, 30, and 20 percent of revenues, respectively.)

COMPENSATION

In assessing the need to restructure CI's compensation policies, Ryder and Gull had to consider several factors. First, they had to balance the realities of past growth — unevenly distributed among the three lines of business — against some coherent plan of action to foster future growth. Particular emphasis was placed on the subscriptions because these had grown more slowly than expected. They needed to build a compensation structure that would promote the subscription service while sustaining the consulting and direct mail services at current levels. As shown in Table 7-13, CI's revenue goal was just under $4 million for 1984 and $6.3 million for 1985. This 60 percent growth rate was to be attained primarily through promotion of the subscription service, which was to account for 80 percent of the growth; consulting would account for 15 percent, and direct mail for 5 percent.

Second, the founders had to deal with some generic compensation problems. Employees could make good money in the firm by bringing in new business or by entering the partnership. However, working full-time was not lucrative and often involved picking up the pieces that part-time employees had left half-done. Further, some part-time employees made more money per hour than some full-time employees. Bonuses for full-time people were unpredictable, fostering a sense that individual performance was inadequately measured and rewarded.

Gull and Ryder had taken in the three junior partners — Marke, Kozinski, and Carter — with a promise that they would be made part of the bonus structure and rewarded appropriately for their contributions to the milestones within their line of the business and to the company as a whole. In 1983, Gull and Ryder drew up the salary and bonus plan, shown in Table 7-15. Gull had a salary of $95,000 and a $50,000 bonus, while Ryder had an $85,000 salary and a $40,000 bonus. The company's remaining after-tax income was used to buy office and computer equipment for approximately $65,000 and to start a money-market fund. The other employees were given raises for 1984 at a rate of 5 percent higher than the increase in the consumer price index for 1983, a decision made solely by Ryder and Gull. Only four or five of the key employees were given higher percentage raises but did not know why or how the percentages were determined.

The fringe benefit package at CI was easy to communicate. It consisted of health insurance provided by a major supplier, with the employer paying 80 percent and the employee providing the remainder. Everyone was given a life insurance policy that paid the equivalent to a year's salary. Holidays were given for each of the eleven federally mandated days, and everyone but the

TABLE 7-15   Salary and Bonus Plan

	Salary	Bonus
Marke	$65,000	$10,000
Kozinski	$75,000	$20,000
Carter	$75,000	$10,000

partners was given two weeks' paid vacation. The partners took three weeks each. Gull, however, liked to spend a good portion of the summer away from the office, writing and thinking at his seashore home.

Each employee, when hired, was told by the hiring partner (at least one was involved in each hiring decision) that the company's communication policy was fully open. They were told to feel free to walk into the boss's office at any time or to make an appointment to discuss a personal or business-related problem.

Finally, the role of the partner remains more or less mysterious to non-partners in the firm. The prevailing sense is that each partner fulfills entirely different functions and has wholly distinct expectations of his or her job and of the firm as a whole. Nonpartners have no way to judge their chances of becoming a partner, which in turn increases their frustration with the overall compensation system.

Questions for Discussion

If you were charged with presenting Gull and Ryder with a proposal to revise CI's compensation system, what would you suggest with respect to

1. hiring practices and salaries/wages for part-time employees, including business students?
2. the company's mechanism for promoting its employees from within, specifically eligibility for partner status?
3. the compensation package for the senior managers and the employees in CI's various business lines?
4. communication of the features of the compensation plan(s) for CI employees?

8

Labor Relations

The major characteristics of the United States system of collective bargaining and the ways in which the actions and reactions of the actors in the system have influenced its evolution are described in this chapter. It opens with an overview of the evolution of the roles of management, unions, and government in collective bargaining. We build on this historical foundation in summarizing the steps managers go through to prepare for, conduct, and evaluate the results of contract negotiations.

This material serves as background for the Kramer Trucking case, an exercise in solving procedural and substantive challenges that employers and unions face in adjusting to the more competitive economic environment of the 1980s. Finally, the appendix to this book contains a collective bargaining simulation to illustrate the processes of negotiation and conflict resolution.

Evolution of Collective Bargaining in the United States

Since the early 1800s when the American labor movement first began, six distinct phases have emerged in the history of United States labor relations, each characterized by a unique set of strategic approaches on the parts of the actors and by particular political and social contexts for those strategies.* By understanding the evolution, one can understand many of the changes that currently are under way in the United States industrial relations system.

The Early Years: 1800 to 1935

Founded in 1794, the Philadelphia Cordwainers' union struck in 1806 for higher wages. As a result of this action, the union was brought to

---

*We wish to thank our colleague, Harry C. Katz, for preparing this historical overview. Harry Katz is an Associate Professor of Industrial Relations, Sloan School of Management, MIT. The piece was written for this book.

trial on criminal conspiracy charges, including the charge of being an illegal combination in order to raise wages and injure others. The union was found guilty and assessed fines that were heavy enough to cause its bankruptcy and ultimate dissolution. The charge of criminal conspiracy was used routinely against unions in this era. This experience of the Philadelphia Cordwainers' union typifies the conditions under which unions were operating and fighting for their existence.

Early unions most often were organized according to craft and followed the organizational patterns of the European Guild System where many immigrant craftsmen were trained. Workers such as shoemakers, typesetters, hatters, carpenters, and tailors were among those who formed the first labor organizations.

An enduring national organization, the American Federation of Labor (AFL), emerged in 1886 under the elected leadership of cigar-maker Samuel Gompers. Within this federation, however, national unions were autonomous and bargained almost exclusively through local affiliates in a small area or sometimes in plants. Gompers and the AFL sought compromises with management in the negotiation of collective bargaining agreements. This willingness to compromise reflected their opposition to the strategies of more radical unions and political reformers.

During this period radical unions and radical political parties occasionally did play crucial roles. In the West, the Industrial Workers of the World (colloquially known as the Wobblies) emerged as a significant organizing force in mines and timberlands. Radical movements were never strong, however, and later declined in influence as the government made efforts to suppress their activities. In addition, workers became more reluctant to identify their interests with a revolutionary political platform.

The courts' attitude toward labor unions followed the lines of the conspiracy doctrine (based on common law), which held that unions and their activities (e.g., strikes) violated property rights and the freedom of contract. Toward the end of this period, the courts' approach shifted to a more laissez-faire position that was more like the federal government's position.

Management also typically viewed labor unions as a basic infringement of property rights. Thus, management opposed — sometimes violently — both union organization and strike activities. Management's stance was supported at times by both the courts and the police.

As union organization spread and the courts and government came to exert less opposition, however, some companies adopted a new strategy toward employee representation. In the 1920s, company unions and independent unions were created within many of the more rapidly growing, sophisticated companies. Firms could both respond to employee concerns and deflect the demand for more aggressive unions.

The defining feature of labor from 1800 to 1935 was that union activity remained largely unregulated and uninstitutionalized. The dearth of regulations and procedures to structure collective bargaining led to some violent struggles between labor and management, which characterized the period as the time of the labor wars.

The Formative Years: 1935 to 1949

In 1937, an almost forty-day sit-down strike by the United Auto Workers at GM's Chevrolet plant number four precipitated a crisis. Strictly speaking, the strike was illegal — an infraction of property rights. The media touted the dangers of such dramatic union actions and spread news of a coming revolution. Governor Frank Murphy of Michigan stated in an official order to the union that if the strikers did not leave the plant, the National Guard would force them out. Through hard bargaining and the judicious negotiating skills of John L. Lewis, head of the newly formed Congress of Industrial Organization (CIO), the governor backed down, and GM agreed to many of the workers' demands. The events surrounding this strike set the precedent for pattern bargaining in the auto industry and others, and captured the tone of labor's growing strength during this period.

During this period, a new labor federation, the Congress of Industrial Organization (CIO), split from the AFL and began to organize all skilled and unskilled production workers in the manufacturing industries. Major organizing strikes led by these new industrial unions followed in the late 1930s and early 1940s in the nation's major industries, including steel, auto, and textiles. The emergence of the CIO industrial unions marked an important shift within the ranks of American labor away from the dominance of craft unions. Other factors shaping and influencing labor included numerous pieces of New Deal legislation that the Roosevelt administration offered in response to the Great Depression.

A key actor in the late 1930s and 1940s was the federal government, which provided a structure for labor-management relations through national legislation. In 1935, Congress passed the National Labor Relations Act (sometimes called the Wagner Act), which to this day is the centerpiece of the country's labor laws. In 1937, the U.S. Supreme Court upheld the constitutionality of the NLRA in the Jones and Laughlin Steel case. The NLRA gave unions the statutory right to exist, made strikes legal, established election procedures to determine representation rights and union jurisdiction, created the National Labor Relations Board (NLRB) to administer the act, and banned various unfair labor practices that management might commit, such as firing union organizers (see Box 8-1 for details).

The government continued to play a dominant role during the war years, when the War Labor Board functioned as an important regulator

BOX 8-1
Key Terms and Principles in
United States Labor Relations

1. *Exclusive Jurisdiction.* When the majority of workers in a specific bargaining unit vote to be represented by a union, that union becomes the sole and exclusive representative for all workers in the unit for the purposes of negotiating a contract.

2. *Bargaining Unit.* A group of workers certified by the National Labor Relations Board (or an equivalent state agency), eligible to vote in an election and to be covered by a bargaining agreement if the union wins the election by a majority vote.

3. *Scope of Bargaining.* The idea that employers and unions are required to negotiate in good faith on *mandatory* subjects of bargaining (those pertaining to wages, hours, and working conditions). Employers and unions may also, but are not required to, negotiate over *permissive* subjects that are outside the mandatory scope.

4. *Unfair Labor Practices.* Actions taken by either an employer or a union that are found by the National Labor Relations Board to be in violation of the duty to bargain in good faith, or of some other specific provision of the NLRA.

5. *Secondary Boycott.* A union puts pressure on employer X so as to induce X to put pressure on employer Y to end a labor dispute involving Y. Secondary boycotts are illegal under the NLRA.

6. *Union Shop.* A workplace in which a worker is required to join the union *after* being hired. This requirement is relatively common.

7. *Closed Shop.* A workplace in which a worker is required to be a union member *before* being hired. The closed shop was outlawed by the Taft-Hartley Act, except in the construction industry.

8. *Right-to-Work Laws.* State laws that make any bargaining provisions that impose a union shop illegal. Twenty states have such laws.

9. *Free Collective Bargaining.* There is a strong preference within the United States system to let the parties central to any dispute or set of issues determine their own fate with only limited government interference. At times, this preference is more rhetorical than real, given significant governmental involvement in the determination of employment conditions.

10. *Decentralized Bargaining Structure.* Most collective bargaining occurs at the plant or corporate level (or some combination of the two). There is relatively little industrywide bargaining involving employer associations (exceptions include trucking, railroads, maritime, clothing, coal mining, and basic steel).

11. *Detailed Labor Contracts.* Comprehensive labor agreements regulate shop floor practices. The strong presence of the local union on the shop floor is associated with the administration of these agreements.

12. *Due Process through Arbitration.* The United States system displays a strong preference for recourse to grievance procedures and binding third-party arbitration for dispute resolution during the term of a contract. However, management is provided with the initiative within that system

through application of the principle that "management moves and the workers grieve."

13. *Business Unionism.* Most unions accept the capitalist system of private property and pursue fairly narrow political objectives. This approach evolved in part as a consequence of the absence of a labor party and a limited radical political tradition within labors' ranks.

14. *Pragmatic Employer Opposition.* On philosophic grounds, employers generally oppose the existence of unions but try to accommodate them where they exist. This stance combines with the business unionism of most of our unions to produce adversarial relations in the negotiation of contracts, but also periodic cooperation between labor and management when clear, joint interests can be identified.

---

of labor-management relations. In its activities the board tended to favor a number of basic principles that emerged as key features of the United States labor relations system. These included (1) a grievance procedure with binding third-party arbitration for dispute resolution during the term of a contract as a quid pro quo for a no-strike guarantee; (2) detailed labor contracts specifying many of the rules that guide shop floor production; and (3) fringe benefits as an element of bargaining. The U.S. Supreme Court sanctioned this last principle by ruling in the Inland Steel case (1949) that pensions were a mandatory subject of bargaining.

In 1947, the Taft-Hartley amendments to the NLRA outlawed certain unfair labor practices by the unions. The amendments prohibited secondary boycotts and closed shops, allowed for the states to pass right-to-work laws, and created national emergency dispute-resolution procedures to govern strikes that threatened the health and safety of the nation.

Management during the 1940s began to respond to the spread of collective bargaining, which had been spurred both by successful union organizing drives and by the policies of the War Labor Board. Among other responses, many firms upgraded and expanded the power and professionalism of their labor relations staff.

Managerial responses to collective bargaining varied. Firms such as Thompson Products (now called TRW) and DuPont successfully helped create independent unions that were not affiliated with the AFL or the CIO. The work forces in other firms, such as the auto and steel industries, were completely organized by the CIO. Managerial strategies in these industries centered on trying to contain and stabilize the collective bargaining process. Still other companies sought to adapt their policies and strategies to unions where they had won representation rights, but to pursue policies to avoid further union organization in unorganized plants.

The Drive to Maturity: 1950s

The 1950s were marked by the solid establishment of a number of the features of today's labor relations system. (Box 8-1 defines these features). The defining characteristic of this decade was the creation of institutions and procedures that brought regularity and stability to collective bargaining.

For unions, that stability was provided by the negotiation of long-term contracts in a number of major industries. The GM-UAW contract of 1948 emerged as the model for many of these agreements. This agreement, which lasted two years, instituted cost-of-living and annual-improvement-factor (productivity) wage increases; it included grievance and arbitration dispute resolution procedures; it contained pension, health insurance, and life insurance benefits; and it was followed in 1950 by a five-year agreement including these clauses and providing the union with the security of a union shop and dues deduction from paychecks (checkoff). A tradition of pattern bargaining also emerged in this and other industries; the terms of master agreements were slightly modified and extended to supplier and related industries. Pattern bargaining satisfied workers' equity concerns by preserving "orbits of coercive comparisons," thus bringing further stability and regularity to contract negotiations (Ross, 1948). Union membership also grew automatically because the agreements combined union shops with employment expansion.

Collective bargaining demonstrated its adaptability in response to the periodic, cyclical economic flux, which marked the 1950s, with the introduction of supplementary unemployment benefits (SUB) and other job security measures. The comprehensiveness of the collective bargaining agreements of the period is illustrated in the table of contents of a typical national contract (see Box 8-2). The merger of the AFL and CIO in 1955 furthered the stability of the collective bargaining system by establishing procedures for resolving disputes that arose between unions competing for the same members.

During this period the federal government was generally inactive and the initiative shifted to the two other major actors — labor and management. Exceptions included the occasional use of Taft-Hartley emergency dispute-resolution procedures, as well as emergency boards created under the guidelines of the Railway Labor Act. Further publicity was created by the McClellan hearings in Congress, which concerned union racketeering. The hearings were followed by the passage of the Landrum-Griffin Act in 1959, which regulates internal union finances and affairs.

When bad economic times and concurrent inventory surpluses weakened labor's strike threat and bargaining power, management periodically tried to gain greater control over work rules. During the 1958–59 recession, managers in the steel industry made such an attempt, resulting in the famous industrywide "long strike" of 1959,

BOX 8-2

Standard Provisions in Collective Bargaining Agreements

Establishment and Administration of the Agreement

Bargaining unit and plant supplements
Contract duration and reopening and renegotiation provisions
Union security and the checkoff
Special bargaining committees
Grievance procedures
Arbitration and mediation
Strikes and lockouts
Contract enforcement

Functions, Rights, and Responsibilities

Management rights clauses
Plant removal
Subcontracting
Union activities on company time and premises
Union-management cooperation
Regulation of technological change
Advance notice and consultation

Wage Determination and Administration

General provisions
Rate structure and wage differentials
Allowances
Incentive systems and production bonus plans
Production standards and time studies
Job classification and job evaluation
Individual wage adjustments
General wage adjustments during the contract period

Job or Income Security

Hiring and transfer arrangements
Employment and income guarantees
Reporting and call-in pay

Plant Operations

Work and shop rules
Rest periods and other in-plant time allowances
Safety and health
Plant committees
Hours of work and premium pay practices
Shift operations
Hazardous work
Discipline and discharge

Paid and Unpaid Leave

Vacations and holidays
Sick leave
Funeral and personal leave
Military leave and jury duty

Employee Benefit Plans

Health and insurance plans
Pension plans
Profit sharing, stock purchase, and thrift plans
Supplemental unemployment benefit plans
Regulation of overtime, shift work, etc.
Reduction of hours to forestall layoffs
Layoff procedures, seniority, recall
Work sharing in lieu of layoff
Attrition arrangements
Promotion practices
Training and retraining
Relocation allowances
Severance pay and layoff benefit plans
Special funds and study committee
Bonus plans

Special Groups

Apprentices and learners
Handicapped and older workers
Women
Veterans
Union representatives
Nondiscrimination clauses

Source: Joseph W. Bloch, "Union Contracts: A New Series of Studies," *Monthly Labor Review,* 87 (October 1964), 1184–85.

---

which lasted 114 days. The final settlement of this dispute included no major amendments to work rules, but reflected a general, widespread effort to maintain the stability of the collective bargaining system, even in the face of severe conflicts in specific cases. This emphasis on stability characterized the entire decade.

The Decade of Rank and File Turmoil: 1960s

In December 1966, Walter Ruether, president of the UAW and an outspoken advocate of the civil rights movement, sent a letter to his local unions, calling on them to become more deeply committed "in the ongoing struggle for equal rights and equal employment opportunity, not only at the opportunity level and through legislation but within the labor movement itself." (*New York Times*, December 30, 1966). Ironically, it was within Reuther's union that the most vocal and radical of the black militants set out to change the de facto segregation among union members within the auto industry. The group started an organization called the Dodge Revolutionary Union Movement (DRUM), which, among other things, referred to the UAW as "scum" in a well-publicized poem. This series of incidents pointed to the disparity between union rhetoric and actual shop floor discrimination and segregation. These issues were to remain important in the labor movement for many years.

The civil rights movement, urban riots, the war in Vietnam, and campus protests created an environment of social turmoil and unrest in the 1960s. This environment combined with the strong economic growth that followed President Kennedy's tax cuts and the Vietnam buildup to produce tighter labor markets and to increase worker power and militance on the shop floor. The rate of contract rejections in union ratification processes reached a record high of 14 percent in 1967. The incidence of both contractual and unofficial (wildcat) work stoppages also rose dramatically. In some industries, unrest on the shop floor was revealed by the complex issues emerging in local negotiations that sometimes led to wildcat strikes. Another new development was the emergence and success of militant public sector unions, a movement that began in large urban areas where so many other social movements were flourishing.

Managements responded in two fashions, which led in opposite directions. On the one side was the accommodative approach that managers took in heavily organized industries that were working to restore stability to collective bargaining processes. Sometimes these managers were faced with union leaders on whom they counted but who were unable to control their rank and file or to assure the smooth operation of the institutional bargaining procedures that had been created and nourished in the previous decade. On the other side were managers in newer and growing firms who were determined to develop an alternative to the bargaining system reigning in older firms. Their approach centered around efforts to avoid unionization by using more sophisticated human resource and behavioral science practices. The growth of nonunion firms later emerged as a major development in the United States industrial relations system, though it remained a largely experimental effort in the 1960s.

Meanwhile, the federal government increased its direct involvement in collective bargaining. The Taft-Hartley emergency procedures were more frequently applied; federal pay guidelines, although technically voluntary, were often fostered by the "jawboning" tactics of Presidents Kennedy and Johnson; and Congress passed civil rights legislation that tried to ensure "equal pay for equal work" regardless of race, creed, religion, and, later, sex. In addition, local governments increased their involvement in union affairs in response to the rapid spread of public-sector bargaining.

Stability and Atrophy: 1970s

Though the parties engaged in collective bargaining perceived changing environmental pressures on their relationship, the 1970s saw them continuing to behave as they had in the 1960s. Representatives of both management and labor continued to be preoccupied with maintaining stability and continuity in the bargaining process.

Events in the steel and auto industries provide good examples of this pattern of behavior. In steel, the Experimental Negotiating Agreement, adopted in 1970, provided automatic wage-rate escalation in exchange for giving up the right to strike during contract renegotiation. GM, in turn, initially set out in a 1970 strike to abolish the use of an uncapped cost-of-living escalator, but later it consolidated its relationship with the new UAW president, Leonard Woodcock, and settled the strike by preserving the traditional wage formulas. In both of these industry sectors, the parties had the advantage of oligopolistic industry structures that allowed for the pass-through of wage settlements. In both industries, management decided to stay with tried and true practices. The data in Table 8-1, drawn from a Conference Board survey (Freedman, 1979), illustrate management's conservative, status quo

TABLE 8-1   Management Nonwage Goals in Collective Bargaining

Areas of Negotiations	Number with Goal	Tighten Existing Provision (%)	Keep Status Quo (%)	Trade Improvement for Other Items (%)	Achieving Goals (%)
Pensions	463	11	43	46	88
Life insurance	427	7	52	40	91
Health insurance	453	11	47	41	87
Dental insurance	410	5	70	25	91
Time off with pay	478	12	55	33	85
Subcontracting	388	17	80	2	94
Layoff and recall procedures	387	33	58	9	87
Flexibility in assignment of employees	467	55	42	3	76
Income security (SUB, severance pay, etc.)	282	6	84	10	89
Cost-of-living clause	441	13	76	10	86
Length of agreement	428	23	64	11	92
Union security	315	10	86	4	94

Source: Thomas A. Kochan, *Collective Bargaining and Industrial Relations: From Theory to Policy and Practice* (Homewood, Ill.: Richard D. Irwin, 1980). Copyright © 1980 by Thomas A. Kochan. Reprinted by permission of Richard D. Irwin, Inc., publishers.

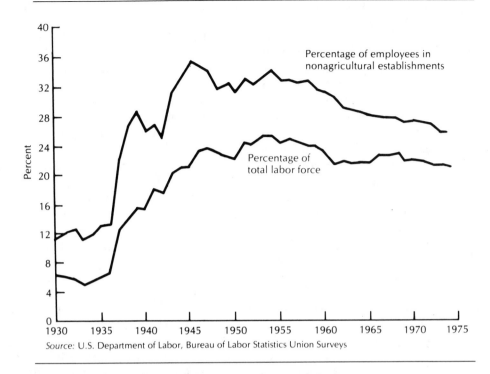

Percent

Percentage of employees in nonagricultural establishments

Percentage of total labor force

Source: U.S. Department of Labor, Bureau of Labor Statistics Union Surveys

FIGURE 8-1 Union Membership as a Percentage of Total Labor Force and of Employees in Nonagricultural Establishments, 1930–1974

approach during the 1970s. Management made little effort to modify significantly the provisions of their collective bargaining agreements.

Private-sector union growth had halted by this point, as revealed in Figure 8-1. At the same time, nonunion firms were proliferating, particularly in the new service and high-tech industries where most unions made few attempts to organize. In the public sector, new union organization continued until the middle of the decade when it was slowed by a taxpayers' revolt. As of 1976, union organization was higher in the public sector, at 39.2 percent, than in private industry, at 28.3 percent.

The terms of private sector contract settlements reflected the status quo orientation. The use of cost-of-living formulas grew in response to high inflation, and fringe benefits also continued to expand. The unorganized sector, however, experienced the full effects of the deep recessions of 1970, 1974–75, and at the decade's end. Concurrently, the number of new labor market entrants, including women, teenagers, and the baby-boom cohort, increased rapidly. Both high inflation and the oversupply of labor resulted in a fall in real earnings for many unorganized workers. Given that unionized workers continued to receive wage increases, including cost-of-living adjustments plus other gains, a widening gap emerged between the earnings of union and nonunion workers.

Within the union movement, the 1970s are marked by a general rejection of worker participation efforts and other programs that might fundamentally alter the collective bargaining system. In the aftermath of the well-publicized strike at GM's Lordstown plant and partly in response to shop-floor unrest, a number of workplace experiments were undertaken in the early 1970s. With only a few exceptions (such as Irving Bluestone in the UAW's GM department), most unionists were skeptical of these endeavors.

The federal government's involvement in the labor market of the 1970s had become more significant as a consequence of a number of income policies that emerged, including the Nixon administration's wage and price controls and the Carter administration's voluntary pay guidelines. In addition, regulatory legislation concerning health and safety (OSHA), pensions (ERISA), age discrimination, and retirement also increased the government's role.

During the late 1970s, a debate emerged over labor law reforms that many unionists and liberal politicians were proposing. The impetus for reform sprang from the recognition that United States industrial relations were changing, and that the rules of the game had to change as well. The debate produced a labor law reform bill that won the support of President Carter and an apparent majority in Congress, but to the frustration of labor supporters, the bill died in a filibuster in the conservative-controlled Senate. Conservative senators were afraid of giving labor any advantage in the union representation election process.

By the end of the decade, economic pressures were increasing. Yet, the decade ended with no serious adjustment in the approaches of the major actors in the collective bargaining arena.

The Need to Experiment: 1980s

By 1980 and 1981, heavily unionized industries in the United States were facing a deep, protracted recession, heightened international competition, domestic nonunion competition, and deregulation (the latter particularly affected the trucking and airline industries). Some analysts argued that structural shifts in the world economy foretold long-term economic problems for these industries. These structural changes included the emergence of sophisticated, and in some cases superior, competition from Japanese and other foreign producers. In part as a result of these pressures, many unions were steadily losing members (Tables 8-2 and 8-3).

Since 1980, the unions in the auto, rubber, steel, and airline industries, among many others, have been forced to make wage and benefit concessions. These concessions produced contractual bargains

TABLE 8-2 Labor Organizations Reporting 100,000 Members
or More, 1980[1] (in thousands)

Labor Organizations	Members	Labor Organizations	Members
Teamsters (Ind.)	1,891	Retail, Wholesale	215
National Education Association (Ind.)	1,684	Government (NAGE) (Ind.)	200
Automobile Workers	1,357	Transportation Union	190
Food and Commercial	1,300	Iron Workers	184
Steelworkers	1,238	Nurses Association (Ind.)	180
State, County	1,098	Railway Clerks	180
Electrical (IBEW)	1,041	Fire Fighters	178
Carpenters	784	Painters	164
Machinists	754	Transit Union	162
Service Employees	650	Electrical (UE) (Ind.)	162
Laborers	608	Sheet Metal	161
Communications Workers	551	Bakery, Confectionery, Tobacco	160
Teachers	551	Oil, Chemical	154
Clothing and Textile Workers	455	Rubber	151
Operating Engineers	423	Police (Ind.)	150
Hotel	400	Boilermakers	145
Plumbers	352	Bricklayers	135
Ladies Garment	323	Transport Workers	130
Musicians	299	Postal and Federal Employees	125
Paperworkers	275	Printing and Graphic	122
Government (AFGE)	255	Woodworkers	112
Postal Workers	251	Office	107
Mine Workers (Ind.)	245	California (Ind.)	105
Electrical (IUE)	233	Maintenance of Way	102
Letter Carriers	230		

[1] Based on reports to the Bureau. All organizations not identified as (Ind.) are affiliated with the AFL-CIO.
   Note: Table is based on preliminary union survey data.
   Source: Bureau of Labor Statistics survey.

that were different from those yielded during the previous three decades. The pattern of regular, continuous gains on all dimensions encompassed by collective bargaining was broken, or at least interrupted.

The election of Ronald Reagan to the presidency both signaled and exacerbated political pressures on the union movement. Reagan's election demonstrated a popular conservative drift, and conservatives blamed unions in part for the country's poor economic performance. The Reagan administration undertook actions that weakened the labor movement. The new administration's attitude toward organized labor was demonstrated early when Reagan fired striking air-traffic controllers. The president also appointed conservative representatives to the National Labor Relations Board and to the staffs that administered OSHA and other programs within the Department of Labor.

When AFL-CIO President Lane Kirkland heard that Raymond Donovan had been appointed Secretary of Labor, he said, "I look for-

TABLE 8-3   Labor Organizations Having Membership Changes
of At Least 25,000 in 1978–80[1] (in thousands)

Labor Organizations	Membership		Change	
	1978	1980	Number	Percent
Automobile Workers	1,499	1,357	−142	−9.5
Steelworkers	1,286	1,238	−48	−3.7
Clothing and Textile	501	455	−46	−9.2
Teamsters	1,924	1,891	−33	−1.7
Musicians	330	299	−31	−9.4
Rubber Workers	r 178	151	r −27	r −15.2
Oil, Chemical and Atomic	180	154	−26	14.4
Ladies Garment	348	323	−25	7.2
Service Employees	625	650	25	4.0
Electrical Workers (IBEW)	1,012	1,041	29	2.9
Machinists	r 724	r 754	r 30	r 4.1
Communications Workers	508	551	43	8.5
Teachers	502	551	49	9.8
Food and Commercial[2]	1,236	1,300	64	5.2
State, County	1,020	1,098	78	7.6

[1] The United Mine Workers was excluded from this table as reported 1978 and 1980 data were not comparable.

[2] Membership figure for 1978 was derived by combining the pre-merger membership of the Retail Clerks International Union and the Amalgamated Meat Cutters and Butcher Workmen of North America.

r = revised.

Source: U.S. Department of Labor announcement, September 1981 (Bureau of Labor Statistics Union Survey).

ward to meeting him." Kirkland's statement symbolized the administration's poor relations with labor leaders. Before Reagan's election, national labor leaders had consulted regularly with the president and other members of the executive branch. Typically, labor leaders were informed of important federal appointments before their announcement. The new administration pursued a quite different course.

Reagan's federal budget cutbacks in social programs also placed labor unions on the defensive. Funds were cut for employment and training programs, equal employment opportunity efforts, OSHA programs, and federal minimum-wage regulations. The Reagan administration was not committed to — indeed often was opposed to — many of the New Deal policies that formed the political backbone of the labor movement.

Meanwhile, management had become a catalyst for change at all levels — corporate, bargaining, and workplace — of the industrial relations system. At the corporate level, human resource policies were being more closely integrated with basic business decisions. In some firms new strategic planning groups were created within the labor relations staff to encourage this integration. A number of companies restructured and broadened the responsibilities of their human resource staff, which also had acquired new responsibilities for enforcing OSHA and EEO regulatory requirements. In some cases, the restructuring grew from efforts to integrate operating managers into contract negotiations. In other cases, reorganization meant replacing or demoting industrial relations staff who had become identified with traditional bargaining and planning styles.

At the collective bargaining level, which is the middle tier in corporate labor relations management, a number of major changes affected both the processes and results of collective bargaining. In many cases, the locus of the negotiations and the scope of a contract's coverage were decentralized to account for specific economic circumstances of a given firm or plant. This trend is associated with a decline in pattern bargaining.

Bargaining outcomes in a number of major industries were affected by the many contract concessions to which unions were agreeing, including pay freezes or cuts and work-rule revisions. This kind of concession bargaining is illustrated in Table 8-4, which shows a variety of trends across industries that suggest the erosion of collective bargaining stability and continuity.

Finally, changes were under way at the workplace level during this era of experimentation and adaptation. Noteworthy are the many worker participation programs that sprang up. Some of these changes appeared to be faddish attempts to imitate the Japanese use of quality circles, but others held more serious and lasting potential. Management also began to establish more direct channels of communication with employees, which sometimes bypassed union representatives, who traditionally have served as a liaison between management and union members. The interesting feature of these new efforts is the linkage created between changes in work rules and new forms of worker involvement. In some collective bargaining relationships, the parties have sought new forms of shop-floor labor relations that are based on principles alien to the traditional United States model of collective bargaining.

Unions responded in different ways to these changes. Economic crises and concession bargaining induced a defensive posture in some of them. The threat to standard union practices was strongest where labor was asked for major pay and work-rule concessions in conjunction with management's appeals for a more open and participatory relationship. Fears that these developments will inevitably lead to a further weakening of the labor movement are heightened where firms are expanding their nonunion operations while requesting more conciliation from their unionized workers. Where the United States labor relations system is heading is unclear, except that an era of experimentation and challenge is under way.

TABLE 8-4 Collective Bargaining in the 1982–83 Bargaining Round

Industry	Environmental Economic Pressures			Bargaining Process			Bargaining Outcomes					
	International Competition	Domestic Nonunion Competition	Regulatory Change	Changes in Degree of Centralization	Shift in Role of IR Function	New Forms of Communication or Tactics	Compensation Level Concessions	Changes in Pay Criteria	Work Rules	Job Security	Union Jurisdictional Issues	Labor Management Cooperation
Auto	X	X		X	X	X	X	X	X	X	X	X
Steel	X	X		X		X	X	X	X			X
Trucking		X	X	X	X	X	X		X		X	
Airlines		X	X		X	X	X	X	X			
Rubber	X	X				X	X		X	X		X
Meatpacking		X		X			X	X	X	X		
Clothing	X	X		X								X
Electrical products										X		
Oil refining						X						

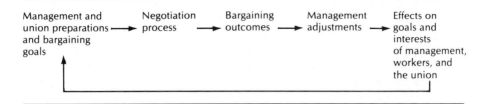

FIGURE 8-2 Sequence of Events in Collective Bargaining from Preparation to Effects

Contract Negotiations: From Preparations to Results

The evolution of collective bargaining suggests that the 1980s have been a period of experimentation and fundamental change in the process and results of negotiations.* This section details current practices in labor negotiations and shows how the process differs from previous patterns. Figure 8-2 outlines the sequence of events in contract negotiations that we review; the sequence begins with management and labor representatives preparing for negotiations and ends with their evaluating the effects of the contract on their respective goals.

Where employees are represented by a union, the design and implementation of many human resource policies take place through collective bargaining. The negotiation process in these situations is a bilateral forum where both unions and employers seek to advance their strategies and policies and to reach an agreement that is responsive to each other's underlying needs and interests. Just as line managers and human resource planners must consider the practical constraints that labor market pressures and employee expectations impose on compensation systems, so also management must recognize that collective bargaining affects a firm's ability to implement its human resource policies and objectives. Most firms only recently began to examine ways to integrate their human resource planning and collective bargaining processes. This section describes the linkages among broad business policies; human resource management strategy and planning; and the preparation, conduct, and results of collective bargaining negotiations.

Preparations for Contract Negotiations

Primary responsibility for preparing to negotiate and conducting the research to establish management's goals and targets usually rests with the labor relations staff. However, line managers from the plant level to the highest executives in the organization participate in important

*This section is based in part on material from Thomas A. Kochan, *Collective Bargaining and Industrial Relations: From Theory to Policy and Practice* (Homewood, Ill: Richard D. Irwin, 1980), 177–343.

ways at various stages in this preparation and decision-making process. Indeed, as management views collective bargaining more as a strategic activity within the firm and less as merely a defensive response to union proposals, line managers and top executives become more active. Moreover, the interplay between the interests of labor relations professionals and line managers, often called *intraorganizational bargaining* (Walton and McKersie, 1965), is often as intense as the bargaining that occurs between the union and management.

Perhaps the best way to describe the process of preparation and the interplay of line and staff roles and interests is to review the way in which a typical large, multiplant firm prepares for negotiations. Preparation for a new round of negotiations in this multiplant firm typically begins at the plant level six to eight months before the start of negotiations. Labor relations staff representatives in each plant meet with plant supervisors to discuss all problems in administering the existing collective bargaining contract. From these meetings comes a list of contract changes that the supervisors want to see in the negotiations. At the same time, the labor relations staff conducts (1) a systematic review of employee grievances that arose during the term of the contract, and (2) an external survey of labor market conditions and wage rates in competing firms in the community. Plant-level activity culminates in a meeting between the labor relations staff in the plant and the plant manager. They attempt in this meeting to screen suggestions for contract changes and to eliminate issues that can be handled either administratively or through informal discussions with local union leaders outside of negotiations; the remaining suggestions are sent to corporate officials as priority items for negotiation.

The second phase of preparation typically involves division-level meetings between labor relations staff and division line managers. Outside industrial relations consultants often attend these meetings. Plant-level priorities for contract changes are compared in division-level meetings and discussion of those items that realistically can be achieved in negotiations are separated from those that are generally unachievable.

While plant- and division-level discussions are taking place, the corporate labor relations staff is formulating its economic proposals on the basis of (1) wage adjustments and collective bargaining settlements in other firms in the industry, and (2) other key settlements that traditionally are used for comparison. The corporate staff works closely with the vice-president of finance to develop the economic parameters or targets for wage adjustments; these are based on comparative labor costs, corporate earnings, and the financial prospects of the firm and the industry. The corporate staff is also responsible for monitoring the political developments within the union and for keeping abreast of national trends and patterns in collective bargaining.

The final step in the preparation involves formulating for the chief executive officer's approval a proposed wage "target," or maximum settlement position, on the economic items and other proposed contract changes. Often two sets of contract outcomes are formulated for the CEO: One, referred to in the literature as "target" settlement points, includes wages and other outcomes that the firm *would like to achieve* in bargaining; the other, called "resistance" points, includes contract outcomes over which the firm *would take a strike* rather than concede (Walton and McKersie, 1965). For example, management might set its target for wages at a 3 percent increase plus a modest improvement in pension benefits, but decide that it would take a strike if wages could not be settled below a 5 percent increase with equivalent increases in pension or other fringe benefits. In this firm, as in most major corporations, the chief executive officer approves before the start of negotiations the parameters within which the negotiating team will bargain.

The above description accurately reflects the traditional pattern of management's preparation for bargaining, but the process changed dramatically in the 1983 round of bargaining in this firm as well as in many others. The more important changes included greater involvement of line managers much earlier in the process and more intensive efforts to introduce the concepts of strategic planning into the preparations. Both of these developments reflect the increased competitive pressures facing many unionized firms and the more proactive efforts of employers to negotiate major changes in the economic terms and conditions governing their unionized employees. In the multiplant firm described above, for example, a team of operating or line managers began meeting to discuss proposed changes in contract provisions governing work rules and subcontracting almost two years before the scheduled start of formal negotiations in 1983. Another large firm — in the auto industry — restructured its corporate human resources staff and created an office of strategic planning for labor relations. The new group spent a year developing new analytical techniques for modeling labor costs, for watching demographic changes in the labor force resulting from industry layoffs and contractions, and for simulating the consequences of alternative labor-cost packages on the short- and long-run competitive position of the firm. The group's new processes met with considerable skepticism and resistance among the more experienced labor relations pros within the corporation; they had worked their way up through the ranks of labor relations and were used to traditional, give-and-take adversarial bargaining and to the politics of union-management relations.

These examples demonstrate the interplay among management, unions, and human resource professionals. The latter must recommend to top executives bargaining parameters that are responsive to the economic and organizational interests of the firm, yet realistic enough to be achievable in negotiations with union representatives. The credibility of labor relations professionals within the firm depends on their willingness both to bargain hard to achieve a collective bargaining agreement that responds to the firm's business strategies and to develop and maintain sound professional relationships and feelings of trust with union representatives. It is this dual role that makes the job of labor relations representatives both interesting and, at times, stressful.

Management's Goals in Bargaining

What criteria guide the choices of target and resistance points for negotiations? As suggested, these criteria must consider not only the *utility* of alternative wages and other contract outcomes, but also the *ability* of the firm to achieve the desired targets or resistance points.

A 1977 Conference Board survey of 668 major corporations found that the criterion ranked most influential on management's wage targets was the wages paid by competitors in the industry or product line of the firm. Wages and conditions in the local labor market were ranked second, followed by the expected profits, productivity, and labor costs trends within the firm (Freedman, 1979; Kochan, 1980). That survey was conducted during the final stage of the post-World War II period of relative stability or incremental adjustment in private-sector collective bargaining. Much of that stability occurred because of the importance given to wage comparisons, or more generally, to the ability of collective bargaining to take wages out of competition by achieving relatively standardized wages across competitors.

The more turbulent, competitive environment of the 1980s has changed the relative importance given to these wage criteria. A 1983 follow-up to the 1977 study found that the rankings have been inverted in industries and companies experiencing the greatest increases in competition. That is, most of the concession bargaining described in the historical overview has occurred because firms have elevated concern over labor costs, profitability, and productivity within their bargaining units to a top priority in their wage targets, while industry standardization and comparisons have been downgraded (Freedman, 1985). The dominant shift in criteria has been from a reliance on external industry- or economy-level comparisons and trends to a concern for the economic conditions of specific units or plants, or of the whole firm.

A similar shift in management goals and behavior occurred on nonwage issues. Again, 1977 Conference Board data showed that the predominant objective of employers on nonwage issues was to maintain the status quo and not negotiate further union-initiated improvements in contract language governing fringe benefits, working conditions, and plant personnel practices. Specifically, the survey found that only a small minority of firms had established specific goals to tighten or pursue management-initiated changes in contract provisions governing fringes such as vacations, health insurance, and subcontracting. The exception to this pattern was that a slight majority (55 percent) of the firms were seeking greater flexibility in job assignment procedures.

Management's status quo orientation on nonwage issues has been replaced in the 1980s with a more aggressive posture. The 1983 Conference Board survey found, for example, that the majority of firms were seeking concessions from employees on health insurance costs and several other fringe benefits. Management also has taken the initiative in seeking changes in a variety of work rules, such as assigning and classifying jobs, and moving people across jobs in layoff, transfer, and promotion situations. These managerial initiatives reflect greater pressures to improve productivity, to lower labor costs, and to increase flexibility in managing human resources under collective bargaining.

Dynamics of Negotiations

To understand how either employers or unions achieve their objectives in negotiations requires an analysis of the dynamics of the negotiation process. Most theoretical models of negotiations rely on the following key sets of concepts: the *bargaining zone* and the *bargaining cycle*.

The Bargaining Zone

A bargaining-zone framework is diagrammed in Figure 8-3. The parties to the process establish target and resistance points before negotiations begin. In addition, both the union and the employer begin formal negotiations with opening offers that overstate their true intentions; that is, the employer's initially stated offer is assumed to be less than its bottom-line position or resistance point and considerably less than the union's resistance point and stated demands. The bargaining process involves a series of compromise offers by each party until the gap between their positions is closed and an agreement is reached. The essence of the process is (1) to discover an opponent's resistance point without divulging one's own, and (2) to induce one's opponent to change a resistance point until it overlaps with one's own.

Where a gap between the resistance points of the two parties exists such that the employer's bottom-line position is less than the union's bottom-line demand, and the union will not settle without calling a strike, a negative contract zone is said to exist. Where resistance points overlap, a positive contract zone exists. Obviously, although it will be

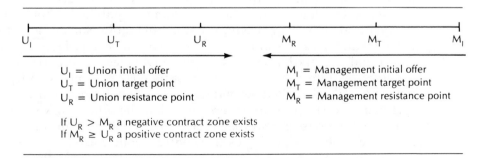

U_I = Union initial offer
U_T = Union target point
U_R = Union resistance point

M_I = Management initial offer
M_T = Management target point
M_R = Management resistance point

If $U_R > M_R$ a negative contract zone exists
If $M_R \geq U_R$ a positive contract zone exists

FIGURE 8-3 Contract Zone Model of the Bargaining Process

more difficult to reach agreement in negative contract zone disputes, in positive contract zone cases it is not a foregone conclusion that settlements will always be achieved without a strike or an impasse. The parties must communicate to each other their bottom-line positions in a way that both recognize the potential for an agreement. Also, both negotiating teams must be sure that their constituents are ready to accept an agreement. Often, the parties at the negotiating table recognize where a settlement can or must occur, but neither the union members nor the corporate executives are ready to accept these terms. It is for these reasons that we often get the ritualistic cycle of negotiations that will be briefly described below.

The Bargaining Cycle

Most typical labor negotiations move through several identifiable states before reaching an agreement. In the earliest stages, a large number of people are often represented on the formal negotiating committees of each party, and large numbers of demands are introduced that both sides know will be whittled to a small number of key issues. Each side overstates its real positions in order to demonstrate to the other, and perhaps more importantly to its internal constituents, its determination to negotiate a hard bargain and to vigorously represent its positions. These early stages of bargaining, therefore, are as much a ritual for constituents as they are for substantive bargaining across the table.

As bargaining moves toward the middle stages, more serious consideration is given to the various proposals of the parties, and the search for a framework for reaching an agreement begins. In these crucial middle stages, both parties sort their relative priorities on the outstanding issues and estimate the probability of an agreement being reached without an impasse or a strike. Further, each party identifies and signals to the other where compromises might be possible. Often in this stage, many nonwage issues are resolved or tacitly removed from further consideration. The parties often follow a dictum, however, that "no issue is finally settled until all issues are settled."

The final stage of bargaining emerges as the contract, or strike, deadline approaches. In this stage, the number of key decision makers on each side tends to dwindle, and the principals often hold off-the-record discussions away from the bargaining table. Sometimes a third-party mediator assists in these off-the-record talks and helps structure the formal negotiation process. In the final stage, each party seeks to convince the other of the credibility of its position and its willingness to take a strike if pushed beyond its resistance-point positions. Further, each party works hard to understand what the other party's real bottom-line positions are, so that they do not back into an unnecessary strike, i.e., one in which a positive contract zone exists.

In the final stage, negotiators on each side must make the strategic choice of deciding whether to put their best and last offer on the table in anticipation of reaching a successful agreement, or to hold back some compromises if putting them on the table would not achieve an agreement without a strike or an impasse. Also in this stage, the talents of the negotiators and any third-party neutrals undergo their most severe test. Every effort must be made to overcome any interpersonal conflicts or personality clashes between the negotiators and to ensure that the communication process is not blocked by feelings of mistrust and misunderstanding. The stakes of misjudgment at this final hour are crucial. Misjudging the other party's resistance point may lead the parties to miss an opportunity for an acceptable agreement and impose an unnecessary strike on both workers and the firm. Alternatively, miscalculating the views of one's constituents and reaching a tentative agreement that is later rejected by either the workers or the executives merely delays the timing of the impasse and brings what was an intraorganizational conflict out into the open.

The dynamics of contract negotiations illustrate why it often appears that so much bargaining goes to the eleventh hour of the contract deadline. Many outside observers have criticized this crisis, or deadline, orientation of collective bargaining. In the past, however, it has been clear that, unless exceptional circumstances prevailed, the political needs of both labor and management negotiators and the real economic differences in interests over which they were negotiating often could be resolved only under the intense pressure of an immediate strike threat and contract deadline.

The Dynamics Change

Exceptional conditions in the 1980s have prevailed in many collective bargaining settings and have modified the dynamics of the negotiation process. In major industries such as trucking, airlines, longshoring, autos, steel, and meatpacking, for example, we have seen contract reopenings before their scheduled revision dates. We also have seen employers not only introduce more proposals for contract changes of their own (rather than react to union proposals), but also justify their proposals for economic concessions by sharing competitive financial information with union representatives and employees. Recently many employers have engaged in direct communications with employees in an effort to explain to them the competitive environment facing the firm and to lower their expectations for the wage settlement.

Management's frankness has led to two types of reactions among labor leaders. In cases such as the bargaining between the United Auto Workers (UAW) and Ford Motor Company, union leaders saw this openness as a positive development, as illustrated in the following statement of Donald Ephlin, the UAW vice-president who headed the union negotiating team at Ford in 1982:

> The entire agreement is structured to facilitate a new and different approach to joint problem solving. While we still disagree from time to time and will likely continue to do so, we are trying to develop "win-win" solutions. To Ford's credit, the company, from the chairman on down,

has made a real commitment to the success of our efforts. For the first time in the history of UAW-Ford bargaining, both the chairman, Philip Caldwell, and the president, Donald Petersen, came to the bargaining table to meet with our rank-and-file bargaining committee. As director of the national UAW-Ford department, I will address the company's board of directors twice annually. That spirit of communication and joint decision making is increasingly present in the day-to-day efforts of the union and the company on the shop floor (Ephlin, 1983, 64–65).

In contrast, the union has perceived management's efforts in other situations as bad-faith bargaining because management bypasses the official union representatives and deals directly with the rank and file.

It remains to be seen whether these changes in the negotiation process represent a lasting shift away from the historic give-and-take pattern of bargaining, or merely a temporary deviation from established traditions because of severe economic pressures. Where the environment has experienced a lasting shift toward a higher degree of competition, some of these recent patterns may continue both in the negotiation process and in bargaining outcomes. To predict patterns of bargaining results, we need to understand that elusive concept of *bargaining power*.

Sources of Bargaining Power

Because collective bargaining involves the interplay of two sets of conflicting interests, the outcome of negotiations can be viewed as the product of the relative power of the parties to achieve their objectives (Chamberlain and Kuhn, 1965). What, then, determines the relative bargaining power of the parties? Most models of collective bargaining assume that bargaining power is established by the economic environment in which the parties operate and by the structural and organizational properties of the bargaining relationship. A general model of the sources of power that affect collective bargaining outcomes is presented in Figure 8-4.

All theories of collective bargaining start by assessing the economic sources of power that bring about wage and compensation decisions. In microeconomics, the ability of a union to increase wages depends heavily on the inelasticity of the demand for labor. More than fifty years ago, economist Alfred Marshall identified four factors that influence the inelasticity of labor demand: (1) the inelasticity of the demand for the final product, (2) the essentiality of labor to the production process, (3) the inelasticity of the supply of other factors of production that could substitute for labor, and (4) the ratio of labor costs to the total costs of production. The first three of these factors are expected to relate positively to union bargaining power, while the latter should be negatively related to union power.

Also more than a half-century ago, labor economist John R. Commons noted that unions must be able to organize a sufficient proportion of the workers employed in a given product market in order to "take

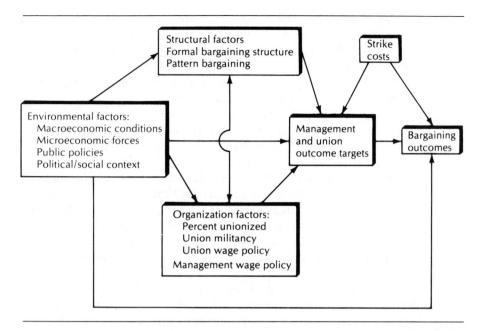

FIGURE 8-4   Sources of Power Affecting Collective Bargaining Outcomes

wages out of competition." This is another way of interpreting Marshall's conditions. That is, if unions are unable to organize large portions of the product market or to engage in some form of pattern bargaining to spread a common wage across the industry, demand will fall for those employees with higher wages and increase for those with wages below the standard rate. Thus, union bargaining power should decline in periods of rising competition from domestic nonunion firms or from foreign producers who operate with lower labor costs. Alternatively, union bargaining power tends to increase with the rate of unionization in an industry, and particularly in industries where both unionization is high and economic concentration significantly bars the entry of new firms. High rates of unionization and economic concentration, for example, enabled unions to increase wages and improve working conditions in the auto, steel, airline, trucking, and railroad industries before competition increased.

In the legal sphere, legislation can affect the power of the bargaining parties. The history of U.S. labor legislation demonstrates the importance of having a secure legal foundation for unionization if employees are to achieve positive results through collective bargaining. Between 1935 and 1947, for example, first line supervisors or foremen were eligible for protection under the National Labor Relations Act (NLRA); foreman unions grew as supervisors saw the benefits of organizing and benefited from the protection of the law. After 1947 and passage of the Taft-Hartley amendments to the NLRA, foremen were excluded from coverage under the law, and their unions subsequently disappeared. Similarly, wages and other terms of employment for public employees improved most rapidly after the passage of state legislation granting them the rights to organize and bargain collectively. Legal protection for organizing, which is free of employer discrimination and retaliation, is probably a necessary but insufficient condition for union power in collective bargaining.

Technology also affects power; it has an obvious effect on a union's ability to engage in a strike to halt the production process. For example, a strike by firefighters or automobile workers can effectively curtail services or production. On the other hand, strikes by telephone workers, workers in chemical plants or oil refineries, or those in many electrical utilities have less of an impact; production can continue with a skeleton supervisory labor force because technology has been used to automate these operations. It is only over a prolonged period, as equipment breakdowns tax the capacity of the supervisory work force, that the unionized labor force's essentiality to these firms and industries increases.

Additional structural and organizational characteristics of the bargaining relationship also affect the power of the parties. For example, the militance of rank-and-file workers and the extent to which management holds some hard-line position will influence the credibility of a strike threat. These more situation-specific aspects of bargaining power are determined in part by the external economic, legal, technological, and other environmental forces. Still, however, the militancy of the rank and file and the strategic decisions and behavior of management and union leaders are crucial determinants of both the dynamics of the negotiation process and the results negotiation produces.

Effects of Collective Bargaining

It is extremely difficult to make general statements about the *average* effect that unions and collective bargaining have on the terms and conditions of employment and on the economic welfare of workers and employers. Collective bargaining in American society is characterized by its *diversity* of results and effects, which is not surprising given its decentralized nature. More than 190,000 separate collective bargaining agreements exist in the United States, and each year roughly one-third of these contracts are renegotiated. Thus, the following overview of the effects of unions in collective bargaining captures only a few of the major long-term effects that unions have had on employment relationships. The presence of a union sets off a dynamic chain of events that causes a wide array of economic and behavioral results of interest to employees and employers.

Wages and Benefits

The primary, initial effect that unions have on the employment relationship is to increase wages. Although the magnitude of the union's effect on wages has varied over time, the most recent studies from the

1970s suggest that on average, unions have raised the wages of unionized workers 15 to 20 percent above the wages paid to nonunion workers in the same occupation with similar personal characteristics. The wage effect is considerably higher for entry-level and lower-skilled positions than for higher-skilled workers whose wages are driven up by labor market shortages. Unions also appear to have had greater positive effects on the wages of nonwhite workers rather than whites, of young and older workers rather than workers in their prime, and on blue-collar rather than white-collar workers. The evidence is also quite strong that unions have had a positive effect on fringe benefits. In fact, the magnitude of these effects on fringe benefits appears to be greater than the magnitude of the union wage effect. Some estimates put the union premium on fringe benefits at 30 percent (Freeman, 1981).

Job/Employment Security

Unions have negotiated for their members a wide range of improvements in job and employment security. The most prominent union effect on job security is the protection of workers from arbitrary discharge or discipline through the grievance and binding arbitration provisions found in almost all private-sector collective bargaining agreements. Seniority provisions in union contracts further protect the economic security of longer-service union members. A minority of unions (mainly in the auto, steel, and other durable-goods manufacturing industries) have successfully negotiated a variety of income security provisions to supplement federal unemployment compensation during temporary layoffs. A smaller minority of unions has negotiated provisions protecting employees from the effects of permanent job loss due to technological change or plant shutdowns; these agreements provide severance pay, retraining and relocation allowances, and, in 10 percent of these agreements, advance notice of plant closings. Although these are important accomplishments, the inability of unions to achieve similar provisions in a majority of contracts has led the labor movement to advocate national and/or state legislation governing plant closings, and to call for a broader role for labor when technological change is introduced than unions have been able to achieve through decentralized collective bargaining.

Safety and Health/Work Environment

Unions have negotiated improvements in health and safety through a combination of provisions for (1) labor-management safety and health committees, (2) protection against exposure to hazardous substances and working conditions, (3) compensation for injured workers, and (4) pay premiums for hazardous work, which raises the cost of unsafe work. In addition, the labor movement has been the central voice in lobbying for passage and strict enforcement of the Occupational Safety and Health Act.

Although many American unions resisted the experiments of the early 1970s in employee participation and the quality of working life

(QWL), much joint union-management experimentation with QWL and related forms of work-organization change has emerged in the early 1980s. Now a diversity of views is found within the labor movement over the merits of union-management QWL projects (Kochan, Katz, and Mower, 1984). Unions such as the Communications Workers of America, the United Steelworkers, the United Auto Workers, and the Newspaper Guild participate with employers in a large number of jointly run QWL projects, and top leaders of these unions generally encourage and support their locals in these efforts. In the majority of unions, however, joint projects are under way at the local level, but national officers neither endorse nor oppose the efforts. The top leaders of a few unions such as the International Association of Machinists and the United Electrical Workers have voiced strong criticism of QWL efforts and view them as efforts by employers to undermine the process of collective bargaining and the role of the union in the workplace. Even in these unions, however, one finds a number of locals participating with employers in various joint efforts. We are clearly in an era of experimentation with greater union-management efforts to change the work environment and improve the quality of working life, productivity, and product quality through employee participation processes.

The task of examining the contents of collective bargaining agreements and identifying areas where unions have achieved improvements in the wages, hours, and working conditions of their members is straightforward. It is much more difficult to assess the contributions (or the lack of contribution) of unions to the psychological well-being of their members and to the general work environment. Empirical evidence from surveys of worker satisfaction suggest that, on average, unionized workers report higher satisfaction with wages and with the bread-and-butter aspects of their jobs than nonunion workers. Part of this is due to the positive effects that unions have had on workers' wages over the long run. On the other hand, union members, on average, report less satisfaction with some of the nonwage aspects of their jobs — particularly job content, challenge, and opportunities for personal growth. This discontent, however, may be changing as unions become more active in working with employers through QWL and other forms of worker participation to improve the work environment. Overall, the evidence suggests that unions and unionized employers have a long way to go in improving the psychological climate of the workplace. Unionized workers clearly rate their firms and their unions more positively on bread-and-butter aspects of their jobs, but less positively on the more intrinsic or task-specific aspects of their work environment (Kochan, Katz, and Mower, 1984).

Management Practices and Organizational Performance

Finally, unions have had an important effect on the evolution of the personnel and human resource practices of American employers. More than forty years ago, a well-known labor economist and management expert noted that one of the most significant effects that unions have on a firm is to create a "shock effect" on employer personnel practices (Slichter, 1941). That is, because unions increase wages, put pressure on the cost structure of firms, and remove some of the arbitrary authority from employers, firms are required to establish more clear-cut personnel policies and standards and to take steps to ensure that these policies are implemented in a consistent, equitable fashion. Further, to the extent that unions increase wages and other labor costs above those of competitors, firms must seek in nonwage areas efficiencies that can increase productivity to compensate for the higher labor costs.

This need for balance leads to a series of managerial adjustments. These adjustments may include greater capital investment and technological change to conserve on the labor required, more careful use of human resource planning to minimize the tendency to overstaff, and higher standards of hiring to increase the quality of workers (since higher wages and better working conditions are being offered). Alternatively, improvements in wages and fringe benefits lead employers to seek union cooperation and/or to negotiate harder in future rounds of bargaining over work-rule and work-organization changes, which can improve productivity and further economize on the use of human resources. The ultimate effect of collective bargaining on a firm's bottom-line concerns for productivity and profitability depends on the interaction between the union's effects on wages and other terms of the contract and the managerial adjustments made in accordance with the contract changes. Because of these interactive effects, unions and collective bargaining are unlikely to have any stable, long-term, average effect on the bottom-line goals of employers. The history of collective bargaining has moved through various evolutionary stages that net some positive and some negative effects on employers' goals. Ample evidence from case studies of employer practices suggests that, from 1930 to 1960, unions had a rationalizing effect on employer policies, which not only improved standards of living for union members but also improved productivity in unionized firms (Slichter, Healy, and Livernash, 1960; Freeman and Medoff, 1979). This shock effect created a *spillover* effect; nonunion firms matched many of the personnel practices of unionized firms and, to some extent, introduced further innovations in personnel practices and processes to counter the threat of unionization. Since the 1960s, new forms of human resource management that emphasize individual differences and small group motivation have been used widely in nonunion firms and have produced more flexible forms of work organization. When combined with lower wages and cheaper fringe benefits, these new systems have given nonunion competitors a productivity and profitability edge over their unionized counterparts. Thus, in the 1980s, unionized firms are engaged in experimentation and tumultuous change in an effort to catch up with innovations in nonunion firms. If history is a guide, we can expect the dynamic interplay between the union and the nonunion sectors of our economy to continue.

References

Barbash, Jack, et al., *Collective Bargaining: Contemporary American Experience,* Gerald G. Somers, ed. (Madison: Industrial Relations Research Association, 1980).

Bernstein, Irving, *The Lean Years; A History of the American Worker, 1920–1933* (Boston: Houghton Mifflin, 1960). Also, *Turbulent Years: A History of the American Worker, 1933–1941* (Boston: Houghton Mifflin, 1969).

Burton, John, "The Extent of Collective Bargaining in the Public Sector," in *Public-Sector Bargaining,* B. Aaron, et al., eds. (Washington, D.C.: BNA, 1979).

Chamberlain, Neil W., and James W. Kuhn, *Collective Bargaining* (New York: McGraw Hill, 1965).

Freedman, Audrey, *Managing Labor Relations* (New York: The Conference Board, 1979), and *Changes in Managing Employee Relations* (New York: The Conference Board, 1985).

Freeman, Richard B., "The Effect of Unionism on Fringe Benefits," *Industrial and Labor Relations Review,* 34, July 1981, 489–509.

Freeman, Richard B., and James L. Medoff, "The Two Faces of Unionism," *The Public Interest,* Fall 1979, 69–83.

Harris, Howell John, *The Right to Manage* (Madison: University of Wisconsin Press, 1982).

Hoxie, Robert F., *Trade Unionism in the United States* (New York, London: D. Appleton and Company, 1923).

Kerr, Clark, John T. Dunlop, Fredrick H. Harbison, and Charles A. Myers, *Industrialism and Industrial Man: The Problems of Labor and Management in Economic Growth* (Cambridge, Mass: Harvard University Press, 1960).

Kochan, Thomas A., *Collective Bargaining: From Theory to Policy and Practice* (Homewood, Ill.: Irwin, 1980).

Kochan, Thomas A., Harry C. Katz, and Nancy Mower, *Worker Participation and American Unions: Threat or Opportunity?* (Kalamazoo, Mich.: The W. E. Upjohn Institute for Employment Research, 1984).

Lenz, Sidney, *The Labor Wars: From the Molly Maguires to the Sitdowns* (Garden City, N.Y.: Doubleday, 1973).

Millis, Harry A., and Royal E. Montgomery, *Organized Labor* (New York: McGraw-Hill, 1945).

Pelling, Henry, *American Labor* (Chicago: University of Chicago Press, 1960).

Rayback, Joseph G., *A History of American Labor* (New York: Macmillan, 1959).

Ross, Arthur, *Trade Union Wage Policy* (Berkeley: University of California Press, 1948).

Slichter, Sumner H., *Union Policies and Industrial Management* (Washington, D.C.: The Brookings Institution, 1941).

Slichter, Sumner H., James J. Healy, and E. Robert Livernash, *The Impact of Collective Bargaining on Management* (Washington, D.C.: The Brookings Institution, 1960).

Strauss, George, "The Shifting Power Balance in the Plant," *Industrial Relations,* May 1962.

Taft, Philip, *The A.F. of L. in the Time of Gompers* (New York: Harper, 1957).

Walton, Richard E., and Robert B. McKersie, *A Behavioral Theory of Labor Negotiations* (New York: McGraw-Hill, 1965).

Suggested Readings

For a comprehensive summary of the evidence of the effects of unions on the goals of individual workers, firms, and the larger society, see Richard B. Freeman and James L. Medoff, *What Unions Do* (New York: Basic Books, 1984).

For a discussion of the effects of changes in the American industrial relations system on the labor movement, see Thomas A. Kochan (ed.), *Challenges and Choices Facing American Labor* (Cambridge, Mass.: MIT Press, 1984).

For a more general discussion of the process of negotiations and ways to improve it, see Howard Raiffa, *The Art and Science of Negotiations* (Cambridge, Mass.: Harvard University Press, 1982).

Collective Bargaining in 1982

This case illustrates how in 1982 bargaining in one company represented a turning point in the conduct of industrial relations and human resource management. The case is about a trucking firm that has experienced severe economic pressures and has developed new business and human resource management strategies during the past several years. In 1982, the company faced the task of negotiating a new labor agreement with the International Brotherhood of Teamsters.

The experiences of Kramer Trucking illustrate the links between business strategy, the process and results of collective bargaining, and human resource management in the workplace. Further, the changes the company was attempting to introduce were stimulated in part by increased competition, which developed gradually in this industry in the 1970s and exploded in the 1980s after passage of the Trucking Industry Deregulation Act. The case allows us to assess the effects of environmental change on industrial relations within the firm.

The day-to-day events that transpired between the summers of 1981 and 1982 vividly illustrate the fundamental changes that occurred during the process of bargaining — from the development of management strategy and preparations for negotiations, to the structure of negotiations, to the criteria used to establish targets and guide the tentative settlement, to the union-management interactions in negotiations, and finally to the process used to ratify the agreement.

CASE
Kramer Trucking Company

The Kramer Trucking Company has been in the trucking industry for more than thirty years. Its most rapid growth occurred in the 1960s and 1970s, and currently it employs approximately one thousand drivers.

From the beginning, the company was a paternalistic employer that attempted to establish close relations with employees and treat them well. As the company grew, it acquired a number of Teamster contracts and eventually was covered under the National Master Freight Agreement (NMFA). This is the national agreement between the Teamsters and an industry association currently called Trucking Management, Inc. (TMI). After it was included in the NMFA, Kramer added a new position, director of industrial relations, to its management structure.

EVOLUTION OF LABOR RELATIONS

The first real labor relations difficulties for Kramer occurred in the 1976 negotiations. The industry association developed a new method of compensation for drivers and included it in the agreement negotiated with the Teamsters that covered Kramer's drivers. The agreement changed the pay system from payment for miles and hours to payment based on a percentage of the shipment revenue. In addition, a concept called comparison pay was included in the agreement to provide a safety net for the drivers if their pay under the new system fell below what they would have earned under the old. In actuality, the new system paid less than the old one, and drivers were upset. As if to confound the problem, neither the Teamsters nor the company had prepared the drivers for the new system; they simply announced it after the bargain was settled. The drivers had no knowledge that a new system would be brought to them for ratification. As a result, they struck, but they ended their brief walkout when the company assured them that it would pay the difference whenever warranted.

The years 1976 to 1979 gave Kramer a mixed set of labor relations experiences. A high level of grievances occurred because the drivers distrusted both the company and the union under the new pay system. Yet, the company grew rapidly because of the general prosperity of the firms whose products it shipped.

The climate of low trust and high conflict continued through the 1979 negotiations. In 1978, a group of disgruntled drivers organized a rival faction within the local union that culminated in another wildcat strike after the 1979 contract was negotiated with the Teamsters.

CHANGES IN BUSINESS AND HUMAN RESOURCE STRATEGIES

In the late 1970s, management concluded that, if relations with the Teamsters continued to deteriorate and if the industry was headed for deregulation, the company would have to set up independent contracting firms to survive. Under this arrangement, nonunion subsidiaries are established in which the drivers own their own tractors and are more loosely affiliated with the company. Management considered the following facts: (1) A large number of independent contracting firms had always existed in the industry. (2) The company estimated that its labor costs were approximately 30 to 50 percent above the costs required to run an independent contractor firm. (3) Deregulation would create an influx of independent contractors, and the ability of Teamster companies both to control entry into their routes and to pass on the costs of labor or other increases to their customers would be inhibited. Thus, Kramer proceeded to establish a number of independent contractor firms. By 1982, several such firms were in place and had grown rapidly in their initial years.

With the new organizational structure came a new management structure. The president of the company decided to develop a more professional management group and hired (1) an experienced executive to serve as the chief operating officer, (2) an experienced professional as the vice-president of human resource management, and (3) an organizational development (OD) specialist. The hiring of these professionals signaled a new approach to managing employees in the firm.

The key ingredients of the new strategy included the following:

1. Develop new communication systems and processes between the company and drivers, and the company and the union.
2. Develop a more employee-centered high-commitment work system for managing the work force.
3. Develop greater driver and union awareness of the competitive conditions facing the company and its work force, and the relationship between those conditions and job security.
4. Reduce the company's labor costs through a combination of a reduction in pay for nonproductive time, the implementation of a new percentage pay or some equivalent system, and the movement away from the National Master Freight Agreement to an individual contract which better fits the Kramer operation.

The first step in implementing this new strategy centered on developing a variety of conferences and training sessions for drivers. One session, for example, was a three-day offsite program in which drivers were given extensive technical training and told how to set goals and calculate their fuel usage before and after the program. On the first day of training, drivers were given a large amount of information about the costs of the business, most of which was on fuel costs (See Tables 8-5; 8-6; Figures 8-5; 8-6; and Exhibit 8-1). For example, they were shown that a 0.1 mile-per-gallon fuel savings resulted in a savings of six hundred thousand dollars per year to the company. Drivers also were encouraged to stay within the 55-mile-per-hour speed limit to conserve fuel. On the third day, the company's chief operating officer discussed in more detail other aspects of the business. One item was the reasons for developing the independent contractor companies. Again, cost comparisons and rate structures in the industry were discussed, and the role of wages and labor costs in the overall competitive structure of the firm were described in detail. This information was also sent directly to drivers in a letter from the president (see Exhibit 8-2). Further communication regarding competitive cost problems was transmitted through letters sent by top executives to drivers and to local union offices (see Exhibits 8-3; 8-4; and 8-5).

TABLE 8-5 Information Provided to Drivers at Training Sessions in 1981

| | Revenue Comparison Revenue (millions) | | | Cost Advantage Versus Kramer Per Mile |
Carrier	1979	1980	% Change	
Grid	$6.4	$9.3	45	
Conway	17.4	24.3	37	23¢ less
Marr	23.9	33.3	39	14¢ less
Hale	14.9	25.5	71	24¢ less
Hartley	52.7	65.8	25	24¢ less
Redd	160.0	190.0	19	19¢ less
Mazzarelli	16.9	20.2	20	19¢ less
Herrity	15.7	20.0	27	N/A
Kramer	142.5	159.0	12	N/A

TABLE 8-6   Kramer Transport Annual Investment in Revenue Equipment

	1978	1979	1980
Tractors			
Quantity	275	509	435
Cost	$9,848,000	$18,442,000	$21,032,000
Trailers			
Quantity	339	362	209
Cost	$2,616,000	$4,280,000	$5,764,000
Total annual investment			
in revenue			
equipment	$12,464,000	$22,722,000	$26,796,000
Net income	$ 3,712,000	$ 4,107,000	$ 3,305,000

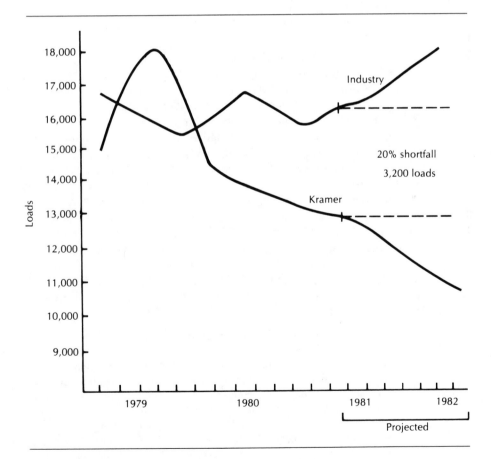

FIGURE 8-5   Kramer Loads versus Industry Forecast
Old Line Customers

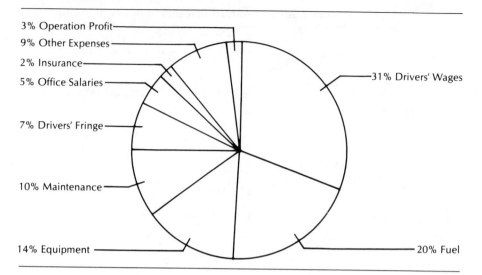

FIGURE 8-6   Kramer Transport, Inc.
1980 Operating Costs as Percentages of Revenue

Another program to take information on the competitive cost problems into the field involved sending key managers, for a week at a time, to selected truck stops around the country. Small groups of drivers could meet and discuss with the managers the effects of industry deregulation, fuel costs, and other competitive aspects of the business and industry.

In another innovation to strengthen the role of operating management and to provide stronger first-line supervisors and drivers, Kramer established a field coordinator system. A company assessment center was opened and drivers were encouraged to undergo assessment for possible promotion into first-line management and supervision. Six supervisors had come up through this system by 1981, and six more were in the process of doing so in mid-1981. This new system also provided a role for drivers in screening new job applicants for the company and providing input into employee selection.

All of these efforts at communication were occurring in 1980 and 1981. The human resource management vice-president described it as an information-sharing process that was "not a democratic process, but an educational process." He continued:

> We are trying to make the best of a deteriorating market situation by involving employees as much as we can in what we are doing. We would like to be in a situation where we could become even more employee-involvement centered, but that will have to wait until we overcome our competitive problems. Unfortunately, we are not in the game (solid financial position) we would like to be, but instead we are in a rapidly deteriorating market position. Our long-term intent is to become more employee involved and to develop a high degree of commitment among our drivers. Specifically, we would like to develop teams of drivers and managers that are organized around the various parts of our business. In this way we would like to recapture the personal involvement and

EXHIBIT 8-1
Some Business Facts

1. Our competitors are not *dumb* — they know our weakness — cost. (I would do the same thing if I was working for Redd, Marr, etc.)
2. Kramer Transport customers are fair game for all other motor carriers.

   Our customer/prices are public knowledge.
   Our customers like the increased number of options they have.

3. Excess capacity will continue to exist in the truckload market through 1983–1985 because of:

   Reduced empty miles because of operating authority
   Private fleets filling up empty miles
   New carriers
   Successful companies will expand

4. Bigness (corporate size) is no guarantee of survival — only competitive costs and responding to customer needs.
5. Laws of economics cause industries to change (and move).

   Supply/demand — excess demand causes prices to rise; excess capacity causes prices to fall.
   Customers will pursue low cost options that meet their service needs.

   Examples: Textile industry moved to the South from the New England area; T.V. sets produced overseas; Armour plant in Central City.
6. Many shippers have severe cost pressures — their survival requires *lower cost* transportation services. If not, *they will be out of business.*
7. A significant portion of the shippers have gone "generic" (like housewives in the supermarket) — their customers are demanding it. Why pay a premium when brand "x" will do the job?
8. Deregulation is causing a permanent change to our lives, jobs, company. The "good old days" are gone and are being replaced by more competitive and *challenging* opportunities.

---

close interpersonal relations that characterized the firm in the past. We know we can't simply return to the old-style paternalism in human relations that existed before, but we want to capture some of its benefits in new ways.

This executive described the nature of this new strategy as developing a form of tough trust based on sharing hard information about the competitive realities facing the firm and the drivers. He contrasted this with the soft trust that has been associated with the organizational development field in the past. He summarized their approach as follows:

What we are doing here might be described as building "tough trust." We are not talking about soft pollyannaish types of trust building but tough trust built on substantive discussions of our problems. This is different from the emphasis on communications for process-oriented change or psychological climate improvement. It is communications designed to get the real problems into the forefront of the minds of the workers, our managers, and union leaders. If we get through this it may be a sign of a real change in the way in which we conduct labor relations in our company and industry and maybe even the country. It means that we are attempting to move from a short-term tactical basis where power rules completely to focus on longer-run concerns.

PLANS FOR THE 1982 NEGOTIATIONS

In the fall of 1980 the chief operating officer of the company formed a new group for planning the 1982 negotiations. The group was labeled the "Industrial Relations & Human Resource Planning Group." The members of the group included the three managers of the operating divisions of the corporation, the director of industrial relations, and the vice-president of human resource management. Their central task was to think about "where we had to be at the point where the contract expired and to determine what needed to be achieved in these contract negotiations." The group defined its task as having three parts: First, they were concerned with the amount and type of knowledge and communications that drivers needed to have prior to the beginning of formal negotiations. Second, they were concerned about the type of knowledge and communications that various managers and supervisors needed. Third, they focused on developing an analytical base for assessing all relevant costs associated with their operations and with the operations of their competitors.

From the planning process came a negotiation strategy that focused on several objectives, including (1) the ability to negotiate a separate contract outside of the NMFA between the company and the Teamsters, and (2) the installation of a new pay structure and system that allowed the company to compete with independent contractors more effectively.

The company formally requested separate negotiations authority from the international union. The president of the company met with the leaders of the international union to present the case for separate negotiations. He laid out the competitive situation directly, with data on the differential labor costs, trends in revenue and erosion of the business, and other pertinent data. He also presented the case that the Kramer operation was distinctly different from the companies covered by the NMFA. The union agreed to allow separate negotiations.

The negotiations were conducted with the team that included the company's chief operating officer, director of industrial relations, and attorney. These negotiations were different from those of previous years. One management negotiator saw the process as shifting from the previous emphasis on power bargaining to a process that was focused more directly on the economic realities of the marketplace and what was right for the people.

It was an economically oriented process this time — a logic-based negotiations. It was also a very calm set of negotiations. It was characterized by: "Here are the data. They are unmistakably clear and here are some things we need to deal with." The president of the company presented the data to emphasize the importance of these points.

EXHIBIT 8-2
Confidential Letter to Kramer Transport Drivers

July 9, 1981

Dear Employee:

I've committed to many of you in a variety of group information and
training sessions and in personal conversation to keep you appraised
of where we stand in our very competitive and often cut-throat
business environment. I believe in telling it as it is. The truth is
that despite the cost reduction work accomplished over the last 18
months we are still not cost and, therefore, rate competitive. The
truth is that our competitors, a mixture of low-cost nonunion owner-
operator companies and union companies with much lower wage-fringe
packages, are taking us on — head on. They are openly stating they
are after us and our customers. They are taking significant business
from us. The truth is that the marketplace is setting the rate that
will move the freight. The shipper has more choice than ever before
and is using it to reduce his transportation costs. The truth is
that the shipper is finding that the nonunion owner-operator company
and the union company with the lower cost base are delivering the
required level of service and flexibility. The truth is that this
rate cutting, shifting of business by shippers, and growth of lower-
cost competition is happening much faster than anyone had
anticipated. The truth is that we are losing important business
rapidly because we are simply <u>not</u> cost competitive. Our position in
the marketplace is not good. The truth is that we need to act and
act now. We have built something very good; now we need to defend
it. It's a battle.

We are seriously questioning each and every aspect of our
noncompetitive cost base including our current method of operation
and our historical strategy of company-owned equipment.

We have to take aggressive action to survive in this battle.
Consider the following facts:

1. Nonunion companies and union companies with different wage-
    fringe packages are able to operate at 15¢–20¢–25¢ per mile
    under where we are — even with our superb cost reduction
    work. Many nonunion owner-operator competitors have wage-
    fringe packages 15¢ per mile less than Kramer Transport. In
    addition, most of our competition has a 5¢/mile advantage
    over us because of their methods of operation and
    individual productivity. They are putting significantly
    more miles on their equipment each year — 110,000–120,000
    driver/equipment miles per year.

2. Low cost competition has made significant inroads on
    Teamster company-owned equipment businesses like ours. It
    has been reported that close to 25 percent of the Teamster

drivers are currently not working. Many companies are out of business. Several are trying to sell. Most of our competition is nonunion.

3. We have reduced prices to keep business. You know this. We have reached the point at which further price reductions to meet competition without lowering our costs would cause substantial (in the millions of dollars) operating losses this year.

4. Owner-operator companies are providing good service right along with the low rates. Shippers are quick to point this out to us. This includes on-time pickup and delivery, good customer service at the docks, trailer pools in a lot of cases, and hassle free performance.

The enclosed information is in support of the points I have made in this letter. I could have enclosed one hundred other articles, business facts, and shipper comments. Reread this letter and study the enclosed material. I'm telling each and every Kramer Transport employee that our situation is very serious! We are a target. We must, and will, take decisive action to defend what we have built together. We have concluded that our company in its present form with its present cost per mile position cannot be successful in this new business environment. I thought it very important to openly share this conclusion with you.

We are currently utilizing all of our resources to develop comprehensive action steps to defend our position in the truckload business. We will openly and candidly keep you informed of the changes required.

Sincerely,

Max Taylor

Max Taylor
President

Enclosures

Enclosure 1

EXAMPLES OF COMPETITORS' COST PER MILE ADVANTAGE
OVER KRAMER TRANSPORT

	COST PER MILE
REDD	24¢ less
HALE	24¢ less
CONWAY	23¢ less
CHANDLER	21¢ less
COBURN	21¢ less
MAZZARELLI	19¢ less
LAWRENCE	18¢ less
MARR	14¢ less

SOURCE: 1980 Trinc's.

EXAMPLES OF LOADS LOST TO LOWER-COST CARRIERS

Loss of Loads from Long-time Customers:

1. Forty-three (43) carriers have approached a long-time customer in Maryland with prices 15¢ to 20¢ per mile below ours. Goldbert, Belmont, PA, will provide more service than we can provide for 20¢ a mile less. This means a loss of 50 to 70 loads per week.

2. Approximately 170 carriers have come in at prices considerably lower than ours for our major customers to a point where only major price change will retain loads.

3. Lawrence has taken all freight from a consumer products manufacturer, which means a loss of 10 to 15 loads per week to Kramer Transport.

4. A large container manufacturer in Ohio has removed Kramer Transport from its routing guide because of lower rates provided by competitors led by RBN. This means 300 loads per week to Kramer Transport.

5. A label company located in Texas has gone from 25 loads per month to zero. Lyle Transit has rates 30¢ a mile lower than ours and is now serving them.

6. A building supply manufacturer's loads have been lost to Boston Transport and Bosie. This means we have lost as much as 30 loads per week from them.

7. A paper manufacturer in Ohio — we have lost 10 loads per week to a company called Travellors out of Minneapolis, MN, who trip leases the freight to other carriers at a cost of 20¢-to-30¢ per mile below us.

8. We have lost 5 loads per week from a paper bag manufacturer in Indiana to RBN, Timeway, and King Freight.

9. A printed material company in Indiana is tendering freight to Hartford Distribution, Mike Ross, Meenen, and Moore at prices 15¢-to-20¢ per mile lower than us. This results in a loss of 5 loads per week for Kramer Transport.

10. We have lost 10 loads per week from a corrugated materials company in the Midwest to a lower cost carrier named Champion Carriers.

11. Hale, at prices 20¢-to-25¢ per mile below us, has taken 3 loads per week from a heating/ventilating company in the Midwest.

Loss of Business from New Accounts:

1. A new account, a major food manufacturer, has developed four more house carriers; among them are Ice Box Transport, Mighty Mike's (high-cube division), and Kuper Systems of America. These are all nonunion, owner-operator companies, who are now sharing in business that was solely served by Kramer Transport two months ago.

2. A new kitchen products customer in Ohio is now using Marr, a nonunion, owner-operator company, to haul loads for 23¢ a mile less than we can.

3. We can't get into a large manufacturing company in Wisconsin because they utilize Eastern, Mazzarelli, and Fairfield at rates 20¢-to-40¢ a mile lower than ours.

SHIPPER COMMENTS

Please note: our loss of business is not the fault of our
customers. As good businessmen, they need to act where they can to
lower the cost of their product in the marketplace. We must focus on
our competition. They are the ones taking us on — the enemy.

The following are actual cases from many others like them. Each
one illustrates some marketplace realities. We are told that our
service is not necessarily unique — but our prices are.

HEAVY GOODS PRODUCER — When questioned about the value of being able
to depend on Kramer in the long run and perceived debt relative to
past service responses, the traffic manager commented: "Kramer is no
better than any other carrier serving us. If you get your rates down
to the competitive level, we will use you; otherwise, we will get
sufficient and satisfactory service from your competition. We must
control our costs to compete in our markets."

CONSUMER PRODUCTS FIRM — After failing to get business back all
other ways, we offered to match Lawrence's price, and even better in
a few instances (about a 25¢-per-mile reduction). The traffic
manager responded: "Lawrence saved us during your strike; they are
providing good service at a big savings in cost, and I am not going
to replace them."

BUILDING AND SUPPLY MANUFACTURER — After Redd Lines was brought in
to share about 50 percent of the business at prices 40¢-per-mile
lower than ours, we questioned at which level above Redd Lines could
we get the business back based on our superior service. The traffic
manager responded: "You have done a great job for us, and for that,
I will give you 60 days to get your prices in line with Redd's;
otherwise, I will have to give them as much of the business as they
can handle. Their service has proven to be just as good as yours."

HEAVY GOODS MANUFACTURING COMPANY — In early 1980, our business was
cut in half from 70 loads per week to 35, and the traffic manager
called us in to present the competitive facts. He related we must
cut our prices 20¢-to-25¢ per mile to keep the 35 loads. We did. In
early 1981, he again came to us and said we had to come down to
RBN's level, which was another 8-to-9 percent per mile. We said we
couldn't, that our service was worth this small differential. The
traffic manager replied: "RBN and Hartford are providing
satisfactory service," and he proved it by cutting us out of that
traffic completely for the last four months.

CAN MANUFACTURER — We were told many times during late 1980 and
early 1981 that our prices were too high. We lost 60 percent of our

previous year's volume with them systemwide. The traffic manager
indicated that Marr Transit on a nationwide basis, and Boston
Transport on a regional basis, is responding service—wise like we
used to six and seven years ago and are totally satisfied with them.
They will only use us if our price is lower, or to the extent those
two carriers can't handle the business. The latter has not happened
often in the past year.

HEAVY GOODS COMPANY — When pointing out to their top Transportation
Manager that the competition was serving them with predominantly
trip—leased equipment and obviously poor service, he strongly
rebutted by saying: "We have had no problem with your competitor's
service and our customers are tickled pink with their rates."

NOTE: The above examples are real and are happening in the
marketplace. You should know, however, that many other excellent
customers want to continue to or start to use Kramer Transport, Inc.
— but only when we become cost competitive.

EXHIBIT 8-3
Letter to Management Employees

September 4, 1981

Dear Kramer Transport Management and Administrative Employee:

I want to share the content of the attached letter with you. Although primarily intended to communicate to our driver group, the content is of pertinent interest to our whole organization.

I want to applaud the work that is taking place on all fronts to improve the cost and service position of our company in the marketplace. I am impressed with the dedication and solid thinking that is being demonstrated.

I want to impress on each of you the importance of change and improvement. Our potential is unbelievably great. We have made the investments in all of the needed areas. We have a solid organization, the right operating concept and a strong presence in the marketplace.

We have one undeniable problem to correct. We must lower our unit cost (¢ per mile). It is up to us . . . each of us. We grew up in a protected, regulated environment. This environment has changed. We understand what is required to be successful in the '80s. We now must accomplish it.

Each of us must be questioning every cost category and everything we do each day. We need to be looking for "New Ideas." We must streamline our company by improving that which needs to be done and eliminating the nonessential. If each of you is not on an active "New Ideas" team, I want to hear from you. If any one has an idea to improve our effectiveness that is not being heard . . . speak up. Our main task in the remaining months of 1981 is to get cost competitive while improving our service offering. This won't happen automatically. It will require creative change, solid thinking and risk. It will be fun! A successful result will position us for an exciting roller coaster ride through the 1980s. Let's do it together.

Sincerely,

Max Taylor
President

Enclosure

September 2, 1981

CONFIDENTIAL LETTER TO KRAMER TRANSPORT DRIVERS

Dear Fellow Employee:

The purpose of this letter is to openly and candidly keep you
informed on where we stand in our marketplace and in our efforts to
get cost competitive so we can win the battle in which we find
ourselves. This is a tough time for all of us. We need to keep
communicating (talking and listening) and problem-solving together.

I hope by now those of you who have attended the business
information meetings and/or talked through our competitive situation
with your manager have recognized that Kramer Transport is not a
typical trucking company. We are different in many ways. The most
important difference is our business philosophy around our
employees. We care. This is what puts us a notch above the others.

We have a serious business problem, and we plan on solving it and
becoming an important part of the motor carrier transportation
picture. We want to take the appropriate decisive actions that will
allow us not only to survive but to win in the long pull. We need to
openly and honestly face up to our serious situation before it is
too late. However, this won't be done hastily or without your
understanding and involvement. To plunge ahead with a series of
short-range decisions could lead to even greater problems. The very
fabric of our company, of our business philosophy, is that people
and good relationships count. Many of you have called or written
Mark Kramer and me asking that we not "lower ourselves" to doing
business like some of our competitors. Mark and I don't plan to do
this, nor do we have to.

We can keep Kramer a good place to work. We can be a successful,
cost-competitive carrier without deviating from our philosophy that
our people count and our people want to do what is right for the
company to win. This is why we have held over 50 separate meetings
and communicated with over 1,200 drivers. This is why we have
initiated information programs, promotion to management, regular
communication meetings in the shop, and kicked off our companywide
cost-reduction program called "New Ideas." Our goal is to win with
our people and not fail and let down our people like over 400
carriers have since deregulation.

But, let me tell you, our business and our business philosophy are
being put to the test right now. The marketplace remains "hostile."
Lower cost, nonunion and union competitors continue to come at us —
head on, and with a rate-cutting business strategy. We are a target.

The marketplace continues to tell us and show us (by giving our
freight to others) that we are 15-20¢ per mile too high on costs/

rates. The shippers know what it costs to operate trucks and are not willing to pay a premium for moving their freight. They are <u>also</u> caught in competitive struggles in <u>their</u> marketplaces. No matter how hard we try, we can't "wish" this problem away. The cold, hard reality is that we are 15–20¢ per mile too high and the business world is cruel to those who aren't cost competitive and service sensitive.

One of the messages that has come through very clearly in our meetings has been: "Why is all of this falling on just the driver?" The answer is that there are a number of reasons <u>and</u> solutions to our 15–20¢ per mile cost problem. Believe me we are looking at each and every one of our cost categories for reductions. <u>Impressive</u> progress has already been made in a number of areas:

- Load ratio is up
- Maintenance cost per mile has been dramatically lowered
- Fuel, equipment, and tire purchasing have yielded savings
- Reduced insurance rates have been negotiated
- Hiring freezes have been imposed
- Call length is down
- Three-way calls have started
- Maintenance employees have absorbed a 20 percent reduction in hours worked
- Paperwork and mailing costs are down
- A new vehicle registration plan was instituted
- Out-of-route miles are receiving high attention
- The impressive fuel results (MPG) are a result of a well-thought-out program
- We've gone to each of our suppliers and demanded reductions
- A "New Ideas" savings program is in effect
- Lower performers are being identified and are/will be dealt with more aggressively

I could go on and on. The focus goes well beyond driver wages and fringes. It is an undeniable fact, however, that our wage-fringe costs are 15¢ higher than most of our competitors. This is the major part of our cost problem and a repositioning <u>must</u> be a part of the solution.

This is not a popular conclusion, but it is honest. We know the cost of living/standard of living issue is a difficult one. However, it is our judgment that our company can't and won't survive in its present form, with its present cost-per-mile position, in this new business environment. We will continue to aggressively work on improving our position in <u>all</u> cost categories. We will continue to look for changes in the way we operate which will improve our efficiency.

Some of you have asked, "If action is called for now, why are we waiting so long and having all of the meetings?" The answer is that we wanted and needed your understanding and input. We read the situation early enough to take the time to communicate. Additionally, we have been talking to and working with the union to define our problem and look at potential solutions.

Thank you for your interest, involvement, and valuable input in our decision making. This is a difficult period. Nations, families, and companies have grown <u>stronger</u> by "coming together" and dealing with such tough problems. Kramer can win and continue to be a good company to work for. It's up to us.

Sincerely,

Max Taylor
President

cc: Local Unions

EXHIBIT 8-4
Letters to Union Officers

March 6, 1981

Teamsters' Union Locals

Gentlemen:

In an article from the February 23, 1981, issue of <u>Transport</u> <u>Topics</u>, the author indicates that a surviving carrier during this industry shakeout will have the following characteristics:

1. can alter his operation to the needs of his shippers
2. can talk to employees
3. can tailor his labor costs

He also indicates that both labor and management have the responsibility to explain the economics and cost realities of the marketplace to the driver.

Sincerely,

KRAMER TRANSPORT, INC.

Peter Gray
Director of Industrial Relations

March 31, 1981

Teamster's Union Locals

Gentlemen:

An article from the March 15, 1981, edition of <u>Traffic</u> <u>World</u>
summarized a recent seminar for Motor Carrier Personnel. At that
meeting the panelists made the following observations:

1. There will be more bankruptcies in the trucking industry
    after business turns up than there are now. Banks today
    can't afford to pull the plug because equipment is selling
    about 50 percent below normal market value.
2. The industry is currently going through a difficult
    adjustment period.
3. With increased emphasis on price, many large shippers will
    know as much about the carrier's cost as the carrier does.
4. The main victim of the Motor Carrier Act has been the
    Teamsters Union, which has seen declining membership in the
    trucking industry. "Over a period of time it sucked too
    much blood out of the goose that laid the golden egg and
    weakened her."

Enclosed is a copy of the article for your information.

Sincerely,

KRAMER TRANSPORT, INC.

Peter Gray
Director of Industrial Relations

Enclosure

As Business Increases So Will Truck Bankruptcies, Says Investment Banker

There will be more bankruptcies in the trucking industry after business turns up than there are now, in the opinion of William Legg of the investment banking firm of Alex Brown and Sons. He made the prediction in an informal panel discussion held in the course of "A Seminar for Motor Carrier Executives" conducted March 5 in Chicago by Kearney Management Consultants.

Mr. Legg continued by saying that "banks today can't afford to pull the plug," the reason being that terminals and equipment are selling about 50 percent below market value. When business picks up, banks will be able to get back a higher percentage of market value or book value, he said. Today, he explained, there are more sellers than buyers. Mr. Legg made this suggestion:

"Before the bankers nail you, you merge. You can merge or you can liquidate."

Another panel member, Richard E. Edwards, chief executive officer and president of Hemingway Transport Inc. of New Bedford, Mass., said, "It seems to me the real purpose of the Motor Carrier Act was to reduce the number of carriers." But Richard Klem, of the Interstate Commerce Commission, also a panel member, denied that that was the purpose of the act.

"Despite the recession and the dropping of tonnage, the motor carrier's rate of return is not as bad as it has been in other recessions, such as in 1975," said Mr. Klem. "In part, I think that is due partly to the freedom motor carriers now have to react."

He said that prior to passage of the act, the Commission had been concerned by how it would affect the industry especially since its passage would coincide with the recession.

The panel moderator, L. L. Waters said:

"We will never be able to determine whether deregulation worked or didn't work because it occurred during a recession."

Mr. Waters is university professor emeritus of Transportation and Business History at Indiana University, a consultant, and a member of numerous boards of directors.

After a most difficult adjustment period, a certain amount of order should develop in the industry after about 10 years, he said.

Mr. Waters predicted that in the future there will be six to eight LTL carriers serving the country, a number of regional carriers, and about 5,000 more small carriers than now exist.

Mr. Edwards agreed with his prediction regarding national carriers. There are 13 national carriers today, he said.

Mr. Waters said that if antitrust laws apply, "it will be extremely difficult for regional carriers to interline."

He said the future will be "extremely difficult" for the medium sized truck companies, and will bring about a lot of turnovers in the smaller companies.

Maurice M. Thiebeault, vice-president and general manager of Interstate System, another panelist, commented on the regional carriers, saying he does not see them "sticking together. I see them fragmenting and each regional carrier doing whatever makes sense to it."

Mr. Legg said, "I think the trucking industry will be better managed in five years, and that will help profitability."

The moderator said that he thinks the well-managed companies will survive.

"I regard the Motor Carrier Act as full employment for old-fashioned rate clerks; lawyers, especially if we get into antitrust; cost accountants; auditors of freight rates, and brokers." Regarding the latter, Mr. Waters said he expects a lot of large companies will know as much about the carrier's cost as the carrier does.

Commenting further on the act, he said the main victim of it has been the Teamsters Union.

"Over a period of time it sucked too much blood out of the goose that laid the golden egg and weakened her," said he. "I'd estimate there are 15,000 fewer Teamster jobs in Chicago than there were 10 years ago."

Mr. Klem commented on rate bureaus, saying:

"There is a good chance they will collapse on their own weight. The ICC, though, has no plans to kill them."

Mr. Klem also said:

"I personally feel that the class-rate structure probably will die. Rates will be based on costs. I view that as a good thing. I think it will improve efficiency."

In the course of another session, Russell W. Scalpone of the Kearney consulting firm spoke on "From Terminal Manager to Regional Manager."

"How do you determine who to promote to regional manager?" he asked.

Mr. Scalpone then answered:

"Results are one method. The persons' track record, however, can be misleading because of resources, the environment of terminal, and the people and labor climate."

Mr. Scalpone listed the following as important skills for a regional manager to have:

— Problem solving capabilities, interpersonal skills, labor relations style listening, error correcting coaching, oral communication, and administrative and written communications.

His firm, Mr. Scalpone said, identifies promotable managers by their past performance and by how they do on a test which consists of a number of management exercises. The person is judged on his performance by a team of evaluators.

He stressed the importance of identifying and developing people within an organization.

"Anyone can go out and pay top dollar but that person probably won't be very loyal," he said. Someone promoted from within the company would be more loyal, he said.

"People development must be a part of business planning," he added.

The seminar also included talks by Kearney personnel on these subjects: "The Changing Environment," Les Koss; "Developing a Successful Business Plan," John Throckmorton; and "Pricing in the New Environment," Angelo Valentine.

Source: From Midwest Bureau of *Traffic World,* March 16, 1981. Reprinted by permission.

EXHIBIT 8-5

Letters to Employees on Status of Negotiations

February 4, 1982

Dear Fellow Employee:

We have committed to keeping our channels of communication open and to keep all employees informed on items of mutual importance. It is the purpose of this letter to do so on several items of interest.

NEGOTIATIONS

As you no doubt have heard, the accelerated negotiations for the national contract have proceeded to the point of a tentative agreement. As we understand, the negotiation results did recognize the highly competitive nature of the truckload industry.

It is important for you to know that we have indicated, to the union, our desire to participate in negotiations but to do so on an individual or separate basis, not represented by any employer association.

It is our belief that this approach to negotiations will better allow us to meet our mutual needs. It is our desire to reach an agreement which will

1. meet the distinct needs of our company and, therefore, our drivers. We are a relatively unique company and type of operation in the truckload industry — company equipment, company drivers, high—service market segment, dedicated to working together to make our whole system efficient.
2. fairly compensate our drivers and, importantly, ensure your job security.
3. allow us to meet the increased levels of competition in the new truckload marketplace.

We will be negotiating with the union's selected representative. We are hopeful that negotiations will be resolved satisfactorily in the not too distant future. We will, consistent with the laws and rules governing this period, keep you advised as to the progress on a regular basis. Some of you might have questions. We will, of course, attempt to answer questions so long as you recognize we are in bargaining with your union. Questions concerning the balloting and ratification process and its impact on you should be directed to your local union. We wanted you to know that we are negotiating separately. It appears, at this time, that your bargaining agents are aware of the problems we are facing and are willing to work with us, at this point, to find solutions.

RUNNING OUR BUSINESS

In the meantime, we must continue to "run our business" and run it well. Our customers have more choices of carriers than ever before. They are demanding and expecting excellent service at very competitive rates. During this period it is imperative that each of us concentrate on meeting these clearly stated shipper needs. If we don't, in this environment, someone else will.

WINTER 1982

On a separate topic, the winter has been challenging to say the least. We've told our customers that we are the "winter carrier". We commend each of you who has, during this period, provided a high level of customer service and driven cautiously. During times like this, even with the extreme level of excess motor carrier capacity, we have the opportunity to demonstrate to people that we are a dedicated, unique company. Thank you.

COMPETITION

Our competitive atmosphere, which we discussed with you last summer, if anything, has worsened. The effects of deregulation, a very poor economy, excess capacity, new carriers, and rate cutting to gain new business combine to put a real severe business pressure on us. We honestly do not see any significant help from an improved economy in 1982. It appears that our country's economy, much like our industry, is in a turbulent transition period. The economy, hopefully, is in transition from a high-inflation, over-borrowed economy to one of sustainable growth in an environment of lower inflation and interest rates. Our industry is in transition from a period of regulated competition where costs were of limited to moderate concern, to an era of free competition where high unit cost (cents per mile) is devastating. We must make it through this transition period. A return to the "good old days" is not possible. We can make it if we each realize we are in this together.

WINNING

As each of us knows, we do have something unique going for us. Our company's most important asset is people, good people. We care about each other. We have a growing mutual respect and are continually working on ways to work more effectively _with_ each other. This is relatively unique in the trucking industry! We understand our business and know how to do it well. This is sensed and experienced by our customers through our many transactions with them. This is what makes a business. We are good. We really are! Kramer Transport can be a real winner — one of the survivors of this "shakeout period." What we have worked so hard to build is worth struggling for.

What's required? As I said in my Christmas letter, we must lower our unit cost/price (cents per mile). This message from the new marketplace is very clear. We must also consistently deliver the level of customer service we are capable of. The transition required must be faced and made. Each of us needs to know that our personal security is tied directly to having our company be successful.

Max Taylor

April 2, 1982

Dear Fellow Employee:

This letter is to provide you with an update on the progress of our contract negotiations. I am pleased to report that the Company and the Teamsters' designated collective bargaining representatives have reached a tentative agreement. Your bargaining representatives have recommended the agreement to the National Negotiating Committee.

In the near future, you will be contacted regarding meetings to be held to explain the terms of the new labor agreement. Following the meetings the agreement will be subject to your ratification.

The current labor agreement has been extended beyond March 31, 1982.

The agreement reached meets our mutual objective of having a Kramer contract which not only fits our operation as a company equipment truckload carrier, but takes into consideration many of the needs and concerns you have expressed.

We have negotiated with two major goals in mind: (1) to position our company to survive. As we all know, there is a major industrywide adjustment taking place due to deregulation; and (2) to provide you with continued employment and benefits.

We sincerely appreciate your patience and understanding during this period. We will continue to keep you informed.

Sincerely,

Max Taylor
President

The negotiations resulted in a tentative agreement that incorporated many of the changes in the pay system that the company proposed. It did not establish a complete or pure percentage-of-revenue system, but it eliminated much of the nonproductive pay of the old miles-and-hours system. The new system was expected to produce approximately a 15 percent savings in labor costs. Whether this translated into an equivalent reduction in drivers' pay would depend on how the drivers adjusted to the new system. There was earn-back potential for those who increased their weekly miles.

The bottom line of the new system is that it provides approximately 26 percent of the freight rates to the driver. This new arrangement was more costly than the one negotiated under the part of the NMFA that would have covered the company had it negotiated within the industry association. Indeed, the company counted on this fact to help sell the agreement to its drivers, because the association agreement served for comparison as the next-best-alternative settlement.

RATIFICATION STRATEGY

The company developed a comprehensive, new approach to ratifying the contract. It should be noted that this was the first time that the Teamster drivers in the company had the opportunity to ratify their own agreements; in the past they were only one very small part of the voting group under the NMFA. The company decided, therefore, that it needed an active communication program to carry through the ratification process. They stressed that this was important not only because the new agreement contained so many changes in the pay system, but also because the Teamsters "only had experience in getting concurrence on improved contract terms. They had little or no experience in dealing with reductions or major changes in operations."

The development of a strategy for ratification was largely the responsibility of the organizational development specialist. A summary of his description of this process (provided in an interview before the ratification process began) is reported below.

> Meetings will be held in the field with approximately twenty-five to one hundred drivers present at each meeting. The primary communicator at each meeting will be a line manager from the division in which these drivers work. The business agent for the Teamsters will be present at each of the meetings. We want the business agents to take supportive roles in this process; however, they will not be required to take an active role. Their approach will vary depending on the individual involved. Some will be neutral, and some will take a more supportive approach. The business agent is not expected or required to be a primary advocate of the agreement at these meetings.

> These meetings are expected to last approximately one and one-half hours. They are designed as a one-way communications process. The manager will run down the dollar items in the contract and make comparisons to the national contract and to pay systems and differences between our contract and those competitors we deal with. Specific comparisons will be made to the rider agreement that we would have been covered under had we stayed within the Master Freight structure.

These meetings will take place in a three- to four-day period in up to twelve different locations around the country. The meetings will be scheduled near the drivers' homes and on weekends whenever possible.

Our objective is to present a credible explanation of the new agreement rather than to make a hard sales pitch. The drivers will be looking to test our credibility along the way. Throughout the presentation the manager will be stressing comparisons to the present situation rather than making comparisons of the new pay levels with the provisions of the past agreement. This is designed to focus on the present economic conditions and to change expectations since any comparisons with past agreements will illustrate the pay cuts these drivers will be taking.

The business agent will, hopefully, provide a supportive statement at the end of the program. But we know this will not happen in all cases and that we will have some agents who want to keep a distance. At a minimum, the business agent will explain the voting process to the drivers.

A lot of work has gone into setting this process up. Basically, we see it as a continuation of the communications process that we had ongoing with the drivers over the last year and a half. The competitive reality meetings laid the groundwork for these types of meetings. As a result, we have developed a much better understanding of our industry. Our workers have developed relationships at the divisional level with our managers. We also have a better understanding of where our trouble spots will most likely be.

We had to work hard on the role of the managers at these meetings and on what they would say. Since the process is one in which we present the material — a one-way communications process — we had to provide a number of anchor points for managers so that they could minimize any questions during their presentation. After the presentations the managers will stay around to answer individual questions on an informal basis.

At each location two or three people will stay in the field to answer questions during the period of time after the meetings up until the ratification vote takes place. In addition, at company headquarters, we will have six or seven key operating managers on call to answer questions of people in the field.

Essentially we have segmented the work force so we can deal directly with our drivers. We have developed a script and framework for dealing with confrontations that may arise. We have also developed a plan to ask union stewards and union locals for support. We also set up procedures to keep track of all information gathered from conversations.

NEGOTIATIONS AND HUMAN RESOURCE STRATEGY

The conduct of the negotiations was an integral part of the broader human resource management strategy unfolding in Kramer Trucking. In turn, the human resource management strategy is an integral part of the larger business strategy of the company. The heavy emphasis on direct communications about the business and the industry with individual drivers before the negotiations process helped to lay the groundwork for changing expectations, for gaining trust and credibility and for getting the drivers to focus on the competitive realities facing the company. The emphasis on developing a stronger line management and supervisory structure was also consistent with the desire to develop more open lines of communications, closer working relationships, and better trust within the firm from the rank-and-file drivers through the entire management structure. It was part of an effort to "get line management to understand its new role and take responsibility for its relationships with individual workers." The vice-president of human resources described the overall approach as follows.

> Generally the human resource plan involves a more direct role in managing and communicating with our people. This has come as a real education to our line managers and we would not have gotten their cooperation and involvement had we not prepared them for this role. Our approach does not involve a soft approach to human resource management. This is a program that is focused on the tough reality. We want to discover what we have to do in human resource management in order to win for the company and for our employees in this new competitive environment. We know that success will rely on drivers choosing to take a pay reduction. We feel that we have to be frank about it and deal with it through an open, fact-based process. In the past the negotiations process was much too detached from our workers and from the economics of our part of the industry. Our approach throughout this has been to bring a basic honesty to the process by showing the drivers exactly how our costs are affected by deregulation and how their compensation relates to the compensation paid by nonunion competitors.

Where does this strategy fit into the larger business strategy? As noted, in the 1970s the company moved to a strategy of establishing and nourishing independent contractor operations. The company showed in the material presented to the drivers that it operates betwen 10¢ and 30¢ per mile above the costs of nonunion independent contractors that have entered the industry since deregulation. The goal of the company is to reduce this differential to between 5¢ and 10¢. Management believes the company can be a "10¢ premium carrier" and describes its business strategy as follows.

> The reality is that there is a fair number of people out there who will go with a premium carrier because of the quality of services, the reliability, and other aspects of the dependability that we can provide. Therefore we will not be the lowest cost carrier in the business. The success of Kramer Trucking will depend on the viability of this strategy and on our ability to get our costs down to an acceptable premium above the low-cost competitors. In a lot of cases we are the low-cost carrier, given the range of total services that we provide. The problem, however, is that the industry is going to a commodity price basis of choosing a carrier rather than use a differential cost structure dependent on the services provided.

> The extent that the Kramer Trucking Company gets its costs down to a level at which it can compete with other companies in its business will determine how fast that company will grow relative to independent contractor companies. There is no question that independent contractor companies will continue to grow more rapidly if the Teamster operations are not viable. In any event, we will continue to expand the independent contractors in those regions and markets where that is the only way of doing business. In the long run, we think we can have a relationship with the Teamsters and under the organization of the Kramer

Trucking Company that will be viable. We think there are great strengths in having our own employee drivers and equipment rather than operating through the independent contractors. We can provide excellent customer services. In addition, we can have the kind of organization that we would like. It is more fun; that is, there is a more human operation and a more highly motivated management team when we have our own employees. Besides, it is a very tenuous type of business for the independent contractors. We do not develop a long-term employment relationship with these people and we do not think that it is as good a way to establish and maintain an organization. Finally, there is not as healthy a development of assets for the long term under an independent contractor strategy. It doesn't take much capital to set up one of these operations. It only costs between $12,000 and $15,000 to put a trailer on the road. The tractor ($50,000) belongs to and goes with the contractor.

In short the key question for the future is how do we best utilize our assets — both equipment and human assets. The difference between the contract that we are operating under and the one that we have negotiated and hope to have ratified is approximately $500,000 per month.

The vice-president of human resource management described how the new contract would position the firm to take the next step in the development of its human resource management strategy and to achieve the type of organization that the company seeks.

We think this contract will position us to build the type of high-commitment work system that we want to establish. We realize this is a very different environment than the typical manufacturing organization. We are very decentralized but we still think we can use the concept of work teams based around the driver, the supervisor, and direct associates. We are working hard to integrate human resource management and organization development into the management process. Our goal is to develop *general managers* by breaking down many of the functional lines and eliminating much of the superstructures that separate managers, supervisors, and drivers. This contract is only one piece of that total picture. We want to first deal with people around the real issues and eliminate a lot of the contract language that has created problems without creating benefits either for the company or for the workers. All of this requires the development of different patterns of behavior by employees and supervisors. This is why we have to work closely with supervisors and drivers to get them to understand the new environment, to react to it in a way that will better contribute to the viability of the company, and to maximize their own earnings and performance under the new system.

Questions for Discussion

The results of the ratification vote on the contract have been tallied. The drivers rejected the contract by a vote of 30 percent for ratification and 70 percent against ratification. What should Kramer management do next?

IV

Human Resource Management and Industrial Relations at the Workplace

PREVIEW

The human resource management and industrial relations system in which individual managers and employees most often interact is the workplace. The central question facing managers at this lowest level of the three-tiered framework introduced in Chapter 1 is the following: How well can human resource management policies and strategies be translated into on-going practices? That is, what effects do they have on the bottom-line objectives of the firm, its employees, labor organizations, and the public policies that govern the employment relationship? If current policies are not deemed effective, a second question becomes relevant: What are the best strategies for changing human resource management practices?

We explore these questions in the followong three chapters. In Chapter 9 we present four short readings that focus on the measurement of human resource outcomes and their relationships to various measures of organizational effectiveness. We begin with measurement issues to reinforce the point that managers need to develop information systems capable of monitoring and evaluating human resource management performance and its effects on the goals of the various parties to the employment relationship. In Chapter 10 we introduce grievance, complaint, and other due process and conflict resolution mechanisms. Chapter 11 is devoted to the organization of work and alternative strategies for introducing changes in the design, organization, and compensation of work.

The organization of these chapters is guided by the generic functions that a workplace system must perform. Workplace systems must (1) provide due process and effective management of conflicts that arise in the course of the day-to-day employment relationship; (2) organize and structure work through a series of principles, rules, or policies; and (3) motivate employees to perform effectively as individuals and as members of their work groups and the larger organization.

These three functions are *interrelated* in a causal cycle. Because workers and managers bring different goals and expectations to the employment relationship, all organizations need procedures and processes for resolving differences of opinion or disputes over employee rights and responsibilities. These disputes can arise over questions of interpretation or application of rights established by formal employment contracts, public policies governing the employment relationship, or organizational norms, rules, and policies. However, unfulfilled expectations of one or more parties can also cause a breakdown in the "psychological contract" (Barnard, 1938; March and Simon, 1958; Schein, 1979) that employees and employers tacitly make with each other. Failure to resolve or effectively manage these conflicts or disputes can lead to a breakdown of trust in the relations between the individual and the organization. Low trust may lead to more written rules that attempt to clarify the rights and obligations of supervisors and employees, which, in turn, may lead to a further breakdown in trust at the workplace.

British sociologist Alan Fox (1974) referred to this cycle as a high-conflict/low-trust syndrome. He argued that work systems that rely on strict lines of demarcation between supervisors and employees, those that structure jobs narrowly into tasks with little individual discretion, and those that allow employees little opportunity for participation or influence are particularly prone to low-trust, adversarial relationships. Although his data were drawn from Britain, his descriptions of workplace relations and the organization of work fit the type of factory and bureaucratic management systems that emerged in most American firms using the principles of scientific management. These principles later became embodied in formal job-evaluation systems and in the detailed collective bargaining contracts negotiated in many industrial settings in the post–World War II period. Thus, an important part of a contemporary manager's job is to avoid falling into this self-perpetuating cycle of low trust, or, if it already exists, to break the cycle with strategies that can promote and sustain higher levels of trust.

Only recently have researchers begun to recognize the interrelationships among these three workplace dimensions of the human resource management system. If Fox (1974) is correct (and the evidence in the Katz, Kochan, and Weber reading in the next chapter supports Fox's argument), then managers must view the management of due process, the organization of work, and the motivation and management of individual employees as interrelated responsibilities.

Thus, what follows in these next chapters can be interpreted as an exploration of the strengths and limitations of two contrasting workplace human resource management systems. The traditional system relies on clear and relatively tight divisions of labor and lines of authority. Formal rules govern the rights and responsibilities of labor and management. Formal systems of due process and conflict management are used to interpret these rules and resolve disputes over the interpretation of written contracts or public policies. Individual employees have clearly specified rights but little discretion over how work is organized or how they are to perform their assigned tasks.

The alternative system encourages greater employee participation over task-related decisions and work organization, relies on fewer written rules or statements of employee and management rights and responsibilities, and is based on more informal, flexible systems for resolving conflicts or achieving due process.

The traditional system has been associated with blue-collar factory settings, while the latter has been used more widely in professional, managerial, and white-collar settings. In recent years, however, while some offices have become more routinized and bureaucratic in organization and management style, others have experimented with the more flexible, high-trust, or high-commitment systems in blue-collar factory settings (Walton, 1980). It remains to be seen whether this more flexible workplace system can remain flexible and maintain high commitment, while still protecting employee rights and promoting due process over a sustained period. The question to keep in mind as we explore these systems is, which pieces of each system will be best suited to the long-term needs of the parties to the employment relationships of the future?

References

Barnard, Chester I., *Functions of the Executive* (Cambridge, Mass.: Harvard University Press, 1938).

Fox, Alan, *Beyond Contract: Work, Authority, and Trust Relations* (London: MacMillan, 1974).

March, James, and Herbert Simon, *Organizations* (N.Y.: John Wiley, 1958).

Schein, Edgar, *Organizational Psychology* (Second Edition) (Englewood Cliffs, N.J.: Prentice-Hall, 1979).

Walton, Richard E., "Establishing and Maintaining High Commitment Work Systems," in J. R. Kimberly and R. A. Miles, eds., *The Organizational Life Cycle: Issues in the Creation, Transformation and Decline of Organizations* (San Francisco: Jossey Bass, 1980), 208–290.

9

Performance Measures and Models

Rapid advances in information technology are rendering quantitative information a routine, low-cost aid to managerial decision making. Yet, before an adequate human resource information system can be designed, standard measures of human resource performance must be identified and their relationships to other measures of organizational effectiveness must be modeled. In this chapter, we use four readings to introduce a number of such measures and review the evidence on their relationships to other measures of organizational effectiveness. The first reading is a short primer on techniques for measuring the most widely discussed but least understood indicator of organizational effectiveness: productivity.

To be useful, the data collected in an information system must be guided by one or more theoretical models that relate performance measures to effectiveness and efficiency measures. The second reading examines the association of the generic functions of a human resource management system to two specific measures of organizational effectiveness: product quality and labor efficiency or productivity. This reading demonstrates the utility of developing models and measures of performance that fit the needs of managers working in a particular organizational setting.

The third reading summarizes the various uses of attitude surveys. It also examines the behavioral science evidence on the relationships among employee attitudes, performance measures, and organizational effectiveness.

Finally, the chapter ends with a reading that discusses the measurement processes and responsibilities that *all managers* must periodically administer — performance appraisals. Unlike the other measures discussed, performance appraisals provide feedback on *individual employee* performance, not the performance or effectiveness of some human resource policy or practice. The line manager or supervisor is directly responsible for conducting performance appraisals. Human resource professionals can provide only the technical expertise needed to design the appraisal system, and perhaps the training needed to ensure its proper use. Line managers and supervisors carry out the appraisals and use them to enhance individual employee development, performance, motivation, and satisfaction. Thus, this last reading focuses not on the many technical issues associated with the design or evaluation of performance appraisal systems, but on their appropriate uses by line managers and supervisors.

Suggested Readings

Aft, Lawrence S., *Productivity Measurement and Improvement* (Reston, Va: Reston Publishing Company, 1983).

Bernardin, H. John, and Richard W. Beatty, *Performance Appraisal: Assessing Human Behavior at Work* (Boston: Kent, 1984).

Greenberg, Leon, *A Practical Guide to Productivity Measurement* (Bureau of National Affairs, 1973).

Guzzo, Richard A., *Programs for Productivity and Quality of Work Life* (New York: Pergamon Press, 1983). This is one of a series of studies of productivity published by the Work in America Institute. All entries in the series are available from this publisher.

The Handbook of Methods for Surveys and Studies (Bureau of Labor Statistics, 1982).

Henderson, Richard I., *Performance Appraisal* 2nd ed. (Reston, Va: Reston Publishing Company, 1984).

Kendrick, John, and David Creamer, *Measuring Company Productivity* (National Industrial Conference Board, 1965).

A Primer on Productivity Measurement

Productivity measures can signal to managers to reassess the labor and capital requirements and costs of their businesses, but too few managers adequately measure the productivity of their various divisions and business units. In small businesses, productivity measurement is more rare than in larger firms, because the measurement and improvement of productivity seem confusing, inefficient, and ineffective. Managers typically think of productivity measurement as being both costly and unnecessary. Thus, we begin by examining several widespread myths about productivity; it should become apparent that when productivity itself is considered in a less mystical light, its measurement becomes less formidable and more obviously worthwhile.

Myths about Productivity

Many people believe that everyone knows what productivity is and why it is important. In fact, although productivity is one of the more commonly used business terms in the manager's vocabulary, it is probably one of the least understood. It is also widely believed that everyone wants to improve productivity. In fact, improving productivity mostly entails the management of *change* within an organization, so this myth seems patently overstated. In fact, the tendency to maintain the status quo is one of the most durable, though often most damaging, features of any organization. It is natural for people in organizations to fear change, but productivity improvement necessarily implies change.

Source: Thomas A. Barocci and Kirsten R. Wever. Kirsten Wever is a Ph.D. candidate at MIT in Political Science and Industrial Relations. The piece was written for this book.

Another frequently touted myth is that productivity can be improved only at the cost of quality, but the following simple example debunks this notion. If a company produces one thousand products a week, of which one hundred are returned because of defects, the problem is obviously poor quality. Yet, by enhancing the quality of the product to reduce the defect rate from 10 percent to 5 percent, that company is simultaneously raising productivity by 5 percent. (It should be noted that assessment of the costs of raising quality is necessary to determine if this is a cost-effective short-run strategy.) A similar process works in many, more intangible operations within a firm, from the level of shop-floor production or the rendering of services to that of top management and its strategic and operational decisions. Contrary to popular belief, quality is a *subset* of productivity, not an obstacle to it.

That technology is the single key to improved office productivity is another myth. Even in high-technology manufacturing industries, new technology should be introduced only after management has measured the productivity of the work being performed. When this has been accomplished, management can see if the new technology is appropriate. If the sequence of events is reversed, the new technology may prove to be inappropriate, thus causing inefficiency and low productivity.

The most damaging myths center on who or what is responsible for declining productivity growth in the United States. Typical scapegoats include unions, government regulation, oil price hikes, foreign competition, and misdirected investments. No doubt, each of these factors has contributed to productivity problems but none is solely accountable for all of the country's productivity ills.

A less-frequently blamed but certainly equally involved party is management.

The managers of America's firms are ultimately responsible for dealing with unions, for responding to — and even initiating — regulatory legislation, for deciding how energy-intensive their facilities should be, for meeting the challenges of internationally competitive markets, and for deciding on long-term investments.

The importance of management's impact on productivity is intensified by an ongoing change in the ratio of factory assembly-line employees to administrative-support employees in the typical United States manufacturing corporation. In the early 1960s, that ratio was 65 or 70 percent to 35 or 30 percent; at present, the ratio is reversed: 40 or 30 percent to 60 or 70 percent. This shift has occurred because managers have increased the numbers of controls and productivity indicators in the factory to align employees with changing product demand, but they have been slower to apply similar controls to the administrative side. Management now needs to focus on its own productivity, as well as that on the shop floor. White collar and managerial productivity is likely to be a major human resource issue in the coming years.

Measures of Productivity

Nonetheless, to place all of the blame for falling productivity on the shoulders of U.S. management is only to perpetuate the myths that surround the issue of productivity. The point is not *who* is responsible for the problem, but *what* can be done about it. The answer presupposes an understanding of how to measure productivity. Such understanding comes in the context of two basic questions: How does management define productivity? How can people be sensitized to appreciate the importance of productivity within the organization? The definition of productivity and the sensitivity of management and employees to its importance are closely connected with its measurement. Moreover, productivity cannot be measured accurately or effectively unless the people

responsible for producing a firm's goods and/or services are willing to cooperate.

Broadly defined, productivity is the relationship between what goes into producing some product or service and the output — the product or service itself. For example, productivity can be defined as the price of the product divided by the number of employee hours and the amount of intermediate goods and/or capital spent to produce it. Assuming, for the sake of simplicity, that the amount of physical inputs into the production process is constant, the productivity of a corporation could be measured by comparing the number of products or services sold to customers with the number of employees in the corporation.

The inputs and outputs of productivity can be categorized, as shown in Figure 9-1. These factors should be considered in measuring any given type of productivity, but will vary from one situation to another. Total productivity measures account for the effects of all inputs — capital, labor, intermediates (purchased goods and services), and (more recently) energy — on aggregate output.[1] To make a comparison, the value of the inputs must be translated into dollars, which can be compared to the price of the goods or services; the difference between the value of the inputs and the value of the outputs is the gross margin. *Changes* in that difference represent changes in the level of productivity.[2]

[1]The equation used to calculate this kind of productivity is:

$$\frac{Q}{K + L + I + E}$$

Where Q = quantity produced
K = capital
L = labor
I = intermediates (purchased goods and services)
E = energy

[2]To measure productivity it is necessary to compare the period of interest to you (say, a three-month period beginning now) with some other period. In this way, it is possible to determine whether productivity has improved or declined. The period that is used as a reference is usually called the base period.

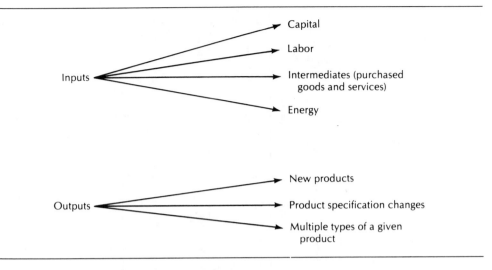

FIGURE 9-1   Productivity Inputs and Outputs

Sometimes it is inappropriate to measure all the inputs and outputs involved in the production process. Partial measures are used to assess the productivity of specific inputs, such as labor.[3] Table 9-1 provides an example of measuring labor productivity. The labor productivity measures of the three producers illustrate the results of different levels of inputs and outputs. Producer A has product unit increases in each of the three years, while direct production hours have decreased and indirect hours have increased; overall productivity has increased by 26 percent. Producer B has unit increases in each of the three years, but both direct and indirect hours have remained constant; overall productivity has increased by 24 percent. Producer C has the same number of units in the three years, while direct hours have decreased and indirect hours have increased; the overall productivity increase is just under 3 percent. Keep in mind that these productivity increases are probably not solely a result of work force improvements. Any perceived change in labor pro-

ductivity could reflect a series of factors, such as an increase in orders, lower interest rates, price changes, more efficient equipment, and so forth.

Another approach to partial measurement, often used for administrative staff, is to identify a specific goal or productivity target against which performance can be measured. An example appears in Figure 9-2. Productivity in this example is measured by identifying the percentage of people hired within a goal of sixty days and calculating from the date when the human resource department received the hiring department's request to when a candidate accepted an offer. As illustrated, for an average of 83 percent of the people hired, the goal was met. In September 1983, the goal of 100 percent was reached for 100 percent of the hiring tasks.

Productivity Indices and Data

Productivity can be measured by using a variety of indices and techniques, as well as a number of data types. The latter include statistics and information from the United States government, from the private sector, and from the individual firm (e.g., self-collected data). Because many

[3]In this case, the equation would read simply Q/L, where Q = quantity produced and L = labor.

TABLE 9-1 Sample of Partial Labor Productivity Measures

	Units Produced			Production Hours Worked (Direct)			Hours Worked (Indirect)			Total Hours Worked (Direct, Indirect)			Direct Hours/Units Produced			Indirect Hours/Units Produced			Total Hours, Direct, Indirect/Units Produced		
	1981	1982	1983	1981	1982	1983	1981	1982	1983	1981	1982	1983	1981	1982	1983	1981	1982	1983	1981	1982	1983
Producer A	4000	4500	5250	60000	56000	53000	10000	12000	15000	70000	68000	68000	15	12.4	11	2.5	2.6	2.8	17.5	15.1	12.9
													% Δ	from 1981		% Δ	from 1981		% Δ	from 1981	
													0	17	33	0	−4	−12	0	13.7	26.2
Producer B	4000	4500	5250	60000	60000	60000	10000	10000	10000	70000	70000	70000	15	13.3	11.4	2.5	2.2	1.9	17.5	15.1	13.3
													% Δ	from 1981		% Δ	from 1981		% Δ	from 1981	
													0	11.3	24	0	12	24	0	11.4	24
Producer C	4000	4000	4000	60000	56000	53000	10000	12000	15000	70000	68000	68000	15	14	14	2.5	3	3.75	17.5	17	17
													% Δ	from 1981		% Δ	from 1981		% Δ	from 1981	
													0	6.6	6.6	0	−20	−50	0	2.9	2.9

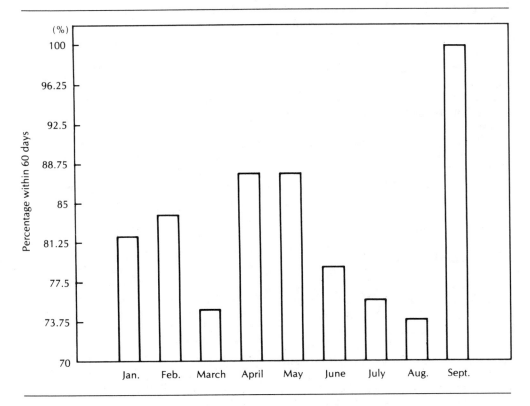

FIGURE 9-2   Receipt-to-Accept Days (Percentage) within Goal, 1983

factors other than the inputs mentioned can cause changes in the level of productivity, no single index or data set will be appropriate for all situations. Various approaches are necessary to account for the effects, for instance, of decreasing demand, higher interest rates, or inflation, all of which can lower productivity. Two general indices are described.

Because productivity must be measured over time to see improvements or declines, some time period must serve as the base of reference. If, for example, the base year is also the initial year of the index, that index is base-year weighted; in other words, a given year's data are considered in terms of the conditions during the base year. To calculate productivity, one would multiply the price of a product or service in some given period by the quantity produced in the present period,

and divide by the present price times the present quantity.[4] If, on the other hand, the current year is always the base year, the index will shift each year to reflect changes in the rates of price movements and in productivity efficiencies. In this case, one would multiply price in any given period by quantity in that period, and divide by present price times quantity in the given period. This type of index reflects the dynamics of the environment, and thus is helpful when inputs and outputs change frequently.[5]

[4]Laspeyres: $\frac{p_i q_i}{p_o q_o}$; Paasche: $\frac{p_i q_i}{p_o q_i}$, where

p is the price of goods and services represented by quantity q, in the present period o, or in some other period i.

[5]Bureau of Labor Statistics, *The Handbook of Methods for Surveys and Studies.*

Traditionally, labor is measured according to hours worked or hours paid. The input of salaried employees can be estimated by calculating the ratio of indirect (salaried) to direct (hourly) workers, and multiplying by direct labor input. Differences in the quality of various labor inputs might also be taken into account. Factors such as age, education, or experience can be measured directly, whereas others, such as motivation or intelligence will be judged more subjectively. Caution must be exercised, however, because the more of these determinants of productivity change are included in the actual measure, the more that potential strategies for improving productivity may be confused with the measures of their effects.

Productivity also can be affected by changes in the type of labor used to produce a service or product. For example, if a recession leads a firm's management to lay off production workers but not salaried employees, then administrative overhead costs will increase proportionally, resulting in an inevitable decrease in *measured* overall labor productivity. This decrease would bear no relation to the actual productivity of the remaining workers. The productivity of all the workers is measured partly in terms of overhead costs; therefore, an increase in the ratio of salaried to hourly employees will affect the productivity measure, which would not reflect the real productivity of either group.

Steps for Measuring Productivity

The measurement of productivity is not the formidable task most managers consider it to be. The following steps provide the basis for an effective measurement system.

1. Determine the objectives, the quantities to be measured, and the reasons for measuring them.

2. Consider the costs and benefits of various indices.
3. Include intangibles that affect or are affected by productivity and the measurement process in (a) the creation of measurements, (b) the measurement process, and (c) the interpretation of the data.
4. Where incentive schemes or other programs might raise productivity, allow management style to include and involve the *people* affected in (a) the program's formation, (b) its maintenance, and (c) its evaluation.

The last step is of particular importance to the line manager, whose job it is to see that a firm's employees both understand and accept the general importance and the specific applications of productivity measures, whether labor-specific or all-encompassing. When used in conjunction with more traditional financial reporting systems, productivity measurements can provide managers with the knowledge required to pinpoint areas and processes that require particular attention.

Summary

The measurement of productivity should be undertaken only after conducting a cost-benefit analysis. A manager's decisions about the use of various measures, different types of data, and appropriate indices will have to reflect his or her individual experience and discreet judgment. This element of subjectivity carries through all stages of measurement and also pervades the interpretation of results. A clear initial understanding of how a particular measurement system works is essential for its flexibility and usefulness. The ability to communicate that understanding to the people affected by the measure will then help ensure its success and lay the foundation for improving productivity.

Questions for Discussion

1. Why have managers often been reluctant to measure the productivity of their operations?
2. Suppose you were the newly appointed manager for productivity of a large multi-divisional corporation. The chief executive officer just created this position in order to encourage development and use of productivity measures throughout the company. Your first assignment is to speak at the annual meeting of division executives and plant/office managers to discuss your plans and objectives. What would you say to them? What questions and concerns would you expect them to raise about your plans? How would you address their concerns?
3. Using any previous employment experience, construct a series of productivity measures. Justify the base period method employed.
4. For the above measures, list at least five intangibles that may affect the observed changes.
5. What factors should determine the frequency of change in measures and base periods?

Assessing the Effects of Industrial Relations Performance on Organizational Effectiveness

The increased competitive pressures experienced by many firms in recent years have drawn managers to examine more carefully the performance of their industrial relations systems. This is leading to a new era of experimentation with various worker participation programs, new local bargaining agreements, and changes in employment practices that are designed to improve both industrial relations and organizational effectiveness. Various pressures are also leading management to apply strategic planning techniques to the industrial relations function, as firms and unions begin to recognize the interdependence among broad business policy decisions and industrial relations performance at the workplace level. Consequently, industrial relations professionals, within management and within unions, are being called upon to critically examine their prevailing practices and to assess alternative strategies that satisfy organizational and worker goals.

Unfortunately, the industrial relations profession has been slow in developing the type of analytical capacity required to support these experimentation, planning, and evaluation processes. Historically, there has been an aversion among many industrial relations managers to the idea of quantitative assessment of industrial relations practices and performance. Few

Source: Harry C. Katz, Thomas A. Kochan, and Mark R. Weber. Harry C. Katz is an associate professor of Industrial Relations, Sloan School of Management, MIT. Mark Weber is Manager of Salary Compensation at General Motors. Portions of this paper are drawn from a larger study by the authors that will appear in the *Academy of Management Journal*, Vol. 28, September, 1985). Partial support for this research was provided by the Alfred P. Sloan Foundation.

firms, for example, systematically collect and analyze industrial relations activity or performance data. Even fewer attempt to relate variations in industrial relations outcomes over time or across locations to indicators of organizational effectiveness or worker well being. To illustrate the potential of this type of measurement, modeling, and analysis of industrial relations systems performance, we draw on data gathered over an eleven-year period from twenty-five manufacturing plants in one company.

Industrial Relations Systems and Performance

While popular accounts often admonish the American industrial relations system for being too "adversarial," this term is seldom clearly defined. Indeed, the dimensions of the industrial relations system and its performance at the workplace are not well specified in the theoretical or empirical literatures.

In this reading, we demonstrate that the three interrelated dimensions of a workplace industrial relations system, introduced in the Preview to Part IV, are related to organizational effectiveness. Specifically, we explore the relationships between measures of productivity and product quality and (1) the effectiveness of the management of conflict in union-management relationships, (2) the motivation, commitment, and behavior of individual workers and work groups, and (3) the rules and practices governing the allocation and use of human resources. The links expected between these aspects of workplace industrial relations and organizational effectiveness are outlined more fully below.

Conflict Resolution Systems

One essential function of an industrial relations system is to establish procedures and processes for addressing and resolving conflicts or problems that arise between employees and management. In the United States, unions and employers rely heavily on formal contract negotiations and grievance procedures for conflict management. The effectiveness of these formal mechanisms is directly related to organizational effectiveness for at least three reasons.

First, these formal representative procedures require considerable amounts of time, people, and resources to manage. Thus, the sheer volume of grievance and bargaining demands that arise will have an effect on the costs of managing a plant. To the extent that management and union resources (time and people) are devoted to managing these formal adversarial procedures, fewer resources are available for training, problem solving, communications and other productivity, human resource management, or organizational development activities. This might be described as the displacement effect of conflict management activities (Katz, Kochan and Gobeille, 1983).

Second, the volume of grievances and bargaining demands can be symptomatic of the success or failure of the parties to resolve differences on a more informal basis or at early steps of the formal procedures. The number of grievances or bargaining demands, and the inability to settle issues without frequent threatened or actual work stoppages most likely signal more deeply seated problems in the conflict-resolution/problem-solving systems of an organization. We expected that measures of grievance rates, the number of bargaining demands, the length of negotiations, strike threats, and strike occurrence would be systematically related to other measures of industrial relations performance and to organizational effectiveness. Much previous research on the determinants of grievance rates is consistent with this argument (Peach and Livernash, 1974; Thomson and Murray, 1976; Knight, 1978; Katz, Kochan, and Gobeille, 1983).

Third, because the formal grievance and bargaining processes focus on distributive issues, they inherently entail some degree of political posturing, gamesmanship, bluffing, and commitment-building tactics (Walton and McKersie, 1965; Schelling, 1960). To the extent that these tactics escalate, are perpetuated over time, and spread across the entire range of issues the parties confront, a high-conflict/low-trust syndrome (Fox, 1971) — or what Boulding (1962) described as a "conflict trap" — can set in. That is, the patterns of conflict may overshadow the potential for integrative bargaining or cooperation even on those issues regarding which the parties share common interests. The belief that this is a common feature of current American industrial relations is what gives rise to the criticism that our system is "too adversarial" (Barbash, 1980).

For these three reasons, we hypothesized that indicators of greater conflict between labor and management at the workplace will be associated with higher costs, poorer quality, and generally poorer organizational performance. Second, we hypothesized that strong interrelationships will exist between the various indicators of industrial relations performance.

We are not implying that these conflict resolutions systems do not serve important, useful functions for labor and management. They are natural and necessary procedures that have endured the test of time for resolving conflicts, which will arise in any employment relationship, and for protecting the rights of employees. It is not their existence, per se, but their poor performance, that is expected to lead to lower levels of organizational effectiveness.

Worker Attitudes and Behavior

Although the conflict resolution system reflects the broad *institutional* features of an industrial relations system, the motivation, attitudes, and behavior of *individuals* and informal work groups can exert an independent effect on organizational performance. Yet, a longstanding (Brayfield and Crockett, 1955; Herzberg, *et al*, 1959; Schwab and Cummings, 1970) and to date unresolved (Dyer and Schwab, 1982) debate continues on the direction and strength of the causal relationships between these individual attitudinal and behavioral characteristics, and organizational performance. On the one hand, abundant evidence suggests that no consistent or simple causal relationship exists between individual worker satisfaction and individual worker performance (Schwab and Cummings, 1970). On the other hand, a wide range of theoretical arguments suggest that individual worker ability, motivation, and participation in job-related decision making will affect both organizational effectiveness and individual worker satisfaction (Hackman and Oldham, 1976; Goodman, 1979; Walton, 1980; Lawler and Ledford, 1981–82). To the extent that workers have the ability and willingness to make suggestions and to participate in the search for ways to improve job performance, and to the extent that these efforts can be maintained over time, high levels of individual motivation and commitment should lead to organizational effectiveness. These positive links between individual attitudes and behavior and organizational effectiveness can be maintained over time only if the larger economic and institutional environments maintain support for high levels of individual involvement and labor management cooperation (Walton, 1980; Kochan and Dyer, 1976). Unless the larger union-management relationship and management systems remain supportive, and workers experience tangible rewards from their involvement, high levels of commitment are likely either to atrophy gradually (Walton, 1975) or to end abruptly in response to some visible conflict (Goodman, 1979).

Another aspect of individual behavior that is expected to relate to other industrial relations outcomes is the rate of absenteeism. Although the evidence on the strength of the relationship between job satisfaction and frequency of absence is mixed (Dyer and Schwab, 1982), it has been argued that voluntary absenteeism should be related to employee motivation (Steers and Rhodes, 1978). Others have suggested that the relationships between the organizationwide rate of absenteeism and worker attitudes, commitment, and other aspects of industrial relations should be stronger than the relationship between absenteeism and individual worker attitudes (Nicholson, Brown, and Chadwick-Jones, 1976). In any event, the costs imposed by high rates of absenteeism should exert an independent effect on organizational performance (Hackman and Lawler, 1971), regardless of the relationship between absenteeism and other industrial relations outcomes.

We expected measures of employee participation in suggestion programs, worker attitudes, and absentee rates to be related to other industrial relations performance measures and to measures of organizational performance.

Human Resource Management Rules and Practices

The substantive rules and practices governing the organization of work, the allocation of workers, the compensation system, and the adaptability to change serve as a third important channel through which the industrial relations system of a workplace influences organizational effectiveness and employee goals. Work rules, their administration and modification, have historically been recognized as important factors influencing labor costs and productivity (Slichter, 1941; Slichter, Healy, and Livernash, 1960; Hartman, 1973; McKersie and Hunter, 1973). These rules and practices developed over time both formally, through collective bargaining agreement provisions, and informally, (Roy, 1952; Dalton, 1959; Kuhn, 1961; Sayles, 1958; McKersie and Klein, 1982) in both union and nonunion situations. Rules are necessary to bring about stability and equity in work practices and to protect the rights and responsibilities of both workers and their employers. However, work practices and rules accumulate, and become outmoded because of technological or other changes in the industry.

Yet, company rules are difficult to change because change often threatens job security by affecting such areas as the jurisdiction of work, seniority and transfer rights, and the number of workers required to perform the given volume of work. Thus, work practices discussions are inherently mixed motive in nature — all parties share an interest in eliminating inefficient work practices, yet revision of work practices may require changes that threaten job security or alter promotion prospects. The flexibility with which the industrial relations system manages and adjusts work rules and work practices at the plant level influences organizational effectiveness and worker objectives. As with bargaining processes and grievance procedures, establishing policies and rules to govern the organization and distribution of work opportunities is a necessary and essential function of the industrial relations system (Dunlop, 1958). Yet the buildup of rules and the inability to modify work practices can reduce organizational effectiveness. To reemphasize the point, it is the ability to *manage* and *adjust* work practices to meet the productivity needs of the firm and the interests of the work force that is critical, and not the presence of rules, that influences organizational effectiveness.

In summary, the quality of conflict management or resolution, individual worker attitudes and behavior, and the flexibility within substantive work rules are three key dimensions of an industrial relations system that will have important effects on organizational effectiveness. Over time these dimensions become interrelated in a reinforcing cycle. Worker dissatisfaction or lack of trust may lead to a higher level of grievances and bargaining demands, and to a more adversarial relationship between workers and management. Inability to effectively resolve conflicts usually leads to greater emphasis on legalistic rules, strict enforcement of contract terms, and a buildup of rules that one or both parties will resist changing. The high conflict/low trust cycle reinforces management's belief in the necessity of rigid, authoritarian styles of supervision; and employee motivation, job performance, and commitment to work declines.

Data and Analysis Plan

The data used to illustrate the power of this model were obtained from the information system of a large durable goods manufacturer in the United States. The data, collected from 1970 through 1980, are observations from the company's twenty-five manufacturing plants; these employ roughly 50,000 people and have annual sales in excess of $1 billion. The technology and the product in all of the plants are similar; and hourly workers belong to the same industrial union.

The data set provides a pooled cross-section sample of 275 observations for most of the industrial relations and organizational effectiveness measures. Missing data reduce this sample in some of the analyses.

Industrial Relations Performance Measures

The industrial relations performance measures included in the analysis and their respective variable names are:

1. The number of grievances filed per one hundred workers (grievance).
2. The number of disciplinary actions per one hundred workers, actions that involve a suspension or more severe penalty (discipline).
3. The number of demands submitted by the union in tri-annual local contract negotiations; these local agreements are supplemental to the companywide contract (demands).
4. The number of days it took to reach a settlement in local contract negotiations before or after settlement of the company's master agreement. Four rounds of bargaining occurred in our sample (1970, 1973, 1976 and 1979), thus the maximum sample size for data

relating to the negotiating process is one hundred (negtime).
5. A survey asked salaried employees a number of questions regarding compensation and benefit levels, working environment, relationships with supervisors and subordinates, and career progress. Low score responses indicated dissatisfaction. A summary score was derived from these surveys for each plant. The variable we utilized is the percentage of respondents in each plant that had an overall survey score greater than 3.2 on a 1 to 5 scale. We had survey data for the years 1977 to 1980 (attitude).
6. The number of suggestions submitted per employee in the company's suggestion program (superemp).
7. The percentage of employees who submitted at least one suggestion during the year. The suggestion program data available was from 1976 to 1980 (sugpct).
8. The absentee rate as a percentage of straight time hours excluding contractual days off (absentee).

The first four of these variables capture aspects of the formal conflict resolution systems in the organizations. The last four measure aspects of individual attitudes and behaviors that are expected to influence organizational effectiveness. Unfortunately, no measures of plant work rules or practices are available for this study.

Organizational Effectiveness

The organizational effectiveness measures available for this study describe two key dimensions of the economic performance of each plant.

1. A product quality index is derived from a count of the number of faults and demerits that appear in inspections of the product. A higher quality score is associated with better product quality. This index is available for 1975–80 (quality).

2. A measure of labor efficiency compares the actual hours of direct labor input to standardized hours calculated by the company's industrial engineers. The labor standards used in this index are adjusted for product attributes. A higher direct labor index is associated with higher efficiency and lower costs. This is the key labor productivity indicator used by the managers of these plants (direct).

Results

Table 9-2 illustrates the importance of examining the diversity of outcomes that are produced by the industrial relations system procedures and policies in different workplaces. Despite the common technology, union, and employer, a wide variation is evident across plants in grievance rates, discipline rates, absenteeism, and other industrial relations and economic performance measures. Note, for example, that in 1980 grievances varied from a low of 5.5 percent in one plant to a high of 121.1 percent in another plant. Absenteeism varied between 4.6 percent and 8.8 percent. The number of contract demands introduced in the local negotiations for the 1979 agreement varied from a low of 66 percent to a high of 690 percent. Direct labor effi-

ciency varied from 20.4 percent above standard to 23.7 percent below standard.

The measures of worker participation in suggestion programs and employee attitudes also reveal wide variation across plants. In 1980, the number of suggestions per employee ranged from .13 percent to 1.04 percent, and the percent of employees with highly positive attitudes is 40 percent in one plant to 74 percent in another.

Relationships Among the Measures

The correlations among the measures of industrial relations performance across plants and years are presented in Table 9-3. The table reveals a high degree of intercorrelation between the various measures of industrial relations performance, thus supporting our hypothesis regarding the interconnected nature of the industrial relations system. For instance, the data show a strong correlation between the various indicators of the level of conflict within the plants. The higher the grievance rate in a plant the higher the discipline rate ($r = .34$), the more demands introduced into local negotiations ($r = .22$), the longer the negotiating time required to reach an agreement ($r = .38$), and the more strike letters issued ($r = .25$).

TABLE 9-2 Mean, Minimum, and Maximum Values of Variables in Plants Across the Company in 1980

Variable	Mean	Minimum Value	Maximum Value	Standard Deviation
Grievance	45.9	5.5	121.1	25.7
Absentee	6.3	4.6	8.8	1.1
Discipline	.180	.045	.401	.075
Demands[a]	283.4	66	690	137.3
Negtime[a]	24.1	−49	210	54.6
Attitude	54.4	40	74	7.9
Sugperem	0.38	0.13	1.04	.24
Sugpct	17.8	8.0	37.3	7.6
Direct	−2.32	−23.7	20.4	9.6
Quality	129.3	119.0	140.0	6.8

[a]These data are for 1979, there were no negotiations in 1980.

TABLE 9-3 Interrelationships Among Industrial Relations Performance Variables as Measured by Simple Correlation Coefficients[a]

	Grievance	Absentee	Discipline	Demands	Negtime	Attitude	Sugperem	Sugpct
Grievance	1.00							
Absentee	.26**	1.00						
Discipline	.34***	.32***	1.00					
Demands	.22**	.08	.33**	1.00				
Negtime	.38***	−.01	.30***	.34***	1.00			
Attitude	−.47***	−.51***	−.25**	−.22**	.02	1.00		
Sugperem	−.15*	.12	.16*	.09*	.24*	.43***	1.00	
Sugpct	−.20**	−.10	.11	.22**	.43***	.91***	1.00	

[a]The number of observations for correlations involving measurers of grievance and discipline rates is 275. There are 250 observations involving the absentee rate. The number of observations involving participation in the suggestion program is 125. The number of observations involving attitudes, the number of contract demands, and negotiating time is 100.

  * = significant at .10 level

 ** = significant at .05 level.

*** = significant at .01 level.

All of these correlations are statistically significant at the 5 percent level.

The data also reveal strong connections between indicators of the level of conflict and measures of employee attitudes and participation. Better attitudes are associated with lower grievance rates (r = .47), lower discipline rates (r = .25), fewer contract demands (r = .22), fewer strike letters (r = .29) and fewer strikes (r = .06). Again, except for strike occurrence, these correlations are statistically significant at the 5 percent level. The connection between individual behavior and the level of conflict also is revealed in the associations that absentee rates and employee participation in suggestion programs have with grievance rates, discipline rates, the number of demands, negotiation time, and the issuance of strike letters.

Relationships Between the Measures

Correlations between measures of direct labor efficiency and product quality are presented in Table 9-4. These correlations provide strong support for our hypotheses that the level of conflict and individual behavior can affect organizational effectiveness. For example, higher grievance

TABLE 9-4 Correlations Between IR Performance and Economic Performance[a]

	Direct	Quality
Grievance	−.41***	−.30***
Discipline	−.22***	.07
Demands	.01	.05
Negtime	−.34***	−.13
Absentee	−.22***	.07
Attitude	.40***	.48***
Sugperem	.21**	.53***
Sugpct	.22**	.53***

[a]The sample size for the correlations involving the direct labor variable ranged from 225 to 100. The sample size involving the quality variable ranged from 150 to 100.

  * = significant at .10 level.

 ** = significant at .05 level.

*** = significant at .01 level.

rates are associated in a statistically significant manner with lower direct labor efficiency ($r = -.41$) and poorer product quality ($r = -.30$). A connection between individual attitudes and behavior and economic performance is also seen in a number of the correlations. More positive employee attitudes are associated with higher direct labor efficiency ($r = .40$) and better product quality ($r = .48$). Similarly, the more suggestions offered per employee, the higher the direct labor efficiency ($r = .21$) and the better the product quality ($r = .53$). These six correlations are statistically significant at either the 1 percent or 5 percent level.

In addition to supporting our hypotheses, evidence of a connection between plant level industrial relations and economic performance lends further strength to our argument that the systematic collection of this type of data has great value for managers. These data provide a way to assess current performance and to identify problem areas.

Conclusion

Industrial relations performance can have significant effects on organizational performance, and these effects can be measured and assessed if a consistent industrial relations information data base is developed and maintained over time. While not every firm will face the commonality of technology, union structure, and contract provisions in its various locations as found in this example, it is clear that standard measures of industrial relations system performance can and should be developed. Grievance, absenteeism, accident, turnover, strike, and organizational climate measures can be standardized and computed for multiple locations. Measures of economic performance, or more generally, organizational effectiveness, may be more difficult to standardize. However, as the previous primer on productivity measurement suggested, valid and reliable indices that allow comparison of performance of the same unit over time are often feasible. The analysis of industrial relations system performance, and the effects of efforts to improve it, needs to become part of the standard tools of both HRM/IR professionals and line managers.

References

Barbash, Jack, "Values in Industrial Relations: The Case of the Adversary Principle," *Industrial Relations Research Association Proceedings*, 1980, 1–7.

Boulding, Kenneth B., *Conflict and Defense* (New York: Harper and Row, 1962).

Brayfield, Arthur H., and Walter H.J. Crockett, "Employee Attitudes and Employee Performance," *Psychological Bulletin*, 50, 1955, 396–424.

Dalton, Melville, *Men Who Manage* (New York: Wiley, 1959).

Dunlop, John T., *Industrial Relations Systems* (New York: Holt, Reinhart and Winston, 1958).

Dyer, Lee, and Donald P. Schwab, "Personnel/Human Resource Management Research," in Thomas A. Kochan, Daniel J.B. Mitchell, and Lee Dyer, eds., *Industrial Relations Research in the 1970s: Review and Appraisal* (Madison, Wis.: Industrial Relations Research Association, 1982), 187–220.

Fox, Alan, *A Sociology of Work in Industry* (London: Collier-MacMillan, 1971).

Goodman, P. S., *Assessing Organizational Change: The Rushton Quality of Work Experiment* (New York: Wiley-Interscience, 1979).

Hackman, J. R., and E. E. Lawler, III, "Employee Reactions to Job Characteristics," *Journal of Applied Psychology* 55, 1971, 259–86.

Hackman, J. R., and G. R. Oldham, "Motivation Through The Design of Work: Test of a Theory," *Organizational Behavior and Human Performance*, 16, 1976, 250–279.

Hartman, P. T., *Collective Bargaining and Mechanization* (Berkeley: University of California Press, 1973).

Herzberg, Frederick, Bernard Mauser, and Barbara Snyderman, *The Motivation to Work* 2nd edition (New York: Wiley, 1959).

Katz, H. C., "Assessing the New Auto Labor Agreements," *Sloan Management Review*, 23, 1982, 57–68.

Katz, Harry C., Thomas A. Kochan and Kenneth R. Gobeille, "Industrial Relations Performance, Economic Performance and Quality of Working Life Programs: An Inter-Plant Analysis," *Industrial and Labor Relations Review*, 37, No. 1, 1983, 3–17.

Knight, Thomas R., *Factors Affecting the Arbitration Submission Rate: A Comparative Case Study* M.S. thesis, Cornell University, 1978.

Kochan, Thomas A. and Lee Dyer, "A Model of Organizational Change in the Context of Union-Management Relations," *Journal of Applied Behavioral Science*, 12, 1976, 59–78.

Kuhn, J. W., *Bargaining and Grievance Settlement* (New York: Columbia University Press, 1961).

Lawler, Edward E., III, and Gerald E. Ledford, Jr., "Productivity and the Quality of Work Life," *National Productivity Review*, 1, 1981–82, 25–36.

McKersie, R. B., and L. C. Hunter, *Pay, Productivity and Collective Bargaining*, (London: MacMillan, 1973).

McKersie, R. B., and J. A. Klein, "Productivity: The Industrial Relations Connection," manuscript.

Nicholson, N., C. A. Brown, and J. H. Chadwick-Jones, "Absence from Work and Job Satisfaction," *Journal of Applied Psychology*, 61, 1976, 728–37.

Peach, David, and E. Robert Livernash, *Grievance Initiation and Resolution: A Study in Basic Steel*, (Boston: Graduate School of Business, Harvard University, 1974).

Roy, Donald, "Quota Restriction and Goldbricking in a Machine Shop" *American Journal of Sociology*, 56, March 1952, 427–42.

Schelling, Thomas C., *Strategy of Conflict* (Cambridge, Mass.: Harvard University Press, 1960).

Schwab, Donald P., and Larry L. Cummings, "Theories of Satisfaction and Performance: A Review," *Industrial Relations*, 9, 1978, 408–30.

Slichter, S. H., *Union Policies and Industrial Management*, (Washington, D.C.: Brookings Institution, 1941).

Slichter, S. H., J. J. Healy and E. R. Livernash, *The Impact of Collective Bargaining on Management* (Washington, D.C.: Brookings Institution, 1960).

Steers, Richard M., and S. R. Rhodes, "Major Influences on Employee Attendance: A Process Model," *Journal of Applied Psychology*, 63, 1978, 518–21.

Thomson, A. J. W., and V. V. Murray, *Grievance Procedures* (London: Saxon House, 1976).

Walton, Richard E., "The Diffusion of New Work Structures: Explaining Why Success Didn't Take," *Organizational Dynamics* (1975).

Walton, Richard E., "Establishing and Maintaining High Commitment Work Systems," in J. R. Kimberly and R. A. Miles, eds., *The Organizational Life Cycle: Issues in the Creation, Transformation and Decline of Organizations* (San Francisco: Jossey Bass, 1980), 208–290.

Walton, Richard E., and Robert B. McKersie, *A Behavioral Theory of Labor Negotiations* (New York: McGraw Hill, 1965).

Organizational Surveys: The Purposes

This reading discusses several reasons for conducting organizational surveys. They are grouped into four categories: (1) feedback; (2) diagnosis; (3) communication; and (4) training. In addition, two sections at the end of the reading explain how surveys can be used as an expression of an organization's concern for its employees and as a means of quantifying the financial impact of employee attitudes on organizational effectiveness.

Feedback Function

Surveys can provide management with knowledge about the organization that is not readily available by other means. Since this information is obtained directly from workers, it should be subject to relatively small amounts of distortion if a survey is designed well. The feedback function is especially important for executives of large, decentralized organizations because it is virtually impossible for them to have any current knowledge of how policies are being administered or accepted by workers.

In one sense, surveys are analogous to the audit function. Whereas an audit provides a systematic examination of corporate records, an organizational survey provides a systematic assessment of employees' perceptions of the state of organizational health. This information can prove invaluable for organizational planning and can often reduce some of the ambiguity involved in making management decisions. For example, knowledge of worker attitudes toward various forms of compensation can aid management in designing or changing a compensation system. Similarly, knowledge of worker attitudes toward various job characteristics can help with the design or redesign of jobs.

The use of systematic surveys can sensitize the organization to changes in employee preferences or reactions over time. It can also be valuable for monitoring or evaluating workers' immediate reactions to organizational changes. By focusing attention on the "good" and "bad" aspects of changes, the survey helps the manager to "fine-tune" change procedures and to maximize the effectiveness of future changes.

In the following three examples, based on actual survey data, organizational surveys were used primarily for (1) auditing, (2) planning, and (3) assessing organizational change, respectively.

A Survey as an Audit Device

In 1975, Sears, Roebuck, and Company conducted a survey of 784 buyers, assistant buyers, and assistant sales managers from eight units of the corporate branch of the company. It was designed to measure the executives' satisfaction with six specific elements of the work and work environment (job satisfaction facets) as well as their general job satisfaction levels. Measures were also made of critical job characteristics, organizational environment characteristics, and certain individual characteristics of these executives. Table 9-5 lists the variables included in this audit.

The results of this survey (summarized in Dunham 1975) were used to examine the relative levels of satisfaction with different facets and to determine which of the individual, job, and organizational environment variables were related to these satisfaction levels. Figure 9-3 summarizes the overall relationships of these sets of variables to the job satisfaction variables. On the average, individual characteristics accounted for only 2 percent of the varia-

Source: Adaptation of Chapter 3 of *Organizational Surveys* by Randall B. Dunham and Frank J. Smith. Copyright © 1979 by Scott, Foresman and Company. Reprinted by permission.

TABLE 9-5 Variables Included in Survey

Job Satisfaction Facets	Individual Characteristics
Supervision	Sex
Career future	Age
Financial	Race
Amount of Work	Education level
Kind of work	Company tenure
Company policies and practices	
Overall satisfaction	

Job Characteristics	Organizational Environment Characteristics
Task significance	Company support level
Skill variety	Leadership: Interpersonal orientation
Task identity	Leadership: Task orientation
Autonomy	Work-assignment favorableness
Task feedback	Career favorableness
	Organizational climate
	Work-group climate

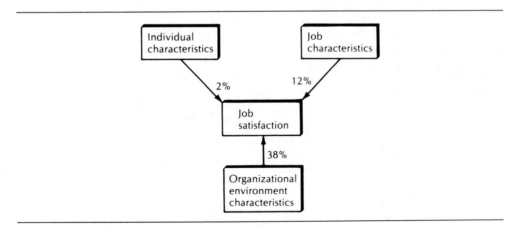

FIGURE 9-3 Average Amount of Predicted Job Satisfaction Variance

tion in job satisfaction scores, while job characteristics and organizational environment characteristics explained 12 percent and 38 percent of the variation, respectively.

The Sears analysis provided some important observations:

1. Of the individual characteristics, only tenure and age were related to any of the satisfaction variables, and even these were related only to satisfaction with career future and with company policies and practices. Older workers with longer tenure with the company were more satisfied than were younger, newer employees.

2. All five job characteristic variables were related to the job satisfaction variables. By far the strongest relationship was between job characteristics and satisfaction with the kind of work. In general, as the significance, variety, identity, autonomy, and feedback perceived in a job increased, satisfaction with the kind of work increased also — as did, to a lesser extent, satisfaction with supervision and satisfaction with company policies and practices.

3. All organizational environment characteristics were related to one or more job satisfaction variables. Satisfaction with supervision and career future had the strongest relationships to organizational variables, while satisfaction with financial aspects and with amount of work had the weakest relationships. Organizational and work-group climate both had a positive impact on satisfaction with company policies and practices. Company support level positively influenced satisfaction with career future more than any other variable. Both interpersonal and task-oriented leadership behavior were very strongly related to satisfaction with supervision. Descriptions of current work assignments were highly related to satisfaction with the kind of work. Finally, positive descriptions of the career were indicative of satisfaction with career future and with company policies and practices.

Although these data cannot prove cause-effect relationships, they do provide a comprehensive overview of the current state of the organization. Such a perspective is valuable for understanding the interaction of employees, jobs, and elements of the organization.

A Survey as a Planning Tool

In 1977 and 1978, Integrity Mutual, a small midwestern insurance company, surveyed 43 employees, from the first-level supervisor to the president (see Dunham 1978). The primary purpose of the survey was to help the company make decisions about the design for a new compensation plan. Workers were asked to describe the various duties that their jobs required, their perceptions of performance-reward contingencies, and their satisfaction with their pay. Supervisors of each job also described the job requirements for these employees.

Using results of this survey, an estimate of the relative value of each job — a process known as job evaluation — was made. A survey of the appropriate labor market provided an estimate of the market value of each job. By comparing the actual pay level for each job to the relative job value (determined by the survey) and to the market value, it was possible to determine whether discrepancies in these comparisons influenced the job satisfaction levels of the employees. . . . The critical results of this analysis are listed below:

1. Although there was a wide range in actual pay among jobs, there was only a weak relationship between level of pay and satisfaction with pay.

2. There was a strong relationship between perceptions of performance-reward contingencies and satisfaction with pay. Satisfaction with pay was significantly higher for workers who felt that their level of pay was a function of their performance level, even if their level of pay was relatively low. Apparently, they were satisfied as long as their low level of pay reflected their own relatively low level of performance.

3. Discrepancies in pay among jobs in the company had a moderately strong influence on satisfaction with pay. Workers

who felt that they were underpaid in comparison to other employees in the company (considering the various job requirements or inputs) had relatively low levels of satisfaction with pay.

4. For lower level employees, satisfaction with pay was not significantly influenced by comparisons to jobs outside the company. Apparently, these comparisons were not made or were not considered important by these employees.

5. For managers at the highest levels of the company, however, comparisons to jobs outside the company did have a significant influence on satisfaction with pay. Managers who felt underpaid in comparison to managers with similar jobs in other companies had relatively low levels of satisfaction with pay.

The results of this survey were useful for planning the new compensation system. Because of the importance of strong performance-reward contingencies, a compensation program based on merit was instituted. To support this decision, a comprehensive system was designed to appraise performance. Organizational policy was modified to encourage effective use of the merit-based compensation system. Because of the importance of job comparisons within the company, the new compensation structure was based on the relative level of worker requirements for each job. In view of the importance of managers' comparisons of their jobs to similar jobs at other companies, adjustments to the salary structure were made to reduce inequitable comparisons. It is too soon to evaluate the effects of these changes, but the initial survey results can now serve as a basis of comparison for future evaluative surveys.

A Survey to Assess Organizational Changes

In 1975 and 1976, surveys were conducted in two branches of a large insurance company (see Dunham, Newman, and Blackburn 1978). The organization's executives had decided to replace a paper-record file system used by clerical and semitechnical workers with a computerized microfiche system, but they were concerned that increases in technological efficiency might be counterbalanced by negative worker responses to the new system. Thus, the purpose of the survey was to determine whether the introduction of this automated system would cause changes in worker attitudes.

The 118 employees involved in the survey were divided into two groups. A control group of 75 employees from one division of the regional office used the old filing system. An experimental group of 43 employees from another division of the same regional office used the new system. A survey questionnaire was administered to both groups of employees one week before the new system was installed. Three months after the change another questionnaire was administered to both groups.

The survey attempted to measure employee satisfaction with the work, with job involvement, and with motivation from the work itself. It evaluated employees' intentions to be absent or to resign as well as attitudes toward absenteeism and resignation. Finally it assessed perceived job complexity (a combination of variety, autonomy, identity, significance, and feedback). In all cases, employees voluntarily provided individual identification for follow-up purposes.

The control group provided a comparison standard and eliminated many possible incorrect explanations of the results. For example, if some factor other than the technological change influenced the responses of the experimental group, this extraneous factor might have been falsely interpreted as an effect of the technological change. Most extraneous factors, however, would also influence the control group since the two groups were highly similar. Thus, the organization wanted to know if there were changes in the experimental group that did not occur for the control group.

The results of this series of surveys showed that there were no significant changes in the average responses of the experimental group to questions about satisfaction, motivation, or behavioral intentions after the introduction of the new microfiche system. Furthermore, the average responses of the experimental group were not significantly different from those of the control group. Thus, on the average, the anticipated negative effects of the change did not occur.

Another interesting result was detected, however, upon a closer examination of the data. Although on the average there were no significant effects, many workers did perceive changes in job complexity. Because some workers perceived an increase while others perceived a decrease in complexity, there was no average change. The fact that more of these changes occurred in the experimental group than in the control group suggested that the new system did have some effect. Furthermore, those people who perceived decreases in the complexity of the job became less satisfied with the work, less motivated by the work, and more likely to resign. These negative effects were offset by persons who perceived increases in complexity. They became more satisfied with the work, more motivated by the work, and less likely to resign.

Overall, the results of these surveys indicated that the introduction of the new filing system would have inconsistent effects on workers. The company could proceed to install the system, knowing that it would probably not have major impact on average worker responses. Because some employees would probably react negatively to these changes, however, the organization would have to be prepared to deal with these individual cases.

Diagnostic Function

Surveys can serve an important diagnostic function for organizations. That is, they can explain or predict critical organizational events such as turnover, absenteeism, tardiness, union activity, and possibly even productivity. Managers who understand the causes of these events may be able to influence them. This section provides an overview of the research on the relationship between satisfaction and each of these critical organizational events.

Unfortunately, many organizations fail to exploit the predictive value of surveys by using them only to diagnose a problem after it has emerged. It is of course quite legitimate to use organizational surveys to solve problems and to address questions such as:

1. Why are our workers dissatisfied with their pay?
2. How can we increase satisfaction with supervision?
3. How can we reduce turnover?
4. Why did our employees form a union?

It is also possible, however, to use surveys to prevent such problems or at least to identify them before they erupt into a crisis. For example, early detection of employee dissatisfaction with compensation or with company policies could permit a careful evaluation of these policies and their impact on employees *before* a union action is required. By identifying many employee concerns at a relatively early stage, surveys allow management to work toward maintaining organizational "well-being" rather than fighting to remove "illness."

The three basic potential problems that diagnostic surveys can identify require different kinds of solutions. The first type is relatively simple to solve: It requires only a "snap of management's fingers." The washroom that needs painting, the machine that needs repair, or the thermostat that needs adjustment are examples of this type of problem. The hardest part of solving these kinds of problems is often simply identifying them. The second type requires policy changes to obtain solutions. These may be as simple as a change in the dress code or as complex as a change in organizational structure. The third type necessitates the creative efforts of both management and employees to solve because there are no prescribed solutions.

In the following overview, we examine a number of organizational problems:

turnover, absenteeism, union activity, and low levels of performance. As stated earlier, managers who use surveys to obtain information about these problems may be able to minimize their negative effects.

Turnover

In the past 25 years there have been four classic reviews of the relationship of turnover to job satisfaction (Brayfield and Crockett 1955; Herzberg, Mausner, Peterson, and Capwell 1957; Vroom 1964; and Porter and Steers 1973). The results of these reviews have been fairly consistent in showing that there is an inverse relationship between satisfaction and turnover. This research has demonstrated that workers who have relatively low levels of job satisfaction are the most likely to quit their jobs and that organizational units with the lowest average satisfaction levels tend to have the highest turnover rates.

Figure 9-4 shows the Heneman and Schwab model (1975) of turnover theory,

which is based on the March and Simon model (1958). According to the theory, the decision to quit the organization is based on perceived desirability of leaving and on perceived ease of movement. Desirability of leaving is primarily a function of job satisfaction but is also influenced by opportunities for transfer or promotion within the company. Thus, low satisfaction and few opportunities for movement within the company will make movement out of the company more desirable to the worker. Perceived ease of movement to other organizations depends on the availability of opportunities for such movement. This availability is, in turn, a function of the general level of business activity, the number of organizations that the worker views as possible job sources, and the worker's level of skill. The greater the perceived ease of movement, the more likely it is that the worker will leave the company.

The two main factors in this model can be restated as: (1) Does the worker want

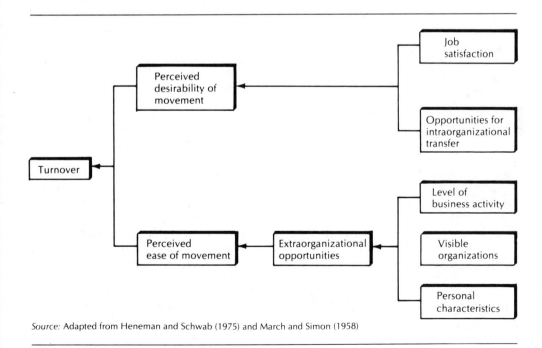

Source: Adapted from Heneman and Schwab (1975) and March and Simon (1958)

FIGURE 9-4 Turnover Theory

to leave? and (2) Does the worker have anywhere else to go? Note that satisfaction should thus have its greatest impact on turnover under conditions in which perceived ease of movement is high. Heneman and Schwab concluded that "by piecing together the evidence . . . there appears to be substantial support for many March and Simon hypotheses."

Table 9-6 contains a summary of the relationship between overall job satisfaction and turnover from 15 studies reviewed by Porter and Steers (1973). It is important to note that these studies included different groups of employees, such as clerical workers, salesmen, manual workers, managers, and even Air Force pilots. Each of these studies possessed methodological rigor, virtually all actually predicted turnover, and most used sound measures of job satisfaction. Thus, these findings should be reliable. An examination of Table 9-6 reveals that in 14 of 15 studies, significant negative relationships were found between job satisfaction and turnover.

Other studies reviewed by Porter and Steers (1973) focused on specific organization, work unit, job, and individual factors as they related to employee turnover. In 8 of 10 studies involving over 3,000 workers from a wide variety of jobs, satisfaction with pay and promotion had significant negative relationships with turnover. In six out of seven studies that assessed satisfaction with supervision, those workers with the lowest satisfaction levels were most likely to quit their jobs, and in four out of six cases satisfaction with co-workers was negatively related to turnover. Similarly, satisfaction with job content was negatively related to turnover in all but one of nine studies. Overall, many different aspects of the work environment seemed to cause turnover.

Hulin (1966) investigated the relationship between satisfaction and turnover by sampling female clerical employees in a large manufacturing company in Montreal. We examine this study and discuss its follow-up (Hulin 1968) to illustrate how a survey can be used both to assess and to act on a turnover problem.

Turnover among the female clerical staff at the company had averaged about 30 percent each year, compared to about 20 percent in other large companies in the area. A cost accounting analysis showed that, at a cost of $1,000 for hiring and training each new clerical worker, direct turnover costs were $130,000 per year. Surveys were administered to 350 clerical workers to obtain basic demographic information about the workers and to assess levels of satisfaction with pay, promotion, co-workers, supervisors, the work, and the work "atmosphere."

TABLE 9-6 Relation of Satisfaction to Turnover

Employee Population	Sample Size	Relation of Satisfaction to Turnover
Insurance agents	990	Negative
Insurance agents	474	Negative
Departmental workers	n.a.	None
Insurance salesmen	n.a.	Negative
Female clerical workers	129	Negative
Female clerical workers	298	Negative
Student nurses	1,852	Negative
Office workers	660	Negative
Lower level managers	1,020	Negative
Military academy cadets	1,160	Negative
Retail store employees	475	Negative
Computer salesmen	Varied	Negative
Female manual workers	236	Negative
Female clerical workers	160	Negative
Air Force pilots	92	Negative

Note: n.a. = Not available.

Source: Adapted from Porter and Steers (1973).

In the six months following the survey, 26 of the workers who had completed the survey quit their jobs. A comparison of the satisfaction scores of the terminators and nonterminators was made, as shown in Table 9-7. A statistical test for overall differences showed that the terminators had significantly lower satisfaction scores than the nonterminators. In fact, the terminators had lower satisfaction on five of the six satisfaction facets. Because the employees who left the company were younger than most of the nonterminators, a new group of nonterminators whose ages, education, and native language matched the terminators was established. The same satisfaction differences were found when this comparison was made. A follow-up analysis identified another 17 workers who quit 7 to 12 months after the survey. This data revealed that the same satisfaction variables had a tendency to predict turnover as long as one year after the survey.

Following this study, the organization instituted various policy changes. After these changes were made, Hulin surveyed the company's clerical workers again. He found that satisfaction was still significantly related to turnover but that satisfaction levels had increased for four of the facets. Perhaps more importantly, the increases in satisfaction were accompanied by a decrease in turnover from 30 percent to 12 percent.

Absenteeism

The relationship between satisfaction and absenteeism (or attendance, to use a positive term) has not been investigated as thoroughly as the relationship between satisfaction and turnover. Moreover, many studies have failed to differentiate between intentional and unintentional absenteeism, illness and nonillness causes, and paid and unpaid absenteeism.[1] De-

[1] It seems important to focus on voluntary absenteeism. Unless one wishes to accept the unlikely possibility that dissatisfaction causes illness which in turn leads to absenteeism, it is futile to attempt to predict absenteeism resulting from illness with satisfaction data.

TABLE 9-7 Satisfaction Scores for Terminators and Nonterminators

Facet Satisfaction	Nonterminators (n = 319)	Terminators (n = 26)
Work	35.87	28.69
Pay*	30.00	30.30
Promotions*	21.80	18.70
Co-workers	41.13	37.40
Supervisors	41.81	38.15
Atmosphere	34.78	32.92

*Scores adjusted for number of items.
Source: Adapted from Hulin (1966).

spite these problems, some meaningful conclusions can be drawn. Vroom (1964) found significant relationships between satisfaction and absenteeism in seven of the nine studies that he analyzed. Porter and Steers (1973) identified significant negative relationships between overall satisfaction and absenteeism in the two recent studies they reviewed. They also found studies in which satisfaction with pay, satisfaction with co-workers, and satisfaction with job content had an impact on absenteeism. In general, it appears that various satisfaction components do influence absenteeism, but the full scope of this effect has not been well documented.

The greatest impact of job satisfaction on absenteeism should be expected under conditions where the worker is relatively free to act (see Herman 1973) and where there are few penalties for being absent. Thus, job satisfaction is more likely to influence absenteeism for salaried employees than it is for hourly workers. A recent study (Smith 1977) examined a situation in which a group of salaried employees were free to attend work or to be absent on a particular day without financial penalty and without social or work-group pressures for being absent. This study involved a group of 3,010 salaried employees who held various administrative, professional, and technical jobs in a company in Chicago and a second group of 340 employees who held similar jobs at the company's New York headquarters.

On April 2, 1975, an unexpected blizzard hit Chicago, greatly hampering the city's transportation system. Attendance on April 3 required not only the decision to attend, but also considerable personal effort to get to work. Attendance ranged from 39 percent to 97 percent in Chicago (median = 70 percent) and from 89 percent to 100 percent in New York (median = 96 percent), where no storm had occurred. (Persons absent because of travel, vacation, or prior illness were not counted.)

The correlations between group satisfaction[2] and group attendance are presented in Table 9-8. It is clear that all six satisfaction facets were significantly and strongly related to attendance in Chicago, where it was both socially and organizationally acceptable to be absent because of the snowstorm. Those groups of workers with the highest satisfaction levels were most likely to exert the high level of effort necessary to get to work. For the New York group, where these conditions (permissive absenteeism) were lacking, there were no significant relationships.

Union Activity

Job satisfaction can have an impact on two major aspects of union activity: (1) the tendency to form or join a union and (2) the tendency to take action within the union, such as filing grievances or striking. Traditionally, pay has been the primary consideration of union activity, but recently there has been added emphasis on medical and retirement benefits, work scheduling, and even the design of jobs. Survey data can be used to attend to critical issues that may influence union activity. This does not imply that surveys are antiunion devices. Indeed, surveys and unions have the same

TABLE 9-8 Correlations Between Satisfaction and Attendance

Satisfaction Facet	Chicago*	New York
Supervision	.54†	.12
Amount of work	.36‡	.01
Kind of work	.37‡	.06
Pay	.46†	.11
Career future	.60†	.14
Company policies and practices	.42‡	.02

*Group following snowstorm.
† $p < .01$ (highly significant).
‡ $p < .05$ (significant).
Source: Adapted from Smith (1977).

purpose: concern for worker needs and feelings. In fact, some union organizations often utilize surveys among their own employees and members to identify the issues that are most important to workers.

Early studies (Smith 1962) indicated that workers who are dissatisfied with their pay or their work tend to feel more positively toward unions and are more likely to join a union. It is widely accepted now that dissatisfaction with organizational policies and practices also encourages workers to seek union assistance in correcting what they view as undesirable conditions.

Herman (1973) reported on two studies (see Getman, Goldberg, and Herman 1976 for more complete information) of elections held to determine union representation. The first study involved an election sponsored by the Retail Clerks Association at two stores of a large discount department store chain; the second was based on an election sponsored by the United Steel Workers of America in a Chicago manufacturing company. Using structured interviews, Herman surveyed a sample of employees. She obtained measures of attitudes toward the union and measures of satisfaction with pay, hours of work, and type of work. Preelection interviews revealed that workers with favorable attitudes toward the union and low satisfaction with the company were most likely to

---

[2]Survey data had been collected from all of these employees in November and December of 1974. Satisfaction with supervision, amount of work, kind of work, pay, career future and company policies and practices were assessed. Average satisfaction levels for each of 27 functional groupings in Chicago and 13 groupings in New York were calculated for this study.

sign a card to authorize the election. Employees who expressed satisfaction with working conditions were not likely to support the union and in most cases voted against the unions. Using only measures of attitudes to predict how the workers would vote led to accurate predictions for 82 percent of the voters in the first study and 83 percent in the second study.

Hamner and Smith (1978) attempted to predict level of union activity by using measures of job satisfaction. A sample of 61,428 salaried employees from 188 units across the United States were studied. In 94 of these units, some union activity — from distributing handbills to losing a union election — had taken place after the administration of an attitude survey. Another 94 units, which had experienced no union activity, were chosen to match these on the basis of size, location, and function. The results indicated that 30 percent of the variance in union activity could be predicted from the measures of job satisfaction. The most important job satisfaction variable was satisfaction with supervision, although satisfaction with co-workers, career future, company policies and practices, amount of work, physical surroundings, and kind of work each had a significant impact. A study of another 31 units showed that these findings were consistent and to some degree generalizable.

It is not surprising to note that strikes and grievances are often a function of dissatisfaction (see Fleishman and Harris 1962; Fleishman, Harris, and Burtt 1955). It is important to recognize, however, that although the majority of strikes are related to wages, hours, and fringe benefits, other factors such as safety and management behavior often contribute to strike decisions as well as to the filing of grievances. Each of these factors, of course, can be evaluated by surveying employees before the grievance or strike decisions are made.

Performance

For years there has been an implicit assumption that job satisfaction influences performance. Actually, there is very little evidence to support this contention. Several reviews of the literature (e.g., Brayfield and Crockett 1955; Herzberg, Mausner, Peterson, and Capwell 1957; and Vroom 1964) have analyzed a large number of studies and concluded that they fail to support a significant link between satisfaction and performance. Table 9-9, adapted from Vroom's (1964) review, presents evidence to support the idea that there is no simple relationship of satisfaction to performance. There is little or no correlation between the two in all but a couple of the 20 studies listed. The median correlation of .14 suggests that only about 2 percent of the variance in performance is related to satisfaction scores.

There are two viable explanations for the absence of a strong relationship of satisfaction to performance.[3] First, Vroom (1964) and Porter and Lawler (1968) argued that this "nonfinding" is quite consistent with a number of theories. For example, expectancy theory suggests that performance has a direct impact on satisfaction (due to outcomes received for performance) but that any effect of satisfaction on performance is quite indirect and therefore not very strong.

The second type of explanation focuses on situational factors that may influence the relationship of satisfaction to performance. Herman (1973) has developed the idea that situational contingencies limit the strength of this relationship. She argued that workers do not have much freedom to vary performance levels because the possible range of performance is often determined by dependence on machines, on other workers, or on the worker's ability level. The acceptable range of performance is typically limited at the top by peer pressure and at the bottom by company policy. Thus, if the range of performance levels available to workers is small, satisfaction cannot have an impact on performance because the worker is not free (or able) to alter his or her output to any substantial degree.

---

[3]An excellent discussion of these explanations can be found in Schwab and Cummings (1970).

TABLE 9-9   Correlational Studies — Job Satisfaction and Job Performance

Worker Population	Correlation	Type of Criterion of Productivity	N
Insurance agents	.23	Ratings	233
	.26	Objective	
Air Force control tower operators	.01	Ratings	109
Hourly paid workers	.05	Ratings	890
Female office employees	.14	Ratings	231
Plumber's apprentices	.20	Ratings	55
Farmers	.12	Ratings	50
Production employees on piecework	.68	Objective	40
Work groups in an equipment manufacturing plant	−.31	Ratings	58
IBM operators	.08	Ratings	193
Departments in mail-order company	.19	Objective	25
Insurance agents	.22	Objective	552
Bus drivers	.31	Objective	144
Departments in an office	.86	Ratings	14
Administrative-technical personnel	.12	Ratings	124
Truck drivers —	.14	Ratings	28
large work groups	−.21	Objective	
Positioners —	.18	Ratings	24
small work groups	.02	Objective	
Female sales-clerks	−.03	Ratings	94
Employees in an electronics firm	.11	Ratings	377
Supervisors in an electronics firm	.13	Ratings	145
Supervisors in a package delivery company	.21	Ratings	96

Source: Adapted from Vroom (1964).

Communication Function

The organizational survey can serve as a communication device in two ways. First, the survey can provide a direct communication channel from workers to management. Since surveys typically guarantee anonymity to respondents, workers should feel free to communicate information that would not normally be expressed directly to management. Thus, the survey can sometimes function as a catalyst and almost always as a "safe" channel for upward communication.

Second, surveys can stimulate downward communication. The feedback session provides a situation in which it is socially and organizationally acceptable for management and workers to discuss issues. Numerous problems can be addressed, but more importantly, many imagined problems can be avoided. For example, a manager may learn that workers support a recent restructuring of their work but resent the manner in which it was explained. In such a case, resolution of a minor problem could salvage the effectiveness of a major organizational change.

Training Function

This function is often overlooked by many organizations although it can be one of the most important products of the survey procedure. The involvement of managers in survey procedures can be an extremely enlightening experience for them and can provide both an opportunity for development of skills and for the attainment of important insights. In some organizations, managers work with survey specialists at the survey development stage to explore critical incidents in the work situation that demand further study in the survey program. By participating in the survey process, they can learn how to isolate critical incidents and how to phrase relevant questions in a language appropriate to the workers.

In other cases, survey involvement can occur at the follow-up stage. Here, managers usually work under professional guidance to help other managers interpret survey results and devise appropriate ways of reporting these results to workers. This experience can be of great value to young managers, since they are able to observe the reactions of both senior executives and employees to survey findings.

Finally, managers can participate in supervised survey teams. Managers who are trained as interviewers have the opportunity to interview workers in units other than their own. This system is a key element in many survey programs and can be a very enriching experience for most managers. It is an almost universal feeling that time spent on a survey team produces more insights into human behavior than any other developmental experience.

Corporate Value Function

Although most organizations are concerned about the welfare of their employees and often state this as an organizational objective, there is seldom any tangible and consistent measure of how well this goal is met. In some cases, it is measured indirectly and after the fact, therefore stressing negative incidents such as strikes, sabotage, or high turnover. A well-designed survey program, however, can serve as tangible evidence of an organization's concern for its employees and can provide a yardstick by which management can measure its performance. Thus, it serves as a statement of a corporate value and as a report card for guiding management behavior.

Wiggins and Steade (1976) discussed a number of issues relating to this survey function and concluded that job satisfaction is a legitimate social concern. They argued that until recently workers were willing to tolerate job dissatisfaction as long as the job was lucrative enough to allow them to enjoy off-the-job events. In other words, the quality of work life could be sacrificed for the quality of life away from work. Wiggins and Steade claim that this is changing. Because workers are no longer willing to segment their lives this way, the quality of work life is becoming central to workers.

> One's future quality of life will depend on an acceptable total-life pattern that includes increased satisfaction in the job segment.

> In this scheme, the development of people and their satisfaction in meaningful jobs will become a corporate social goal that parallels the proper uti-

lization of other resources to meet society's needs. This will represent a corporate commitment to the humanization of work and the opportunity to grow and advance in rewarding jobs (Wiggins and Steade 1976, 50).

A special task force created in 1971 by Elliot Richardson, then secretary of health, education, and welfare, to examine "health, education and welfare problems from the perspective of one of the fundamental social institutions — work" indicates a growing interest in the quality of work life. The rather dramatic conclusion reached by this task force was presented in its report, *Work In America* (1973), as follows:

> Our analysis on work in America leads to the conclusion: Because work is central to the lives of so many Americans, either the absence of work or employment in meaningless work is creating an increasingly intolerable situation. The human costs of this state of affairs are manifested in worker alienation, alcoholism, drug addiction, and other symptoms of poor mental health. Moreover, much of our tax money is expended in an effort to compensate for problems with at least a part of their genesis in the world of work. A great part of the staggering national bill in the areas of crime and delinquency, mental and physical health, manpower and welfare are generated in our national policies and attitudes toward work (p. 86).

Or, in the words of Albert Camus, "Without work all life goes rotten. But when work is soulless, life stifles and dies."

Financial Impact of Employee Attitudes

Although the results of organizational surveys are usually somewhat subtle, attempts have been made recently to document these results by using hard figures. Likert (1961) applied the term *Human Re-source Accounting (HRA)* to a category of methods for developing indicators of the state of organizations. While there have been a number of efforts to develop HRA systems for organizations (e.g., Alexander 1971; Flamholtz 1974; Herrick 1975; Macy and Mirvis 1976), the systems developed by Likert (1973) and Likert and Bowers (1973) can serve as an example. Their system assesses the relatively short-term costs of worker behavior. By correlating attitude scores with costs of these behaviors, it predicts changes in unit cost from changes in attitudes.

Using a variation of the HRA method, Mirvis and Lawler (1977) empirically evaluated the financial impact of job attitudes for 160 tellers at a midwestern bank. Their study — an application of Likert's ideas — measured the tellers' job satisfaction and the tellers' beliefs about which levels of performance would lead to which outcomes. They related these measurements to absenteeism, turnover, and performance (tellers' balance shortages) and evaluated them to reflect short-term costs. Their analysis indicated that an improvement in the tellers' job satisfaction of one half of a standard deviation (a moderate increase) would lead to a predicted direct savings of $17,664 and a potential total-cost savings of $125,160 over the course of a year. This is a potential savings of $782 per teller per year.

The reader should be cautious in evaluating Human Resource Accounting techniques. These methods are fairly new and still need considerable developmental work. They do hold promise, however, for substantiating the economic value of worker attitudes. Although this approach seems to ignore the growing social concern for the quality of work life, these two positions are not mutually exclusive. It is entirely appropriate to value worker attitudes from both a social and an economic perspective. In fact, in one sense, the HRA approach does little more than quantify in financial terms a dividend that the socially concerned organization is likely to receive for improving worker attitudes.

References

Alexander, M., "Investments in People," *Canadian Chartered Accountant* 98, 1971, 1–8.

Brayfield, A. H., and W. H. Crockett, "Employee Attitudes and Employee Performance," *Psychological Bulletin* 52, 1955, 396–424.

Dunham, R. B., "Affective Responses to Task Characteristics: The Role of Organizational Functions," Ph.D. dissertation, University of Illinois, 1975.

——, "Two Job Evaluation Techniques and Determinants of Pay Satisfaction," Paper presented at the convention of the American Psychological Association, Toronto, Ontario, Canada, 1978.

——, J. E. Newman, and R. S. Blackburn, "Employee Reactions to Technological and Organizational Changes," Paper presented at the convention of the Midwest Psychological Association, Chicago, 1978.

Flamholtz, E. G., *Human Resource Accounting*, Dickenson Publishing, 1974.

Fleishman, E. A., and E. F. Harris, "Patterns of Leadership Behavior Related to Employee Grievances and Turnover," *Personnel Psychology* 15, 1962, 43–56.

——, and H. E. Burtt, *Leadership and Supervision in Individuals*, Ohio State University, Personnel Research Board, 1955.

Getman, J. G., S. B. Goldberg, and J. B. Herman, *Union Representation Elections: Law and Reality*, Russell Sage Foundation, 1976.

Hamner, W. C., and F. J. Smith, "Work Attitudes as Predictors of Unionization Activity," *Journal of Applied Psychology* 63, 1978, 415–21.

Heneman, H. G., III, and D. P. Schwab, "Work and Rewards Theory," in *Motivation and Commitment*, Bureau of National Affairs, 1975.

Herman, J. B., "Are Situational Contingencies Limiting Job Attitude–Job Performance Relationships?" *Organizational Behavior and Human Performance* 10, 1973, 203–24.

Herrick, N. Q., *The Quality of Work and Its Outcomes: Estimating Potential Increases in Labor Productivity*, Academy of Contemporary Problems, 1975.

Herzberg, F., B. Mausner, R. O. Peterson, and D. F. Capwell, *Job Attitudes: Review of Research Opinion*, Psychological Series of Pittsburgh, 1957.

Hulin, C. L., "Job Satisfaction and Turnover in a Female Clerical Population," *Journal of Applied Psychology* 50, 1966, 280–85.

——, "Effects of Changes in Job Satisfaction Levels on Employee Turnover," *Journal of Applied Psychology* 52, 1968, 122–26.

Likert, R., *New Patterns of Management*, McGraw-Hill, 1961.

——, "Human Resource Accounting: Building and Assessing Productive Organizations," *Personnel* 50, 1973, 8–24.

——, and Bowers, "Improving the Accuracy of P/L Reports by Estimating the Change in Dollar Value of the Human Organization," *Michigan Business Review* 1973, 15–24.

Macy, B. A., and P. H. Mirvis, "A Methodology Assessment of Quality of Work Life and Organizational Effectiveness in Behavioral-Economic Terms," *Administrative Science Quarterly* 21, 1976, 212–26.

March, J. G., and H. A. Simon, *Organizations*, John Wiley & Sons, 1958.

Mirvis, P. H., and E. E. Lawler, III, "Measuring the Financial Impact of Employee Attitudes," *Journal of Applied Psychology* 62, 1977, 1–8.

Porter, L. W., and E. E. Lawler, III, *Managerial Attitudes and Performance*, Richard D. Irwin, 1968.

——, and R. M. Steers, "Organizational, Work, and Personal Factors in Employee Turnover and Absenteeism," *Psychological Bulletin* 80, 1973, 151–76.

Schwab, D. P., and L. L. Cummings, "Theories of Performance and Satisfaction: A Review," *Industrial Relations* 7, 1970, 408–30.

Smith, F. J., "Problems and Trends in the Operational Use of Employee Attitude Measurements." Paper presented at the convention of the American Psychological Association, 1962.

———, "Work Attitudes as Predictors of Attendance on a Specific Day," *Journal of Applied Psychology* 62, 1977, 16–19.

Vroom, V., *Work and Motivation* (New York: John Wiley and Sons, 1964).

Wiggins, R. L., and R. D. Steade, "Job Satisfaction as a Social Concern," *Academy of Management Review* 1, 1976, 48–55.

Work in America. Report of a special task force to the secretary of health, education, and welfare. MIT Press, 1973.

Split Roles in Performance Appraisal

In management circles, performance appraisal is a highly interesting and provocative topic. And in business literature, too, knowledgeable people write emphatically, pro and con, on the performance appraisal question.[1] In fact, one might almost say that everybody talks and writes about it, but nobody has done any real scientific testing of it.

At the General Electric Company we felt it was important that a truly scientific study be done to test the effectiveness of our traditional performance appraisal program. Why? Simply because our own experience with performance appraisal programs had been both positive and negative. For example:

Surveys generally show that most people think the idea of performance appraisal is good. They feel that people should know where they stand and, therefore, managers should discuss an appraisal of their performance with them periodically.

In actual practice, however, it is the extremely rare operating manager who will employ such a program on his/her own initiative. Personnel specialists report that most managers carry out performance appraisal interviews only when strong control procedures are established to ensure that they do so. This is surprising because the managers have been told repeatedly that the system is intended to help them obtain improved performance from their subordinates.

We also found from interviews with employees who have had a good deal of experience with traditional performance appraisal programs that few indeed can cite examples of constructive action taken — or significant improvement achieved — which stem from suggestions received in a performance appraisal interview with their boss.

Source: "Split Roles in Performance Appraisal" by Herbert H. Meyer, Emanuel Kay, and John R. P. French, from *Harvard Business Review*, January-February 1965. Copyright © 1965 by the President and Fellows of Harvard College; all rights reserved.

[1]Douglas McGregor, "An Uneasy Look at Performance Appraisal," HBR May-June 1957, p. 89; Harold Mayfield, "In Defense of Performance Appraisal," HBR March-April 1960, p. 81; and Alva F. Kindall and James Gatza, "Positive Program for Performance Appraisal," HBR November-December 1963, p. 153.

Traditional Program

Faced with such contradictory evidence, we undertook a study several years ago to determine the effectiveness of our comprehensive performance appraisal process. Special attention was focused on the interviews between the subordinates and their managers, because these are the discussions which are supposed to motivate people to improve their performance. And we found out some very interesting things — among them the following:

Criticism has a negative effect on achievement of goals.

Praise has little effect one way or the other.

Performance improves most when specific goals are established.

Defensiveness resulting from critical appraisal produces inferior performance.

Coaching should be a day-to-day, not a once-a-year, activity.

Mutual goal setting, not criticism, improves performance.

Interviews designed primarily to improve a man's performance should not at the same time weigh his salary or promotion in the balance.

Participation by the employee in the goal-setting procedure helps produce favorable results.

As you can see, the results of this original study indicated that detailed and comprehensive annual appraisals of subordinates' performances by their managers is decidedly of questionable value. Furthermore, as is certainly the case when the major objective of such a discussion is to motivate the subordinate to improve performance, the traditional appraisal interview does not do the job.

In the first part of this article, we will offer readers more than this bird's-eye view of our research into performance appraisal. (We will not, however, burden managers with details of methodology.) We will also describe the one-year follow-up experiment General Electric conducted to validate the conclusions derived from our original study. Here the traditional an-nual performance appraisal method was tested against a new method we developed, which we called Work Planning and Review (WP&R). As you will see, this approach produced, under actual plant conditions, results which were decidedly superior to those afforded by the traditional performance appraisal method. Finally, we will offer evidence to support our contention that some form of WP&R might well be incorporated into other industrial personnel programs to achieve improvement in work performance.

Appraising Appraisal

In order to assure a fair test of the effectiveness of the traditional performance appraisal method, which had been widely used throughout General Electric, we conducted an intensive study of the process at a large GE plant where the performance appraisal program was judged to be good; that is, in this plant —

... appraisals had been based on job responsibilities, rather than on personal characteristics of the individuals involved;

... an intensive training program had been carried out for managers in the use of the traditional appraisal method and techniques for conducting appraisal interviews;

... the program had been given strong backing by the plant manager and had been policed diligently by the personnel staff so that over 90% of the exempt employees had been appraised and interviewed annually.

This comprehensive annual performance appraisal program, as is typical, was designed to serve two major purposes. The first was to justify recommended salary action. The second, which was motivational in character, was intended to present an opportunity for the manager to review a subordinate's performance and promote discussion on needed improvements. For the latter purpose, the manager was required to draw up a specific program of plans and goals for subordinates which would help them improve job performance and to qualify, hopefully, for future promotion.

Interview Modifications

Preliminary interviews with key managers and subordinates revealed the salary action issue had so dominated the annual comprehensive performance appraisal interview that neither party had been in the right frame of mind to discuss plans for improved performance. To straighten this out, we asked managers to split the traditional appraisal interview into two sessions — discussing appraisal of performance and salary action in one interview and performance improvement plans in another to be held about two weeks later. This split provided us with a better opportunity to conduct our experiment on the effects of participation in goal planning.

To enable us to test the effects of participation, we instructed half the managers to use a *high participation* approach and the other half to use a *low participation* technique. Thus:

Each of the "high" managers was instructed to ask the appraisee to prepare a set of goals for achieving improved job performance and to submit them for the manager's review and approval. The manager also was encouraged to permit the subordinate to exert as much influence as possible on the formulation of the final list of job goals agreed on in the performance improvement discussion.

The "low" managers operated in much the same way they had in our traditional appraisal program. They formulated a set of goals for the subordinate, and these goals were then reviewed in the performance improvement session. The manager was instructed to conduct this interview in such a way that his/her influence in the forming of the final list of job goals would be greater than the subordinate's.

Conducting the Research

There were 92 appraisees in the experimental group, representing a cross section of the exempt salaried employees in the plant. This group included engineers; engineering support technicians; foremen; and specialists in manufacturing, customer service, marketing, finance, and purchasing functions. None of the exempt employees who participated as appraisees in the experiment had other exempt persons reporting to them; thus they did not serve in conflicting manager-subordinate roles.

The entire group was interviewed and asked to complete questionnaires (a) before and after the salary action interview, and (b) after the delayed second discussion with their managers about performance improvement. These interviews and questionnaires were designed to achieve three objectives:

1. Assess changes in the attitudes of individuals toward their managers and toward the appraisal system after each of the discussions.
2. Get an estimate from the appraisees of the degree to which they usually participated in decisions that affected them. (This was done in order to determine whether or not previous lack of participation affected their response to participation in the experiment.)
3. Obtain a self-appraisal from all subordinates before and after they met with their managers. (This was done in order to determine how discrepancies in these self-appraisals might affect their reactions to the appraisal interview.)

Moreover, each salary action and performance improvement discussion was observed by outsiders trained to record essentially what transpired. (Managers preferred to use neither tape recorders nor unseen observers, feeling that observers unaffiliated with the company — in this case, graduate students in applied psychological disciplines — afforded the best way of obtaining a reasonably close approximation of the normal discussions.) In the appraisal for salary action interviews, for example, the observers recorded the amount of criticism and praise employed by the manager, as well as the reactions of the appraisee to the manager's comments. In the performance improvement discussions, the observers recorded the participation of the subordinates, as well as the amount of influence they seemed to exert in establishing their future success goals.

Criticism and Defensiveness

In general, the managers completed the performance appraisal forms in a thorough and conscientious manner. Their appraisals were discussed with subordinates in interviews ranging from approximately 30 to 90 minutes in length. On the average, managers covered 32 specific performance items which, when broken down, showed positive (praise) appraisals on 19 items, and negative (criticism) on 13. Typically, praise was more often related to *general* performance characteristics, while criticism was usually focused on *specific* performance items.

The average subordinate reacted defensively to seven of the manager's criticisms during the appraisal interview (that is, he/she reacted defensively about 54% of the time when criticized). Denial of shortcomings cited by the manager, blaming others, and various other forms of excuses were recorded by the observers as defensive reactions.

Constructive responses to criticism were *rarely* observed. In fact, the average was less than one per interview. Not too surprising, along with this, was the finding that the more criticism employees received in the performance appraisal discussion, the more defensively they reacted. People who received an above-average number of criticisms showed more than five times as much defensive behavior as those who received a below-average number of criticisms. Subordinates who received a below-average number of criticisms, for example, reacted defensively only about one time out of three. But those

who received an above-average number reacted defensively almost two times out of three.

One explanation for this defensiveness is that it seems to stem from the overrating each employee tended to give to his/her own performance. The average employee's self-estimate of performance *before* appraisal placed him/her at the 77 percentile. (Only 2 of the 92 participants estimated their performance to be below the average point on the scale.) But when the same employees were asked *after* their performance appraisal discussions how they thought their bosses had rated them, the average figure given was at the 65 percentile. The great majority (75 out of 92) saw their manager's evaluation as being less favorable than their self-estimates. Obviously, to these employees, the performance appraisal discussion with the manager was a deflating experience. Thus, it was not surprising that the subordinates reacted defensively in their interviews.

Criticism and Goal Achievement

Even more important is the fact that employees who received an above-average number of criticisms in their performance appraisal discussions generally showed *less* goal achievement 10 to 12 weeks later than those who had received fewer criticisms. At first, we thought that this difference might be accounted for by the fact that the subordinates who received more criticisms were probably poorer performers in general. But there was little factual evidence found to support this suspicion.

It was true that those who received an above-average number of criticisms in their appraisal discussions did receive slightly lower summary ratings on overall performance from their managers. But they did not receive proportionally lower salary increases. And the salary increases granted were *supposed* to reflect differences in job performance, according to the salary plan traditionally used in this plant. This argument, admittedly, is something less than perfect.

But it does appear clear that frequent criticism constitutes so strong a threat to self-esteem that it disrupts rather than improves subsequent performance. We expected such a disruptive threat to operate more strongly on those individuals who were already low on self-esteem, just as we expected employees who had confidence in their ability to do their jobs to react more constructively to criticism. Our group experiment proved these expectations to be correct.

Still further evidence that criticism has a negative effect on performance was found when we investigated areas which had been given special emphasis by the managers in their criticisms. Following the appraisal discussion with the manager, the employees were asked to indicate which one aspect of their performance had been most criticized by the manager. Then, when we conducted our follow-up investigation 10 to 12 weeks later, it revealed that improvement in the most-criticized aspects of performance cited was considerably *less* than improvement realized in other areas!

Participation Effects

As our original research study had indicated, the effects of a high participation level were also favorable in our group experiment. In general, here is what we found:

Subordinates who received a high participation level in the performance interview reacted more favorably than did those who received a low participation level. The "highs" also, in most cases, achieved a greater percentage of their improvement goals than did their "low" counterparts. For the former, the high participation level was associated with greater mutual understanding between them and their managers, greater acceptance of job goals, a more favorable attitude toward the appraisal system, and a feeling of greater self-realization on the job.

But employees who had traditionally been accustomed to low participation in their daily relationship with the manager did not necessarily perform better under the high participation treatment. In fact, those who had received a high level of criticism in their appraisal interviews actually performed better when their managers set goals for them than they did when they set their own goals, as permitted under the high participation treatment.

In general, our experiment showed that those who usually worked under high participation levels performed best on goals they set for themselves. Those who indicated that they usually worked under low levels performed best on goals that the managers set for them. Evidently, employees who usually do not participate in work-planning decisions consider job goals set by the manager to be more important than goals they set for themselves. Those accustomed to a high participation level, on the other hand, may have stronger motivation to achieve goals set for themselves than to achieve those set by the manager.

Goal-Setting Importance

While subordinate participation in the goal-setting process had some effect on improved performance, a much more powerful influence was whether goals were set at all. Many times in appraisal discussions, managers mentioned areas of performance where improvement was needed. Quite often these were translated into specific work plans and goals. But this was not always the case. In fact, when we looked at the one performance area which each manager had emphasized in the appraisal interview as most in need of improvement, we found that these items actually were translated into specific work plans and goals for only about 60% of our experiment participants.

When performance was being measured 10 to 12 weeks after the goal-planning sessions, managers were asked to describe what results they hoped for in the way of subordinate on-the-job improvement. They did this for those important performance items that had been mentioned in the interview. Each manager was then asked to estimate on a percentage scale the degree to which the hoped-for changes had actually been observed. The average percent accomplishment estimate for those performance items that *did* get translated into goals was 65, while the percent estimate for those items that *did not* get translated into goals was about 27! Establishing specific plans and goals seemed to ensure that attention would be given to that aspect of job performance.

Summation of Findings

At the end of this experiment, we were able to draw certain tentative conclusions. These conclusions were the basis of a future research study which we will describe later. In general, we learned that:

Comprehensive annual performance appraisals are of questionable value. Certainly a major objective of the manager in traditional appraisal discussions is motivating the subordinate to improve performance. But the evidence we gathered indicated clearly that praise tended to have no effect, perhaps because it was regarded as the sandwich which surrounded the raw meat of criticism.[2] And criticism itself brought on defensive reactions that were essentially denials of responsibility for a poor performance.

Coaching should be a day-to-day, not a once-a-year, activity. There are two main reasons for this:

(1) Employees seem to accept suggestions for improved performance if they are given in a less concentrated form than is the case in comprehensive annual appraisals. As our experiment showed, employees become clearly

[2]See Richard E. Farson, "Praise Reappraised," HBR September-October 1963, p. 61.

more prone to reject criticisms as the number of criticisms mount. This indicates that an "overload phenomenon" may be operating. In other words, people seem to have a tolerance level for the amount of criticism they can take. And, as this level is approached or passed, it becomes increasingly difficult for them to accept responsibility for the shortcomings pointed out.

(2) Some managers reported that the traditional performance appraisal program tended to cause them to save up items where improvement was needed in order to have enough material to conduct a comprehensive discussion of performance in the annual review. This short-circuited one of the primary purposes of the appraisal program — that of giving feedback to the subordinates as to their performance. Studies of the learning process point out that feedback is less effective if much time is allowed to elapse between the performance and the feedback. This fact alone argues for more frequent discussions between the manager and the subordinate.

Goal setting, not criticism, should be used to improve performance. One of the most significant findings in our experiment was the fact that far superior results were observed when the manager and the employee *together* set specific goals to be achieved, rather than merely discussed needed improvement. Frequent reviews of progress provide natural opportunities for discussing means of improving performance *as needs occur,* and these reviews are far less threatening than the annual appraisal and salary review discussions.

Separate appraisals should be held for different purposes. Our work demonstrated that it was unrealistic to expect a single performance appraisal program to achieve every conceivable need. It seems foolish to have a manager serving in the self-conflicting role as a counselor (helping employees to improve their performance) when at the same time presiding as a judge over the same employees' salary action cases.

New WP&R Method

This intensive year-long test of the performance appraisal program indicated clearly that work-planning-and-review discussions between employees and their managers appeared to be a far more effective approach in improving job performance than was the concentrated annual performance appraisal program.

For this reason, after the findings had been announced, many GE managers adopted some form of the new WP&R program to motivate performance improvement in employees, especially those at the professional and administrative levels. Briefly described, the WP&R approach calls for periodic meetings between the manager and the subordinate. During these meetings, progress on past goals is reviewed, solutions are sought for job-related problems, and new goals are established. The intent of the method is to create a situation in which manager and subordinate can discuss job performance and needed improvements in detail without the subordinate becoming defensive.

Basic Features

This WP&R approach differs from the traditional performance appraisal program in that:

There are more frequent discussions of performance.

There are no summary judgments or ratings made.

Salary action discussions are held separately.

The emphasis is on mutual goal planning and problem solving.

As far as frequency is concerned, these WP&R discussions are held more often than traditional performance appraisal interviews, but are not scheduled at rigidly fixed intervals. Usually at the conclusion of one work planning session the employee and manager set an approximate date for the next review. Frequency depends both on the nature of the job and on the manager's style of operating. Sometimes these WP&R discussions are held as often as once a month, whereas for other jobs and/or individuals, once every six months is more appropriate.

In these WP&R discussions, the manager and the subordinate do not deal in generalities. They consider specific, objectively defined work goals and establish the yardstick for measuring performance. These goals stem, of course, from broader departmental objectives and are defined in relation to the individual's position in the department.

Comparison Setting

After the findings of our experiment were communicated by means of reports and group meetings in the plant where the research was carried out, about half the key managers decided they would abandon the comprehensive annual performance appraisal method and adopt the new WP&R program instead. The other half were hesitant to make such a major change at the time. They decided, consequently, to continue with the traditional performance appraisal program and to try to make it more effective. This provided a natural setting for us to compare the effectiveness of the two approaches. We decided that the comparison should be made in the light of the objectives usually stated for the comprehensive annual performance appraisal program. These objectives were (a) to provide knowledge of results to employees, (b) to justify reasons for salary action, and (c) to motivate and help employees do a better job.

The study design was simple. Before any changes were made, the exempt employees who would be affected by these programs were surveyed to provide baseline data. The WP&R program was then implemented in about half of the exempt group, with the other half continuing to use a modified version of the traditional performance appraisal program. One year later, the identical survey questionnaire was again administered in order to compare the changes that had occurred.

Attitudes & Actions

The results of this research study were quite convincing. The group that continued on the traditional performance appraisal showed no change in *any* of the areas measured. The WP&R group, by contrast, expressed significantly more favorable attitudes on almost all questionnaire items. Specifically, their attitudes changed in a favorable direction over the year that they participated in the new WP&R program with regard to the —

. . . amount of help the manager was giving them in improving performance on the job;

. . . degree to which the manager was receptive to new ideas and suggestions;

. . . ability of the manager to plan;

. . . extent to which the manager made use of their abilities and experience;

. . . degree to which they felt the goals they were shooting for were what they *should* be;

. . . extent to which they received help from the manager in planning for *future* job opportunities;

. . . value of the performance discussions they had with their managers.

In addition to these changes in attitudes, evidence was also found which showed clearly that the members of the WP&R group were much more likely to have taken specific actions to improve performance than were those who continued with the traditional performance appraisal approach.

Current Observations

Recently we undertook still another intensive study of the WP&R program in order to learn more about the nature of these discussions and how they can be made most effective. While these observations have not been completed, some interesting findings have already come to light — especially in relation to differences between WP&R and traditional performance appraisal discussions.

Perceived Differences

For one thing, WP&R interviews are strictly one-to-one in character, rather than having a parent-to-child flavor, as did so many of the traditional performance appraisals. This seems to be due to the fact that it is much more natural under the WP&R program for the subordinate to take the initiative when performance on past goals is being reviewed. Thus, in listening to the subordinate's review of performance, problems, and failings, the manager is automatically cast in the role of *counselor*. This role for the manager, in turn, results naturally in a problem-solving discussion.

In the traditional performance appraisal interview, on the other hand, the manager is automatically cast in the role of *judge*. The subordinate's natural reaction is to assume a defensive posture, and thus all the necessary ingredients for an argument are present.

Since the WP&R approach focuses mainly on immediate, short-term goals, some managers are concerned that longer range, broader plans and goals might be neglected. Our data show that this concern is unfounded. In almost every case, the discussion of specific work plans and goals seems to lead naturally into a consideration of broader, longer range plans. In fact, in a substantial percentage of these sessions, even the career plans of the subordinates are reviewed.

In general, the WP&R approach appears to be a better way of defining what is expected of an individual and how he/she is doing on the job. Whereas the traditional performance appraisal often results in resistance to the manager's attempts to help the subordinate, the WP&R approach brings about acceptance of such attempts.

Conclusion

Multiple studies conducted by the Behavioral Research Service at GE reveal that the traditional performance appraisal method contains a number of problems:

1. Appraisal interviews attempt to accomplish the two objectives of —
   ... providing a written justification for salary action;
   ... motivating the employee to improve his work performance.
2. The two purposes are in conflict, with the result that the traditional appraisal system essentially becomes a salary discussion in which the manager justifies the action taken.
3. The appraisal discussion has little influence on future job performance.
4. Appreciable improvement is realized only when specified goals and deadlines are mutually established and agreed on by the subordinate and the manager in an interview split away from the appraisal interview.

This evidence, coupled with other principles relating to employee motivation, gave rise to the new WP&R program, which is proving to be far more effective in improving job performance than the traditional performance appraisal method. Thus, it appears likely that companies which are currently relying on the comprehensive annual performance appraisal process to achieve improvement in work performance might well consider the advisability of switching to some form of work-planning-and-review in their industrial personnel programs.

Questions for Discussion

1. What is the purpose of the appraisal interview?
2. How much effect does it have on job performance?
3. Why is it in conflict with salary action?
4. How else can workers be motivated to improve?

10

Due Process Systems

Our introduction to the concept of due process at the workplace starts with a description of the evolution and current status of grievance procedures and arbitration systems commonly found in United States collective bargaining contracts. These procedures are the centerpiece of the day-to-day collective bargaining relationship and also the forerunner of many appeal procedures and due process systems now found in nonunion settings.

Structure of Union Grievance Procedures

A typical multistep grievance procedure is outlined in Box 10-1. A grievance usually begins when an employee believes his or her rights under the collective bargaining contract have been violated, or when a union representative believes that management has misinterpreted or failed to apply correctly a provision of the collective bargaining agreement. Initially, the individual employee or union representative discusses the complaint or problem with a first-line supervisor. Although accurate records are not kept of such discussions, it is believed that more than 90 percent of all grievances are resolved informally at the initial oral stage without filing a written grievance. If no oral resolution is achieved, however, the employee ordinarily contacts a union steward. The grievance is then put in writing and either resubmitted to the first-line supervisor or, more commonly, given to a management representative at the next level of the organizational hierarchy. A meeting is then held to discuss the written grievance. Management has a specified period of time in which to respond to the union and the employee. Sometimes management agrees that the employee's rights were violated or that the contract was misinterpreted and proposes a remedy that is acceptable to both the employee and the union. Alternately, management might disagree with the union's and the employee's interpretation of the situation, thereby denying the grievance. The union then can appeal to a higher management level. Usually, by the fourth step of this type of appeal process, unresolved grievances go to a neutral

BOX 10-1
Steps in a Typical Grievance Procedure

A. Employee-initiated Grievance

Step 1

a. Employee discusses grievance or problem orally with supervisor.
b. Union steward and employee may discuss problem orally with supervisor.
c. Union steward and employee decide if (1) problem has been resolved or (2) if not resolved, whether a contract violation has occurred.

Step 2

a. Grievance is put in writing and submitted to the production superintendent or other designated line manager.
b. Steward and management representative meet and discuss grievance. Management's response is put in writing. A member of the industrial relations staff may be consulted at this stage.

Step 3

a. Grievance is appealed to top line management and industrial relations staff representatives. Additional local or international union officers may become involved in discussions. Decision is put in writing.

Step 4

a. Union decides whether to appeal unresolved grievance to arbitration according to procedures specified in its constitution and/or bylaws.
b. Grievance is appealed to arbitration for binding decision.

B. Discharge Grievance

a. Procedure may begin at step 2 or step 3.
b. Time limits between steps may be shorter so as to expedite the process.

C. Union or Group Grievance

a. Union representative initiates grievance at step 1 or step 2 on behalf of affected class of workers or union representatives.

Source: Thomas Kochan, *Collective Bargaining and Industrial Relations* (Homewood, Ill. Irwin, 1980). Copyright © 1980 by Thomas Kochan. Reprinted by permission of Richard D. Irwin, Inc.

---

third-party arbitrator for a binding decision. Most arbitrators are chosen jointly by union and company representatives from lists supplied by independent organizations such as the American Arbitration Association or by government agencies such as the Federal Mediation and Conciliation Service.

Union officials are not required to appeal a grievance to a higher step of a procedure or to take all unresolved cases to arbitration. But they must decide whether the grievant has a valid claim which could be won upon appeal. At the same time, a union is required by law to represent all members of the bargaining unit fairly (whether they are union members or not). Employees can sue a union in federal court if the union breaches its "duty of fair representation" (McKelvey, 1984).

Grievance arbitrators use well-established criteria to decide cases. The primary criterion centers on the written terms of the contract. If the relevant terms of the agreement are clear and can be applied unambiguously to the dispute, the arbitrator looks no further, because his or her basic function is to interpret and apply the contract's provisions (Elkouri and Elkouri, 1973; Zack and Bloch, 1983). If the contract is ambiguous, or where the circumstances that led to the dispute were not completely anticipated by the contract provisions, arbitrators will turn to criteria such as the past practices of the parties in similar situations, normal custom and practice in the industry or occupation, previous arbitrator rulings in similar cases, and oral testimony on the intent of parties who initially negotiated the contract language in dispute. Finally, an important part of the arbitrator's task is to judge the credibility of witnesses and to choose among conflicting testimony in establishing the "facts" of the case. For this reason, arbitrators rely on rules of evidence similar to those used by judges in courts of law (Zack and Bloch, 1983).

Normally, the burden of proof in arbitration lies with the grievant. That is, the grievant must convince the arbitrator that the contract was in fact violated. Discipline and discharge cases are the major exceptions to this rule. When an employee appeals a discharge to arbitration, the burden is on *management* to prove "just cause" for firing the employee. Just cause is seldom explicitly defined in a collective bargaining agreement. But specific offenses that result in automatic discharge — such as fighting or sleeping on the job — may be itemized in the contract or in company rules. Principles of just cause have evolved over the years as part of the "common law" of arbitration. One of the central principles of just cause, for example, is that progressive discipline (warnings, suspensions, and so on) should precede dismissal.

History of Grievance Arbitration

Grievance procedures were introduced in the late nineteenth century in industries such as clothing and coal mining. But grievance arbitration did not become a common practice in collective bargaining until after it was actively endorsed during World War II by the War Labor Board (WLB) (Fleming, 1964). In 1947, the Taft-Hartley Act made grievance arbitration a part of our national labor policy by endorsing it as the final method of resolving conflicts during the term of a collective bargaining agreement. Although the act did not make grievance arbitration mandatory in collective bargaining, it did encourage further public support for this innovative method of resolving disputes that occur during the term of an agreement. Then, in 1960, the U.S. Supreme Court issued three grievance-related decisions known as the Steelworkers' Trilogy. These three decisions further endorsed grievance arbitration as the preferred method to resolve disputes about the interpretation of collective bargaining agreements. The court held that judges must defer to the decisions of arbitrators on the substantive merits of a dispute, confining any judicial review to whether the arbitrator followed due process procedures. Further, the decisions stressed that in cases where it is unclear whether a particular issue should be taken to arbitration or through the court system, the claim must go to arbitration. Finally, these decisions reinforced the view that arbitration serves as a quid pro quo for giving up the right to strike during the term of an agreement.

Although the Steelworkers' Trilogy continues to define the basic roles of arbitration and the courts where the issue is interpretation of collective bargaining provisions, the status of arbitration has eroded somewhat in the 1970s, with the growth of public policies regulating individual rights at the workplace. Arbitration continues to be the central mechanism for resolving disputes that fall solely within the scope of privately negotiated collective bargaining contracts. But issues involving workers' rights that are regulated by public policies, such as equal employment opportunity and safety and health in the workplace, are also subject to the jurisdiction of specific government regulatory agencies, and ultimately to the enforcement powers of the courts (see chapter 12 for further discussion on this issue). In a landmark case in 1974 — *Alexander* v. *Gardner-Denver* — the Supreme Court departed from its Steelworkers' Trilogy doctrine for cases involving employment discrimination. The court ruled that an arbitrator's decision involving a claim of discrimination covered by federal statutes does not preclude judicial review of the substantive merits of the claim. Further, the grievant may bypass arbitration and go directly to the appropriate government agency or to the courts. When a claim is taken to court, the judge will hear the evidence independently, whether or not an arbitrator has given a decision. The court does not need to give weight to an arbitrator's decision.

Since the *Gardner-Denver* decision, the arbitration community has engaged in a professional debate about whether the decision criteria for arbitrators should expand to interpret the provisions of the statute or statutes relevant to a given case. Traditionally, arbitrators are bound only to interpret what the parties have written into their own contracts. They are neither expected nor encouraged to create new contractual terms by considering other factors. Those who argue that interpretation of the public law lies outside both the responsibility and the expertise of arbitrators apply the traditional logic that led to the acceptance of arbitration as an effective administrative and due process tool for employees, employers, and labor unions. Others who argue that arbitrators should consider the intent and requirements of public policies believe that unless arbitrators do so, they risk reducing the relevance of arbitration to workplace problems and conflicts.

This brief review illustrates both the important contributions and current limitations of arbitration to United States industrial relations. Arbitration was introduced into collective bargaining as a cheap, fast, and more efficient and responsive system to insure due process and peaceful resolution of conflicts at the workplace. As such, arbitration could provide more efficient and acceptable methods for resolving conflicts than those available through the courts or through strike actions. In the early years, many arbitrators played an important role in helping the parties to develop a "common law of the shop." But as the parties became more sophisticated in their relations with each other, and as collective bargaining contracts became more complex, the process has become more legalistic, slower, and quite expensive. To counteract that trend, a number of efforts have been introduced to expedite the arbitration process by skipping one or more steps of the grievance procedure and using a more informal hearing procedure and written awards (Zalusky, 1976).

At the other extreme, some arbitration procedures today may follow very rigid legalistic rules of evidence in which lawyers represent the employer and the employee, written transcripts of the arbitration hearing are required, and hearings involve multiple challenges and objections to witness testimony. The flexible and informal conflict resolution system envisioned by the early advocates of arbitration has in some situations been transformed into a legalistic quasi-judicial proceeding.

Although grievance procedures and arbitration generally have become more formal and legalistic, these mechanisms for resolving conflicts in the workplace have demonstrated a record of achievements that would not have been possible by relying solely on public agencies and the courts. Criteria have developed under which professionals can judge the effectiveness of grievance procedures and other due process mechanisms. These criteria are a useful checklist for managers to use in monitoring the effectiveness of the grievance arbitration and other due process systems within their control.

Evaluation of Grievance Procedures

Evaluation of due process procedures ordinarily begins by considering operational criteria, such as the delays between the initiation of a grievance and its resolution, and the costs to the parties of resolving the grievance (Kochan, 1980; Goldberg and Brett, 1983). Another useful indicator of the operational effectiveness of grievance procedures is the extent to which disputes are resolved effectively at early stages of the procedure. The general philosophy guiding this criterion stresses the desirability of resolving disputes at levels closest to the workplace so that the individuals most directly involved have the greatest control over the outcome. Therefore, a high rate of dependence on outside arbitrators usually is taken as an indicator of ineffective conflict management.

Absence of any grievances, however, does not necessarily indicate effectiveness. A lack of grievances may signal low confidence in the procedure or a fear of retaliation for raising problems or complaints at the workplace. Indeed, perceptions of credibility and freedom from retaliation are perhaps the two most important criteria for evaluating the effectiveness of due process systems. It is generally agreed, however, that an extremely high rate of grievances also indicates ineffective conflict management and probably a low-trust or highly adversarial climate in the employment relationship (see the paper by Katz, Kochan, and Weber in chapter 9). Although the number of grievances provides some useful information, the absence of grievances should be viewed with caution and perhaps concern.

Finally, one of the most important and least examined indicators of the effectiveness of a grievance procedure is the effect that resolutions of conflicts have on the subsequent behavior of the parties. Organizations and individuals should learn from the process of settling grievances and find better and more equitable ways of applying organizational rules, policies, and contracts (Argyris and Schon, 1978; Knight, 1984). This principle is as simple as the basic notion that people should learn from their mistakes. However, there is often a residue of tension, mistrust, and resentment by the "losers" of a grievance, which remains after the conflict has been resolved officially. Therefore, managers need to monitor the climate that follows the resolution of grievances to ensure that no individual receives discrimination for asserting his or her rights at the workplace and to reestablish a hospitable work environment among grievant, supervisors, and peers.

Due Process Procedures for Nonunion Employees

Under current United States law, access to the courts to resolve work-related disputes is guaranteed only when a specific law, such as a law barring discrimination in employment, has been violated. (See Box 10-2 for a list of legal prohibitions against discharge.) Thus, in the absence of a collective bargaining contract, protective civil service procedures or tenure provisions enjoyed by most government employees and teachers, employers are free to discharge their employees "at will." No reason or "just cause" for dismissal is necessary for these nonunion, nongovernment employees, who account for approximately two-thirds of the workers in the United States.

Over the last century, however, various scholars and social reformers have argued that *all* employees should have access to due process or dispute resolution procedures on a broad array of issues including unfair discharge. In 1910, for example, Louis Brandeis issued a plan,

BOX 10-2
Legal Prohibitions against Discharge

Discrimination based on race, color, national origin, sex, or religion; Age (40 to 69); Union organizing or collective bargaining efforts; Handicaps (if the company has federal contracts);

Filing a complaint regarding discrimination, unequal pay, job safety or health, pension rights, or coal mine safety; Entering military service (or within a year after return); Pregnancy; Refusal to do a life-threatening or dangerous task; Wage garnishment for indebtedness; Exercising a right under a pension plan; Refusing sexual advances.

Source: Robert Ellis Smith, *Workrights* (New York: E.P. Dutton, 1983). Copyright © 1983 by Robert Ellis Smith. Reprinted by permission of E. P. Dutton.

"The Protocol of Peace," which was adopted briefly by the New York cloak industry. The plan provided for arbitration of both individual work-related disputes and disputes over certain wage issues. During World Wars I and II and the Korean War, the federal government established a variety of procedures to resolve disputes that might hamper wartime production.

Most recently, several prominent industrial relations experts (Summers, 1976; Stieber, 1984) have called for legislation modifying the employment-at-will doctrine by giving all employees the right to press claims of unfair discharge. Several court decisions offer support for this position, as indicated by the following statement in a 1978 West Virginia Supreme Court decision:

> The rule that an employer has an absolute right to discharge an at-will employee must be tempered by the principle that where the employer's motivation for the discharge is to contravene some substantial public policy principle, then the employer may be liable to the employee for damages occasioned by this discharge (Smith, 1983).

Nevertheless, federal and state governments have not chosen to implement such protections as public policy. Nor has there been strong interest in establishing labor courts to resolve disputes about employment rights disputes, as many European nations have done. Thus, most employees depend on the mechanisms their employers provide to resolve employee complaints and to ensure due process.

Until recently, dispute-resolution procedures have been available only to the small minority of nonunion employees whose employers were strongly committed to progressive personnel policies. For example, IBM's communications system, entitled "Speak-Up," and its formal Open Door program, have been in existence for several decades. Increasingly, however, dispute-resolution procedures are being established for other nonunion employees.

Nonunion dispute-resolution systems have many of the same objectives as union grievance procedures. Thus their performance should be judged against criteria similar to those outlined for evaluating grievance procedures. In addition, these systems have expanded in nature and function in recent years in an attempt to serve a broader scope of communication, problem-solving, and due process needs.

Varieties of Dispute-Resolution Procedures

Rowe and Baker (1984) identify as many as thirty-one types of complaint systems. The most common are: (1) mechanisms for answering employee questions; (2) provisions for supervisor/employee communications; (3) mechanisms for senior managers or personnel officers to investigate complaints; (4) various forms of employee counseling; (5) ombuds services; and (6) formal adjudication where the final decision rests with a higher-level manager, hearing officer or panel working for the employer, a jury of peers, or a neutral outside arbitrator.

Of these structures, the first three are the most common. As Ewing (1977) notes, these structures are all relatively informal, unpredictable, and potentially very effective. Aram and Salipante (1981) also argue that while formal adjudication procedures are best for handling certain disputes for nonunion as well as union employees, even highly formal union grievance procedures depend on informal relations between supervisors and stewards or employees. Thus, it is not surprising that formal and informal procedures often exist side by side.

Mechanisms for Answering Employee Questions.   Many employers answer employee questions and complaints through in-house publications, question boxes, and (somewhat less frequently) special question lines. Sometimes an employer will offer more than one of these services, such as the written question line and the telephonic Q-line at Security Pacific National Bank. Most of these services carry the advantages of assuring confidentiality and revealing trends in the frequency and types of problems. They are useful, however, only for disputes that involve simple questions of fact or policy.

Provisions for Supervisory/Employee Communications.   Most employers report having an open-door policy, allowing complaints to be raised with an immediate supervisor or, in some cases, with a higher-level manager. IBM is one of a handful of organizations that established formal procedures to insure an effective open-door policy. Generally, however, management has a tendency to endorse its own decisions when complaints involve supervisory actions, discouraging employees from entering what they see as a revolving door (Rowe and Baker, 1984). An additional problem with this form of supervisory/employee communications as a mechanism for dispute resolution is that it is hard to assure consistent solutions throughout the organization.

Other forms of supervisor/employee communication include skip-level meetings, sensing sessions, and various types of employee participation groups. Although such mechanisms often encompass goals larger than dispute resolution, they invariably help to identify workplace problems and to establish a climate of trust intended to minimize future disputes. Such procedures feature more formal mechanisms for raising complaints than most open-door systems. Nevertheless, even they may not preclude inconsistent solutions, and they may not provide formal mechanisms for resolving disputes that involve either individual employee rights or broad organizational policies. Employees may choose not to use these procedures for issues with which management is likely to disagree. Even where a procedure does exist for raising issues, resolution is not guaranteed.

Mechanisms for Investigating Complaints. Informal procedures often use senior managers or personnel officers to investigate employee complaints. Sometimes these mechanisms are combined with open-door policies to create multistep procedures. Like open-door systems, however, the use of senior managers or personnel officers to investigate complaints may lead to inconsistent results and an employee perception of bias towards management's interests.

Employee Counseling. Counseling, often confidential, is a more formal program intended to assist employees with work-related problems and disputes. The role of a counselor is typically that of a neutral resource. For example, Control Data Corporation sees counselors in its Employee Assistance Resource (EAR) program as advocates for the resolution of problems, rather than as advocates for the employee or employer. Thus, counselors often direct employees with complaints to a particular manager or to a separate company appeal procedure (Westin, 1984).

Some counseling programs focus on specific issues such as equal employment opportunity or drug and alcohol assistance. Others, such as the one at the National Broadcasting Corporation (NBC), use a professional counselor. At NBC, the professional counselor is viewed as the most effective vehicle for addressing a diverse and idiosyncratic array of disputes that arise in what one NBC vice-president characterized as a "free-wheeling corporation, with lots of high egos" (Westin, 1984).

Ombuds Services. In contrast to counseling, ombuds services are established specifically to provide employees with an advocate. Although this service is most common in government, universities, and customer relations, a few companies such as American Optical, Boeing-Veritol, Singer, and General Electric's aircraft engine division have established ombuds offices.

Most ombuds procedures were first adopted during the turbulent 1960s, when students were challenging campus administrators aggressively, and when society in general awakened to the need for protection against the arbitrary exercise of authority in various organizational settings. Like many counseling services, ombuds programs are often a complement rather than an alternative to formal complaint procedures. However, American Optical and some other firms view the ombuds service as preferable to a formal complaint system, because employees who use it are less likely to risk their career prospects.

Formal Adjudication Procedures.   Increasingly, employers are establishing formal procedures to adjudicate disputes. Like union grievance procedures, formal procedures generally have three to five steps, beginning with formal notification of the supervisor and/or a higher-level manager. Three key criticisms have been directed at nonunion grievance procedures: (1) not enough assistance to employees in preparing and presenting their cases, (2) inadequate employee protection against recrimination for initiating the procedure, and (3) too little independence from management of the decision maker at the last step of the procedure.

Ombuds officers, and sometimes counselors or personnel staff, may have formal responsibility for representing employees. Usually, however, representation is not available to employees, prompting some observers to conclude that outside unions provide employees with a level of support and self-confidence that is "the irreplaceable element inherently absent from the most enlightened attempts by management to devise a nonunion grievance procedure" (Tripp, 1963).

A second criticism that nonunion grievance or complaint systems must overcome is that they provide less protection against reprisal for participating in the procedure. This hazard, of course, is most significant when the employee's complaint becomes public knowledge or when a complaint becomes a part of the employee's personnel files. Often, psychological or social pressures, such as peer pressure among managers to avoid pressing grievances publicly, also inhibit full use of due process procedures. Although this criticism is more commonly made about nonunion grievance procedures, it is also a concern in unionized settings where employees who win grievances still may be subject to various forms of harassment.

The third criticism is perhaps the most serious. Although the last phases of nonunion grievance or complaint procedures differ considerably, the final decision rests most commonly with senior management rather than a neutral third party. Hearing officers or panels working for the employer are much less common, except in civil service procedures. A jury of peers or a panel including peers, managers and personnel officers, is even less common and often limited to disputes involving statutory issues such as discrimination. In addition, Balfour (1984) notes that procedures featuring peer review carry greater risks of misapplied standards and substantively incorrect decisions. Employees, comparing the various sources of decision, are more likely to perceive the final decision as credible if it is reached outside of the management hierarchy (Rowe and Baker, 1984).

Outside arbitration of nonunion employee grievances represents the most independent form of such decision making, but it is also the least used. Nevertheless, a handful of employers that includes Trans-World Airlines, American Electric Power, Northrup Aviation, Eastern Airlines, Kraft, Polaroid, American Airlines, and the Life Saver division of Squibb Corporation do use outside arbitration as the final step of their complaint or grievance procedures. The American Arbitration Association (AAA) recently has taken an active role in assisting employers to establish nonunion arbitration procedures that address the common criticisms of these systems. And as Box 10-3 shows, the Federal Mediation and Conciliation Service asks employers to demonstrate that their procedures meet a series of due process standards before it will provide a list of arbitrators from its panel.

In 1977, Ewing identified a trend toward greater use of due process procedures such as these. He also noted an increased willingness by executives and managers to hear employees speak out on controversial issues. However, he also reported that the vast majority of organizations responding to his survey — approximately two thousand subscribers to the *Harvard Business Review* — had informal rather than formal complaint procedures. There were also indications that the use of more formal procedures declined during the 1970s. Some of the more formal procedures that arose during the crisis atmosphere of the 1960s apparently were abandoned in the more conservative and economically troubled 1970s.

BOX 10-3
Due Process Standards for Nonunion Grievance Arbitration

---

1. Is the grievance-and-arbitration procedure spelled out in a personnel manual or an employee handbook?
2. Do employees have access to the grievance-and-arbitration procedure as a matter of right?
3. Does an employee have a voice in the arbitrator selection?
4. Does an employee have a right to representation of his or her choice in the grievance-and-arbitration process?
5. Is the arbitrator's award binding and enforceable?

All of these questions must be answered in the affirmative in order for the Federal Mediation and Conciliation Service to send the parties a list of arbitrators.

Source: Federal Mediation and Conciliation Service, Office of Arbitration Services.

Among formal procedures, Balfour (1984) argues that ombuds systems are preferable because of their simplicity and emphasis on resolving disputes at the lowest possible level. Considering the range of problems that can arise and the differing needs of various types of employees, Rowe and Baker (1984) claim that "multifaceted systems offer the best chance for supporting nonunion employees and . . . managers to find constructive options for problem-solving."

Compared with union grievance procedures, nonunion procedures feature a broader variety of structures and a capacity to address a broader array of issues. Nevertheless, with a few exceptions, nonunion procedures do not provide employees with the same degree of independence or professional support for raising grievances or neutral judgment for resolving disputes. It is clear that through organizations such as the American Arbitration Association and the Federal Mediation and Conciliation Service, nonunion procedures increasingly are able to incorporate the best features of union systems. The extent to which these procedures spread to larger numbers of organizations and prove durable and successful in delivering due process to otherwise unprotected employees will undoubtedly influence whether public-policy makers and the courts allow the employment-at-will doctrine to prevail.

References

Aram, John D., and Paul F. Salipante, Jr., "An Evaluation of Organizational Due Process in the Resolution of Employee/Employer Conflict," *Academy of Management Review*, 6, April 1981, 197–204.

Argyris, Chris, and Donald A. Schon, *Organizational Learning* (Reading, Mass.: Addison-Wesley, 1978).

Balfour, Alan, "Five Types of Non-union Grievance Systems," *Personnel*, 61, March–April 1984, 67–76.

Elkouri, Frank, and Edna Elkouri, *How Arbitration Works*, 3rd ed. (Washington, D.C.: Bureau of National Affairs, 1973).

Ewing, David W., "What Business Thinks About Employee Rights," *Harvard Business Review*, September–October 1977, 81–94.

Fleming, Robert W., *The Labor Arbitration Process* (Urbana, Ill.: University of Illinois Press, 1964).

Goldberg, Stephen B., and Jeanne M. Brett, "Grievance Mediation: An Alternative to Arbitration," in Barbara D. Dennis, ed., *Proceedings of the Thirty-Fifth Annual Meeting of the Industrial Relations Research Association* (Madison, Wis.: Industrial Relations Research Association, 1983), 256–59.

Knight, Thomas R., "Toward a Contingency Theory of the Grievance-Arbitration System," in David B. Lipsky and David Lewin, *Advances in Industrial and Labor Relations*, vol. 2 (Greenwich, Conn.: JAI Press, 1984).

Kochan, Thomas A., *Collective Bargaining and Industrial Relations* (Homewood, Ill.: Irwin, 1980).

McKelvey, Jean, ed., *The Changing Law of Fair Representation* (Ithaca, N.Y.: ILR Press, 1984).

Rowe, Mary P., and Michael Baker, "Are You Hearing Enough Employee Concerns?" *Harvard Business Review*, May–June 1984, 127–35.

Smith, Robert Ellis, *Workrights* (New York: Dutton, 1983).

Stieber, Jack, "Employment at Will: An Issue for the 1980s," in Barbara D. Dennis, *Proceedings of the Thirty-Sixth Meeting of the Industrial Relations Research Association* (Madision, Wis.: Industrial Relations Research Association, 1984), 1–13.

Summers, Clyde, "Arbitration of Unjust Dismissal: A Preliminary Proposal," in *The Future of Arbitration in America* (New York: American Arbitration Association, 1976), 159–96.

Tripp, L. Reed, "Collective Bargaining Theory," in Gerald G. Somers, ed., *Labor, Management, and Social Policy* (Madison, Wisc.: University of Wisconsin Press, 1963).

Westin, Alan, ed., *Proceedings of the National Conference on Resolving EEO Disputes Without Litigation* (New York: Educational Fund for Individual Rights, 1984).

Zack, Arnold M., and Richard I. Bloch, *Labor Agreement in Negotiation and Arbitration* (Washington, D.C.: Bureau of National Affairs, 1983).

Zalusky, John, "Arbitration: Updating a Vital Process" in *The American Federationist*, Volume 83, November, 1976.

Suggested Readings

Frank Elkouri and Edna Asper Elkouri, *How Arbitration Works*, 3rd ed. (Washington, D.C.: Bureau of National Affairs, 1973).

James R. Redeker, *Discipline: Policies and Procedures* (Washington, D.C.: Bureau of National Affairs, 1983).

Christopher A. Barreca, Anne Harmon, and Max Zimmy, *Labor Arbitrator Development: A Handbook* (Washington, D.C.: Bureau of National Affairs, 1983).

Arbitrating Disputes

The arbitration problem presented here illustrates a typical discharge case. We have presented the first part of the arbitrator's award, in which the facts of the case are summarized as the arbitrator interpreted them based on the testimony of the witnesses, the oral and written arguments of the attorneys, and the written transcript of the hearing. The questions for discussion then ask you to first act in the role of the arbitrator to issue a binding decision and then in the role of the company's manager to suggest what actions should be taken after the decision.

CASE
Great Lakes Boat Company

In the matter of arbitration between:

Great Lakes Boat Company and Metal Trades Council of New County, Wis., AFL-CIO

Opinion and award of the arbitrator Ira Block

Grievance #2100-83

Discharge of Edward Fields

Hearings were held on this matter in Green Bay, Wisconsin, on February 10 and March 7, 1984. A full transcript was taken, and briefs were filed with the arbitrator within five working days of the end of the last hearing, in accordance with the provisions of the expedited grievance procedure under the existing contract (JX-1). Representing the company was Joseph W. Amber, Esq; representing the union was Albert L. Silverman, Esq. Present at the hearing on one or both days were the following:

For the Company:

Joe Amber, attorney
Al Jones, E.B. division
Donald Enright, E.B. division
Rodney C. Sawyer, E.B. division
Charles A. Peterson, Labor Relations, E.B. division
John H. Brazilian, E.B. division
Monica Radvany, Labor Relations

For the Union:

Albert L. Silverman, attorney
Richard Woods, steward

Paul Shearson, steward
Robert B. Black, steward
Carlos Bravo
Craig Brown
Edward Fields, grievant
Kathryn Otis, boilermakers chief steward

The issue agreed upon by the parties is as follows: Was the discharge of Edward Fields on or after September 12, 1983, for just cause? If not, what shall the remedy be?

FACTS AND ISSUES

This case concerns Mr. Edward Fields, a welder at the Boat Company, who has been in the employ of the company for twenty-six years. Fields is a member of the bargaining unit and is therefore subject to the rights and responsibilities accorded members of the unit under the collective agreement in force at this time (JX-1). Therefore this dispute, having moved in a timely manner through the steps of the grievance procedure required by the contract, is appropriately before this arbitrator. Fields, according to testimony, has never been disciplined or given a warning slip prior to September 9, 1983.

Donald Enright is a foreman on the third shift and had been Fields's supervisor for approximately three weeks. As a foreman, he is responsible for directing his crew and inspecting their work, among other things.

On Friday evening, September 9, 1983, Fields violated company welding standards by welding downhill. (Welding "downhill," or on an angle that allows the hot metal to run before setting, can produce faulty welds which may later cause the final product, in this case a small military boat, to fail to meet required stress tests.) Through a series of events, his foreman, Donald Enright, saw this weld and informed Fields the following Monday morning, September 12, that Fields should come to the "super's shack" (the superintendent's office) around lunchtime (4:00 a.m.). The purpose of the meeting was to give Fields the warning slip (C-2) and a one-day suspension for the welding violation. Enright had previously discussed the violation and proposed suspension with his supervisor, Mr. Brazilian, who concurred with Enright.

The events surrounding the scene in the super's shack when Fields received the warning slip are in dispute. The interchange between Fields and Enright prior to Fields's post-lunch appearance at the super's shack, and the actions and conversations during and after, confirm that it was not a pleasant situation but these events do not go directly to the heart of the issue and will not be fully recounted here. Suffice it to say that the company alleges that Fields did not want to accept the warning slip but was told by his union steward, Robert B. Black, that he had no choice; subsequently, he did accept it. Moreover, Fields allegedly indicated that he wanted Enright to "prove it" (the bad weld). Fields later admitted doing the weld and that the technique used violated company rules and regulations.

Sometime after the interchange at the super's shack, at approximately 6:15 a.m., Foreman Enright was walking down the dock signing time cards when he was called by Fields. Enright either stopped or slowed down while Fields approached him. Fields's purpose was to tell Enright that the new job to which he had just been assigned had an excessive "root gap" and thus could not be done. The interchange that followed is the event that gave rise to the discharge and this grievance. Enright told Fields to go back to the job and that he (Enright) would come and look at it. At this point, the company maintains, Fields threatened to pull out Enright's mustache hairs, "one by one," do him other bodily harm, and hinted that he would harm Enright's family. Then, according to the company, Enright told Fields he was going to convey the alleged threat to Enright's supervisor, Brazilian. The two then parted and Fields walked over to a coworker, Brown, who was standing nearby. Brown was standing out of hearing range but was reasonably close. Carlos Bravo, a union member, was walking by while Fields and Enright were talking and indicated that Enright was smiling and that he (Bravo) tapped him (Enright) on the shoulder (in friendly jest, according to Bravo's testimony). Neither indicated in testimony (and both were sequestered) that any heated exchange was taking place, nor did either hear threats being made. No one was able to corroborate Enright's testimony about the exact nature of the exchange with Fields. Only Brown and Bravo were in the area, and their testimony neither supports nor definitely contradicts Enright's version. It must be added that the management personnel who did see Enright shortly thereafter did indeed testify that Enright was shaken and disturbed.

It must also be pointed out that Fields indicated that he did not know that security was picking him up for allegations that he threatened a supervisor, while at the same time it appears that steward Black recalled that Fields did know that he was accused of having made such a threat. The inconsistency in the testimony could be due to memory problems, but it is the arbitrator's opinion that Fields was probably aware of the reason for the security pickup. Certainly after twenty-six years in the shipyard, Fields must have realized that the security pickup was for more than his one-day suspension for welding downhill. This adds credibility to the company's claim that the exchange between Enright and Fields involved more than just a simple "go back to your job" order with no response from Fields.

The threats that Enright alleges were reported to the local police department the morning after the incident. Because Enright's testimony in the police report was never questioned by the union, it must be credited as true. Again, this leads the arbitrator to conclude that the Enright/Fields exchange was not nearly as soft as presented by the union. This fact alone, however, will not give full credibility to the company's position offered via Enright's testimony.

The issue that must be addressed here is to confirm, via the testimony offered and the facts submitted at the hearing, whether Fields actually did threaten Enright on this September morning. No one questioned the policy of the company to discharge a person immediately, regardless of the circumstances, for threatening the supervisor. Whether we can find fully convincing evidence to confirm the threat is the question on which the decision must turn; the company bears the burden of proof.

The company, in trying to prove its case, has concentrated on finding inconsistencies in the testimonies of Fields, Brown, Bravo, Black, and others who offered to testify at the union's request. Indeed, as shown in the transcript and brought out clearly in the brief, the company has shown that there are inconsistencies and conflicting testimony concerning the actions and words that surrounded the event on the dock where Enright and Fields had their conversation/confrontation. Whether the contradictions and inconsistencies are the result of bad recall, deliberate distortion of the truth, or human error, in this arbitrator's judgment, cannot be decided with full certainty.

Moreover, the company brought witnesses in to testify that the grievant had a reputation of being a "bully." On cross-examination by the union, the company stated that Fields's personnel file contained no record of being warned or disciplined for insubordination or any other violation of rules since he was hired.

Questions for Discussion

If you were the arbitrator in this case,

1. Would you uphold the company's discharge of Fields, reinstate him without any disciplinary penalty, or decide that he should be reinstated but penalized in some way for his misconduct?
2. What standards or reasons would you use to support your decision?
3. What weight would you give to the reputation of the grievant as a "bully"? What weight would you give to the lack of any record of prior disciplinary warnings or actions on the grievant's personnel record?
4. If you were the manager in charge of this shipyard, what actions would you take if the arbitrator
   a. reinstated Fields?
   b. upheld the discharge?

11

Work Organization and Employee Participation

In this chapter we explore alternatives for designing and modifying systems of work organization, a topic that dates back to the origins of scientific management and industrial engineering. Early designers of jobs and work systems operated on simple models of motivation and engineering and traditional principles of management. Workers were assumed to be motivated by the economic compensation received for job performance; efficiency was maximized by dividing work into simple and narrow tasks; supervisors or engineers decided how the work was to be done, while employees executed the specific tasks.

This system was designed for mass production and similar long production runs that characterized so much of the industry emerging after 1900 (Piore and Sabel, 1985). Later, job evaluation techniques were applied to attach wage rates to these jobs. Detailed collective bargaining agreements after the 1930s codified many of the job design and work organization principles of scientific management and job evaluation, and emphasized seniority in layoff, work assignment, and promotion decisions.

From this background emerged what we might label a "traditional" system of work organization. This system arrays jobs into a hierarchy of distinct, often multiple classifications, each of which is assigned a distinct wage rate. Individuals are paid the wage associated with the specific job performed on a given day; movement in the hierarchy occurs as jobs become vacant. The rules governing promotion or job assignment are specified either in a personnel·policy handbook or in a collective bargaining contract.

Newer Views of Job Design

In the 1960s, experiments with new forms of job design and work organization began to emerge. These were intended to introduce greater motivation and flexibility into the organization of work. Initial discussions of these alternatives focused on job rotation and job enlargement — techniques for introducing more variety, challenge, or interest into individual work assignments (Hulin and Blood, 1968), and for reducing alienation and enhancing motivation (Blauner, 1964). Traditional job design principles, it was argued, had produced too fine a division of labor to motivate workers and avoid boredom on the job. By the end of the 1960s, a good job was defined as one that provided high degrees of task variety, feedback, challenge, and autonomy, as well as the opportunity to learn new skills (Hackman and Oldham, 1980).

Advocates of worker involvement argued that designing jobs in this way would lead to higher levels of both job satisfaction and job performance. A minority of union leaders also viewed this approach to job design as according appropriate respect to the skills of workers and fostering a form of shop-floor democracy consistent with the union's broader social mission. Critics of this design theory asserted that workers' evaluations of their jobs would be filtered by the social setting of the work and the subjective perceptions or interpretations of the workers. This "social information processing" school argues, therefore, that it is not the objective attributes of the job that influence motivation, but rather the employees' perceptions, interpretations, and definitions of their work (Salancik and Pfeffer, 1977).

The evidence to date does not resolve this debate, but it suggests that, on average, broader job designs are associated with higher levels of job satisfaction and with less turnover. Whether broad job designs also lead to higher levels of job performance is less clear; the evidence suggests that performance depends largely on how well the job design fits the technology and the task of the job (Thomas and Griffin, 1983). That is, contemporary theories of job design recognize that motivational, economic, and engineering principles must be considered in organizing work. A broad, multitask job may increase motivation but, beyond a certain point, may lose the economic efficiencies of specialization and division of labor.

Social and Technological Dimensions of Work

As new views emerged about designing individual jobs, another group of behavioral scientists argued for a better fit between the technological and the social dimensions of work and for the need to organize work not around individuals and specific jobs, but around work groups or teams (Trist, 1981). The team approach grew from post–World War II European experiments with group decision-making, which were interpreted in the United States in light of both an emerging set of open systems theories and a growing interest in industrial democracy. Box 11-1 presents an overview of General Motors' application of the sociotechnical approach to plant design or redesign. The proposition underlying the sociotechnical approach holds that productivity and job satisfaction are optimized by integrating the social needs or interests of workers with the technical demands of the work. Proponents of a sociotechnical approach have observed that social scientists too often

BOX 11-1
Participative Plant Design and Redesign:
The Socio-Technical Systems Approach at General Motors

Socio-Technical Systems (STS) is a method for understanding the operation of organizations and for designing and redesigning them. It has been used and refined for about thirty years in England, Scandinavia, Europe, and North America. GM began using this approach in the mid-1970s. It is a step-by-step process for analyzing the factors — human and technical — that must be considered in the design of a work setting. STS considers the self-esteem and skills of people who work with machines as at least as important as the technical functioning of the machines.

Social and Technical Systems

The technical system in an industrial manufacturing facility usually includes:

Machines
Plant layout
Computers and software
Manufacturing procedures
Gauges and other measuring devices
Process-control feedback loops in the technology

The social system in most organizations includes:

Ways in which decisions are made
Departmental boundaries
Reporting structure
Ways of adapting to change
Organizational culture and norms

These social and technical factors are intimately interrelated. It is impossible to design a technical system that does not have implications for the social system and vice versa.

A New Plant Design Process

To design a new plant with complementary social and technical systems that are effective, it is important to bring in a variety of key people at early stages of the design process. The process begins with what we call a sanction group. They are usually division staff heads. The purpose of the sanction group is just that — to provide sanction — not to design.

It is the plant design team that creates the design. They begin with an analysis of the market niche for the product to be manufactured and the characteristics of the work culture they want to create in the plant. The operating philosophy and business goals are based partly on this analysis.

Source: Excerpted from William Duffy, "Participative Plant Design and Redesign: The STS Approach," in *The Work Life Review,* Volume II, Issue 1 (March 1983).

The plant design team typically includes not only senior plant management and engineering, but union representatives and hourly workers — a critical policy change for the General Motors Corporation.

Once the design team is in place and its initial work is done, it can begin an in-depth analysis of proposed social and technical systems.

Conducting Technical Systems Analysis

The technical systems analysis is a simple manufacturing process-control technique designed to identify and eliminate "key variances" in the process. Key variances could be bad incoming parts, parts damaged in transportation, or bad parts made by machines unable to produce to specification. These variances cause further variances from quality or cost standards in other operations downstream in the production process.

Once the key variances in a manufacturing process have been identified, there are a number of options for eliminating them: (1) design them out of the product or of the manufacturing process; (2) precontrol, a form of process control in which knowledge of the process, set-up methods, and preventive maintenance is so comprehensive that little checking of parts is needed; (3) short feedback loops that check parts at each stage of manufacture and provide feedback on the variance data so that the manufacturing process can be corrected. This can be done manually or through automation.

Conducting Social Systems Analysis

The goals of a social system analysis are to develop data needed to design a plant organization that will

1. achieve the organizational philosophy and business goals of the organization, e.g., eliminate variances or control them as close to the source as possible.
2. integrate the interdependent functions of the organization around common goals — production groups with their in-plant customers, service functions with production, and service groups with other service groups.
3. meet the reasonable needs of the organization's members.
4. become self-correcting in terms of performance against goals and be able to adapt to change with minimal disruption.

When designing plant 55, the Pontiac Motor Division set up a special sanction group of substaff heads. They worked together to integrate division staff decisions that have an impact on a plant's goals. In other words, the group is there to ensure that engineering staff and personnel staff at the division level do not set conflicting priorities for the plants. In the plant, meanwhile, the management team is also set up so that they can easily communicate with each other and thus coordinate resources in order to best meet plant goals — decisions do not have to go up one hierarchy and down another to be resolved.

This integration of staff functions at the top allows for the design of floor-level work units where there is a high level of employee participation in problem solving and planning.

Social systems analysis has led to the creation of "work units" at the shop-floor level. Work units have the following characteristics:

1. They have the resources and training to control quality, cost, and schedule performance at the floor level.
2. They have a quality check and feedback loop at the output end of the unit to control quality.
3. They have the capability to repair defects so that only known good pieces go to the next work unit.
4. They have extensive training in:
   problem solving
   variance control
   use of computerized performance feedback
   working together effectively
5. Each work unit is a cost center. It gets feedback on controllable costs. Some work units get group rewards for cost improvements.

---

ignore the technical parameters of jobs and that engineers too often ignore social needs. Although these principles have generated a strong following among some practitioners, no conclusive evidence supports or rejects the theory.

These ideas on job design and sociotechnical systems have spawned much innovation and experimentation with different types of job designs and work systems, particularly in "greenfield" sites — new plants located in areas separate from old plants. (See the case studies by Verma and McKersie that follow.)

Flexible Work Systems

While job-design and sociotechnical theorists were stressing the motivational aspects of these new work systems, managers were gaining experience using them. With use, the new systems were seen as more flexible means of allocating work and potentially of overcoming the work-rule rigidities of the traditional system. For managers, the flexibility and concurrent lower costs in these new systems were at least as important as their motivational potential. The advantages of flexible work systems are becoming more apparent as changing technologies and market structures also require greater flexibility and adaptability; new work systems must allow for a more variable product mix (Piore and Sabel, 1985). In addition, recent computer-based advances in manufacturing technology allow for greater flexibility in the use of machinery and, in turn, demand greater flexibility in the allocation of human resources.

To make this kind of flexible manufacturing system work efficiently, a work organization system is needed that simultaneously promotes flexibility, adaptability, and a work force that has the skills, ability, and experience to perform multiple tasks and to analyze problems that arise in a constantly changing work environment.

In sum, the rise of flexible work organization systems started with concerns for the psychological growth and motivational needs of employees. While these concerns are still important from the standpoint of individual workers and some unions, senior managers' interests in these flexible work systems are driven more by their belief that flexibility is crucial to enhancing productivity and product quality in the modern workplace.

Preview of Readings and Cases

In the two readings and three cases that follow, we explore alternative strategies for introducing new systems of work organization.

The first reading presents the most frequent, most difficult challenge management encounters in introducing new principles of work organization, namely, doing so in the context of a preexisting plant or office and work force. Janice Klein explores the difficulties that first-line supervisors and middle managers experience in adapting to organizational changes, particularly those designed to increase the involvement and participation of rank-and-file workers. The second reading, an abridged version of a United States General Accounting Office (GAO) report, provides an overview of productivity and gains-sharing programs and their impact on efficiency in various work settings.

In the first case, Anil Verma describes the nature of a team-oriented workplace design. The company chose to introduce this innovative design in a greenfield site with a newly recruited work force. Although this is the easiest strategy to follow, since it does not require changing the rules that govern the organization of work among an existing work force, it is not always economically feasible or socially desirable to abandon an existing location and work force. Accordingly, in the second case, Robert McKersie describes a hybrid strategy — a new plant using a new work-organization design is constructed where an old, traditional plant was closed; laidoff workers had the option to transfer to the new plant. The strategy provides for a technologically innovative physical setting and requires workers to accept and to be trained in a new work system. This case also requires that management and union successfully negotiate a collective bargaining agreement that is suited to the plant's technology and new work system.

The chapter closes with a third case that explores the evolution of a quality-of-working-life experiment. Like many such experiments, this one began as a narrow quality-circle program designed to improve the work environment for employees and the relations between workers and management. Over time, it expanded to address the basic concerns of the parties for higher productivity, lower costs, more flexible work organization arrangements, and employment security. As it expanded, it encountered a number of organizational obstacles to its continuity. Whether the experiment is worth saving, or indeed, whether saving it is possible given the environment in which the parties found themselves after two and one-half years' experience, should provide for lively discussion.

References

Blauner, Robert, *Alienation and Freedom* (Chicago: University of Chicago Press, 1964).

Hackman, Richard, and Greg Oldham, *Work Redesign* (Reading, Mass.: Addison-Wesley, 1980).

Hulin, Charles L., and Milton R. Blood, "Job Enlargement, Individual Differences, and Worker Responses," in *Psychological Bulletin*, Vol. 69, 1968, 41–55.

Piore, Michael J., and Charles T. Sabel, *The Second Industrial Divide* (New York: Basic Books, 1985).

Salancik, Gerald R., and Jeffrey Pfeffer, "An Examination of Need-Satisfaction Models of Job Analysis," in *Administrative Science Quarterly*, Vol. 22, 1977, 427–56.

Thomas, Joseph, and Ricky Griffin, "The Social Information Processing Model of Task Design: A Review of the Literature," in *Academy of Management Review*, Vol. 8, October 1983, 672–82.

Trist, Eric, *The Evolution of Socio-Technical Systems* (Toronto: Ontario Quality of Working Life Centre, 1981).

Suggested Readings

Reward Systems and Productivity. A Final Report for the White House Conference on Productivity (Houston: American Productivity Center, 1983).

Inge, Sud, and Nima Ingle, *Quality Circles in Service Industries* (Englewood Cliffs, NJ: Prentice Hall, 1983).

Patchin Robert I. *The Management and Maintenance of Quality Circles* (Homewood, Ill.: Dow-Jones-Irwin, 1983).

Metzer, Bert L., *Profit Sharing in 38 Large Companies* (Evanston, Ill.: Profit Sharing Research Foundation, 1978).

Simmons, John and William Mares, *Working Together* (New York: Alfred A. Knopf, 1983).

First-Line Supervisors and
Shop-Floor Involvement

We were so worried that the employees would not accept the program that we spent all our time trying to convince them of the benefits. On the other hand, we assumed that since supervisors are managers they would just accept the program. What we found was that it was much easier to sell it to the employees than the supervisors. (A plant manager)

When change occurs at the workplace, many parties are involved, but first-line supervisors are central to facilitating the change process. As the plant manager quoted above indicates, upper management too often assumes that the most resistant group of employees will be hourly workers. The extensive efforts to secure this group's cooperation often ignore the attitudes of middle- and lower-level managers and supervisors.

Because supervisors are usually considered members of management, the top management assumes that they will comply with directives and support any change. On the surface, supervisors often appear supportive, but later, doubtful questioning or negative attitudes often emerge and tend to undermine the change process. This resistance may become overt defiance, but more often supervisors remain silent or show only mild enthusiasm, which workers translate into questionable support. Because most workers look to their supervisors for guidance or direction, the supervisors' lack of support can affect negatively the shop workers' response to organizational change.

This article discusses one change, the

Source: Janice A. Klein, Assistant Professor, Harvard Business School. The piece was written for this book. (See footnote 10 for additional source information.)

introduction of shop-floor employee-involvement programs, and one subgroup of lower management, first-line supervisors. The analysis is based on a recent study of first-level supervisors in eight plants, where programs were introduced to encourage more participation by shop-floor workers. The programs ranged from quality circles to quality-of-working-life (QWL) programs to semiautonomous teams in plants that were both new (seven years) and old (fifty-five years), both large (1,600 employees) and small (265 employees), both union and nonunion. Seven of the programs were aimed at changing attitudes and behaviors in existing plants, while one was a start-up operation (albeit more than fifteen years ago). Three to five years after the initial change, the programs involving semiautonomous teams prospered, but four out of the five quality circle programs were phased out because of lack of support at all levels of the organization. Supervisory responses to these various programs were mixed, but many supervisors were less than totally supportive, especially during the initial stages.

Although first-line supervisors appear to be the natural facilitators of such change, some managers have looked at shop-floor involvement as a way to reduce the ranks of lower management. Therefore, the first question to address is whether a need for first-line supervisors exists in participative work settings.

Need for Supervisors

In 1973, when the *Work in America* task force recommended participatory management as a solution to declining worker satisfaction and productivity, they noted:

Some managerial jobs, however, do tend to be eliminated such as some of the lower- and middle-management positions as well as foremen. . . . Without retaining opportunities for individuals in these jobs, however, either they would be put out of work or, with the threat of that possibility, oppose the redesign of work.[1]

Much of the literature on quality of working life parlays this theme and emphasizes that, as a major benefit of QWL programs, they eventually eliminate the first layer of management.[2] Is it realistic to expect the complete elimination of an intermediate role between management and workers? Experience tends to indicate the opposite. First, Cole found that in Japan — the model for much of this effort — there was "no diminution" and, if anything, an "increase in the authority and role of the foreman."[3] Second, a plant manager in one of Schlesinger's case studies noted: "It was also clear that our notion of running without supervisors was either premature or infeasible. The management staff simply could not adequately stay in touch with our workers to the extent that appeared necessary."[4]

The experiences in this study support these observations. In one plant, the management team initially was divided on whether a need would exist for supervisors over semiautonomous work teams, so they devised a new support role. After a short trial with a new coordinator role as a staff position, however, productivity declined because the teams were unable to function on their own.

First-Line Supervisor as Facilitator

Research has shown that first-line supervisors who are competent and perform their jobs properly are instrumental in influencing worker attitudes and behaviors.[5] Therefore, it follows that supervisory support should be a key factor in any successful program involving the work force. However, this study indicates that some organizations have by-passed the lower levels of management in their enthusiasm to encourage employee involvement at the workplace. As a result, many supervisors view their new role with trepidation for fear of not understanding their new assignment, or of not wanting or being able to perform it.

First-line supervisors have been called the "men in the middle," caught between the conflicting needs of management and labor.[6] As such, they have become a buffer in the effort to supply a product or service. As companies embark on shop-floor involvement activities, however, many of the commonly used supervisory powers and behaviors are becoming obsolete.

A fundamental basis for supervisory influence has been the foremen's or supervisors' power to reward or penalize workers in exchange for increased output.[7] Before the rise of industrial trade unions and personnel departments, foremen had almost total control over the workplace; they could use either the threat of dis-

[1]*Work in America* (Cambridge, Mass.: MIT Press, 1973), 104.

[2]Reference to this can be found in articles such as Richard E. Walton and Leonard A. Schlesinger, "Do Supervisors Thrive in Participative Work Systems?," *Organizational Dynamics*, Winter 1979.

[3]Robert E. Cole, *Work, Mobility, and Participation: A Comparative Study of American and Japanese Industry* (Berkeley, Calif.: University of California Press, 1979), 209.

[4]Leonard A. Schlesinger, *Quality of Work Life and the Supervisor* (New York: Praeger, 1982), 16.

[5]See S. M. Sales, "Supervisory Style and Productivity: Review and Theory," *Personnel Psychology*, Volume 19, 1966, 275–86.

[6]Burleigh B. Gardner and William F. Whyte, "The Man in the Middle: Position and Problems of the Foreman," *Applied Anthropology*, Vol. 4, No. 2, Spring 1945; Thomas H. Patten, *The Foreman: Forgotten Man of Management*, American Management Association, 1968; Donald E. Wray, "Marginal Men of Industry: The Foremen," *American Journal of Sociology*, Vol. 54, 1949.

[7]Leonard A. Schlesinger and Janice A. Klein, "The First Line Supervisor: Past, Present, and Future," in *Handbook of Organizational Behavior*, J. Lorsch, ed. (Englewood Cliffs, N.J.: Prentice-Hall, 1984).

missal or the favor of hiring a friend or relative in exchange for increased production. With the development of workplace rules and union contracts, exchanges became informal one-on-one arrangements, or deals such as: "Meet the production quota for the shift, and you're free to do as you like until the bell rings." Another supervisor-employee exchange involves job assignments: Supervisors may hand out good assignments as rewards to their better workers, but bad assignments as informal punishments.

New Forms of Supervisory Influence

Shop-floor involvement is altering many of the exchange powers available to supervisors. Instead of interacting one-on-one with employees, many supervisors now must manage through a team or group. The day-to-day tasks of supervisors, such as job assignments, are now being performed by teams. Another major change is also occurring in the flow of communications. In the past, supervisors were the prime conduit for information between management and workers on the shop floor. Now, with quality circles and other forms of QWL programs, communications often flow directly from top management to the shop floor, at times by-passing supervisors altogether.

What mechanisms for power and influence are left for supervisors? Many consultants have used the words "coach," "support," and "teach" to describe supervisors' new role. Are these the new bases of influence? Workers at one plant were asked to describe the ideal team manager. The following is a representative response:

> The best team manager is one who is fair and stands up for the team. That kind of person will support us with upper management and help get us the resources we need to make the job better.

The phrases "help" and "get resources" sound very much like new forms of ex-

change. A team manager can use these as leverage to get the teams to perform. Similarly, workers have their own form of reciprocity, as two of them explained:

> You help new team managers learn, because you figure that you may want some help in the future when one of them becomes "the boss."

> It becomes a kind of give-and-take relationship. Supervisors learn that we (the employees) are the ones who really know the operation best and can either make or break them.

What are the stepping stones to help supervisors move from the traditional "power through retaliation" style to a "power through participation and caring"? One senior supervisor at the plant with semiautonomous teams offered a clue when he complained about supervisors' current state.

> You know, when this whole thing started I was basically against it, but now I've been converted. I see that it can work, and the employees can handle many of the repetitive, day-to-day activities. But upper management still has one thing wrong. They tell us to totally get out of the day-to-day activities and that's impossible. Somebody still needs to do the "firefighting," and that's where we can be most effective.

This supervisor's comment is similar to a description of the supervisor's role in General Motors' QWL program:

> A new support system [is] made up of experienced supervisors who now take on new responsibilities such as planning, plantwide problem solving, interfunctional coordinatiion, and general "trouble shooting."[8]

[8]D. L. Landen and Howard C. Carlson, "Strategies for Diffusing, Evolving, and Institutionalizing Quality of Work Life at General Motors," in *The Innovative Organizations: Productivity Programs in Action*, Robert Zager and Michael P. Rosow, eds. (New York: Pergamon Press, 1982), 307.

Delving deeper into what firefighting or trouble shooting entails revealed a one-on-one problem-solving practice not very different from the supporting or coaching role. Problem solving itself is not a new task for supervisors; often it has been identified as a primary function of management.[9] What has occurred is a delegation of many of the routine problem-solving tasks to work teams. As a result, the firefighting has moved to a different level. As a way to reward or punish, supervisors now can pick and choose the individuals or teams they will support or help. The reciprocity may be more subtle, but it is there in the form of helping or training exchanges. A plant manager involved in a QWL program described the process as follows:

> The strong foremen have an ability to manage people. They do this through three tools: (1) they ask for advice from their people, (2) they give recognition and positive feedback, and (3) if they can't answer a question, they admit it and then get back to their people with a response. In this way they make a contract. If they break it, they lose [people's] confidence.

Another new form of reciprocity described was helping or working side by side with employees. For example:

> One supervisor fills in on the line when employees need to take a break.

> Another supervisor noted that he makes it a habit to try to either carry over a box of supplies or help operators in loading a machine while chatting with them, in order not to appear to be watching or spying on them.

These new supervisory functions were delineated formally in a document proposed in one of the plants included in this study (see Exhibit 11-1).

[9]See Chester I. Barnard, *The Functions of the Executive* (Cambridge, Mass.: Harvard University Press, 1938) or Henry Mintzberg, *The Nature of Managerial Work* (New York: Harper & Row), 1973.

Supervisors' Views of Shop-Floor Involvement

The supervisors in the eight plants studied had mixed reactions to shop-floor involvement; some were positive, some negative, and some neutral.[10] Several themes highlighted common concerns or issues.

Supervisors were asked, via an attitude survey, several questions concerning shop-floor involvement programs within each of their plants.[11] These questions focused on three distinct dimensions of the programs: whether the program was good for the company, good for employees, and good for supervisors. Table 11-1 shows that almost three-quarters of the supervisors (72 percent) in these plants viewed shop-floor involvement as a program that was generally good for the company. More than half (60 percent) saw the program as helpful for their subordinates, but less than a third (31 percent) viewed it as helpful to themselves.[12]

These findings lend support to a generally held belief that shop-floor involvement programs are merely "the top telling the middle to do something for the bottom." As one supervisor noted:

> For five years we have been beaten over the head with the need for more participation by workers. By this time we know we'd better believe, or at least

[10]The remainder of this article is adapted from Janice A. Klein, "Why Supervisors Resist Employee Involvement," *Harvard Business Review*, September/October 1984. Copyright © 1984 by the President and Fellows of Harvard College; all rights reserved.

[11]The questions were given to all first-line supervisors in the seven plants that had implemented a shop-floor involvement program in an effort to change attitudes and behaviors of its existing work force. This was followed by ninety-minute, small group interviews with all survey respondents.

[12]The rank order of these three categories held true across all seven plants, regardless of type and success of program, manufacturing technology, or plant culture.

EXHIBIT 11-1
Duties of First-Line Supervisors
in a Plant with Semiautonomous Work Teams

1. *Commitment* — Supervisors must promote teamwork and convey a genuine interest in and support for the concept. They should encourage cooperation and work with the employees in developing team competence and cooperation.
2. *Communications* — Supervisors are the major link in the communications channel between management and hourly employees. Supervisors must learn to relay daily instructions through the team to reach team members.
3. *Training* — Supervisors are in a good position to assess the training needs of their employees. As such, they are responsible for identifying, coordinating, and, where possible, conducting the necessary training.
4. *Human Relations* — Since supervision is key to maintaining positive employee attitudes and high morale, supervisors must develop good human relations skills. This means becoming employee-centered by showing an interest in employee problems, emphasizing communications and team spirit, and demonstrating a sincere concern for workers' welfare.
5. *Motivation* — Supervisors must learn to be motivators, not just disciplinarians. They can motivate by giving employees responsibility (with accountability) and a sense of contribution. Supervisors should learn to use such phrases as "What's your opinion?" "What can I do to help?" and "Thank you."
6. *Delegation* — This allows supervisors to take on additional duties and pass on to employees many of the routine details that they can handle effectively. Delegation helps to bolster both individual and team morale by giving everyone an opportunity to share responsibilities and rewards.
7. *Decision Making* — Supervisors' performance ultimately hinges on the outcome of decisions. Teams can be allowed to make routine decisions, but supervisors must set priorities and explain why some decisions take precedence over others.
8. *Discipline* — Supervisors must always remember that employees are individuals as well as members of a group. Most employees will respond to techniques aimed at motivating them, but a few may not. In those cases, the supervisor may have to administer discipline.
9. *Feedback* — There are times when every team needs guidance, support, and reinforcement. Both oral and written feedback is necessary to make individuals and teams aware of their strengths and weaknesses.

Source: Janice A. Klein, "Why Supervisors Resist Employee Involvement," *Harvard Business Review,* September/October 1984. Copyright © 1984 by the President and Fellows of Harvard College. Reprinted by permission.

---

say, that it is good for the company and for employees. However, no one has really stressed that it would be good for us, except that we either should believe it or we don't have a job. Since whether it is good for supervisors is a more personal thing, we were probably more honest.

TABLE 11-1 Supervisors' Views of Shop Floor Involvement Programs (sample size = 139)

Good for company	72%
Good for employees	60%
Good for supervisors	31%

Negative supervisory attitudes eventually will surface to affect worker attitudes and participation adversely. In several plants, supervisors were directed to form quality circles despite their personal opposition to the concept. As a result, they merely held meetings to appease their managers, but most of the circles ultimately faded away because of lack of support or because of infrequent meetings. In another plant, several supervisors criticized the program to peers and workers behind the backs of upper management.

First-Line Supervisors as Victims

Supervisory interviews in each of the plants in this study helped to unravel several underlying concerns of first-line supervisors who became involved with shop-floor activities. Three overriding issues emerged as factors leading to negative attitudes, and often to resistance, toward worker involvement programs among the lowest layer of management. These are concerns most supervisors share, regardless of their background, leadership style, or other differences.

The first overall fear pertains to the basic need for job security. The popular press has raised the question of whether supervisors are made redundant with the use of participative management, and it is a prime concern of all supervisors to know whether management intends to reduce the supervisory work force or does not intend to eliminate any line personnel.

Once job security issues are alleviated, the next concern is job definition. In the plant that reorganized the work force into semiautonomous teams, the management team took more than three years to articulate clearly the role and their expectations of first-line supervisors. On a lesser scale, supervisors involved with quality circles must find a way to balance their egalitarian position one hour per week within the circle with their ongoing, day-to-day interactions with their employees.

Lastly, the burden of these programs ultimately falls on the supervisor, which

TABLE 11-2 Potential Supervisory Resisters of Shop-Floor Involvement Programs

Who Resists	Why They Resist
Theory X proponents	Counter to belief system
Status seekers	Don't want to lose prestige
Skeptics	Doubt support of upper management
Equality seekers	Why not us?
Deal makers	Interference with use of reciprocity

means additional work. This work may be short-term, as in team development and training, or ongoing, as in those quality circles where supervisors are assigned responsibility for leading and administering the circle activities.

Even within plants where these three concerns were addressed, some supervisors were still reluctant to accept fully the concept of participation. The evidence gathered in these plants further indicates that there are five types of supervisors who tend to hold negative attitudes toward shop-floor involvement programs and may resist such efforts.[13] Table 11-2 outlines the five categories of potential resisters and the central reasons they resist.

Managers' Responses to Supervisors' Concerns

Change seldom occurs without some impetus or pressure. This applies to supervisors as much as to anyone else. More often than not, change activities, in this case shop-floor involvement, are directed with the implied threat of "Do it or find another job." This threat only causes su-

[13]These categories are based upon an analysis of the survey data coupled with comments gathered via 264 interviews with managers, supervisors, and workers.

pervisors to view the programs as an order or as a distasteful pill they have to swallow. In contrast, some organizations have found ways to develop support for shop-floor involvement activities by treating participation as a reward rather than as a punishment. (See list of related readings at the end of this article for more in-depth treatment of several of the following recommendations.)

One answer may be to include participation in shop-floor involvement programs as part of the formal measurement and reward system for supervisors. Another possibility is to give supervisors the same type of recognition as workers. One of the plants in this study makes it a practice to have team managers make presentations to upper management. Another plant found that a QWL team for foremen, which meets regularly with the plant manager, was a way to regain supervisory support for its program.

Other aspects of the supervisory role, such as the work load, should also be reviewed. If worker involvement programs are simply added to the many other elements of the job (as quality circles were in several plants), supervisors are apt to view them solely as an extra burden. If supervisory duties are delegated downward, other tasks such as planning activities or special projects need to be added to fill the void left in supervisory positions.

Supervisors also may use shop-floor involvement programs to enhance their reciprocal arrangements with their managers. Besides treating reciprocity as a mechanism to gain the support of their employees, astute supervisors may use this support for the programs as a trade for favors from managers. In addition, by being actively involved with the programs, they can have more control over the process and flow of information up and down the organization.

Finally, a major incentive is to reduce the disincentives that supervisors see. To this end, managers need to address the concerns of the supervisory resisters. In some cases, their complaints can be re-

medied. In others, the supervisors themselves may be a major part of the problem. In either case, the first step in managing supervisor resistance is to understand the various reasons why some supervisors resist.

Theory X Proponents

Probably the most difficult group is supervisors who hold Theory X values; they simply do not believe that workers can be trusted or can have anything valuable to contribute. An organization can sort out its supervisors through the hiring or termination process, or it can provide awareness or behavior-modification training, but it is questionable whether the values of 30-to-50-year-old individuals can be significantly altered by a short-term structural change in the work environment. This is not to say that they are hopeless, but that changing their basic assumptions about workers may be extremely difficult.

These supervisors should be given some basic training and be exposed to some success stories. One plant found it helpful to send some of its disbelieving supervisors to sister plants that had institutionalized shop-floor involvement. This converted several of the hard-liners. However, the number of successful turn-arounds may be limited. This is one case where replacements may be necessary.

Status Seekers

These supervisors comprise the second most difficult group. Status seekers enjoy the prestige of being a supervisor and are reluctant to give this up by sharing their role with others. They may readily acknowledge that workers have something to contribute, but they have to be shown that their employees will contribute more if they are not treated as second-class citizens. They need to be convinced that workers can be viewed as equals but have different jobs to perform.

Corrective actions for status seekers are similar to those used for Theory X proponents — training and exposure to successful shop-floor involvement sites. In addition, time and patience may change their attitudes. This is what happened with several recently recruited team managers at one plant. Recent college graduates, they began work with the self-image of a boss. As one worker explained:

> Some of the new recruits come in really gung-ho, thinking they are the boss. It takes them about six months and they learn if they treat us with respect, we'll perform and they will look better.

Skeptics

Skeptics doubt the sincerity and commitment of top management to the change process. These supervisors need to be shown that upper management is committed to this new way of managing. One way is to explain openly why shop-floor involvement processes are different from other programs that have come and gone. Another is to ask supervisors what it would take for them to believe that upper management is committed. Management can either accept or reject these conditions, but if rejection is necessary, it will create further skepticism unless clear, candid explanations are offered.

All too often middle managers are just as skeptical as supervisors. The key is for managers at all levels to convey their commitment, not only in words, but also through their actions. As one manager noted:

> One of the main problems early on was that we really didn't have the support of the middle managers. Often a manager would walk up to one of the employees and sarcastically say, "Oh, aren't the teams running well!" which would be viewed as the manager making a joke out of the teams. When the supervisors heard this, they questioned the wisdom of supporting the teams if their boss didn't believe in it.

If managers are converted and convey their support, the only formula to win over

supervisors may be a combination of time and patience. Experienced supervisors have gone through too many short-term programs to be convinced quickly that this one is permanent. At one plant, even after five years of success with quality circles some foremen were still concerned that with changing priorities the program may be on the way out. Only after shop-floor involvement becomes institutionalized as a way of managing will skepticism finally cease.

Equality Seekers

Equality seekers can be grouped according to (1) those who want to be part of the design process, and (2) those who want a program for themselves. The key to the first group is to get them involved early. The definition of the supervisory role can be a participatory process with those who will be affected. This also applies to the total shop-floor involvement process. However, by involving the supervisors, managers must risk giving up some of their power, just as supervisors do with the introduction of the shop-floor involvement programs. As in the case of the skeptics, much of the problem lies with the middle managers. Many of the issues raised by first-line supervisors are identical one level up.

The second group of equality seekers, those who want equal treatment with the workers, are basically asking, "Aren't supervisors as important as workers?" As one manager recalled:

> In the design process we decided we should take the reserved parking spaces away from the foremen as a show of good faith to the union. However, the foremen made an issue out of it and we had to reverse our decision. In essence, they were asking where the quality of work life was for them.

The concern is not that workers are getting recognition or respect, but that it is happening at supervisors' expense. Establishing a supervisory QWL team, or support group, may solve many of these concerns.

Equality seekers also need to see some reward for their support of the program. The answer may lie in the incentives discussed earlier. In addition, supervisors need to see the programs as helpful to themselves as supervisors. Several comments made by supervisors in this study are relevant:

Many foremen have found quality circles useful on two counts. First, they have found they can get things done through quality circles, which would never get a high enough priority to get attention otherwise. Second, they use the circles as a two-way communication vehicle. They can gather information on the work force through the circle members and they can also use the members to pass on information to their peers.

Teams are particularly helpful for new supervisors because the operators usually know more than the supervisor. By getting the teams to make decisions, it helps the supervisor, and you get better decisions.

Teams build up an expectation that team members should put their inputs into decisions. This is extremely helpful for the supervisors because it gets employees to help them with their job.

The best mechanism for conveying this message is for equality seekers to learn from their more enthusiastic peers just how the programs are helping them perform their job. Management can try to convey some of this, but it can backfire. As one supervisor recalled:

The main problem was that they [upper management] kept telling us how helpful it would be for us. They built up our expectations and then we found out that it wasn't all that good for us. It would have been better if they hadn't said anything about how it would help us.

Deal Makers

As noted, a significant source of supervisory power lies in a supervisor's ability to make exchanges. Shop-floor involvement activities require supervisors to relinquish many prior modes of exchange and find new mechanisms of influence. However, some supervisors are unwilling to relinquish their exchange powers, or have yet to develop new ones. These supervisors, referred to here as deal makers, tend to resist worker involvement in decision making. These resisters are unwilling to relinquish their current exchanges because (1) they believe that their deals are superior to any new ones, or (2) they have yet to discover new forms of reciprocity.

Every supervisor uses some form of reciprocity. The key for management is to encourage exchanges that are useful or helpful, in contrast to those that are dysfunctional or compromising. In the first case, deal makers may need the same prescription as the Theory X proponents and the status seekers: train them and provide them with exposure to successes, but if they don't change they may have to be replaced. The second group may just need assistance in seeing how shop-floor involvement programs can be helpful in their one-on-one exchanges with employees. Along this line, several explanations were given by supervisors who viewed the programs as increasing their one-on-one interactions:

Teams help you to get to know everyone better so you just naturally talk with them on a one-on-one basis more often. This is especially true for some of the soft-spoken people who end up showing you how knowledgeable they are. In this way, supervisors start interacting with those individuals they may not have in the past.

They break down the barriers between supervisors and hourly people. By giving us a common reference point, it is easier to communicate with one another.

Teams help primarily in upward communication. The program helps team members communicate with supervisors where in the past they were often reluctant to talk with a supervisor on a particular issue.

As with equality seekers, the best mechanism for helping deal makers recognize potential benefits is through peer assistance from the more enthusiastic supervisors. It may be difficult for management to enlighten supervisors on reciprocity because this is often an unconscious process. And, if reciprocity is discussed as a management tool, it can easily be viewed as manipulative.

Replacement of Supervisors

In some instances, remedial actions will not convince supervisors that shop-floor involvement programs will improve the quality of working life, and training will not succeed in changing supervisory behavior. When all else fails, replacement may be the only recourse. One plant decided to replace its entire supervisory work force (in an effort to remain non-union) but spread the moves over a three-year period. The replacements were slowly accomplished through attrition, lateral reassignments, performance terminations, and promotions. Thus, managers were able to make the changes without undue stress on those involved. In addition, they did it in such a way that supervisors did not feel their job security was threatened. Even supervisors who are totally supportive of shop-floor involvement turn against the program if they perceive a threat to their job security. Therefore, movement to what one company called "less damaging jobs" may be more appropriate than termination.

One issue in replacement is the selection of new supervisors who will fit the new environment. What skills should they have, and is there an ideal supervisor? Several of the plants in this study swung

toward hiring more, or only, college graduates. As in the 1950s, success was mixed when this was the favored way to provide the supervisory skills needed to manage a newly unionized work force.[14] One company in this study is now moving in the direction of filling 100 percent of its supervisory positions with management trainees hired directly out of college, while another has gone back to promoting employees who acquired further education on a part-time basis. The optimal solution is most likely a blend of the two.

Conclusions

The evidence clearly indicates that supervisors are needed and that the position is just as essential as it always has been. The role has changed, however, and supervisors in transition will need assistance in learning new skills. They will need to know what is expected of them and how they will be measured. They must be provided the necessary training and support (both morally and in the form of resources) and given time, within reasonable limits, to make the transition to their new role. Above all, they need to know that their job is real, and that they are not being used merely to set up the teams, after which they will be declared redundant.[15]

Experience shows that neglecting supervisory concerns leads to some resistance, which is true for any change at any level. The issues raised by first-line supervisors appear to be similar among managers one or two levels higher. In addition, the introduction of new technology at the workplace may lead to a similar kind of

[14]Kenneth Hopper, "The Growing Use of College Graduates as Foremen," *Management of Personnel Quarterly*, Volume 6, Number 2, Summer 1967.

[15]These conclusions are similar to those found by a Work in America Institute task force. See Jerome M. Rosow, and Robert Zager, eds., *Productivity Through Work Innovations* (New York: Pergamon Press, 1982).

resistance. Several companies are beginning to find as much or more resistance among supervisors as among the rank-and-file workers. However, corrective action may not be as overwhelming as some managers now view it to be. By giving adequate management attention to the five types of potential resisters, supervisory opposition can be transformed into active support.

Suggested Readings

Rosow, Jerome M., and Robert Zager, eds., *Productivity Through Work Innovations* (New York: Pergamon Press, 1982).

Sasser, W. Earl, Jr., and Frank S. Leonard, "Let First-Level Supervisors Do Their Job," *Harvard Business Review*, March–April 1980.

Schlesinger, Leonard A., *Quality of Work Life and the Supervisor* (New York: Praeger, 1982).

Schlesinger, Leonard A., and Janice A. Klein, "The First Line Supervisor: Past, Present, and Future," in *Handbook of Organization Behavior*, J. Lorsch, ed. (Englewood Cliffs, N.J.: Prentice-Hall, 1983).

Walton, Richard E., and Leonard A. Schlesinger, "Do Supervisors Thrive in Participative Work Systems?," *Organizational Dynamics*, Winter 1979.

Westley, William A., *Quality of Working Life: The Role of the Supervisor* (Ottawa, Ontario: Minister of Labour, Government of Canada, February 1981).

Questions for Discussion

1. Why do you think that first line supervisors tend to be the "forgotten people in the middle" in many organizations?
2. What advice would you give to a friend right out of an MBA program that was about to take a job as a first line supervisor in a company known for its commitment to employee participation processes? What if the friend was a forty-five year old skilled blue collar worker just about to accept a promotion to first line supervisor?
3. Suppose you were called in as a consultant to a firm about to embark on a major employee participation process. What actions would you advise to maximize the support of first line supervisors and middle managers in this process?

Productivity Sharing Programs: Can They Contribute to Productivity Improvements?

Introduction

A 1975 National Science Foundation supported study at New York University investigated worker motivation, productivity, and job satisfaction. According to the study, the principal factor in creating highly productive and satisfied workers was recognition and reward for effective performance. The study concluded that the reward should be meaningful to the employee, whether it is financial, psychological or both. Managers have increasingly recognized not only that employee incentives can result in greater productivity, but that workers often know more about their jobs than anyone else, and can make valuable suggestions for improvement.

The oldest incentive plans are oriented towards individuals. Individual incentives, such as piecework, reward an employee directly for the amount of work done. Group incentive plans, on the other hand, are gain-sharing plans in which a bonus or percentage of profits is paid to a group of employees based on its overall performance. Other approaches that do not provide financial incentives, but seek to motivate by improving the work environment, are known as quality of work life (QWL) plans.

One form of group incentive that has received attention recently is productivity sharing. Productivity sharing plans are designed to measure the productivity of a plant or firm and to share benefits of productivity gains with all participating employees. The three commonly used plans are Scanlon, Rucker, and Improshare.

Productivity sharing plans differ in the formula used to compute productivity savings and in the implementation method employed. Both Scanlon and Rucker plans generally measure the payroll of the plant or firm against total dollar sales, and compare it to the past average of several years. The Improshare plan measures output against total hours worked. Hence, while the Scanlon and Rucker plans use dollars as the measurement unit, Improshare uses hours. These plans are modified by adjusting the formulas used for bonus calculations to factor out increases or decreases in the selling prices of the product.

All three productivity plans are flexible regarding the make-up of the group involved in the plan. Direct and indirect production workers, as well as management, may be included. Engineered standards are not necessary for the functioning of any plan. Scanlon plans rely heavily on labor-management productivity committees as the focal point for worker involvement and plan implementation. Rucker plans also use labor-management committees, and Improshare plans allow for, but are not built around, such committees.

Although the exact number of firms involved with productivity sharing plans is not known, it is thought to be about 1,000. Through contacts and visits with consultants and productivity organizations, we developed a list of seventy-eight firms believed to have productivity sharing plans, and eighteen firms said to be considering such plans.

The Evolution of Productivity Sharing Programs

Individual Incentive Systems

The earliest and simplest type of incentive plan was direct payment for work done, or piecework compensation. Such plans tied pay directly to performance, to achieve

Source: Adapted from a Report of the General Accounting Office of the U.S. Congress, March 3, 1981.

significant labor productivity gains. Over the years these incentive plans have been refined and modified. The modifications were heavily influenced by "scientific management," a school of thought established under the leadership of Frederick Taylor in the early 1900s. However, even before Taylor's work, Frederick Halsey recognized that employees were reluctant to increase productivity under individual piece rates because they feared management would raise standards.

The Halsey plan was perhaps the first to recognize the unworkability of straight piece rates in most settings. Plans developed since that time commonly have a base rate plus an incentive premium for above normal time. For example, the Bedaux plan was similar to Halsey's, but based on engineered standards with the benefits shared between the direct (production) and indirect (support) workers. The Gantt plan also guaranteed a base rate to those who produced below the standard and a high piece rate premium to those who produced above the standard.

Currently, some industrial firms use a method called measured daywork, which may be combined with an incentive system. Measured daywork is used to encourage good performance or to reprimand poor performance, and normally includes work study techniques such as time studies and methods measurement. When coupled with an incentive system, the worker is normally paid the standard base rate when beginning employment. Subsequently, the worker's actual performance is compared with the standard, and the hourly rate increases or decreases according to the past relationship between actual and standard performance — as performance increases, so will the incentive payment. Although such an incentive plan is promoted because it avoids short term fluctuations in production, it also hides inefficiencies and may not motivate as well as more direct systems. In practice, the application of measured daywork as an incentive system is very flexible, and thousands of companies undoubtedly use it in some form.

At least three characteristics underlie most of the individual-oriented incentive systems: (1) they normally have a base rate of pay with an incentive premium; (2) they are based on engineered standards, at least in industrial settings; and (3) their use, although widespread, appears to be declining. There are a number of reasons for the decline:

Many people question the ability of a company to maintain a fair, equitable, and motivating incentive system for either individuals or small groups.

Workers often resist new equipment or methods because of the possible impact on their earnings. Hence, the plan may become dysfunctional to the goal of productivity improvement.

Unions frequently oppose individual incentive plans because they may pit one employee against another, and ,if not accurately maintained, they often lead to grievances.

The systems often ignore indirect workers and can therefore create conflicts between these and direct workers who are under the incentive plan.

Accurate maintenance of the standards is costly; also, new tasks and processes can be hard to integrate.

Since only labor costs are normally considered, waste and inefficiency may actually escalate material and equipment costs.

Peer pressure or fear of management's upgrading standards may restrict output.

The systems have less applicability as the nation moves toward more automation.

Individual Suggestion Systems. Individual suggestion systems reward employees for suggestions that reduce costs. The reward is normally a percentage of the first year's savings, up to a maximum amount. The award is approved through a formal submission, review, and approval process. Many organizations have installed such plans with varying degrees of success. Results, as measured by cost savings or productivity improvements, often depend on the extent of management's commitment to the plan and the opportunity for fair and rapid feedback. But the success of these programs is often hampered by the presence of any of the negative conditions outlined above for individual incentives.

Group Incentive Systems

Management's need for increased productivity expanded the gain sharing concept beyond individual incentives. Although group sharing — including profit sharing — has been in existence for many years, especially at higher managerial levels, only recently has it attracted considerable interest as an organizational incentive system. Many managers believe that if group plans can help obtain and keep competent managers, they can have the same effect with other employees. Furthermore, some managers believe that all employees can contribute significantly to organizational performance, and most group plans encourage this. Others believe that such plans recognize the interdependencies of various functions and, consequently, are the only plans that will work. Finally, the increased promotion and availability of literature on gain sharing have contributed to the growing interest in group incentive programs.

Profit Sharing. Profit sharing is the oldest type of gain sharing plan. Managers and employee groups have long participated in profit sharing, which has a certain underlying appeal to managers, since bonuses will be paid only through increased profits. Profit sharing is distinguished from productivity sharing in that the former is not based on sales performance or output per hour. But it is similar to productivity gain sharing in financial terms; both plans provide benefits on either a cash or deferred basis.

As of December 31, 1978, 282,397 deferred profit sharing plans were registered with the United States Treasury. In addition, there are about as many cash plans. Where profit sharing has been applied on a cash basis, numerous firms have cited significant improvement in performance. Some managers believe that this success results from emphasis on cost reduction, integration of personal and organization goals, ease of administration, unlikelihood of undermining employee security, and payment of bonuses only when profits exist. However, problems include the inability of employees to relate to the system, the unwillingness of management to share information with employees, the lack of a relationship between profit sharing and productivity performance, the difficulty in stimulating employee involvement, and delays in payment because profit is not determined until the end of the period.

Besides profit sharing, the three most commonly cited group gain sharing plans are Scanlon, Rucker, and Improshare. Their similarities include: (1) frequent bonuses, (2) use of a production- rather than a sales-based formula, (3) emphasis on employee involvement, and (4) elimination of individual incentive systems. In addition to the above plans, many firms have had plans custom designed.

Scanlon Plan. Joseph Scanlon developed the Scanlon plan in the 1930s to save a failing company. Three general principles underlie the plan: employee involvement, bonus payment, and identity with the firm. Employee involvement is accomplished through a formalized suggestion system and two overlapping committee systems. Elected employee representatives meet at least monthly with their departmental supervisors to review productivity, cost reductions, or quality improvement suggestions. These committees, often called production committees, have certain decision-making authority for less costly suggestions. Considerable work can occur in any area affecting costs or quality. More costly suggestions, or those affecting another department, are referred to a higher level committee.

The higher level committee — normally called the screening committee — meets monthly to discuss suggestion activity, bonus results, and other items such as backlogs and quality problems. Membership normally includes elected employee representatives from the production committees and appointed management representatives.

The second principle involves the payment of bonuses to participating employees, for increased productivity. Traditionally, many Scanlon plans start with the following ratio calculation:

$$\text{Base ratio} = \frac{\text{Payroll costs to be included}}{\text{Value of production}}$$

Normally, a historical study is made to determine the proper base ratio. In any month when actual labor costs are less than the established base ratio, a bonus is earned. For example, if the base ratio is 20 percent, and in month $\times$ the value of production (sales plus or minus inventory) equals $1,000,000, then allowed labor equals $200,000 (1,000,000 $\times$ .20). If actual labor costs equal $160,000, then a bonus pool of $40,000 is generated ($200,000 − $160,000).

Some of this bonus pool is reserved for deficit months and for a year-end jackpot to reward continued high performance. Normally a certain percentage is taken by the company to pay for capital expenditures. The remainder is paid to all participating employees as a monthly bonus based on a percentage of their wages.

This calculation was established because it is simple and easy to understand. Furthermore, it recognizes the interdependencies of the different labor areas. However, other variables also affect its equitability in measuring productivity, such as the product mix and capital expenditures. Some plans adjust the percentage allowed each time a major change occurs in wages, or when major investments are made in capital expenditures. Other plans factor out the effects of changes in selling prices or product mix. Many firms have also installed plans that consider alternatives, such as:

using a different labor percentage for each major product line

increasing the percentage to include more costs

becoming more specific by considering primarily physical outputs and inputs

electing to employ return on investment

The key to the Scanlon success does not rest on the particular calculation, but rather on the congruence of management and employee objectives and their commitment to the success of the plan as long as it is reasonably equitable to customers, company, and employees. The plan is normally voted in by the employees for a trial year; a vote on whether to renew the plan is taken at the end of that year.

Identify with the firm — the third Scanlon plan principle — is developed through education, communication and discussion concerning the plan's goals, objectives, problems, and opportunities. Considerable management development is often necessary, especially at the supervisory level, along with better managerial planning and information systems.

Commonly cited accomplishments of the Scanlon plan, in addition to increased productivity, include better team work and cooperation, faster responses to problems, better product quality, less resistance to change, more employee involvement, and lower rates of absenteeism and turnover. When the plan is unsuccessful, not only are those accomplishments not achieved, but the level of trust in management is lowered and bonus earning opportunities are limited.

In reality, the Scanlon plan, in its most successful form, is more a management philosophy to improve performance than an incentive plan. Although probably fewer than 400 such plans exist, they have attracted considerable interest from behaviorists because of their heavy emphasis on quality of work life variables, including employee involvement, recognition, and a feeling of achievement.

Rucker Plan. This plan also evolved during the Depression, when Allen W. Rucker noted the existence of a historical relationship between payroll costs and what he called production value (actual net sales plus or minus inventory changes minus outside purchased materials and services).

The plan, for which an employee vote is considered optional, emphasizes employee involvement through the establishment of a suggestion system, Rucker committees, and improved labor-management communications. It is a group plan where everyone, excluding top executives, shares a percentage of gains. Individuals are granted recognition for suggestions and other activities, but are not rewarded financially. A thirty percent reserve is normally established for deficit months. The processes used to elicit commitment and suggestions are, in many ways, similar to those underlying the Scanlon plan.

The Rucker bonus calculation establishes a historical relationship between labor and value added. For example:

Net sales		$ 900,000
Inventory change (increase)		100,000
		1,000,000
Less material and supplies used		500,000
Production value (value added)		500,000

$$\text{Rucker standard} = \frac{\text{Payroll costs included}}{\text{Production value}}$$

Assuming that labor costs in the base period(s) were $300,000, the Rucker standard becomes:

$$\frac{\$300,000}{\$500,000} = .60$$

Hence, in any month in which the actual labor costs are less than 60 percent of production value, a bonus is earned.

This calculation partially accounts for variables such as product mix. It should also encourage employees to save on materials and supplies, allowing them to obtain more of the benefit. If a 5- to 7-year

historical analysis indicates an unstable relationship between labor and production value, the Rucker plan is not appropriate. The number of Rucker plans in effect is unknown because of limited research on the use of this and similar plans.

Improshare Plan. Improshare (IMproved PROductivity through SHARing) is relatively new, and is apparently growing quite rapidly in popularity because of the ease of its installation, and its lack of emphasis on employee involvement. The goal of Improshare is to produce more products in fewer labor hours. Management retains all rights, and a vote is not normally used. Improshare measures performance rather than dollar savings.

The plan is based on the number of work hours saved for a given number of units produced, compared to the number of hours required to produce the same number of units during a prior base period. The savings realized by the reduced actual hours are shared by the firm and the employees involved directly and indirectly with producing the units.

The plan is not affected by changes in sales volume, technology, or capital equipment. The Improshare plan can easily be divided according to product lines and adapted to small groups and departments in a company without being affected by changes in product mix.

Two aspects are key to the program — work hour standards, and the base productivity factor. For forty production and twenty non-production workers, the situation might be as follows:

Base period

Work hour standard

$$= \frac{\text{Total production work hours}}{\text{Units produced}}$$

$$\text{Product A} = \frac{20 \text{ employees} \times 40 \text{ hours}}{1,000 \text{ pieces}}$$

$$= 0.8 \text{ per piece}$$

$$\text{Product B} = \frac{20 \text{ employees} \times 40 \text{ hours}}{500 \text{ pieces}}$$

$$= 1.6 \text{ per piece}$$

Product A = .8 × 1,000 =   800
Product B = 1.6 ×   500 =   800
Total standard value hours 1,600

(Note: Total standard value hours could be simplified to be standard time in the base period.)

Base Productivity Factor (BPF)

$$= \frac{\text{Total production and nonproduction hours}}{\text{Total value standard hours}}$$

BPF = (40 production + 20 nonproduction employees) × 40 hours
= 2400/1600 = 1.5

(Note: Nonproduction workers are now added.)

Bonus calculation

Bonus calculation (month X)

Product A = 0.8 hours × 600 units × 1.5
= 720
Product B = 1.6 hours × 900 units × 1.5
= 2,160

Improshare hours (standard hours for
actual units produced)   2,880
Less actual hours   2,280
Gained hours   600

Employee share of gained (saved) hours

$$= \frac{\frac{1}{2} \text{ gained hours}}{\text{actual hours}}$$

$$= \frac{300}{2,280}$$

$$= 13.1\% \text{ bonus}$$

Improshare includes the time worked by both direct and indirect workers, and can be easily established because it uses existing records and, at least in the beginning, places little emphasis on employee involvement or organizational development. The size of bonuses is subject to a ceiling. A buy-back provision is normally included, which essentially gives employees a cash award to raise standards. The time allowances are changed only for capital expenditures and method changes. The goal is clear — more output for fewer hours of either direct or indirect labor.

Proponents of the plan argue that while no formal labor-management structure is required, the operation of the program results in improved interaction between employees and management. The reason for this improvement is that under Improshare, management and employee goals are the same — improved productivity and reduced production costs. Traditionally, the two groups have had different goals. Under the sharing plan, however, workers share the gains and the losses with management and have an incentive to improve their performances.

Application of Group Incentive Systems to Service Industries

Although many service industry companies use profit sharing, they have tended not to use other types of group incentive plans. Little reason exists for their avoiding productivity sharing; output measures may in fact be easier to develop in many service industry firms than in manufacturing firms because inventories are less of a problem. In fact, many manufacturing firms have more indirect than direct labor employees, and therefore face many of the measurement problems encountered in service industries.

Productivity sharing plans have been successfully applied in a limited number of hospitals, governments, food services, insurance companies, repair firms, and banks. The primary reasons for the limited application include the lack of: (1) productivity measures, (2) dedication to productivity improvement, (3) management sophistication, and (4) knowledge about productivity sharing plans. However, since service industries are increasingly interested in productivity improvement, their use of productivity sharing plans may become more widespread.

Significant measurement problems may occur when output calculations are difficult to determine, as is the case in some government agencies. In such cases, gain sharing might be determined by savings under budget as well as quality monitoring. All of the other quality of work life systems that underlie gain sharing could be applied without difficulty.

Results of Productivity Sharing and Other Incentive Plans

Proponents of productivity sharing plans say these plans can increase a firm's productivity and provide many benefits to both the firm and its employees, including higher wages in the form of bonuses to employees, increased profitability for the company, a spirit of cooperation among employees and between employees and management, and greater involvement and commitment of employees to their work.

The information we obtained from employees and union representatives provided ample evidence of the value of productivity sharing. Many firms achieved significant savings from their productivity sharing plans, and the majority of firms expressed satisfaction with them. Moreover, most officials we interviewed at firms that had other types of incentive plans believed that these plans also resulted in significant cost savings.

Monetary Benefits

Many of the firms included in our review attributed significant workforce savings to their productivity sharing plans. Savings averaged 17.3 percent at the thirteen firms with annual sales of less than $100 million. At the other eleven firms annual sales were $100 million or greater, and savings averaged 16.4 percent.

Among the twenty-four firms providing financial data, those whose productivity sharing plans had been in effect the longest showed the best performance. Firms

that had plans in operation over five years averaged almost twenty-nine percent savings in workforce cost for the most recent five-year period. Individual firms' average savings ranged from 13.5 to 77.4 percent. Those firms whose plans had been in operation for less than five years averaged savings of 8.5 percent.

The majority of firms with productivity sharing plans did not periodically assess savings to determine their source and nature. Only nine firms indicated they made such an assessment, and of these only four could show concomitant documentation. Officials at a number of firms said the source and nature of savings were difficult to measure. When asked what they believed were the most important factors in realizing the increased savings, they gave the following responses:

Number of Firms	Percentage of Responses	Comments
10	14.9	Improved performance of employees
10	14.9	Change in employees' attitudes, job interest, etc.
8	11.9	Increased productivity
8	11.9	Reduction in scrap, rework, and waste
8	11.9	Better use of materials, supplies, and equipment
7	10.5	Cost saving suggestions
6	9.0	Improved processes or procedures
5	7.5	Better product quality
5	7.5	Other
67	100.0	

Improved Satisfaction of Union or Employee Representatives

Several labor union officials have questioned whether productivity sharing plans can provide long term benefits. For example, one official stated that while productivity sharing plans can improve productivity in the short term, productivity begins to taper off as time passes. Our data do not support his claim. In fact, at several of the firms such criticism was directed more often at incentive plans based on engineered standards than at productivity sharing plans.

At most of the firms where an employee or local union representative was interviewed, the productivity sharing plan was stated to have had a positive effect on the workforce. That is, the climate between labor and management was said to have improved since the introduction of the productivity sharing plan.

Employee and union representatives cited increased wages as the most important reason for the improved climate between management and the work force. Other reasons included improved labor-management relations, better communication, a greater voice for employees in management of the company, and better acceptance of employees' suggestions by management.

Improved Satisfaction

The vast majority of firms expressed satisfaction with their productivity sharing plans, and believed that current benefits warranted their continuation. Officials at 22 firms said that the benefits originally anticipated were realized. On the other hand, several firms said that higher bonuses were expected than had actually been realized. For the most part, firms said they had never considered abandoning their plans. They believed that their productivity sharing plans gave them a competitive advantage in marketing their products and/or services.

Difficulties Encountered with Productivity Sharing Plans

Despite the numerous benefits claimed for productivity sharing plans, many pitfalls can mitigate their success. When a firm attempts to establish a productivity sharing plan, it may encounter difficulties trying to develop a workable bonus formula. Firms may have to overcome resistance by employees and management. Once the productivity sharing plan begins functioning, other problems may develop if the plan is not properly implemented or monitored. If financial reverses occur, expected cost savings may not materialize. These and other problems can result in the ultimate demise of a firm's productivity sharing plan.

Three of the seven firms surveyed that were considering productivity sharing indicated that the ability to develop an appropriate bonus formula would have a major influence on whether they ultimately adopted a plan. At one firm, a lack of adequate historical records was making it difficult to develop a base period. An official at another firm said that determination of an appropriate base period was complicated by the firm's product mix, which varied substantially from year to year. A third, highly capital intensive firm, was trying with difficulty to develop a bonus formula which accurately reflected labor productivity gains, and which was not affected by price increases.

Factors being weighted by the firms considering adoption of a productivity sharing plan included developing an appropriate bonus formula, potential rejection of the plan by the union, the need for stronger commitment by management, the need to raise current productivity to acceptable levels, and the need for improving markets for the company's product and increasing profitability so that bonuses could be paid.

Two firms elected not to adopt a productivity sharing plan. The president of a small electric motor manufacturing firm said he decided not to adopt a plan because of an unsatisfactory relationship with consultants. About three years ago a consulting firm gave a presentation to company officials on the benefits of productivity sharing. Company officials were interested but the consulting firm was slow in helping the firm implement a plan. When two years passed and little progress had been made, the president sought the services of another consultant. However, by this time many employees had become frustrated by the long and drawn out process. As a result the president decided not to implement a plan.

The manager of a plant in a multi-million dollar industrial corporation considered a productivity sharing plan to increase productivity and improve labor-management relations. However, officials at corporate headquarters rejected the plant's request to adopt the plan.

Further, fifty percent of the firms we examined said they had encountered obstacles in implementing their productivity sharing plans. The obstacle most often cited was resistance by employees, management or unions. Various explanations were mentioned for employee and management resistance. In some cases, employees on piecework feared a loss of income if productivity sharing was adopted. One firm allayed this concern by guaranteeing the wages of its piecework employees for a specified period of time after productivity sharing was to be implemented. In another firm where coverage under a productivity sharing plan was limited to production employees, resentment arose among the employees who were not included.

Management resistance at several firms was attributed to the difficulty in adjusting to the participative management concept. For example, one firm reported that although employee turnover decreased because of their productivity sharing plan, the turnover among the managers increased.

Why Some Productivity Sharing Plans Are Not Successful

Three firms in our sample had discontinued their productivity sharing plans, and three others did not believe that current benefits warranted their continuation. Numerous reasons were given for the lack of success at these six firms, including:

financial difficulties,
lack of management commitment or dedication,
inadequate design or implementation,
little or no bonus payments,
failure to develop a good communication system between labor and management,
insufficient monitoring of performance, and
use of an inadequate bonus formula.

Examining several cases in more detail is useful in illustrating factors which can lead to the failure of productivity sharing plans.

Case A

A multi-product manufacturing company with annual sales of over $600 million implemented a productivity sharing plan in one of its divisions. Shortly after the plan got under way, the company incurred some major expenses which forced it to shift funds away from that division. This caused the layoff of a number of employees; those remaining feared that the plan would cause them to work themselves out of a job. The program's credibility plummeted, and the plan was finally dropped about six months after it had started. Although bonuses averaged nine percent during the period in which the plan was in effect, management was not convinced that the bonus formula was adequate.

Case B

A small manufacturing company with annual sales of about $24 million set up a productivity sharing plan for all its employees. The plan was discontinued about fifteen months later because of serious financial reverses. According to a company official, the plan also failed because it was implemented without sufficient planning. Goals were not clearly established and management was not fully committed to the plan. A union official said that participative management meetings never had high priority. Employees could not understand why they received a bonus some months but not others. When financial problems developed, the plan was abruptly dropped. As a result, the union official found relations between management and labor to be twice as bad as they were before the program started.

Case C

A manufacturer of specialized parts established a productivity sharing plan two years ago. According to a company official, expected benefits never materialized. Management assumed that once the program was in place, it would take care of itself. Furthermore, no adequate communication system between labor and management was ever established. The official responsible for the plan favored its discontinuation because bonus payments were never made, and because employees and management interacted only minimally.

Eight other firms noted similar problems with productivity sharing plans. However, at all of these firms officials believed that current benefits outweighed disadvantages. For example:

A metal product manufacturer with approximately $300 million in annual sales operated a productivity sharing plan covering all employees at one of its thirteen facilities. In the first year of the plan's operation, savings of $64,500 were generated during 5 months, while losses of $96,000 occurred in the other seven months. The resulting $31,500 deficit was attributed to a loss of sales due to a slump in the industry. Nevertheless, a company official expects performance to improve once business conditions pick up. The firm had no plans to abandon productivity sharing.

A small manufacturing company included about 900 of its 1,200 employees in a productivity sharing plan. Savings from the plan averaged twenty-seven percent over the most recent five-year period. In addition, a company vice-president said that labor-management relations had improved while employee grievances, turnover, and absenteeism had decreased since the plan's inception. Nevertheless, several top management officials expressed reservations about the plan due to a lack of good criteria to measure effectiveness.

A division of a multi-billion dollar manufacturing corporation established productivity sharing plans at four of its smaller facilities. Most of the other plants in the division used individual incentive plans based on engineered standards. The productivity sharing plans were considered temporary measures to be used until engineered standards could be developed. In the four years the productivity sharing plans had been in effect, savings averaged less than one percent of participating work force cost. The smaller savings were attributed to wide swings in volume and inadequate monitoring of the plan. However, according to a company official, productivity at these plants had improved, and he believed that current benefits warranted continuing the plan.

Conclusion

Most of the problems mentioned in adopting or operating plans were due to internal factors, such as financial difficulties, insufficient commitment by management, and inadequate design or implementation. Despite these problems, the benefits of increased profitability and of improved employee morale and labor-management relations resulting from productivity sharing plans were thought by almost all firms to outweigh the concomitant difficulties.

Questions for Discussion

1. Should the United States government take steps to encourage the adoption and broad diffusion of various gains-sharing or profit sharing plans? Why or why not? If yes, what government strategies would be effective in encouraging broad diffusion?
2. Should employees be given a vote on the question of whether or not to adopt a gains-sharing plan or should this be a management decision? The Scanlon Plan strongly recommends a vote. The Improshare Plan does not.
3. What are the differences and similarities between the forms of participation designed into the Scanlon Plan and the participation that is built into most quality circle or quality of working life programs?
4. Some argue that a form of gains-sharing will be required in order to keep quality of working life or quality circle programs alive over an extended period of time. Do you agree or disagree?

Exploring the Team Form of Work Organization

The following case describes the work organization system installed in a small manufacturing plant opened in 1977 in the midwest by a large diversified manufacturing firm. In designing the plant managers were encouraged by corporate executives to incorporate as many flexible work system features as possible.

We present this case in order to acquaint students with the basic human resource dimensions of these new flexible work organization systems and to consider questions about how they might look as they age over time.

CASE
Electrical Cable Plant

Planning for the new plant began in 1974 when an East Coast cable manufacturing division of a large multidivision manufacturing firm began to consider options for opening a new facility. While business plans were being developed, the corporate and division industrial relations managers encouraged the designated plant manager to try "something different" in the work organization of the plant: an innovative, nontraditional system of work organization and industrial relations.

The plant's managers and several corporate managers visited other plants within the company and in other firms to study nontraditional ways of organizing a factory. The plant manager reported: "I came back excited at the prospect of opening a new plant where workers would participate fully in decisions taken to run the plant." Many external and internal consultants worked on the project until four months after start-up. One corporate-office consultant stayed another two years. By 1978, the company had four plants in other divisions that were organized along nontraditional systems of industrial relations and work organization.

PRODUCT AND PROCESSES

The plant manufactures electrical cables for supplying power to submersible pumps used for oil wells. The process starts with coiled copper rods that are purchased from copper-rolling mills and drawn to smaller diameters. One large machine draws, anneals, and adds a tin-lead protective coating to the wire. Another machine braids several strands of the wire, and the cable is

Source: Anil Verma is an assistant professor of industrial relations on the Faculty of Commerce and Business Administration, University of British Columbia. This paper is drawn from his Ph.D. dissertation, Union and Nonunion Industrial Relations at the Plant Level, Sloan School of Management, MIT, 1983, and is used by permission.

covered with rubber or synthetic insulation through an extrusion process. Finally, several of these insulated cables are braided and covered with synthetic tape and nylon braiding. Most cables also are covered with galvanized iron armor, a process in which strips of iron are helically wound over the assembled cables. Both drawing and extrusion machines are large and take considerable time and skill to set. Production runs must be large to be economical. The extrusion machine, in which cables travel a thousand feet at speeds of up to 2,100 feet per minute between incoming and take-up rolls, is run by five to six operators. The machine itself occupies six hundred square feet of the shop floor. The other machines are smaller and typically need one operator.

MARKET CONDITIONS FOR THE PRODUCT

The output from this plant reportedly meets 80 percent of the domestic market demand. Cables are sold through the manufacturers of submersible pumps. Another division of the company, which makes these pumps, is a leading source for marketing the cables. As the primary customer is the oil industry, demand varies directly with world oil production.

WORK ORGANIZATION AND INDUSTRIAL RELATIONS

By 1983, the plant had 150 employees. The work organization system used a team concept, whose underlying philosophy is that all employees — managers and workers — are treated similarly. Managers are paid for their knowledge or skills, as are workers. Wages are not tied to output; all workers are salaried and work in teams rather than on individual jobs.

The plant is divided into four production, one maintenance, one administrative, and several resource teams that handle finance, personnel, and marketing (see Table 11-3). Each team has eight to ten members and a team manager. In most cases, team managers are team members who have been promoted. (In another plant, team coordinators are team members who fill the job in rotation for a few months at a time.) Team managers act as their group's facilitator in helping teams make day-to-day decisions. The plant has no first-line supervisors. All coordination across teams is provided by one foreman responsible for the entire plant. The plant does not use a direct/indirect classification of workers. All personnel are treated as direct employees.

The plant has nine job levels, and workers may start from level 1 and work their way up to level 9. Upward movement, in principle, is contingent on learning extra skills. Workers must learn to operate, set, or maintain another machine to move up a level. Each of the nine levels is set ten points apart and all skills in the plant are calibrated in terms of points. A sample of skill calibrations is shown in Table 11-4. A new hire must learn one of the skills worth ten points within the first thirty days to qualify as a level 1 worker. He or she may learn any of the skills that are worth ten points. For example, learning to operate either the vulcanizing machine I, the strander, or the

TABLE 11-3 Team and Subgroup Work Units

Team	Subgroup
Armoring	Braiders, armoring machines, lacquer
Extrusion	Strander, bow-twister, plastic line, continuous vulcanizing
Metals	Wire drawing, rubber insulation compound, taping
Test and repair	Test, repair, lead press
Administration	
Shipping and receiving	
Technical	
Utility	Boiler, electrical, mechanical
Resource	Area Managers, resource, professionals
Management	

TABLE 11-4 Examples of Skill Levels and Pay-Point Worker Teams

I. Extrusion Team
Vulcanizing machine I	10 points
Vulcanizing machine II	20 points
Plastic lining machine	20 points
Strander	10 points
Twisting machine	10 points

II. Armoring Team
Armor machine rounds	20 points
Armor machine flats	10 points
Lacquer machine	10 points
Braiders	10 points

III. Metals Team
Rubber insulation mixer 1st floor	10 points
Rubber insulation mixer 2nd floor	25 points
Rubber insulation mixer 3rd floor	5 points
Wire drawing machine	20 points
Taping machine	10 points

IV. Test/Repair Team
Test I	15 points
Physical dimensions	10 points
Repair I	10 points
Repair II	15 points
Lead press	10 points

braider would earn a worker 10 points and, therefore, a move up to level 1. After being promoted to the next level, a worker must wait four months before learning another skill. If a worker at level 1 were to learn another skill worth ten points, he or she would move to level 2, but if the skill learned is worth twenty points (e.g., vulcanizing machine II or the rounds armor machine), the move would be two steps up, to level 3. Such schemes are sometimes referred to as pay-for-knowledge compensation systems. The plant manager described the system as follows:

> Our philosophy here has been to let the evolutionary process mold our systems rather than adhere sharply to defined work rules. For example, when we started the plant, we wanted to train all workers on all jobs. Soon we discovered that we were spending too much time on training and not enough on production. So we moved to a system where workers primarily concentrate on learning other jobs within their own teams. Also, we created two paths along which workers could move up. One of them, of course, is by learning an extra operation, and the other is by improving proficiency on the same job. A number of proficiency levels have been defined for each job in the plant by the teams themselves.

Currently, about 70 percent of the plant's 130 workers have attained the highest level (level 9). The remaining 30 percent are distributed through levels 5 to 8. The responsibility for training is left to the current operator, who must exhibit a high degree of proficiency as an operator. Initially, any operator could become a trainer, but it was discovered that some operators made better trainers than others. Thus, a trainer level beyond level 9 was established with a higher wage.

ROLE AND AUTHORITY OF THE TEAMS

The principle underlying the plant's design is to decentralize decision making at the shop-floor level. Workers participate in a range of decisions affecting their immediate jobs, including the scheduling of production, assigning work to team members, monitoring production and scrap levels, determining overtime requirements, providing feedback to other teams, and making personnel decisions such as hiring and promoting. At the beginning of every month, each team projects how much work will be done and the resources it needs. These calculations include the number of standard and overtime hours, manpower requirements, support services, and so on, followed by estimates of total labor costs, percentages of labor utilization, and other productivity measures (see a sample calculation in Exhibit 11-2). An outline of the role, responsibility, and authority of the autonomous team is shown in Exhibit 11-3, and a statement about the team manager's role is shown in Exhibit 11-4.

Promotion decisions also are made by the team in a highly programmed format. Individuals must meet predetermined skill and performance levels. Skill must be demonstrated in quality and quantity, and in a number of functional areas such as teamwork, problem solving, and housekeeping. A sample of the evaluation form and its use in one individual's case is shown

EXHIBIT 11-2
Team Work Sheet for Projecting
Monthly Labor Requirements and Costs

March 82 ___ Final
_19.5_ × _20_ × 8 hours = _3120_ hours

overtime	+ 30.25
total	3150.25
absents	155.75
total	2994.5
loaned hours	- 397
total	2597.5
borrowed hours	+ 9
total	2606.5
vacations	- 42.5
Total Actual Hours	2564

Unit code	Pieces	Standard Hours	
8555	1825	373	
8078	3058	165	
8642	99	33	
8767	111	35	Total 606

Level	Rate	Number of People	Cost
1	4.15 × ___	= ___	
2	4.34 × ___	= ___	
3	5.08 × 4.5	= 22.86	
4	5.39 × 5	= 26.95	
5	5.70 × 4	= 22.80	
6	6.00 × 1	= 6.00	
7	6.30 × 1	= 6.30	
8	6.60 × 4	= 26.40	

Total 111.31

Total Cost ÷ Number of People = Average Hourly Rate
$111.31 | 19.5 | $5.71
Average Hourly Rate × Total Actual Hours = Labor Cost
$5.71 | 2564 | $14,640
Labor Cost ÷ Standard Hours Earned = Labor Cost Per/Standard Hour
$14,640 | 606 | $24.16
Total Labor Cost + Total Supply = Total Cost
$14,640 | $3,921.59 | $18,561.59
Total Cost ÷ Total Standard Hours Earned = Total Cost Per Standard Hour
$18,561.59 | 606 | $30.83
Supplemental Cost ÷ Standard Hours Earned = Cost Per Standard Hours
$3,921.59 | 606 | $6.47
Total Standard Hours ÷ Total Actual Hours = % of Labor Utilized
606 | 2564 | 24
Total Pieces Projected ÷ Total Pieces Ship = % of Goal Attained
7000 | 5093 | 73
% of Absenteeism ___ 5

Projections *March 82*
_19.5_ × _20_ × 8 hours = _3120_ hours

overtime	+ 25
total	3145
absents	- 89
total	3056
loaned hours	- 300
total	2756
borrowed hours	+ 0
total	2756
vacations	- 0
Total Actual Hours	2756

Unit code	Pieces	Standard Hours	
8555	3000	613	
8078	4000	215	
			Total 828

Level	Rate	Number of People	Cost
1	4.15 × ___	= ___	
2	4.34 × ___	= ___	
3	5.08 × 4.5	= 22.8	
4	5.39 × 5	= 26.5 (1 person for 2 wks)	
5	5.70 × 4	= 22.8	
6	6.00 × 1	= 6.0	
7	6.30 × 1	= 6.3	
8	6.60 × 4	= 26.4	

Total 111.8

Total Cost ÷ Number of People = Average Hourly Rate
$111.31 | 19.5 | $5.71
Average Hourly Rate × Total Actual Hours = Labor Cost
$5.71 | 2756 | $15,737
Labor Cost ÷ Standard Hours Earned = Labor Cost Per/Standard hour
$15,737 | 828 | $19.01
Total Labor Cost + Total Supply = Total Cost
$15,737 | $3,500 | $19,237
Total Cost ÷ Total Standard Hours Earned = Total Cost Per Standard Hours
$19,237 | 828 | $23.23
Supplemental Cost ÷ Standard Hours Earned = Cost Per Standard Hours
$3,500 | 828 | $4.23
Total Standard Hours ÷ Total Actual Hours = % of Labor Utilized
3,500 | 828 | $4.23
Total Pieces Projected ÷ Total Pieces Ship = % of Goal Attained
828 | 2756 | 30
% of Absenteeism ___ 3

---

in Exhibit 11-5. Although the plant manager has a veto on promotion decisions, this veto has never been used.

In many of these decisions, a blending of management inputs and team decisions appears to be the norm. The plant manager stated:

> Recently two separate teams went through the same exercise of deciding who moves to another job that came open in another team. At first, asked to make the decision themselves, they picked the worst performer in the team. Since we did not perceive this to be in the best interests of the plant, we intervened. My reasons for intervention were that I wanted them to deal with the problem themselves rather than to unload it on some other team. They reacted to my intervention by trying to unload the decision on the management.

EXHIBIT 11-3
Autonomous Team Role, Responsibility, Authority

I. Team Performance (final product, quantity and quality)
   1. Job method performance and evaluation (individual and team)
      A. Oversee job design and approved method
         a. Job procedures (set-up, operation procedures, put away)
      B. Job standardization and method compliance
         a. Product flow
         b. Method compliance
            1. Performance levels goals
            2. Training, retraining, and coaching
            3. Job tools
            4. Job supplies
            5. Method improvement recommendations
            6. Specific FR procedures (core shill, etc.)
      C. Recommend policies and/or procedures for effective operation of a given department or team
II. Team planning and scheduling
   1. Monthly volume forecast
      A. Beginning of month, estimate L.U., overtime, supply and labor cost per standard hour, potential problems, casting availability, casting quality (yield), and required manning
      B. Middle of month, make final projection of what they plan to ship and L.U.
      C. End of month, submit *actuals* report
      D. End of month, hold evaluation and product control meeting
   2. Monitor schedule for variances and take corrective actions
      A. Meet weekly and monthly goals
         a. Plan daily work assignments (allocate personnel based on need)
      B. Monitor daily production
         a. Evaluate key information document (daily, written)
            1. Identify variances and substandard performance
            2. Determine cause and take corrective action
            3. Schedule overtime
            4. Communicate bottlenecks out of teams' control to shift manager (yields, quality, management, etc.)
III. Materials and supply control
   1. Ensure timely ordering of needed supplies
   2. Keep accurate account of required supplies
   3. Maintain elective waste control
   4. Know and control costs
IV. Team discipline
   1. Oversee adherence to work hours, breaks, and lunch time
   2. Maintain safe work conduct
   3. Respect the rights and resources of others
   4. Manage personality conflicts and shared equipment
V. Salary administration
   1. Perform rate study and recommend performance goals
   2. Monitor pay raises
      A. Conduct equal and unbiased evaluations of all team members
   3. Recommend pay changes

VI. Team skill development
  1. Team work
     A. Participate actively in team meetings
     B. Perform administrative function effectively
     C. Discuss problems with each other in an open, consistent manner and give constructive criticism to core management
     D. Perform all required tasks
     E. Coordinate work assignments
     F. Collaborate rather than compete
  2. Problem solving/trouble shooting
     A. Identify operations problems
     B. Anticipate future potential operating problems
  3. Housekeeping/safety
     A. Enforce plant safety rules and norms
     B. Clean work area daily
     C. Keep assigned equipment and tools in proper working condition by performing simple maintenance where qualified or contracting other responsible persons
     D. Prevent accidents by correcting safety hazards, if qualified, or reporting hazards to persons responsible for making corrections

---

EXHIBIT 11-4
Role, Responsibility and Authority of Team Coordinator

---

1. Serve as communications link between the team and core management
2. Coordinate and maintain team administrative responsibilities
3. Coordinate team planning and scheduling
4. Attend assistant operations manager's daily production meetings

---

> That too was unacceptable because it was a sort of abdication. Next, they wanted to draw lots to make the decision. Two managers worked together with this team over two weeks. Over time, they began to explore the implications of the move in terms of opportunities, etc. Finally, the position of "what if I move" was developed for each member of the team. This was in contrast to the earlier position they took by way of "let's see who will be asked to leave." Once a self-examination note was struck, we immediately had a volunteer for the move.

One of the more important personnel tasks for the team is to appraise team members' performance on the job and advise management on promotion decisions. Performance on the job is appraised every four to six months. Evaluators are drawn from team peers, as well as from management. The process includes taking skill tests developed by the team members. When promotions are being considered, the team rates the candidates on the basis of attendance records, indicators of proficiency, and performance on a written test. The plant manager described the role of seniority in promotion decisions.

EXHIBIT 11-5
Evaluation Form

Evaluation of _Doug Jones_ Master # ___38068___ Date _4-20-82_

Promotion to pay level: ___8___

Date requested: _4-70-82_

4/20/82
P. D.

Goals	Skill		Quantity/Quality	Demonstration Time
05	Hardwheel	8530	125/95%	
03	Belt	8530	67/90%	720
03	Goye	8530	40/98%	Hrs.

Actual	Skill		Quantity/Quality	Demonstration Time
05	Hardwheel	8530	125/95%	720 Total hrs.
03	Belt	8530	67/90%	
03	Goye	8530	40/98%	

Comments: _____

Has individual met required goals? ___✓___ Yes _____ No

Has individual met demonstration times? ___✓___ Yes _____ No

Skill level required:	Level 1	Level 2	Level 3	Level 4
Teamwork				✓
Problem solving				✓
Housekeeping/safety			✓	

Have these levels been met according to the attached sheet? _____ Yes _____ No

If levels have not been met, state recommended action:

_____ OK on Tr - 8530 Sam George _____

Promotion approved ___✓___ Rejected _____

Committee   _Ricardo Dube_   _Joe Mahoney_ Team member
             Anthony Castle   _Pat Coppola_ Team member
             Anne Tolpe   _Ned Turner_ Team member

When speaking of promotions, one needs to distinguish between the employee-initiated movement from levels 1 through 9 as different from the personnel needs of other teams, which require promotion from production teams to maintenance team or management to other resource teams. Movement through the levels (1 to 9) are initiated by the employee. The only constraint on movement is time. Once an employee moves to a new level, he or she must stay with the newly acquired skill at least for four months before moving on to learn newer skills. These upward movements may be strongly correlated with seniority simply for the reason that the employee with more seniority has been in the plant that much longer to learn new skills. The other kind of promotion, i.e., from production to maintenance and management, would have a much lower correlation with seniority because promotions are based entirely on ability.

WAGES AND THE WAGE-SETTING PROCESS

Wages are comparable to those paid by other area employers. The entry-level wage rate is relatively low ($4.15 per hour in March 1982), whereas the average wages of workers in the plant tend to be higher because the pay-for-knowledge system allows workers to progress through the point and pay levels more rapidly than in the traditional system. Thus, average wages in the plant are among the top three in firms in the area. These rates, however, are approximately 15 to 20 percent lower than the average wages paid comparable unionized workers in other plants of this firm. The plant manager explained some of the difficulties in setting competitive wages.

> One of our problems is that few of our jobs are comparable to those found in a traditionally organized plant. Most of my employees are competent in multiple tasks, which makes comparison with a typical narrowly defined job very difficult. My problem gets even more complex when you consider that many of the office employees can do at least two jobs in the office and one job on the shop floor. How is one to define "comparable wages" for such employees?

EXPERIMENT IN PERSPECTIVE

The first plant manager was promoted to divisional manager in 1980, but because this is the only plant in the new division, he remains the plant's chief operating officer. He has spent eight years in the company as an engineer-manager. Before the plant opened, he worked in plants organized in traditional ways. In explaining why the plant has been a success, he stressed several points.

> We have laid a heavy emphasis on good communication within an organization. Last year we hired two consultants to work with our teams in identifying training needs. Later all employees were put through a program of one-on-one communications skills. Our training groups were vertically integrated. Each group included employees from all levels. Another important point is that we as management have never abdicated our responsibility to manage. I have tried to build a participative structure, not a permissive one where freedom may be misused as license. I have not shied away from using the managerial veto on team decisions that I believed not to be in the best interests of the organization.

We have also let our systems evolve over time, as I suggested earlier. Recently we have realized that there is almost too much cohesion in the teams. Many employees have begun to look at their teams as home turf in a proprietary way. This extreme identification is also a bit unhealthy. So we are now moving toward a system where employees would rotate across teams. This will allow them to identify more with the organization than with just a specific team.

Voluntary turnover at the plant has been low (about 5 percent) in recent years although about 40 percent quit their jobs in 1978, the first year of the plant. The personnel manager described the start-up as a process of sorting for the "right kind" of worker.

There were some with high-absence records. Others who found it difficult to handle all the freedom they had on the job. We had several very young people who didn't have enough work experience and hadn't as a result developed the work ethic. Now our recruitment is more selective and our teams participate heavily in the recruitment process.

When asked to give some examples of serious disagreements within a team the plant manager related the following cases:

One team wanted to fire one of its members. The team had done a good job of documenting the various stages of indiscipline before coming to me. They had given this individual several warnings. They had his absence record, performance record, results on tests, etc., all of which were not good. Meanwhile, the individual approached me with an appeal that he be given another chance. I decided to ask the team to reconsider their decision and keep the man. The team complied with extreme reluctance. This man's performance is still marginal months later. I may have to admit that I was wrong in this case, but then that's what this plan is all about. In another case, we had a well-qualified minority female candidate for an opening who was rejected by the team. Candidates spend a day with the teams on the shop floor. The team was acting on not what she had on paper, but how she responded to the work situation. Again, I insisted we hire her. Her performance was so bad she didn't even last through the probation period. Again, in retrospect I should have listened to the team, but some disagreement provides a healthy tension. Ours has to be a system of checks and balances. I cannot run the plant all by myself, nor can they.

Questions for Discussion

1. The design of the jobs and the compensation system in this plant seem to violate many of the principles of work organization that have guided industrial engineers since the days of Frederick Taylor and the scientifc management movement. On the other hand, the new system appears to provide more of the motivational incentives some behavioral scientists believe are needed to create high-commitment work systems. First, what are the basic differences between the team-concept system and the traditional system? Second, is the team system better suited to the needs of current technology and to the current labor force than the traditional system, or is the team approach unlikely to be an efficient, equitable system for organizing work and compensating and motivating workers over the long run?

2. What would account for the 40 percent turnover rate in the first year of the plant? What types of workers are likely to do well in this kind of work system?

3. Suppose that three years from now a new plant manager takes over, discovers that 90 percent of the production and maintenance work force has progressed to level 9 of the pay system, and wants to know what, if anything, can be done. Would the labor costs of this plant be out of line with competing plants? What, if anything, should be done about workers who have been at level 9 for a long time?

4. In this plant, workers have much more say than unionized workers in task-related decisions about the organization and conduct of their work and in the personnel decisions governing promotions to higher skill levels and hiring new workers. On the other hand, they appear to have less say in decisions about salary levels, fringe benefits, the design of the overall work system, and the process of resolving disputes between workers and managers. Is this an acceptable trade-off for workers over the long run? Will participation in task-related decisions lead to worker demands for greater participation in decision making on traditional bread-and-butter issues? To worker demands for participation in other areas of management decision-making?

Putting an Existing Work Force in a New Plant

The following case describes the issues a firm faces in designing new work systems into a new plant that is to be staffed with workers from an old plant who are used to traditional forms of work organization. It is based on the experiences of a large corporation that recently opened a technologically advanced assembly plant.

CASE
Start-Up of a New Plant: Some Procedural Issues

Firms have followed two different strategies to restructure and modernize their operations. On the one hand, some have abandoned old facilities, moved to new greenfield sites, equipped them with the latest technology, recruited a new work force, and oriented that work force to the new work system. Most firms following this strategy also have chosen to open the plants on a nonunion basis. On the other hand, some have chosen to retrofit existing plants by introducing new physical capital and a new social technology or work system.

The plant described in this section falls between these extremes. The company built a new plant and equipped and designed it with the newest technology. The workers and the union were moved from other plants that the company had closed in the area.

Source: Robert B. McKersie, Professor of Industrial Relations, Sloan School of Management, MIT. The piece was written for this book.

BACKGROUND

Several years ago, the company closed a major midwestern plant, a large complex employing more than ten thousand workers, and decided to build a new plant nearby that would employ three thousand workers at full capacity. Equipped with the latest in technology (see Exhibit 11-6), the plant was intended to assemble products of the most advanced design.

In establishing the plant, the company decided at the division level to introduce new forms of work organization, given their experience at other plants in the corporation. Management wanted to organize the work force into teams led by supervisors (in this sense, they would not be completely autonomous, as was the case in some other new plants). Management also wanted a pay-for-knowledge system, which would promote workers as they acquired different skills within the team. Traditional job classifications and movement based on seniority would not be used.

By mid-1983, the plant had been operating for two years with approximately one thousand workers. In this start-up phase, only prototypes were being produced to allow for correcting design problems. The date for introducing the new product had been postponed several times, the latest being 1985.

The plant operated with only one shift. These workers had been recruited from the layoff list of the closed plant and were hired on the basis of seniority among those who applied. The salaried workers, who were not unionized, were assigned to the plant, rather than being given an option.

In addition to innovations in work design, management emphasized many ideas regarding equality within the plant. For example, executives were given no special parking spots; all employees ate in the same cafeteria; and managers did not wear ties. More important, a plant council was organized and quality-of-working-life (QWL) coordinators were invited to attend regularly.

Shortly before the plant was to employ its first workers, division management requested the regional office of the union to assign union representatives to the plant. It is the practice of this union to allow the regional office to assign representatives to a new plant, pending the recruitment of the work force. After the work force is up to full force, an election of union officers is held and a first contract is negotiated. Management is free to design the plant and its work system and to operate the plant accordingly during the start-up; contract negotiations later give the union the opportunity to propose changes in the work and compensation systems.

The union assigned three QWL coordinators who had been active in the former plant's QWL system. They participated actively in the plant's start-up, attended the plant manager's council, and made many suggestions about personnel procedures and policies. For example, they recommended a stringent disciplinary approach to workers with poor attendance records.

The start-up period entailed extensive training; employees at all levels of the organization attended numerous training sessions about the new technology and the new work organization. For example, all supervisors received five weeks of training in methods to encourage participation. Some supervisors

EXHIBIT 11-6
Plant Design

The $600-million plant bristles with robots, computer terminals, and automated welding equipment, including two massive $1.5 million Robogate systems that align and weld assemblies of body panels. Unmanned forklifts, guided by wires buried in the floor, will carry parts directly from loading docks. In its flexibility, this plant will set new standards; for example, the products built on the same assembly lines will have almost no exterior sheet-metal parts in common. A new loading dock will receive truckload deliveries of many smaller and more frequent shipments on the just-in-time model.

Source: A journalist's description of the plant.

---

also attended a Dale Carnegie course on how to communicate effectively with members of their teams.

Everything was progressing well, except for the technical problems with the new product; but these delays gave the organization more time to work on the human and industrial relations issues central to the start-up. Two years into the start-up, the union's regional office assigned an acting president and a seven-member committee. Shortly after arriving, this group took a strong position against the new work organization — especially the pay-for-knowledge system — and withdrew cooperation from the plantwide council. Group members said they would withhold judgment about the system until they had had an opportunity to negotiate the first agreement. It was clear from their position, however, that they intended to press for the return to a traditional work organization at the new plant.

MANAGEMENT'S VIEWS

Management believed the start-up had been progressing reasonably well; the plant manager used the term "evolving steadily." The organizational development specialist thought that attitudes were becoming more and more positive.

One of the plant superintendents said that most workers liked the team concept and the pay-for-knowledge system, and that he had heard many people say "We'll never go back to the old way." However, several of the superintendents identified problem areas they had encountered in the start-up phase. For example, the superintendent of the maintenance department indicated that the process of persuading craftsmen, who were used to thirty or forty different skill areas, to work with as few as six or seven classifications and to put the emphasis on cross-training were meeting with resistance. The maintenance workers knew that cross-utilization would mean fewer jobs and less overtime; the maintenance superintendent felt handicapped in having no incentive to offer beyond the statement: "It's better for productivity and better for the company to have fewer categories and more flexibility across the categories."

The superintendent of the body shop noted: "People should know how much time the new system takes, since we are spending a lot of time in consultation and discussion." He thought that the new system was much better than the traditional method, but that it required a lot of management time to ensure that the process worked effectively.

UNION'S VIEWS

No one view dominated within the union regarding the work system being installed at the plant. Perspectives formed at various levels of the union organization illustrate this uncertain position.

Neither the international nor the regional office of the union had assumed a policy position on the use of new work systems or, for that matter, on the QWL approach used in the company since the early 1970s. In a discussion with the union's director of education, it was made clear that the union was unfamiliar with the concept of pay for knowledge, and that no extensive discussions had been held among union officials about such new work systems, which were increasing in the United States.

The local union was familiar with QWL programs, as it had supported the concept of QWL since the early 1970s. For the most part, QWL meant weekly meetings for problem solving and communication; it did not mean the pay-for-knowledge system, broadened job classifications, or any of the other attributes of the plant's new system. Those concepts, in fact, carried a negative connotation within the union, because the company had used them in the mid-1970s at a new plant in the south, which initially was nonunion. After organizing that plant, the union negotiated the return to a more traditional approach to the organization of work.

The union vice-president, who had taken over as director of the union's branch at the company, agreed that the issue was, What does quality of work life mean in the 1980s? At an offsite meeting of plant managers and the local union committee in the summer of 1983, union representatives stated that to them quality of working life meant: People should be treated right and then productivity will follow. They also emphasized the need to focus on product quality. Several local representatives noted, however, that to them quality of working life should not become mingled with the question of how jobs should be structured and compensated in the new plant. These were collective bargaining issues to be addressed by the elected union leaders and the bargaining committee, not the QWL coordinators. QWL had brought more dignity to the workplace and a better climate to the worker-supervisor relationship, but to broaden QWL to include work system issues risked negating these gains and their benefits.

The QWL coordinators were perplexed, for they had participated in discussions about the new work system but then were forced to withdraw when the committee was appointed. They generally agreed with the narrow view of QWL. One QWL coordinator, for example, described the new work system as "cannibalistic" because it combined jobs and created a smaller work force.

The positions of the union president and the seven committee members were varied. The president held a negative attitude toward several key aspects of the new work system and also indicated that he would attempt to have the old system installed when local negotiations started. Several other committee members, however, noted that certain aspects of the new system were preferable to traditional systems.

Some of the grievance committee members thought that the new system posed problems for their roles and functions. One of them commented:

> What do I do when a worker comes up and says that he would like to file a grievance because he is not being advanced to the next step in the pay-for-knowledge system, and then when I go and start investigating the grievance I hear from all of the other members of the team that the individual is not qualified for the next step. This is a situation that I do not know how to handle. In a traditional operation I focus on the foreman, and we go at it, and perhaps I can get the problem resolved. Here the focus is not on the foreman but on the whole work team.

A member of management made the same point:

> Traditional union leaders are very good at meeting the needs of the 5 percent who are the outspoken, grievance-prone individuals. This new system requires them somehow to relate to all workers, and they are having difficulty establishing their role and function in this new context.

It should be noted that several of the committee members believed that the union might have a role if there were some benefits to take back to the rank and file.

SYSTEM PARAMETERS

As the work system was completely designed and under way when the union leaders arrived at the plant, they saw little they could do. What other dimensions that might benefit the rank and file *could* they influence? Among the several possibilities, one concerned the question of employment levels and employment assurances. Several General Motors and Ford plants, for example, had introduced Pilot Employment Guarantee (PEG) programs, wherein workers were assured that 85 percent of the work force would not be laid off. This particular company, however, was reluctant to give such an assurance in a start-up situation with a product whose marketability was not yet tested.

Another potentially valuable benefit would be access to information; union leaders could be in a position to know as much as possible about the plant's economic prospects. Access to such information would be of limited use in this case though, because the plant manager admitted that he knew little about the plans for employment build-up, about specifically when a second shift would be hired, or about the outlook for the new product.

The upcoming negotiations for the local agreement would bring some of these system issues into focus. The manager of labor relations discussed the inevitable tension between the union's need to deal with seniority and job security issues, and some of the countervailing realities of the new work organization. For example, in a traditional plant workers can transfer between shifts and between jobs, indulging their preferences for schedules and work types and minimizing their chances of being laid off during a downturn. In this case, plant management had indicated that it would not allow the movement of workers out of teams, across shifts, and to other departments. Consequently, the manager of labor relations was giving considerable thought to alternative work-force management concepts and procedures so that seniority would have some weight and so that the stability needed in a team-organized work environment could be maintained.

Another difficult design issue had to do with the respective roles of teams, the QWL committees, labor-management meetings, and the plant council. In some plants the rule was that no contractual matters were ever discussed within the QWL meetings. This reflected the desire to separate integrative from distributive bargaining issues. Although workers realized that many topics entailed aspects of both kinds of bargaining, they believed they lacked a sufficient basis for coordinating and appropriately relating these different issues.

Questions for Discussion

This start-up case raises a number of important issues for management and union officials and for those interested in the process of designing and implementing industrial relations and human resource management systems in new plants.

1. How and when does a company bring union leaders into the decision-making process for the design of a new plant?
2. Should the company have insisted on having the president and grievance committee assigned from the start? Or, given the lack of policy support for the new system at the regional and national union levels, was it inevitable that early involvement would have resulted in union resistance to the system from the start?
3. Is it too much to expect union leaders who come out of traditional plants to be able to define a viable role for the union in these new team and pay-for-knowledge systems?
4. What benefits, if any, can a union take back to its membership if it is brought in after the new design has been implemented and when workers are already operating under the new system? If the union comes in at this late stage, how can its leaders avoid pressures to focus more heavily on the grievances of those dissatisfied with the new system than on the positive reactions of those who prefer the new system?
5. Are there better ways to deal with the union's need for more information about how the new plant design and the new work system will actually work and with the union's need for stronger assurances on adequate employment levels? These two issues are not fully within the control of plant managers but must be dealt with if the new system is to be effective.
6. One ground rule that has been adopted to guide the QWL process is to separate negotiations and adjudication of contractual matters from the deliberations of QWL teams. Can this principle be maintained in the start-up of a new plant? More specifically, what should be the relationship between the plantwide council, the collective bargaining process, and the grievance procedure?
7. Can an accommodation be found between the new system and the traditions and expectations of workers who have come out of traditional plants?

Experimenting with Quality of Working Life

Many quality-of-working-life (QWL) experiments begin as narrow efforts focused on involving individuals and small groups of workers in decisions affecting their jobs. Over time the experiments tend to expand and influence collective bargaining relationships and high-level management decisions. This case describes the dynamics of a QWL process and its relationship to employer and union strategies. In doing so, it illustrates how a specific QWL process can affect the general economic, managerial, and collective bargaining contexts in which the process is embedded.

CASE
APEX Corporation

BACKGROUND AND ENVIRONMENT

Local 1 and APEX have had a long-standing, cooperative, collective bargaining relationship. The company voluntarily recognized this international union in the late 1940s when the firm was a small manufacturer of a single product line. From the outset, the relationship was influenced by the strong philosophy of the firm's founder, who believed in the desirability of maintaining cooperative, highly professional relationships between the union and the company. His commitment has carried through the relationship to the present, and his philosophy was passed to his various successors, largely through the continued leadership position of the corporate director of industrial relations.

In the 1950s, APEX capitalized on technological breakthroughs, which transformed the firm from a small, unknown business to one of the leading Fortune 500 corporations. The company continued to enjoy rapid growth and high profits through the 1960s; technological advances continued to provide it with a near monopoly in its major product line. As the company expanded, new plants were opened and the union was recognized voluntarily on the basis of card checks or uncontested representation elections in each new facility. The major manufacturing facilities of the corporation are located in one medium-sized city in the Northeast. Smaller facilities are located in other cities in various regions of the country. During the 1970s, the company acquired several smaller firms, as it sought to diversify into related product lines with high-growth potential.

The competitive environment for this company changed dramatically in the 1970s. Both domestic and foreign competition intensified, while growth in the market for its products began to decline. The market declined more rapidly during the recession of the early 1980s. By 1982, the company announced the necessity to reduce its blue- and white-collar labor forces by at least 30 percent in an effort to regain its competitive position in its basic product line. It also intended to shift its new product development resources to the newer, more promising lines of business developed through its recent acquisitions.

ORIGIN AND STRUCTURE OF THE QWL PROCESS

The idea for a QWL program came from the chairman of the board. Because of his interest, the 1980 collective bargaining agreement negotiated with Local 1 included provisions for employee involvement (see Exhibit 11-7).

The structure of the QWL process consisted of several joint committees and groups. At the top was the planning and policy committee of four union officers and four management representatives. The latter were the vice-president of manufacturing, the manager of personnel, the director of industrial relations, and the manager of QWL services. This committee met every four to six weeks and was responsible for establishing broad guidelines and policies for the QWL process. Each plant in the company had an advisory committee of ten union and ten management representatives to develop plans for implementing the QWL process, monitoring its progress, and coordinating its activities with other developments in the plant. Within each plant the various business centers also had steering committees of an equal number of management and union representatives. The task of these committees was to support the QWL teams as they trained in problem-solving techniques.

The basic unit of the process was the QWL team of six to eight employees from the same work area. Participation was voluntary; both bargaining unit and other employees were encouraged to participate. Each team elected a leader who may or may not be the supervisor for that work group. Approximately 50 percent of the leaders in these groups are not supervisors.

Each team underwent a ten-week, forty-hour training program, of which the employer paid for twenty-eight hours and the employee contributed twelve hours. The training emphasized problem-solving skills and team building. Exhibit 11-8 outlines some of the material covered. At the end of a training program, a graduation ceremony was held in which each team presented its analysis of workplace problems and suggested solutions to plant managers. Union representatives usually spoke at these ceremonies.

After graduating, each QWL team met for an hour each week to discuss problems and to review the status of suggestions for improvements made at previous meetings. The groups could not make changes that would conflict with the provisions of the collective bargaining agreement.

The efforts of these teams were supported by eight full-time union and eight full-time management QWL coordinators who provided technical advice and helped train the teams. Each coordinator agreed to remain in the position for at least two years. In addition, a full-time manager of QWL services monitored the program for the corporation. He was assisted by an outside consultant who initially worked four days a week but later scaled his involvement to one day a week. The consultant was hired jointly by the local union representatives and the company.

The QWL teams can be described accurately as quality circle groups, as they focus on solving job-related problems. As of June 1982, no changes had been made in the organization of work, the roles of supervisors, the compensation structure, or other structural aspects of the plant-level work organization. The manager of QWL services, however, saw this as only the first phase of a more ambitious process of change. In addition to increasing the number of workers trained for the QWL process (his goal is to train and involve 80 percent of the work force by the end of 1985), this manager

---

EXHIBIT 11-7
Employee Involvement

A Joint Company-Union Employee Involvement Committee shall be established to investigate and pursue opportunities for enhancing employees' work satisfaction and productivity. To this end, the Joint Committee shall meet regularly to undertake the following responsibilities:

A. Review and evaluate ongoing programs, projects, and experiments, both within and outside the Company, designed to encourage employee involvement.
B. Develop programs, projects, and experiments that might ultimately be broadly applied.
C. Establish subcomittees to develop suggested programs for specific areas. Hear and review reports from these subcommittees.
D. Submit reports and recommendations to the Company and Union regarding the implementation and subsequent progress of specific programs.

EXHIBIT 11-8
Putting QWL into Practice
Problem-Solving, Team — Education, and Training

QWL/EI Concepts

Problem-Solving Skills
Data gathering techniques
Cause and effect analysis
Pareto analysis and histogram
Check sheets and control charts
Using statistics

Team Building and Functioning
Interpersonal communications
Effective team meetings
Team records and reports
Work on real problems
Using technical staff support
Presentation skills

Program = 40 hours (28 paid, 12 voluntary)
        :   4 hours over 10 weeks

Graduation — Team presentations on real problems

Presented to: Steering committee and management

---

envisioned the process progressing so that workers and QWL teams would address a wider array of issues related to work organization, job design, work layout, and work group management. The QWL process would become the kind of organization associated with autonomous work groups. By mid-1982, however, none of the teams had moved to this stage, nor had the company and the union agreed to this objective.

By the summer of 1982, approximately 25 percent of the members of the bargaining unit had been trained and were participating in a QWL team. Layoffs and seniority movement had disrupted the teams since mid-1981 so that many who had completed training were not participating in teams.

INITIAL UNION RESPONSE

According to the union's international representative, the officers and members of Local 1 were unsure how the QWL process would affect them. He stated:

> We weren't making a quality product and we knew if we could produce a better product it would enhance job security. But the stewards were skeptical, the shop chairmen didn't want to get involved. They didn't know what QWL meant and it was a gimmick to them. The company has had so many programs, each beginning and ending at various points in time. At the same time, the union's perception of the company's goals at the outset of the program was that this was an honest approach to get workers involved in improving efficiency and quality. We thought that the top executives of the corporation (the chairman of the board and the president and chief executive) were sincere.

Despite some initial apprehension, the union decided to participate actively in developing the QWL program. A year after its initiation, union representatives reviewed their position and found a positive change. The international union representative stated:

> This has been a real eye opener to me. Management wanted to make certain changes and produce more to meet their schedules. The workers agreed to cooperate. They understand the competitive threat better now. They see the relationship between their work and the success of the product they make.

The business agent for Local 1 had been with the company for more than fifteen years and was also skeptical of the program at first. He assessed the program's status when it was a year old as follows:

> Management is really sharing information with us. This would not have been possible three or four years ago, and I see this as a result of the QWL program. At a meeting yesterday, for example, the vice-president of manufacturing shared all the numbers on costs and future orders that he has so we could really get behind this layoff problem. [The union representatives and the company had met to try to avoid the layoffs of approximately thirty people and had succeeded.]

Another long-term company employee and union official was the general shop chairman, a full-time employee union representative paid by the company. In addition to coordinating the shop stewards, he was the key union overseer of the QWL process. He was highly skeptical of the QWL program but later became a vigorous advocate, as his statement shows:

> At first I saw little point in all of this. We worried that this sort of program would make the shop stewards superfluous. But we have had no regrets. The program is running very efficiently. The management director of the QWL program is very fair in his dealings with the union. We have had great confidence in the consultant the company hired to work with us, and we trust him. The key is that we are considered to be equals by management. It's not like a short-lived program run by management where we will be left to pick up the crumbs.

The support of the shop stewards was slower in developing, as in most cases, but by the time interviews were conducted two years into the process, none of the shop stewards voiced opposition to the program, and none saw serious overlaps or jurisdictional conflicts between the QWL process and grievance procedures or provisions of the collective bargaining agreement. Further, all agreed that the union should continue to support the QWL process and to be active in it.

The first two and a half years of the QWL process saw growing support and commitment on the part of top union leaders and union stewards. In addition, the union representatives serving as QWL facilitators were emerging as another important group of union support for the process.

EVOLUTION OF MANAGEMENT SUPPORT

Within a year of the negotiations over the 1980 agreement, the chairman was replaced by the current president of the corporation who shared the chairman's strong commitment to developing the QWL process. Thus, corporate commitment remained strong through the process's initial implementation phase.

Despite the support of top management, support among first-line supervisors and middle managers, as reported by both company and union representatives, was more variable and problematic. Lack of this group's support is one of the major reasons QWL and other worker participation processes often fail. Turnover and promotions also erode management's commitment. In this case, a number of job changes had occurred among the plant managers, the personnel director for the manufacturing division in which the program was located, and the vice-president of manufacturing, the highest management official with line responsibilities directly involving the QWL plants.

The first test of the continuity of management's support for the QWL program came near the end of the first year. APEX was undergoing a major corporate reorganization and a shift in business strategy to become more competitive with Japanese and domestic manufacturers. A new vice-president of manufacturing had been hired, and the budget for the QWL program's second year was under review. Layoffs would be coming in that second year.

The chairman of the company was quoted in a business periodical as saying:

> This isn't a crash program for 1981 or 1982. It's an attempt to restructure the entire business. We're talking about ways to get leaner and tougher throughout the company.

The article about APEX continued with the following description of corporate changes:

> Operations will be split into smaller groups, decision-making will be decentralized and its 125,000-strong work force will be reduced as part of a cost-cutting drive intended to boost productivity in every aspect of the company's business, from manufacturing to marketing.

Layoffs were a major part of the plan to make APEX more competitive, as the president emphasized in the article:

> We have too much manpower generally in the company, and we've got to drive up productivity at a much faster rate. There are too many people and too many layers of management.

The issue of funding the QWL program's second year erupted in a meeting that involved the managers of the four plants in the manufacturing complex, the vice-president of manufacturing, the QWL consultant, the director of QWL services for the corporation, and the three union officials. The meeting began with the vice-president indicating that the estimated $6 million price tag for the program's second year was too high, that such money was unavailable for the program. The consultant reported the meeting as follows:

> The dynamics of this meeting were interesting in two respects. First the general shop chairman (who is the union representative on the QWL program) took on the new vice-president of manufacturing and challenged him directly by asking him if the company was "decommitting" to the program. Second, the plant managers took a much more active role in challenging the new vice-president as well and in trying to look for alternative solutions. The general shop chairman initially brought up issues that the plant managers should have raised themselves, such as, what's the consequence of backing off the program the first time money becomes an issue?

These discussions ultimately produced an agreement: The plant managers first would absorb some of the QWL program's costs within their line budgets, and second would look for ways to lower the program's cost without slowing its progress. Eventually, the cost of the second year was pared to $3 million. With the joint support of the local union representatives and the line managers, the QWL program survived its first test: the turnover of a management decision maker.

Lack of support for the program among middle managers and first-line supervisors was another problem. After two years of experience with the program, the vice-president of manufacturing asked the director of QWL services to develop a strategy to confront the problem. They titled their new strategy "Changing the Management Culture."

Local union representatives estimated that 80 to 85 percent of the line managers above the first-line supervisor and below the plant managers were opposed to the QWL process. Opposition of these managers was attributed to their fears of losing power and of having their roles changed. At the same time, they failed to see the leadership styles and decision-making processes of managers above them changing in ways that were consistent with the QWL process.

Opposition also appeared from some support groups, such as the manufacturing engineering personnel. This group felt threatened by having hourly workers suggest changes in work practices or layouts that heretofore had been within the jurisdiction of engineering.

VIEWS OF THE RANK AND FILE

Rank-and-file employees explicitly agreed to initiate the QWL process when they voted to ratify the 1980 collective bargaining agreement. Although that agreement was ratified by an overwhelming majority, the QWL provision was insignificant in their discussions of the contract and in the vote itself. Thus, the first evidence of rank-and-file reactions to the QWL process came from the response to initial requests for volunteer participants. According to both the manager of QWL services and union representatives, most employees initially were reluctant. As the union representatives had stated, the rank-and-file also had witnessed a number of management initiatives to improve productivity, to try out new communications programs, and to enhance attitudes. They were afraid that the QWL process was another gimmick. A number of groups, however, were persuaded to consider the process, and after the first several groups responded positively to the QWL training, interest in the concept spread more rapidly. The manager of QWL services reported that after the program was initiated and several teams had completed training, most requests for volunteers resulted in positive responses from 50 to 70 percent of the employees addressed.

In mid-1982, surveys were conducted of 218 workers participating in the QWL process and of 167 workers not participating. The surveys were intended to assess the workers' interest in gaining a say in QWL-type issues and to assess whether experience with the QWL process in its first twenty months had had any effects on workers' views of their jobs, on the *actual* amount of say or influence they thought they had on QWL-type issues, and on their assessment of the effectiveness of their local union in dealing with QWL issues.

The results showed a continued strong interest in gaining a say in QWL issues (more than 80 percent of the respondents indicated they wanted "some" or "a lot" of say in how work is done and the quality of the work produced). Conversely, workers who were involved in the QWL process *did not* report having significantly more say over workplace decisions related to QWL issues, *did not* rate their jobs more favorably, and *did not* rate the effectiveness of their union higher on QWL issues than did the comparison group of nonparticipants.

Thus, there was no evidence that the QWL process had achieved significant improvements in the work environment in its first twenty months of operation. Some evidence, however, suggested that the rank and file were becoming more disillusioned with the QWL process as time passed. For example, some of the most negative assessments came from the earliest volunteers who participated. Moreover, only 25 percent of the nonparticipants indicated an interest in getting involved in the QWL program.

In commenting on these data, the general shop chairman stated:

> Those numbers seem to coincide with what I thought was going on. Those who got involved early are saying to us "We took some big risks in getting involved early. Then we see that we are improving productivity and quality in our shops. At the same time layoffs are occurring all around us and the work force continues to shrink. We are now asking, What are we getting out of this process?"

Thus, the interview and survey data suggested that the QWL process was greeted at the start with an initial degree of rank-and-file skepticism. This was replaced quickly by a favorable response and a burst of enthusiasm. After experience with the process, worker interest appeared to have reached a plateau, followed by a period of questioning and some degree of disillusionment. Their disillusion may not have derived as much from the development of the QWL process as it did from their increasing concern for job security when confronted with layoffs and permanent work force reductions.

LINKS TO THE COLLECTIVE BARGAINING RELATIONSHIP

Two sets of experiences illustrate the relationship between the QWL process and collective bargaining. The first concerns a high labor-cost operation that the firm was threatening to subcontract to outside vendors; the second, the process and results of negotiating the 1983 labor agreement, the first agreement to be negotiated after the QWL process had been in effect.

High-Cost Operation

One of the most difficult and controversial issues to arise between the company and Local 1 had been what to do with approximately two hundred workers engaged in manufacturing wiring harnesses, an electronic component of the company's final product. When APEX first developed the technology for its major product line, no other firms had the capability of manufacturing these wiring harnesses. The company had developed this capability in-house and had always produced its own wiring harnesses. As the technology became more routine and the market for these parts grew, many small firms entered the market and sold the components to larger firms for use in their final products. Almost all of these newer, smaller firms were nonunion and paid wages considerably below the rate under the Local 1 agreement. The 1982 average total compensation for Local 1 employees in this particular operation was approximately $19 per hour, compared to estimates of $8 from one vendor and $12 from another. Productivity comparisons also failed to show any significant offsetting advantage of using Local 1 employees. Thus, the cost of wiring harnesses was considerably higher for APEX than for its competitors. Consequently, many APEX managers had been arguing that the wiring harness operations should be subcontracted. The pressure to do so was intensified because the firm's domestic competitors, who had entered the market much later than APEX, subcontracted this work.

The corporation and the local union had recognized this problem and agreed before 1980 to phase out the wiring harness operations through attrition without laying anyone off. The agreement became unworkable, however, as the market for the firm's products began to deteriorate in 1980. The union and the company recognized the need for an alternative arrangement. Although management was applying strong pressure to contract the work, the local union strongly opposed this proposal. The vice-president of manufacturing described the discussions in 1981 as follows:

> Management three levels above me made a decision to close down this operation. The international representative of the union responded to that decision by pointing out that his shop stewards were just livid about this decision because it contradicted an earlier negotiated effort to reach an accommodation on this problem. As a result, several of us within management said, Let's not just put these people out on the street but let's give the problem to them to see if something can be worked out. Let the people themselves select a team to decide what is needed in this area. So this is what we did.

A group of workers and supervisors organized a task force to examine alternative ways of reducing the costs of the wiring harness operations. After one year of study and research, the group reported their recommendations to a union and management steering committee. The vice-president of manufacturing described their proposals as "astonishing recommendations"; the following is his description of what the task force recommended.

> The group found that management was doing a number of things wrong. The layout of the plant was wrong and they showed how it could be redesigned. The amount of overhead allocated to this area of the plant was also found to be wrong. They found lots of things that could be done differently. For example, they want to alter the contract language governing transfers and promotions to slow down the movement of people across jobs. They would like to have a separate seniority unit for people working in this area to also cut down on the number of moves in and out of the operation. They would like to make the jobs more flexible and interesting so that people don't desire to rotate out of them. They would like to use more part-time workers at peak periods of production to smooth out the work force and to allow the payment of lower wages and fringe benefits. They propose eliminating a number of supervisors and working as a semiautonomous work group. Overall, they have come up with a 29 percent cost reduction proposal. Companies can't get 29 percent cost reductions these days through management studies alone.

The changes being proposed, if implemented, would have modified significantly the terms of the collective bargaining agreement. After studying the recommendations, both union and company representatives agreed to add them to the agenda for the next contract negotiations, which were due to start a month later.

1983 Contract Negotiations

Contract negotiations for the first agreement since beginning the QWL experiment started in late 1982 to meet the contract expiration date of March 31, 1983. Both parties realized that these negotiations would determine whether the QWL process would survive, and each deferred taking a position on the process until it had reviewed the other side's initial proposals.

Significantly, both parties knew that these negotiations would be the most difficult they had faced in more than thirty years. Since the 1980 contract had been signed, the market for the firm's products had shrunk drastically, the recession of 1981–83 had depressed sales across the industry, and the firm's new business strategy required it to compete on the basis of price for the first time in history. These changes in competitive conditions and strategy necessitated deep price cuts, which put intense pressure on manufacturing costs. The firm also had decided to reduce permanently its blue- and white-collar labor forces by more than thirty percent, concentrating the reductions in the manufacturing facilities where the QWL process was in place. Although many of these layoffs had occurred already, there was evidence to suggest that the shrinking process was not yet complete.

Two central issues for negotiations were job security and income security. Further, the concession bargaining that had dominated negotiations in many other industries in 1981 and 1982 meant that many of the industries and unions traditionally used as bases of comparison had implemented contract concessions and wage deferrals. The union representatives realized that this environment of concession bargaining, along with the financial problems of the company, would not support as large an economic settlement as had been achieved in the past.

Finally, accompanying the transition to the new business strategy and the increased pressure on manufacturing and labor costs was a shift in the distribution of power within top management. The power of the cost-conscious financial managers had increased at the expense of the industrial relations department. The industrial relations staff lost much of its autonomy over the planning and strategy formulation for labor negotiations. Meanwhile, the union representatives recognized that other management officials were in direct control of the negotiations and that the industrial relations staff would be under intense pressure to negotiate labor cost reductions and tighter contractual language.

As the negotiations opened, it was entirely unclear just how highly management valued the QWL process. The union representatives believed that the hard-line position management negotiators were advocating signaled that the company really did not care whether the QWL process survived. They thought the company was being hypocritical in its approach to the negotiations. On the one hand, during the term of the 1980 agreement, the company had been preaching the values of QWL with its stress on openness, problem solving, high trust, and information sharing. On the other hand, the company's initial proposals for negotiations called for major concessions subcontracting language, in job transfers, several promotions, and other sensitive areas. In addition, to the union negotiating team, the employer representatives appeared unwilling to consider alternatives in a problem-solving fashion.

The union opened negotiations by making two basic points. First, it stressed that it had cooperated with the company throughout the term of the agreement to develop and sustain the QWL process and that it wanted to maintain and strengthen that process. Second, it stressed that for the process to be sustained through a second term of the contract, some provisions for job security and for sharing the gains of the QWL process needed to be included in the new agreement. Specifically, the opening statement to the union's written proposal was as follows:

> As employees of APEX Corporation and members of Local 1, we are extremely concerned about the stability of employment and income in [our plants]. We realize that much of APEX's problems can be attributed to competition in [this industry]. We also realize, however, that the Bargaining Unit has been adversely affected by other, more controllable factors: ineffective management styles, inefficiencies, underutilization of our manufacturing capabilities, and subcontracting. The result of these hindrances has been to the detriment of both the Company and the Union. They have contributed greatly to the Company's inability to compete; and they have thusly resulted in horrendous losses to the Bargaining Unit.
>
> The Company need not be reminded of our major problems of late. Our membership has encountered staggering levels of employment reductions. Hundreds of our members have realized the loss of their jobs and the sacrifice of their earnings. While still more fortunate than those that have been laid off, thousands of others have been cut back to lower classifications with eventual lower pay levels.
>
> In 1980 the Company came to us during contract negotiations and asked for our help . . . urged us to participate in making APEX more competitive. The Union enthusiastically accepted the Company's employee involvement concept. We whole-heartedly pledged ourselves to the challenge, and the months that followed have demonstrated our commitment to serve the Company's best interests.
>
> We are very proud, as we should be, for the many refinements that have been developed through our participation in problem solving. Advancements have been realized in cost reductions, quality improvements, safety, equipment utilization, and manufacturing methodology.
>
> In 1980 the Company voiced a need for our help . . . a need for our commitment . . . and we responded. We vowed our support to meet your need.
>
> With these negotiations, it is time for the Company to favorably respond to our essential needs. It is now time for the Company to make a commitment.
>
> Now is when the Company must realize the necessity of providing job security and income protection. If we are to continue as cooperative partners in making APEX Corporation a stronger organization, we must be given assurances that our livelihood is secure. It is an absolute requirement that these negotiations provide to our members certainty of job security and income protection.

Questions for Discussion

1. What should management's objectives be for these negotiations? Specifically, should it try to save and strengthen the QWL process? If so, what should management try to achieve in the negotiations? If not, what should it try to achieve?
2. What should the union's objectives and strategies be
   (a) if management indicates a willingness to continue and strengthen the QWL process?
   (b) if it becomes clear that management is no longer committed to the QWL process?

V

Government's Role in Human Resource Management

PREVIEW

The government assumes an active role in the human resource management and industrial relations system of any industrialized country. As noted in Chapter 2, the government must balance its role as an interested party with goals of its own (e.g., full employment, price stability, economic growth, productivity, labor peace) against its responsibility to mediate and regulate conflicting interests and potential imbalances of power in employment relationships. Thus, managers must treat government policy as another external factor to consider in designing and implementing human resource management policies. Moreover, managers are increasingly called upon to work directly with government policy makers and administrators in designing and executing various public-private partnerships. Such coordination is meant to reduce the adversarial nature of the relations between business and government concerning human resource management and industrial relations issues and to help clarify more efficient ways of achieving both public policy and management objectives.

In this section we review the alternative strategies that different United States administrations have followed in regulating various aspects of the employment relationship. We describe the evolution and current status of government policies that affect two vital human resource management activities: health and safety, and equal employment opportunity. We end with a safety management case that illustrates how, notwithstanding government regulation, management retains much responsibility and discretion in carrying out its human resource management functions.

453

12

Alternative Government Strategies

Governments can use four different approaches when dealing with industrial relations or human resource management issues (see Table 12-1). The various roles a government can assume, ranging from no intervention to direct regulation, entail the following strategies:

1. taking a laissez-faire approach, allowing the outcomes of issues to be determined by market forces and/or the discretion of private decision-makers
2. taking various measures to improve the performance of market forces
3. regulating the process of managerial and/or labor decision-making
4. directly regulating the substantive outcomes or the terms and conditions of employment relationships

Table 12-1 displays several functional areas of human resource management that may be subject to governmental intervention. The table illustrates an important point: the general absence of government regulations affecting the *strategic* level of managerial decision-making. This absence is consistent with the tradition in the United States of a relatively limited governmental role in the industrial relations arena. Unlike the governments of many European nations (see Chapter 13), government regulations in the United States have tended to be limited to the bottom two tiers of the three-tiered framework introduced in Chapter one. Because of the free-enterprise orientation of the American political economy, direct federal control of fundamental business strategy decisions has been rare.

Nonetheless, the long-term historical trends indicate a shift toward a more active, interventionist government strategy with respect to a growing array of human resource management issues. Commentators are not equally sanguine about this trend, but the growing role of government increasingly requires human resource managers to de-

TABLE 12-1   Examples of Alternative Strategies of the Role of Government

	Free Market	Improve Market Performance	Regulate Decision-Making Process	Regulate Substantive Outcomes
Selection and Staffing	Employment at will Technological change Plant closings	Unemployment compensation taxes Training subsidies or incentives	Equal employment opportunity laws Jobs Partnership and Training Act	Affirmative action goals/quotas Mandatory retirement restrictions
Compensation and Benefits	Health insurance		Employee Retirement and Income Security Act	Minimum wage laws
Labor and Employee Relations			National Labor Relations Act	
Working Environment and Conditions	Employee participation/ involvement	Workers' compensation taxes	Hazardous substances communications rules	Safety and health standards

vise policies and practices for coping with government regulations and for working with government representatives to achieve their underlying policy objectives. These processes embody the essence of the often-touted goals of overcoming the adversarial relations between business and government and increasing business-government cooperation.

Overview of Federal Strategies

Role of the Free Market

As noted, the United States traditionally has promoted free enterprise with limited government intervention. For example, Table 12-1 lists several issues that are subject to legislation in most European countries, but left to market forces and private decision-making in the United States. These include plant closings, health insurance benefits, employee participation rights through work councils or similar forums, and decisions to discharge employees. In the absence of specific federal legislation on these issues, the private contractual relationships between employers and employees are circumscribed by the common law and specific provisions of civil and criminal laws.

Improving Market Performance

Economists who specialize in government regulation have argued that government intervention is justified when markets fail to produce efficient solutions. Sometimes market failure derives from a lack of adequate information. Other times market failure occurs when private decision makers fail to consider the costs borne by society (or a specific subsegment thereof) as a result of discrete market-based decisions. Alternately, the peculiar nature of public goods can cause market failure: Public goods benefit all consumers equally, but because no individual party is sufficiently motivated to produce them in the absence of equitable cost-sharing mechanisms, the free market usually will not provide these goods or services (the classic example of such a good is a lighthouse).

When one or more of these conditions holds, the solution most economists prefer is government intervention geared toward correcting the market's imperfections. For example, if adequate information is unavailable about certain health hazards, the government can sponsor research to produce the information needed and disseminate it to workers, unions, employers, and the general public. In cases where eliminating market imperfections is unfeasible, economists may recommend adopting policies that create incentives for private decision makers to behave in ways that will attain the desired outcomes. Workers' compensation and unemployment compensation taxes are examples of this approach. Employers are taxed at a rate that reflects their injury and layoff experiences, which gives them an incentive to minimize these experiences and lower their tax liabilities. The process requires no direct government involvement in organizational decision-making or government inspection of compliance with a given performance standard. Employers are left to choose the optimal strategy for minimizing their costs by investing in injury and/or layoff reducing practices.

The theory behind this regulatory strategy is that employers will invest in such practices to the point where the marginal costs of additional investments equal the marginal benefits achieved (costs foregone) from reduced injuries and/or layoffs. The obvious public policy problem associated with this approach is how to set tax rates and levels high enough to compensate for the costs of injuries or spells of unemployment. Neither workers' compensation nor unemployment compensation taxes escape this difficulty. In fact, it is unclear whether it would ever be politically feasible to set tax rates in this fashion. Finally, only certain public policy issues are amenable to this type of tax incentive or market correction approach. Many issues require a more active government role.

Regulating Decision-Making Processes

When intervention in the employment relationship is required, the United States government has tended to favor the establishment of equitable rules of the game by encouraging the private parties in the employment relationship to create solutions tailored to their own situations. Specific legislation of this type often emerges when government representatives find an imbalance of power in the employment relationship.

The National Labor Relations Act (NLRA) is a prime example of this approach. The NLRA does not dictate the terms of settlement between management and labor, for example, but establishes the rules of conduct governing the rights of each party. Similarly, the Employee Retirement and Income Security Act does not guarantee every employee a pension, but instead seeks to establish standards protecting the pension rights of individuals who have been promised a pension by their employers. Two more recent examples of this approach are the Jobs Partnership and Training Act and the Occupational Safety and Health Administration (OSHA). Among numerous other items, the latter's regulations govern the rights of workers to be informed of toxic substances to which they may be exposed in the workplace.

Regulating Outcomes

The federal government always has been reluctant to intervene directly in substantive outcomes of the employment relationship, although this type of regulation has increased steadily over time, particularly between 1960 and 1980. Between 1960 and 1975, for example, the number of substantive regulations governing employment relationships that were administered or enforced by the Department of Labor more than tripled, from 43 to 134 (Dunlop, 1976). It was during that era that Title VII of the 1964 Civil Rights Act took effect, significantly expanding the role of the federal government in promoting and enforcing equal employment opportunity. The federal regulatory role in occupational safety and health began in 1970 with passage of the Occupational Safety and Health Act (OSHA). These and similar regulations signaled a move away from the view that the labor market can produce desirable employment conditions simply as a result of the government-established economic incentives or collective bargaining rules. The more recent, more direct strategy of government intervention comes closer to mandating the specific standards to be met by employers and labor organizations.

Since the late 1970s, government regulations affecting employment have not expanded much. The Reagan administration since 1981 has cut back the resources for enforcing existing regulations. These developments may represent only a short-run deviation from a longer-term trend toward a more active governmental role. Or, they may represent a lasting pattern in which private decision makers are expected to internalize public policy objectives and take responsibility for their implementation, with the government assuming a more consultative or passive role. It remains to be seen which of these interpretations will prevail.

For management, it can be dangerous to speculate on the future direction of the United States government's labor and human resource policies. It can be even more dangerous for firms to establish policies or practices based on such political forecasts. Managers, however, need to develop a stable set of policies and practices for managing human resource issues of interest to both their firms and the society. These policies should be responsive to the interests of the firm, its employees, and the government's public policy objectives; they also must be able to withstand variations in the political philosophies and enforcement strategies of different political leaders.

As our discussion turns to the management of health, safety, and equal employment opportunity, we emphasize two themes: first, how managers adapt to public policy regulations, and second, how they supplement these regulations through internal organizational policies and practices that suit the needs of the firm and its employees.

Health and Safety

The responsibility for health and safety in the workplace is shared by managers, government officials, labor unions, supervisors, and individual workers. It is a highly visible arena for examining the extent to which the efforts of these various parties complement each other or become tangled in a web of adversarial relationships.

The magnitude of the health and safety challenge is clear. Each year, between four and five thousand workers are killed on the job, more than five million are injured, and approximately forty million workdays are lost due to on-the-job injuries or illnesses. Moreover, these safety statistics may represent only a small percentage, for no reliable data exist on the number of occupational illnesses and deaths due to exposures to toxic substances in the workplace. For years some occupational health professionals have estimated an annual one-hundred thousand deaths due to occupational illnesses. No consensus emerges, however, around a single number because of disagreements over the definition of occupational illness. The following example illustrates this point.

It has been well known for some time that exposure to asbestos in the workplace increases the probability of lung cancer (Gunderson and Swinton, 1981), and that cigarette smokers have a higher probability of contracting lung cancer. Workers exposed to asbestos who smoke are significantly more likely to develop cancer than similarly exposed workers who do not smoke. One study (Reasons, Ross, and Paterson, 1981) estimated that asbestos workers who do *not* smoke are *eight* times as likely to develop lung cancer than the general unexposed population, but exposed workers who *do* smoke are *ninety-two* times as likely to contract this disease. The question becomes, who should be counted in the occupational disease and fatality figures — all asbestos workers or only nonsmoking asbestos workers? The measurement problem is made more complex by the long latency period of many occupational diseases. For example, it normally takes ten to thirty years for asbestos-related diseases to be detected.

Regardless of the measurement problems, it is clear that the rapid rate at which new chemicals and substances of yet unknown effects are being introduced to the workplace will increase the necessity of reducing the risks of occupational diseases and coping with the consequences of past exposures. A long-standing debate rages over the responsibilities of chemical suppliers and/or purchasers for investigating the effects of exposures to new substances, and over the rights of workers to be informed of the contents and risks associated with such substances in the workplace (Ashford and Caldort, 1983).

Causes and Remedies

Some disagreement is evident in the safety and health literature about whether the preponderance of injuries are caused by the unsafe acts of workers or by unsafe working conditions and environmental hazards. The controversy arose from a study carried out in the 1960s by Hindrich (see Hindrich, Peterson, and Roos, 1980), who reviewed 12,000 insurance claims and 63,000 accident records and concluded that 83 percent of the accidents were caused primarily by unsafe acts, and 10 percent were due to unsafe conditions. Since that study, four separate studies have found that the distribution of causes is more evenly divided (Hagglund, 1979), supporting a general conclusion that both factors are significant contributors to injuries.

Table 12-2 shows that injury rates vary widely across industries, reflecting variations in the hazards associated with different types of work. At the other extreme, an examination of the accident data for specific companies often shows that the probability of injury varies considerably across workers doing similar jobs. New and low-seniority workers tend to have higher accident rates than their more experienced colleagues. At the same time, injury rates tend to increase with age (Hagglund, 1966).

It seems evident from this research that a comprehensive strategy for improving safety and health performance must address causal forces embedded in both the work environment and worker behavior. Further, although safety is a more tangible, visible, and measurable phenomenon, occupational health issues may pose the bigger, more complex challenge and require greater government, management, and union attention in the future. With this in mind, we explore strategies that each of these actors has followed in recent years regarding safety and health in the workplace.

Government Policy

Since passage of the Occupational Safety and Health Act in 1970, OSHA, the administration responsible for the act's enforcement, has been one of the most visible and controversial governmental agencies.

TABLE 12-2   Occupational Injury and Illness Incidence Rates by Industry Division, 1982

Industry	Incidence Rates per 100 Full-time Workers[1]			
	Total Cases[2]	Lost Work Day Cases	Nonfatal Cases Without Lost Days	Lost Work Days
Private sector[3]	7.7	3.5	4.2	58.7
Agriculture, forestry, and fishing[3]	11.8	5.9	5.9	86.0
Mining[4]	10.5	5.4	5.0	137.3
Construction	14.6	6.0	8.6	115.7
Manufacturing	10.2	4.4	5.8	75.0
Transportation and public utilities	8.5	4.9	3.6	96.7
Wholesale and retail trade	7.2	3.1	4.1	45.5
Wholesale trade	7.1	3.4	3.7	52.1
Retail trade	7.2	2.9	4.3	42.6
Finance, insurance, and real estate	2.0	.9	1.1	13.2
Services	4.9	2.3	2.6	35.8

[1]The incidence rates represent the number of injuries and illnesses, or lost workdays per 100 full-time workers and were calculated as: (N/EH) × 200,000, where:

  N = number of injuries and illnesses, or lost workdays
  EH = total hours worked by all employees during calendar year
  200,000 = base for 100 full-time equivalent workers (working 40 hours per week, 50 weeks per year).

[2]Includes fatalities. Because of rounding, the difference between the total and the sum of the rates for lost workday cases and nonfatal cases without lost workdays may not reflect the fatality rate.

[3]Excludes farms with fewer than 11 employees.

[4]Data for some independent contractors who perform services or construction on mining sites are also included.

Source: Bureau of Labor Statistics, U.S. Department of Labor.

(See Box 12-1 for a summary of the act.) Employers have criticized OSHA for overzealous enforcement of often frivolous safety standards (the most famous was a regulation, rescinded by the Carter administration in the late 1970s, governing the appropriate height of toilet seats). The labor movement has criticized OSHA for having an inadequate inspection force and being slow to develop new standards governing toxic substances known to be prevalent in the workplace. Most recently, labor has criticized the Reagan administration for reversing or relaxing earlier regulations, for placing too much reliance on abatement cost considerations in issuing new standards, and for abandoning government's general responsibilities as an advocate of worker rights and interests.

Economists, too, have criticized the approach toward regulation embodied in the act and its enforcement. Reliance on the enforcement of numerous specific standards via OSHA inspections is considered an inefficient system for improving the performance of the private market.

BOX 12-1
Overview of the Occupational Safety and Health Act of 1970

Coverage

All federal agencies and private employers engaged in interstate commerce. Excludes self-employed, farmers who employ only members of their immediate family, and other workplaces not covered by federal statutes.

Administration

Occupational Safety and Health Administration (OSHA) within the U.S. Department of Labor. OSHA's purposes are to:

Encourage employers and employees to reduce workplace hazards and to implement new or improve existing safety and health programs;

Establish rights and responsibilities for employers and employees for achieving better safety and health conditions;

Maintain record-keeping and reporting systems for monitoring job-related injuries and illnesses;

Develop and enforce mandatory safety and health standards;

Provide for development, evaluation, and approval of state occupational safety and health programs.

Standards

The *General Duty* standard provides that employers "must furnish . . . a place of employment which is free from recognized hazards that cause or are likely to cause death or serious physical harm to employees."

Specific standards covering a wide variety of equipment, toxic substance exposure levels, and work practices are issued for general industry, maritime, construction, and agricultural establishments.

Inspections

OSHA has the authority to enter and inspect establishments to determine if the employer is in compliance with the Act. A 1978 U.S. Supreme Court decision (*Marshall v. Barlow's, Inc.*) requires OSHA to obtain an adminstrative search warrant from a federal magistrate before entering the workplace except in cases of imminent danger to workers' lives or where the employer gives consent to enter and inspect. Because OSHA's inspection staff can visit only a minute fraction of the five million workplaces covered, it generally allocates its inspection resources in the following order of priority:

1. Imminent danger situations (usually based on complaints)
2. Catastrophes and fatality follow-up investigations
3. Employee complaints
4. High-hazard general schedule inspections
5. Reinspections as follow-ups to serious violations

Source: Adapted from *All About OSHA*, U.S. Department of Labor, Occupational Safety and Health Administration, 1980.

Citations and Penalties

Nonserious violations: less than $1,000 for each
Serious violations: $300 to 1,000 for each
Repeated violations: up to $10,000
Willful violations: up to $10,000 for each and possible imprisonment if
death of an employee results

Employer Responsibilities

General duty to provide workplace free from recognized hazards and in
compliance with OSHA standards and regulations
Inform employees of OSHA and keep, post, and provide access to OSHA
records and standards upon request
Provide and maintain safe tools and equipment
Cooperate with OSHA inspectors, allow authorized employee
representatives to accompany inspectors during walkaround, and pay
employees for time spent on inspections
Not to discriminate against employees for exercising their rights under
the act

Employer Rights

Seek advice and consultation from OSHA
Appeal OSHA citations to the Occupational Safety and Health Review
Commission and then to the federal courts
Request a variance from a standard by demonstrating that an
alternative method of compliance is equally effective

Employee Responsibilities

Comply with all applicable OSHA standards and cooperate with OSHA
inspectors
Follow employer safety and health rules, wear protective equipment,
report hazardous conditions to the supervisor, and report promptly
any on-the-job injury or illness to the employer

Employee Rights

No discrimination for exercising rights under the Act such as
complaining to an employer, union, or OSHA about a safety or health
hazard, filing a safety or health grievance, participating in a safety
and health committee or union activity relating to safety and health,
or participating in OSHA conferences, inspections, or hearings
Review copies of OSHA standards, rules, toxic substance data, or
personal medical records an employer may have on file, observe any
monitoring or measuring of hazardous substances and request
information from the employer, OSHA, or the National Institute for
Occupational Safety and Health on hazardous substances in the
workplace
Have name withheld from the employer for any written complaint
submitted to OSHA

Instead, some economists would prefer to shift OSHA's emphasis from safety standards to health standards, from enforcement via inspection to greater dissemination of information to workers and managers, and from the setting of standards to the creation of stronger economic incentives or "injury taxes" (Smith 1976). Finally, economists from the U.S. Office of Management and the Budget (OMB) have long urged OSHA to make more explicit use of cost/benefit analyses when setting standards.

Safety and health professionals within firms generally have welcomed the added influence they have gained in managerial decision-making because of OSHA. However, some also have argued that the detailed regulations omit the real causes of injuries and illnesses, and therefore divert management's attention and resources from problem solving and policy development to compliance and reporting.

Since 1970, various OSHA administrations have responded to these diverse criticisms in a number of ways. Approximately one thousand specific safety standards were dropped in 1978 because they were unnecessary, obsolete, or unworkable. Inspection targeting policies, whereby OSHA inspections focus on firms and industries with above average accident rates, were implemented during the Carter Administration and continued in the Reagan years. More resources have been devoted to generating information, training union and management industrial hygienists and other health professionals, and expanding the role of state and federal government consultative services. Various proposals have encouraged voluntary compliance, offering employers the option of establishing comprehensive safety and health policies and labor-management safety and health committees in return for the promise not to inspect the employer's facilities. So far, however, few employers have shown an interest in participating. For example, the Reagan administration offered three different types of voluntary compliance programs, but could boast only twenty-two employer participants after a year.

One of the biggest challenges OSHA faces is staying current with health and safety hazards as new technologies emerge or new substances are introduced into production processes. The dynamics of technological change and the development of new processes probably will keep OSHA in the limelight and will afford the agency ample opportunity to experiment with alternative strategies for fulfilling its responsibilities.

When the law was first passed, few offices or factories used video display terminals (VDTs). Even less knowledge existed about their potential health hazards. The widespread introduction of VDTs in recent years has produced controversy over radiation exposure, eye and back strain, and emotional stress associated with prolonged work with these machines. Should OSHA set standards for VDT equipment or its use? Should this be left to collective bargaining, employer policies, and the private market? Is there enough knowledge to know what to do? (Some of these questions are addressed in greater detail in Chapter 3.)

Union Strategy on Health and Safety

United States trade unions historically have followed a three-pronged strategy for dealing with the safety and health needs of their members: (1) lobbying for the passage and enforcement of state and federal legislation; (2) negotiating collective bargaining provisions that protect workers against and/or compensate workers for the risks associated with hazardous work; and (3) establishing joint union-management plant committees to deal with safety and health issues on a continuing basis. Union activity recently has increased in all three of these areas. The labor movement was the driving force in lobbying for the passage of the Occupational Safety and Health Act, and continues to be the most aggressive lobbyist for the rigorous enforcement and administration of the act. Also, since 1970 the number of safety and health provisions in collective bargaining agreements has rapidly expanded. Table 12-3 summarizes the types of provisions currently found

TABLE 12-3   Collective Bargaining Provisions on Safety and Health

	Percentage in All Major Contracts	Percentage in Manufacturing Industry Contracts	Percentage in Mining Industry Contracts
Some provision on safety[a]	82	87	100
General statement of responsibility[a]	54	64	75
Company to comply with laws[a]	27	25	58
Company to provide safety equipment[a]	46	51	100
Company to provide first aid[a]	20	23	42
Physical examination[a]	30	30	83
Hazardous work provisions[a]	25	25	58
Accident investigations[a]	17	23	58
Safety committees[a]	45	57	83
Dissemination of safety information to employees[b]	16	18	38
Dissemination of safety issues to union[b]	19	21	44
Employees to comply with safety rules[b]	47	50	67
Right of inspection by union or employees safety committees[b]	20	30	56
Wage differentials for hazardous work[b]	15	6	6

[a]Source: *Collection Bargaining Negotiations and Contracts*, May 26, 1983, Bureau of National Affairs, Vol. 2, Section 95.

[b]Source: *Major Collective Bargaining Agreements: Safety and Health Provisions*, BLS Bulletin #1425-16 (Washington, D.C., 1976).

in bargaining agreements and the frequency of these provisions in agreements in the mining industry. A comparison of survey data collected in 1970 and 1983 by the Bureau of National Affairs (BNA) indicates the rate of growth of these provisions. By 1983, 82 percent of the contracts included in the survey had some provision for safety and health. This compares to 65 percent of the contracts in the 1970 survey. The number of safety and health committees also increased from 31 percent to 45 percent. The data in Table 12-3 suggest that safety committees are more frequent in manufacturing than in nonmanufacturing firms and, not surprisingly, most frequent in the hazardous mining industry.

The growth in union activity concerning health and safety can be traced to the late 1960s when unions began reacting to increased worker consciousness about occupational injuries and illnesses. The generalized increase in lobbying, bargaining, and joint committee activities also reflected a recognition among union leaders that its three strategies were mutually interdependent. For example, safety and health have always been issues of moderate importance to American workers, but for the majority covered under bargaining agreements, safety has not been of high enough priority to sustain the pressure of a strike. Partly this is due to the high variations in the degree of exposure to unsafe working conditions among different workers in the same bargaining unit.

The diversity of exposure and interest was documented in a 1977 nationwide Quality of Employment Survey. Only 17 percent of hourly wage earners indicated that they would be willing to trade a 10 percent increase in wages for improved safety and health conditions in their jobs. Safety and health ranked eighth among eleven alternative job improvements that workers were asked to rank according to preference for trade-offs. Union members on average were slightly more willing to make this trade-off than nonunion workers. In contrast, workers who indicated they were exposed to above-average job hazards were considerably more willing to make the trade-off. Among this group, approximately 42 percent were willing to forego a 10 percent wage increase for improved safety and health conditions. Thus, unions seeking to improve safety and health only via the collective bargaining process faced the dilemma of having some of their members extremely concerned about these issues, while the majority were unwilling to bear the cost of a strike to achieve significant gains along these lines.

Consequently, unions at the workplace turned to their second strategy: forming safety and health committees to deal with issues continually during the term of the contract. Safety and health committees have been included in a number of collective bargaining contracts since World War II, but most union officials have been skeptical of the potential of union-management committees of all kinds, including safety and health committees. (See Box 12-2 for a summary of the results of a study of the effectiveness of these committees.) Before passage of the Occupational Safety and Health Act, union leaders re-

BOX 12-2
Operational Features and Effectiveness of Union-Management Safety and Health Committees

The most difficult problem that the joint safety and health committees have is maintaining their continuity. This is an age-old problem for all joint union management committee efforts. In our study we found a wide variation in the survival rate and the frequency of committee meetings. Most committees, it should be noted, do survive on paper. We found no examples of unions and employers removing a clause providing for safety and health committees out of their contracts. On the other hand, a good number of the committees simply failed to meet frequently enough to have any significant effect. For example, the standard contract provision normally calls for monthly meetings, yet about 45 percent of the committees in our sample failed to meet that frequently. A full 18 percent had not met at all in the previous six months. We found the committees that were most effective in staying active over time were ones that (1) combined the monthly meeting with a walk-around inspection of the plant a day or two prior to the meeting, (2) kept written minutes of committee recommendations, (3) spent some time at each meeting going over old committee recommendations and reviewing progress made on implementing them, (4) had a diverse array of skills and sections of the plant represented within the union group on the committee, (5) had first-line supervisors on the committee, (6) had management safety representatives with sufficient authority to make decisions, and (7) had a regular procedure for reporting the results of committee recommendations to both the rank and file workers and to top management.

Union-management committees are often described as problem solving cooperative efforts. We found, however, that these safety and health committees could better be described as a mixture between negotiating and problem-solving ventures. Those committees that were most successful were ones where union representatives were willing and able to exert pressure for action (often by pointing out the consequences of failing to work effectively through the joint committee). Here is where the pressure of using the procedures in the Act has an important role to play in ensuring that joint committees are effective. We also discovered that these joint committees served as supplements to the changes that the Act and its enforcement were bringing out in these plants. For example, the effect of the law was much more important than the recommendations of these committees in influencing capital investments in new equipment or plant renovations. The committees, on the other hand, played a key role in monitoring general housekeeping, fire protection, materials handling, and environmental problems (e.g., heat, air, dust, coal). This finding reinforced our view that safety and health committees are only one small component of a comprehensive or integrated strategy for delivering safety and health improvements at the workplace. It would be a mistake to believe that these committees can operate in isolation from an effective law and a comprehensive management safety and health program.

Source: Summary of key findings from Thomas Kochan, David B. Lipsky, and Lee Dyer, *The Effectiveness of Union Management Safety and Health Committees* (Kalamazoo, Mich.: The W. E. Upjohn Institute for Employment Research, 1977). Reprinted by permission.

ported that employees did not take such committees seriously because they had no effective sanctions against their employers' failure to implement committee suggestions (Kochan, Lipsky, and Dyer, 1977).

Consequently, the labor movement turned to the passage of federal legislation to provide a more effective framework for strengthening their efforts in the workplace. The unions believed that federal laws not only would provide the standards and enforcement that were lacking under the prior state-by-state legislative approach, but also would help unions at the local level to improve safety and health contract provisions and gain a stronger management commitment to joint committees.

Employer Health and Safety Policies

Effective employer safety and health policies in an environment characterized by comprehensive government regulation and intensive labor union interest requires the coordination of efforts at all three levels of the employment relationship: strategic, functional, and workplace.

Strategic-Level Considerations.

The highest level of management is crucial to safety and health policies for the same reason top management is important to all other human resource management functions: It determines the importance of, organizational commitment to, and resources for safety and health policies. Without strong top management commitment to improving safety and health performance, lower-level line and staff managers will not give these issues the priority or attention needed to sustain effective practices. In addition, top management assumes a key role in deciding the appropriate strategy for relating to government and/or union efforts to improve safety and health. Top management can encourage active cooperation with OSHA, unions, and employee groups, or it can hold these groups at arm's length and do only what is necessary to comply with its legal obligations.

Again, as with other policies, top management must decide how much weight to give safety and health criteria when making strategic decisions, such as investing in new equipment and machinery. For example, the Tennessee Valley Authority (TVA) has an explicit policy of annually reviewing its capital budgeting plans against a list of capital improvement priorities drawn up by its safety and health engineers. The TVA goes further than most organizations by having safety and health professionals review its major engineering designs before management's approval. These reviews show how top management's commitment to safety and health can be translated into standard, tangible policies and actions.

Functional-Level Considerations.

Safety and health professionals traditionally have not occupied positions of high status or influence in management. The external threat of OSHA enforcement, however, has served to upgrade their status and influence because of the increased potential for noncompliance penalties and public exposure. Field studies of management and union practices have found that OSHA's presence has strengthened the role of management health and safety professionals (Kochan, Lipsky, and Dyer, 1977; Freedman, 1981).

OSHA also has provided the impetus for developing more comprehensive organizational data on safety and health experiences. As a by-product of OSHA's record-keeping requirements, an increasing number of firms have developed standard data bases that link accident and illness data with production, personnel, and other management information systems. These data allow for analysis of individual and organizational factors that cause variations in accident and illness rates and in costs across locations and over time. Maintaining these data systems can be valuable for diagnosing the causes of safety and health problems, for experimenting and evaluating potential remedies, and for analyzing the relationships between safety and health performance measures and various measures of organizational effectiveness. A recent study (Ichniowski, 1983), for example, found a significant negative relationship between accident rates and productivity across a sample of paper mills. The lost production in the mill with the worst accident record translated into an operating income of approximately 17 percent below its potential, had it performed at the median accident rate of all the mills. These data are needed to provide evidence for the often quoted but seldom documented adage that "safety pays."

Workplace-Level Considerations.   Achieving a safe, healthy work environment depends on the motivations and behavior of supervisors and workers. Accident data often show variations in accident rates across groups and individuals doing similar work. Data also show seasonal and time-of-day patterns of accidents. Knowledge of these variations is the first step toward their elimination. Unless good safety and health performance is rewarded, or poor performance punished, a wide variance probably will continue in the attention paid to safe work practices. Those supervisors and workers who place a high priority on safety probably will take the proper precautions, whereas the less conscientious will overlook precautions or will have insufficient knowledge or training to recognize potential hazards or dangerous practices. Consequently, adequate communication, reward systems, and training are essential workplace level components for a comprehensive safety and health policy. Finally, because motivation must be reinforced periodically in order to be maintained at high levels, safety awareness programs and bonus or incentive systems for meeting safety objectives form part of an ongoing, comprehensive safety and health program.

Conclusion

Clearly, we can never live or work in a risk-free environment, as resources for improving occupational safety and health conditions are limited. The task of management is to assure that sufficient public and private resources are devoted to achieve a level of safety and health that the public judges to be acceptable, that affected workers consider to be fair, and that firms and consumers find to be economically viable. Managers, labor representatives, and individual workers, in turn, need to complement the federal government's efforts to help achieve these objectives as efficiently as possible.

Equal Employment Opportunity

The median female full-time employee earns approximately 60 percent of her male counterpart. To eliminate underrepresentation of women in certain jobs and overrepresentation in others would require job changes by about 66 percent of the women employed in 441 occupations (U.S. Commission on Civil Rights, 1978; Blau and Hendricks, 1979). The unemployment rate for blacks and other minorities consistently has hovered around double the rate for whites since the 1960s, with only small, temporary cyclical deviations. On the other hand, there is strong evidence (see Table 12-4) that considerable progress has been made since 1964 in reducing the gaps in earnings, employment, and occupational status between blacks and whites (Freeman, 1978; Brown, 1981).

Although no one should interpret the above facts as conclusive evidence of the current magnitude of employment discrimination against women and minorities, the numbers help underscore why equal employment opportunity (EEO) is among the most volatile and complex human resource management issues of our time. In this section, we outline the various laws and regulations that govern EEO, summarize the evidence on their effects, and relate them to the management of EEO within organizations.

Federal Policies

The roots of EEO policy can be traced to the Fifth, Thirteenth, and Fourteenth Amendments to the U.S. Constitution which, respectively, provide for due process of law, abolish slavery, and ensure equal protection under the law. In 1941, as part of the nation's defense build-up, President Franklin Roosevelt signed Executive Order 8802 establishing the Fair Employment Practices Committee. Thereby, he began a policy of nondiscrimination among defense contractors and federal agencies; post-1960s legislation and executive orders have reinforced what he began by stating specific rules governing discrimination in employment.

Table 12-5 summarizes major EEO-related laws and executive orders. The Equal Pay Act of 1963 outlaws discrimination on the basis of sex and establishes the key standard that males and females must receive "equal pay for equal work." The most important, far-reaching, and comprehensive statute, however, is Title VII of the Civil Rights Act of 1964, which outlaws discrimination on the basis of race, sex, national origin, color, and religion. In 1967, the Age Discrimination Act was

TABLE 12-4 Evidence on the Black Economic Progress Since 1964

(1) *Has the income gap between nonwhites and whites narrowed as measured by the ratio of black to white earnings, and has the rate of reduction in these earnings ratios accelerated? The answer to both questions is "yes," with the biggest improvements between 1964 and 1976 for younger, more educated, and female blacks.*

Group and Measure	Earnings Ratios (Nonwhites/Whites)				Changes in Earnings Ratios	
	1959	1964	1969	1976	1949–59	1964–75
Median wages/salaries of all workers	.58	.59	.67	.70	0.6	0.9
Median wages/salaries workers age 20–24	.64	.70	.82	.82	−0.2	1.3
Median earnings for young men by education						
High school graduates	.70			.77	−0.3	0.4
College graduates	.70			.94	0.3	1.4
Median wages/salaries of females	.53	.58	.79	1.01	1.8	3.6

(2) Have blacks and other minorities made progress in penetrating higher status occupations as measured by the percentage of nonwhites in various occupations to the percentage of whites in these occupations and has the rate of change in these ratios increased? The evidence suggests that nonwhites have made progress in penetrating higher status jobs since 1964.

Relative Penetration into Selected Jobs	Position				Annual Change in Position	
	1950	1964	1969	1977	1950–64	1964–77
Professional, male	.39	.45	.48	.64	0.4	1.5
Managers, male	.22	.22	.28	.43	0.0	1.6
Managers, male college graduates only	.42	.41	.49	.72	0.0	2.4
Craftsmen, male	.41	.58	.68	.72	1.2	1.1
Professionals, female	.47	.60	.70	.89	0.9	2.2
Clericals, female	.15	.33	.55	.72	1.3	3.0

Source: Data derived from the U.S. Bureau of Labor Statistics and the Census of Population as reported in Richard B. Freeman, "Black Economic Progress Since 1964: Who Has Gained and Why," National Bureau of Economic Research, Working Paper No. 282, November 1978, Tables 1 and 2, 8–9.

passed, outlawing discrimination in employment decisions for those between the ages of 40 and 70. Subsequent amendments to this act banned mandatory retirement before the age of 70 for most employees. The major exceptions are tenured college professors and executives earning more than $27,000 per year.

TABLE 12-5 Major Equal Employment Opportunity Statutes and Executive Orders

Laws or Orders	Human Resource Management Requirements
1. Equal Pay Act of 1963	Prohibits discrimination on basis of sex — requires "equal pay for equal work."
2. Title VII of the Civil Rights Acts of 1964 as amended in 1972	Prohibits employers engaged in interstate commerce, unions, and employment agencies from using race, sex, national origin, color, or religion as a basis for employment practices. A 1979 amendment made it illegal to discriminate against pregnant women because of childbirth-related medical reasons.
3. Age Discrimination Act of 1967 as amended in 1978	Prohibits discrimination in employment on the basis of age for those between the ages of 40 and 70. Mandatory retirement rules are illegal for all but tenured faculty and executives earning more than $27,000 per year.
4. Executive Order 11246 as modified by Executive Order 11375	Requires employers with government contracts to refrain from discrimination in employment and to take affirmative action to end any underutilization of women or minorities. Work-force analysis data must be collected and reported along with plans (e.g., recruitment, training, and promotion) for remedying underutilization where it exists.
5. Vocational Rehabilitation Act of 1973	Prohibits discrimination of handicapped people and requires affirmation of government contractors. Employers must make reasonable accommodations to remove obstacles that would keep handicapped workers from performing jobs for which they are qualified.
6. Veterans Readjustment Act of 1974	Government contractors must develop affirmative action plans to hire Vietnam-era veterans.

These EEO statutes are accompanied by several statutes and an important executive order of the president, which establish *affirmative action* requirements for firms holding federal government contracts. Affirmative action implies a duty to refrain from discrimination and to take specific actions to achieve a more equitable representation of women, minorities, and other protected groups in an organization's work force. Executive Order 11246 requires federal contractors to develop affirmative action plans and file them with the Office of Federal Contract Compliance (OFCC), an agency within the U.S. Department of Labor. An affirmative action plan consists of three key components: (1) an analysis of the *availability* of minorities and females in the relevant labor markets in which the firm operates; (2) statistical data showing the *utilization* of these workers across the various job categories within the firm; and (3) a plan that specifies *targets and timetables* for redressing underutilization of these covered workers. Similar affirmative action requirements for government contractors grow out of the Vocational Rehabilitation Act, which requires the removal of obstacles that impede disabled workers from access to jobs they are otherwise qualified to perform, and out of the Veterans Readjustment Act, which requires contractors to have an affirmative action plan for hiring Vietnam-era veterans.

Administration and Enforcement

The responsibility for administering and adjudicating these laws and regulations is shared by the Equal Employment Opportunity Commission (EEOC), an independent agency of the federal government; the OFCC within the Labor Department, which is responsible for monitoring compliance of government contractors; and the Justice Department, which is responsible for enforcing a broad range of civil rights laws outside the employment arena (e.g., fair housing, voting rights). The Justice Department also has filed suits against (or in support of) state and local governments, which are outside the jurisdiction of the EEOC.

Since 1978, the EEOC has been the leading federal agency for EEO matters. It is responsible for administering the Equal Pay and the Age Discrimination acts as well as Title VII. Many state and local governments also have EEO legislation and ordinances that are enforced by their own fair employment practices agencies.

The enforcement and adjudication processes that these agencies use can be long and slow and can end in charges being dropped, in the imposition of penalties and back-pay awards, or in negotiated consent decrees. The ultimate penalty for government contractors found guilty of discrimination is cancellation of existing contracts or disbarment from future bidding on government contracts. This penalty rarely has been imposed. Only twenty-five companies were disbarred between 1965 and 1980, and none between 1980 and 1984. Although the EEOC was given enforcement powers in 1972 and has litigated a number of cases, it has also used negotiations and consent decrees to narrow or resolve disputes between parties.

Consent decrees are negotiated settlements between employers and the federal government. Where a union is present, it also can be a party to the negotiation of the agreement, as in the case of the steel industry consent decree (Ichniowski, 1983), or it can choose to stay out of the negotiations. These agreements typically are approved and overseen by a federal judge or by a special court-appointed master or mediator. Consent decrees represent one attempt by the federal government to apply the well-developed industrial relations techniques of negotiation, mediation, and third-party adjudication as alternatives to protracted litigation.

Although the most publicized parts of major consent decrees are the back-pay awards firms agree to make, these agreements are equally important for the changes in personnel policies they introduce. Wallace (1982;16) noted, for example, that major decrees have provided for such things as job evaluation studies (NBC decree), modification of personnel assessment techniques (Merrill Lynch decree), across-the-board adjustment in base salaries and revision of seniority, training, and transfer policies (Steel Industry decree). The 1973 AT&T consent decree, which instituted affirmative action in this telecommunications conglomerate, has served as a model for later decrees. Its major provisions and accomplishments are summarized in Box 12-3.

Not all cases can be resolved through negotiations or consent decrees. Indeed, EEO litigation has been a growth industry for lawyers, and, because of the growing use of statistical analyses in these cases, for social scientists with expertise in quantitative analysis. A sampling of major court decisions shaping the evolution of EEO law is in Box 12-4.

In attempting to prove or refute a charge of discrimination, both plaintiffs and defendants increasingly have chosen to introduce complex analyses of statistical data. The introduction of statistical data into these court proceedings has made EEO litigation one of the most complex legal and analytical tasks confronting human resource management professionals. The models used are variants of human capital (Mincer, 1962) theories of wage determination. These models use multiple regression analysis to estimate an earnings equation that controls for measures of workers' education, experience, training, and job-level or job-evaluation scores. The unexplained portion of the variation in wages is attributed to the effects of discrimination. The validity of this approach depends on the extent to which all legitimate determinants of wages are captured by the model.

Comparable Worth

The typical wage discrimination suit addresses one source of discrimination: unequal pay for people doing the same work. Recently, however, more attention has been given to the effects of discrimination caused by the sex stereotyping of jobs, that is, the segregation of women into occupations that typically pay less than male-dominated jobs. The controversy is about comparable worth.

Eleanor Holmes Norton, a former EEOC chairperson, has called comparable worth the most controversial EEO issue of the 1980s. The comparable worth criterion fundamentally attempts to modify the doctrine of "equal pay for equal work" (endorsed in the 1963 Equal Pay Act) by arguing that men and women should be paid equally for jobs of a *comparable nature and value* to the employer. This subtle but profound difference has generated a number of major disputes and court cases and remains an entirely unsettled area of EEO policy. So far, the EEOC has not endorsed the comparable worth concept, and the Justice Department under the Reagan administration has announced that it will actively oppose this doctrine in future court proceedings where it becomes a test issue.

BOX 12-3
The AT&T Consent Decree

The Consent Decree signed in January 1973 between the twenty-three operating companies of the American Telephone and Telegraph Company (AT&T)
and the federal agencies responsible for employment discrimination regulations and laws (EEOC, Department of Labor, and Department of Justice)
established a model for changing the internal labor market and enabled
women to move into jobs that had not previously been available to them.

The heart of the January 1973 Consent Decree, which lasted six years, was
AT&T's Model Affirmative Action Plan, Upgrading and Transfer Plan, and Job
Briefs and Qualifications. All jobs were classified into fifteen major categories
known as Affirmative Action Program Jobs. These AAP Jobs comprised groups
of jobs having similar content, opportunities, and wage rates. Then a
utilization analysis was made to determine where deficiencies existed for
women and minorities. Ultimate goals and intermediate targets for one-,
two-, and three-year time frames were set for the establishments of each of
the telephone operating companies. Under the modified seniority provisions
of the Transfer Plan, women in nonmanagement and noncraft jobs could
transfer to better-paying craft jobs on the basis of their operating company
net credited service (seniority). The "affirmative action override" was used to
promote women and minorities who met the basic qualifications
requirements into vacancies where members of their group were not
adequately represented. Thus, career ladders were publicized and relevant
labor pools were redefined.

By January 1979, when the decree ended, management had developed a
sophisticated model to track all of its employees (Goal 2); the unions had lost
their legal battle over whether the affirmative action override undermined
the seniority provisions of their collective bargaining contract, and the
utilization of women had improved significantly. For example, prior to the
Consent Decree, AAP Job category 10 (craft inside, semiskilled) had been an
entry-level job primarily for young males. In the restructured internal labor
market of the decree, operators, office clerical, and all predominantly female
occupations served as the relevant labor pool from which vacancies in the
craft jobs were filled.

Progress was uneven throughout the Bell System due to the severity of the
1974–1975 recession in some regions and to the introduction of technology,
which displaced a number of women, especially telephone operators.
Although there was a decrease in the number of women in the system and a
slight decline in their share of total employment, there was a noticeable shift
away from the traditional female occupations (clerical, operator,
administrative) into nontraditional jobs (management and crafts). The
number of women who had reached middle management and above (general
managers) had quadrupled, and women accounted for 59 percent of the
increase in all managerial jobs. The implementation of the upgrade and
transfer segments of the decree was mainly responsible for more than tripling
the number of women in craft jobs.

Source: Phyllis A. Wallace, "Increased Labor Force Participation of Women and
Affirmative Action," in Phyllis A. Wallace, *Women in the Workplace* (Boston: Auburn
House, 1982), 16–20. Reprinted by permission.

BOX 12-4
Key Court Decisions on Equal Employment Opportunity

Case	Decision
1971 a. *Griggs* v. *Duke Power*	An employer was prohibited from requiring a high school diploma or the passing of a standardized intelligence test as a condition of employment in or transfer to jobs when (1) neither standard is shown to be significantly related to job performance, (2) both requirements operate to disqualify black applicants at a substantially higher rate than white applicants, and (3) the jobs in question formerly had been filled only by white employees as part of a long-standing practice of giving preference to whites.
b. *Contractors Association of Eastern PA* v. *Secretary of Labor*	The court ruled that requiring contractors to achieve goals pertaining to minority employment was a proper remedy for low participation rates by minorities in construction. Further, this did not interfere with the National Labor Relations Act regulation of union hiring halls.
1974 *Alexander* v. *Gardner Denver Company*	Arbitrator's decision on a claim involving discrimination covered under Title VII of the Civil Rights Act does not preclude judicial review of the award nor does it preclude the employee from pursuing legal remedies through federal agencies or the federal court. A court will hear the case *de novo* and decide it on its merits and will give the arbitrator's decision whatever weight the court deems appropriate.
1977 *International Brotherhood of Teamsters* v. *United States*	Persons cannot be compensated (either through back pay or constructive seniority) for discrimination that occurred before the Civil Rights Act of 1964. Further, the routine administration of a bona fide seniority system is not unlawful after the act unless it is "the result of an intention to discriminate because of race . . . or national origin . . . ."
1979 *Weber* v. *Kaiser Aluminum*	A union and management could negotiate into the collective agreement an affirmative action plan that created a quota system for admitting black craftsmen to a training program.

| 1981 | *Gunther* v. *County of Washington* | Gave Title VII protection to claims of wage discrimination even if the jobs are not "equal" as the term is used under the Equal Pay Act of 1963. |
| 1984 | *Fire Fighters* v. *Stotts* | Exempted bona fide seniority systems governing layoffs from Title VII. The specific case involved the court overturning the use of an affirmative action plan established by the City of Memphis to protect low-seniority black firefighters from layoffs. Whether this decision will be interpreted broadly to make it illegal to establish affirmative action plans that modify previously established seniority provisions cannot be determined until the courts apply the ruling from this case to cases that arise in the future. |

Box 12-5 reports a landmark study of the use of comparable worth to restructure the compensation system covering employees of the state of Washington. The study produced recommendations that would cost the state an estimated $18 million to implement. The state initially refused to implement the recommendations, and the state employee's union filed a discrimination suit and received a favorable ruling in federal court. The case is now under appeal, but the state has implemented a new compensation plan that provides targeted salary increases, for certain job classifications, above the normal increases granted to state employees. These targeted increases are to be phased over a ten-year period to eliminate the salary differentials that violate the comparable worth standard.

Several issues in the comparable worth controversy strike at the heart of compensation theory and practice. Opponents of the use of comparable worth argue that no independently valid measure exists of the worth of a job, except the wages required by the supply-and-demand forces of the external marketplace. Job evaluation as typically used in industry is simply a means of creating a rational internal job and wage hierarchy that is linked to the external labor market through the wages of key jobs. Salaries for all other jobs are set according to these externally grounded key job salaries (Schwab, 1980).

The arguments against the development and use of comparable worth focus on two points. First, there are no workable definitions of the concept, nor administrative procedures capable of comparing the worth of jobs requiring *dissimilar* skills. People may disagree in their value judgments regarding the worth of nurses compared to plumbers, for example, but no accepted scientific procedure exists for comparing jobs requiring such disparate skills and training. Second, the substitution of some comparable worth criterion for valuing jobs would work

BOX 12-5
State of Washington Study of Comparable Worth

In the state of Washington, the state government employees' union requested that a study be undertaken, using job evaluation techniques, to compare jobs held mainly by men (for example, traffic guide, construction coordinator, electrician) with those held mainly by women (for example, secretary, clerk typist, nurse practitioner). The study found that for jobs rated equally by the job evaluation system, those held mainly by men were paid 20 percent more on the average than those held mainly by women: The difference occurred largely because the state's pay scales had been developed by using area wage surveys.

The Washington study utilized a "factor point analysis" of job content to determine comparable worth.

Initially, the study team selected "benchmark" classifications for evaluation. These benchmarks consisted of classifications that were "sex dominated" (classes were defined as male or female dominated if the respective classes consisted of 70 percent male or 70 percent female employees).

Using the guide charts prepared by the consultant, the team evaluated the 121 benchmark classifications by subjecting the selected questionnaires to a factor-point analysis of the knowledge and skills, mental demands, accountability, and working conditions required. A table of evaluations was established, ascribing points to the classifications evaluated. These points are the measurement of job content for the purpose of establishing comparable worth.

Using the points the team assigned to the classifications evaluated, the consultant analyzed the state's salary practices with respect to those classifications. The consultant concluded:

> The conclusion can be drawn that, based on the measured job content of the 121 classifications evaluated as part of this project, the tendency is for women's classes to be paid less than men's classes, for comparable job worth.
>
> Overall, comparing both salary systems, the disparity is approximately 20 percent. This degree of differences varies noticeably by salary system, by classification level, and by individual classification.

Source: *The Comparable Worth Issue,* Special Bureau of National Affairs Report, 1981, 46–47. Reprinted by permission.

---

against the value dictated by external market forces. In the end this would be counterproductive, because the result would be higher levels of unemployment among those competing for the upgraded jobs (Hildebrand, 1980).

Proponents of comparable worth argue that market-based wages are simply the result of decades of sex stereotyping and the segregation of women into low-paid jobs. Moreover, they argue that modifications of the job evaluation process, such as the approach used in the state of

Washington study, can contribute to an assessment of the extent of systematic undervaluation of jobs predominantly filled by women.

Whatever the outcome of this debate, three things are clear. First, no administrative procedure can ignore the workings of the external market. Second, the ultimate solution to discrimination because of sex-segregated occupations is to break down the barriers to occupational mobility and placement and thereby achieve a more equitable sex (and race) distribution across all jobs. Third, even if comparable worth proves to be found wanting in its present form for either legal or economic reasons, its proponents will achieve a partial victory. The issue of pay equity has been raised to the forefront of the debate over equal employment opportunity and compensation practice. The debate is forcing critical analyses, as well as some reform of internal wage structures, career ladders, and recruitment practices.

Effects of Federal EEO Policies

How have two decades of federal EEO policies affected the economic and employment status of women and minorities? Although the evidence is mixed (as usual) and the leading experts do not completely agree (as always), the preponderance of evidence suggests the following general conclusions. (For more detailed summaries of the evidence see Brown, 1981; Freeman, 1978; Blau, 1982; Leonard, 1983.)

1. The income and employment status of blacks and other minorities increased at a faster rate after 1964 than in previous decades. The strongest relative gains occurred for younger and more educated blacks and for black women. Some of this progress is due to a general rise in educational attainment among blacks and to the favorable economic growth rates of the 1960s and early 1970s. Younger and college-educated blacks did better than older and less-educated blacks. Another part of the relative improvement is due to affirmative action policies and their enforcement through employer and government contractor reporting, auditing, consent negotiations, and legislation. The most recent and best-designed study of the specific effects of the enforcement efforts of the OFCC and the EEOC supports this conclusion (Leonard, 1983).

2. Less progress is observed in the data on the status of women. Despite isolated examples of the movement of women into key public- and private-sector positions, neither the aggregate data on income differences nor those on occupational distributions showed significant change since the mid-1960s. Because women and minorities are disproportionately concentrated at lower seniority levels, they are especially vulnerable to the threats of layoffs and permanent displacement during recessions. Thus, although the data have not yet been analyzed, many experts fear that some of the progress made by minority workers in the 1970s was set back by the deep recession of 1981–83.

TABLE 12-6   Changes in Personnel Practices Due to EEO

	Percentage of Companies
Have *formal* EEO program	86
Include affirmative action plans (those subject to OFCCP regulations)	96
Have had investigation or other action under Title VII	63
Have made changes in selection procedures because of EEOC	60
testing procedures	39
revised job qualifications	31
application forms	30
recruiting techniques	19
Have special recruiting programs	
for all minority workers	69
for minorities in professional/managerial positions	58
Have programs to ensure EEO policies	
communications on EEO policy	95
follow-up personnel or EEO office	85
training sessions or EEO office	67
periodic publications of EEO results	48
EEO achievements included in performance appraisals	33
Have special training programs	
for entry-level jobs	16
for upgrading	24
for management positions	16

Source: Bureau of National Affairs Personnel Policies Forum, *Equal Employment Opportunity: Programs and Results,* BPF Survey No. 112, March 1976, as cited in Richard B. Freeman, "Black Economic Progress since 1964: Who Has Gained and Why?" National Bureau of Economic Research Working Paper No. 282, November 1978, 47.

3. As shown in Table 12-6 and discussed below, considerable evidence shows that government policies have changed many organizational human resource policies and practices. The long-term effects of public policies will depend on how these organizational changes are translated into expanded opportunities for women and minorities in the future.

Summary: Implications for Human Resource Management

The growth of a federal EEO policy has had a profound impact on the human resource management profession and has helped elevate it closer to top management. The potential costs of EEO adjudication, the increased consciousness of women and minorities of their rights, the continuing gaps between the income and employment status of women and minorities compared to white men, the sensitivity of discrimination as a political issue, and the growing demands for sophisticated data collection, analysis, and reporting all have contributed to the rise in status and influence of human resource professionals within the management hierarchy (Janger, 1977; Kochan and Cappelli, 1984). EEO regulations and guidelines have encouraged organizations to collect more extensive demographic data, to develop human resource models and plans, to use more comprehensive job evaluation techniques, to renegotiate and restructure seniority systems, to validate selection procedures, to expand training and career development, and to modify promotion criteria. Table 12-6 reports the numerous effects that federal EEO policy has had on a number of these and other human resource management practices. Many of the changes have been expensive for organizations to implement; yet, little doubt exists that they have upgraded the professional standards of the human resource management function.

Two points are worth future consideration. First, whether the influence that human resource management professionals gained from the pressures of government regulation and enforcement efforts in the first two decades of EEO policy will be maintained during the current period of less vigorous federal enforcement remains to be seen. Second, no one knows if top executives have internalized EEO values so that their organizations will continue to upgrade the status of women and minorities when enforcement is less vigorous.

Much of the progress women and minorities made in the 1960s and 1970s was due to a combination of favorable labor market conditions and explicit laws and orders from the legislative and executive branches of the federal government. The degree of progress in the 1980s, however, will depend on the combination of court rulings, state and local policies, top management's values, and human resource professionals' advocacy within their organizations. The outcomes, in turn, will depend on the pressure and support these actors receive from their ultimate constituents — the men and women who have a direct stake in the attainment of equal employment opportunity.

References

Ashford, Nicholas, and Charles G. Caldort, "Framework Provides Path Through Right-to-Know Law," *Occupational Health and Safety*, October 1983, 11–27.

Blau, Francine D., "Discrimination Against Women: Theory and Evidence," in William A. Darity, Jr., ed., *Labor Economics: Modern Views* (Boston: Nijhoff, 1982).

Blau, Francine D., and Wallace E. Hendricks, "Occupational Segregation by Sex: Trends and Prospects," *Journal of Human Resources*, 14, Spring 1979, 197–210.

Brown, Charles, "The Federal Attack on Labor Market Discrimination: The Mouse that Roared," National Bureau of Economic Research Working Paper No. 669, Cambridge, Mass., 1981.

Civil Rights Commission of the United States, *Civil Rights, Social Indicators of Equality for Minorities and Women* (Washington, D.C.: U.S. Government Printing Office, 1978).

Dunlop, John T., "The Limits of Legal Compulsion," in *Labor Law Journal*, Vol. 27, February 7, 1976.

Freedman, Audrey, *Industry Response to Health Risk* (New York: The Conference Board, 1981).

Freeman, Richard B., "Black Economic Progress Since 1964: Who Has Gained and Why?" National Bureau of Economic Research Working Paper No. 282, 1978.

Freeman, Richard B., "Public Policy and Employment Discrimination in the U.S.," National Bureau of Economic Research Working Paper No. 282, 1978.

Gunderson, Morley, and Katherine Swinton, "Collective Bargaining and Asbestos Dangers at the Workplace" (Ontario: Royal Commission on Asbestos, December 1981).

Hagglund, George, *Some Factors Contributing to Wisconsin's Occupational Injuries*, Ph.D. dissertation, University of Wisconsin, Madison, 1966.

———, "Approaches to Safety and Health Hazard Abatement," in Proceedings of the *Symposium for Labor Educators on Occupational Health and Safety*, School for Workers, University of Wisconsin, Madison, 1979.

Hildebrand, George, "The Market System," in E. Robert Livernash, ed., *Comparable Worth* (Washington, D.C.: The Equal Employment Advisory Council, 1980), 79–106.

Hindrich, Herbert, Dan Peterson, and Nestor Roos, *Industrial Accident Prevention*, 5th ed. (New York: McGraw-Hill, 1980).

Ichniowski, Casey, "Have Angels Done More? The Steel Industry Consent Decree," *Industrial and Labor Relations Review*, Vol. 36, January 1983, 182–93.

Janger, Alan, *The Personnel Function* (New York: The Conference Board, 1977).

Kochan, Thomas A., David B. Lipsky, and Lee Dyer, *The Effectiveness of Union-Management Safety and Health Committees* (Kalamazoo, Mich.: The W. E. Upjohn Institute for Employment Research, 1977).

Kochan, Thomas A., and Peter Cappelli, "The Transformation of the Industrial Relations and Personnel Function," in Paul Osterman, ed., *Internal Labor Markets* (Cambridge, Mass.: MIT Press, 1984), 133–61.

Leonard, Jonathan S., "Anti-Discrimination or Reverse Discrimination: The Impact of Changing Demographics," Title VII and Affirmative Action on Productivity, National Bureau of Economic Research Working Paper No. 1240, 1983.

Mincer, Jacob, "Labor Force Participation of Married Women," in *National Bureau of Economic Research: Aspects of Labor Economics* (Princeton, N.J.: Princeton University Press, 1962), 3–24.

Reasons, C. L., et al., *Assault on The Worker: Occupational Health and Safety in Canada* (Toronto: Butterworths, 1981).

Schwab, Donald P., "Job Evaluation and Pay Setting: Concepts and Practices," in E. Robert Livernash, ed., *Comparable Worth* (Washington, D.C.: The Equal Employment Advisory Council, 1980), 49–78.

Smith, Robert S., *The Occupational Safety and Health Act* (Washington, D.C.: The American Enterprise Institute, 1976).

Wallace, Phyllis A., "Increased Labor Force Participation of Women and Affirmative Action," in Phyllis A. Wallace, ed., *Women in the Workplace* (Boston: Auburn House, 1982), 1–26.

Suggested Readings

Freedman, Audrey, *Industry Response to Health Risk* (New York: The Conference Board, 1981).

Gold, Michael E., *A Dialogue on Comparable Worth* (Ithaca, N.Y.: ILR Press, Cornell University, 1983).

Gould, William B., *A Primer on American Labor Law* (Cambridge, Mass.: MIT Press, 1982).

Hammer, Willie, *Occupational Safety Management and Engineering* (Englewood Cliffs, N.J.: Prentice-Hall, 1981).

Livernash, E. Robert, *Comparable Worth* (Washington, D.C.: The Equal Employment Advisory Council, 1980).

McCulloch, Kenneth J., *Selecting Employees Safely Under the Law* (Englewood Cliffs, N.J.: Prentice-Hall, 1981).

Morris, Charles J., ed., *The Developing Labor Law* 2nd edition, (Washington, D.C.: Bureau of National Affairs, 1983).

Schlei, Barbara Lindemann and Paul Grossman, *Employment Discrimination Law* (Washington, D.C.: Bureau of National Affairs, 1983).

Smith, Arthur B., Jr., *Employment Discrimination Law: Cases and Materials* (New York: Bobbs-Merrill, 1976).

Wallace, Phyllis A., *Women, Minorities, and Employment Discrimination* (Lexington, Mass.: D. C. Heath, 1977).

Hidden Profitability in Safety

The following case illustrates that beyond humane considerations, adequate safety provisions also can be reflected directly in a company's or business unit's profits. At Boiler Corporation, these hidden advantages are explored through comparisons across business units within the organization and between the firm and various industry averages. Perhaps the most important theme of this case is its simplest one: Paying attention to the various diverse costs of poor safety conditions can and does pay off in profits and productivity.

CASE
Boiler Corporation

District managers in Boiler Corporation, Inc. were having some trouble adjusting to new profit-center rules and procedures that had been instituted the previous year. Under a new management, each of the districts was to become a full profit center and to be rewarded (or taxed) incrementally for performance above or below the average profits of the districts. The new cost-control and reporting measures were working well now that the five district managers had survived their initial shock and had been trained in basic accounting.

BACKGROUND

Boiler Corporation is a subsidiary of a multinational conglomerate, Conglom, Inc., which bought the company ten years ago. Boiler's main business is to install and service large heating systems in office buildings and other large structures. It is a unionized company with a long history of intense bargaining and a complicated contract with the Boiler and Heating Installation Union (BHIU). All union members are skilled and have participated in a formal apprenticeship program. The union maintains a ratio of one apprentice per fifteen journeymen.

Sam Spade, manager of the central district for six months, believed he had made some significant accomplishments in cutting costs and increasing productivity. He began a series of weekly half-hour meetings with his workers in groups of five to eight craftsmen with a leader, usually a foreman, presenting problems and suggestions. Several suggestions had brought substantial savings, and Spade expected that these savings would be reflected in the bonus his district would receive from corporate headquarters. He decided to distribute some of the bonus money among those who worked with him and formulated a plan for merit or productivity pay increase. This would not be built into salaries or wages, but would rather be a one-time merit increase, awarded with much fanfare.

One evening Spade spent three hours at the hospital awaiting the results of tests on an eye injury one of his craftsmen had sustained on the construction site. Although the injury was not serious, the man would be out of work collecting workers' compensation for at least two weeks. The injury prompted Spade to examine the company's safety records to see if something could be done to avoid such injuries and to link safety improvements to his overall effort to improve productivity and control costs.

Spade studied the relevant data the next morning and was appalled. During the previous year, corporate headquarters had charged his district $196,720 for workers' compensation premiums, partially reflecting accidents within his district and branch offices. He found that corporate headquarters, when computing the profitability of each district, simply added to the district average the total cost of workers' compensation payments and other direct safety and health costs. Spade thus became keenly aware that these costs directly affected his own bottom line. Besides the direct effect on his district's profits, Spade was concerned that the total cost of accidents was much higher. In addition to the payments to the employee for medical expenses and rehabilitation, most accidents caused lost supervisor time, lost time for other employees, and damage to equipment and tools. (Refer to Tables 12-7, 12-8, 12-9, 12-10, and 12-11 for accident statistics.)

OUTLINE OF COSTS

In attempting to estimate costs, Spade had at his disposal various guidelines that other companies used. The following areas appeared to be relevant to his situation:

1. Compensation administration and legal expenses
2. Time lost, salaried personnel

TABLE 12-7   Sources of Accident Costs

Visibility Level	Source
1	Medical, hospital and workers' compensation cases

2	Time lost by supervisor
	    assisting the injured person
	    securing a replacement
	    supervising repairs to equipment
	    investigating the accident

3	Time lost by other employees
	    assisting the injured person
	    employees standing and watching
	    waiting for materials
	    safety engineer's investigation
	    administration costs

4	Damage to work in process, damage to machine
	    damage to equipment
	    damage to tools
	    loss of production
	    loss of use of machine during repair work

3. Time lost, hourly personnel
4. Net income loss due to items 2 and 3
5. Damage to equipment: repair, replacement
6. One-half time productivity of injured for first forty hours after return to work
7. Lost income due to inefficiency of replacement worker(s)

From historical data, he estimated the cost of legal and administrative fees to be $1,000 per incident when a worker's compensation claim is contested. In his district, four cases had required the use of company lawyers during 1982. He estimated that salaried personnel spent at least forty hours investigating an incident, writing reports, attending meetings, and replacing the injured worker; their time was valued at $550. The time that hourly personnel spent expressing sympathy and curiosity and conducting the union investigation was approximated at thirty-five hours per incident; given the average union rate of $10 per hour, the cost was $350.

To quantify the impact of accidents on net income, Spade used the following procedure. The district's net income of $1,800,000 was divided by the total hours worked (659,000). This gave a contribution to net income of $2.73 for every productive hour. Next, the seventy-five hours that salaried and hourly employees expended on each incident was multiplied by the total number of lost workday cases and then by the hourly contribution to net income.

Damage to equipment was estimated to average $1,500 per lost workday accident.

TABLE 12-8   Number of Lost-Time Accidents[1], 1982

Northern district	22
Southern district	24
Eastern district	18
Western district	22
Central district[2]	32

[1]Man-hour exposure in each district was equivalent.
[2]Sam Spade manages the Central district.

TABLE 12-9   Central District's Accidents by Branch, 1982

	Accidents	Number of Employees	Man-hour Exposure
Branch A	8	105	209,000
Branch B	6	50	100,000
Branch C	8	50	100,000
Branch D	10	125	250,000
Total	32	330	659,000

TABLE 12-10 Cause of Accident

Branch	Employee No.	Cause	Body Part	Days Lost
A	1	Carrying/holding	Back	20
	2	Lifting/lowering	Back	25
	3	Fall from elevation	Leg	23
	4	Struck by moving object	Eye	10
	5	Fall down the stairs	Back	25
	6	Carrying/holding	Arm	10
	7	Hand-power tool	Finger	10
	8	Struck against stationary object	Head	5
			Total	128
B	1	Injured repairing	Arm	15
	2	Miscellaneous	Back	12
	3	Struck by falling object	Foot	20
	4	Lifting/lowering	Back	25
	5	Lifting/lowering	Back	25
	6	Fall from moving object	Finger	4
			Total	101
C	1	Motor vehicle accident	Neck	30
	2	Struck by falling object	Toe	8
	3	Injured repairing	Hand	7
	4	Pushing/pulling	Back	30
	5	Lifting/lowering	Back	20
	6	Caught in equipment	Leg	45
	7	Carrying/holding	Arm	10
	8	Struck by moving object	Foot	15
			Total	165
D	1	Lifting/lowering	Back	20
	2	Struck by falling object	Eye	15
	3	Fall from elevation	Foot	20
	4	Electrical burn	Arm	15
	5	Struck by moving object	Eye	10
	6	Struck against moving object	Eye	10
	7	Lifting/lowering	Back	20
	8	Motor vehicle accident	Neck	35
	9	Struck by handtool	Finger	5
	10	Struck by moving object	Eye	10
			Total	160

According to the guidelines Spade was using, each disabled employee is only half as productive during the first forty hours after returning to work. This seemed a reasonable number to incorporate into his analysis.

Last, the cost of replacement involved either training a new worker or using experienced workers on overtime. This cost was equal to total days lost times eight hours times the hourly contribution to net income.

In outlining the above costs, Spade realized that the impact of accidents on his district's profits picture was much greater than originally expected, and his analysis did not include first-aid injuries or property damage that did not

TABLE 12-11   Breakdown of Selected Factors by Accident, 1982

Branch	Employee	Age	Date of Accident	Time of Day	Year of Hire	Length of Time on Present Job
A	1	30	2/18/82	1:20 P.M.	1978	4 years
	2	25	4/13/82	11:30 A.M.	1980	2 years
	3	28	6/24/82	1:10 P.M.	1981	2 weeks
	4	45	7/05/82	10:30 A.M.	1970	1 month
	5	26	7/21/82	9:00 A.M.	1979	3 years
	6	28	7/29/82	1:30 P.M.	1979	1 week
	7	22	8/11/82	3:40 P.M.	1982	2 months
	8	33	11/17/82	1:45 P.M.	1977	5 years
B	1	28	1/14/82	10:40 A.M.	1976	3 weeks
	2	32	5/10/82	1:30 P.M.	1980	2 years
	3	21	7/28/82	2:00 P.M.	1980	1 week
	4	35	8/09/82	4:30 P.M.	1981	1 year
	5	33	8/25/82	1:15 P.M.	1978	4 years
	6	22	10/07/82	8:30 A.M.	1982	1 month
C	1	24	1/17/82	4:50 P.M.	1980	2 years
	2	38	3/11/82	1:15 P.M.	1972	5 years
	3	31	6/07/82	1:30 P.M.	1981	1 year
	4	33	6/07/82	7:35 A.M.	1982	1 month
	5	37	7/08/82	1:05 P.M.	1970	2 weeks
	6	22	7/29/82	1:40 P.M.	1982	3 months
	7	28	9/03/82	4:00 P.M.	1982	6 months
	8	40	12/17/82	10:10 A.M.	1975	3 years
D	1	40	2/04/82	4:15 P.M.	1973	7 years
	2	21	3/09/82	1:25 P.M.	1981	1 year
	3	29	3/25/82	1:05 P.M.	1979	1 month
	4	20	7/21/82	10:35 A.M.	1978	4 years
	5	34	6/24/82	4:20 P.M.	1980	2 years
	6	22	7/05/82	1:10 P.M.	1982	3 weeks
	7	25	7/21/82	10:35 A.M.	1978	4 years
	8	29	8/11/82	4:00 P.M.	1975	3 months
	9	23	8/17/82	1:40 P.M.	1980	2 years
	10	23	11/18/82	3:30 P.M.	1981	1 year

result in injury. Spade was unsure how to measure these costs for Boiler, Inc., but other companies used the following two checklists:

A. First-aid injuries resulting in lost workdays

1. Time away from job while first aid is being administered
2. Time spent investigating the incident
3. Time spent revisiting the dispensary, if this proves necessary
4. Time spent by first-aid personnel and cost of equipment used on first-aid cases
5. Time spent by injured worker's fellow employees rendering assistance and extending sympathy

B. Property damage that does not result in personal injury

1. Damage to materials in storage or process
2. Damage to buildings, overhead doors, equipment, etc.
3. Damage to vehicles whether repaired or not
4. Damage to overhead cranes and related equipment

Using these lists, Spade conservatively estimated that a first-aid injury costs $150 and that a property damage accident with no injury costs $100. In attempting to calculate the number of incidents involving first-aid or property damage without injuries Spade used a standard ratio (see Exhibit 12-1).

EXHIBIT 12-1
Foundation of an Accident

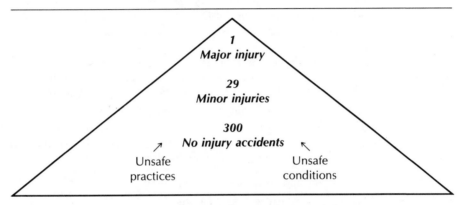

00.3 percent of all accidents produce major injuries
08.8 percent of all accidents produce minor injuries
90.9 percent of all accidents produce no injuries

The ratios above — 1–29–300 — show that in a unit group of 33 similar accidents occurring to the same person, 300 will result in no injury, 29 will produce minor injuries, and 1 will cause a serious injury.

These ratios apply only to the average case. The major injury may result from the very first accident or from any other accident in the group.

Underlying and causing all accidents, including those resulting in no injury or in either minor or major injury, there is an unknown number of unsafe practices or conditions, often running into the thousands.

Note: The determination of this no-injury accident frequency followed a study of over 5,000 cases. In the accident group (330 cases) shown above, a major injury is any case that is reported to insurance carriers or to the state compensation commissioner. A minor injury is a scratch, bruise, or laceration such as is commonly termed a first-aid case. A no-injury accident is an unplanned event involving movement of a person, an object, or a substance (slip, fall, flying object, inhalation, etc.), having the probability of causing personal injury or property damage.

Source: H. W. Heinrich, Dan Peterson, and Nestor Roos, *Industrial Accident Prevention,* 5th edition (New York: McGraw-Hill, 1980). Reprinted by permission.

OTHER CONSIDERATIONS

Because no one plans to get hurt, Spade was uncomfortable with the idea of forecasting the cost of accidents for the following year. Still, his district had the highest accident rate in the region, and this was costing him money. Spade decided to talk with his region's safety administrator to become familiar with safety programs in other districts. After a lengthy meeting, Spade returned to his office to study the materials the safety administrator had given him and to consider the points that had been raised. First on his mind were the requirements of the Occupational Safety and Health Act. He wondered whether his district could pass a safety inspection. Given the frequency of accidents, he was apprehensive.

Having recently read about the lawsuits filed against the Manville Corporation (relating to health problems caused by working with asbestos), Spade wondered if the products or techniques used at Boiler Corporation, Inc. should be investigated to guard against any possible long-term liabilities for the company.

Next Spade probed the construction industry statistics published by the U.S. Department of Labor (Exhibits 12-2 and 12-3). He noted that "lost workday cases" (column 2, Exhibit 12-3) under Special Trade Construction (plumbing, heating and air conditioning) was 5.8 in 1980 and 5.9 in 1981. Although he did not have equivalent figures for his district, he suspected that his rate was much higher than the industry average. The U.S. Department of Labor uses the following formula to derive incident rates:

$$\frac{\text{Number of injuries} \times 200,000}{\text{Employee hours worked}} = \text{Incidence rate}$$

The 200,000 hours shown in the formula represent the equivalent of 100 employees working 40 hours per week, 50 weeks per year and provide a standard base for incident rates.

EXHIBIT 12-2
Occupational Injury Incident Rates for the Three General Categories of Contractors in the Construction Industry

Industry	Total Cases (Thousands)	Injuries Lost Workday Cases (Thousands)	Average Lost Workdays Per Lost Workday Case
Construction	530.4	222.1	18
General building contractors	134.7	54.5	18
Heavy construction contractors	122.7	49.4	18
Special trade contractors	273.1	118.2	18

EXHIBIT 12-3

Occupational Injury Incidence Rates per 100 Full-Time
Workers for the Subcategories of the General Contractors
in the Construction Industry 1980, 1981

	Incident Rates per 100 Full-time Workers*							
	Nonfatal							
	Total Cases		Lost Work-day Cases		Cases Without Lost Workdays		Lost Workdays	
Industry	1980	1981	1980	1981	1980	1981	1980	1981
Construction	15.5	14.9	6.5	6.3	9.0	8.6	116.1	112.1
General Building Contractors	15.4	15.0	6.4	6.1	8.9	8.9	112.1	106.6
Residential building construction	11.8	11.7	5.7	5.5	6.1	6.2	99.6	98.7
Operative builders	12.3	11.3	5.2	5.1	7.1	6.2	74.1	76.9
Nonresidential building construction	19.2	18.3	7.2	6.7	11.9	11.6	128.9	117.2
Heavy Construction Contractors	16.0	14.7	6.2	5.9	9.7	8.7	116.8	105.2
Highway and street construction	15.4	13.8	6.1	5.7	9.2	8.0	122.0	112.6
Heavy construction, except highway	16.9	15.0	6.3	6.0	9.9	9.0	114.6	102.5
Special Trade Construction	15.3	15.0	6.6	6.5	8.7	8.5	117.9	118.0
Plumbing, heating, and air conditioning	16.1	15.5	5.8	5.9	10.3	9.6	94.8	97.4
Painting, paper hanging, and decorating	9.5	8.9	5.0	4.8	4.5	4.1	114.3	102.4
Electrical work	14.1	13.7	5.1	5.1	9.0	8.6	85.5	90.8
Masonry, stonework, and plastering	15.9	15.6	7.6	7.4	8.3	8.2	135.9	137.3
Carpentering and flooring	12.6	12.5	6.9	6.3	5.7	6.1	115.0	106.9
Roofing and sheetmetal work	20.5	19.8	11.2	10.2	9.2	9.6	216.0	200.0
Concrete work	14.5	13.2	6.9	6.7	7.6	6.5	118.5	126.2
Water well drilling	15.5	13.1	8.4	7.1	7.1	6.0	143.1	146.0
Miscellaneous special trade contractors	16.0	16.8	7.3	7.4	8.7	9.4	133.9	137.0

*Formula: $\dfrac{\text{Number of injuries} \times 200{,}000}{\text{Employee hours worked}} = \text{Incidence rate}$

Note: The 200,000 hours shown in the formula represent the equivalent of 100 employees working 40 hours per week, 50 weeks per year, and provides the standard base for the incidence rates.

WORKERS' COMPENSATION PROCEDURE

At present, each office reports a monthly expense to indirect cost for workers' compensation premiums. This "accrual" is based upon a fixed percentage of new payroll and is an estimate of what actual premiums will be. Under this system, the relative safety of one branch versus another will not reflect a difference in operating efficiency. Variances between accrued expenses and actual costs are shown as an adjustment to indirect cost at the district headquarters level.

The actual premiums paid each year to headquarters are comprised of three components: actual medical and indemnity (payments to employees while out of work) costs up to $300,000 per case; a fee for insurance coverage in cases higher than $300,000; and a fee for administrative burden.

SUMMARY

Spade decided that he would like to improve his district's overall safety record by identifying problems that were specific to each of his branches and by formulating plans to reduce them. He realized that the present system of allocating safety costs on the basis of direct expense provided little incentive to do so. Yet, formulating a plan appeared to be imperative because of the high indirect costs and the resultant loss in productivity.

Questions for Discussion

1. Which branches would you want to investigate and why?
2. What specific questions would you ask the field supervisors in these offices?
3. What safety programs would you suggest?
4. What innovations/programs would you suggest the Boiler Corporation adopt? How would you justify the investment?

VI

Looking Abroad
and into the
Future

PREVIEW

Up to this point we have focused on the evolution and contemporary nature of human resource management and industrial relations in the United States. Now we broaden the horizon by examining how other countries design and manage employment relationships and by considering the kinds of challenges United States managers are likely to encounter in the future.

In Chapter 13 we explore the similarities and differences between American, Japanese, and European industrial relations systems. We thereby point out the broad array of options that United States management, labor, and government leaders might consider in shaping future strategies. In Chapter 14 we use the conceptual framework and material discussed throughout the book to explore some of the major challenges and strategic adaptations that may be required of all the parties to employment relationships in the years ahead.

13

Alternative Industrial Relations Systems

Comparing the industrial relations systems of different countries allows us to step back from the detailed practices and issues we have been examining and to assess the overall effectiveness of a given system's design. An industrial relations system must be evaluated against a variety of criteria reflecting multiple objectives. Among the most prominent are the system's abilities to (1) resolve conflicts and promote cooperation among workers, employers, labor organizations, and government; (2) contribute to economic growth and improved standards of living for the work force; and (3) adapt to changes in its larger economic and social environment. A comparative perspective also illustrates a variety of ways in which different industrial relations systems work toward the same objectives. These differences often require various types of managerial behavior that would seem alien to managers who are used to contemporary United States practices.

It is interesting to note how the limelight has shifted over time across different industrial relations systems. For example, in the postwar environment of the late 1940s and 1950s, the United States system of free collective bargaining with a limited role for unions was considered the model for governments in Western Europe and Japan to follow as they reconstructed their economies and political systems. In Japan, the American occupation government introduced many concepts from United States labor law into Japanese society. Similarly, through the Marshall Plan in Europe, efforts were made to ensure that free trade unions and the principles of collective bargaining were incorporated into the rebuilding of West Germany and other European nations. In the 1950s, much research explored the exportability of the United States model of industrial relations to other democratic states, as part of a larger United States effort to limit the growth of communism. In the 1960s, attention turned to the Swedish industrial relations and labor market system as a model for achieving a high level of labor peace, comprehensive labor market adjustment and human resource development, and a rate of economic growth that produced one of the highest standards of living in the world. In the 1970s, some of the credit for the West German "economic miracle" was attributed to its mechanisms for worker participation and codetermination at the level of the firm and to the government's consultation of labor and business in economic policy making. By the 1980s, the Japanese human resource management system had become the model for producing labor-management consensus and cooperation, steady growth in productivity, high quality goods, individual worker commitment and motivation, and adaptability to the changing world economy. In contrast, by the end of the 1970s, the American system was being criticized widely for being too adversarial, slow to adapt to the world economy, and unable to fully use its human resources.

This shifting focus should caution us against believing that one optimal design prevails for a nation's human resource management system. Instead, we need to recognize that each system must fit the unique culture and values of its society and adapt through time to adjust to changes in its external and internal economic and social environments. Thus, the differences observed across systems at any point in time generally reflect differences in culture, history, values, and political structures. To attempt to import attributes of another system without understanding how these relate to the larger environment, therefore, may be patently counterproductive.

Yet, it is sometimes possible to adapt practices developed in other systems to the needs of one's own. The Japanese, for example, demonstrated this point by adapting and integrating quality control techniques from American engineers into their human resource management systems. It is also extremely helpful to compare the quality of the fit between the overall structure of different systems with current and future characteristics of their environments. That different systems have performed particularly effectively at different periods suggests that certain features perform best given a specific, time-bound set of environmental characteristics.

Industrial relations systems are relatively slow to adapt to changing environments and often continue to follow policies and practices long after environmental changes render them obsolete. One historical example of this lag in the United States was the unwillingness to abandon outmoded common-law principles for regulating human resources until catastrophic conditions during the Great Depression demonstrated the need for unemployment insurance, workers' compensation, and collective bargaining legislation. A contemporary example might be the lack of adequate joint labor, management, and government analyses and planning for the human resource consequences associated with advances in microelectronics technology. Precisely because industrial relations systems are so slow to change, it is important to examine the process of adaptation by comparing industrial relations traditions and practices throughout the world.

The opportunity to learn and to transfer innovations from different systems is increasing as more managers gain experience in managing multinational enterprises, in doing business across international boundaries, and in forming joint ventures with foreign firms. Therefore, we need a framework for comparing the designs of alternative industrial relations systems and the expectations they place on managers working within them. Kennedy's summary of European industrial relations and Shirai's and Inagami's articles on Japan were chosen with this objective in mind. These articles provide concise overviews of strategic decision making, of human resource policy making, and of workplace practices in the respective nations.

Strategic-Level Comparisons

The main differences among American, European, and Japanese practices at the strategic level of organizations reflect variations in relationships among business, labor, and government. Traditionally, the United States government has not assumed an active role in strategic business decision making that affects human resource management within a firm. Moreover, except in periods of wage and price controls, business has seldom interacted directly with the United States government in shaping the course of national economic policy. Similarly, the United States labor movement traditionally has opposed formal union participation in corporate decision making via membership on boards of directors. European industrial relations systems, by contrast, have much more experience with corporatist or tripartite (labor, business, and government) consultation on broad economic policy and planning (Crouch, 1980), as well as with worker representation on boards of directors through such arrangements as the German system of codetermination. Although Japan has no formal structure for worker participation in corporate decision making or in government policy making, the Ministry for International Trade and Industry (MITI) has assumed a strategic role in allocating capital and influencing the growth and decline of various industrial sectors. In addition, as Shirai and Inagami point out, most large Japanese firms engage union leaders in informal consultations about broad corporate strategies.

Important differences also exist across these systems in management values that guide human resource management. Shirai makes this point by describing the values in Japanese firms that underlie top management policies toward human resource management and the characteristics of Japanese enterprises that support these values (long-term organizational tenure of top executives, low rate of stockholder pressure, etc.). These managerial and cultural differences are important to understand if we are to consider the conditions necessary to import practices found in Japanese firms at lower tiers of the framework.

Neither European nor Japanese managers display as deep an antipathy toward unions as is embedded in the value systems and ideologies of United States managers and top executives. It has been hypothesized that top executives in Japan accept the role of enterprise unions but would strongly resist unions of a more radical nature. Enterprise unions can represent effectively the interests of their members without challenging the underlying organizational values top executives want to perpetuate (Shirai, 1983). In Europe, the effects of the long-standing political power of labor movements and the stronger working-class consciousness of the labor force combine to help explain the greater acceptance of unions by society at large and, in turn, by business leaders.

In at least one sense, it is ironic that unions are more readily accepted among European than United States managers. Unlike many of their European counterparts, the United States trade union movement traditionally not only has accepted the values of the capitalist, free enterprise system, but also has been one of its most vocal supporters. Yet, United States managers continue to strongly resist unions, whereas many European unions that adopt a socialist ideology are more readily accepted as legitimate partners of management.

Functional-Level Comparisons

Equally important differences in these industrial relations systems are visible in the middle tier of our framework. The industry-level collective bargaining structure in Germany and the enterprise-level structure in Japan (with its links to the nationwide spring wage offensive) can be contrasted with the more diverse assortment of plant, area, firm, and industry bargaining structures and firm-specific personnel practices found in the United States. Similarly, whereas most European countries and Japan have had longer traditions of government provided or required fringe and social welfare benefits (vacations, health care, etc.), the United States historically has left the provision of these benefits to private firms and the collective bargaining process. Only since the 1960s have we seen in the United States an incremental growth in the role of the federal government in regulating the substantive terms of employment contracts.

Differences in broad human resource policies also are visible. Compared to their United States counterparts, most large Japanese firms place a higher priority on employment continuity for their permanent work forces, and they rely on a larger network of temporaries and subcontractors as buffers against economic downturns. In Europe, the 1970s produced expansion in legislation governing layoffs, discharges, and plant closings. In contrast, in the United States these issues are again left to the discretion of employers and/or the collective bargaining process. As we saw in Chapter 6, only a small (though growing) number of leading firms are committed to policies explicitly designed to stabilize employment. Layoffs and voluntary mobility across organizations are more frequently used options in the United States than in either Japan or most European countries.

Workplace-Level Comparisons

Several unique aspects of United States industrial relations stand out when we compare practices at the workplace level of these systems. Neither most European countries nor Japan exhibits as strong a presence of local unions and detailed contractual regulations of working conditions and practices as that found in the United States. This job-control tradition of United States labor unions now is clearly under stress as employers seek greater flexibility in work organization and employee involvement through the various experiments with quality-of-working life programs and new forms of work organization, described in earlier chapters. In many European countries, work councils substitute for detailed contracts and strong local unions. A similar reliance on consultation rather than negotiation and legal, contractual enforcement mechanisms is found in Japan, in such devices as quality circles, production advisory committees, and union-management communication at the plant level. Thus, at the workplace level we see some movement on the part of United States firms to adopt parts of both the Japanese and the European patterns, in the hope of achieving more flexibility and less adversarial relationships.

All of the above statements about the "American," "Japanese," and especially "European" approaches obviously oversimplify a wide diversity of practices found within these systems. Yet, by abstracting to these generalized statements, we are led to question many of the traditions and patterns that practitioners in the United States otherwise might take for granted. Although we must be careful about the limits of piecemeal efforts to import practices that appear to work well in other contexts, this kind of comparative perspective can help us see a range of new possibilities for improving the performance of human resource management in the United States. Our task in considering the use of these options in the United States is constantly to ask, How would this practice fit into our larger set of human resource management policies, and what else would we have to change for these alternatives to work effectively in our settings? Conversely, the challenge to United States managers working abroad is, How much of the tradition and practices of the host industrial relations system should be followed? How much of the American heritage and experience should be imported into this foreign context? The case and the readings that follow provide more background for discussing these questions.

Suggested Readings

Blanpain, Roger, ed., *The Vredeling Proposal: Information and Consultation of Employees in Multinational Enterprises* (Boston: Kluwer, 1983).

Crouch, Colin, and Alessandro Pizzorno, eds., *The Resurgence of Class Conflict in Western Europe Since 1968* (London: MacMillan, 1980).

Industrial Democracy in Europe Study Committee, *European Industrial Relations* (Oxford: Oxford University Press, 1980). See also *Industrial Democracy in Europe*, a 1981 book written by the same study committee and published by the same press.

Kamata, Satochi, *Japan in the Passing Lane: An Insider's Account of Life in a Japanese Auto Factory* (New York: Pantheon Books, 1983).

Ouchi, William, *The M Form Society* (Reading, Mass.: Addison-Wesley, 1984).

Shirai, Taishiro, ed., *Contemporary Industrial Relations in Japan* (Madison, Wis.: University of Wisconsin Press, 1983).

Some Major Issues in
European Labor Relations

Employee Representation
on Company Boards

It is in West Germany that the important pioneering developments in worker partic- ipation have occurred, both at the com- pany level in the form of employee repre- sentation on supervisory boards and at the plant level in the form of works councils. It is significant, we believe, that worker participation in West Germany has devel- oped at the two levels of industrial rela- tions where West German unions have not played important roles. Although West German unions have been active politi- cally at the national level and economi- cally (through collective bargaining) at the industrial level, there has been little or no union presence at the company and plant levels. As a result, vacuums existed with respect to effective representation of em- ployees at these two lower levels. Worker participation was developed to fill these vacuums.

The company board structure in West Germany is by law two-tiered, consisting of a supervisory board and a management board. The supervisory board has control over broad company policies and also elects the members to the management board. The day-to-day operation of the company is in the hands of the manage- ment board. Employees are represented only on the supervisory board.

Employee board representation in West Germany takes place under one of three different laws passed in 1951, 1952, and 1976. The 1951 law applies only to the coal, iron, and steel sector; the 1952 law applies to companies in other industries

Source: Thomas Kennedy, *European Labor Re- lations: Text and Cases* (Lexington Books, D. C. Heath and Company). Copyright © 1980 by D. C. Heath and Company. Reprinted by per- mission.

with from 500 to 2,000 employees; the 1976 law applies to companies in other industries with more than 2,000 employ- ees. The basic differences in the laws con- cern: (1) parity, (2) union nomination of employee representatives, and (3) selec- tion of the company director of labor. Un- der the 1951 law in coal, iron, and steel industries, the employee representatives are equal in number and power to the owner representatives. Under the 1952 law, the employees elect only one-third and the owners elect two-thirds of the members of the board. Under the 1976 law, although the employees elect one-half of the board members, parity is not achieved because the chairman, who is an owner-representative, has two votes in case of a tie. Under the 1951 law, the union has the right to nominate a majority of the employee representatives, whereas under the 1952 law it has no right to nominate any of them, and under the 1976 law it has the right to nominate only a minority. Un- der the 1951 law, the company's labor di- rector must be approved by the employee representatives of the board, but under the 1952 and 1976 laws he is selected by a simple majority vote of the board.

At the center of the struggle over changes in employee board representation in West Germany have been the three is- sues that distinguish the present West Ger- man laws as outlined in the previous par- agraph. Unions have proposed and management has opposed: (1) parity, that is, that worker representatives should be not only equal in number, but also equal in power to the owner representatives on the supervisory board, (2) an increased union role, whereby employee represen- tatives would be selected through or at least nominated through the union institutions, and (3) a requirement that the director of labor on the management board must be approved by the employee representatives on the supervisory board.

In sponsoring the 1976 employee board representation legislation, the West German unions hoped to achieve these three objectives in all industry. But the employers strongly resisted these changes and were successful in having the union proposal weakened to the point where the new legislation accomplished none of them. The unions, of course, were disappointed. Heinz-Oscar Vetter, chief of the DGB, stated that the new law makes a joke of parity.[1] The struggle, however, did not end with the passage of the 1976 legislation. Achievement of the three goals in worker directorships remains an important part of the long-run legislative program of the West German labor movement.

West German companies report that employee board membership has not prevented management from functioning effectively, and indeed, has provided company management with a good avenue of communication with its employees. The West German managers with whom we spoke indicated that the employee representation system has contributed to a much better comprehension of management problems by the leaders of the employees, and in turn, by the employees themselves. It is the general opinion that the time spent by management in educating and dealing with employee board representatives has been time well spent.

During the sixties and early seventies, the West German industrial system with its high gross national product per person and relatively low inflation and unemployment rates became the envy of other countries, both in Europe and elsewhere. It was believed by many that much of the West German success could be attributed to the high degree of industrial peace and cooperation that prevailed in the country and that employee board membership was an important factor contributing to that peace and cooperation. As a result, in the early seventies, several other European countries passed legislation that required employee board representation. Although for more than twenty years employee board representation had been a purely West German phenomenon, in the two-year period 1973–1974, four other European countries — Austria, Sweden, Denmark, and Norway — adopted employee board representation plans, and in the Netherlands legislation became effective that gave the Dutch works councils the right to nominate and veto candidates for company supervisory boards. Then in 1975, the European Commission published a revision of its proposed directive which would require adoption of employee board representation plans in all of the countries in the European Economic Community. The Commission also recommended in its proposed statute for a European company that all such companies be required to have employee board participation.

The expansion of employee representation plans to other countries in Europe did not continue after 1974. Since then, no other European country has adopted such plans except Ireland, where in 1977 legislation was enacted that entitles the employees of seven state-owned companies to elect one-third of the board members from candidates nominated by the unions.

The failure of employee board representation plans to continue to be adopted in other European countries has been the result of several factors. First, there has been a growing body of opinion that such plans have not been the basic cause of labor peace in West Germany and increasing doubt concerning their possible effectiveness in countries where the labor relations structure and ideology are quite different from that of West Germany.[2] Second, man-

[1] Craig R. Whitney, "Labor's Voice Heard in West Germany," *New York Times*, January 25, 1976.

[2] P. Brannen, et al., *Worker Directors* (London: Hutchinson of London, 1976), 229.

agement organizations and conservative political groups have vigorously opposed employee board representation which they argue would erode the decision-making power of managements and the owners to the detriment of the whole community. Finally, strong opposition has developed from many labor leaders who perceive employee board representation as interfering with the development and maintenance of an effective labor movement.

No employee board representation plans have been adopted in Italy, Belgium, or Switzerland. In Italy and Belgium, they have been vigorously opposed by the left-wing labor unions on the basis of ideology. In Switzerland, a proposed plan was defeated in 1976 in a national referendum. In France, it is generally agreed that the present plan, which allows the works councils to send four observers to board meetings, is completely illusory; but the major French unions, like their Italian and Belgian counterparts, oppose the adoption of an effective employee board representation plan for ideological reasons.

In Great Britain, there was much debate of the issue before and after the publication of the Bullock report in January, 1977. In May 1978, however, the Labor government issued a White Paper which placed the emphasis on the development of union joint representation councils (JRCs) rather than employee board representation. However, it did provide that after three or four years, if a JRC so desired and the majority of the employees so voted, the company would have to accept employee representatives on its supervisory board. There is no indication that the new Conservative government in Great Britain will support even the watered-down proposal of the former Labor government. Finally, the European Commission has not issued a directive that would force the member countries to adopt an employee representation plan. Now that the West Germans and Dutch have lost their dominance in the European Trade Union Confederation as a result of the expansion of that organization, there will be

less pressure on the Commission to issue such a directive or to insist upon employee board representation as an integral part of the European company legislation.[3]

It may be, of course, as W. W. Daniel states, that in the long run the tide of employee board representation as an element of industrial democracy in Europe is irresistible. But as Daniel has said, it appears now that it "will not be realized quickly or easily."[4]

Works Councils

A works council is a plant committee (composed of employees, or employees and company representatives) with which the management must consult, and in some cases, reach agreement before taking action on certain matters that affect the workers. After World War II, works councils were established by legislation in a number of European countries: France (1945), Sweden (1946), the Netherlands (1950), West Germany (1952), and Italy (1953). Thus, West Germany, which had a pioneer role in enacting legislation involving workers on company boards, was not the first country to adopt works council legislation. However, over the years works councils have played a much more important role in West Germany than in any of the other countries. The number of employees covered by works councils, the number of employees serving as councillors, the scope of the issues considered by the works councils, and the power of the councils have been greater in West Germany than in any of the other countries in this study. In a study by Bluechen in 1966, 88 percent of the West German workers stated that the works council in their plant had secured important concessions from management and had been important to

---

[3] Emil Joseph Kirchner, *Trade Unions as a Pressure Group in the European Community* (England: Saxon House, 1977), 47.

[4] W. W. Daniel, "Industrial Democracy," in *Comparative Industrial Relations in Europe*, by Derek Torrington (London: Associated Business Programs, Ltd., 1978), 49.

them individually in their relations with management.[5]

As indicated earlier, the West German labor movement has not been important at the plant level. While some of the West German unions, such as IG Metall, have made attempts to develop power at the local level, generally such development has not been significant. Under West German law, management is not required to deal with union representatives at the plant level and, in fact, has vigorously opposed any attempt on the part of the unions to force it to do so. On the other hand, the law does require West German management at the plant level to recognize and deal with a works council. As a result, the works council has become the body through which West German workers are represented at the local level. In the other European countries where works councils have been important, the unions have been weak at the local level. By comparison, in Great Britain and the United States where unions have had strong plant organizations, works councils have not developed.

Although works councils have received far less publicity than representation of workers on company boards in West Germany, the former have had more effect than the latter on West German employees and on the West German industrial relations system. The number of employees who participate as works councillors is much larger than the number who participate as board representatives, and the number of hours spent on council work is much greater than the number spent on board work. Many of the councillors now spend full time on council matters. Although it is true that the boards sometimes deal with issuses that have a profound impact on the employees, the issues covered by the works councils are much more extensive in scope and of more immediate concern to the workers. Moreover,

employee representatives are likely to be more knowledgeable about the issues discussed in works council meetings than about many of the items that come before the supervisory board. As a result, participation by employee representatives is more meaningful at the council level. Finally, on a number of issues the works council possesses parity of power with management. In other words, codetermination exists and management cannot take action unless the council agrees. Only in the coal, iron, and steel industries do employee board members have parity of power. In all other industries, they can be outvoted by owner representatives.

The 1972 amendment to the West German Works Constitution Act greatly increased the scope and power of the works council. The number of issues that management must discuss with the council was greatly enlarged, and many issues were moved from consultation to codetermination. On the other hand, the 1976 board representation legislation did not provide the employee representatives with parity of power. In light of these developments, it is expected that the future impact of the works councils will be even more important in comparison with employee board representation.

In the other five European countries in our study, the importance of the works councils varies from being practically nonexistent in Great Britain to being very significant in the Netherlands. In Great Britain, there is no law requiring works councils, and although some companies did have them in the past, such organizations have been largely replaced by shop stewards councils which now represent British employees quite effectively at the local level. In France, although a 1945 law, as revised in 1966, required a plant with fifty or more employees to have a works council (comité d'entreprise), a government study in 1975 found that the committees had been set up in less than half of the plants. In Italy during the fifties, the national unions and the national industry association (Confindustria) agreed upon a plan to

[5] Ivor L. Roberts, "The Works Constitution Acts and Industrial Relations in West Germany, Implications for the United Kingdom." *British Journal of Industrial Relations* 11 (1973): 354.

establish works councils (internal commissions) in each plant. In recent years, however, the commissions have been replaced by union factory councils (CDFs) which engage in local bargaining. In the Netherlands, since the revision of the law in 1971, works councils have been very important and a new law which became effective September 1, 1979, further increases the scope and power of the councils. Swedish works councils became operative in 1946 as a result of an agreement between the national union confederation (LO) and the national employers' association (SAF). In 1966 and again in 1975, the scope of the councils was enlarged. However, in 1976 the LO cancelled the agreement on works councils and opened up the whole matter for collective bargaining. It is expected that the bargaining will result in a continuation of the works council system, but its nature may be altered considerably.

Debate over the future role of works councils continues in the European countries where they have been operating. The debate concerning their future has centered around four topics: (1) the role of management, (2) the role of the union or unions, (3) the scope of issues that management must discuss with the council, and (4) the power of the council, that is, the authority to codetermine with management rather than simply to advise management.

In West Germany and in the Netherlands the works council is composed entirely of employees. However, in Sweden the works council is a joint body, consisting of an equal number of management and employee representatives.

The West German unions have no formal role in the nomination or election of members to the works councils. The employees in each plant draw up lists of candidates from among the employees, and then vote for them in secret elections. Non-union as well as union members can and do serve as councillors. However, a study in 1972 found that 78 percent of the coun-

cillors were union members,[6] and an earlier study found that 98 percent of the council chairmen were union members.[7]

In Sweden, the employee members of the works council are elected from the union ranks only. In addition, the chairman of the factory union committee is an ex-officio member of the works council. Since 95 percent of the blue-collar workers in Sweden are union members, very few workers are excluded from council participation. Nevertheless, it is significant that in Sweden the works councils exist within the union system.

In the Netherlands, the unions have the right to propose lists of candidates, but groups of non-union employees may also propose lists. As a result, non-union as well as union members may be elected to the Dutch works councils.

There appears to be no move at present by the West German unions to get formal control over the nomination and election of councillors. In Sweden, the works council system is now the subject of collective bargaining, but it is highly unlikely that the Swedish unions will give up control of the works council election process. In the Netherlands, the 1979 legislation did not change the unions' role in the nomination and election of councillors. Thus, in the three countries in our study where works councils are important, the formal role of the unions is likely to remain as it has been in the past — very weak in West Germany, very strong in Sweden, and somewhere in-between in the Netherlands.

West German works councils are not permitted to deal with certain matters, such as general wage increases and job evaluation schemes, which are reserved for collective bargaining between the union and the trade association. However, as previously indicated, the scope of works council matters has been very broad and was greatly expanded in the 1972 legisla-

---

[6] Solomon Barkin, *Worker Militancy and Its Consequences* (New York: Praeger Publishers, 1975), 251.

[7] Roberts, "Works Constitution Acts," 352.

tion. West German management has objected to this expansion because it means that management can make fewer and fewer decisions without first consulting with the works council.

In Sweden, the scope of issues under the jurisdiction of the works council was expanded in 1966 and again in 1975. It is possible that the unions will attempt to further expand the scope in the collective bargaining that will replace the old system. Swedish management may be expected to oppose such expansion.

The 1979 Works Council Act in the Netherlands expanded the scope of the councils' work to include: hiring of temporary workers, setting up of new firms, entering into or withdrawing from cooperation with another firm, and seeking advice from outside experts. Dutch management opposed the expansion.

The strongest opposition by management to changes in existing works council laws in West Germany and the Netherlands has concerned the attempt to increase the power of the works councils by moving items from consultation to codetermination. Both the West German and the Dutch laws have provided that management must only consult with the works council on certain items, but must reach an agreement (codetermine) on certain other items. Under consultation, management loses the right unilaterally to make an immediate decision, but may retain the right to make the final decision. However, under codetermination, management loses not only the right to make the immediate decision, but also the right to make the final decision. Under West German law, if the management and works council cannot agree on a matter that is subject to codetermination, the issue may be referred to a concilation committee on which a neutral party casts the tie-breaking vote. The decision of the conciliation committee is binding on both parties. Under Dutch law, if management and the union cannot reach agreement on a matter that must be codetermined, the issue may be referred to

an industry council and, if necessary, to the Minister of Social Affairs for a final decision.

The 1972 amendments in West Germany greatly expanded the area of codetermination. Many items, which prior to that time were subject only to consultation, became subject to codetermination under the new law. As a result, the power of the works council was increased and by the same token, management's decision-making authority was eroded.

Under the 1971 works council law in the Netherlands, codetermination was limited to a small number of items: work rules, pensions, profit-sharing or savings schemes, working hours and holiday arrangements, and safety and health measures. Under the 1979 act, codetermination rights were expanded to include: wage scales and remuneration schemes, hiring and dismissal policies, promotion policies, training, personnel rating systems, welfare services, and grievance procedures. Dutch management strongly opposed this loss of decision-making authority.

In Sweden the works councils, which are composed of an equal number of company and employee representatives, have been purely consultative and are likely to remain so. The unions have been more interested in increasing the power of the plant union representatives than in giving the works councils codetermination authority.

Asset Formation and Employee Ownership

Asset formation accomplished through employee stock ownership, which could result in worker participation in company decision making, is an issue that has been hotly debated by management and labor in Western Europe in recent years. To date, however, no legislation incorporating the provisions of such a plan has been enacted.

As has been indicated in earlier chapters, in West Germany, France, and the

Netherlands, laws have been passed that provide for bonus-savings plans or profit-sharing plans. Under the West German law, employees may save tax free up to 624 deutsche marks per year to which government adds a bonus of 30 percent to 64 percent, depending on the employee's marital status. Under the French law, companies are required to share profits with employees. Under the Dutch law, employers, if they wish, may adopt either a bonus-savings plan or a profit-sharing plan for their employees. British companies also may provide savings or profit-sharing plans for their workers, and legislation has been suggested to make such plans more attractive in the tax realm. However, none of the plans contemplates participation by the employees in corporate decison making through stock ownership. In fact, most of the plans do not involve stock ownership, and in the West German plan, which does permit employees to invest their savings in company stocks or bonds, only about 1 percent have opted to do so.

The French and Italian communist and socialist unions are opposed on the basis of ideology not only to the existing asset formation schemes, but also to any other type of asset formation plan. Both French and Italian labor leaders have condemned such plans as being contrary to the immediate interests of the employees and to the long-run goals of their union organizations.[8] On the other hand, although British, Dutch, West German, and Swedish unions are critical of current plans, they do support a system of asset formation that would: (1) secure its funds through profit sharing rather than worker savings, (2) invest the funds in company stock, and (3) place control of the stock in the unions rather than in the individual workers. The British, Dutch, West German, and Swedish unions see in asset formation, based on these three principles, a device whereby employees through their unions might attain a role, and perhaps eventually a controlling role, in company decision making.

During the 1970s the West German, Swedish, and Dutch union have sponsored legislation in their countries based on the three principles set forth in the previous paragraph. In 1974, the West German unions sponsored a plan that would have required companies to contribute up to 10 percent of their profits to the employees in the form of stock, which although held individually by the employees, would have been controlled jointly by the union and the company.

In 1973, the Swedish Confederation of Trade Unions published its first version of a proposed asset formation plan, which has become known as the Meidner plan after its author who is an economist for the LO. The most recent version of the Meidner plan provides that Swedish companies would pay 20 percent of net profits in the form of shares into a workers' fund. Individual employees would have the right to vote 20 percent of the shares, but a coalition of unions in the area would have the right to vote the other 80 percent.

In 1964 in the Netherlands, the union federations published a compulsory profit-sharing plan (VAD) which would have established a national fund financed by "excess profits" and managed entirely by union representatives. In 1977, the union proposal was changed to provide that 23 percent of company profits be used to buy shares, one half of which would go to the workers and one-half of which would be paid to the national pension fund.

In each of the three countries, West Germany, Sweden, and the Netherlands, the asset plans proposed by the unions have met with severe criticism and vigorous opposition from management. As a result, none of the plans has been adopted. In West Germany, the government has moved instead to strengthen the workers' premium savings plan. In Sweden, industry has proposed as an alternative a voluntary profit-sharing and savings plan for individual employees. In the Netherlands, the new government in 1978 proposed a

---

[8] Norris Willatt, *Multi-National Unions* (London: Financial Times, Ltd., 1974), 40.

watered-down bill which contains both individual and collective features. Under the new proposal, a 12 percent tax on company "super profits" would be used to give extra benefits to employees, and an additional 12 percent tax would be paid into a special fund for pensions to be administered by twelve members nominated by the unions and eight members nominated by the government.

Dismissals

One of the most significant and dramatic changes in labor relations in Europe in the last ten years has been in the area of dismissal of employees — dismissal of individual employees for alleged misconduct, and dismissal of groups of employees for economic reasons, that is, redundancy.

During the last ten years, in every one of the six European nations that we have studied, legislation has been enacted that has severely curtailed management's rights in this area. The new legislation has been based on the concept of the employee's property right in the job; the notion that since an employee works on a job, he invests his "assets" in it; and that these assets should not be destroyed by the employer unless he has good cause and is willing to compensate the employee for the loss.[9]

Although the elements of the legislation differ from country to country, the trend is toward a program that requires management to:

1. demonstrate reasonable cause for the dismissal,
2. specify such causes in writing to the employee,
3. consult with the representatives of the employee before dismissal,
4. provide the employee with a period of notification prior to dismissal,

[9] Michael Rubenstein, "Dismissals and the Law," in *Comparative Industrial Relations in Europe*, by Derek Torrington (London: Associated Business Programs, Ltd., 1978), 147.

5. keep the employee at work until the court determines if dismissal is justified,
6. compensate the dismissed employee for the loss of his property rights in the job,
7. reinstate the employee, if he has been dismissed and the court determines the dismissal was not for just cause.

Not all of these seven components are in effect in all six countries. Likewise, in the countries where a particular item is in effect, the requirements under it may vary. For example, prior notification is required in all six countries, but the length of notification varies considerably. Notification reaches a maximum of six months under certain conditions in Sweden and the Netherlands; whereas it is limited to a maximum of twelve weeks in Great Britain. Likewise, the amount of compensation varies but can be as high as 3,000 pounds in Great Britain and forty-eight months of pay in Sweden. In all six countries, management is required to consult with representatives of the employees before action is taken, but in most of the countries, after consultation, management is free to dismiss the employee or employees prior to a court decision on the merits of the case. However, in France, redundancy dismissals may not occur without the approval of the regional department of labor, and in West Germany, the court may order the company to continue to employ the worker or workers until the court decides whether dismissal is reasonable.

Reinstatement of employees who have been found to have been unjustly discharged is still not required in most European countries. Instead, it is contended that compensation for loss of a job is a more desirable and practical solution. However, in at least two of the six countries, reinstatement is now provided in the legislation. The current Italian legislation requires that an employee who has been unjustly discharged must be reinstated as well as be paid damages of at least five months' pay. Effective April 1, 1978, British labor tribunals were given the power to order employers to reinstate employees who had been unfairly discharged. (Prior to that date, the British tribunals could recommend reinstatement but could not order it.)

Employee dismissal is not only an area where advances through national legislation are being made, but also an area where the EEC has been active and will probably continue to be active. In 1975, the European Council adopted a directive (effective in February, 1977) which requires that no company in the European Economic Community may make redundant ten or more employees without proper consultation with workers' representatives and public authorities. In 1976, the European Commission sent to the Council a preliminary draft on "Protection of Workers in the Event of Individual Dismissals." A final draft on this aspect of job security is expected to come before the Council in the near future. The thrust of EEC action is to bring about harmonization of dismissal policies among all the countries in the European Economic Community.

Under the new legislation, management is still free to dismiss redundant employees. However, employees are provided considerable protection and must be given compensation for the loss of their "job assets." As a result, management finds that it now has much less flexibility to adjust to a decrease in demand for its product. At the very time when it needs to cut costs most, management may either have to continue to employ workers whom it does not need or give them sizeable termination payments. As a result, labor has become much less a variable and much more a fixed cost.

Absenteeism

Absenteeism among workers in Western Europe is very high compared with absenteeism in the United States or Japan. A study by the Swedish employers' association showed that in 1973 sickness absenteeism among industrial workers in Europe ranged from a high of 10 percent in Sweden to a low of 5 percent in the United Kingdom, compared with only 4 percent in the United States and 3 percent in Japan. It is believed that since 1973 the rate has continued to climb. In each of the European countries in this study, the production loss resulting from absenteeism was many times the loss resulting from strikes. For example, in 1976 in Great Britain, workers lost 350 million man days as a result of "certified sickness" absences compared with 6 million man days as a result of strike action. In France, the Heilbronner report stated that in 1975 time lost as a result of absenteeism was almost one hundred times that lost as a result of strikes.

The high rate of absenteeism is believed to be primarily a result of the very liberal sick-pay plans in effect in most of the European countries. The basic provisions of the sick-pay laws in 1974 in the six countries are shown in Table 13-1.

In France and Italy, the sick pay as required by law is heavily supplemented by collective agreements. Under the Italian agreements, it is almost universal practice to pay 100 percent of earnings for the first three days of absence because of sickness. Moreover, under many Italian agreements, the 100 percent is extended for a much longer period than the three days. In a survey of twenty Italian companies in 1978, it was found that all twenty had agreed to supplementary sick pay, which most commonly provided employees with full pay for the first several months of absence resulting from illness.[10] In France, the mensualization agreements not only provide monthly pay for blue-collar workers, but also extend to them the supplementary sick-pay benefits that formerly were available only to white-collar workers. As a result, the total percentage of earnings received by French workers who are absent because of illness is much higher than the legislative requirement, as set forth in Table 13-1.

[10] *European Industrial Relations Review*, No. 55, July-August, 1978, 14.

TABLE 13-1   Sick Pay Provisions

Country	Duration of Benefits	Amount of Benefits
Great Britain	Flat rate benefit limited to 312 days, if less than 156 contributions have been paid; otherwise replaced by invalidity benefit after 168 days entitlement. Earnings-related supplement limited to 156 days.	Flat rate of £8.60 per week plus earnings-related benefit at 33⅓% of earnings between £10 and £30, and 15% of earnings between £30 and £42, plus family supplements.
France	12 months over a three-year period.	50% of earnings, plus family supplements.
Italy	6 months per year.	50% of earnings, 66⅔% after 21 days.
The Netherlands	12 months.	80% of earnings.
West Germany	78 weeks over a three-year period.	100% of earnings for first 6 weeks, thereafter 80%, plus family supplements.
Sweden	Unlimited.	90% of earnings.

Rights and Benefits for Women Employees

During the last ten years, major changes have been made in the rights and benefits of women employees in all six of the European countries in this study. The governments have moved to provide greater protection and benefits to women by enacting three types of legislation: maternity rights and benefits laws, equal pay laws, and equal opportunity laws.

All six countries now have legislation that provides that a woman employee may not be dismissed because of pregnancy and also must be reemployed without loss of acquired job rights following childbirth. In addition, the legislation provides that for a certain number of weeks before childbirth and a certain number of weeks after childbirth, the woman worker must be given time off with pay. The number of weeks of maternity leave varies from twelve weeks in Great Britain and the Netherlands to nine months in Sweden, and pay varies from 80 percent in Italy to 100 percent in the Netherlands and West Germany (see Table 13-2).

In addition to paid maternity leave prior to and immediately following confinement, several of the acts provide for leave to take care of the child. The French 1975 law requires that an employer grant an employee an unpaid leave of up to one year after giving birth, with reemployment and acquired job rights guaranteed. Moreover, the French 1977 Parental Leave Act permits either parent to stop work at any time for two years without pay to care for children, with reemployment and acquired job rights guaranteed. Italian law provides for maternity leave at 30 percent pay for up to six months during a child's first year, plus another six months when a child under three years old is sick. Reemployment and acquired job rights are guaranteed in both situations.

Since 1974, the Swedish law has permitted a father as well as a mother to take time off with pay to care for a young child. As revised in 1976, a total of nine months' parental leave with pay may be taken, eight months at 90 percent of pay, and one month at about $6 per day. (The nine months include maternity leave prior to childbirth, which, of course, must be taken

TABLE 13-2 Maternity Protection and Benefits Acts in Six Western European Countries

Country	Legislation	Protection against Dismissal Resulting from Pregnancy	Reemployment and Protection of Acquired Job Rights	Length of Paid Leave	Pay during Leave as % of Prior Pay
Great Britain	1975 Employment Protection Act (as amended)	Yes	Yes, provided worker returns within 29 weeks after child birth	12 weeks	90% including social security
The Netherlands	Sickness Benefit Act and 1976 Protection Against Discrimination Act	Yes	Yes	12 weeks	100%
West Germany	1972 Act for Protection for Women in Employment	Yes	Yes	14 weeks	100%
France	1975 Maternity Protection Act (amended July 1978); 1977 Parental Leave Act	Yes	Yes	16 weeks	90%
Italy	1971 Act for Protection of Working Mothers	Yes	Yes, job must be held for one year	20 weeks	80%
Sweden	1976 Parental Benefits Act	Yes	Yes	9 months	90% for first 8 months and about $6/day for ninth month

by the mother.) The percentage of eligible fathers participating in the program has risen rapidly as follows:

1974   2.4%
1975   5.2%
1976   7.5%
1977   over 10.0%[11]

The five countries that are part of the European Economic Community (Sweden is not a member of the EEC) have been under pressure from the EEC to enact and make effective equal pay legislation. The treaty of Rome which established the EEC in 1957 provides in paragraph 119 that, "Each member state shall . . . ensure and subsequently maintain the application of the principle of equal remuneration for equal work as between men and women workers."

In 1975, the European Commission issued a directive to the member countries ordering them to implement the equal pay provisions of paragraph 119, and in 1976 the European Court of Justice issued its first decision on this issue. In 1968, Miss Gabrielle Defrenne had brought a suit against Sabena Airlines claiming that she had been paid less than male workers for the same type of work. Her plea was rejected by the Belgian labor tribunal and on appeal by the Belgian labor court and council of state. She then appealed to the European Court. The European Court ruled that "the principle of equal pay for women as set forth in Article 119 is enforceable. . . ."

In West Germany, equal pay has been the law since 1959 when a federal court ruled that the constitution required the same pay for men and women doing the same work. In 1975, new laws requiring equal pay became effective in Great Britain and the Netherlands. (The British law had been passed in 1970 but was not fully effective until 1975.) In Italy, an act implementing the constitutional provision for equal pay become effective in 1977.

Despite such constitutional provisions, legal decisions, and legislative enactments, the European Commission found in late 1978 that its directive ordering equal pay under paragraph 119 of the treaty of Rome "has still not been completely implemented in any of the Member States of the Community." The Commission proposed a European-level meeting of employer and employee organizations to discuss the elimination of indirect discrimination through job classification systems and initiation of infringement proceedings against certain member states before the Court of Justice.[12]

In Sweden, which is not covered by the Commission directive, the move toward equal pay has resulted largely from collective bargaining aided also by a Council on Equality (1972) and later a Parliamentary Equality Committee (1976). In 1979, a new law requiring equal pay was passed, but it was a watered-down version of the original proposal and its effectiveness is much in doubt.

Equal opportunity legislation generally has been more recent than equal pay legislation. For example, equal opportunity legislation in Great Britain was not passed until 1975, five years after the equal pay legislation. The 1975 British Sex Discrimination Act provides that it is unlawful for an employer to discriminate against women in hiring or dismissal or "in the way he affords her access to opportunities for promotion, transfer or training or to any other benefits, facilities or services." In West Germany, the 1972 Works Council Act provides that there shall be no discrimination because of sex, and in Italy the 1977 Anti-Discrimination Act prohibits discrimination because of sex with respect to hiring, training, promotion, and career development.

In December, 1975, the European Coun-

---

[11] "Swedish Promotion Blitz Tries to Lure Dads into the Nursery," *International Herald Tribune*, April 21, 1978, 6.

[12] *European Industrial Relations Review*, No. 58, November 1978, 5–6.

cil issued an equal opportunity directive which became effective for all EEC countries on July 1, 1978. Article 3 of the directive requires that: "There shall be no discrimination whatsoever between men and women on grounds of sex in the conditions, including selection criteria, for access to all jobs or posts, whatever the sector or branch of activity, at all levels of the professional hierarchy." It is still too soon to determine how effective the directive will be in promoting equality of opportunity for women employees.

In Sweden, the Equal Treatment in Working Life Act, which was enacted in 1979 and became effective January 1, 1980, provides for equal treatment for women in hiring, promotion, and training. However, as stated earlier, the new law is a watered-down version of the original proposal and its effectiveness in bringing about equal pay and equal opportunities is much in doubt.

In November, 1978, the European Council adopted a directive that requires equalization of social security benefits for men and women. The directive applies to retirement, sickness, invalidity, industrial injury, and unemployment benefits. The directive is not immediately effective, but instead, allows the member nations until 1985 to bring their systems into compliance with all its provisions.

In summary, during the last ten years, major progress has been recorded in providing Western European women with maternity rights and benefits. Sweden has surpassed all of the other nations in this respect. Within the countries in the European Community, there are considerable differences in the rights and benefits. This appears to be an area that will lend itself to harmonization by directives of the European Council.

Much progress has been made also in the areas of equal pay and equal opportunities. However, in these areas, especially in the area of equal opportunities, much still remains to be done to implement the national legislation and the directives of the European Commission. A 1978 directive of the European Commission will attempt to bring about equality in social security benefits by 1985.

Questions for Discussion

1. The various formal structures of representation (works councils, codetermination, etc.) found in some European countries were adopted prior to the 1980s. Do you believe they will be an advantage or a disadvantage to the management and employees of these firms in the environment of the 1980s and beyond?

2. What lessons might American managers learn from the experience their European counterparts have had with the legislation described in this paper governing employee benefits, hours of work, and other working conditions?

3. Are trends in human resource management and industrial relations in the United States leading us to adapt more or fewer of these European legislative and corporate policies and practices?

4. What are the major cultural, political, and legal barriers to adapting European structures of representation in American firms?

5. What are the major cultural, political, and legal barriers to adapting American human resource management strategies and practices in European firms?

Characteristics of Japanese Managements and Their Personnel Policies

Postwar Reforms and the Power Structure of Enterprises

In this chapter we will confine our discussion for the most part to the management organization and practices of large Japanese enterprises, because labor union organization is concentrated in this sector and the system of union-management relations that has evolved over the years between the enterprise unions and the managements of the major corporations has had a strong influence on labor relations in all the other sectors. However, we cannot ignore the management and union structures that prevail in the small and medium-sized enterprises: they employ more than 70 percent of all Japanese workers, and among the difficult problems that remain to be resolved is how to establish and stabilize industrial democracy in this sector.

It was the large enterprises that commanded the attention of the American Occupation Forces immediately following World War II and a number of reforms were implemented: the zaibatsu were dissolved; the large monopolistic companies were split into smaller units; the stock holdings of these companies were liquidated and stock ownership "democratized" — that is, these stocks became available for purchase on the open market; top company executives who had played leading roles during the war were purged; and property taxes were levied, precipitating the downfall of wartime corporation magnates. All of these reforms had very strong

Source: Taishiro Shirai, ed., *Contemporary Industrial Relations in Japan* (Madison, Wis.: University of Wisconsin Press, 1983). Reprinted by permission of The University of Wisconsin Press and Taishiro Shirai.

effects on the management structure of large enterprises as well as on their industrial relations philosophy and policies.

One result of these reforms is that the ownership and management of companies in Japan is now more distinctly separate than in most other capitalist countries in the world. "Capitalist control," of course, does not exist in the national enterprises or public corporations (the Postal Service or the National Railways, for example), but it also can be said to be virtually absent in the leading private-sector enterprises. Because company stock is widely dispersed among a large number of owners, each with only a few shares, the stockholders are, in practical terms, virtually deprived of any power over the day-to-day decisions of company managements, and only in extraordinary situations have they had the power to appoint or remove top management personnel. The inevitable consequence is that the general meeting of stockholders has only nominal power and that even the boards of directors of the major corporations have come to be monopolized by the companies' full-time managing directors. Thus, it can be said that a "managerial revolution" has materialized in Japan to the extent that the power of the company management exceeds that of company stockholders.

It may be useful to begin our examination of the management power structure in Japanese companies and the characteristics of their decision-making mechanisms by comparing the functions of inspectors in Japan with those of the West German *Aufsichtsrat*, inspectors' organizations representing shareholders and employees of the company. The German inspectors have the power to appoint members of the board of directors, to control its activities, and to approve or reject some major business decisions. The Japanese inspectors, in contrast, have no such powers and their function traditionally has been limited to auditing a company's accounts. The 1974 revision of the Commercial Law authorized inspectors to review how the executive board members performed their duties, but even here their inspection is confined to whether or not the activities of the board members are legal and does not consider whether they are proper or reasonable. Thus, it cannot be said that this change in the law had any visible effect on company power structures. The Commercial Law was again amended in 1981, which further reinforced the authority of the inspectors in that they could ask not only executive board members but also general managers to provide them with necessary information concerning business conditions of the company. This amendment went into effect on October 1, 1982, and the impact on the power balance between inspectors and boards of directors is yet to be seen.

More important than the function of inspectors in any discussion of the management power structure in Japan is the role of the stockholders' general meeting. Its position and power were defined in a 1950 revision of the Commercial Law as being limited to the determination of conditions fundamental to a corporation's existence, such as its establishment or dissolution, its merger with another company, the appointment or dismissal of executive board members, and changes in the amount of authorized capital. The power to make all strategic business decisions is in the hands of the board of directors. Although the boards do report these decisions at the stockholders' meetings, the meetings themselves are largely ceremonial and it is most unlikely, except in emergency cases, that stockholders would disapprove any decision previously made by a board of directors. As far as appointments or dis-

missals of board members are concerned, they are usually reported ex post facto and are routinely approved.

The point being emphasized here is that more than merely the law and custom prevail and that control of corporations through a concentration of stock ownership, as is often seen in the United States and Western Europe, operates in only a limited sense in large Japanese enterprises, for the following reasons:

First, as stated earlier, the postwar reforms of the large corporations enabled the "employee managers" to gain the power and authority to function as top management. Another factor that operated to curtail the stockholders' influence and their share of profits was the growth of the enterprise unions.

Second, there has been a great change in the composition of corporation stockholders, with the stock of any one corporation now being owned by a large number of individuals as well as by banks, insurance companies, and other corporations. In 1980, more than 70 percent of the total number of shares of stocks listed on the stock exchange was owned by corporations and slightly less than 30 percent was owned by individuals. It actually is fairly common in Japan for large corporations to own stock in other large corporations, but that does not mean that any of them will exercise the right to control another's management. Rather, the situation compels them to respect each other's autonomy and to refrain from intervening in the business management. Also, a large corporation may have a considerable number of corporate stockholders who may find it difficult to agree among themselves on the need to intervene or on what type of intervention would be appropriate. Furthermore, many of the corporate stockholders have invested in other corporations only for the profitable utilization of their assets; therefore, their investments may be only on a short-term or temporary basis. Thus, if they are dissatisfied with the management of a particular company, a wiser move would be for them to sell their stock.

Third, the capitalization of large Japanese corporations is probably unique in that owned capital is, on average, no more than 20 percent of total capital. This proportion is lower than that among companies in most developed countries. Thus, a high percentage of a Japanese corporation's financial demands must be met by borrowed capital. So far, the corporation managements have been successful in securing the funds they need by persuading the banks to support their long-term investments in plant and equipment. As a result, their need to rely for this capital on stockholders, who are generally concerned with short-term profits, has lessened, and this, in turn, has weakened the stockholders' power to control the corporation managements.

These three factors have worked to expand the scope of top management's discretion in formulating corporate policies and making decisions so that it might be said that large corporations in Japan have realized not only the separation of management from ownership, but also the establishment of a system in which management enjoys almost unrestricted power over the owners.

I should make it clear that when I am speaking about the company's top management, I am referring to a small group of full-time executives, the *Jōmukai*, who actually have the power to make decisions on matters that are discussed by the corporation's board of directors. As a rule, members of this group are the president, the vice-president (unlike U.S. companies, Japanese companies have very few vice-presidents), the senior managing director (*senmu*), and the managing director (*jōmu*). This executive board is kind of an "inner cabinet" of the board of directors which assists the president in the day-to-day operation of the business. The responsibilities vested in this group lead to what we call the "loosening of the checking function of the board of directors" and, consequently, to further concentration and internalization of decision-making power within the corporation.

The Development of Managerial Personnel through "Promotion from Within"

The obvious next questions, then, are: What kinds of people are these top managers, and where do they come from? Generally, the establishment of management control means that professional managers, independent of corporate ownership, come to the fore and assume the responsibility and power to run the business. In the case of Japan, however, it should be noted that when we speak of professional managers, we are referring to something different from what the term means in the United States and other advanced industrialized societies. Top professional managers in the United States frequently move from one company to another, demonstrating their managerial expertise beyond the boundaries of any one corporation. In other words, they are capable of performing their managerial functions as professionals in an open labor market where there is high mobility among firms. As such, they are often scouted and hired away by rival companies. Accordingly, they tend to be free from any commitment to or any identification with a particular corporation, nor do they feel obliged to do more than what is required by their contracts.

An overwhelming majority of Japanese managers have advanced to their present positions from the ranks of general employees through the system of internal promotion, or "promotion from within" the particular company. Rather than being a postwar innovation, this system of regular career paths for all employees was well established among large Japanese corporations, both public and private, before World War II. The companies hire groups of new university or college graduates and, as they climb the managerial ladder, they accumulate experience in various jobs, not confined to any specialized field, through job rotation at regular intervals. Finally, those who survive this extensive training and screening process are promoted to top management positions.

The organization of white-collar employees into enterprise unions after the war not only reinforced their employment security, but entrenched more solidly than ever before the practice of developing managers within a particular company by this system of promoting long-service employees. Of course, a system of this kind could not operate successfully in the new and rapidly growing firms, in those companies that have gotten into financial difficulties, or in those companies closely related to public corporations and government agencies. In these latter cases, the probabilities are that they have had to hire managers from outside. These imported managers constitute only a small share of the total in Japan, the overwhelming majority of the managers having been promoted within their particular companies.

Management Philosophies and Personnel Policies

The fact that the top management of most Japanese corporations are long-service employees who have been promoted from within their companies undoubtedly affects their management philosophy and especially their industrial relations policies. Five principal features of their philosophy, as it relates to industrial relations, can be summarized: First, their primary concern is the continued existence and further development of their corporation. Second, they regard all company employees, including themselves, as members of the same corporate community. Third, they take an egalitarian view of income distribution between labor and management within the company. Fourth, they are crucially concerned with maintaining stability and peace in the company's industrial relations. (In other words, they strive to avoid industrial disputes and strikes, often at any cost.) Fifth, they tend to reject the intervention of outside labor groups in any negotiations over internal labor problems, an attitude that

might be described as exclusionist. Let me discuss each of these points in more detail.

First, it would seem to be quite natural, and understandable, that the top executives of a Japanese firm would attach the utmost importance to its continued existence and development. This concern is rooted in a sense of identification with the company that results from their own long service with it as well as in a sense of responsibility for the continued employment and improved conditions of their fellow employees. Moreover, only by keeping the company prosperous and expanding can they ensure their own influential positions and prestige both within and outside the corporation. The fact that managers motivated by such a value have been given real power in their companies has contributed to the creation of a highly competitive market economy in Japan, and the positive entrepreneurship of these people is an important factor in the rapid growth of the Japanese economy. These managers have been progressive and enterprising in promoting technological change and innovations, in pioneering in new industrial areas, in adjusting to changing industrial structures, in reorganizing industrial locations, and in expanding international trade and investment overseas as well as in many other corporate activities. Such entrepreneurship is possible only because management has primacy over ownership in Japanese corporations, which enables the managers to make plans and decisions from a long-term perspective, unrestricted by short-term considerations of profits and dividends.

Second, the firm conviction on the part of these managers that company employees are members of a corporate community seems to be quite different from views of employers in the United States and some Western European countries. For those Japanese managers who have climbed the promotion ladder within their companies, it is not extraordinary to consider other employees as colleagues, or subordinates or juniors, in the ranks in which they themselves spent many years. At the same time all these employees belong to the enterprise union of which the managers once were members, and perhaps officers. Since most of the older regular employees have been with the company for most of their working lives and the younger ones expect to follow the same pattern, they and the managers tend to feel that they are "in the same boat." Their relationship, thus, is friendly and respectful rather than formal and contentious. However, it was the bitter labor disputes during the 1950s and the first half of the 1960s that firmly established the now prevailing principle that the maintenance and improvement of the employees' working conditions was a more important management responsibility than the maintenance and improvement of stockholders' dividends. The stockholders never benefit at the expense of the employees, but the employees may avoid layoffs at the expense of the stockholders.

When Japanese managers have to deal with redundancy — called an "employment adjustment" in Japan — because of a business slump or a financial problem for the corporation, their first move is to reduce or suspend the payment of dividends and to cut the salaries of the top management. Next, if necessary, they would reduce the salaries of middle management personnel and the amount of the semiannual bonuses that all company employees receive. If further cutbacks are needed, they usually take the form of a reduction in hours of work, termination of the employment contracts of temporary workers, job transfers or rotation of employees, and/or a temporary release from employment. Additional adjustments may include suspension of employees' wage increases, reduction in their monthly compensation or bonuses, and a call for the voluntary retirement of older employees. Management's last resort, if all other efforts fail to solve their problems, would be the dismissal of some employees. Thus, at

the heart of management's view of the employees as fellow members of the corporate community is a commitment to provide the regular employees with job security under the so-called lifetime employment system in Japan.

There are at least three factors that underlie the third feature of Japanese management philosophy — the managers' view that income distribution between labor and management should be egalitarian. These factors are (a) that they themselves have come up through the ranks via the system of promotion from within and are familiar with the financial needs of the employees; (b) that both the blue- and white-collar workers belong to the same enterprise union; (c) that the union, in the collective bargaining process, is able to exert a strong regulatory influence on the distribution of wages and salaries within the company. The result is that over the years the income differentials between labor and management have tended to narrow. In 1927 the before-tax annual compensation of company presidents in Japan was 110 times the annual starting salaries of new college graduates, but in 1980 the presidents were paid only 14.5 times as much as the newly hired college graduates.

Fourth, it would seem to be almost inevitable that the labor policies of Japanese managers, in keeping with their management philosophies and their attitudes toward their fellow employees, would place primary emphasis on maintaining stability and peace in the labor-management relations within the company. These managers are acutely aware that industrial disputes are most detrimental to the continued existence and progress of any company in a highly competitive market. Needless to say, conflicts of interest between unions and managements do occur in Japan, as elsewhere, and the managers have to deal with them. However, if a strike or other industrial action develops out of one of these conflicts, in Japan it is taken to mean not only that a group of employees has dared to make public their distrust of or hostility toward management within the corporate community, but also that the managers have somehow failed or been clumsy in administering their labor relations policies; this perception will have a decidedly negative effect on their authority and prestige both within and outside the company.

Yet the fact that Japanese managers emphasize the maintenance of industrial peace and stability does not necessarily imply that all of them respect the basic rights of workers and labor union autonomy or that they favor industrial peace based upon the idea of industrial democracy. Like employers in other countries, most Japanese managers would prefer not to have the limits on their decision-making and on management prerogatives that unions and collective bargaining bring to their firms, and Japanese managers generally rate nonunion companies higher than unionized companies. The employers in small and medium-sized companies are the ones who are particularly disconcerted by unions in their establishments, and they often resort to rather extreme measures in their attempts to drive them out.

In postwar Japan, of course, it is unlawful for any employer to deny a labor union recognition or to refuse to bargain, as such actions are unfair labor practices. Therefore, if these employers have to recognize a union as a representative of their employees, they would prefer that it would be one whose membership was confined exclusively to their own employees, and they would make every effort to prevent an outside union from intervening in the labor-management relations within their companies.

Fifth, as has been suggested in the paragraphs above, Japanese managers tend to try to keep their industrial relations with their employees a private affair, confined to the corporation. Such an exclusionist policy takes a variety of forms. For example, managers attempt to avoid any negotiations with a higher labor organization to which their enterprise union might be affiliated, or, if they are forced into such negotiations, they will try to limit the scope of bargaining with that organization. If an outside union does succeed in organizing some of the company employees, the management frequently will try to force those employees to disaffiliate, will deliberately disfavor them on their jobs, or will intervene in the union's affairs. If there are two or more unions representing groups of employees, the management may favor one by taking a moderate approach in dealing with it while adopting a hostile attitude toward the others. All of these actions are unfair labor practices, of course, and are strictly forbidden by law. And, although they seem to be used most frequently and blatantly by the smaller companies, they also can be observed as part of the labor policies of large companies, including those in the public sector.

Human Resource Management
at the Workplace in Japan

Lifetime employment is often cited as being one of the pillars of human resource management systems in large Japanese enterprises. Indeed, given the steady increase in lifetime employment practices since the end of World War II, it is hardly surprising that Western scholars and managers have been so struck with their role in Japanese industrial relations as a whole. But the success of the lifetime employment system hinges on several other prominent characteristics of Japanese labor-management relations. The purpose of this brief overview is to consider the relationship between these various qualities of the Japanese system, which also include the promotion of extensive internal career paths, a qualification evaluation system that links seniority with merit criteria, flexibility in the creation and maintenance of work groups, several formal and informal channels of labor-management communication, and a set of conditions that mitigate toward extensive contact between labor and management.

Long-Term Employment and Internal Career Paths

Long-term employment in Japan has increased steadily since the end of the Second World War, particularly among male white-collar employees, but increasingly among male blue-collar workers as well. Among male workers employed in large enterprises (over 1,000 employees) the development of internal labor markets within the firm has steadily increased the

Source: Abridged and adapted from Takeshi Inagami, *Labor-Management Communications at the Workshop Level*, Japanese Institute of Labor, 1983, with permission of the author and the Japanese Institute of Labor.

average length of employment in a given organization. The length of service by age of white-collar and blue-collar workers is depicted in Figure 13-1.

The success of long-term employment depends on an enterprise's ability to create extensive channels for the internal movement and promotion of their employees over time. Traditionally, promotion to managerial positions in Japan has been correlated with an employee's length of service with the firm and educational background. But because both of these have increased significantly for the population as a whole over the last few decades, it became necessary to find a new set of criteria for promotion. Because ability and merit ratings are not completely correlated with length of service, these factors have come to play an increasingly important role in management promotion decisions. This shift in promotion criteria in turn mandated a change in human resource management techniques, with decreasing emphasis on managing people in groups according to education and length of service, and a greater focus on individual employees' talents and abilities (commonly referred to as ability-based management).

Ability-based management and promotion decisions are based in part on formal promotion criteria, and in part on more informal arrangements that have sprung up since the 1970s.

Most white-collar employees are still promoted formally on the basis of job-related skills and work performances. Comparatively few companies explicitly consider educational background in promotion decisions. Educational attainment and the reputation of the schools attended do, however, play important roles in the initial recruitment and selection decisions

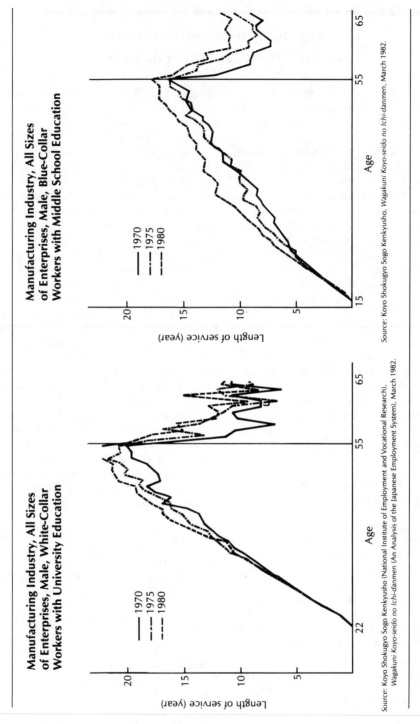

Manufacturing Industry, All Sizes of Enterprises, Male, White-Collar Workers with University Education

1970
1975
1980

Length of service (year)

Age

Source: Koyo Shokugyo Sogo Kenkyusho (National Institute of Employment and Vocational Research), Wagakuni Koyo-seido no Ichi-danmen (An Analysis of the Japanese Employment System), March 1982.

Manufacturing Industry, All Sizes of Enterprises, Male, Blue-Collar Workers with Middle School Education

1970
1975
1980

Length of service (year)

Age

Source: Koyo Shokugyo Sogo Kenkyusho, Wagakuni Koyo-seido no Ichi-danmen, March 1982.

FIGURE 13-1 Trends In the Average Length Of Service by Age

of major companies. And less than 5 percent of large-scale manufacturing companies emphasize length of service in such decisions for white-collar workers. For blue-collar workers, length of service is also a considerably less important promotion criterion than job-related knowledge and skills. That is, the seniority-based promotion system is declining in importance for both kinds of employees. This development is paralleled by the fact that job transfers within the firm are also increasing for both blue- and white-collar employees.

Flexible Labor-Management Communication Channels

At the level of the enterprise, joint consultation between labor and management representatives is the most widespread and important channel of communication. This type of consultation occurs at the firm level, where it is usually attended by union leaders and top management, and at the workshop level, where production procedures and work schedules are discussed. The higher level consultations are generally held three or four times a year, where, management usually discusses business strategies and plans in some detail with union representatives. If personnel problems arise from management's plans, it is not uncommon for the parties to establish a joint technical committee to consider potential solutions to such issues.

Production committees meet more often. In these meetings, management usually presents production and work schedule plans, and union representatives voice the positions of their members on the shop floor. These meetings usually conclude in consensus because their substance has generally been agreed upon previously by the lower-level production committee. The success of this sort of consultation hinges primarily on the thorough familiarity of both labor and management with the details of the production process. Foremen, for example, often attend production committee meetings as management representatives, since they are closest to the processes being discussed.

Because of the emphasis on familiarity with the actual substance of these consultations, decision making tends to be of a "bottom-up" nature, at least *de facto*. Thus, this system attempts to reflect the views of the workers themselves. These views, in turn, are clarified and consolidated in various forms of work groups, and by the comparatively broad scope of many job definitions.

Employee and Work Group Characteristics

Job descriptions tend to be relatively vague and function more as guidelines than rigid standards, particularly for white-collar employees. Thus, employees' careers are developed through exposure to a wide variety of job tasks, or even jobs. This breadth of exposure is complemented by the relatively flexible relationship between employees and their jobs. That is, if an employee misses work on a given day, his or her co-workers are familiar enough with the job's substance to pinch hit temporarily in order to maintain the performance of the workshop unit. Interpersonal relations are therefore quite important in the work group. People with particularly keen interpersonal skills are often promoted to foreman from within their work groups, at which point they take on a role that represents both management and employees.

Labor-management communication is thus promoted at this relatively low level by the identification of workers with their foremen, and thus with management goals. Foremen both take up the grievances of their subordinates at formal workshop meetings, and advise them informally and personally. Foremen are often simultaneously union representatives, again casting them in their dual role, bridging the concerns of the employee and the employer.

Because of the above-mentioned emphasis on merit and ability-based management and promotions, there does exist a certain amount of competition among employees working at the same level. But at the same time, the ability-based management system formally acknowledges employees' progress in such a way as to raise their status even in the absence of formal promotion. Therefore, employee competition remains relatively latent and commitment to the work group and to coworkers remains relatively high.

Quality Circles and Suggestion Systems

The group orientation of the Japanese human resource management system at the workshop level is supported by the widespread use of quality circles (QCs) and suggestion systems. Together, these participative mechanisms have contributed significantly to the widely publicized productivity and quality control successes of the Japanese economy. Ironically, QCs were actually imported from the United States after World War II when the Americans were still closely involved in reconstructing the Japanese economy. In the 1960s, QCs became increasingly popular in Japan, as foremen and their workers took much of the initiative in perpetuating, and even in establishing them. By 1980, more than a million Japanese employees were active QC participants. Other kinds of "small group activity" are also widespread, particularly in the major companies.

The philosophy underlying QCs is that if quality comes first, profits will follow, at least in the long run. Production is oriented primarily toward customers and/or consumers; satisfaction with product quality is thus considered to be crucial. As a consequence, various work groups have a great regard for each other, since quality hinges on their aggregate performance. Further, many employees are trained in statistical and other methods of quality control and take on a good deal of so-called

management responsibility in turning out a quality product.

QCs are most common in manufacturing, followed by maintenance and equipment control operations, general office management, and sales and service operations. They usually involve about eight members each and meet about every two weeks. In the cases where QCs meet at times other than during regularly scheduled working hours, members generally receive some sort of financial or other compensation for their time. Company-level meetings with reports from QC leaders are held once or twice a year; plant level meetings of this type occur two or three times annually.

The suggestion system fosters employee involvement in a more individually oriented fashion, yet it is in some ways closely related to QCs. Suggestion systems are usually enacted for relatively short periods of time when a specific need or problem arises. Since the first oil crisis of 1973, the number of suggestion systems has dramatically increased in Japan: in 1973, the average annual number of suggestions submitted per company was just under 25,000; by 1980, that number had more than doubled to top 55,000. Meanwhile, the percentage of suggestions actually adopted reached an average of 70 percent.

The success and popularity of both QCs and suggestion systems in Japanese enterprises are closely connected with their roles as mechanisms for constant and in-depth communications between management and labor. As such, they both support and derive support from the other aspects of Japanese human resource management described above.

Summary and Conclusions

We have tried here to emphasize the integrated and interdependent natures of various pieces of the human resource management systems that cover permanent employees in large, private-sector Japanese enterprises. It should be clear that lifetime or long-term employment policies are contingent on a much broader system of management, which plays up extensive management-labor communication from high-level consultation to suggestions submitted by low-level production workers. This system of communications is in turn dependent on and supportive of extensive efforts to deepen and widen internal career paths through promotion policies and job rotation, which increasingly emphasize ability-based management.

The group emphasis that permeates Japanese enterprises of all kinds fosters not only communication, but also a certain measure of competition. But, as noted above, the aggregate environment at a typical Japanese enterprise tends to render competition among employees relatively latent, by rewarding merit not only through promotions, but also with other implicit and explicit status increases. The regular assessment of employees, together with the visible acknowledgment of their improvements, further strengthens the basis for communication, quality-enhancing suggestions, and work group productivity.

Questions for Discussion

1. The major features of the Japanese human resource and industrial relations system evolved in the post World War II environment of steady economic growth and an expanding export sector. To what extent will the system continue to perform well in the future if the rate of economic growth slows? If competition for exports from lower wage developing nations intensifies? As the labor force and population of Japan ages?

2. At the encouragement of the occupation government immediately after World War II, Japan enacted labor legislation patterned after the United States' National Labor Relations Act. What features of the "American model" are visible in Japan today? What features are not present?

Japanese Management in an American Setting

The following case illustrates some of the unique issues involved in implementing a Japanese management system and culture in a traditional American workplace. The case raises numerous questions about the degree to which new human resource management standards can and should be imposed in a setting quite different from that for which the practices were created.

CASE
Ishida Corporation

In January 1983, the Japanese tire producer, Ishida, bought a radial tire manufacturing facility in Marshall, Ohio. The Marshall facility came under the management of Nakano, who served for ten years as president of Ishida's largest manufacturing facility in Japan. Nakano was chosen to manage the Marshall operations because of his excellent record in Japan; he had raised productivity by 90 percent during his last six years by investing in new technology and because of his outstanding ability to nurture good relations with his work force.

In Japan, Nakano had been able to guarantee formally that his employees would have employment security, regular pay raises, and annual bonuses. In return, they gave the company their loyalty and their commitment to a steady increase in plant productivity. Ishida accomplished these goals despite the ongoing introduction of new technology, which required flexibility in organizing the work and in deploying the work force.

The diffusion of quality circles (QCs) throughout Ishida's plants aided the company's success.

Nakano also had maintained excellent relations with the union in Japan. He held monthly meetings with local union leaders to discuss productivity and to share information on the company's financial situation. These accomplishments were due also in part to the fact that the Japanese plant was run by only three layers of management, and there were extremely effective horizontal communications between managers in different functional areas, as well as close ties with the union.

Ishida's acquisition of the Marshall facility fell within a larger strategic plan that included general corporate expansion and growth. The corporation's goal was to become one of the three largest tire manufacturers in the world by the mid-1980s. This strategy was divided into the following goals:

1. Supply the specific quality and quantity of tires required in each geographical region in which the corporation operates, with a view to establishing local subsidiaries in cases where rapidly growing demand is projected.

2. Largely because of cost considerations, buy existing plants overseas instead of building new ones, except in cases where market growth is ensured and expansion will be necessary.
3. Produce the highest quality tires and maintain the highest standards of service to customers. (The importance of these goals is illustrated by Ishida's refusal to give its name to a company and its products until productivity and quality levels met corporate standards.)
4. Gain productivity advantages through investment in advanced tire-production technology and through high-volume production.

The Marshall facility employed 250 people when Ishida took over. The number of employees had peaked at 750 before the tire industry slump in the late 1970s and early 1980s, and production had dropped to about 400,000 tires per year. Productivity was approximately 33 percent of Ishida's most productive Japanese plants, a rate attributed to comparatively inefficient technology and work practices.

Within a week of the acquisition, 170 laid-off workers were rehired. The first few years would be problematic in Marshall; although production was projected to rise to a million tires per year, the company would operate at a loss of about $10 million per year for the first two years after the acquisition. In part, this was due to the fact that the company planned to invest $30 million to $50 million in new machinery and equipment, which would raise profitability in the long run, but not the short run.

Within the first four months of Nakano's tenure as president of the Marshall facility, productivity rose by approximately 20 percent. He attributed most of this increase to the employee's increased sense of job security. Labor relations practices had changed significantly since the takeover, despite a contract with the United Rubber Workers (which was patterned after the industrywide agreement) that continued after Ishida's takeover. Nakano's approach to labor relations was based on the following goals:

1. Accept the union and operate on the basis of building an atmosphere of trust and cooperation.
2. Try to stabilize and increase the work force, although in the absence of formal job guarantees.
3. Work toward minimizing costly, inflexible work rules built into the master contract, so as to increase management's flexibility in the deployment of human resources.
4. Streamline not only the hourly work force, but also the management structure.

The centerpiece of Nakano's new labor relations strategy was clearly a commitment to furthering job security and increasing discretion with respect to job design and work rules. The company intended, for example, to diversify into the production of truck radials, which Marshall had never manufactured, thus expanding job opportunities and increasing job stability. The successful attainment of that goal, however, depended on Marshall's becoming competitive with a nearby, nonunionized Michelin facility. This would require an overall productivity increase of 30 percent. Nakano made these requisites clear to his managers and hourly employees when he took over.

To further Ishida's larger strategy for growth and expansion, the Marshall facility's management agreed with the local union leaders on the following amendments to the master contract:

1. The existing contract included seniority clauses that caused concern about the movement of employees across jobs. The contract was amended to allow the company to assign two primary work activities to each employee, thus clarifying the jobs to which any given employee could be assigned.

2. Because of anticipated construction and the introduction of new technology, Nakano was concerned about a clause mandating that all overtime be on a voluntary basis. The clause was amended to read that the company would try to find volunteers when overtime was necessary, but that it would be able to assign compulsory overtime when not enough volunteers could be found.

3. The contract contained shift preference clauses that allowed employees to transfer across jobs any time they wanted, which could disrupt the company's investment in training aimed at achieving higher levels of productivity. The clauses were altered to allow shift preference changes only twice a year.

After six months as president of the Marshall facility, Nakano confronted several dilemmas with respect to the institutionalization of a coherent, regularized human resource management strategy. The overriding questions revolved around how many of his Japanese management practices he should follow in managing the United States plant, and which of the plant's prior practices should be continued. He was also concerned about how to implement appropriate Japanese practices without alienating his United States managers and workers, or the union.

Questions for Discussion

1. In Japan, Nakano had shared financial information regularly with local union leaders as part of an overall strategy of maintaining open lines of communication with the workers and their representatives. At the Marshall facility, he had instigated monthly meetings with the local URW leaders within two months of his presidency, but recently his American lawyers had advised him that such an approach could be dangerous in the long run. These lawyers had warned him that the union might use such information to the company's disadvantage in the next round of bargaining and advised him to stop the meetings immediately. Nakano was uncomfortable with this advice, however, because he was accustomed to open relations with organized labor and he believed that much of his past success had been founded on such communication. What would you do?

2. In contrast to the operations he had headed in Japan, Nakano found that vertical communication in Marshall was better, but horizontal communication among his managers was considerably worse. He was uncertain as to how he might improve

horizontal communication across functional areas without endangering vertical communication. What would you suggest?

3. As part of his plan to streamline the organization in Marshall, Nakano wanted to eliminate two or three management levels; currently, there were six levels of management. To carry out this plan, however, he anticipated the need to downgrade several of the managers' job descriptions and salaries. He was concerned about the feasibility of this move and did not know exactly how to approach the problem. How would you approach Nakano's problem?

4. Nakano wanted to introduce quality circles throughout the Marshall plant but did not know if by doing so he would infringe on the terms of the URW contract, or jeopardize relations with the union. Among other things, the contract's seniority clauses hampered his plans for introducing quality circles, as well as other aspects of his long-term plans for the Marshall operations. His concern with these clauses was that the investment in training he wanted to make as part of the QC process would be lost because of the frequent transferring and bumping that the current seniority clauses produced. Nakano was uncertain as to how he should approach the union leadership on the matter of amending these clauses. What approach would you recommend?

5. The former management of the Marshall facility had belonged to the Tire Producers' Industry Association, which had coordinated collective bargaining with the URW among the major firms. Management representatives from each firm met before and during negotiations to reach a general agreement on targets and goals. After a pattern agreement was signed, other firms in the association were expected to sign agreements with equivalent terms. If Nakano joined the industry association, he would be maintaining a continuity that might stabilize the company's position in the industry. At the same time, he was wary about joining the association because he feared that such a move might jeopardize both his relations with the union local and his ability to negotiate a degree of flexibility into his plant's contract, which he considered necessary to the successful introduction of new technology and product lines. What advice would you give to Nakano on this issue?

14

Preparing for the Future

Throughout this book we have stressed the dynamic nature and historical foundations of policy and practice in human resource management and industrial relations. We have also noted that while the specific procedures and practices used to manage the employment relationship vary through time and across occupational groups, organizations, and societies, the parties involved bring some basic generic concerns to any employment relationship. In this final chapter, we speculate on the shape some of the generic concerns are likely to take in the years ahead.

Our purpose here lies less in forecasting the future than in providing a framework for students and professional managers to apply at various points in their professional careers. Although time may change the problems of the moment and the parties' responses to them, the framework presented here should serve as a checklist of basic concepts and issues through which future events and developments can be interpreted. We begin our analysis of future developments in the same way as we started the process of human resource planning, by analyzing environmental trends.

Economic Conditions

Of the various environmental conditions that shape a company's human resource management, none is more pervasive or dominant than the market conditions of the firm's products and its own labor markets. The trend toward increased competition within product markets that began in the first half of the 1980s is likely to continue, because the phenomenon is not limited to the United States; in part, it also reflects the growing interdependence of the world economy.

Competition always presents a dilemma for human resource management. On the one hand, competition can foster innovation and open new market opportunities for entrepreneurs, and in the process create new jobs and sources of income for their employees as well as society as a whole. Even large enterprises are attempting to create the conditions that foster creativity, entrepreneurial spirit, and economic incentives needed for successful new ventures. Thus, supporting the start-up and subsequent evolution of small teams of dedicated professionals will be an increasingly important human resource management challenge.

On the other hand, in mature markets with fewer opportunities for growth and market expansion, increased competition leads to pressures for the control of human resources and increases competition for scarce job opportunities. With these pressures comes the need to prepare employees and employers for career transitions, job losses, and organizational restructuring.

Clearly, both effects will be important features of the competitive environment in the years ahead. Because those benefiting from new job opportunities created by a more competitive environment are unlikely to be the same people who will be displaced by the effects of competition, problems of economic dislocation and adjustment will continue to pose important concerns to public and private decision makers. Managing this adjustment process is likely to occupy much of the attention of human resource planners both within and outside the firm in the years ahead.

Technological Innovations

No single generalization can capture the diverse effects that ongoing advances in microelectronics and its various offshoots will have in the future. In factories, new technology is clearly displacing large numbers of direct production workers and requiring greater analytical skills of maintenance and technical workers. The effects of new technology in the office, however, are more diverse. For example, surveys of the effects of office automation demonstrate that although some jobs may become more narrowly defined and "deskilled" (secretaries becoming word processing specialists) others may be broadened to incorporate work previously done by higher-level personnel (secretaries may use spreadsheet technology to update and produce reports). Moreover, as we have stressed throughout this book, ways in which new technologies are incorporated into the workplace have more to do with managerial discretion than with the technologies themselves. Will future managers build the concerns of human resource management into their decisions about the design and implementation of new technology? Or will technological investment and design decisions continue to be made on narrow engineering and economic efficiency grounds by professionals and executives who are several steps removed from the consequences their decisions hold for current and future employees?

The history of United States industrial society suggests that workers are seldom content to leave to the sole discretion of others issues that directly affect their own vital interests. Thus, if history is any guide, we are likely to see pressures to forge a closer link between decisions about the design and implementation of new technology and their human resource management consequences. The central question will be whether such links will be created through management, employee, or government initiative.

Regardless of how the participation in such issues occurs, increased competition and more rapid technological change will demand greater attention paid to *flexibility* and *adaptability* in employment relationships. We will return to this argument as we explore future developments in other aspects of industrial relations and human resource management.

Demographics and Work Values

If, as suggested, workers commonly aspire to gain some influence or control over the forces affecting their basic interests, how can we expect this aspiration to influence future employment relationships? As Rosabeth Kanter hypothesized in Chapter 2, workers during the past several decades have had rising expectations about their right to individual (if not collective) influence over work environments, careers, and economic security. The shift in the American labor force toward more professional, service-sector, and white-collar work implies that these expectations of greater control in the workplace will be manifested in a wide variety of ways. Moreover, the decisions in which professionals and other highly educated employees expect to participate extend far beyond concerns about wages, hours, and working conditions, which traditionally have been the primary focus of United States collective bargaining.

Contemporary employees are equally interested in participating in task-related decisions that shape how their work is to be performed. Although workers who share common interests may continue to turn to collective forms of organization and participation, organizations of the future increasingly may be composed of shifting coalitions of informal interest groups, task forces, problem-solving groups, and other interactive and fluid decision-making bodies (Bacharach and Lawler, 1981). Moverover, individuals with scarce skills and sufficient alternatives in the external labor market will continue to assert their interests individually, either by raising their voices in the workplace or by taking their skills to other employers. Thus, forms of organization and group interaction are likely to be more diverse than in the past; consequently, the need for managers with skills in negotiation, team building, organizational change, and problem solving is likely to be stronger than ever.

Political and Social Developments

Environmental changes in the workplace cannot be divorced from the political and social contexts in which they occur. Periods of economic change and turmoil often lead to shifts in political attitudes and power configurations. Indeed, increasing evidence illustrates that business, labor, and government leaders in the United States are now openly questioning many of the labor policies that have provided the foundation for the United States industrial relations system since the 1930s.

However, the reasons for raising questions about labor policy and the preferences among alternatives for the future expressed by labor and management are dramatically different. Many employers believe government regulation of the workplace went too far in the 1960s and 1970s; they therefore applauded the policies of the Reagan administration in the first half of the 1980s. By contrast, labor leaders are nearly unanimous in their belief that current labor law is insufficient, ineffective, and inadequately enforced.

Clearly, the outcomes of current and future political debates about the basic direction and content of policies in areas such as union organizing, equal employment opportunity, safety and health, plant closings, and industrial policy will all have an important bearing on human resource management and industrial relations policies in the United States. Moreover, these debates are likely to transcend the traditional political line separating labor from management. Not only are changes in the occupational mix making it more difficult to draw a clear distinction between "labor" and "management," the interests and political preferences within these two groups are becoming more diverse.

Regardless of the direction of future swings in the political balance of power, one thing is certain: Political and social forces will continue to influence the basic structure of the industrial relations system in their historic fashion, by defining the rights and obligations of employers, employees, labor organizations, and government.

Choices for the Parties

The environment sets the context and limits the discretion decision makers have in influencing the course of human resource management, but managers, employees, and labor leaders can and do respond to their environments in different ways. The model guiding the organization of this book adopted a strategic-choice perspective designed to encourage decision makers to consider the effects of their actions on human resource policies at three levels within the firm: at the level of strategic decision making where business strategies and human resource management policies are set by top executives; at the functional level of the firm, where professionals and line managers design and implement specific human resource policies; and at the level of the workplace where individual employees and supervisors experience the actual implementation and effects of these policies.

Few organizations systematically consider the relationships between or the consistency among policies and practices across all three of these levels. Even fewer consider what effects policies enacted at one or more levels of their organizations will have on the needs and interests of other actors in the industrial relations system. In many organizations, internal contradictions in the strategies advocated at different levels are commonplace. Further, adversarial strategies continue to dominate interactions among most employers, labor organizations, and government agencies (Kochan and McKersie, 1983).

To the extent that contradictions remain in the policies and practices found at different levels within an organization, high levels of conflict among organizational participants can be expected to surface in the future. When the actors have differing goals and expectations, negotiation and alternative means for resolving interparty conflicts are essential. In the years ahead, professionals within management, labor, and government must discuss and perhaps modify these internal contradictions and adversarial relationships. How the key actors currently respond to their environments may forecast future developments.

Employer Strategies

Employers generally focus human resource strategies around goals such as controlling costs and maintaining high levels of productivity, flexibility, adaptability, control, and employee commitment, but the relative importance of these goals has varied from one firm to another and through time with changing business conditions and other environmental factors. In recent years, however, an increasing number of firms have attempted to link explicitly their strategic business objectives and their human resource management policies.

Much attention has also focused recently on the values top executives bring to their management roles and on the effects these values have on how employees are treated. Some firms judged to be among the best managed often are described as having strong organizational cultures that reflect the values and managerial philosophies of the entrepreneurs who founded or led them through early, critical periods of their histories (Schein, 1983). As a firm grows and its markets mature, or cost competition becomes a major threat to continued success, the challenge of maintaining commitment to traditional values while economizing on human resources intensifies. Indeed, reassessing the mix of values and business strategies driving an organization may become imperative during periods of major organizational transitions or shifts in the external environment.

At the functional level of a firm, line managers have begun to play, and are likely to continue to play, more active roles in the translation of broad strategic-level objectives into concrete human resource management and workplace-level activities. This role also reflects an increased awareness of how effective human resource management contributes to the overall performance of a firm. In return, human resource professionals have had to adjust to this new strategic orientation and responsibility of line management. Demands are made upon them to respond to the concerns of line managers by ensuring that human resource management policies contribute to productivity, quality, and cost objectives.

In organizations going through transitions from one set of business strategies and/or managerial values to another, the human resource professional often is challenged to simultaneously facilitate adaptation to new policies and to integrate these with the traditional practices that must endure to meet legal requirements, and contractual obligations, or to perpetuate overriding organizational policies. Thus, during transition periods, human resource managers spend much time mediating between those who advocate major changes and new approaches and those who prefer to remain with customs and practices that worked well in the past. Managing organizational transitions will continue to be an important joint function of line managers and human resource professionals in the future.

Although important changes in the management of human resources have taken place at the strategic and functional levels, change has been particularly dramatic in the workplace. Management desires for improvements in productivity, product quality, labor costs, flexibility, and employee commitment have unleashed an unparalleled spate of innovations and reappraisals of traditional work practices and organizational arrangements. The diffusion of various forms of employee involvement and participation, the move toward more flexible forms of work organization, and increased investing in new technologies all reflect an increasing managerial willingness to take the initiative to meet generic human resource management goals and practices.

One question raised by this renewed management interest and activity is whether changes introduced at the workplace level to enhance productivity and flexibility are consistent with functional and strategic decision-making policies that maintain employee trust and employment security. Or are the workplace changes implemented as quick, short-run solutions in a crisis atmosphere that are not matched by the type of top managerial values and higher-level strategies needed to sustain employee trust?

For example, high commitment from employees at the workplace level often requires a corresponding strategic commitment by top management to reinvest in the business so as to ensure employment security in the foreseeable future. It might also imply, as the discussion of various profit and gain-sharing plans suggested in Chapter 11, that compensation policies be adjusted to reward employees in some direct and explicit fashion for their contributions to the firm. Many other examples illustrate the key point that employers must examine how the practices they advocate relate to all three levels of the firm. Failure to do so risks encountering strong initial resistance to change, as well as disillusionment and distrust as employees perceive the organization's failure to reinforce workers' contributions with compatible strategies at higher levels of decision making.

Relations with External Actors

The dominant human resource management development of our era is the drive to adapt human resource practices to the strategies and objectives of a firm. But there is a real danger that as human resource policies are revamped to become more responsive to the concerns of top management and the internal needs of the firm, managers lose sight of the effects of their policies on the other key actors in industrial relations. Of specific interest are the effects of corporate policies on labor organizations, other associations of employees, government, and the society at large.

At no time since the 1920s have labor unions in the United States been more on the defensive than in the first half of the 1980s. The concessions extracted from union members during the deep recession of 1981–83 and the steady decline since 1960 in the proportion of the labor force represented by unions have convinced many union leaders that United States managers still do not accept unions as legitimate and permanent institutions in society. This, in turn, has produced an intense internal debate among union leaders over the fundamental direction of unions' political and collective bargaining strategies. Indeed, managers, union leaders, government officials, and other commentators are asking more basic questions about the future role of the labor movement than perhaps at any time since the 1930s. Simultaneously, more experimentation is occurring now with alternative forms of labor-management relations within the collective bargaining framework than there has been in many years.

This experimentation represents a piecemeal search for a "new industrial relations system." Most of that effort has focused on the quality of life in the workplace and/or cooperative strategies to reorganize work and/or adapt to new technologies. Clearly, this type of experimentation is likely to continue as the unionized sectors of the economy attempt to adapt to the pressures of a more competitive, technologically changing economy, and to a more demanding, better educated work force.

Yet, only a small fraction of contemporary experiments have been institutionalized to the point where they can be viewed as stable new forms of labor-management relations at the workplace. Moreover, even fewer of the executives and labor leaders overseeing these workplace experiments have adapted their relationships at the collective bargaining level, or at the highest levels of strategic decision making, in ways that will maintain the trust and cooperation they seek to cultivate at the workplace. Until changes are forthcoming at these higher levels, it is premature to herald the arrival of a new industrial relations system. For example, it is unlikely that cooperative relations can survive at the workplace level in bargaining relationships if union leaders are unwilling or unable to adapt their collective bargaining goals to the specific economic conditions facing the firm, or if top executives continue to practice union-avoidance policies. In short, a new industrial relations system that is capable of withstanding the test of time is likely to emerge and diffuse only as both labor and management integrate their practices into basic organizational strategies and value systems.

Labor unions, however, are not the only form of employee organization that employer policies need to consider. Indeed, as the professional, technical, and white-collar segments of the workforce grow, employers are likely to confront an increasing array of professional associations seeking to represent their members' interests in employment relations. The Institute for Electrical and Electronic Engineers (IEEE), for example, has proclaimed employment security as the most important goal it seeks to promote for its members (IEEE, 1984). IEEE has embarked on a series of studies to determine the extent to which employer policies have changed to promote this objective. Other interest groups representing the concerns of women, minorities, and other employee groups lacking formal representation through collective bargaining also are likely to increase in popularity and activism in the future. Thus, we will probably see more varied forms of quasi-representation and more demands for participation in the setting of human resource management policies and objectives as the work force becomes more professional and white-collar. The form these relationships will take depends as much on the managerial reception they receive as on the objectives of the new employee groups.

Relations with Government and Society

It seems appropriate to conclude our discussion of contemporary human resource management and industrial relations by considering one of the most uncertain aspects of the industrial relations environment in the United States today: the federal government's labor and human resource policies. We have witnessed what many observers believe is a fundamental shift in the direction of national labor policy in the first half of the 1980s. In the process of implementing its general strategy of reduced government regulation of business, the Reagan administration scaled back enforcement activities of the Occupational Safety and Health Administration and the Equal Employment Opportunity Commission, reversed several key National Labor Relations Board decisions that had limited management's freedom to reallocate work from union to nonunion plants, and cut back public resources supporting employment, training, and human resource development programs. In return, employers are being asked to assume more of these responsibilities by engaging in a new spirit of partnership with the government and with their employees, and thereby to demonstrate that a less adversarial business-government-worker relationship is in the best interest of labor, management, and society.

Not surprisingly, the labor movement sees this approach to labor policy as a direct attack on its role in society and is attempting to reverse these policies. Thus, the role of government in industrial relations and human resource management is likely to continue to shift in response to the balance of political power in American society. In the long run, such flux simply increases the need for line managers and human resource professionals at all levels to develop and implement policies and practices that meet the basic needs of all the parties to the employment relationship — the firm, its employees, labor organizations, and the larger society. Satisfying these needs will continue in the years ahead to serve as a good working definition of effective human resource management and industrial relations.

References

Bacharach, Samuel B., and Edward J. Lawler, *Power and Politics in Organizations* (San Francisco: Jossey Bass, 1981).

Kochan, Thomas A., and Robert B. McKersie, "Collective Bargaining: A Time for Change," *Sloan Management Review*, Vol. 24, Summer 1983, 59–66.

"Professional Practices for Enginerers, Scientists, and Their Employers," pamphlet of the Institute of Electrical and Electronics Engineers, Inc. (IEEE), 1111 19th St., N.W., Suite 608, Washington, D.C., 20036, 1984.

Schein, Edgar, "The Role of the Founder in Creating Organizational Culture," *Organizational Dynamics*, Summer 1983, 13–28.

Appendix
Collective Bargaining Negotiations

Introduction

The materials included in this Appendix (General I–VI sections) provide the basic data for a collective bargaining game. Your class will break into the following negotiating units or teams:

Company Negotiators

Walter Dickens, Personnel
Mark Fort, Production
Anne Follett, Finance
Curtis Evens, Foreman

Union Negotiators

Arthur Showe, International Representative of the UMP
William White, President of Local 245
Harris Ford, Steward and senior employee with D. G. Barnhouse
Jenny Jansen, Steward and junior employee with D. G. Barnhouse

Your instructor has been provided with the company and union information you will need after you have been assigned a role.

General I: D. G. Barnhouse Co., Inc.

At the turn of the twentieth century, Donald Grayson Barnhouse, a highly skilled lathe craftsman, opened a small shop in which he made specialty machine tools. With little financial capital — he had only $1,000 from savings and small personal loans — but a great deal of entrepreneurial stamina, he gathered enough used tools to open his shop on the outskirts of Grandville, Illinois. After ten years in operation, D. G. Barnhouse's business was steady enough to support him and his small family, but he could afford only one apprenticed employee.

By 1915, Barnhouse's luck turned, as small auto companies opened plants near Grandville. His company, D. G. Barnhouse Co., Inc., had a reputation for quality, which soon led nascent area auto companies to buy tools from him. Thus, after 15 years of modest performance, D. G. Barnhouse Co. (DGB) became one of the foremost suppliers to the emerging auto industry.

By the mid-1920s, DGB began diversifying into several new kinds of lathes, for which demand strongly increased as the decade progressed. These lathes were produced in the machine tool plant DGB built during the previous decade. DGB also had maintained the older plant, in which auto parts continued to be the primary product. By early 1929, DGB's success led Barnhouse to allow the company to go public and capitalize on a rapidly expanding market. The capital thus generated was used in a new shop devoted solely to the production of machine tools. This shop was just beginning production when the stock market crashed and the Great Depression began.

In 1932, Barnhouse was forced to close his older auto parts plant. The depression was only one factor in that decision. The plant also would have required upgraded machinery and buildings, and its maintenance costs were unreasonably high. Most of the company's skilled workers — its most senior employees — were moved to the machine tool plant. DGB hoped to keep all of these workers throughout the depression. The decision to close the auto plant instead of the machine tool facility was also based on the belief that demand would grow first and faster in the machine tool industry as economic conditions improved.

As the depression drew to a close, demand for machine tools did increase, and DGB's work force once again grew. Success in producing quality machine tools led Barnhouse to abandon plans to reopen the auto parts facility.

The business thrived throughout the period between World War I and World War II. At the end of World War II, Donald Grayson Barnhouse, Sr. turned the firm over to his son, D. G. Barnhouse, Jr., who had been intimately involved in the company's successes after the depression. At the time of the succession, DGB employed 600 workers, and sales totalled more than $10 million. Some of the firm's success had hinged on the booming war-time economy, however, so that in 1947 DGB had to lay off 18 per cent of its work force because of the drop in defense-oriented demand. Because many of the firm's war-time customers were retained after 1945, the transition to the production of exclusively civilian goods was not prohibitively difficult.

Nevertheless, the firm's postwar growth was sporadic. Attempts to diversify into a greater variety of industrial products were not uniformly successful. By the late 1950s, DGB was in a tenable but not comfortable position within the industry.

In the late '50s, D. G. Barnhouse III took over from his father as president and chief executive officer. Under the son's leadership, the company's strategy shifted toward greater emphasis on research and development, as well as diversification and expansion into new markets. The company grew rapidly throughout the '60s and early '70s, as a combined result of his leadership and of growth in the international economy. The employees at the Grandville plant gained respectable wage and benefit increases annually, and the company sustained a reasonable profit margin.

By the mid-'70s, a new plant was opened in nearby Newton, Indiana, a rural area offering low-cost labor. This plant finished and assembled several types of low-cost machine tools. It employed 90 women and 60 men; these nonunion employees were grouped into five job classifications, from production and assembly workers to a single general mechanic for maintenance. Blue-collar employment in the Grandville plant numbered 500 at the time.

By the early 1980s, DGB once again considered a new strategic direction. Under consideration was the possibility of investing in new, automated manufacturing equipment, which would allow for a 10 percent work-force reduction in the Grandville plant. Alternately, the new equipment could be installed in the Newton plant, while the older Grandville plant could be phased out slowly. This latter option would entail moving some of the Grandville plant's equipment to Newton, and increasing the number of employees at the newer plant.

Labor Relations at D. G. Barnhouse Co., Inc.

Because the Barnhouse family was so integral to the company's history, DGB's labor relations were characterized from the beginning by paternalism. The company had always been careful to protect senior employees against shifting economic conditions. During the depression, several skilled employees were given jobs sweeping the floors of the Grandville plant to avoid being laid off. Before the war, boom times were characterized by overtime work and subcontracting to keep the number of employees low and stable.

The firm's paternalism was also reflected in fringe benefits; its employees were granted life insurance pensions and hospitalization insurance long before these became standard benefits even in unionized companies. Partly as a result of these long-standing paternalistic policies, the Steelworkers, the Machinists, and the Auto Workers had been unable to unionize DGB's employees throughout the '30s.

By the beginning of World War II, as business increased dramatically, workers went on a seven-day work schedule, and morale was strained severely. As a result, the employees of DGB decided to form a union of their own. Substantial encouragement came from several first-line supervisors, and a local of the United Metal Products Workers of America (UMP) gave its help. The company was certain that this effort at unionization simply reflected the work of a handful of radicals, and it was completely surprised when the National Labor Relations Board (NLRB) representation election resulted in a substantial majority in favor of unionization.

Even before the union became official, DGB had paid wages more or less equal to those paid in competing unionized plants in the area. It had regularly participated in industry-wide wage surveys to remain apprised of the going rates. At the same time, DGB had always been reluctant to grant long-term or automatic cost-of-living increases, or to appear to be following the bargaining pattern set in any particular industry. This aversion to automatic wage/benefit increases and to following pattern bargains was reflected in the contracts negotiated with the union from the end of the war until the early 1980s. Not until 1982, and even then only reluctantly, did DGB negotiate a cost-of-living clause in its contract with the UMP.

DGB has always given liberal fringe benefits. Its life insurance plan provides at least two years' pay, as well as double indemnity, with the company paying half of the premium. DGB also pays for half of its employees' Blue Cross–Blue Shield insurance. The company's policy has always been to pay regular employees half-pay during sick leave.

Until several years ago, DGB kept pace with industry levels of pension benefits. Currently, its plan provides retiring employees with 2 percent of average earnings based on their last five years of service for each year of service up to thirty years; employees contribute half the cost of the pension. The combined weekly employee contribution for pension and insurance is $8.50.

The 1984–85 Negotiations

The 1984–85 contract was difficult to negotiate, because the union was unhappy about lagging wages and benefits, and because the company was facing difficult market conditions. The union was unable to gain anything approaching workers' demands. By a 400 to 890 vote (with 20 members not voting), the membership rejected a contract with the following general features:

1. 12 cents per hour increase to unskilled, 18 cents to skilled workers
2. A modest cost-of-living (COLA) clause
3. An agreement to study ways of upgrading the pension plan
4. An agreement to consider modifications in work rules and job and pay classifications

After another unsuccessful week of negotiations, the workers began a strike. Three days later, all of the skilled workers and some of the unskilled employees went back to work voluntarily, and DGB was operating at close to full capacity again. Finally, a two-year agreement was signed on March 31, 1984.

The Aftermath

After the strike, all of the employees at DGB were discontented. Old divisions between skill groups flared. Unskilled workers were angry with both the company and their union. All the workers began to feel it was time for some kind of change.

Two months after the abortive strike, a young drill press operator, Bill White, challenged and narrowly defeated the incumbent local union president; White's campaign emphasized the need for more worker input into plant operations and control over technology and investment. The younger workers were pleased in general with White's approach, but the older employees (with less fear of losing their jobs) were not so sanguine, particularly since White seemed to be uninterested in pension plan improvements.

All the workers shared anxiety about their job security, however, reacting to increasing publicity about automation in machine tool plants and sluggish demand for machine tools themselves. DGB did nothing to allay the employees' fears of layoffs or replacement by robots.

The Community

Grandville, Illinois has a population of 160,000. The nearest large city is Chicago. The working population is approximately 70,000, of which 10 percent are unemployed. The unemployment rate is significantly higher for minorities and women. Some of the unemployed population secure a nominal income from sales of small farm produce.

Aside from DGB's Grandville plant, nine organized firms are in the city. Their products, unions, and employee statistics are shown below:

Company	Principal Products	Union	Number of Employees
1	Hoists	United Steel Workers	315
2	Pumps	Machinists (IAM)	712
3	Controls	Machinists (IAM)	342
4	Electronics	I.U.E.	2,498
5	Truck Bodies	Allied Industrial Workers	2,902
6	Metal Parts	U.A.W.	1,240
7	Structural Steel	Iron Workers	1,198
8	Bakery	Bakery Workers	202
9	Trucking	Teamsters	79

Building construction employees also are organized extensively in Grandville, but no other company is organized by the UMP. The largest of a number of unorganized plants manufactures office equipment and employs about 1,000 people. This group of workers has been subject to three unsuccessful organization drives during the last decade.

The Upcoming Negotiations

Employee recommendations about the substance of the union's position in the upcoming negotiations were being considered by the UMP local leadership. The union had notified DGB that it wished to renegotiate the contract and would send a list of negotiating proposals to the company. Donald Grayson Barnhouse III responded that he would send the company's counter-proposals to the union as soon as he received their negotiating demands.

General II: Collective Bargaining Agreement

Parties to the Agreement

This Agreement, made and entered into this first day of April 1984 is made by and between D. G. Barnhouse Co., Incorporated, of Illinois, hereinafter called the "Company", and Local 245 International Union, United Metal Products, Machinery and Related Equipment Workers of America, hereinafter called the "Union."

Article I: Intent and Purpose

Section 1 — The parties hereto intend and propose herein to set forth and comply with an agreement concerning pay rates, work hours and employment conditions, and to set procedures for the prompt and equitable adjustment of alleged grievances.

Section 2 — The Company shall in no way discriminate against any employee on the grounds of membership in or affiliation with the Union.

Article II: Recognition

Section 1 — The Company recognizes the Union as the sole and exclusive bargaining agent representing the employees in the Grandville, Illinois plant of the Company for the purpose of collective bargaining with respect to rates of pay, wages, hours of work and other conditions of employment.

Section 2 — The term 'Employees' for the purposes of this Agreement shall mean all of the employees of the Company except office employees, foremen, watchmen and guards, timekeepers, and supervisors who have and exercise the authority to recommend the hiring, promoting, discharge, disciplining of employees, or otherwise effecting changes in the status of employees.

Article III: Strikes and Lockouts

Section 1 — The Company agrees there shall be no lockout of its employees and the Union agrees that neither it nor any of its members shall cause, permit, or take part in any strike during the term of this Agreement.

Article IV: Hours of Work

Section 1 — The normal work hours for all employees shall be eight (8) per day and forty (40) per week and, for production employees, shall be limited to the period from Monday through Friday.

Section 2 — Hours worked in addition to the normal work hours shall be according to the following schedule: forty (40) to forty-five (45) shall be limited to five (5) days; over forty-five (45) to fifty-five (55) hours shall be limited to five and one-half (5½) days; fifty-five (55) to sixty (60) hours shall be limited to six (6) days. All other work schedules shall be mutually approved by the Company and the Union.

Section 3 — All time worked by an employee in excess of eight (8) hours in any one day and forty hours (40) hours in any one week and all time worked on Saturday shall be paid for at the time and one-half rate; provided, however, employees shall not receive time and one-half for Saturday as such if they were absent during the week except for one of the following reasons: sickness, accident or death in the family, jury duty or subpoena to court. In cases when an employee was absent due to one of the above reasons, he/she shall turn in a slip stating the reason for that absence, not later than Saturday of the week in which he/she was absent. All time worked on Sunday shall be paid for at the double-time rate.

Section 4 — The Company will attempt to distribute overtime as equitably as possible among affected employees; and shall allow Union officials to verify same.

Section 5 — The Company shall allow Union Bargaining Committee members first priority for working the first shift; and when feasible employees with the greatest seniority within their job classifications shall be granted second priority to work the first shift, and those next in seniority, the second shift. Further, once an employee exercises seniority rights to obtain a transfer from one shift to another, he/she shall not return to the original shift until a period of six (6) months after the transfer shall have elapsed.

Section 6 — All employees shall be granted two (2) fifteen (15) minute rest periods, at a time to be mutually agreed upon by the Company and the Union, and with pay at their hourly base rate. Smoking, other than during rest periods, is prohibited, and then only in the designated places.

Section 7 — Employees shall not be absent from work without permission except for good and sufficient reason and an employee must, except in an emergency, notify the Company no later than three (3) hours after the scheduled starting time, when he/she cannot work.

Section 8 — Penalty for violation of Sections 6 and 7 of this Article will be:

1st Offense — Caution by foreman and a written report to Union and Personnel Department
2nd Offense — One-day suspension without pay
3rd Offense — Two-day suspension without pay
4th Offense — Cause for dismissal

Article V: Wages

Section 1 — The rates for all employees shall be in accordance with the "Rate Classification of Jobs," which shall be appended hereto as Appendix "A" and made a part of this Agreement.

Section 2 — All employees shall receive a cost-of-living adjustment in pay, as of January 15, 1985, of one (1) cent per hour for each 0.3 point rise in the U.S. Bureau of Labor Statistics All-Cities Consumer

Price Index for the period covering January 1984 to January 1985. However, if the Consumer Price Index declines to levels below those of January 1984 there shall be no pay reduction.

Section 3 — Newly hired employees with less than thirty (30) days of employment to their credit shall be considered probationary employees: provided, however, the Company may request an extension of the probationary period not to exceed thirty (30) days for employees whose qualifications or capabilities are in doubt. Any employee remaining in the service of the Company beyond his/her probationary period shall automatically receive an increase of five (5) cents per hour and every fourth (4th) week thereafter, until the minimum of his/her classification is reached.

Section 4 — Any employee who is placed in his/her regular occupation after a layoff or transfer for reasons beyond his/her control shall be paid the wage rate applicable at the time of the layoff or transfer, plus or minus any general wage increases or decreases effective during that period.

Section 5 — Except for the above provisions, no employee's wage rate shall be changed except by mutual agreement between the Company and the Union.

Article VI: Seniority, Layoffs, and Rehiring

Section 1 — The Company shall notify the Union at such time as any newly hired employees who have completed their probationary period.

Section 2 — An employee's seniority rights shall be measured on a plant-wide and departmental basis, starting from the first day or hour worked. If, however, an employee is rehired after having quit voluntarily or after having been duly discharged, that employee's seniority will be measured as of the time of rehiring.

With respect to the scheduled hours of work per week, the Company shall conform with the following provisions:

a. The hours of work shall be reduced to forty (40) hours a week before any such employees are laid off.
b. The schedule of hours per week may be increased from between forty (40) to forty-five (45) inclusive without any employee being called back.
c. The schedule of hours per week may be increased to more than forty-five (45) for a maximum period of four (4) weeks, after which time enough employees who have been laid off will be recalled in order to revert to a maximum forty-five (45) hour work week.

Section 3 — In the event of a layoff employees with the least plant-wide seniority will be laid off first, and employees with the most seniority will be retained, subject to their ability to perform the available work without being trained.

Section 4 — In the event that workers shall be recalled after having been laid off, the last to have been laid off shall be the first to be recalled, as per the conditions noted in Section 2 of this Article, above. Any laid off employee shall accrue seniority, to be credited after his/her return to work, for a grace period of up to three (3) months. However, no employee shall surpass any other employee in seniority solely as a result of the provisions of Section 2 of this Article, above. An employee shall be considered to have quit voluntarily if he/she does not return to work within five (5) days of receiving notification of recall by registered letter to his/her last known address by the Company.

Section 5 — On any layoff or return to work the Company shall notify the Union and the employee affected not less than two (2) working days before such layoff or return to work occurs. Any grievances involving such layoff or return to work shall be submitted to the Company no later than five (5) working days after the Company has given due notice of the fact.

Section 6 — The Company shall post an updated seniority list on all bulletin boards at the workplace, shall furnish the Union with such lists, and shall consider such lists to be a matter of mutual approval with the Union. Such lists will include the names, hiring dates, and seniority positions, on a plant-wide and departmental basis, of all employees.

Section 7 — In case of layoff, the president of the Union shall have seniority over all other employees during his/her term of office, regardless of length of service with the Company.

Article VII: Discharge

Section 1 — If the Company discharges an employee, such action will be taken for good and sufficient reason, and shall be taken after notifying the Union Bargaining Committee of the action and reasons therefore. If investigation of such an action leads the Union to conclude that the employee affected was discharged unfairly, that employee shall have the right to lodge a grievance against the Company in accordance with the grievance procedure established in Article XII of this document.

Article VIII: Promotion, Transfers, New Jobs, and Merit Rating

Section 1 — The Company shall notify the Union president when any vacancy or a new job of any occupation occurs which is under the jurisdiction of the Union, and which results in the need for additional help in the department affected. Such notification shall include a statement of the required job qualifications, of the approximate wage rate and of any other pertinent information. Upon receipt of such notification the Union will post the job opening on the designated bulletin board(s), after which time interested applicants shall submit written bids for the position to the Union president, who shall send a copy of these bids to the Company's Personnel Office. Any such jobs shall be awarded on the basis of seniority when the qualifications of applicants are approximately equal.

Section 2 — All employees accepting promotion or transfer shall be granted a reasonable period of time for training, during which time they shall receive no less pay than the minimum established in Appendix A. Any higher rate of pay shall be determined on the basis of experience, application and general qualifications for the job in question, at the time of the employee's reclassification.

Section 3 — With the exception of trainees, each employee on rate ranges shall be considered for a merit raise six (6) months after employment in his/her classification, and at six (6) month intervals thereafter until he/she reaches the maximum rate in the classification. Trainees shall receive merit consideration six (6) months after completion of the ninety (90) day training period. Foremen shall submit written reports of all employees' progress to the Personnel Department at six (6) month intervals, with copies of such reports being furnished at the time of their receipt to the president of the Union.

Article IX: Military Service

Section 1 — When an employee with seniority is called or volunteers for service in any of the Armed Forces of the United States, he/she shall, upon termination of such service, be restored to his/her former position, or to a position of similar status and pay; provided, however, that he/she has received honorable discharge, is physically and mentally competent, notifies the Company of his/her intention to return to work at least 90 days prior to his/her discharge, and reports for work not more than ninety (90) days after release from service; and provided further, that the Company's circumstances have not been changed so as to make it impossible or unreasonable to do so.

Section 2 — Any employee who is rehired in accordance with the provisions of this Article shall advance in seniority in the same manner as though he/she had remained in the Company's service.

Article X: Vacations

Section 1 — All employees shall receive a vacation with pay in accordance with the following schedule:

a. All employees with between six (6) months' and one (1) year's service at the start of the vacation period shall receive a two (2) week vacation with forty (40) hours' straight time pay, provided they have worked at least 125 hours in each month following the month in which they were employed. The latter provision with respect to the number of hours worked per month may be modified upon mutual agreement between the Union Bargaining Committee and the Company.

Vacation for all other employees shall be computed from the following table:

b. All employees will receive vacation according to the following criteria, in which the time of service is to be measured at the start of the vacation period. More than one (1) but less than ten (10) years of service — two (2) weeks' vacation with eighty (80) hours' straight time pay; more than ten (10) but less than twenty (20) years' service — three (3) weeks' vacation with one hundred twenty (120) hours' straight time pay; more than twenty (20) but less than twenty five (25) years' service — four (4) weeks' vacation with one hundred sixty (160) hours' straight time pay; twenty five (25) or more years' service — four (4) weeks' vacation with one hundred sixty (160) hours' straight time pay.

Section 2 — Employees voluntarily terminating their service to the Company shall receive vacation pay earned during the previous year at the time of separation. Vacation pay earned the current year shall be paid not later than March of the following year.

Section 3 — The vacation period shall be the first two (2) weeks in August at which time the plant shall shut down; provided, however, that when August 1 occurs later in the week than Wednesday, the vacation period shall start the following Monday.

Section 4 — Upon request, any employee with ten (10) to twenty (20) years of service shall be granted a third week of vacation. Employees with more than twenty (20) years of service shall be granted a third and fourth week of vacation. For these additional weeks, eligible employees will have the right to select their vacation dates on the basis of seniority provided it does not interfere with the operation of the business.

Section 5 — Employees are not permitted to postpone their vacations from one year to another or to omit vacations and draw pay allowance in lieu thereof.

Article XI: Holidays

Section 1 — The following days shall be considered work holidays:

New Year's Day
Memorial Day
The Fourth of July
Labor Day
Thanksgiving Day
Christmas Eve
Christmas Day

The Union shall be able to determine one further floating work holiday per year.

Section 2 — When employees perform no work on a holiday, as defined in Section 1, above, they shall receive eight (8) hours' pay at their base rate for each such holiday, unless such a holiday occurs on a day not regularly scheduled for work, and unless an employee has not completed his/her probationary period with the Company as of the date of such a holiday.

   a. Employees shall receive pay for each holiday not worked, as outlined above, if they worked the scheduled work days immediately before and immediately after the holiday. If the schedule of work hours exceeds fifty (50) hours per week at the time of a holiday, an employee shall receive holiday pay in accordance with the above provisions if he/she has worked at least 80% of the scheduled hours on the scheduled work days immediately preceding and immediately following the holiday. An employee is also qualified for holiday pay if his/her failure to work on the days immediately preceding and following the holiday is caused by any of the following:
      (1) The employee is excused from working because he/she is ill;
      (2) The employee is injured in the plant;
      (3) The employee suffers a death in his/her family;
      (4) The employee must serve on a jury or attend court pursuant to subpoena;
      (5) The employee becomes a parent.
   b. Any employee required to work on a holiday shall be paid at his/her straight time hourly rate for all hours actually worked plus straight time at his/her hourly rate for eight (8) hours.

Article XII: Grievance Procedure

In the event any employee feels that he/she has a just complaint or grievance with respect to any employer-employee matter, an earnest effort shall be made by the parties thereto to settle such differences at the earliest time and in the following manner:

   a. Between the aggrieved employee and his/her foreman or between the Department Steward and the foreman.
   b. If no satisfactory agreement is reached, the matter in dispute shall be referred in writing to the president of the Union, and the Bargaining Committee shall then bring the matter to the attention of the duly designated representative of the Company.
   c. If no satisfactory agreement is reached by the Union and the Company representatives, the matter in dispute may be referred by either party to the American Arbitration Association for final and binding arbitration by an arbitrator to be designated by the Association. The proceedings shall be conducted in accordance with the rules of the Association.

Article XIII: Insurance and Pensions

The Company will continue in effect the existing insurance covering death and accidental death or dismemberment of full-time regular employees and hospitalization and surgical care of regular full-time employees, except as the terms and conditions of such insurance may be altered by the carrier.

The Company will also continue in effect the existing Pension Plan. (See Appendix C.)

Article XIV: Union Business

Section 1 — Any employee who is a member of the Union and who may be called upon to transact Union business, shall, upon application to the proper representatives of the Company and the Union, be allowed to leave work for sufficient time to transact such business or to attend such meetings as may be necessary.

Section 2 — Any member of the Union who may be elected or appointed to any office in the Union that requires a leave of absence shall, at the expiration of such term of office, be reinstated to his/her former or equivalent position, including all rights previously held, provided that the Company's circumstances have not changed so as to make it impossible or unreasonable to do so.

Section 3 — The Union shall be allowed to collect dues, sign membership application cards, ballot for Union officers and distribute the regular monthly Union publications after working hours on Company property.

Section 4 — The Company shall install and maintain bulletin boards for the Union in places mutually agreed upon by both parties. No material shall be posted thereon except that pertaining to the activities and business of the Union.

Article XV: Duration of Agreement

This Agreement shall be effective April 1, 1984. It shall remain in full force and effect from April 1, 1984, to and including March 31, 1985, and thereafter it shall be automatically renewed from time to time for further periods of one (1) year unless either party at least sixty (60) days prior to March 31, 1985, or any subsequent expiration date, serves on the other party written notice of its desire to amend or terminate the Agreement. If the notice given is one expressing an election to terminate, then the Agreement shall expire upon such ensuing expiration date. If the notice given is one expressing a desire to amend the Agreement, the party serving such notice to amend shall, within thirty (30) days from the date such notice to amend is served, transmit to the other party in writing the specific amendments proposed for negotiation amd mutual agreement. If the party upon whom such notice to amend is served also desires to amend the Agreement, it also shall serve written notice to amend not later than ten (10) days after receipt of the other party's notice to amend; and within thirty (30) days from the date its notice is served shall transmit to the other party in writing the amendments it proposes for negotiation and mutual agreement. Negotiations between the parties on the amendments so proposed shall begin as soon as possible after the above mentioned notices have been given, but pending consummation of an Agreement on the proposed amendments, the terms and conditions of the old Agreement shall continue in effect.

IN WITNESS WHEREOF, we hereunto set our hands at Fort Jefferson, Indiana, on this 31st day of March, 1984.

(Signed)

Company: _____
D. G. Barnhouse Co., Incorporated
Donald G. Barnhouse III, President

Union: _____
U.M.P. LOCAL 245
William White, President
James LaPierre, Secretary

Appendix A: Rate Classification of Jobs

Labor Grade	Job Title	Rate Range*
1	Tool and Die Maker	$10.20–$12.08
2	Machinist	$ 9.97–$11.64
	All-Around Mechanical Inspector	"
	Plant Electrician	"
	Plant Mechanic	"
3	Machine Specialist	$ 9.59–$11.33
	Gauge Inspector	"
4	Tool Grinder	$ 9.52–$11.25
5	Electrician	$ 9.22–$11.09
6	Carpenter	$ 8.91–$11.03
7	All-Around Instrument Assembler	$ 8.91–$11.03
8	Mechanical Inspector	$ 8.91–$11.03
	All-Around Mechanical Assembler	"
9	Turret Lathe Operator	$ 8.83–$10.79
	Engine Lathe Operator	"
	Handscrew Machine Operator	"
	Milling Machine Operator	"
10	Drill Press Operator	$ 8.76–$10.72
	Final Asembler	"

*A newly hired employee may be paid a rate no more than 23 cents per hour below the minimum of the classification for which he was hired and the rate shall be increased to the minimum in accordance with Article V, Section 2.

Labor Grade	Job Title	Rate Range*
11	Set-up Man	$ 7.85–$10.11
	Welder (Tool Room)	"
	Grinder Operator	"
12	Production Tester	$ 7.85–$10.11
13	Receiving Inspector	$ 7.78–$ 9.96
	Instrument Assembler	"
14	Production Inspector	$ 7.69–$ 9.89
15	Shear Operator	$ 7.69–$ 9.89
	Resolver Asembler	"
16	Punch Press Operator	$ 7.69–$ 9.89
17	Outside Truck Driver	$ 7.56–$ 9.73
	Expeditor–Machine Shop	"
	Shipper and Receiver	"
	Painter	"
	Storekeeper	"
	Expeditor–Assembly	"
18	Fireman	$ 7.46–$ 9.66
	Expeditor–Tooling	"
	Subassembler	"
19	Oiler	$ 7.41–$ 9.52
	Bonding and Spraying	"
	Tool Keeper	"
20	Power Trucker	$ 7.31–$ 9.36
	Timekeeper	"
	Bonding Man	"
	Store Clerk	"
21	Groundskeeper	$ 7.10–$ 8.98
	Basic Assembler	"
	Routine Assembler	"
22	Sweeper	$ 6.94–$ 8.91
	Assembler	"

Appendix B: Distribution Table

Job Grade	Number of Employees
1	5
2	10
3	11
4	17
5	22
6	26
7	30
8	34
9	36
10	36
11	39
12	38
13	35
14	32
15	32
16	29
17	26
18	14
19	10
20	6
21	7
22	5
Total:	500

Appendix C: Illinois First Life Insurance Co. Life Insurance and Retirement Benefit Agreement Summary

The employees covered under this agreement include all full-time employees of the Company; new employees become eligible after the probationary period of employment, or immediately if they are over 55 years old. At the option of the Company employees can remain insured after layoff or become reinsured upon rehiring but with no credit given for the period during which they were not insured.

Life Insurance. In case of the death of an employee, except by suicide or while serving in the Armed Forces, the beneficiary will receive a death benefit of double the annual salary of the employee, i.e., 2,080 times the employee's last base hourly wage rate. Upon proof that death occurred as a result of accidental injury, this benefit will be doubled. The employee can change his/her beneficiary by notifying the Company in writing. If he/she dies with no beneficiary on record, the benefit will be paid to his/her estate. The beneficiary may elect to be paid the benefit in equal installments of an amount determined by the Insurer and based on the age of the beneficiary.

If an employee terminates his/her employment with the Company, he/she may automatically purchase from the Insurer insurance providing coverage up to the level of that in force at the time of such termination at the Insurer's individual premium rates.

Pensions.   Upon retirement at age 65 or later eligible employees with at least 10 years of service with the Company will receive pension benefits monthly for life of 2 percent of the average monthly base wage during the 60 months prior to retirement, multiplied by the number of years of service (to a maximum of 30), and reduced by 20 percent of the amount the employee would normally receive under the Social Security Act.

Employees with more than 10 years of service who terminate employment with the Company before retirement will receive pensions as per the above, calculated on the basis of the 60-month period prior to termination.

Premiums.   The total weekly premium of $20.00 times the number of employees covered will be paid within 7 days of the end of each calendar week of coverage, and will be allocated to insurance coverage (20 percent) and pension coverage (80 percent). This rate will remain in effect for the first 5 years of the agreement, after which the Insurer may change it, after providing at least 90 days' notice as such, on any anniversary of the agreement.

Interest will start to accrue on unpaid premiums on the 8th day after the end of the calendar week of coverage. After 26 weeks of failure to pay premiums the agreement will be terminated as outlined below.

If the Company pays less than the full premium per employee, it must collect the balance from the employees and pay the full premium to the Insurer. Employees working full time will pay no more than 50 percent of the premium. Employees on layoff or Company-approved leaves of absence can pay up to 100 percent of the premium. All employees within each of these categories will pay the same percentage of the premium.

Employees who have contributed as above and who terminate employment with the Company can receive a refund for their payments with 6 percent annually compounded interest, after which point they lose all rights to future retirement benefits.

Funding.   The Insurer will apply the premiums received to the purchase of term life insurance and permanent annuity coverage sufficient to provide the stipulated benefits for service credited to covered employees before or after the date of the agreement, as appropriate.

Administration.   The Company will be responsible for maintaining records for each covered employee, showing the following data on the employee: name and current address; date of birth; name and address of beneficiary; current base hourly rate; number of years and months of credited service both before the date of the agreement and after the date of the agreement; wages received during the preceding 60-month period; and amount and date of each employee contribution to pension coverage premiums.

These records will be available to the Insurer for inspection or audit at any reasonable time.

Upon notification from the Company of the death of a covered employee, the Insurer will be responsible for making payment of the death benefit to the beneficiary.

The Insurer will be responsible for regular payment of retirement benefits to retiring employees upon Company notification of retirement by a covered employee or upon notification by a terminated employee with vested retirement benefits. The Insurer will not be responsible for payment of that portion of a benefit which results from the employee's service to the Company prior to the date of the agreement and/or for which the Company has not paid sufficient premiums.

Upon notification from the Company within 7 days of the termination of a covered employee, the Insurer will be responsible for notifying the employee of his/her options, if applicable, to receive refund of pension benefit premiums, if any, with interest, or if eligible, to vest his or her rights to future retirement benefits under the plan; and to convert to a regular individual life insurance policy available from the Insurer.

Within 30 days of the end of each calendar year or other Company designated fiscal period, the Insurer will provide the Company with the following information: Premiums paid by the Company and by employees during the year for current coverage; premiums paid during the year for coverage prior to the agreement date; contingent liability for unpaid premiums for prior coverage; interest paid on late premiums for current coverage and premiums for prior coverage; interest on premiums for prior coverage which has accrued and has not been paid; and other appropriate information.

Applicable Law.   The terms of this plan are governed by the laws of the State of Illinois.

The Company is responsible for securing approval for the agreement from the Internal Revenue Service.

Termination.   The plan may be terminated by either party on any anniversary date, provided that at least 60 days' written notice has been given and received. The agreement will terminate automatically if at any time there are less than 100 covered employees.

Upon termination of the agreement, all covered employees will be given the options normally provided, as if they had terminated employment with the Company.

The Insurer will not be released by termination of this agreement from the responsibilities (1) to continue paying retirement benefits to those who have already retired and (2) to initiate retirement benefits to those employees with a vested right to retirement benefits at the date of such termination.

For the Insurer: For the Company:

/s/ James Gordon   /s/ D. G. Barnhouse III

CLU   President
Illinois Cooperative Life Insurance Co.   D. G. Barnhouse Co., Inc.

December 30, 1983

Illinois Cooperative Life Insurance Company
D. G. Barnhouse Co., Inc. Pension Plan
Computation of Retirement Benefit for 1980 Retirement

Name of employee _____ (sample) _____

Date of hire ____5/1/59____ Date of Retirement ____1/16/80____

Months employed __252__ Less uncredited months __36__ Credit Service _216_

Wage History

Year	Gross Pay	F.I.C.A. Pay	Year	Gross Pay	F.I.C.A. Pay	60 Month Base Pay
1959	4560	4560	1970	6270	6270	
1960	4530	4530	1971	7110	7110	
1961	4640	4640	1972	7810	7810	
1962	5140	4800	1973	8510	8300	
1963	5200	4800	1974	9105	8900	
1964	5510	4800	1975	9834	9400	8900
1965	5720	4800	1976	10719	10300	10000
1966	5940	4940	1977	12636	12400	11800
1967	6020	6020	1978	14040	13600	13400
1968	6410	6410	1979	15600	15000	14800
1969	6490	6490				

Computation of Primary Social Security Benefit

17 years of highest credited FICA earnings ____1963–1979____

Earnings in that period ____$137,350____

Average monthly earnings ____$673____

Primary monthly benefit amount ____$343.60____

Computation of Basic Monthly Retirement Benefit

Base pay during final 60-month period _____ $58,900
Average monthly earnings _____ $981.66

Service factor _____ 18 _____ years service × 2% = _____ 36%
Average monthly earnings × Service factor equals Basic
Monthly Benefit _____ $353.40

Appendix D: Consumer Price Index

All-Cities Index, 1967 = 100

January 1972	123.2	
January 1973	127.7	+ 4.5
January 1974	139.7	+12.0
January 1975	156.1	+16.4
January 1976	166.7	+10.6
January 1977	175.3	+ 8.6
January 1978	187.1	+11.8
January 1979	204.7	+17.6
January 1980	233.3	+28.6
January 1981	260.5	+27.2
January 1982	282.5	+22.0
January 1983	293.5	+11.0
January 1984	305.2	+11.7

Source: U.S. Dept. of Labor Bureau of Labor Statistics

General III: D. G. Barnhouse Co., Inc.
Statement of Financial Position

	Last Year	Two Years Ago
Assets		
Current Assets		
Cash	$ 1,160,206	$ 1,102,813
Accounts Received (Net)	3,027,476	3,895,825
Inventory	12,040,281	11,707,781
Other	144,506	104,497
Total Current Assets	$16,372,469	$16,810,916
Fixed Assets		
Investments (at cost)	$ 114,092	$ 114,092
Plant, Property and Equipment	22,021,031	21,010,980
less: Accumulated Depreciation	11,976,945	11,784,645
Plant, Property and Equipment (net)	10,044,086	9,226,335
Total Fixed Assets	$10,158,178	$ 9,340,427

Other Assets

Intangible Assets (net)	$ 156,448	$ 164,654
Deferred Charges	281,198	307,184
Total Other Assets	$ 437,646	$ 471,838
Total Assets	$26,968,293	$26,623,181

Liabilities and Equities

Current Liabilities

Accounts Payable	$ 1,293,630	$ 915,195
Notes Payable	2,212,900	3,162,500
Accrued Expenses	382,689	501,993
Accrued Taxes Payable	57,859	501,237
Other	744,172	727,480
Total Current Liabilities	$ 4,691,250	$ 5,808,405
(Net Working Capital)	$11,681,219	$ 11,002,511
Total Liabilities	$ 4,691,250	$ 5,808,405

Shareholder Equity

Common Stock (par value $1.00, 5,800,000 shares authorized and issued)	$ 6,670,000	$ 6,670,000
less: Treasure Stock (200,000 shares)	230,000	230,000
Common Stock Outstanding (5,600,000 shares)	$ 6,440,000	$ 6,440,000
Retained Earnings	$15,837,043	$14,374,776
Total Shareholder Equity (per common share)	$22,277,043	$20,814,776
Total Liabilities and Equities	$26,968,293	$26,623,181

Statement of Income and Retained Earnings

	Last Year	Two Years Ago
Income Statement		
Net Sales	$30,579,826	$31,025,621
Cost of Goods Sold	22,023,587	21,292,887
Gross Profit on Sales	8,556,239	9,732,734
Selling and Administrative Expense	4,754,001	6,080,616
Net Operating Profit	$ 3,802,238	$ 3,652,118

Other Income and Expense

Income	10,977	61,280
Expense	134,240	175,285
Net Other Expense	$ 123,263	$ 114,005
Net Income Before Taxes	3,678,975	3,538,113
Income Tax Expense	1,765,908	1,698,294
Net Income (per common share)	$ 1,913,067	$ 1,839,819

Retained Earnings Statement

Retained Earnings, beginning of year	$14,374,776	$12,985,757
Net Income for the Period	1,913,067	1,839,819
less: Dividends Paid	450,800	450,800
Retained Earnings, end of year	$15,837,043	$14,374,776

Statement of Sources and Uses of Funds (Last Year)

Sources of Funds

Net Earnings for the Period	$	1,913,067
Depreciation		192,300
Decrease in Intangible Assets and Deferred Charges		34,192
	Total $	2,139,559

Uses of Funds

Increase in Working Capital	$	678,708
Property, Plant, Equipment Additions		1,010,051
Cash Dividends Paid		450,800
	Total $	2,139,559

Analysis of Increase in Working Capital

Increase (Decrease) in Current Assets

Cash	$	57,393
Accounts Receivable		(868,349)
Inventory		332,500
Other Current Assets		40,009
	$	(438,447)

Decrease (Increase) in Current Liabilities

Accounts Payable	$	(378,435)
Notes Payable		949,600
Accrued Expenses		119,304
Accrued Taxes Payable		443,378
Other Current Liabilities		(16,692)
	$	1,117,155
Net Increase in Working Capital	$	678,708

General IV: Quarterly Sales and Earnings per Share Record

Sales by Quarters	Last Year	2 Years Ago	3 Years Ago	4 Years Ago	5 Years Ago	6 Years Ago
First	$ 8.51	$ 8.55	$ 6.95	$ 5.67	$ 5.12	$ 5.07
Second	$ 7.82	$ 8.38	$ 6.20	$ 5.78	$ 4.07	$ 5.59
Third	$ 7.52	$ 7.49	$ 6.34	$ 5.53	$ 5.39	$ 5.50
Fourth	$ 6.73	$ 6.60	$ 5.69	$ 5.37	$ 5.29	$ 5.03
Earnings/Share	$ 0.33	$ 0.32	$ 0.30	$ 0.32	$ 0.04	$ 0.20
Dividends/Share	$ 0.09	$ 0.09	$ 0.09	$ 0.09	$ 0.09	$ 0.09

(Sales in $ million, earnings and dividends in $)

General V: D. G. Barnhouse Co., Inc. Employee Age Groups

Age	Number of Employees
Under 30	164
30–39	112
40–49	90
50–59	73
Over 60	61
Total:	500

General VI: D. G. Barnhouse Co., Inc. Seniority List

Term of Service	Number of Employees
0–2 Years	71
3–9 Years	160
10–14 Years	49
15–20 Years	122
Over 20 Years	98

Name Index

Subject Index